Purchasing and Supply Chain Management

The McGraw-Hill/Irwin Series in Operations and Decision Sciences

SUPPLY CHAIN MANAGEMENT

Benton
Purchasing and Supply Chain Management
Third Edition

Burt, Petcavage, and Pinkerton
Supply Management
Eighth Edition

Bowersox, Closs, Cooper, and Bowersox
Supply Chain Logistics Management
Fourth Edition

Johnson, Leenders, and Flynn
Purchasing and Supply Management
Fourteenth Edition

Simchi-Levi, Kaminsky, and Simchi-Levi
Designing and Managing the Supply Chain: Concepts, Strategies, Case Studies
Third Edition

PROJECT MANAGEMENT

Brown and Hyer
Managing Projects: A Team-Based Approach
First Edition

Larson and Gray
Project Management: The Managerial Process
Fifth Edition

SERVICE OPERATIONS MANAGEMENT

Fitzsimmons and Fitzsimmons
Service Management: Operations, Strategy, Information Technology
Eighth Edition

MANAGEMENT SCIENCE

Hillier and Hillier
Introduction to Management Science: A Modeling and Case Studies Approach with Spreadsheets
Fifth Edition

Stevenson and Ozgur
Introduction to Management Science with Spreadsheets
First Edition

MANUFACTURING CONTROL SYSTEMS

Jacobs, Berry, Whybark, and Vollmann
Manufacturing Planning & Control for Supply Chain Management
Sixth Edition

BUSINESS RESEARCH METHODS

Cooper-Schindler
Business Research Methods
Twelfth Edition

BUSINESS FORECASTING

Wilson, Keating, and John Galt Solutions, Inc.
Business Forecasting
Sixth Edition

LINEAR STATISTICS AND REGRESSION

Kutner, Nachtsheim, and Neter
Applied Linear Regression Models
Fourth Edition

BUSINESS SYSTEMS DYNAMICS

Sterman
Business Dynamics: Systems Thinking and Modeling for a Complex World
First Edition

OPERATIONS MANAGEMENT

Cachon and Terwiesch
Matching Supply with Demand: An Introduction to Operations Management
Third Edition

Finch
Interactive Models for Operations and Supply Chain Management
First Edition

Jacobs and Chase
Operations and Supply Chain Management: The Core
Third Edition

Jacobs and Chase
Operations and Supply Chain Management
Fourteenth Edition

Jacobs and Whybark
Why ERP? A Primer on SAP Implementation
First Edition

Schroeder, Goldstein, and Rungtusanatham
Operations Management in the Supply Chain: Decisions and Cases
Sixth Edition

Stevenson
Operations Management
Eleventh Edition

Swink, Melnyk, Cooper, and Hartley
Managing Operations across the Supply Chain
Second Edition

PRODUCT DESIGN

Ulrich and Eppinger
Product Design and Development
Fifth Edition

BUSINESS MATH

Slater and Wittry
Practical Business Math Procedures
Eleventh Edition

Slater and Wittry
Practical Business Math Procedures, Brief Edition
Eleventh Edition

Slater and Wittry
Math for Business and Finance: An Algebraic Approach
First Edition

BUSINESS STATISTICS

Bowerman, O'Connell, Murphree, and Orris
Essentials of Business Statistics
Fourth Edition

Bowerman, O'Connell, and Murphree
Business Statistics in Practice
Seventh Edition

Doane and Seward
Applied Statistics in Business and Economics
Fourth Edition

Lind, Marchal, and Wathen
Basic Statistics for Business and Economics
Eighth Edition

Lind, Marchal, and Wathen
Statistical Techniques in Business and Economics
Fifteenth Edition

Jaggia and Kelly
Business Statistics: Communicating with Numbers
First Edition

Purchasing and Supply Chain Management

Third Edition

W. C. Benton, Jr.

The Max M. Fisher College of Business
The Ohio State University

Mc Graw Hill Education

PURCHASING AND SUPPLY CHAIN MANAGEMENT, THIRD EDITION

Published by McGraw-Hill Education, 2 Penn Plaza, New York, NY 10121.

Some ancillaries, including electronic and print components, may not be available to customers outside the United States.

This book is printed on acid-free paper.

1 2 3 4 5 6 7 8 9 0 QVR/QVR 1 0 9 8 7 6 5 4 3

ISBN 978-1-259-09543-6
MHID 1-259-09543-6

Cover credit: *Nikada/Getty Images*

www.mhhe.com

To my colleague Linda F. McHenry

W. C. Benton, Jr.

Brief Contents

Contents

PART FOUR
PRICE/COST ANALYSIS AND NEGOTIATION STRATEGIES 285

Preface

The material in this book is intended as an introduction to the field of purchasing and supply chain management. It is suitable for both undergraduate and graduate students. The field of purchasing has turned over many times during the past 35 years. The traditional purchasing function has evolved from a narrowly defined activity into a professional supply chain management function driven by people and technology. The role supply chain management is concerned with is cost containment, profitability, and relationship building. The discipline of supply management is the core component of an effective supply chain. This book is based on more than 25 years of practice, teaching, research, and consulting experience. This book is different from other purchasing textbooks in that it focuses on an *analysis-driven purchasing practice*.

Interest in purchasing/supply chain management both in industry and in academia is growing at an increasing rate. There are several factors that have driven the *purchasing revival*. First, many companies are becoming more profitable by increasing throughput, lowering inventories, and minimizing operational expenses. Second, supply chain information is becoming the primary driver throughout the supply chain management system. Third are the recent trends in outsourcing and, finally, buying organizations are using *power* to manage their supply chain. The information in this book provides state-of-the-art concepts, analysis, and supply management solutions. The topical matter includes *purchasing decisions and business strategy, the legal aspects of purchasing, materials management, inventory management, just-in-time (lean) purchasing, purchasing procedures, e-purchasing, systems contracting, supplier selection and evaluation, strategic outsourcing, global sourcing, purchasing supply partnership, supply chain power, total quality management (TQM) and purchasing, price determination, bargaining and negotiations, purchasing transportation services, equipment acquisition and disposal, health care purchasing, and purchasing professional services*. Most purchasing, logistics, and supply management students will be directly employed in purchasing or related supply chain management areas. The book focuses on the interrelationships of purchasing with the rest of the functional and system areas of the organization, with particular emphasis on the interface with marketing, logistics, supply chain management, and operations management. However, each chapter is designed to be self-contained, so that the reader can easily refer to the topic of interest. There are numerous *real-world* cases and exercises based on practical organizational situations. Each case has been refined through in-class usage. The cases are intended to *reinforce* the lessons learned from the chapters.

The treatment of purchasing and supply chain management in this book is extensive and complete. The contents in the book can be covered in a one-semester course. The textbook is intended to be used for undergraduate and graduate level courses in purchasing management, supply management, procurement management, contract management, logistics, and supply chain management. The book is also an excellent resource for executive education and training seminars. Depending on the pedagogy, the book also could be used in operations management and industrial engineering courses. The book is an excellent resource for the Certified Purchasing Manager (C.P.M.) program sponsored by the Institute of Supply Management (ISM) and the certification program sponsored by The Association for Operations Management (APICS).

CHANGES TO THIS EDITION

The third edition of *Purchasing and Supply Chain Management* focuses on the next generation of purchasing and supply professionals. This is the best time for the next generation of managers to pursue careers in purchasing supply chain management. Today, supply professionals must possess a comprehensive skill set. They must have excellent technology and negotiations skills in order to add value to their organization. Supply professionals must also be analytical problem solvers. In today's global arena, purchasing and supply professionals must be able to interact with potential sources of materials and services throughout the world. This edition is a comprehensive, easy-to-follow authoritative guide to state-of-the-art purchasing and supply methods, perfect for both students and supply professionals.

Some of the highlights include the following new and expanded topical coverage:

- An increased emphasis on supply chain integration
- New coverage on managing complex global outsourcing services
- Expanded coverage of health care purchasing and supply chain management
- New coverage on purchasing strategy and the development of strategic purchasing plans for competitive advantage
- Expanded coverage of E-procurement technology
- New coverage on service sector procurement
- New coverage on markup versus margin
- New coverage on professionalism, ethics, and the law
- Expanded coverage of supply chain relationship management
- New coverage on project pricing
- Six new *real-world* cases
- A comprehensive set of new exercises and problems

The third edition is both timely and topical and intended to help the new generation of students and supply professionals to become more effective supply management professionals.

BOOK STRUCTURE

The structure of this book is motivated by new developments in the field of purchasing and supply chain management. An example of the coverage is given in Parts One through Five below.

Part One. Introduction to Purchasing and Supply Chain Management

Chapter 1 establishes the purchasing function's contributions to profitability. This is the best time for the next generation of managers to pursue careers in purchasing and supply chain management. Supply professionals must possess a comprehensive skill set. They must have excellent technology and negotiations skills in order to add value to their organization. To become a competitive strategic weapon, purchasing has abandoned the fragmented approaches of the past. The purchasing function is an integral part of the transformation of raw materials and component parts into finished goods by utilizing materials, systems, information, and people. Supply professionals must also be analytical problem solvers. In today's global arena, supply professionals must be able to interact with potential sources of materials and services throughout the world.

In general, the business world has become increasingly more interconnected. The European Union's (EU) financial crisis is having a profound effect on North

American and Asian economies. Supply management professionals must learn to adapt to the EU supply chain uncertainty. Given the level of direct investment and the trading relationships between the EU and the two largest economies in the world, which are the United States and China, the world could easily slide into world economic crises. Volatile exchange rates, EU member defaults, worker strikes, and social unrest are possible throughout the EU. In order to manage supply chain risk we must first determine specifically, where the risk exists in the supply chain. Any company with a global footprint must evaluate and adapt their supply management function based on the EU realities. The effective supply chain organization with critical strategic EU suppliers and customers must devise a plan for qualifying alternative strategic supply chain relationships. There is also an urgent need to conduct site visits and keep a watchful eye on inventory levels.

In **Chapter 2**, a framework for linking purchasing decisions with the firm's competitive strategy is presented. The framework offers a systematic approach for designing purchasing strategies consistent with a firm's competitive strategy. Supply management can play a significant role in making a firm competitive. Today, purchased inputs offer a potential source for helping a company develop leverage against its competitors. Purchasing actions designed to reinforce the firm's competitive priorities can give the firm advantages over its competitors. In essence, firms must design their purchasing actions to emphasize their competitive strategy. Both students and professionals will also learn about the elements required to develop a strategic sourcing plan. The legal aspects are presented in **Chapter 3**. The purchasing professional in an organization must be able to understand the legal aspects of the purchasing function. The relationship between ethics and the law is complex. Many violators of ethical conduct maintain that their actions are perfectly legal under the law. The societal norms must also be considered. Perhaps the most significant change of the legal aspects of purchasing is the impact of the information age.

Part Two. Materials Management

Chapter 4 focuses on materials management in support of the transformation of raw materials and component parts into throughput (sales). The functions included in the materials management concept include (1) materials planning and control, (2) production scheduling, (3) receiving, (4) stores, (5) traffic, (6) disposal of scrap, (7) quality control, and (8) inventory control. Inventory management is presented in **Chapter 5**. Inventory is the life blood of any business. Most firms store thousands of different items. There are many inexpensive supply or operating type items. The type of business a firm is in will usually determine how much of the firm's assets are invested in inventories. Hospitals carry beds, surgical instruments, and food, pharmaceutical, and other miscellaneous items. On the other hand, manufacturing firms carry office supplies, raw materials, component parts, finished products and many other industry-related items. Just-in-time (JIT) or lean purchasing is introduced in **Chapter 6**. The current shift toward the so-called "Lean Thinking" manufacturing environment is one of the major motivations for JIT purchasing. JIT has changed the role of purchasing from merely placing orders to investigating the supplier's technical and process capabilities. Perhaps the most important realization is the fact that suppliers should become an extremely important consideration for the purchasing function, wherein they should be viewed as partners and not adversaries.

Part Three. Fundamentals of Purchasing and Supply Chain Management

Chapter 7 focuses on purchasing procedures, e-purchasing, and systems contracting. Online or e-procurement technology has become an important part of purchasing and supply chain management and the rate of adoption has increased significantly. The world of business-to-business commerce has become essential to the purchase of ORM and MRO items. E-purchasing has fundamentally transformed the traditional indirect purchasing function. E-purchasing has led to significant cost saving and coordinated efficiency. Online driven indirect purchasing reduces the day-to-day waste in the manual purchasing system. Direct materials tend to be purchased in quantities based on complicated production planning and control systems. Some direct material purchasing situations involve long intricate negotiations. Many high technology manufacturing firms purchase fully assembled component systems electronically. The new information age will force both large and small firms to consider the competitive advantages of online reverse auctions and RFID technology. Businesses that use reverse auctions have made testimonials of savings of more than $800 million from online bidding.

Supplier selection is addressed in **Chapter 8**. The selection of suppliers is a complex and demanding question that has no real correct answer. Each firm must weigh the benefits and risks of single and multiple sourcing. If it is clear to proceed with a reduction of the supply base, numerous methods can be used. However, in this it is recommended that a strategic approach be incorporated into the supplier selection process. A strategic match between buyer and supplier can allow an easier cooperative relationship to exist and flourish. Buyer and supplier relationships have become increasingly important for a number of reasons. There is a trend toward specialization away from manufacturing an entire product and to more contract manufacturing and purchasing. In some market segments, it is estimated that 80 percent or more of total product revenue often passes directly to suppliers as payment for labor, materials, and equipment. This significant transfer of value downstream emphasizes the importance and significance of supply chain relationship management. For any buying organization to stay competitive in today's aggressive market sectors, it is essential that they maintain strong relationships with their best contract manufacturers and suppliers. The criterion of net price is emphasized more heavily in the apparel and the electronic industries than in the chemical and construction industries. In the electronics industry, this is due to the assumption that both quality and delivery are inherent in the product. By deciding which criterion to emphasize, firms will be able to select the suppliers from which they will benefit the most.

Strategic outsourcing is addressed in **Chapter 9**. Outsourcing is the complete transfer of a business process that has been traditionally operated and managed internally to an independently owned external service provider. A complete transfer means that the people, facilities, equipment, technology, and other assets are no longer maintained once the business process is outsourced. Strategic outsourcing has rapidly become the building block for globalization. Fueled by the Internet, outsourcing has evolved into the most pervasive business paradigm in the past 50 years.

The anticipated economic implications of outsourcing initiatives are complex. There are significant hidden outsourcing costs that are sometimes not accounted for. The motivation for outsourcing is commonly driven by the savings in direct labor and other tangible operating costs. Yet, significant hidden costs are often overlooked when preparing a financial business case for outsourcing. Hidden costs include relationship management costs, quality costs, implementation- or transition-related expenses, and internal coordination costs, among others. If not considered, these financial implications can eat away at the anticipated gains from outsourcing.

In the coming decade, more and more firms will be expanding their operations into international markets. The subject of **Chapter 10** is global sourcing. As firms' competition heats up, firms will become more global minded. To be a global firm, management must be able to critically evaluate foreign markets. In the current business environment, firms are beginning to develop global procurement strategies. The electronic, chemical, and metal industries are leading the global procurement charge. The North American Free Trade Act and the European Economic Community will fuel global sourcing in the next decade. In this chapter a detailed total cost analysis is presented to show the hidden costs associated with global sourcing. The buying firm must also know how to negotiate in foreign countries. There are two germane forms of opportunism associated with both domestic and global outsourcing: shirking and poaching. *Shirking* represents the extent to which the service provider is inclined to deliberately underperform or withhold resources should the customer be unable to detect such action. Shirking is often associated with the problem of moral hazard and is frequently cited as a typical form of passive, yet intentional opportunism. *Poaching* is the extent to which the service provider is inclined to utilize information gained through its relationship with the customer for its own, perhaps unauthorized, benefit should the customer be unable to detect such action.

A brief description of the sourcing environment in the United Kingdom, India, Germany, France, and China is presented.

Chapter 11 is entitled "Supply Partnerships and Supply Chain Power." The intense coordination necessary for effective supply chain integration necessitates a reduced supplier base; where manufacturers were once producing products with thousands of suppliers, successful firms are now manufacturing better products with fewer suppliers. The large pie of purchased parts and materials thus gets divided among fewer players, and more is at stake for the suppliers. The suppliers must strive to develop best practice in order to gain the critical preferred status with the manufacturers, and these preferred suppliers must maintain best practice or face effortless replacement from the large base of competitors. This intensifies the power imbalance within an industry sector. The manufacturers can maintain the attitude that the suppliers must maintain pace with the industry or lose a potentially significant amount of their business.

Interfirm power may be defined as the ability of one firm (the source) to influence the actions and intentions of another firm (the target). Several sources of power, both positive and negative, exist to affect the operational strategies and processes of both the power target and the source. The influences of power affect critical interfirm relationship elements as well as firm performance and satisfaction. Despite such effects, most firms may not be completely aware of the broad scope of power dimensions and thus may not actively manage their power. A relational orientation, though, complicates the role of power within interfirm interactions. For instance, power may interfere with the mutuality and sincerity of interfirm alliances, inducing the power source to more directly use its power. On the other hand, allying firms may expose themselves to further opportunistic behavior by conniving partners, thus increasing the prominence of power within the relationship. This discussion highlights the importance of power awareness as well as recognition of power as a valuable approach for increasing the competitive positioning of the entire supply chain. Beyond its valuable contributions to the inspiration of supply chain management, this chapter only provides an initial glance at power influences within the supply chain.

Chapter 12 is entitled "Total Quality Management (TQM) and Purchasing." Preliminary studies indicate that assembly time is roughly proportional to the number of parts assembled. It has been shown that the number of parts in a design can be decreased by 20–40 percent when engineers are told to design the product to minimize the number of parts. Six Sigma is a way to measure supplier quality. Supplying firms that follow the core philosophy of Six Sigma will make excellent strategic partners. Six Sigma suppliers focus on (1) defects per million as a standard metric, (2) providing extensive employee training, and (3) the reduction of non-value-added activities.

An awareness of the Taguchi philosophy, with a program to integrate design and manufacturing, is the ingredient many manufacturers need to produce high-quality, low-cost products. SPC alone will only determine conformance to design. It will not produce designs that enable firms to compete effectively in the world market in the millennium.

Part Four. Price/Cost Analysis and Negotiation Strategies

Chapter 13 focuses on price determination, which is one of the most important decisions that successful organizations make. The purchasing professional must become an expert on the product or services for which they are responsible. Given the complexity of the buying decision, the purchasing professional must be prepared to analyze each significant buying situation on the basis of the conceptual and economic impact of various buying decisions. The foundations for price determination are rooted in the *economics* and *psychology* disciplines. It is conceivable that a powerful buyer could force a supplier to eliminate its overhead from the ultimate price. Price determination is becoming the most important competitive weapon necessary to ensure survival in today's competitive environment. Companies are spending an increasingly larger percentage of their revenue dollars for the acquisition of goods and services. Finally, in today's competitive construction market, markup and margin are sometimes used interchangeably. However, gross margin and markup are not the same. A clear understanding of markup versus gross margin is an important concept when estimating and bidding jobs in the construction industry.

Chapter 14 examines the important human interactions called bargaining and negotiation in a business setting. Bargaining occurs between individuals, groups, organizations, and countries. In this chapter we considered bargaining between two parties, each possessing resources the other side desires. When two parties are involved in distributed bargaining, the parties are in basic conflict and competition because of a clash of goals: the more one party gets, the less the other gets. Integrative bargaining is a situation where some areas of mutual concern and complementary interest exist. The situation is a varying-sum schedule such that by working together both parties can increase the total profits available to be divided between them. The distributive bargaining situation has been fully explored by psychologists. Economists on the other hand have spent most of their efforts in examining bargaining on integrative bargaining situations. An experiment in distributive bargaining is also included to better illustrate both effects of economic and psychological aspects on the outcome of bargaining situations. The experiment examines the effect of contingency compensation on both buyers and sellers. It also allows speculation about the differences in the power system of buyers and sellers and how they affect the outcome of bargaining situations.

Part Five. Special Purchasing Applications

Chapter 15 provides an in-depth analysis of transportation costs. With JIT systems transportation costs are magnified. Some of the transportation costs include such activities as selecting the mode of transportation to be used in moving a particular shipment. Over the road transportation accounted for approximately 90 percent of total transportation costs. In other words, a large share of the expenditures was associated with moving products from the manufacturing facility to the ultimate consumer. The competition in the trucking industry is fierce, so in order to be successful, a carrier must provide the shipper with high service and low costs. The general consensus is that on-time delivery and price are the key competitive criteria. The chapter concludes with interviews with three Fortune 500 purchasing executives.

In **Chapter 16** a step-by-step capital acquisition process is given. The steps are based on (1) requisition, (2) company objectives, (3) new product ideas, (4) cash flow analysis, (4) an economic evaluation, (5) a financial plan analysis, and (6) expenditure control. Next, an extensive lease-versus-buy decision is discussed and illustrated. When does it make more sense to buy capital equipment? When does it make more sense to lease? A detailed tutorial on the lease-versus-buy decision is given in the chapter supplement.

Chapter 17 is a special feature of the textbook. There are critical differences between the health care supply chain and industrial supply chain, such as the automotive supply chain. One difference is the manner in which revenue is generated. The cost of health care is expected to increase at an exponential rate. Many businesses and health care organizations will be driven from the market because of uncontrollable non-salary costs and declining profits. This radical shift is the result of increased price competition and the regulatory environment. The focus of this chapter is on purchasing day-to-day supplies and capital equipment acquisition. The day-to-day services include dietary, linen, housekeeping, physical plant engineering, pharmacy, laboratory, inpatient treatment (nursing units), surgery, radiology, administration, and others. Each area has specific and often unique materials and supply needs, creating a requirement in these facilities for a supply management system that can provide the necessary supplies when needed. In the current climate of increasing health care costs, systems inventory must be optimized without sacrificing the level of service provided. Finally, businesses spend hundreds of millions of dollars on group health plans every year. At the same time, premiums are increasing rapidly. In 2008 health care costs accounted for approximately 16 percent of GNP. According to the Kaiser Family Foundation Employer Health Benefits Annual Survey, the costs for providing health insurance increased by an average of 14.9 percent in 2012, the fourth straight year of double-digit premium increases. Health care benefits costs have clearly dominated overhead expenditures. Employers are responding to the increased health care benefits costs by moving away from traditional employer-sponsored insurance plans to consumer-driven health care plans.

Chapter 18 focuses on sourcing professional services. The service sector has taken on an increasingly important role in the world economy. The service sector has become the engine of growth for the American economy, fundamental to the health and prosperity U.S. businesses, large, medium, or small. Service companies are engaged in every type of commercial activity—manufacturing, transportation, energy and utilities, retail and wholesale trade, finance and government. In the United States, jobs in the service sector have increased from just under 50 percent to 85 percent of the total jobs. Thus, the purchasing of professional services is gaining exceptional attention. The largest growth has come from the governmental sector. Unlike manufacturing, it is more difficult to measure the performance of design consultants, contractors, and inspectors. The chapter ends with a supplement dedicated to an extensive example of the scope of work for a federal highway administration project.

SUPPLEMENTS

Online Learning Center: www.mhhe.com/benton3e

The Instructor Edition of the *Purchasing and Supply Chain Management, 3/e* OLC is password-protected and a convenient place for instructors to access course supplements. Resources for professors include the Instructor's Manual, PowerPoint slides, solutions to exercises, sample syllabi, sample exam questions, and comprehensive solutions to the case studies. The case solutions are based on the latest research and theoretical developments.

TEGRITY CAMPUS: LECTURES 24/7

Mc Graw Hill tegrity campus

Tegrity Campus is a service that makes class time available 24/7 by automatically capturing every lecture in a searchable format for students to review when they study and complete assignments. With a simple one-click start-and-stop process, you capture all computer screens and corresponding audio. Students can replay any part of any class with easy-to-use browser-based viewing on a PC or Mac.

Educators know that the more students can see, hear, and experience class resources, the better they learn. In fact, studies prove it. With Tegrity Campus, students quickly recall key moments by using Tegrity Campus's unique search feature. This search helps students efficiently find what they need, when they need it, across an entire semester of class recordings. Help turn all your students' study time into learning moments immediately supported by your lecture.

To learn more about Tegrity, watch a two-minute Flash demo at http://tegritycampus.mhhe.com.

AACSB STATEMENT

The McGraw-Hill Companies is a proud corporate member of AACSB International. Understanding the importance and value of AACSB accreditation, *Purchasing and Supply Chain Management* recognizes the curricula guidelines detailed in the AACSB standards for business accreditation by connecting selected questions in the text to the six general knowledge and skill guidelines in the AACSB standards.

The statements contained in *Purchasing and Supply Chain Management* are provided only as a guide for the users of this textbook. The AACSB leaves content coverage and assessment within the purview of individual schools, the mission of the school, and the faculty. While *Purchasing and Supply Chain Management* and the teaching package make no claim of any specific AACSB qualification or evaluation, we have within *Purchasing and Supply Chain Management* labeled selected questions according to the six general knowledge and skills areas.

ACKNOWLEDGMENTS

The following reviewers provided valuable feedback on the manuscript. The reviewers contributed significantly to the final version. They include:

Professional

Robert Hairston, Corning, Inc.
Robi Bendorf, Bendorf and Associates
Carol Marks, Industrial Distribution Group
Sukhmeet Garha, Centas, Inc.
Linda F. McHenry, Esq., W. C. Benton and Associates, Inc.

Special thanks to Linda, who reviewed and contributed significantly to Chapter 3.

Academic

Gopesh Anand, University of Illinois
Chad W. Autry, Texas Christian University
Yong Hoon Choun, The Ohio State University
Kurt Hozak, Indiana State University
Jayanth Jayaram, University of South Carolina
Russell W. Jones, University of Central Oklahoma
Les Kauer, Southern Nazarene University
Laura Meade, Texas Christian University
Frank Montabon, Iowa State University
William C. Moser, Ball State University
Patrick Penfield, Syracuse University
Tobias Schoenherr, Michigan State University
Michael Stodnick, University of Dallas
Dorothy L. Smith, Webster University
Amy Z. Zeng, Worcester Polytechnic Institute

I want to thank Christina Kouvelis, Kaylee Putbrese, Thomas Hayward, and the entire team at McGraw-Hill/Irwin for producing the third edition. I want to also thank Kurt Strand, Senior Vice President, McGraw-Hill, for his support during the early development stages of the project. The McGraw-Hill/Irwin team consists of quiet, battle-tested professionals. Their passion for excellence helped us attain the highest level of quality and excellence. My greatest appreciation goes to the hundreds of students who have shared classrooms with me from whom I have learned more than I have ever taught. If you have any comments or suggestions you would like to share with me, I welcome them.

Email: benton.1@osu.edu
www.supplychain-mgt.com
W. C. Benton Jr.
Semper Fidelis

About the Author

W. C. Benton, Jr. is the Edwin D. Dodd Professor of Management and Distinguished Research Professor of Operations and Supply Chain Management in the Max M. Fisher College of Business at The Ohio State University. Professor Benton teaches courses in supply chain management to undergraduates, MBAs, and doctoral candidates. Dr. Benton received his doctorate in both operations and systems management and quantitative business analysis from Indiana University, Bloomington, Indiana.

Ranked number one out of 753 operations management researchers in terms of quality and quantity, Dr. Benton's vast research and writing accomplishments include more than 120 articles in the areas of health care performance issues, economics of cardiovascular surgery, purchasing management, inventory control, supply chain management, quality assurance, and materials management that have appeared in *The New England Journal of Medicine, Annals of Thoracic Surgery, American College of Physician Executives, Decision Sciences, Journal of Operations Management, Naval Research Logistics, IEE Transactions, European Journal of Operational Research, Quality Progress, Naval Research Logistics, The Journal of Business Logistics, The Journal of Purchasing and Supply Chain Management, Production and Operations Management, Interfaces, Journal of Supply Chain Management,* and *Production and Operations Management.* Dr. Benton has published four textbooks and he has authored "Bargaining, Negotiations, and Personal Selling" for the *Handbook of Economic Psychology.* He currently serves on the editorial boards for the *Journal of Operations Management, Decision Sciences, Journal of Supply Chain Management, Journal of Business Logistics, Business of Service Industries Journal, International Journal of Productivity and Quality Management,* and as a Special Issue Editor for the *European Journal of Operational Research.* For the Engineer and Manufacturing and Service Enterprise Systems Divisions at the *National Science Foundation,* he is a research panel member.

Professor Benton's expert contribution to the business and governmental arena includes consultancy for Grant Hospital, Ashland, IBM, RCA, Frigidaire, The Ohio Department of Transportation, The Florida Department of Transportation, The Indiana Department of Transportation, The South Carolina Department of Transportation, The Alabama Department of Transportation, The Kentucky Department of Transportation, The Federal Highway Administration, Battelle Institute, The United States Air Force, Gelzer Automated Assembly Systems, Bitronics, Inc., The Ohio Bureau of Disability Determination, Bio-Ohio, The Carter Group Canada, and others.

He serves on the board of directors for the Healthcare Accreditation Colloquium, Inc., The Sleep Medicine Foundation, Academic Council for Healthcare Research, The House of Hope, and The Supply Chain Research Group and is a member of the Decision Sciences Institute, The Institute of Management Sciences, The Institute of Supply Management, The Production and Inventory Control Society, the Operations Management Association, American Society for Quality Control, Society of Logistics Engineers, The Mathematical Association of America, and others.

Note to Students

The material contained in this textbook is practical, relevant, and useful. The lessons you learn from this book are based on proven conceptual and analytical principles. The concepts covered in each chapter are relatively simple and highly intuitive.

The primary focus is on the interrelationships of purchasing/supply chain management with the rest of the functional and system areas of the organization with particular emphasis on the interface with marketing, operations management, and supply chain management. The ultimate goal for any for-profit concern is to quickly transform all purchased resources into *sales*.

At the conclusion of a course in purchasing, you should be able to competently buy products or services for profit and nonprofit organizations. In addition, you should be able to view how the purchasing/supply function affects the throughput of the entire operation of the organization and how the purchasing activity fits within the supply chain management field. This textbook is also an excellent preparation for the Certified Purchasing Manager (C.P.M.) program sponsored by the Institute of Supply Management (ISM).

"The ability to achieve any goal is absolutely contingent on the quality of your mind."

Part One

Introduction to Purchasing and Supply Chain Management

Chapter One

Purchasing and Supply Chain Management

Learning Objectives

1. Understand the purchasing function's contribution to profitability.
2. Identify the relationship between the purchasing function and other functional areas.
3. Explore the basic historical development of the purchasing function.
4. Understand the evolution of the basic supply management concept.
5. Differentiate between purchasing, supply management, and supply chain management.
6. Understand the relationship between the purchasing function and inventory, ordering, and transportation costs.
7. Discuss the advantages and disadvantages of centralized purchasing organizational designs.
8. Identify various purchasing organizational designs.
9. Learn about careers in purchasing.

INTRODUCTION

After millennia of unchallenged success, businesses and governments around the world are entering a new era of unprecedented openness. The movement to hold corporate officers and politicians accountable is spurred by three powerful forces: economics, technology, and zeitgeist. The entire world is experiencing a deep recession. The Internet, meanwhile, has revolutionized the speed and power of data analysis and dissemination. And financial institutions are being held responsible.

In general, the business world has become increasingly more interconnected. The European Union's (EU) financial crises are having a profound effect on North American and Asian economies. Supply management professionals must learn to adapt to the EU supply chain uncertainty. Given the level of direct investment and the trading relationships between the EU and the two largest economies—the United States and China—in the world, the world could easily slide into world economic crises. Volatile exchange rates, EU member defaults, worker strikes, and social unrest are possible throughout the EU. In order to manage supply chain risk we must first determine specifically where the risk exists in the supply chain. Any company with a global footprint must evaluate and adapt their supply management function based on the EU realities. Keeping track of the EU financial crises must become a high priority for supply chain professionals. The financial risk of both the EU customers and strategic supplier base must be factored into demand and supply risk. The effective supply chain organization with critical strategic EU suppliers and customers must devise a plan for qualifying alternative strategic supply chain relationships. There is also an urgent need to conduct site visits and keeping a watchful eye on inventory levels.

In certain industries, Asian manufacturers dominate the United States' consumer market. Third-world nations in Central and South America, Southeast Asia, and China continue to attract U.S. manufacturers seeking low wages for laborious tasks. And, in the midst of everything, the United States is a giant consumer base with an enormous command of technology but is steadily losing the infrastructure needed to create jobs.

In addition to significant events that have impacted the world's business environment, individual firms have had to change radically in response to burgeoning technologies. Historically, the management of materials and component parts was the most neglected element in the production process. Only when the cost of materials and subassemblies increased did management attempt to investigate alternative methods to the planning and control of the acquisition and transformation functions in the organization. Instead, most firms emphasized minimizing the cost of capital and labor. The focus on labor was logical because the industrial revolution had generated many labor-intensive manufacturers. Producing large standardized batches represented the norm for some manufacturers. Some firms have embraced new technologies and invested in technology-driven manufacturing systems. Although these new systems are up and running, too frequently they are being operated just like the old models, thus defeating the very purpose the system was designed to achieve. The reality is that technology is rapidly displacing labor. During the next decade, the supply management function is likely to contribute to profits more than any other function in the company.

PURCHASING MANAGERS, BUYERS, AND PURCHASING AGENTS

Supply managers, buyers, and purchasing agents seek to obtain the highest-quality merchandise at the lowest possible purchase cost for their employers. In general, purchasers buy goods and services for use by their business organization. On the other hand, buyers typically buy items for resale. Purchasers and buyers determine which commodities or services are best for the specific requirement, choose the suppliers of the product or service, negotiate the lowest price, and award contracts that ensure that the correct amount of the product or service is received at the appropriate time. In order to accomplish these tasks successfully, purchasing managers, buyers, and purchasing agents identify foreign and domestic suppliers. Purchasing managers, buyers, and agents must become experts on the services, materials, and products they purchase.

Purchasing managers, buyers, and purchasing agents evaluate suppliers on the bases of price, quality, service support, availability, reliability, and selection. To assist them in their search for the right suppliers, they review catalogs, industry and company publications, directories, and trade journals. Much of this information is now available on the Internet. They research the reputation and history of the suppliers and may advertise anticipated purchase actions in order to solicit bids. At meetings, trade shows, conferences, and suppliers' plants and distribution centers, they examine products and services, assess a supplier's production and distribution capabilities, and discuss other technical and business considerations that influence the purchasing decision. Once all of the necessary information on suppliers is gathered, orders are placed and contracts are awarded to those suppliers who meet the purchaser's needs.

All of these—changing economic and political environments, emerging technology versus labor, and the changing nature of purchasing as a discipline—must influence the role of purchasing and supply management. To become a competitive strategic weapon, purchasing and supply management must abandon fragmented approaches. The same company that invests in a technology-based manufacturing system (hard technology) at the same time must invest in result-oriented training programs (soft technology). The purchasing function must become an integral part of transforming raw materials and component parts into finished goods by utilizing materials, systems, information, and people. Innovative sourcing requires companywide strategies with strong executive engagement that is internally driven and customer focused.

THE EVOLUTION OF THE PURCHASING AND SUPPLY MANAGEMENT FUNCTION

To become a competitive organization in today's global economy, the purchasing and supply management function must become world class. The supply management function is the key to unlocking the value within the organization. Organizations must optimize sourcing assets. As can be seen in Figure 1.1, there are three phases in the optimization of an organization's sourcing assets. Stage 1 involves leveraging through volume discounts. It can easily lead to significant reductions in the total purchasing costs. Stage 2 involves focusing on the value proposition throughout the supply chain among customers and suppliers. Finally, stage 3 is

FIGURE 1.1
Unlocking Sourcing Value

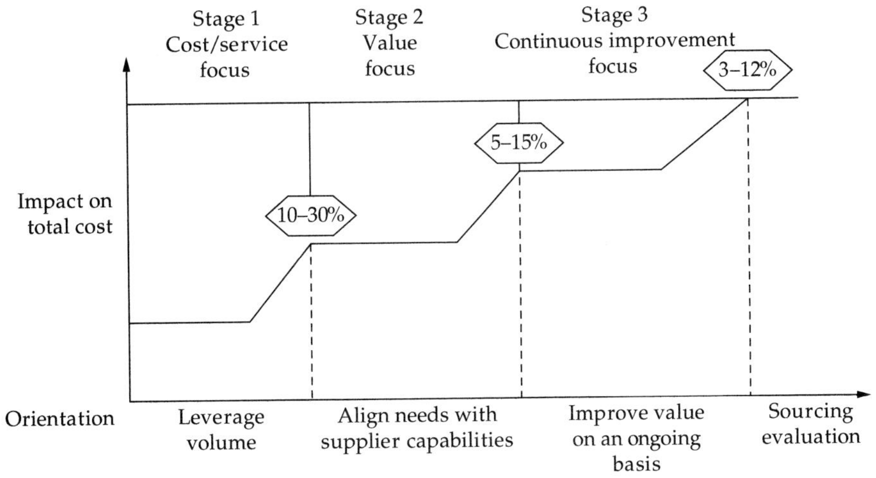

FIGURE 1.2
The Evolution of the Sourcing Function

Traditional Orientation	Current Thinking
1. Focus on prices	1. Focus on value
2. Total cost of ownership	2. Total contribution to ownership
3. Process—driver sourcing approach	3. Strategic intent—driver sourcing approach
4. Compatibility objectives	4. Differentiation objectives
5. Involvement in specification definition phase	5. Involvement in strategic decisions
6. Procurement skills	6. Business skills
7. Sourcing as adversarial zero-sum transaction	7. Sourcing aligned and intrinsically linked with business stakeholders

necessary for sustaining the successes in the previous two phases. Practice and high-quality feedback allow the purchasing professional the ability to make adjustments to stages 1 and 2. The organizations that produce excellence are those that continuously improve. In general the purchasing and supply management function has evolved from a pure cost management function to a competitive advantage. See Figure 1.2.

THE SUPPLY MANAGEMENT PROCESS

The primary focus of this text is integrated purchasing and supply management. See Figure 1.3. In the past 25 years, the supply management function has grown from a tactical function of purchasing/procurement into a key strategic role within organizations. Supply management now:

- Contributes to the bottom line.
- Serves as an information source.
- Increases efficiency and productivity.
- Enhances the continuous improvement process.
- Improves competitive position and customer satisfaction.
- Impacts the organization's image and social policy.
- Develops the organization's future leaders.

Supply management exists to explore business opportunities and implement supply strategies that deliver the most value possible to the organization, its suppliers, and its customers. Strategic supply management is the organization's primary source for collecting market intelligence and developing cost-reduction programs. Given the strategic nature of the supply function, the top supply management professional is usually a member of the organization's senior management team. In this leadership role, supply management professionals must be knowledgeable and understand all areas of the business in order to develop strategies consistent with the organization's goals and successful business procedures.

With the increasing technology and demand for global operations, supply management is often involved in finding sources for products and/or services from international suppliers. An understanding of global business concepts is increasingly important for those in the profession.

In most firms, functional managers within each area make independent decisions using similar techniques. The approach introduced in this chapter proposes that the supply management decision should be integrated. Integrative materials

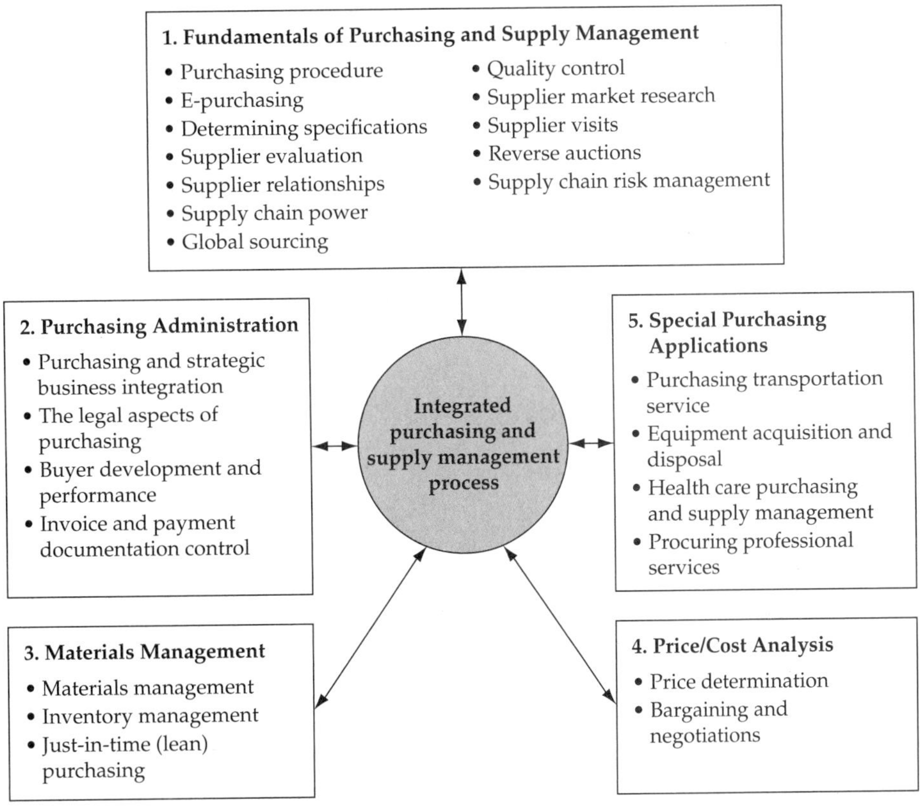

FIGURE 1.3 Integrated Purchasing and Supply Management Process

management consists of the planning, acquisition, and conversion of raw materials and component parts into finished goods. In this scenario, each functional manager reports to the same superior. What's more, the managers should work for the overall purpose of delivering high-quality products to the customer on time. An important objective of this approach is to provide high-quality customer service while minimizing the cost of producing the service.

Integrative supply management is not related to the size of the firm. Realistically, the purchasing subfunctions must first be integrated before the supply function will be synergistic with other business functions.

The purpose of supply management is to support the transformation of raw materials and component parts into shipped or inventory goods. The function of inventory in general is to decouple the entire transformation process. During the transformation process, materials are combined with labor, information, technology, and capital.

The supply planning system is central to the acquisition of part and component needs in an assemble-to-order environment. The material requirements planning (MRP) function is the most important input into a manufacturing planning and control system. Although many productive companies have embraced just-in-time (JIT) philosophies, they continue to use MRP concepts to enhance the effectiveness of the manufacturing mission. Perhaps the most significant change in the past decade has been in the purchasing function. During the time period 1960–1980, most American manufacturing firms fabricated 60–80 percent of the product's value (see Figure 1.4). On the other hand, in the past decade, a large number of manufacturing firms purchased between 60 and 80 percent of the product's

FIGURE 1.4
Manufacturing Process (1960s–1980s)

Source: Srivastava and Benton (1998).

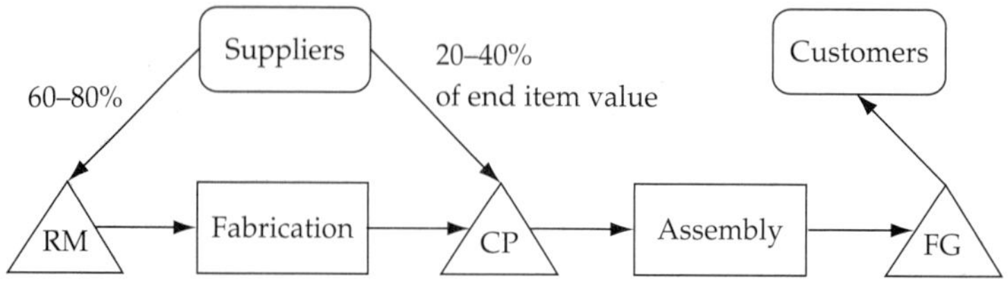

FIGURE 1.5
Manufacturing Process (1980s–now)

Source: Srivastava and Benton (1998).

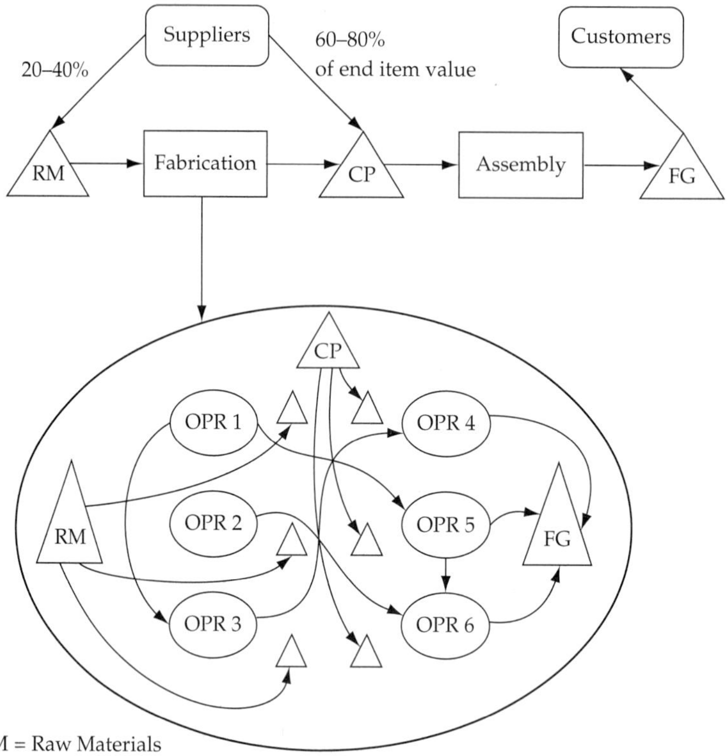

RM = Raw Materials
OPR = Operation
FG = Finished Goods
CP = Component Parts
△ = Inventory Storage

value (see Figure 1.5). Since this impressive shift in percentages, the complexity of the manufacturing system has been greatly reduced. As can be seen in Figure 1.5, the complexity in the fabrication operation has been shifted upstream to the supplier. Under the traditional model, the firm transformed significantly more raw materials and labor into the end product. Today, since industrial firms are purchasing more and more subassemblies (component parts), the manufacturing focus is shifted downstream to the assembly operation. This significant shift has elevated the importance and profile of purchasing professionals.

A vice president of purchasing for a Fortune 500 company suggested that the *discount* acceptance decision cannot be made independently from the open order rescheduling decision. He went on to suggest that inventory record accuracy and open order rescheduling were key inputs into determining whether to accept or reject a specific discount schedule.

The expected economic benefit from the creation and continuous improvement of an integrated purchasing and supply management process is supply chain profit maximization. See Figure 1.5.

The global economy has evolved from exclusively manufacturing to services. Thus, it is important to show how the lessons learned from manufacturing supply management can be applied to service systems purchasing. The differences between service supply management systems and the traditional supply management systems must be acknowledged. In service supply management systems, human capital forms a significant source of the value proposition. In addition it is more of a challenge to measure value in service supply management. Chapter 18 focuses on service supply management.

PURCHASING DOLLAR RESPONSIBILITY

The cost of acquiring, storing, and moving materials is an increasingly large fraction of the *cost of goods sold*. To gain a different perspective about the importance of materials-related expenditures, consider the dollar responsibility of one General Motors materials management group:

1. Parts and materials = 10 times direct labor dollars
2. Supply management expenditures = $100 billion
3. Transportation bill = $3 billion
4. Purchasing buys 97 percent of all component parts.

The mission of the General Motors supply management group is to manage purchasing, planning, scheduling, and the transportation of material required for specific products in a manner that will provide a *significant competitive* advantage to the division in the production of quality trucks and cars. Integrative purchasing and supply management make possible the production of vehicles in terms of cost and quality that are competitive in the world.

Thus, we see that the dollar responsibility of supply management is very large in both relative and absolute terms. More importantly, supply management is responsible—it contributes to the competitive stance and long-run survival of the firm.

The following are ratios of materials-related costs that are typically cited in fabrication–assembly industries, for example, consumer durable goods.

Cost of purchase = 80 percent of sales
Cost of marketing (sales) = 10 percent of sales
Cost of transportation = 10 percent of sales

These ratios are increasing for various reasons: material shortages, increased use of synthetic materials, inflation, and thoroughly complex high-value products.

1. *Material shortages*. As natural resources are consumed, more costly methods of exploration, extraction, and processing are necessary. Shortages also result from political events. Former colonies of Western nations, once a low-cost and ready source of supply, have gained their independence. As autonomous nations, these new nations manage their resources to achieve economic, social, and nationalistic objectives.

In the early 1960s, nearly all the chrome in Rhodesia (Zimbabwe) was owned by U.S. firms. Rhodesia was described as a very comfortable, placid little British colony. The United States had almost no domestic sources of chromium, a material essential for manufacturing a wide range of products used in everyday life and military defense. Yet during the struggle for Rhodesian independence, the U.S. government placed an embargo on imports of chromium from Rhodesia. Prior to the second Gulf war and after the first Gulf war, there was a similar embargo on oil from Iraq.

Shortages can occur by depletion and by governments. In 1986, the U.S. government wrestled with the question of economic sanctions against the government of South Africa for its apartheid policy.

2. *Synthetic materials.* In our quest for lighter-weight products with sophisticated capabilities, we have turned more and more to man-made materials. These compounds, fabrics, and crystalline structures are the materials from which the marvels of high-tech products are made. For example, automobiles will soon boast rust-free outer skins made of laminates of ferrous and nonferrous materials. They will be powered by an engine built around a ceramic engine block. The design and production costs of such esoteric materials are reflected in their higher cost structure. There are, of course, offsets to higher purchase prices. The operating costs of the products are expected to be lower and their capabilities greater.

3. *Inflation.* During 2005, the materials buyer experienced periodic increases as material prices were adjusted upward in response to the rising costs of energy and labor. Managing materials during inflationary periods, or in developing countries with triple-digit inflation, results in decisions that would make little sense in stable environments.

4. *Complex, high-value products.* Management in the auto industry frequently hears the complaint, "They don't make them like they used to." The industry's response is, "If we did, you wouldn't buy them." Consumers demand ever more reliable and capable products. Our cars now have microprocessors to monitor the vehicle's operation and tell us everything we would want to know about the state of the car. There are seat and steering wheel heaters. There's an instrument that tells us how many miles we can travel with the gasoline inventory on board. Another device talks to us telling us to shut doors, buckle up, and so on. Recently, vehicles with a communications link that communicates with an Earth-orbiting satellite tell the driver exactly where they are. Maps are displayed on a computer monitor with a cursor showing instantaneously the location of the car. Not all products are so esoteric, but generally today's products (and those of tomorrow) will utilize more complex materials and components in more configurations with higher degrees of customization. For all these reasons, you should expect no reversal in the trends of increased dollar responsibility and the strategic importance of supply management. Where else is the potential for cost reduction and competitive advantage so great?

POTENTIAL FOR PROFIT

All supply management activities have potential for cost reduction and, hence, increased profit. The purchase of raw materials is used to illustrate what is called the "profit leverage" argument. We might just as easily have used the distribution or production activities. Suppose a firm has an income statement such as that illustrated in Figure 1.6.

FIGURE 1.6
Income Statement Example 1

Sales (000s)	$1,000
Direct materials	500
Direct labor	200
Gross Profit	$300
Selling and administrative expense	250
Net Profit	$50

FIGURE 1.7
Income Statement Example 2

Sales (000s)	$1,000
Direct materials	490 (49% of sales)
Direct labor	200
Gross Profit	$310
Selling and administrative expense	250
Net Profit	$60

At this level of activity, direct materials are (500/1,000) × 100, or 50 percent of sales. Direct labor is 20 percent. Suppose the purchasing manager is able to reduce the cost of materials by 2 percent. Perhaps the manager bargains more skillfully, or substitutes standard materials for custom-made materials. Or perhaps a value analysis program resulted in the purchase of functionally equivalent but less costly materials. Many opportunities exist to reduce the cost of purchases. If the firm's sales remained the same, the effect on profit, given the 2 percent reduction of material cost, would look like that in Figure 1.7. For each $1 reduction of material cost, there is a $1 increase in profit. The ratio is 1:1.

What increase in sales would be necessary to increase profit by $10,000 if material costs were not reduced?

Let x be the required sales; then $0.5x$ is the cost of materials and $0.2x$ is labor cost.

$$\text{Sales} = \text{Variable cost} + \text{Fixed cost} \pm \text{Profit}$$

$$x = 0.5x + 0.2x + 250 + (10 + 50)$$

$$x = \$1{,}033{,}333$$

Sales must be increased by $33,333 to achieve the same $10,000 increase in profit. The ratio is 3.3:1. Depending on the market, and the firm's competitive position, a sales increase of 3.3 percent may be possible only by exerting considerable effort. This is not to say that cost reductions in purchasing are achieved at no cost, but before trying to increase market share, we need to get our operating cost well in hand. Profit efficiency, not market share, should be our first concern.

INTEGRATED SUPPLY MANAGEMENT (ISM)

Whatever the appeal and promise of integrated supply management, achieving integration is a challenge. In firms with conventionally organized subfunctions, supply managers are primarily concerned with satisfying their own subfunctional objective. Purchasing managers minimize purchasing costs; marketing managers minimize distribution costs; and so on. These objectives are local, not systemwide. The decisions of a production-inventory control (PIC) manager may maximize utilization of production equipment, yet poorly serve the requirements of the marketing manager.

The decision of the purchasing manager affects not only the purchasing function but other materials functions. It is the objective of ISM to manage the related considerations. Purchasing should consider the nonpurchasing consequences of its decisions.

Suppose a purchasing manager must decide the order quantity for a material with an annual requirement of 200,000 units. The material is consumed by manufacturing at a constant rate. The unit cost of the material is $1. For transportation purposes, 50,000 units are considered a truckload (TL). Shipments less than 50,000 units are charged at a less-than-truckload (LTL) rate, that is higher per unit.

Asked to state their objectives, the subfunctional managers might respond by saying:

Purchasing manager: "Minimize annual ordering cost."
PIC manager: "Minimize work-in-process inventory."
Traffic manager: "Minimize transportation cost."

If the purchasing manager weighs only the purchasing objective, annual ordering cost is minimized when the annual requirement is ordered once a year. Order cost is the cost to place one order. It is incurred each time an order is placed, or part of an order is scheduled for delivery. Placing a single order for 200,000 units minimizes annual order cost but results in an average inventory of $100,000. We assume no safety stock, and receipt of the material is at the beginning of the year.

Average inventory = (Beginning inventory + Ending inventory)/2
= (200,000)/2
= 100,000 units @ $1 per unit, the average inventory value held is $100,000.

The significance of average inventory is that inventory cost is a function of average inventory. Inventory is an asset. Working capital is tied up in material rather than an alternative asset. Opportunity costs as well as costs of storing, insuring, and handling are incurred when inventory exists.

If the purchasing manager considered PIC's objective (minimize WIP inventory), the order quantities would be 4,000 units, with an order going to the supplier once a week. Assume there are 50 weeks in a year. Because manufacturing requires a uniform flow of material, its weekly requirement is 200,000/50, or 4,000, units per week. The reduction in average inventory when order quantity changes from 200,000 to 4,000 units is offset by the 50-fold increase in annual ordering cost.

To satisfy the traffic manager, the order quantity should be at least 50,000 units. With that quantity, the TL transportation rate applies and transportation costs are minimized. At 50,000 units, the average annual inventory is $25,000 and 200,000/50,000, or 4, orders per year are placed.

Each manager can make a strong case for the order quantity selected. If the purchasing manager ignores the PIC and traffic manager, manufacturing will have to live with a year's supply of material in its stockroom. The purchasing manager should try to quantify the inventory and order costs, and ask about other costs that might be relevant.

Suppose the cost of carrying one unit of material in inventory is $1/year, and that the order cost is $100/order. Assume the transportation rates are $20/CWT LTL and $10/CWT TL. CWT means "hundred weight," that is, 100 pounds. The

FIGURE 1.8
Integration Trade-off Example

	Purchasing Cost	Order Quantity	Average Inventory	Orders/Year
Purchasing	$100	200,000	$100,000	1
PIC	$5,000	4,000	$2,000	50
Distribution	$400	50,000	$25,000	4

weight of the material is 1 pound. In tabular form, the annual costs of the order quantities of 200,000, 4,000, and 50,000 are shown in Figure 1.8.

ANNUAL INVENTORY-ORDERING-TRANSPORTATION COSTS

At least in terms of the costs quantified, and assuming realistic estimates of inventory cost/unit/year, and cost to place an order, the order quantity of 50,000 units minimizes annual costs. A word of caution: There are often costs that have not been identified. For that reason we should not label the sum of the three costs as "total annual cost." Later we'll learn that the criterion for decision making in supply management is "total cost of ownership."

Now, what effects if any does the decision in the preceding example have outside the supply management function? Let's sample the reactions of other functional managers to the decision to order 50,000 units of the material in question.

Manufacturing manager: "Sounds good to me. I always feel good when I've got wall-to-wall inventory, but I don't want to be charged with inventory in the raw storeroom."

The point illustrates the manufacturing manager's knowledge that while he needs to worry about a stockout only four times a year, the cost of manufacturing's security blanket (inventory) can be high.

Controller: "$25,000 worth of inventory on the average is just too much. It ties up working capital and money doesn't grow on trees, you know."

Plant engineer: "Where do you guys plan to store 50,000 units? We're already renting warehouse space across town. Besides, this stuff gets liberated (stolen) if it gets out of our sight."

Sales manager: "I really don't have anything to say. Just don't let manufacturing stock out. Keep the stuff coming off the production line. We have backorders by the tons."

So, you see that a rather routine decision about a purchased item's order quantity affects a variety of non-materials management people. How can the *best* decision be made—one that provides the desired *customer service* at *minimum cost*? In this example, the customers are manufacturing, sales, distribution, the final consumer, and, of course, purchasing, which is the supplier's customer. The costs of satisfactory customer service are only partly identifiable and quantifiable. Our knowledge of the opportunity costs of poor customer service is also incomplete. Yet decisions must be made while recognizing that systemwide decision criteria are:

1. Multiple
2. Complex
3. Conflicting

Supply management is a developing discipline and an area of management specialization. Measures of customer service are usually expressed in terms of the *availability* of material. Did the plant ship on time? Was the product on the shelf when the customer entered the shop? While important, availability is only one dimension of customer service.

Purchasing, inventory control, and distribution do not have detailed cost classification and accounting procedures. In manufacturing, we have a history of cost accounting going back to the turn of the century. Elaborate techniques are used to relate costs to output levels. Costs are segregated into variable and fixed portions. Budgeting for manufacturing is done with precision using resource standards produced by work measurement methods perfected many decades ago. Tell us what you want to produce and we'll tell you exactly what amounts of resources you'll need—direct materials, manufacturing supplies, tooling, machining time, setup, and so on.

Standard costs of production are the basis for operating budgets, product prices, and control of production costs. Such is not the case in purchasing, marketing, and transportation. As these areas develop, purchasing and distribution cost accounting will become part of the accounting-information system. Standard costs to create the *time* and *place* utilities will be calculable. Budgeting for materials management activities will have the detail and reliability of budgeting in manufacturing. When supply management costs become more visible, their control becomes more feasible.

ORGANIZING FOR PURCHASING

Supply coordination involves both *structure* and *design* of the organization. Purchasing organizational *structure* is the sum total of the ways in which an organization divides its labor into distinct tasks and then coordinates among them. Organizational *design* is concerned with bringing together a group of interrelated tasks for a common goal. However, organization design alone does not ensure effectiveness or efficiency. It is a well-known fact that most companies' organizational charts do not reflect true lines of authority and responsibility that flow through managers. Too much detail can lead to micro management. On the other hand, a loosely designed organizational structure can lead to a greater risk.

In any purchasing organization, two major problems must first be considered. The first issue, where should the purchasing functions be located in the organization? Second, what level of authority should the purchasing function have? Given the evolution of outsourcing, the purchasing function is expected to gain more authority in the corporate hierarchy.

CENTRALIZED VERSUS DECENTRALIZED PURCHASING

The first issue deals with centralized purchasing of decentralized functions. Centralized purchasing involves coordinating all purchasing activities for the entire plant through one central location. That purchasing department is the only place in the firm where requisitions are processed and suppliers are selected. Decentralized purchasing authority and responsibility for supply-related functions are disposed throughout the organization.

Advantages of Centralized Purchasing

In most cases, centralized purchasing results in lower costs because of the availability of purchase quantity discounts. If all material uses are coordinated into one major purchase, the supplier will work harder to service the buying firm. Large dollar purchase quantities equal buying power. Most manufacturing firms spend more than 70 percent of their total revenue on purchasing materials and component parts. Thus, the effectiveness of a centralized organizational design will have a significant impact on profit. As an example, consider a firm that has several departments that use similar components; they could actually compete against each other for scarce material, resulting in higher prices for each department.

Centralized purchasing promotes the effective use of purchasing professionals because it allows the supply manager more authority and credibility. Each buyer can easily become an expert on associated buys (commodities and noncommodities). Expertise will be developed when there is a critical mass. GM, Dell, Walmart, and IBM all use centralized purchasing and have in-house expertise ranging from engine parts to rental cars to office equipment to pharmaceuticals.

Centralized purchasing enables the buying firm to do a better job of monitoring various changes throughout the industry. Centralized purchasing also lends itself to periodic (1) reviews of purchasing activities, (2) evaluation of suppliers, and (3) development of purchasing training programs. In decentralized purchasing operations, these important strategic activities may not be accomplished.

Centralized purchasing is preferred from the suppliers' point of view. The selling firm can easily determine whom to call on. This will improve efficiency for both parties.

According to a recent Center for Advanced Procurement and Supply (CAPS) study, 59 percent of the firms used a combination centralized–decentralized structure and 28 percent used centralized purchasing. Only 13 percent of the firms responding used decentralized purchasing.

Disadvantages of Centralized Purchasing

There are several arguments against centralization. Most of the resistance is from companies where there are decentralized profit centers. The three main arguments are given below:

1. **High engineering involvement in procurement decision making.** At the early stages of product development, engineering needs to be deeply involved with the design, which can be different with remotely located centralized purchasing.
2. **High need to coordinate purchased parts with production schedules.** This is especially applicable when small amounts are ordered frequently. The supplying firm must be within close geographical proximity or guarantee JIT deliveries. It may not be cost-effective to have centralized purchasing operations in some JIT situations.
3. **High need to buy from local community.** Sometimes it makes good political sense for firms to make purchases in the community where the plant is located.

Because of the profit-leveraging effect, profit center managers feel the need to control purchasing if they are to be held accountable for profits.

Advantages of Decentralized Purchasing

Decentralized purchasing provides for a more streamlined procedure since the department manager's purchasing needs and thus decisions can be made immediately.

TABLE 1.1 The Degree of Centralization Impacts on Purchasing Success

	Completely Decentralized Purchasing System	Hybrid Purchasing System	Centralized Purchasing System
Advantages	Business responsiveness	Business responsiveness, increased leverage, some processes	Increased cost savings, enhanced talent management, consistent processes
Disadvantages	Loss of leverage, lack of consistent sourcing process	Priority given to business requirements, difficult to control and coordinate activities	Significant focus on cost savings, less focus on business requirements
Example Organizations	Heavy highway construction	Universities	Major retailers, automotive manufacturers, and technology

As an example, if a manager needs to purchase 10 laptops for the business unit, the unit manager can easily make the purchase online or from a local computer store.

Disadvantages of Decentralized Purchasing

The disadvantages of decentralized purchasing are duplication of effort in buying, receiving, inspection, and accounts payable. Decentralized purchasing also prevents the buying organization from taking advantage of volume discounts.

Centralized/Decentralized Hybrid Purchasing Systems

Some organizations adopt a hybrid system that combines both centralized and decentralized purchasing. They use centralized purchasing for larger organization-wide contracts, but give individual business units autonomy to make small purchases for their departments or subsidiaries. Table 1.1 summarizes the three approaches.

THE FUTURE ORGANIZATION CONCEPT

The future outlook is that the majority of significant dollar-valued purchases will continue to be centralized. This trend also will be the result of increased computer-based management information systems. As firms become lean, centralized purchasing will become a major focus. Long-term agreements will be more frequently negotiated to stabilize prices. Honda of America is an excellent example of a firm that uses centralized procurement as a competitive weapon. Approximately 75 percent of the sales dollar for each automobile manufactured in Marysville, Ohio, is purchased from Japanese firms. Moreover, as multinational firms continue to expand and grow, the host government's national interest will increasingly become the focal point of a firm's procurement strategies. An example of geographically centralized purchasing is given in Table 1.2.

TABLE 1.2 Centralized Purchasing Examples

A Fortune 500 appliance company is a good example of a company that has great difficulty in centralizing purchasing on a geographical basis. The company has many plants throughout the country. Although each plant makes electrical products, the product lines are diverse. As a result, the company has relatively few common suppliers, and those are widely separated geographically.

In some cases, national pricing contracts have been negotiated on a centralized basis for common items that can be utilized by the individual plants as they see fit, particularly where the vendor has several plants nationwide and can provide adequate delivery. Such items are relatively few, however, and are of a supply rather than a production nature. In no case are actual purchase orders placed from the central location in Cincinnati. At one time, machine tools were purchased in this manner. This practice was later abandoned because of objections by manufacturing.

Even when several plants are located in the same local geographical area, their requirements could be so specialized that they would often prefer to do their own purchasing.

On the other hand, the Columbus, Ohio, plant operates with a centralized purchasing department handling the buying of all raw materials, fabricated component parts, and maintenance repair and operating (MRO) items for four product lines:

Refrigerators and freezers
Room air conditioners
Specialty product (dishwashers)
Compressors

Each division had its own manufacturing, engineering, and sales departments, all reporting to a general manager. Production control reported to the manufacturing manager in each case. Purchasing reported to the general manager.

REPORTING ASSIGNMENT

The status of the purchasing professional in an organization is determined by the capacity structure. In the majority of the Fortune 500 firms, the purchasing professional reports directly to the manufacturing vice president. This is also true for medium-sized firms. In order to be effective, the purchasing function should never report to another major line activity. If this occurs, the purchasing professional does not have the appropriate authority to make a difference. Of course, the reporting structure must be consistent with the capabilities of the specific person in each position. The purchasing organizational structure also should be different for service-based firms. Purchasing services will be addressed in Chapter 18.

A recent Center for Strategic Supply Management (CAPS) study found that in 16 percent of the firms surveyed, purchasing managers report directly to the president. However, in the majority of the firms, the purchasing manager report directly to the V.P. of Manufacturing/Operations. In smaller firms, more than one-third of the purchasing professionals report to the V.P. of Manufacturing. What's more, in firms with sales between $5.1 and $10 billion, 61 percent report to either the President or Executive V.P.

THE SUPPLY MANAGEMENT CONCEPT

The supply management concept is a formal organizational concept that is involved with the flow of materials through a manufacturing firm. The functional areas affected include (1) purchasing, (2) inventory control, (3) traffic, (4) production control,

Careers in Purchasing

Now is the best time for the next generation of managers to pursue a career in purchasing and supply management. Supply management professionals must possess a diverse skill set. First, the successful supply manager must have excellent technology, people, and negotiations skills in order to add value to his or her organization. Supply professionals must also be analytical problem solvers. In today's global business arena, supply management professionals must be able to interact with potential sources of materials and services throughout the world.

ISM SALARY STUDY

The average salary for a supply management professional is $112,404. One of the major factors affecting salary and professional achievement continues to be education. Those with a bachelor's degree earned an average of $99,490, while the average for those with a master's degree was $134,458. Among all degree holders, average salaries were highest for respondents with a technical/engineering degree. They reported an average salary of $126,013.

An increasing number of supply management professionals are earning salaries that exceed $100,000. Almost one-third of the respondents to a 2012 ISM salary survey reported earning a six-figure salary. The median salary was $900,000, with the highest salary exceeded $682,000. Most entry-level (less than 3 years) supply management reported an average of $69,350. The purchasing and supply management salary drivers are job title, experience, education, credentials, annual spend, gender, and size of the organization. A summary of the results of the 2012 ISM salary survey is shown in Table 1.3.

TABLE 1.3 2012 Salary Summary

Overall average for supply management profession	$ 112,404
Average for those with five or fewer years of experience	$ 74,911
Average for those with BS/BA in business	$109,298
Average for those with CPSM certification	$107,534
Average for those with a master's degree	$131,458

Source: *ISM 2012 Salary Survey Results.*

For a more comprehensive discussion of purchasing and supply management career opportunities, see www.ism.ws/CareerCenter.

and (5) stores, as shown in Figure 1.9. Approximately 70 percent of the firms surveyed have adopted the supply management concept. The overwhelming acceptance of the supply management concept has created a need for more technical and managerial sophistication from the supply manager.

Some emerging organization structure examples of the trend toward the supply management concept are given in Figure 1.9. A common feature of all the organizational examples is that people support and adjust the process using technology to increase throughput.

The examples in this section are by no means conclusive. In summary, designing an organizational structure is dependent upon:

- The kind and quality of information it gathers from its customers, suppliers, and partners:
  - How the company gathers the information.
  - How it interacts with each of these constituents.
- How this information flows through the organizational structures:
  - Who has access to it and who doesn't.
  - How the information is utilized in making decisions.
  - How the information is stored for ease of use and analyzed.
- Whether both the organizational processes and systems reflect and mirror information flow.

FIGURE 1.9
Organizational Examples

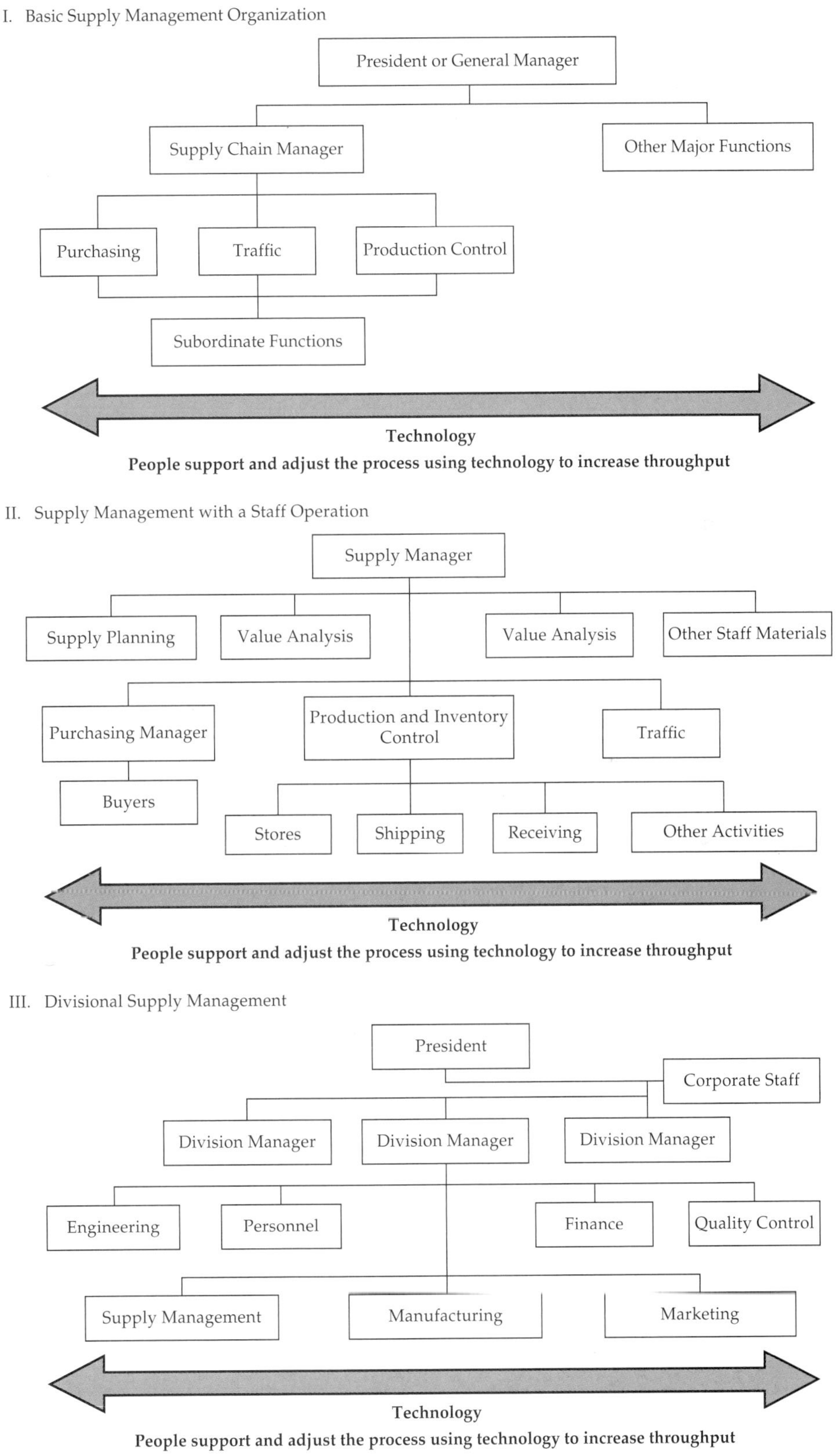

PROFESSIONALISM AND PURCHASING AND SUPPLY MANAGEMENT

As supply chains continue to grow globally, and as products become more complex, the supply chain professional must become more sophisticated. Supply management professionals across all industry sectors must become major players in the organization's decision-making process.

The Institute of Supply Management offers three professional certifications. They are the Certified Professional in Supply Management (CPSM), the Certified Supply Management (CSM), and the Certified Professional Supplier Diversity (CPSD). The CPSM and CSM are similar in that they require the same level of managerial and technical knowledge. The knowledge base for both certifications focuses on effective decision making in an integrated supply management operating environment. Specifically the knowledge base includes financial analysis, strategic sourcing, and international regulations. There are more than 3,700 professionals that have been certified as CPSMs and CSMs. The CPSD was established in 2010. The primary purpose of the CSPD is to show that the organization is committed to diversity throughout the company's supply chain. The 2012 ISM salary survey shows that the average salary for the CPSM credential was $107,534 compared to $99,740 for those without the CPSM designation. A summary of the three professional credentials is given in Figure 1.10.

FIGURE 1.10 A Snapshot of Requirements for ISM's Professional Credentials

	CPSM®	CSM™		CPSD™	
Education Requirement	Bachelor's degree from a regionally accredited institution or international equivalent	No degree requirement	Associate's degree from a regionally accredited institution or international equivalent	No degree requirement	Bachelor's degree from a regionally accredited institution or international equivalent
Experience Requirement	3 years of full-time professional supply management experience (nonclerical, nonsupport)	5 years of full-time professional supply management experience (nonclerical, nonsupport)	3 years of full-time professional supply management experience (nonclerical, nonsupport) with associate's degree	5 years of professional (nonclerical, nonsupport) supplier diversity or supply management experience	3 years of professional (nonclerical, nonsupport) supplier diversity or supply management experience
Testing Requirements	Pass the three CPSM® Exams or, if you are a CPM in good standing, pass the Bridge Exam	Pass the three CSM™ Exams or, if you are a CPM in good standing, pass the Bridge Exam		Pass two Exams—the CPSD™ Exam and CPSM® or CSM™ Exam 1	

Source: *Supply Chain Management*, April 2012.

THE INSTITUTE OF SUPPLY MANAGEMENT EXCELLENCE AWARD

Each year the ISM recognizes organizations that exhibit outstanding achievements within the supply management profession. The winning organizations are recognized in four categories: technology, process, organization/structure, and sustainability. A brief description of each category is given below:

1. **Technology.** Innovative technology is recognized where technology is the key driver and source of substantial contribution to organizational success that is new to the field of supply management.
2. **Process.** Innovation in transforming a supply-related process such as sourcing or supplier relationships, strategic cost management, quality, inventory, transportation, and project management in ways that are new and performance enhancing for the supply management field.
3. **Organization/Structure.** Innovations in organizational change that demonstrate new and more effective supply management roles.
4. **Sustainability.** Excellence and innovation in implementing an organization's sustainability program, including principles of social responsibility.

The 2012 ISM Leaders in Supply Management Excellence are given below:

1. Award category: Technology
   Winner: IBM
   Website: www.ibm.com
   Revenue: U.S. $106.9 billion (full year 2011)
   Number of employees worldwide: 400,000
   Company description: IBM invents and integrates hardware, software, and services to help forward-thinking enterprises, institutions, and people succeed on a smarter planet.
   Project focus: Supply assurance of IBM's multitier supply chain.
   Key successes: Deployment of a global tool and management process to aggregate, monitor, and analyze supply at all levels and nodes in the supply chain; use of the tool to effectively manage supply disruptions.
   Key individuals: Joanne Wright, vice president, global demand and supply management; Claudio Cereda, CPMT project coordinator; Martin Ball, supplier data integration; Ken Rudner, global component supply assurance; Don Journey, consulting supply chain manager.
2. Award category: Sustainability
   Winner: T-Mobile USA, Inc.
   Website: www.t-mobile.com
   Revenue: Service revenues of U.S. $4.67 billion in the third quarter of 2011
   Number of employees worldwide: 42,000
   Company description: Based in Bellevue, Washington, T-Mobile USA, Inc. is the U.S. wireless operation of Deutsche Telekom AG (OTCOX: DTEGY). By the end of the third quarter of 2011, approximately 129 million mobile customers were served by the mobile communication segments of the Deutsche Telekom group—33.7 million by T-Mobile USA—all via a common technology platform.

Multiple independent research studies continue to rank T-Mobile USA among the highest in numerous regions throughout the United States in wireless customer care and call quality.

Project focus: Inventory reduction and associated cash flow release.

Key successes: (1) Closed the ecosystem and now have cradle-to-grave control of handsets and (2) insurance utilization.

Key individuals: Chris Newell, vice president, logistics; Dennis Pettit, director, reverse logistics; Nancy Yee, director, aftermarket services; Scott Carlson, senior manager, demand planning; Michelle Gross, senior manager, analytics; Brian Stoltz, senior manager, supply planning; Kevin Sweeney, senior manager, vendor management.

3. Award category: Process

   Winner: Cisco Systems, Inc.

   Website: www.cisco.com

   Revenue: U.S. $44 billion

   Number of employees worldwide: 64,000

   Company description: Founded in 1984, Cisco Systems is the worldwide leader in networking—transforming how people connect, communicate, and collaborate.

   Project focus: Understanding that Cisco's global supply chain risk exposure was broad and pervasive, the Supply Chain Risk Management (SCRM) team was formed to develop and implement processes to mitigate potential risks from new product introduction through sourcing, manufacture, test, and delivery. As part of this mandate, SCRM also orchestrates incident management teams to ensure measured and effective mitigations of actual supply chain disruptions.

   Key successes: SCRM's embedded end-to-end resiliency processes delivered results through various crises that threatened supply chains worldwide. During the financial crisis from late 2008 to mid-2010, SCRM analytics revealed that five critical suppliers faced high-risk disruptions. "Last-time buys" and second sourcing options were instituted so that Cisco was not impacted when all five of the suppliers eventually filed for bankruptcy. During the first 70 days of the 2011 Japan earthquake and tsunami, Cisco was able to mitigate impacts to its supply base, ensure minimal disruption to customer orders, and avoid a large potential revenue exposure stemming from the crisis.

   Key individuals: John O'Connor, senior director, business transformation, supply chain operations; James Steele, program director, supply chain risk management, supply chain operations.

4. Award category: Organization/Structure

   Winner: The American Red Cross

   Website: www.redcross.org

   Revenue: Not-for-profit

   Number of employees worldwide: 29,000 full-time and part-time employees, and more than 500,000 volunteers

   Number of supply management employees worldwide: 60

   Company description: Largest U.S.-based nonprofit humanitarian organization.

   Project focus: Reinvent and implement a new supply chain management focus and process within a major nonprofit organization.

Key successes: New organizational structure creating synergy with the business units; a simplified way to work with clients and suppliers; and savings in excess of U.S. $40 million for the first two years in operation.

Key individuals: Jill Bossi, CPM, vice president, and CPO; Charles Yopp, senior director, disaster and chapter sourcing and procurement; Pam Baxter, director, enterprise sourcing and SCM services; Robert Kloak, director, biomedical sourcing; Marshall Ellis, director, real estate management; Jeff Yingling, senior director, technology sourcing.

Summary

In this new millennium, the global impact of the purchasing process for individual firms will be revolutionary. The purchasing function is quickly becoming one of the most important contributions to profitability. The "professional purchasing position" is now a viable career path. To become a competitive strategic weapon, purchasing has abandoned the fragmented approaches of the past. The purchasing function is an integral part of the transformation of raw materials and component parts into finished goods by utilizing materials, systems, information, and people.

Purchasing organization design concepts also were presented. In any purchasing organization, two major problems must be considered. The primary decision has to do with where the purchasing function should be located in the organization, and the second consideration is what level of authority the purchasing function should have. Career opportunities and salary data for purchasing professionals also were presented.

Critical to the implementation of integrated supply management is the issue of *business strategy*. Purchasing actions designed to reinforce the firm's competitive priorities can give the firm advantages over its competitors. In essence, firms must design their purchasing actions to emphasize the competitive strategy. A framework for linking purchasing decisions with the firm's competitive strategy will be presented in Chapter 2.

Discussion Questions

1. Compare and contrast the two unique types of purchasing categories in the business world.
2. The purchasing function can easily make a contribution to profitability. Please discuss this statement. What is the profit leverage effect of purchasing?
3. What is meant by "materials management"?
4. What is meant by "supply management"?
5. Describe how purchasing interacts with other functional areas of the firm.
6. Discuss the issue of centralization versus decentralization as it applies to the purchasing function. What are the advantages of centralized purchasing organizations? What are the disadvantages of centralized purchasing?
7. Discuss the specific objectives of purchasing and supply management. Relate these to (1) the automobile industry, (2) a hospital, and (3) a pizza shop.
8. What are some of the careers in purchasing?
9. What are the most well-known professional purchasing associations?

Suggested Cases

Austin Wood Products
Advanced Computer Logic
Carter Systems Canada, Inc.
Great Lakes University

Reference

Srivastava, R., and W. C. Benton Jr. "Purchase Quantity Discounts and Open Order Rescheduling in an Assemble-to-Order Environment: The Hidden Economic Tradeoffs." *European Journal of Operational Research* 110 (1998), pp. 261–71.

Chapter Two

Purchasing Decisions and Business Strategy

Learning Objectives

1. Explain the role of purchasing in corporate strategy.
2. List and explain the most important elements of the strategic planning process for purchasing.
3. Name the components of purchasing strategy.
4. Explain how sourcing is integrated into corporate strategy.
5. Discuss how purchasing strategy is linked to other functional areas.
6. Understand the impact of purchasing decisions on supply chain management.
7. Explain how the sourcing audit can be used to formulate purchasing objectives and strategy.
8. Discuss the supply chain relationship pegging analysis.
9. Learn how to develop a strategic purchasing plan.

INTRODUCTION

Purchasing can play a significant role in making a firm competitive. Purchased inputs constitute a large portion of the company's resources. In most industrial firms, material constitutes 60–80 percent of the total revenue dollars. Purchased inputs offer a potential source for helping a company develop leverage against its competitors. Purchasing actions designed to reinforce the firm's competitive priorities can give the firm advantages over its competitors. In essence, firms must design their purchasing actions to emphasize the competitive strategy.

In this chapter, a framework for linking purchasing decisions with the firm's competitive strategy is presented. Alternate purchasing strategies can be formulated by selecting a unique combination of purchasing actions. The framework offers a systematic approach for designing purchasing strategies consistent with a firm's competitive strategy. This chapter also shows how decision makers can operationalize the linkages between competitive strategy and purchasing decisions.

FIGURE 2.1
Purchasing Strategy Framework

Decision Areas	Decisions	Alternatives
Supply management	Number location	Single or multiple source, close or geographically dispersed
	Size	Small versus large
	Managerial expertise	High or low
	Financial health	High or low
	Amount of purchase	Restrict to a certain percentage of supplier's output or no constraint
	Engineering	Developmental versus experienced supplier
	Length of contract	Long term (annual or larger) or short term
	Relationship	Strategic versus commodity focused
	Extent of computerization	Manual versus information systems
	Communication (integration)	Share production plan versus nonsharing
	Value engineering	Active program versus no program
Buying	Criteria	Cost, quality, delivery or lead time, perceived delivery reliability or reputation
	Purchasing scale	Economies of scale (cost/volume) or economies of scope (joint replenishment)
	Ordering policy	Integrated with supplier information system or nonintegration
Supplier development	New product or substitute product development	Develop supplier or look for new sources
Scope of manufacturing activity	Degree of integration	Make versus buy, outsourcing

Purchasing and Competitive Strategy Linkage

In today's turbulent supply markets, purchasing professionals are expected to develop options that can help business units remain competitive. In doing so, purchasing managers need to devise purchasing actions such that they are consistent with each other and with the firm's competitive strategy. The framework for purchasing strategy given in Figure 2.1 proposes a way of linking the competitive strategy with the purchasing policy. The components and linkages for purchasing strategy are given in Figure 2.2. Competitive priorities are one means of articulating a firm's competitive strategy. The competitive priorities are a key determinant of the importance given to different criteria in purchasing material. However, the purchasing criteria also are influenced by individual buyer performance and reward criteria. The competitive priorities define the intended or desired purchase criteria and the reward criteria determine how closely the objectives are met.

FIGURE 2.2
Components of Purchasing Strategy

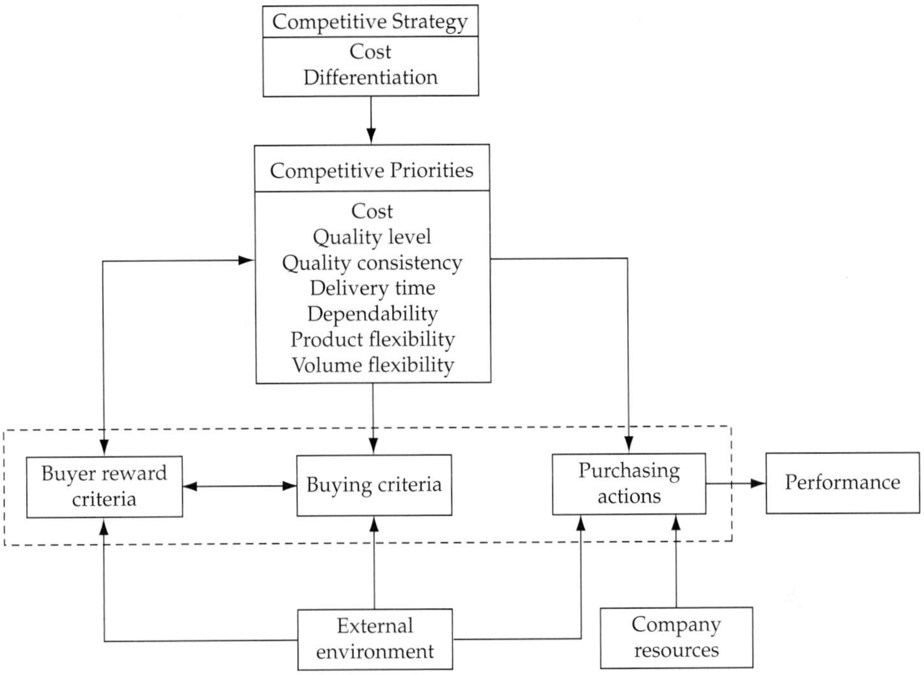

The purchasing decisions or actions that constitute purchasing strategy are determined by the firm's competitive priorities, its resource capabilities, and the environment. In the formulation of purchasing strategy, the organization's competitive priorities, the organization's strengths and weaknesses, and the competitive environment must be considered.

COMPETITIVE STRATEGY

A firm can compete in two broad alternate ways. It can either seek competitive advantages on cost or choose to differentiate itself from its competitors on some attributes of the product or in the way it markets its product. The notion of two generic competitive advantages—cost and differentiation—is important but too broad to be useful for management faced with day-to-day decision making. The competitive strategy is articulated in terms of competitive priorities. Key environmental factors also must be considered.

As an example, low-cost strategies generally imply more product standardization, less flexibility in responding to customer demands, fewer options, acceptable quality, and continuous process technology. A low-cost strategy is mostly concerned with market penetration with a high-volume, low-cost product. On the other hand, a product differentiation strategy is concerned with providing the customer with more selection, which implies higher costs and prices. The higher costs are a result of higher material cost and skilled labor costs. The higher service levels expected also lead to increased finished goods inventories. The impact of purchasing/manufacturing on inventory is given in Figure 2.3.

FIGURE 2.3
Purchasing Strategy and Inventory Investment

Strategy	Inventory Classification			
	Raw Materials and Parts	Work in Progress	Finished Goods	Spare Parts
Low cost—make to stock	Low	Low	Medium	Low
Narrow product line—make to stock	Low	Low	Medium	Medium
Wide product line—make to stock	Medium/high	Medium	Medium	High
Rapid customer response with customized product	High	Low	None	Low
Level production for seasonal demand	Low	Low	High/low	High/low
Quick spare part response	Low	Low	—	High

COMPETITIVE PRIORITIES

The competitive priorities operationalize the firm's competitive strategy. The two generic competitive advantages—delivery speed and reliability—are operationalized in terms of cost, quality performance, quality conformity, product flexibility, volume flexibility, and customer service. By assigning priorities to these dimensions, the firm operationalizes its strategy. The priorities can then be used to generate alternatives that are consistent with the firm's competitive strategy. A company competing on cost should drive the overall costs down. On the other hand, a firm competing on differentiation must devise its actions that enhance its uniqueness on quality or on flexibility or on customer service or on any combination of the three. (See Tables 2.1 and 2.2.)

TABLE 2.1
Cost and Differentiation Strategies

	Cost	Differentiation
Purchasing criteria	Low cost/unit Consistent quality Short lead time Dependable delivery	High quality Short lead time Dependable delivery Unit cost based on freight rates
Bargaining basis	Economies of scale	Economies of scope
Supplier	Multiple suppliers	One or few suppliers
Supplier size	Suppliers with moderate/ large capacities	Suppliers with moderate/ small capacities

TABLE 2.2
Environmental Factors

1. Inflation rate
2. Monetary policy
3. Fiscal policies
4. Technological development
5. Industry capacity
6. Market growth
7. Global stability

PURCHASING CRITERIA

The criteria in buying material must reflect firms' competitive priorities. A firm competing on cost must give high priority to purchasing costs. A firm competing on flexibility must give high priority to lead time in buying material. With short lead times, the company can be more flexible; it can develop the ability to respond to changing situations quickly. Lead times are also important in achieving superior customer service. Suppliers with short lead times and who are reliable in meeting their due dates minimize the problem of material shortages for the manufacturer; as a result, the company's production can be more dependable in meeting the customers' due dates. A company emphasizing customer service will need to carry more inventory to buffer against uncertainties, if the supplier is unreliable. Inventory is an expensive alternative. Purchasing decision makers must consider the firm's competitive priorities in choosing the criteria on which the material is purchased.

The criteria on which the buyer's performance is evaluated can influence the effectiveness of purchasing actions and effectiveness in making the firm competitive. Cost variance seems to be the dominant criterion in evaluating performance of purchasing decision makers. This emphasis on cost can drive purchasing decision makers to take actions that keep material costs low, but other criteria may be neglected, and the purchasing actions may end up being inconsistent with the competitive strategy. The reward criteria determine the firm's actual priorities. The closer the reward criteria reflect the performance on the competitive priorities, the narrower the gap will be between intended and realized objectives. If reward criteria emphasize cost, purchasing decision makers will emphasize cost in making decisions, irrespective of the competitive priority.

SUPPLY CHAIN STRATEGY

As competitive forces increase, customers demand better products, faster delivery, increased service, and decreased costs. As firms become more competitive, a rippling effect is experienced by the suppliers. As a result of increased competition, deregulation, and relaxed antitrust requirements, the supplier partnerships concept has emerged as a competitive weapon. Other secondary reasons for partnerships are the increased use of electronic data interchange (EDI) and just-in-time (JIT) manufacturing. In theory, the newly developed "partnership concept" is adequate; however, in practice, partnerships may result in one-way power moves. One partner usually gains the flexibility and efficiency of quickly responding to the changing marketplace; the weaker partner is left with higher inventories and unstable schedules. As inventory levels are reduced throughout the supply chain,

FIGURE 2.4
Major Characteristics of Industrial Buyer/Seller Relationships

Source: Ellram (1991).

Factor	Open-Market	Partnership	Vertical Integration
Degree of risk/reward	Minimize risk, maximize rewards	Manage/share risk and reward	Absorb or manage risk and reward internally
Relationships	Single contract between firms	Multiple contracts/ levels	Multiple contracts/ levels
Information	Limited—only as needed for transaction	As required for planning, output, processes, technology	Fully integrated
Planning	Short term—transaction	Long term—ongoing	Long term—ongoing
Asset ownership	Completely separate	May be shared, or some financial commitment	Fully owned

each member becomes less insulated from demand variation. As defined by Maloni and Benton (2000):

> . . . the power of a supply chain member [is] the ability to control the decision variables in the supply strategy of another member in a given chain at a different level of the supply chain. It should be different from the influenced member's original level of control over their own supply strategy.

Thus, supplier partnerships are not always beneficial for both buyer and seller.

These new supplier/customer relationships require trust and commitment by both parties, which is in direct contrast to their historical relationships that have been far from cooperative. Traditional purchasing attitudes have always encouraged arm's-length relationships with price as the dominant buying factor. Today, supplier partnerships look for a more cooperative attitude between parties. Although many companies are claiming to be interested in supplier partnerships, the effectiveness of these proposed arrangements is just beginning to be studied.

Companies participate in a variety of supplier relationships and take on a variety of roles. Each company can be a supplier, customer, or end-user of products. As presented in Figure 2.4, supplier partnerships can be categorized using five factors: (1) degree of risk/reward, (2) type of relationship, (3) information, (4) planning, and (5) asset ownership.

The characteristics of buyer-seller relationships exist on a continuum beginning with the traditional approach of *open-market*, with a single short-term contract that presents minimal risk to both parties. The opposite extreme is *vertical integration*, where the parties are fully integrated as one unit. *Partnerships* are a hybrid of these extremes with each party retaining an individual identity. A long-term relationship provides the ability to share assets and integrate planning, technology, and processes. *In theory*, partnership members equally share risks and rewards.

Since supplier-customer relationships have historically been categorized by open-market characteristics, this often-adversarial relationship may be difficult to circumvent when developing a partnership. The movement from one extreme to another requires great trust and cooperation of the parties. This comfort level can be more easily obtained by understanding the dynamics of the relationship, the inherent risks and benefits to each party, and by safeguarding the individual partners from undue burdens or compensation. A real-world example is given in Figure 2.5.

FIGURE 2.5
A Partnership Example

PPG Industries established what came to be known as "Supply City" in Lake Charles, Louisiana, next to its Chemical Plant. This complex consists of nine noncompeting suppliers who supply the plant on a JIT basis with high-use maintenance, repair, and operating (MRO) inventory items.

Before Supply City, the Lake Charles facility operated a warehouse for spare parts and MRO items. This warehouse was linked throughout the plant by computers with item users. Users would order supplies needed through the computer. Orders were printed out in the warehouse and stock pickers would pick the material, load it onto a truck, and deliver it on a prescheduled basis throughout the plant. This system operated effectively; however, operating cost and inventory levels were high. In an attempt to reduce cost and lower inventory levels, the Supply City idea was executed. This new system would set up a supplier stocking program and establish a supplier complex in one location next to the Lake Charles plant.

Supply City is an industrial park created by PPG next to the Lake Charles Chemical Plant. The suppliers in the facility signed five-year agreements ensuring continuity of supply and minimum levels of performance. PPG's side of the contract outlines commodity groups for each supplier, stock levels, pricing, and delivery schedules. These contracts ensure a full scope of commitment from both sides while guaranteeing sales volumes for each supplier.

The Supply City stocking program operates within the existing plant stock-picking warehousing systems. Each supplier is connected to the plant computer system. When plant personnel place an order for an item supplied from Supply City, the order is printed out in the supplier's office instead of the plant warehouse. The supplying firm then retrieves the item and places it on the dock to be delivered to the plant with the next scheduled shipment. The item is then delivered to the plant receiving dock and is immediately transferred to the end-user. This system eliminates duplicate stock storage and handling from middleman stock pickers. Each supplier is paid electronically every two weeks, eliminating invoicing.

In the first two years of operation, Supply City allowed the Lake Charles plant to eliminate 45–50 percent of its plant inventory, resulting in a savings of $3 million. Stock-outs were reduced to 3 percent. In addition, administrative costs were reduced through elimination of POs and invoices, procurement time was reduced, quality was improved through the reduction of suppliers, and the close proximity of technical personnel improved supplier technical and material application support. These savings and improvements can be transferred directly to PPG customers in the form of improved product quality, reduced cycle time to market allowing for quick adjustment to customer demands, and reduced costs for the final products.

SUPPLY CHAIN RELATIONSHIP QUALITY

In dynamic business-to-business environments, maintaining a competitive advantage is a major survival factor. The advent of supply chain management has led to a more complicated operating environment. Not only does the individual firm have to maintain its competitive edge; the entire supply chain must be competitive. Supply relationship quality indexing can be used to drive continuous improvement in competitive supply chains. The individual members of the supply chain cannot function without the economic, quality, and service performance of the other supply chain members. The quality of the relationships between each supply chain member will determine which firms survive in a competitive environment. Many manufacturing firms consider the relationship between themselves and their ultimate customers more important than the relationship between themselves and their suppliers. In the next section, we present the various phases of a competitive ranking system in order to determine how supplying firms evaluate manufacturers (buyers) as customers.

Supply Chain Relationship Quality Indexing Example

The purpose of supply chain relationship quality indexing is to drive the supply chain toward continuous improvement. Each member (i.e., suppliers, buying organizations, customers) of the supply chain is a stakeholder. The objective is to provide a valued product or service to the ultimate stakeholder, the customer, as shown in Figure 2.6.

As can be seen in Figure 2.6, the customer is the endpoint in the value chain. The challenge facing the manufacturer is deciding how to increase the value of the supply chain without sacrificing the interests of the ultimate customer or the various suppliers in the supply chain. *Supply chain relationship quality indexing* is a methodology that may provide the manufacturer with the information needed to make the hard decisions about balancing the needs of the buying organization and the needs of the supply chain itself. The ultimate customer's expectations of performance may not be consistent with the manufacturer's or supplier's expectations. The customer is interested in cost, quality, satisfaction, service, and delivery performance. The customer will engage competing manufacturers and supply chains if their expectations are not met. On the other hand, supplying firms may be just as critical for the manufacturer's survival as the ultimate customer. There is a trend toward outsourcing a larger share of the sales dollar to suppliers. Thus, it is not easy to replace a strategic supplier. In a supply chain environment, changing suppliers can have an adverse effect on the value creation process. More importantly the supplier may choose to service manufacturer B and sever the relationship with manufacturer A (see Figure 2.6). The change in suppliers could easily have a negative impact on the desires and expectations of the ultimate customer. As shown in Figure 2.6, in a supply chain environment, the manufacturer is the suppliers' customer.

Because of the increasing importance of supplier relationship management, many buying firms are implementing supplier relationship management strategies in their business plans to ensure that they maintain their competitive edge. This is especially true in an oligopolistic environment where supplying firms are members of competing supply chain networks. This supply chain relationship disparity is the motivation for the current supplier relationship quality (SRQ) indexing. SRQ indexing seeks to assess the supplier-buyer relationship from the supplier's point of view. Specifically, SRQ indexing is concerned with the extent to which cooperation, trust, commitment, satisfaction, and performance expectations

FIGURE 2.6
Typical Supply Chain Network

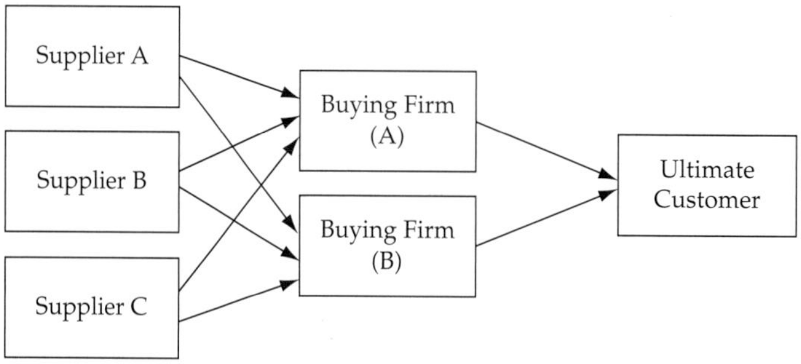

TABLE 2.3
Cumulative Market Share in 2012

Source: *The Wall Street Journal*, August 4, 2012.

Manufacturer	Vehicles Sold in the U.S. Market	Percentage of Total	Cumulative Percentage
GM	1,757,470	18.7	18.7
Ford	1,510,614	15.3	34
Toyota	1,399,514	14.7	48.7
Chrysler	1,108,629	11.6	60.3
Honda	949,347	10.2	70.5
Nissan	774,577	7.7	78.2
Hyundai	479,789	4.8	83
VW	286,751	3.2	86.2
Mazda	185,349	1.7	87.9
Audi	75,256	0.9	88.8
Mitsubishi	41,316	0.3	89.1
Other	1,142,432	10.9	100
Total	9,711,044	100	100

influence the relationship between supplying and buying firms competing in the same industry. An example of the SRQ indexing process for the automobile industry is illustrated in Appendix A, offering insight into the development processes of effective SRQ supplier-buyer relationships.

Critical issues addressed by SRQ quality indexing will provide the purchasing manager with answers to the following questions:

- How does commitment influence the SRQ index of the supplier-buyer relationship?
- How does trust influence the SRQ index of the supplier-buyer relationship?
- How does cooperation influence the SRQ index of the supplier-buyer relationship?
- How does satisfaction influence the SRQ index of the supplier-buyer relationship?
- How does performance influence the SRQ index of the supplier-buyer relationship?

The trends in the automobile industry are used to set the stage for the SRQ indexing methodology. While different industries are in varying stages of implementing supply chain management efforts, one of the more developed efforts is in the automobile industry. The import of high-quality, fuel-efficient, and competitively priced automobiles from Japan in the 1970s and 1980s forced American automobile manufacturers to become more competitive or go out of business. Subsequently, one critical success factor in the industry has proved to be effective supplier partnering. Furthermore, the industry retains a fertile climate for technological integration. Given these two elements, the automobile industry served as an excellent source of study.

Table 2.3 shows the relative state of competition in the U.S. automobile industry. One impression is that relatively few manufacturers account for most of the automobile production for the U.S. market. The Big Three, along with the two primary Japanese transplant manufacturers (Honda and Toyota), sell over 70.5 percent of new automobiles in the U.S. market. Given the high price of automobiles and the fact that over 9.7 million vehicles were sold in the United States in August 2012, a tremendous amount of revenue is associated with just five manufacturers. This indicates a significant supply chain power advantage in favor of the automobile manufacturers because they are an oligopoly.

Given the market share of the larger automobile manufacturers, there are many critical industrywide issues that affect supply chain processes in the United States. This has implications for manufacturer-supplier integration. First, both the U.S. and Japanese transplant firms are attempting to utilize supply chain management as a source of competitive advantage within the industry. Effective supply chain management involves the coordination of suppliers and manufacturers to decrease costs, increase quality, and accept more product design responsibilities.

In the management of an effective/coordinated supply chain relationship between suppliers and manufacturers, there must be a way to assess what constitutes success from the suppliers' and buyers' vantage points. The suppliers' perception is important in spite of the relative difference in power between supply chain partners. One way to assess how suppliers view success is to peg the supply chain relationship on the appropriate criteria.

In the early 1900s, automobile manufacturers transformed the entire manufacturing industry from a craft orientation to mass manufacturing. Half a century later, the same industry revolutionized manufacturing again, steering manufacturing from mass production to lean production. Now these same producers offer the next revolution in e-manufacturing. These automotive giants were not the first to embrace the information economy. However, over the past several years, they have contributed to its development. This development has experienced difficulties and roadblocks at every stage. Nevertheless, the automobile industry can be a leading indicator of what lies ahead for the application of networking and information technology to manufacturing and supply chain management.

The major automakers share the same supply chains. During August 2012, there was a serious shortage of a plastic resin. Resin is crucial because it helps the tubes prevent fuel line deterioration. It is also used in seats and in products for other industries. The shortage was caused by an explosion in March 31, 2012 at a plant in Germany. The resin shortage problem was expected to be resolved during winter quarter 2012. The major automakers could be confronted with an even bigger crisis, running short of parts simply because there will not be enough production capacity to get back on schedule.

As of September 14, 2012, it is not known which plants or models will be affected. Each of the major automakers must attempt to avoid fourth quarter capacity problems. But it may be tough to manage the intricate supply chain of companies that make most of the 3,000 parts that go into every car, from tiny valves and computer chips to heavy metal castings for transmissions. This is an excellent example of the importance of the concept of supplier relationship quality (SRQ).

Global automakers are always vulnerable to such disruptions because of the implementation of "just-in-time" systems in which parts are delivered just days or hours ahead of when they are needed.

The earthquake and tsunami that hit Japan in 2011 knocked out parts plants and forced the industry to scramble for alternatives. The crisis hit Honda and Toyota hardest, but all automakers had to make adjustments. For example, a Japanese factory that was the only source of a unique paint pigment was disabled, forcing automakers to limit color choices.

In 1999, General Motors, Ford, and Chrysler joined together in a venture that attempted to take advantage of the promises of e-manufacturing. The venture was given the name Covisint, COmmunication VISion INTegration. This online marketplace was expected to connect more than 35,000 suppliers, partners, and manufacturers worldwide in a virtual market that would process over $300 billion worth of transactions annually. To date, Covisint has not worked for at least two reasons:

1. A majority of the suppliers were skeptical and did not sign up.
2. The manufacturers themselves did not appear to trust sharing information among themselves.

The major automakers share the same supply chains, creating a "free-rider" situation in which the automakers lack the incentives to invest adequately in their supply bases. That is, if an automaker helps their suppliers develop a new technology, the supplier's other customers will enjoy the same improvements without having contributed.

With the increase in globalization, driven in part by IT, competition has increased at accelerated rates. Increased competition has led to firms focusing more on their core competencies and less and less on vertical integration. This focus has led to increased specialization within the firm, which drives the need for firms to outsource more of their noncore functions. The result is that a firm must build more collaborative business relationships with constituencies beyond its formal boundaries. Moreover, tightly integrated sharing of information facilitates these relationships. As competition increases, the range of integration expands and the need to manage information becomes increasingly critical. The rise of MRP, MRP2, CRM, SCM, and ERP is evidence of the need for information sharing and the fact that e-manufacturing is becoming a reality.

Five automobile manufacturers (Chrysler, Ford, General Motors, Honda, and Toyota) participated in the research project. Telephone interviews were conducted with Ford and Toyota. Field visits were conducted with General Motors, Chrysler, and Honda at their facilities.

The manufacturer meetings, as well as other industry research, showed that the manufacturers had achieved different levels of success in implementing supply chain management. Some manufacturers, such as Chrysler and Honda, were already capitalizing on integrated supply relationships in order to gain competitive advantage in the industry. Others, like General Motors, still struggle, however, to implement effective supply chain integration strategies. Given this disparity, the SRQ indexing methodology was implemented. The results are discussed in Appendix A.

THE INTEGRATED BUYING MODEL

The integrated buying model is shown in Figure 2.7. The decision maker faces multiple goals in making the buying decision. The cost per unit, quality, and lead time are some of the issues that a decision maker faces in making the buying decision.

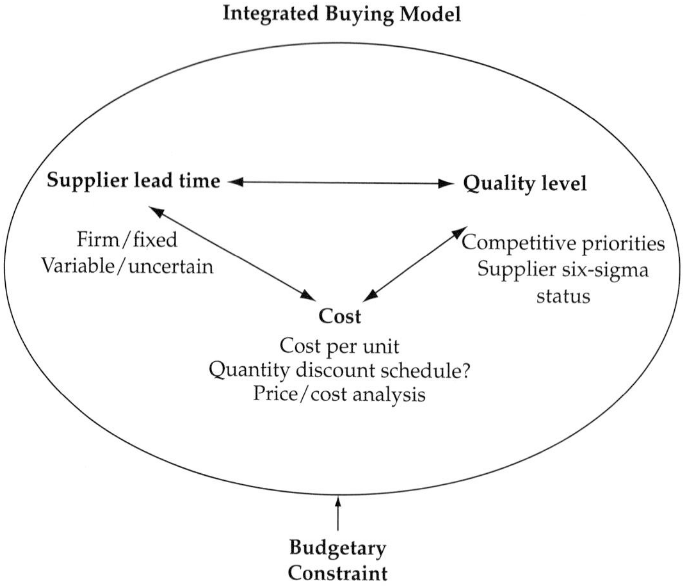

FIGURE 2.7
Integrated Buying Model

In most cases, the purchasing decision calls for buying the right material as specified at an acceptable cost and quality level within a reasonable lead time. The acceptable levels will vary depending on the firm's competitive position. The decision maker has to contend not only with multiple goals but also with several constraints. Firms often have limited resources. Inventory budgets may be limited, or storage space may constrain the quantity that may be purchased at any instant. The multiple goals must be satisfied within the constraints.

Cost

The cost per unit of material depends on the volume or amount purchased, the quality level desired, and the desired lead time. Material procured in larger volume enables the firm to buy at discounts. The discounts drive down the material cost. Higher quality level expressed in terms of lower defect rate usually pushes the purchase price higher. Since the supplier ensures higher quality by absorbing or preventing more defects, it usually charges a premium. To procure material at less-than-normal lead times, a premium price may have to be paid by the buyer. Thus, cost per unit is composed of material volume, quality level, and response time.

Quality Level

The quality level of material purchased must meet the desired objective as defined by the firm's competitive priorities. The lower the acceptable defect rate, the higher the quality level of the material purchased. A firm emphasizing quality may give more importance to achieving quality goals than cost objectives. Six sigma is a way to measure supplier quality. Supplying firms that follow the core philosophy of six sigma will make excellent strategic partners. Six-sigma suppliers focus on (1) defects per million units as a standard metric, (2) provision of extensive employee training, and (3) the reduction of non-value-added activities.

Lead Time

Supplier lead time affects a firm's flexibility and service to its own customers. Firms that compete in volatile markets and face rapidly changing product or technology require greater flexibility than firms competing in stable markets. With short lead times, the company can be responsive to external changes. In these circumstances, firms may desire to pay a premium for quick delivery in order to maintain their competitive edge. The more uncertainty there is in a supplier's lead times, the more difficult it is to manage the production process.

Constraints

A buyer must not only satisfy cost, quality, and lead-time goals but also stay within quantity and budgetary constraints. The buyer must ensure that the right quantity of material is purchased to satisfy the demand; otherwise, shortages may occur, resulting in poor customer service. The budget limitations may constrain the amount of material that can be purchased at any instant. The buyer may have to give up quantity discounts if the storage or budget resource is not available.

THE STRATEGIC SOURCING PLAN

There are a number of important challenges facing supply managers and executives in the future. Perhaps the most significant changes will occur in the purchasing area. More and more firms will be competing for limited supplies of materials. At the same time, stockholders will demand more profitability. In addition, the internationalization of supply markets, manufacturing, and market segments will bring the purchasing function into clear focus. The opportunities, if pursued, will be unlimited; if not pursued, it could be devastating to the firm's survival. In order to take full advantage of the challenges, the purchasing function must be integrated into the firm's overall strategic plan.

Developing a Strategic Sourcing Plan

The development of a strategic sourcing plan requires the following:

1. A complete understanding of corporate strategies and marketing plans in order to provide well-integrated purchasing systems.
2. An extensive evaluation/study of current suppliers, how performance is measured, and the expectation of suppliers relative to the industry.
3. Study of the degree of global purchasing opportunities.
4. Identification of total costs associated with current purchasing department/function, budgets, staffing, and so forth.

Management must devise a data collection instrument in order to provide data to respond to the four issues given above. The strategic purchasing plan must answer questions related to specific sources of supply, technological changes, and the extrapolated costing structure. The four phases of the strategic sourcing plan are given below.

Phase 1. Sourcing Audit

The sourcing audit is used as a diagnostic process that identifies opportunities for increased profitability. The audit should be broad and systematic and will serve to reaffirm company objectives, determine how well the current sourcing strategy is performing, and identify the areas that need immediate managerial attention.

Some of the issues relating to the organization, policies, and procedures that should be addressed are listed below:

1. Evaluation by senior management of the increased profits and benefits from an effective sourcing system.
2. Interdepartmental communication on the benefits from the joint sourcing requirement.
3. Effective participation in long-range planning by the supply management/ purchasing department.
4. Evaluation of the efficiency and cost-effectiveness of existing sourcing policies.
5. Exploration of the cost-effectiveness of the present purchasing organization.
6. Examination of the advantages and disadvantages of a centralized versus decentralized organization.
7. Review of the strategic plans of the purchasing department to determine if they have been carefully developed and documented.
8. Senior management support of the purchasing manager.
9. Assessment as to whether procedures for small purchases are cost-effective.
10. Review of the current purchasing manual to determine whether it is understood and followed in current purchasing decisions.
11. The role of senior management in promoting compliance with the purchasing manual throughout the company.

In addition, questions relating to the requirements process, the selection of the right sources, getting the right price, subcontract administration, and other important issues will be thoroughly investigated.

Phase 2. Organizational Development

This phase involves developing sourcing strategies; setting clearly outlined areas to cut costs and improve profitability; establishing a sourcing control system based on frequent analysis and systematic approach; formulating incentive programs; and making provisions for training by taking advantage of local ISM seminars and in-house sessions on how to establish the purchase of monitoring systems.

Phase 3. Implementation and Evaluation

In this phase, a thorough indoctrination of the company with sourcing strategy, implementation of new procedures, monitoring of sourcing activities, feedback mechanism for evaluation, and refinement of sourcing processes is conducted. The implementation and evaluation plan includes:

1. Thorough indoctrination of the company with the sourcing strategies.
2. Implementation of new procedures.
3. Monitoring of sourcing activities.
4. Development of a feedback mechanism.
5. Refinement of sourcing processes.

Phase 4. In-House Training Sessions

Classes should be conducted in groups of approximately 15 individuals. Appropriate purchasing and other management personnel from the company will attend these sessions to learn state-of-the-art purchasing techniques, negotiation strategies, and cost-containment methods.

Program Objectives by Phase

From work done during Phase 1 of the project, the company can expect to gain valuable insight into the present sourcing system and discover paths that can lead to new opportunities as the company enters the next decade. Information on the relationship with suppliers during the current period compared with the next decade will help chart the course for the future. In addition, the present systems for the control of the sourcing process should be evaluated, as should the compliance with the purchasing manual.

In addition, sourcing objectives should be refined to take advantage of insights gained from Phase 1 of the project. Buyers should be exposed to a reinforcement of the basic skills of their profession, refinement of the technical knowledge required, and a system of effective time management that are necessary to take advantage of sourcing opportunities. Finally, control devices for monitoring and reassuring sourcing activity will be created for ensuring consistency and effectiveness.

During and following Phase 2, "management by objective" systems should be implemented that enable the Purchasing Department to clearly set cost-savings goals. These savings will go straight to the bottom line.

After Phase 3 has been completed, the company can expect to be operating with a more developed organization capable of producing more cost-effective purchases with more profit from the savings. In short, more efficiency from planning and controlling the sourcing operation can be expected. The necessary tools also will be in place for effectively monitoring and refining the sourcing processes and conducting in-house sourcing audits in the future.

Purchasing and supply management has evolved into a strategic business activity and thus also is a potential contributor to the successful development of new products. However, the involvement of purchasing in new product development (NPD) is for the most part informal in most firms. Firms differ in the extent to which they involve purchasing in NPD. Purchasing specialists can be especially useful at the design and engineering phase of the NPD process. See Figure 2.8.

PURCHASING STRATEGY TRENDS

An article entitled, "Research Opportunities in Purchasing and Supply Management" was published in the August 2012 issue of the *International Journal of Production Research.* Panels of eight leading scholars in the purchasing and supply management (PSM) field were the contributors for the study. Among them were several journal editors of highly respected peer-reviewed academic journals publishing PSM research, as well as authors of some of the most successful PSM textbooks. These distinguished individuals provide an opportunity to tap the knowledge of a group of experts with extensive experience in the academic and practical aspects of PSM.

The purchasing and supply management function is crucial for effective business strategy and operations excellence. The PSM function has evolved from being a routine transactional function to a dominant function that delivers true competitive advantage to the business organization. The environment of increased globalization and outsourcing has led to an increased reliance on supplying organizations. This change in status has significantly enhanced the importance of PSM's

FIGURE 2.8
Purchasing's Role in the New Product Development Process

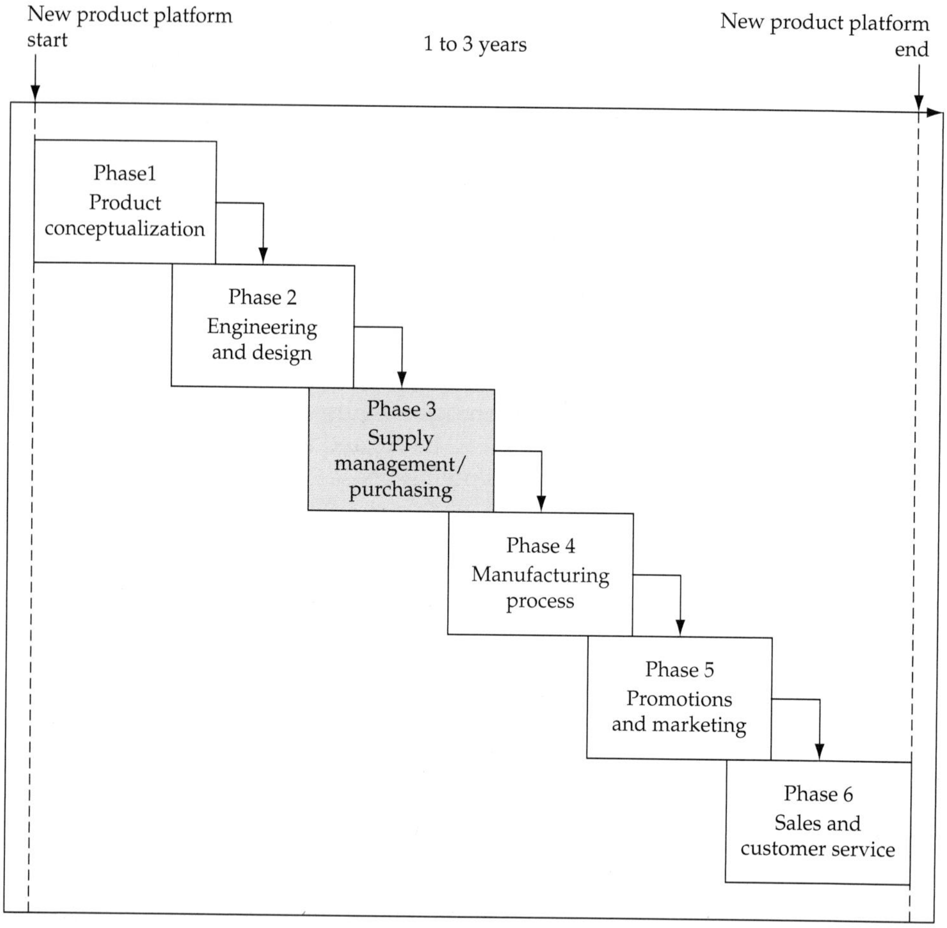

role in the business strategy process. It is therefore crucial to highlight future trends in industry practice. The findings are given below:

1. **Increases in global purchasing with China and India.** Outsourcing from India and China will continue to be important to businesses throughout the world. The products and services that are outsourced will become more sophisticated. Examples include health care, tax consulting services, engineering and design, and high-tech manufacturing.
2. **The strong relationship management between buying and selling organizations.** While the development (creation) of buyer-supplier relationships is well understood (e.g., influence of trust, dependence, communication, etc.), the ending or termination of these relationships warrants additional understanding. Specifically, when do buyers end a relationship, and when do they switch to an alternative supplier? Why do buyers resist switching to an alternative supplier even when there is a "better" alternate supplier? Given the costs involved in forming and maintaining supplier relationships, it is critical to understand factors that influence the termination of a buyer-supplier relationship.
3. **Buyer-supplier relationship life cycles.** It will become critical that buyer-supplier relationships consider the life cycle of the relationship in order to assess new productive relationship insights. For example, supplier development in

early versus late relationship phases needs to be understood. The goals and results of supplier development efforts might be quite different depending on the stage of the relationship.

4. **Purchasing function as a key driver of business strategy.** Supply chain management must be seen as a strategic element, instead of merely a means to managing the flow of products. A fundamental rethinking must occur in order to leverage the supply base to its fullest potential. Supply chain leverages organizational transformation and strategic change, focusing on the issues of strategic procurement, supply chain competence, and supply-chain integration.
5. **Supply-chain culture as a key resource and component of corporate strategy.** A firm's supply-chain culture and its influence on corporate strategy and performance will increase in the coming years. Aspects of supply-chain culture include service to customers, attitudes toward suppliers, adherence to established processes, readiness for and adaption to change, communication styles, and level of respect for members of the extended supply-chain team.
6. **Monitoring buyer or supplier ethical conduct in the supply chain.** The relationship between ethics and the law can be described as complex. Many violators of ethical conduct maintain that their actions are perfectly legal under the law.
7. **Developments in electronic purchasing.** As the market for electronic PSM offerings is expanding, the selection of the most appropriate solution is becoming increasingly challenging. Buying organizations can choose between dedicated software residing on their servers to hosted Software-as-a-Service (SaaS) solutions. Costs and benefits of these two extreme options may depend on firm and industry characteristics, and need to be carefully considered in choosing an electronic PSM execution strategy.
8. **Determining the appropriate electronic purchasing structures.** The notion that electronic procurement is only suited for indirect or maintenance, repair, and operating (MRO) supplies needs reevaluation. Recent developments in electronic procurement solution offerings enable procurement professionals to address management of quality and delivery beyond price-related aspects. These developments are changing the role of electronic procurement systems from a purely cost-based, transactional processing tool to a decision support system. In order to harness this potential, maintaining an alignment between the system capabilities and the practices it supports is critical. For example, a distinction between MRO I and MRO II items depending on their criticality, and subsequent choice of the structure for electronic reverse auctions, is necessary for the successful utilization of this tool, enabling increased value appropriation from the electronic procurement system. Critical MRO items and suppliers may not be suitable candidates for reverse auctions.
9. **The supplier's perspective of reverse auctions.** The use of reverse auctions represents one of the major components of an electronic procurement strategy. From a supplier's perspective, two pressing questions pertain to the relational implications and the supplier's response to, for example, a reverse auction invitation, which is often perceived by suppliers as an antagonistic way of doing business. Within this context, a supplier's perspective of a buying firm's intentions and efforts can significantly influence their level of satisfaction, which in

turn has implications for the buying firm's performance. The supplier's potential retaliation after having been "pressured" to participate in an auction should be expected.

10. **Long-term relationship risk of continuous reverse auction purchasing.** Reverse auctions are a great tool to obtain market price visibility and to obtain the most competitive bids. However, the mechanism has also been criticized for promoting sharp business practices and hurting the relationship. As such, reverse auctions should be used to gain market information, but should probably not be used as a routine sourcing method. To maintain trust and cooperation between buying and supplying firms, reverse auctions should be used carefully. While certain mechanisms can help in preventing the buyer-supplier relationship from deteriorating, negative effects are not unavoidable in all instances. For instance, while suppliers may be willing to bid competitive prices, they may have to achieve these by cutting back on quality, service, or delivery reliability. While this seems likely, no research has been found that empirically or quantitatively investigates this issue.
11. **The role of decision support systems in purchasing and supply management.** While most companies have transitioned to an integrated enterprise resource planning (ERP) system, or are in the process of doing so, the true potential for PSM to truly leverage the wealth of data available for better decision making is likely untapped to a large extent. The presence of a strategy is therefore not sufficient; it also requires effective execution, implementation, and adoption of practices. The value of Decision Support Systems (DSS) and Enterprise Requirements Planning (ERP) systems for PSM is, however, well accepted.

Purchasing and supply management will continue to become more relational focused, rather than transactional with key suppliers. Of course, for commodities, automation will remain the primary focus.

Summary

This chapter suggests there should be more comprehensive integration of the purchasing function with the strategic and competitive goals of a firm. Each firm must take a closer look at the purchasing and strategic interface, if it is to compete in the world manufacturing arena. In the future, corporate goals cannot be achieved by marketing alone. For many years, there has been a missing link between corporate planning and the purchasing process. In this chapter, we have presented a comprehensive framework for linking a firm's purchasing decisions with the firm's overall competitive strategy. The framework for analysis consists of a rich conceptual model. Within the conceptual model, we present the important linkages between the firm's competitive strategy and purchasing decisions. The trend toward supply chain management requires trust and cooperation between buying and selling organizations. The supply chain members cannot function without the economic, quality, and service performance of the other members. The quality of the relationships between each supply chain member determines which firms survive in a competitive environment. An extensive supply chain relationship quality indexing analysis was used to measure the degree of quality relationship between auto manufacturers and their tier-one suppliers.

There is no single strategic goal for any competitive firm. Cost minimization in terms of the buying decision has been the dominant objective of most material managers, but in today's competitive business environment, it should not be the only objective. In fact, the current trend is to place higher priorities on quality and delivery performance than on cost minimization.

The challenges and opportunities for the purchasing professional have never been greater. The next decade will put the purchasing function into the spotlight.

Discussion Questions

1. Why should the purchasing professional be concerned with strategic planning?
2. How does purchasing fit into a firm's overall strategic plans? Give a specific framework for the linkage between purchasing and competitive strategy.
3. What are the components of purchasing strategy?
4. What decision areas are associated with purchasing strategy?
5. What is the impact of purchasing strategy on manufacturing inventory?
6. What is meant by "partnering"? Please categorize the five factors of partnerships.
7. Discuss the elements of the proposed buying model mentioned in this chapter.
8. Describe the elements of a strategic purchasing plan.
9. Describe the supply chain relationship quality indexing process.

Suggested Cases

The Capital State Arena

NEP: The Art and Science of Purchasing Coal

Eastern Waves Case, Inc.

Tom and Jerry Construction

References

Burt, D. N., Donald Dobler, and Stephen Starling. *A Purchasing Perspective on the Supply Chain.* 7th ed. New York: McGraw-Hill, Irwin, 2003.

Chappell, L., Gail Kachadourian. "DCX Drags Suppliers Down Rocky Road: Bernhard Declares End to Era of Good Feeling." *Automotive News* (August 13, 2001), p. 1.

Ellram, Lisa M. "Life Cycle Patterns in Industrial Buyer Seller Partnerships." *International Journal of Physical Distribution and Logistics Management* 21, no. 9 (1991), pp. 12–21.

Maloni, Michael J., and W. C. Benton Jr. "Power Influences in the Supply Chain." *Journal of Business Logistics* 21, no. 1 (2000), pp. 42–73.

Maloni, Michael J., and W. C. Benton Jr. "Supplier Relationship Quality (SRQ) and the Supply Chain Network." Working paper, The Fisher College of Business, The Ohio State University, Autumn 2008.

Maloni, Michael J., and W. C. Benton Jr. "Supply Chain Partnerships: Opportunities for Operations Research." *European Journal of Operational Research* 101, no. 3 (1997), pp. 419–29.

Maloni, Michael J., and W. C. Benton Jr. "Supply Chain Relationship Pegging." Working paper, The Fisher College of Business, The Ohio State University, Summer 2005.

Porter, M. E. *Competitive Advantage*. New York: The Free Press, 1984.

Schoenherr, Tobias, Sachin B. Modi, W. C. Benton, Craig R. Carter, Thomas Y. Choi, Paul D. Larson, Michiel R. Leenders, . . . Stephan M. Wagner. "Research Opportunities in Purchasing and Supply Management." *International Journal of Production Research*, 40, no. 16 (August 2012), pp. 4556–79.

Appendix A

Supply Chain Relationship Quality Study[1]

PHASE I

The assessment phase is represented by the observations during the plant visits.

PHASE II. DATA COLLECTION AND QUESTIONNAIRE DEVELOPMENT

A mailing list for 548 of the most critical tier 1 suppliers in the automobile industry was used as the sample for the study. This list consisted of individuals with high-level, strategically oriented positions, having titles such as president, CEO, and chairman. The data were entered into spreadsheet format and verified twice for entry accuracy. The data were then filtered for problems. Some companies also were removed from the Honda list because they were Honda subsidiaries. Given a total of 548 contact names supplied, 130 were considered usable for the quality analysis study after data cleansing. The response rate for the supply chain quality study was 23.7 percent. This sample allowed for suitable testing of the research question.

Demographics of Respondents

Several standard demographic measures including products/services supplied, percentage and value of sales to the manufacturer, quality certification, and number of employees were taken to obtain a general understanding of respondent attitudes. The ranked frequencies of the products and/or services provided by the suppliers are displayed in Table A.1. Bearing in mind that a respondent may select more than one category, chassis and power train components were found to be the most frequently marked categories. Most of the remaining categories were relatively evenly distributed in frequency, indicating that each of the categories was well represented in the data.

Next, the suppliers were asked to estimate the average percentage of their total sales as well as the total dollar amount of sales purchased by the manufacturer of

TABLE A.1
Categories of Products/Services of Respondents

Category	Count	Percent
Chassis components	54	23.6
Power train components	54	23.6
Interior components	33	14.4
Exterior components	32	14.0
Stamping components	28	12.2
Electrical components	27	11.8
Other	24	10.5
Transportation/logistics	24	10.5
Tooling/equipment/construction	12	5.2
Nonproduction services	6	2.6

[1] The data for this study were collected in 2007. The impact of the current economic crisis in the industry is not reflected in this study.

TABLE A.2
Demographics of Respondents

Category	Percent of Sales	Value of Sales	QS9000 Certified	ISO9000 Certified	Number of Employees
Mean	23.52	3.39	125 yes	112 yes	6,949.11
Standard deviation	26.28	1.50			

interest (Table A.2). The average percentage was 23.52 percent, indicating that the manufacturers accounted for a relatively large proportion of the suppliers' sales. The average dollar amount of sales was found to lie between $5 million and $50 million. The number of employees per firm averaged approximately 7,000.

Finally, information about quality certification with specific regard to ISO9000 and QS9000 was collected. *ISO9000* (International Organization for Standardization) seeks to offer standardization of quality management issues. Firms attempting to register for certification must meticulously map and refine the control of processes such as inspection, purchasing, distribution, and training. One hundred twelve of the respondents report that they currently have or will soon qualify for ISO9000 certification. The steep cost of certification may prevent small suppliers from achieving such certification. Related to ISO9000, *QS9000* was developed by the Big Three U.S. manufacturers (General Motors, Ford, and Chrysler) specifically for the automotive industry.

Supplier Relations Data Collection

This section will serve to establish an assessment of supplier relations in the U.S. automotive industry. This understanding of industry best practice will help the reader to focus on the importance and relevance of the summary statistics to be presented later. Specifically, a segment of the survey given below sought to establish a comparison of supplier opinions about the different major manufacturers in the automobile industry. The statement read, "In considering your relationships with the following firms, please allocate a total of 100 points among them based on their quality as a customer"; Chrysler, Ford, General Motors, Honda, and Toyota were among the e-manufacturers listed. These five manufacturers accounted for over 85 percent of U.S new vehicle sales in 1999.

An assessment of the relative quality of the manufacturers through the eyes of the suppliers was measured with the point allocation. If all the manufacturers supplied by the particular respondent have perceived quality as a customer, the score for each should be equal to 100 divided by the number of firms supplied. Scores differing from this average score would indicate above- or below-average perceived quality. This allowed suppliers to rate their customers, thus offering an *industry relationship standard* of the results of supplier relationship efforts. In order to gain insight into the factors affecting supplier relations pegging responses, respondents also were asked to select important factors influencing their rating of customer quality. They selected one or more among *commitment, cooperation, trust, satisfaction, performance,* and other.

PHASE III. THE CLASSIFICATION AND ANALYSIS

The scores for each response were examined. Any score sets that failed to total to 100 were removed from consideration, as were responses that indicated the respondent supplied only one of the five listed manufacturers. This left 130 usable

TABLE A.3
Index Scores for Usable (n = 130) Responses

	Chrysler	Ford	General Motors	Honda	Toyota
Mean	**1.42**	**0.91**	**0.72**	**1.10**	**0.96**
St. dev.	0.467	0.428	0.405	0.545	0.398
t-stat	8.84	−2.14	−7.25	1.76	−0.86
p-value	< .01	0.03	< .01	0.08	> .10
Count	97	108	113	98	69

supplier responses. The score sets for response were taken as a percentage of the expected response given the supplier considered all its manufacturer customers as equals. For instance, if a respondent supplied four manufacturers, the expected score for each would be 25. If a manufacturer achieved its expected score of 25, its resulting indices would be 25 divided by 25, equaling one. Thus, the quality indices would assume a value of one if the supplier considered the manufacturer to retain average quality as a customer. Subsequently, indices greater than one would indicate an above-average rating for customer quality while a below-average score would be below one. Table A.3 shows summary statistics for these customer quality indices. With an average overall rating of 1.42, Chrysler retained the strongest reputation among the suppliers, while Honda ranked second with a mean score of 1.10. The ranks of the remaining three manufacturers were found to be Toyota (mean of 0.96), Ford (0.91), and General Motors (0.72). Ninety-five percent confidence intervals were constructed for each score and are displayed in Figure A.1 to offer a visual representation of the scores. The scores also were tested for significance in difference from the average value of one. Both Chrysler and Honda showed evidence of significant above-average ratings while Ford and General Motors demonstrated significance in below-average ratings. Toyota demonstrated no significant difference from one.

To gain further insight regarding suppliers' opinions of their customers, this same analysis was conducted for the 41 respondents who indicated that they supplied all five manufacturers. These results (see Table A.4) were similar to the previous ones, finding Chrysler with the highest average rating at 1.40. Honda followed with 1.06, then Toyota with 0.95, Ford with 0.87, and General Motors with 0.72. Figure A.2 displays 95 percent confidence intervals for the mean score for each firm. Also, t-tests run for significance in difference from the average value of one revealed that Chrysler retained a significant above-average rating while Ford and General Motors demonstrated significant below-average ratings. Both Honda and Toyota demonstrated no significant difference from one.

FIGURE A.1
95% Confidence Intervals for Index Scores (n = 130)

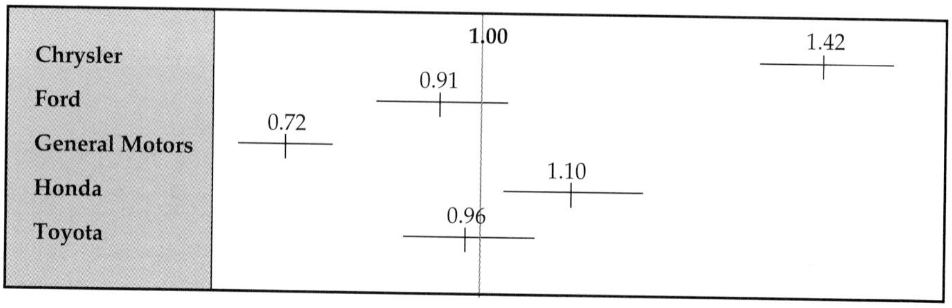

TABLE A.4
Index Scores for Suppliers of All Five Manufactures ($n = 41$)

	Chrysler	Ford	General Motors	Honda	Toyota
Mean	**1.40**	**0.87**	**0.72**	**1.06**	**0.95**
St. dev.	0.561	0.427	0.445	0.565	0.392
t-stat	4.51	−2.01	−3.98	0.72	−0.78
p-value	< .01	0.04	< .01	> .10	> .10
Count	41	41	41	41	41

The above relationship assessment verifies this best practice, indicating that these two firms set the industry best practice for fostering relationships with their suppliers.

IMPORTANT FACTORS IN CUSTOMER ASSESSMENT

The customer assessment results were tallied for the 130 suppliers providing responses to the relationship assessment (Table A.5). Of these factors, commitment (98 out of 130 responses, 75.4 percent), cooperation (107, 82.3 percent), and trust (93, 71.5 percent) were checked most frequently. Both satisfaction (33, 25.4 percent) and performance (56, 43.1 percent) were chosen less, by fewer than half of the respondents, and no consensus replies were provided for the "other" category. These proportions were examined for significance in difference from .50 (50 percent of respondents). Commitment, trust, and cooperation were significantly greater than .50. Furthermore, satisfaction was found to be significantly less than .50, while performance demonstrated no significant difference.

The respondents also were asked to indicate the relationship factors that were most important in evaluating the quality of the automotive manufacturers as customers. The most important relationship factors—cooperation (107, 0.823 percent), commitment (98, 0.754 percent), and trust (93, 0.715 percent)—were selected more frequently. Both performance (56, 0.431 percent) and satisfaction (33, 0.254 percent) were chosen by less than half of the respondents. There were no consensus replies chosen for the "other" category. These proportions were examined for significance in difference from .5 (50 percent of the respondents), and cooperation, commitment, and trust retained significance greater than .50. There is less than .50 significance for performance and satisfaction. An explanation for this finding is the comfort level the respondents had with defining some of the concepts. Cooperation, commitment, and trust can be perceived to be more easily defined. On the other hand, the performance and satisfaction definitions are less clear. Performance and

FIGURE A.2
95% Confidence Intervals for Index Scores for Suppliers of All Five Manufacturers

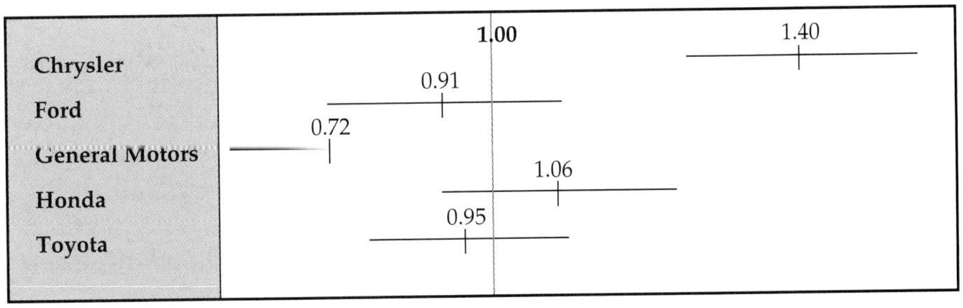

TABLE A.5
Basis for Allocation of Points in Pegging Assessment ($n = 130$)

	Commitment	Cooperation	Trust	Satisfaction	Performance
Count	98	107	93	33	56
Frequency	**0.754**	**0.823**	**0.715**	**0.254**	**0.431**
z-stat	5.79	7.37	4.91	−5.61	−1.58
p-value	< .01	< .01	< .01	< .01	> .10

satisfaction may be confounded with financial and relational elements. Perhaps in future studies, performance and satisfaction can be more clearly defined.

Another explanation for the lack of significance of performance and satisfaction as indicators of customer assessment may be derived from supplier expectations. Because the primary performance measures in the industry are associated with the manufacturer, the suppliers may accept their own performance measures through the manufacturer. Thus, these suppliers seek to maintain their relationships with the best-practice manufacturers as they figure their own success will be inevitable because of their alignment with these manufacturers. This would be especially true over the last few years, as the manufacturers have enjoyed great profitability.

These results show that in judging the quality of the manufacturers as customers, the suppliers are more focused on relational elements such as commitment, cooperation, and trust. Satisfaction and performance seem to carry less weight in such an assessment. This is not to say that the suppliers are not concerned about performance and satisfaction. It merely indicates that the suppliers seem to be more relationally oriented and value those customers that seek to foster sincere and mutual business partnerships.

Overall, the assessment reveals the importance of *manufacturer strategy* toward supplier management. The suppliers value those manufacturers that foster relational exchanges. This indicates that those manufacturers that are focused upon building strong supplier partnerships should place emphasis on enhancing the relationship itself. This yields direct implications for supply chain strategy in practice.

PHASE IV

The purpose of this study was to develop an objective supply chain relationship quality indexing system. The U.S. automobile industry was used as the test industry for *a supply chain relationship quality indexing system.* In general, the respondents believe that Chrysler and Honda are higher-quality customers than the other three manufacturers. The respondents ranked the automotive manufacturers from the highest quality to the lowest as Chrysler, Honda, Toyota, Ford, and General Motors.

These results clearly show that in judging the quality of the manufacturers as customers, the suppliers are more focused on relational elements such as commitment, cooperation, and trust. Satisfaction and performance seem to carry less weight in such an assessment. This is not to say that the suppliers are not concerned about performance and satisfaction. It merely indicates that the suppliers seem to be more relationally oriented and value those customers that seek to foster sincere and mutual business partnerships.

RELATIONSHIP ASSESSMENT SURVEY

I. Estimate the percentage of your sales accounted for by Automotive Industry

____

Please check the approximate category of the overall **value of your sales** to Chrysler.[2]

< $2 mil __	$2–5 mil __	$5–20 mil __	$20–50 mil __
$50–100 mil __	$100–500 mil __	> $500 mil __	

Is your firm QS9000 registered? ________

Is your firm ISO9000 registered? ________

Approximate the number of employees in your firm ______________

II. In considering your relationships with the following firms, please allocate ***a total of 100 points*** among them based on their relationship quality as a customer. If you do not sell to a company, indicate "n/a" (for not applicable).

Chrysler	_____
Ford	_____
General Motors	_____
Honda	_____
Toyota	_____
TOTAL	**100**

In the above ratings, which (more than one may be chosen) are important factors for the basis of your point allocation? The factors and definitions are listed below:

Commitment ___	Cooperation ___	Trust ___
Satisfaction ___	Performance ___	Others _____

- **Commitment.** Commitment is defined as the feeling of being emotionally impelled. The distribution channel literature has found that the relationship between power and commitment is dependent upon the origins of the commitment.
- **Trust.** Trust is defined as a type of expectation that alleviates the fear that one's exchange partner will act opportunistically. It is the firm's belief that another firm will perform actions that will result in positive outcomes for the firm as well as not take unexpected negative actions against the firm that will lead to negative outcomes.
- **Cooperation.** Cooperation is defined as the degree to which two trading partners work together to solve problems, establish strategic directions, and generally work for their mutual goals.
- **Satisfaction.** Supplier satisfaction is defined as the feeling of equity with the relationship no matter what power imbalance exists.
- **Performance.** Performance is defined as the ability to execute intentions and goals.

Thank you again for your time and cooperation in responding.

[2] The same questionnaire was also given to all General Motors, Ford, Toyota, and Honda suppliers. The company names were randomized in order to give each manufacturer equal chances as the first on the list.

Chapter Three

The Legal Aspects of Purchasing[1]

Learning Objectives

1. Discuss the legal aspects of the purchasing function.
2. Review the factors that are involved in the selection of the purchasing manager.
3. Understand the extent of the purchasing professional's legal authority.
4. Explain how contracts and purchase orders are legally executed.
5. Name the essentials of a binding purchasing contract.
6. Define the terms of an enforceable contract.
7. Distinguish between an offer and a nonoffer.
8. State the possible outcomes of an offer.
9. Understand the legal implications of leasing.
10. Understand the legal impact of the information age.
11. Recall the components of electronic contracts and signatures.
12. Discuss the importance of ethics in purchasing.
13. Articulate how to comply with *women business enterprise* (WBE), *minority business enterprise* (MBE), and *disadvantaged business enterprise* (DBE) programs.

INTRODUCTION

Every day parents send their sons and daughters to college. After a difficult examination, Jane text messaged her parents and announced that she needed a new TV and that she needed their permission to make the purchase. Her mother called the local appliance store manager to tell them that Jane had her permission to charge the purchase to her account. Her father informed Jane that she could proceed with the purchase as long as it was within an *appropriate* price range. After evaluating more than 20 TV sets, Jane decided and signed the charge slip. The TV was delivered to her apartment on the same day. At the end of the month, her father

[1]The author expresses appreciation to Linda F. McHenry, Esq., W. C. Benton and Associate, Inc., for her contributions to this chapter.

received a statement for $856. A day later, while still in shock, the father sent the appliance store a check, and the transaction was completed.

At first glance this appears to be a normal transaction between families and retailers. The impressive coincidence of this scenario is that Jane accomplished her mission in the same way the purchasing process is accomplished in a business. A need is requested by a specific department and the purchasing person satisfies the need. The potential source is evaluated in terms of quality, price, and delivery performance. The purchasing manager makes the purchase and the treasurer of the company sends the check after an **invoice** is received.

As can be seen, both Jane and the purchasing agent are able to buy goods and services and have someone else pay the bill. However, the seller must know that the decision maker has given the purchasing manager the authority to make the purchase. This transaction is legally binding through the *agency* concept. An agency relationship requires at least three parties. The first party is the principal, the one with the need. The second party is the agent, who represents the principal. The third party is the one with which the agent conducts business on behalf of the principal.

The purchasing manager is an agent for the firm. The terms *purchasing manager*, *buyer*, and *purchasing agent* will be used interchangeably. The purchasing manager administers the purchasing function. The purchasing function consists of many tasks within the business entity, including supporting the company with the required (1) materials, (2) supplies, and (3) services.

The most important task that the purchasing officer is involved in is representing the principal in the development and **negotiation** of contracts with third parties. The title *purchasing agent* is a generic legal term. Recently, the term has been superseded by vice president of purchasing, vice president of materials management, and vice president of supply management. From a legal standpoint, the term *purchasing agent* accurately defines the individual who deals with a third party for a principal.

The selection of the senior purchasing manager is an important recruitment effort since the person will "inherit" the principal–agent relationship for all the expenditures and commitments of the company made by the purchasing agents. From a legal point of view, the following factors are associated with the appointment:

1. The purchasing manager must be granted the authority to make purchase contracts.
2. The purchasing manager accepts the contracting authority.
3. The employer accepts the commitments that were made to the purchasing manager.

AUTHORITY OF THE PURCHASING MANAGER

The three types of purchasing authority are express authority, implied authority, and emergency authority.

1. *Express authority*. Express authority is conferred to the purchasing manager by the principal. This authority usually occurs automatically when the purchasing manager is appointed. The detail associated with the appointment should reside in the company bylaws. The statement may be a job description for the top procurement officer. It is recommended that the purchasing manager's authority be in writing. If the authority is put in writing, there should be no

misunderstanding of what the manager's express authority is. This will especially be helpful if there are disagreements between any parties in the relationship. As an example, in most states, real estate contracts must be in writing.

2. *Implied authority*. Implied authority is implied by the law at the time the principal grants express authority to the purchasing agent. It gives the purchasing agent the legal authority to carry out the duties for which he or she was appointed. As an example, if the purchasing agent is given the express authority to make a contract, he has the implied authority to negotiate the terms of the contract. This includes:

   - The quantity
   - The quality and other specifications
   - The delivery conditions
   - The price
   - The payment date

   Implied authority is clearly needed in order to complete a transaction. However, the purchasing agent does not have the *implied* authority to sign a promissory note for the principal unless granted the express authority to do so.
3. *Emergency authority*. In cases where the purchasing agent does not have express or implied authority, the purchasing agent may still take action. Emergency authority is rarely used. Emergency authority is used only when the purchasing manager must protect the principal's rights or property when a consultation with the principal is impossible at the time.

In general, most of the purchasing authority is not given in writing or the scope is vague. When purchasing managers are appointed as agents for the company, they are vaguely given the purchasing responsibility. However, written formalities are important when a legal issue occurs.

It is strongly recommended that the authority of the purchasing manager be clearly written and communicated. This is also true for buyers and other purchasing personnel under the purchasing manager. In addition, most buyers are given dollar limitation authorization. Any contract that exceeds the dollar level must be signed by a superior purchasing officer.

EXECUTION OF CONTRACTS AND PURCHASE ORDERS BY THE PURCHASING MANAGER

Purchasing personnel routinely sign **purchase orders** and **contracts** committing the company to the specific terms and conditions of purchase orders and contracts. The purchasing official has no personal liability providing that the following requirements are met:

1. The name of the principal or company is shown on the document.
2. All parties involved know that the purchasing agent is acting on behalf of the company or principal.
3. The agency relation is shown on the document.
4. The purchasing agent is acting within the scope of his or her authority for the transaction.

A legal signature is any type of signature as long as the person who is signing the document intends it to represent his or her authority. Typewritten, faxed, and e-mail signatures are also acceptable for execution.

In some cases, the purchasing agent can become personally liable for signing if a note is signed without an official title. This is true even if the intent was to sign for the company. This is also true when a company official signs a check without an official title listed.

ESSENTIALS OF A PURCHASE CONTRACT

A purchase consists of passing *title* of a product or service to a *buyer* from a *seller*. The title represents the ownership right to the product or service. A *buyer* is a person who contracts to buy goods or services. A *seller* is a person who sells or contracts to sell goods or services. The two parties must agree to the transaction before a sale can take place. This *agreement* is a *contract*. The title of the good or service cannot be passed until an agreement or contract is reached between the buyer and seller.

THE REQUIREMENTS FOR A CONTRACT

The four components of an enforceable (contract) agreement are the following:

1. *The parties must be capable.* Both parties must know what they are doing. This standard clearly eliminates parties who are impaired in any way. Impairment includes an insane person, a confirmed alcoholic, and a confirmed drug addict. It is important to acknowledge that these conditions must be confirmed through adjudication. Of course, if a party entered the company into an undesirable agreement after too many drinks, he or she cannot use impairment as a legal defense. Finally, a corporation itself cannot enter into a contract without a corporate official as an agent.
2. *The subject of the matter must be legal and valid.* The definition of a valid contract is that the product or service contracted must be legal and not against public policy. The court cannot enforce a contract that is illegal. This is usually not a problem for most purchasing officials since most of the products and services are covered.
3. *There must be mutual consideration. Consideration* is a legal term that is easily understood until there is a challenge. The definition of consideration is that something of value passes from one party to a second party in exchange for a promise of the second party. The value must be consistent with the second party's promise. If an auto mechanic is given $1,000 in return for a promise to repair a fender, that is mutual consideration. Mutual consideration makes a contract legally binding and enforceable. In most cases, if there is no consideration, the contract is not enforceable.

   Mutual consideration is important to purchasing managers. One objective of the purchasing manager is to receive the best value for the company. As an example, some of the important purchasing considerations are price, quality, quantity, and delivery.
4. *The parties must reach an agreement by offer and acceptance.* In a purchasing situation, the seller usually makes an *offer* and the buyer accepts, negotiates, or rejects the *offer*. Only when the offer is accepted is there an agreement.

In summary, under the U.S. Commercial Code, an agreement is a legal transaction that requires all four components given above. The absence of any of the components results in an unenforceable agreement in a court of law.

OFFERS

The final requirement for a valid contract is the mechanics of reaching an agreement. In order to have an agreement, there must be an offer and an acceptance of the offer. The definition of an *offer* is a proposal made to someone to enter into a contract. It is also *an invitation to do business*. An offer is also a legal commitment to the other party. In the business purchasing environment, an offer can be initiated by either the buying or selling party. If the buying firm initiates an offer, it is called an *offer to buy*. When selling firms initiate an offer, it is referred to as an *offer to sell*. Of course, throughout an extended negotiations process, there will be numerous *offers* and *counteroffers*.

An *offer* clearly has legal implications. If a person makes an offer, he or she must be prepared to perform if the offer is accepted. The *acceptance* of an offer poses legal obligations. The written contract should immediately follow the *acceptance* of the offer.

Purchasing agents receive numerous offers on a daily basis and must be able to identify complete legitimate offers. The three necessary components of an offer are the following:

1. *Intent to make an offer*. The intent to make an offer must be clearly stated. The purchasing official should require the **supplier** to submit a written quotation form that states precisely what the *supplier offers to sell* or (in the case of the buying firm) *the purchaser offers to buy*.
2. *Communication of the offer intent*. The offer must be communicated to the offeree. The purchasing agent can easily communicate the offer with a purchase order. The seller communicates through a proposal or quotation.
3. *Identification of the specific subject matter*. The product or service must be accurately described. Specifications are especially important when the competitive bidding method of pricing is used. Brand names, quality standards, and specific performance expectations also should be used. The quantity and price are also important when referring to the subject matter.

INVITATION TO DO BUSINESS

In most instances, the purchasing official initiates an invitation to do business. The purchasing official issues a **request for quotation (RFQ).** The RFQ is an excellent way for the buying firm to test the market without making a legal commitment to purchase. The RFQ lacks the *intent* component. When the intent component is missing, the document is merely an invitation to bid.

Suppliers use catalogs as an invitation to do business. The catalog usually illustrates colorful pictures and detailed descriptions. Catalogs fail to meet the *intent* and *identification* requirements necessary for a legal offer. Suppliers usually place a caveat in the catalog that qualifies the stock level and prices of the listed item. Given the rise of the *Internet* revolution, promotional materials are becoming close to a *bona fide offer*. There is also an increased opportunity for fraud and illegal selling activity. There has been a rise in *consumer* protection laws to prevent illegal selling. However, there is little protection for the professional purchasing environment.

COUNTEROFFERS

The negotiations process between the buyer and the seller usually leads to many offers and counteroffers. A counteroffer is legally binding if it contains the components that institute an offer. A more comprehensive treatment of the counteroffer process is given in Chapter 11.

THE TIME LIMITS OF AN OFFER

There are four outcomes of an offer:

1. *The offer may lapse.* The terms of an *offer* can be specified to lapse after a stated period. Suppose you are a purchasing agent who receives a **quote** for 5 tons of rebar and on the face of the quotation you are given seven days to decide whether to accept the *offer*; if you fail to take action during the seven days, the offer no longer exists. The seven-day period is counted from the date typed on the request for quotation (RFQ). The seven days commence when the offer is received and only if the RFQ is undated. If the supplier is attempting to avoid a price increase or offer a quantity discount, the offer may be subject to *immediate acceptance*. The purchasing agent must be careful about acting too often on *immediate acceptances*. It is understood that the experienced purchasing agent is close to being an expert on the items he or she purchases and should be able to distinguish between buying *opportunities* and buying *risks*. In the case of a quantity discount purchase, the buyer not only must consider the cost per item; he or she also must consider the total costs (cost of capital, inventory carrying cost, insurance cost, and the cost of obsolescence) of the purchase. The purchasing agent must be able to analyze the conceptual as well as the economic criteria associated with alternative buying decisions. In any case, the supplying firm's representative should be questioned about the reason for requirement of *immediate acceptance* of the *offer*.

In many cases, an *offer* has no time limits and, in these cases, the law states that the offer should lapse after a *reasonable* period of time, although it usually does not indicate what that is. Thus, the time span may vary. The following factors can serve as guidelines for what is a reasonable period of time:

- The nature of the product or service
- The variability of the market price
- The historical dealings between the two parties
- The industry norms

As an example, if the supplier is selling a perishable commodity, then it is easy to see that an immediate response is needed. On the other hand, if the seller is offering a Hummer to you, there is a wide range of discretion. This is a serious problem in the construction industry. As an example, in March, Apex Trucking firm agreed to haul 100 tons of dirt based on a total cost (costs that included fuel, labor, maintenance, tire replacement, etc.). The prime contractor later informed Apex that the project had been delayed until December. In the meantime, the cost to Apex of diesel fuel increased from $2.30 per gallon to $3.05 per gallon. This is significant since dump trucks get an average of 5 miles to a gallon.

2. *The offer may be rejected*. The rejection of an offer kills it completely. The offer ceases to exist. The rejection of an offer must be communicated to the supplier. The communication can be either verbal or written. If the offer is amended, it becomes a counteroffer.

3. *The offer may be revoked*. In some instances, the offer is revoked. The law permits an offer to be revoked anytime before it is accepted. According to the law, if a company has the free will to make an offer, the company also has the equally free will to revoke the offer before it is accepted. Remember, consideration has not occurred. Revoking an offer is legal, but it should be avoided if possible. It usually causes a hardship on the buying firm. It is the responsibility of the purchasing professional to protect the buying firm. The following approaches can be used to protect against revocation:

- Obtain a firm offer.
- Write an option contract.
- Secure a bid bond.

4. *The offer may be accepted*. The offer is accepted and a contract is made.

FIRM OFFERS

The firm offer question should be raised when quotations are requested. This approach gives the supplier equal opportunity to consider the risks before quoting. As an example, consider the following condition for Apex Trucking:

> Prices quoted in your offer must be guaranteed for 90 days. This assurance must be included in the quotation you submit. Quotations received without such assurances will be returned.

Quotations as a result of this RFQ are enforceable. It must be made clear to the supplier that any supplier that submits an offer without this guarantee will not be considered. The purchasing manager must enforce this condition for each of the suppliers. If the purchasing manager does not enforce this condition, he or she loses credibility. Other suppliers will quickly find out that the purchasing person (the company) is unethical.

OPTION CONTRACTS

In case the supplier is unwilling to give the buying firm a firm offer, the purchasing professional should attempt to offer the seller an option contract. The seller will make an agreement to allow the **buyer** a specific time limit to make the purchase. Consideration will pass from the offeree to the offeror in return for a firm commitment. As an example:

> For the consideration of $1,000, for the next 90 days we will sell you our Centrino mobile integrated computer chip for $12.50 per chip delivered, in units of 1,000 chips, up to a total of 5,000 chips.

This option contract is enforceable because of the payment of the $1,000 *consideration*. The buyer is actually paying for the protection of a firm offer. In the case that the buyer fails to make a purchase during the 90-day period, the seller retains the $1,000. An option contract can be executed for any length of time.

BID BONDS

A bid bond enlists a third party into the transaction. The supplier secures a bonding company to guarantee that the supplier will enter into a contract if it is awarded the contract. However, if the supplier is the successful bidder and fails to perform, the bonding company must pay the buying firm the damages incurred up to the limit of the bid bond. The bid bond approach is used extensively by governmental agencies. A bid bond condition is usually motivated by a federal or state regulation. Bonding is used to protect governmental agencies from unqualified bidders. Therefore, it should come as no surprise that bonding companies are selective in the issuing of bid bonds. The supplying firm must be able to prove that it possesses the managerial, engineering, and financial capability required to perform the contract. Bonding is used when risks are expected. Thus, bonding is widely used in the construction industry.

PROMISSORY ESTOPPELS

The construction industry is unique in that the general/prime contractor accepts offers from subcontractors in expectation of being awarded a project from a third party. As an example, a bridge contractor solicits offers from a structural steel firm for the purpose of preparing an estimate for the department of transportation. It is understood between the prime contractor and the subcontractors that an acceptance cannot be made until the project has been awarded. However, the prime contractor is depending on the promise of the subcontractor to provide steel contracting if the prime is awarded the project. The doctrine of promissory estoppels is enforceable by the prime contractor. There is a famous case in which a prime contractor solicited a telephone bid from a paving contractor. The paving subcontractor failed to perform after the prime contractor was awarded the project. The court ruled in favor of the prime contractor.

ORAL CONTRACTS

Oral contracts occur every day. Ordering a pizza is an oral contract. However, oral contracts have no place in the professional purchasing arena. If a supplier refuses to perform, there is no recourse for the buyer. The courts are silent on enforcing oral contracts that exceed $500.

TERMS OF A CONTRACT

Quantity

An offer must express a fixed quantity of a sale. A contract that does not specifically express quantity is unenforceable. The unit of measure of quantity is unique to the industry. As examples:

1. Concrete is quoted in cubic yards.
2. Lumber in board feet.
3. Number of bales of hay.
4. Barrels of oil.
5. Number of gallons of fuel.

If the quantity terms in the contract are missing, the contract is unenforceable. Please see Chapter 5 for an economic discussion of quantity determination and inventory control.

Quality

The purchasing professional must pay close attention to the quality term of the contract. Quality should not be overspecified or underspecified. There is a wide range of quality factors. The quality factors must be included in the final contract. See Chapter 12 for a comprehensive discussion of the quality dimension.

Price and Credit Terms

The pricing terms of a contract are directly related to value. The purchasing professional must obtain the best value for the firm. Thus, price is the third major term that must be included in an enforceable contract. The price is determined when the offer is accepted. In some cases, price escalation clauses are used in a contract. A price escalation clause is an adjustment that the seller utilizes in order to compensate for variances at delivery. Purchasing professionals should agree to an escalator only as a last resort. See Chapter 13 for a comprehensive discussion on the pricing term. Finally, the purchasing professional should negotiate the credit terms with the supplier. See Chapter 14 for a comprehensive discussion on bargaining and negotiations.

Delivery Terms

Delivery terms are closely related to price terms. The transportation between the buying and selling firm is usually considered as part of the price. The delivery terms formalize the responsibilities of the buying and selling firm for delivery of the goods. As an example, "FOB shipment" means free on board (FOB) at a named place. Please see Chapter 15 for a comprehensive discussion of transportation analysis.

Leasing

Leasing is becoming more attractive for both consumers and businesses. Consumers are leasing automobiles in record numbers. One reason for the increase in consumer leasing is the tax effect of the leased automobile for small businesses. If the automobile is partially used for the business, a portion of the monthly lease payment is tax-deductible.

For a business, the lease payment is fully deductible and there is no need to keep track of depreciation of equipment on the balance sheet. Since the business does not own the plant equipment at the end of the lease, the business has no equity. However, productivity is increased as a result of the continuous modernization of equipment. There is clearly a trade-off. At the current time, there are no laws that specifically address the rights and obligations of the lessee and lessor. See Chapter 16 for a comprehensive discussion on leasing.

THE LEGAL IMPACT OF THE INFORMATION AGE

The Internet has infiltrated every aspect of the world. E-mail has outpaced the postal system as the primary communication mode in the developed world. Nine-year-old kids are buying and selling through eBay.com. In some instances, purchasing professionals are requiring the supplier to meet minimum levels of connectivity, which is not easily done. The investment in business-based information systems and their upkeep are expensive. Walmart and General Motors have mandated their suppliers to become electronically connected. Most governmental agencies also are moving toward connectivity. Electronic contracting is worldwide. An illustration from the automotive industry follows.

A major challenge facing the automobile manufacturing industry is the integration of supply management with information and technology management. As technology continues to develop, automobile manufacturers and their suppliers will have to share more information to help maintain market share. It is important to integrate **supply chain management** with information technology. An excellent example of leveraging information technology in this new reality is the development of **reverse auctions** by the Big Three automotive manufacturers to purchase materials electronically from most of their suppliers. Covisint is the business-to-business (B2B) automotive e-marketplace supported by the major car companies. Covisint implemented reverse auctions for the Big Three automotive manufacturers.

To date it appears that General Motors is the most aggressive user of Covisint (reverse auctions). General Motors purchased approximately $96 billion from suppliers through Covisint. Chrysler purchased approximately $5.2 billion of goods and services through reverse auctions during the same period. Ford saved approximately $350 million during fiscal year 2002 as a direct result of using reverse auctions.[2] While the owners of Covisint reaped benefits from this online transaction space, most auto suppliers did not subscribe to Covisint. Only 3,000 of the 5,000 registered auto suppliers used Covisint. One possible reason for not subscribing is that most suppliers at the time did not have the information technology capabilities required for the Covisint system. Another possible reason was that most suppliers believed that Covisint was not economically beneficial to their firms. At the present time, it is unclear whether the auto suppliers can benefit from using Covisint. However, most managers are enthusiastic about applying information technology in supply chain practices.

More and more consumers and businesses are contracting internationally. The legal difficulties of Internet transactions are apparent. During the next decade, we can expect the case law to be voluminous. Consider the requirements for an *offer* and legally binding contract discussed earlier, and it should be apparent that very little of the current law applies.

Electronic Contracts and Signatures

In 1996, the United Nations Commission on International Trade Law (UNCITRAL) adopted the Model Law on Electronic Commerce, which offers member states of the United Nations methods to address barriers to the use of electronic communications in their commercial law. The Model Law, with a Guide to Enactment, can be found at http://www.uncitral.org/uncitral/zh/publications/publications.html.

The Model Law itself allows legal requirements for a person's signature to be satisfied by use of a method that identifies the person and indicates the person's approval of the signed text. The method must be as reliable as appropriate in all the circumstances. This is a very useful assurance that electronic documents may be signed electronically, and it leaves parties broad flexibility in the choice of technology or method.

[2] See Informationweek.com, August 2002.

"Electronic signature" means a signature (data) in electronic form in, or attached to, or logically associated with, a data message and used by or on behalf of a party in a contract with the intent to identify that person and to indicate that person's approval of the contents of the data message.

A secure signature should be such that it can be used to identify the signer. This does not mean that the signature itself must consist of or include the signer's name. Identification by reference to other sources of information would be sufficient. Thus, for example, a digital signature may identify the signer by reference to a certificate issued by a certification authority. The main requirement is that the identification process must be relatively prompt, objective, and automatic. Thus, for example, while a handwritten signature is presumably capable of identifying the signer, such identification cannot normally be made promptly or automatically, and is frequently not an objective determination. In many cases, the signature itself is not readable. Even where it is readable, that signature may ultimately be capable of identifying the signer, but the timing and certainty of the identification process may not always satisfy the requirements of electronic commerce. Thus, a handwritten signature may not always be reliably identified as the signature of a particular individual (in the absence of an admission of that fact or a witness to the signing) without the testimony of an expert in handwriting analysis who has compared admitted signatures of the purported signer with the signature in question. In such a case, the result is unlikely to be prompt or automatic, and the conclusion of the expert is in many respects subjective rather than objective. By contrast, the use of a personal identification number (PIN) in an automatic teller machine provides the bank with an automatic, objective, and prompt identification of a specific person who is tied to a specific address and a specific account number when the funds are withdrawn. Such a person is not in a position to deny that the request for funds contains his or her signature (although that person may deny having signed the request; that is the subject of the reliability requirement).

A secure signature must be linked to the data message being signed in such a manner that if the message is changed, the signature is invalidated. Such a linkage may be regarded as a crucial requirement for a secure signature, since otherwise the signature could be simply excised from one data message and pasted onto another.

Cryptographic Signatures (PKI)

Cryptography is the science of securing information. The technology is based on scrambling information and then unscrambling it. Many businesses consider the cryptographic signature method known as Public Key Infrastructure (PKI) as the most secure and reliable method of signing contracts online.

The PKI method is used to encrypt online documents so that they will be accessible only to authorized parties. The parties have "keys" to read and sign the document, thus ensuring that no one else will be able to sign the document. The PKI technology is widely accepted by businesses. Many online services offer PKI-encrypted digital signature systems that function much like bank PINs for bank cards.

The Federal Electronic Signatures in Global and National Commerce Act (ESGNCA)

The Federal Electronic Signatures in Global and National Commerce Act (ESGNCA), or E-Sign, went into effect on October 1, 2000. The law made online contracts for a variety of business transactions more clearly enforceable. At the same time, it allows businesses to satisfy their obligation to provide legally required notices to *buyers and sellers* by sending notices electronically, once respondents provide consent for such online communication.

Electronic contracts and electronic signatures are legal and enforceable. The law benefits B2Bs (business-to-business websites) that need enforceable agreements for ordering supplies and services. The law helps them conduct business entirely on the Internet. This results in substantial cost savings to businesses.

PURCHASING AND ETHICS

Ethics can be defined as the standards of right conduct. However, depending on many factors, what constitutes ethical conduct varies. On the other hand, there are many clear examples of unethical conduct. But there are many business practices that are less discernible among business professionals. Some examples in this gray area are as follows:

1. Using a high-pressure sales technique to persuade naive customers to buy
2. Misleading a buyer or seller into thinking he or she is getting a deal
3. Giving a potential client or customer an expensive gift

How do you decide whether these controversial business approaches are acceptable? On the other hand, some of the most egregious examples of unethical conduct are also illegal. Examples include bribery, giving and receiving kickbacks, falsifying costs on private and public contracts, deceptive behavior, and outright dishonesty about attributes of products.

Ethics and the Law

The relationship between ethics and the law can be described as complex. Many violators of ethical conduct maintain that their actions are perfectly legal under the law. The societal norms must also be considered. In a free democracy, the law can only codify and enforce the most egregious violations as defined by society. In democracy governments must not stand between buying and selling organizations. However, fraud should be prevented by law, and ethical conduct must be practiced in order to prevent greed and opportunism. The elimination of fraud and exploitation does not regulate aggressive negotiations and other business practices. Aggressive but honest and effective negotiations may lead to an advantage for the negotiator. The legal system cannot determine the rules of engagement for fairness in negotiations. Ethics does not require an opponent to seek less than the optimum outcome. There are no fast rules on knowing when a negotiation evolves from skillful aggression to exploitation. At what point does bluffing become lying? If a car buyer tells a car seller that she "cannot afford" to pay more than $15,000 for the car even if the buyer has been approved for $20,000, this can be considered a bluff and not a lie. The term "cannot afford" is sufficiently vague enough to prevent the buyer from lying. It should be clear that good business and ethical conduct are equivalent. Successful business conduct requires that both parties are sensitive to differences in culture and situational context. Bluffing in the negotiations process is usually counterproductive and could lead to damaged relationships.

Ethics and the Negotiations Process

Purchasing professionals must strive to conduct honest negotiations. However, there are some situations when honesty is out of the control of the negotiator.

Sometimes veracity can be overruled by company culture. This could cause a serious conflict. Consider a situation where you are speaking for your boss. If it is understood that you are taking your boss's point of view and relying on information supplied by your boss, you may not be lying in saying something false. As a purchasing professional, it must be made clear to the opponent that you are speaking on behalf of your company and not yourself. This could cause serious conflict.

In general, negotiations must not be fraudulent (full of lies and misrepresentations) or exploitive (taking unfair advantage of the opponent). Finally, just because an action is legal does not make it ethical. Chapter 14 will discuss in greater detail the aspects of the negotiations process.

Purchasing agents are governed by the company's ethical policies, the **Uniform Commercial Code,** the *Securities and Exchange Commission*, and many state and local laws. Purchasing agents who violate ethical codes could easily go to jail. Various actual company and government ethical policies are given below.

A Corporate Code of Ethics Example

Big D Purchasing subscribes to the principles of the Institute of Supply Management (ISM). Suppliers should read and understand the guidelines below:

- Avoid the intent and appearance of unethical or compromising practices in relationships, actions, and communications.
- Demonstrate loyalty to the employer by diligently following the lawful instructions of the employer, using reasonable care and only authority granted.
- Refrain from any private business or professional activity that would create a conflict between personal interest and the interest of the employer.
- Refrain from soliciting or accepting money, loans, credits, or prejudicial discounts, and the acceptance of gifts, entertainment, favors, or services from present or potential suppliers that might influence, or appear to influence, purchasing decisions.
- Handle confidential or proprietary information belonging to employers or suppliers with due care and proper consideration of ethical and legal ramifications and governmental regulations.
- Promote positive supplier relationships through courtesy and impartiality in all phases of the purchasing cycle.
- Refrain from reciprocal agreements that restrain competition.
- Know and obey the letter and spirit of laws governing the purchasing function and remain alert to the legal ramifications of purchasing decisions.
- Encourage all segments of society to participate by demonstrating support for small, disadvantaged, and minority-owned businesses.
- Discourage Big D Purchasing's involvement in employer-sponsored programs of personal purchases that are not business related.
- Enhance the proficiency and stature of the purchasing profession by acquiring and maintaining current technical knowledge and the highest standards of ethical behavior.
- Conduct international purchasing in accordance with the laws, customs, and practices of foreign countries, consistent with U.S. laws, your organization policies, and these Ethical Standards and Guidelines.

Big D Purchasing does allow promotional items to be exchanged if (1) the item displays the company logo and (2) the item is of a value less than $25. Payment of meal expenses is an acceptable and common practice in today's business environment. The purchase of meals should alternate between companies.

University Code of Ethics Example

1. Give first consideration to the objectives and policies of my institution.
2. Strive to obtain the maximum value for each dollar of expenditure.
3. Decline personal gifts or gratuities.
4. Grant all competitive suppliers equal consideration insofar as state or federal statute and institutional policy permit.
5. Conduct business with potential and current suppliers in an atmosphere of good faith, devoid of intentional misrepresentation.
6. Demand honesty in sales representation whether offered through the medium of a verbal or written statement, an advertisement, or a sample of the product.
7. Receive consent of originator of proprietary ideas and designs before using them for competitive purchasing purposes.
8. Make every reasonable effort to negotiate an equitable and mutually agreeable settlement of any controversy with a supplier, and/or be willing to submit any major controversies to arbitration or other third-party review, insofar as the established policies of my institution permit.
9. Accord a prompt and courteous reception insofar as conditions permit to all who call on legitimate business missions.
10. Cooperate with trade, industrial, and professional associations, and with governmental and private agencies for the purposes of promoting and developing sound business methods.
11. Foster fair, ethical, and legal trade practices.
12. Counsel and cooperate with NAEB members and promote a spirit of unity and a keen interest in professional growth among them.

National Institute of Governmental Purchasing (NIGP) Code of Ethics Example (short version)

1. Seeks or accepts a position as head or employee only when fully in accord with the professional principles applicable thereto and when confident of possessing the qualifications to serve under those principles to the advantage of the employing organization.
2. Believes in the dignity and worth of the services rendered by the organization and the social responsibilities assumed as a trusted public servant . . .
3. Is governed by the highest ideals of honor and integrity in all public and personal . . . relationships in order to merit the respect and inspire the confidence of the organization and the public being served.
4. Believes that personal aggrandizement or personal profit obtained through misuse of public or personal relationship is dishonest and not tolerable . . .
5. Identifies and eliminates participation of any individual in operational situations where a conflict of interest may be involved.

As can be seen, all three of the plans are specific and easily understood. However, in order for any ethical code of conduct to be effective, there must be enforcement. In most cases, unless the purchasing agent commits egregious violations, it is business as usual.

WOMEN AND MINORITY COMPLIANCE

Government contractors, under certain conditions, must award subcontracts to minority or disadvantaged bidders. Several Fortune 500 companies have implemented measures to encourage purchasing managers to purchase from a variety of diverse suppliers. To be eligible to participate in some federal programs, a company must be certified as at least one of the following:

- *Women-owned business.* A company that is at least 51 percent owned by one or more women or, in the case of a publicly owned business, at least 51 percent of the stock of which is owned by one or more women, and whose management and daily business operations are controlled by one or more women.
- *Minority-owned business.* A company that is at least 51 percent owned, managed, and controlled by one or more minority persons. Minority means being African American, Hispanic American, Native American, or Asian American.
- Small Business Administration (SBA) hub zone.
- SBA disabled veteran.

Qualifying as a disadvantaged business enterprise (DBE) does not guarantee that a company's bid will be accepted.

Summary

The purchasing professional in a firm must be able to understand the legal aspects of the purchasing function. The purchasing function consists of many tasks within the business entity. The tasks include supporting the company with the acquisition of materials, supplies, and services. Purchasing agents also represent the company in negotiations with suppliers. In order to perform the duties, the purchasing professional must be given authority. The authority usually occurs automatically when a purchasing manager is appointed. The detail associated with the appointment should reside in the company bylaws. Purchasing personnel routinely sign purchase orders and contracts committing the company to specific terms and conditions.

The four components of a valid contract are (1) the parties must be capable, (2) the subject matter must be legal, (3) there must be mutual consideration, and (4) the parties must reach an agreement. Of course, oral contracts occur on a daily basis. However, there is no recourse for either party for oral contracts exceeding $500.

The most significant change of the legal aspects of purchasing is the impact of the information age. The Internet has infiltrated almost every aspect of the purchasing function. Recently, Walmart, General Motors, and numerous governmental agencies have mandated that their suppliers become electronically connected. The chapter ends with a discussion on the importance of an ethical code of conduct for purchasing agents.

Discussion Questions

1. What tasks are allocated to the purchasing function? What are the legal issues associated with the purchasing function?
2. What is meant by *purchasing authority*? Give examples of each type of purchasing authority.

3. How does *implied authority* relate to *express authority*? Give specific examples.
4. Discuss the liability issues associated with purchasing agents' actions.
5. What are the requirements of an enforceable contract? Provide specific examples. How is an *offer* related to a contract?
6. Compare and contrast *an invitation to bid* with an *offer*.
7. What are the four outcomes of an *offer*?
8. Explain how the purchasing agent can protect the company against a revoked *offer*.
9. Discuss the legal impact of the information age on the purchasing function.
10. What is an electronic signature?

Suggested Cases

AMD

Butler Systems

Tom and Jerry Construction

References

King, Donald B., and James J. Ritterskamp Jr. *Purchasing Manager's Desk Book of Purchasing Law.* 3rd ed. Englewood Cliffs, NJ: Prentice Hall, 1997.

Uniform Commercial Code. 1994 Official Text. Philadelphia, PA: American Law Institute and National Conference of Commissioners on Uniform State Laws, West Publishing Company, 1995.

Part Two

Materials Management

Chapter Four

Materials Management

Learning Objectives

1. Identify the activities of materials management.
2. List and explain the five functions of inventory.
3. Discuss the relationship between purchasing and materials management.
4. Determine how the materials management concept makes a contribution to profitability.
5. Understand why firms have implemented materials management systems.

INTRODUCTION

The purpose of materials management is to support the transformation of raw materials and component parts into shipped or finished goods. The function of inventory, in general, is to decouple the entire transformation process. During the transformation process, materials are combined with labor, information, technology, and capital. The five functions of inventory are:

1. Pipeline inventories (raw materials/in process)
2. Cycle inventories
3. Buffer stock
4. Seasonal
5. Decoupling

These five basic functions of inventory are fundamental to achieving smooth flow, reasonable equipment utilization and materials handling costs, and maintenance of good customer service. Periodically, an inventory audit of the five functions must be performed to compare the "should have" and the actual investment (units) for each function. Inventory is treated as a current asset for accounting purposes.

Figure 4.1 illustrates a flow diagram of inventory usage in a materials management system.

The supplier is the source of raw materials and component part inventories. Customer service is a concept that applies to all suppliers whether they are external to the company or internal. In the system shown in Figure 4.1, there are both external and internal pairs of suppliers and customers, for example, suppliers-purchasing, purchasing-assembly. Each supply point must meet peak demand or suffer the loss of sales when demand exceeds capacity.

FIGURE 4.1 Production Inventory System

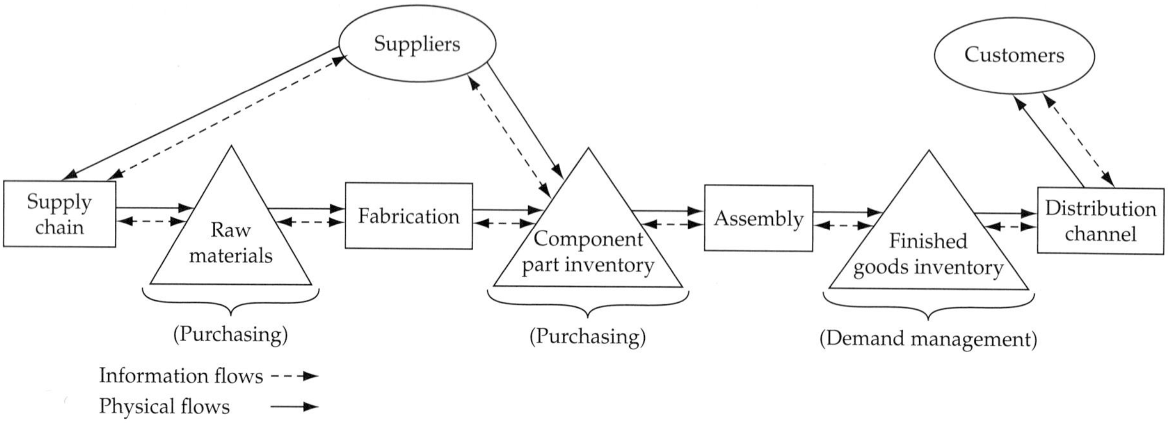

MATERIALS REQUIREMENTS PLANNING AND CAPACITY REQUIREMENTS

When planning to acquire materials, whether raw materials, component parts, or finished goods, the capacity must be considered for both the buyer and seller. Each materials acquisition must be translated into a capacity requirement by the supplier. For example, suppose we have a scenario as shown in this section.

Capacity Planning

Say capacity is the potential to produce 50 assemblies an hour. Although the short-term capacity may be higher, effective capacity is a range of substantial output under normal conditions, that is, a rate. A manufacturing plant is designed to produce 1,000 units of product a day. Is it possible for the plant to operate at a rate of 10, 50, or 120 units a day? There is a lower limit beyond which it is not economical to run. At some point, management will decide to shut down rather than produce indefinitely at a rate that does not generate revenues to cover fixed and variable costs. At low rates of production, fixed costs are borne by small volumes of output resulting in higher unit costs.

The upper level of production is limited by the process technology and/or the disposition of the workforce. Can a plant manager exhort workers to produce, in the short run, at very high levels of production to satisfy a very important customer? Probably yes, but not very often. Pushing the plant (equipment, people, and suppliers) to produce at very high levels of output accelerates wear and tear on machines and people. Machine maintenance, quality, and morale suffer.

Combinations of factors determine lower and upper bounds of capacity. Plant managers are concerned that productive facilities be well utilized. For the economy as a whole, we monitor the utilization of industrial capacity as an indicator of the general level of economic activity.

Capacity and Inventory

In general, inventory is stored capacity. If capacity is insufficient to satisfy peak demand for a product with seasonal sales, finished goods inventory can be accumulated during periods of low demand. In other words, if this inventory did not exist, management would have to invest in additional production equipment and systems to satisfy the demand of customers during peak demand periods. In the age of computer-integrated manufacturing (CIM), computer-aided design and manufacturing (CAD/CAM), flexible manufacturing systems (FMS), and group technology (GT), the burden of specification is changing from the buying organization to the supplying organization. The implications are serious. Buying organizations must be knowledgeable about the new manufacturing technologies so they can make good decisions about their purchase, implementation, and utilization.

THROUGHPUT TIME

The delay between receipt of raw materials and the availability of the finished goods produced from them is *throughput time* (TPT). The concept applies also to single components of the supply chain; for example, we speak of the TPT for the plant or distribution center.

For the whole system, TPT should be as short as possible. Consumers prefer to obtain goods or services in the shortest possible time. If TPTs are long, it is more likely that the customer's requirements will change:

> "I know we ordered 100 units, but now we only need 75."
>
> "Yes, we ordered 50 blues and 50 greens; now we really need 75 blues, 15 greens, and 10 reds!"
>
> "As long as you haven't finished the order, we'd like to change the product specifications."
>
> "The due date we originally agreed to was the first of the month, but now we don't need the stuff until the 15th."

The longer an order for material stays in the plant, the larger the work-in-process inventory will be, the larger the storage area required, and the more likely the material will be damaged, lost, or stolen. Work-in-process inventory has little market value except to the salvage yard. The firm is not in the business of making and inventorying work-in-process. The adage is, "Move it out; ship it; bill the customer."

ORDER CYCLE

The order cycle is both a link and a set of activities. As a link, the order cycle facilitates the flow of information and materials.

Customers communicate orders and inquiries about the status of orders. Suppliers respond and initiate the movement of product to the customer. The link that is the order cycle is sometimes visualized as a conduit or *pipeline*. The pipeline is the means by which various resources flow:

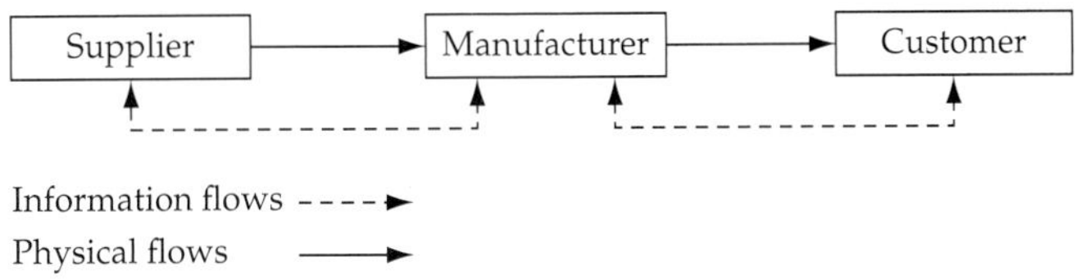

1. Information (orders, billings, inquiries)
2. Material
3. Money (credit)
4. Title

Distribution managers speak of a *distribution channel* when they mean the network of system components from the manufacturer to the final consumer, and the pipeline or linkages that tie the components together. From these notions, the concepts in the following sections can be developed.

Integrated Materials System

It is not necessary that all resource flows between components occur at the same time or in the same manner. This idea is called *channel separation* and is useful when designing supply-distribution systems. It really isn't accurate to say that components are joined by a single link. The pipeline actually has several channels because the transfer of materials, information, money, and title requires separate and specialized channels. Only in the simplest of exchanges would resource flows occur simultaneously.

The order cycle has some important characteristics. First, an order cycle has "length." The distance between supplier and customer determines, in part, how long it takes to transmit data and transport materials. However, the *modes* by which information is sent and material moved also determine the length of the order cycle. A customer may elect to have an order moved by various transportation technologies (modes):

1. Air
2. Rail
3. Truck
4. Water
5. Pipeline

Trade-off involves speed, reliability, inventory, and cost. For lightweight, high-valued items, overnight parcel express might be justified, but this would not be the case for a heavy, low-margin, noncritical item.

Customer orders also may be transmitted by alternative technologies:

1. Telephone
2. Postal service
3. Internet
4. Fax
5. EDI

The prices of these modes vary; although more rapid service usually implies a higher price, technologies such as the Internet have somewhat changed that paradigm. Once the infrastructure investment (e.g., fax machine, Internet, software) is made, the incremental cost is very low despite very high rates of communication. The more rapid, the higher the price. The trade-off considerations are similar to those for transportation.

The shorter the order cycle, the quicker the customer is served and the less inventory the manufacturer needs. If you have a *reliable* supplier who can supply you every day, you would order just enough to satisfy your daily requirement. At the end of the day, your stockroom would be empty. You can manage with a minimum of inventory, and your customer in turn will benefit. All of the activities that comprise the order cycle can be modified (redesigned) to change the time required, but always there are trade-offs to be evaluated—price, inventory, and customer service.

Order Cycle—Activities

The order cycle is not only a link, but a set of activities. The principal activities and the locus of responsibility are:

Activity	Responsibility
Order preparation	Customer
Order transmission	Customer
Order processing	Supplier
Order transportation	Supplier
Order receipt	Customer

Each activity is in turn a bundle of tasks. For example, the receipt of materials by the customer involves:

1. Physical receipt
2. Unloading
3. Inspection
4. Storage location decision
5. Move to storage
6. Documentation

Each of these, in turn, initiates further activity. For example, inspection verifies that the materials were in fact ordered, the condition of the order, and whether the order is complete. If everything is okay, accounts payable is notified so that payment to the supplier is made.

Lead Time

If we represent the order cycle as a set of activities, we can identify an important property of the order cycle—lead time. Some may argue that lead time begins when the order is transmitted. We'll go a step earlier and include order preparation, which begins when the need for material is recognized. See Benton and Krajewski (1990).

CUSTOMER SATISFACTION

The managers of integrated materials systems have two objectives:

1. Customer satisfaction
2. Minimum total materials costs

Earlier we spoke about *customer service*. Whether the term *service level* or *fill rate* is used, the idea is the same: the fraction of customers' demand that is satisfied without delay, or received as promised. Customer service is only one dimension of customer satisfaction. The latter includes material availability and a whole lot more. Customer satisfaction is whatever it takes to make the customer happy. In this sense, it is defined by the customer, may be subject to change, and is subjective. Suppliers cannot say what customer satisfaction is *unless* they have talked with their customers.

Quality, as we'll see shortly, is another concept that's explained in various ways. Good quality is a consumer expectation and a vital part of customer satisfaction. General Motors has adopted what it describes as a "customer-oriented vehicle evaluation" quality audit. Previously, finished vehicles were randomly taken from the assembly line daily and inspected for completeness, fit, and finish. That process is called a *static audit* because the vehicles are not road-tested.

Corporate officials learned from talking with customers that half of their complaints were not detected by the static audit. An enhanced audit was developed that included a road test so that engine and transmission performance, as well as squeaks, rattles, wind noise, and water leaks, could be discovered. The number of discrepancies found during the road test was added to discrepancies noted during static auditing. Discrepancies by vehicle and plant are reported throughout specific General Motors divisions.

The objective of the program is "zero discrepancies." Management describes the enhanced audit as an aid to achieve world leadership in product value and customer satisfaction. General Motors believes this audit process allows a vehicle to be rated through the eyes of the customer. "Our customers decide whether we pass the final audit."

Subjectively, customer satisfaction is what the customer says it is. The following are elements of satisfaction.

Material Availability

Two cases must be distinguished. If a firm makes products *to order*, customer service is measured by the degree to which products are completed and shipped *as promised*. Conceivably, an order may be rescheduled at the request of the customer, in which case the revised date is used to determine whether the order was shipped on time, early, or late.

Many *make-to-order (MTO)* firms faithfully calculate the ratio of on-time to total shipments. When customer service is measured this way, we speak of a firm's *delivery performance*. It's not uncommon to have delivery performances in the 90 percent and higher range. Rather than strive for a particular number, management needs to know what its competitors are doing. High delivery performance may only indicate scheduling inflexibility on the part of the supplier. "You asked for shipment on the 15th, and, by God, that's when we're shipping."

The second case is the firm that produces standard products in anticipation of demand for them—a *make-to-stock (MTS)* firm. The consumer expects to find the product on the shelf, that is, available for immediate shipment. In this case, order processing time does not include purchasing and production delays, unless a stockout is experienced.

If all customer orders are processed without delay, the level of service is 100 percent. Service level (SL) for an MTS firm is the ratio

$$SL = (\text{Orders shipped}/\text{Orders received}) \times 100$$

Unfilled orders are processed in one of three ways:

1. Backorder
2. Substitution
3. Cancellation

A customer who goes on backorder chooses to wait until material again becomes available. It is estimated that processing a backorder (or any special order) is three times more costly than handling routine orders. Backorders are filled; customers are inconvenienced.

There are other ways to express relative availability. Some companies offer "same day service," which means in most cases that orders received today are shipped today. Transportation time then becomes the determinant of delivery delay. Sometimes the service level objectives may be expressed in terms of 90 percent of an order received will be shipped within four days of receipt.

On-Time Shipment

This element of customer service is a variation on the notion of availability. On-time shipment has to do with the delivery promises made, and the ratio of orders shipped as promised to total orders. If an order is shipped on time, it is presumed that the customer is well served. Realistically, customers are more concerned about when the materials are *received*.

On-Time Receipt

Customers place orders based on *need dates*. The more imminent the calendar date, the more urgently material is needed. To say an item is needed on the 10th of the month means that, if the item is not actually in hand on that date, dire consequences ensue. Sometimes the need date is called the "drop dead date." "If I don't receive the order by the 15th of the month, I'm dead."

The customer thinks of material delivery in terms of the date of receipt, not the date of shipment. However, the supplier often has little control and not much information once an order is turned over to a transportation firm. Calls to the supplier are answered with the explanation, "It's on the truck, or plane, or in the mail." Suppliers rarely ask customers about the receipt of an order, using the logic "no news is good news." However, the absence of complaints doesn't mean that customer service is satisfactory. Suppliers need to follow up to determine whether orders were received on time, in good condition, and so on. See Benton and Shin (1998).

Complete Shipment

Orders commonly call for numerous items, sometimes in matched sets. A manufacturer of office furniture receives orders for matched desks, chairs, tables, and file cabinets. An order probably contains the requirements to furnish one particular office. The customer expects to receive all items at the same time. If a complete order cannot be shipped, the customer should be given the choice of a split shipment or rescheduling of the order. If a customer accepts partial receipt of an order, we say that the partial shipment was planned. The customer knows where and when the balance will be shipped. Unplanned partial shipments (actually receipts) result when materials are misrouted, lost, or stolen. The order left the supplier complete but arrived short.

Quality of Receipt

The quality of material can deteriorate between the time it leaves the production floor and the time it arrives at the customer's storeroom. Packaging, loading, transport, and unloading can all take a toll. Although damages can be claimed, materials received in poor condition are unsuitable for processing or distribution. The effect is the same as if a partial shipment were received. One purpose of receiving inspection is to determine damages and begin the procedure to replace, repair, or claim compensation. While the supplier may point an accusing finger at the carrier, the customer service obligation does not end at the supplier's loading dock.

Flexibility

Flexibility is the extent to which a supplier can accommodate a customer's requests. Perhaps the request is for special processing, packaging, or shipment. Even make-to-stock manufacturers receive such requests. The need to be flexible blurs the distinction between *make-to-stock* and *make-to-order*.

The name of the game, whatever the firm's classification, is *customer satisfaction*. Note that the costs of these extras are borne by the customer. The question is not who pays, but the willingness and ability of suppliers to cost-effectively perform nonstandard tasks for the customer.

Some requests for flexibility require that a supplier change its basic mode of operation. A wholesaler may perform processing and packaging—activities we normally associate with production. If such activities are offered to all customers, and become the basis by which the firm competes, the wholesaler has integrated vertically. The steel service center is a good example. What began as occasional requests to perform basic operations (cut to length, form, and grind) now constitutes a major part of the product-service offering of the steel service center. Don't call it a steel warehouse because it's much more than a place to store steel. A more comprehensive discussion about shifting activities forward or backward in the production-distribution network or channel will be given in Chapter 6.

Responsiveness to Inquiry

Customers want assurances that their orders are on schedule, especially as the shipping date nears. This element of customer service is the timeliness and accuracy of the information a supplier provides a customer. Suppliers who can't locate an order on the shop floor, or in the warehouse, or who answer all inquiries with, "It just went out on the truck," inspire little confidence.

Customers don't call to simply chat, but for information on which they can rely. You'll be reminded often in this text not to lie to the customer. Even if the truth is disappointing, or puts the supplier in a bad light, the sooner the customer has the facts, the sooner the necessary adjustments can be made. If, as a customer, you are told by a supplier that its workers have begun a work stoppage, you can begin to plan alternatives immediately. If, however, you learn about the walkout two weeks later when your order's shipping date has come and gone, the consequences for you are more severe—your options are fewer and probably more costly.

Customers want and should get as much notice as possible. Don't tell customers what you think they want to hear, unless it is the truth. Putting an unrealistic shipping date on the order ensures only disappointment.

Customer Satisfaction—The Balance

To summarize, customers want:

- Short lead time
- Good quality
- High value
- Customized products
- Postsale service

The cost of satisfying a customer's delivery time needs may not be entirely known, but we can argue that none of these elements of customer satisfaction are realized without cost. When customers are dissatisfied, other hidden costs are incurred—the costs of customer dissatisfaction. For example, the cost of good-quality materials is the sum of the cost to *prevent* poor quality and the costs to *detect* and respond to poor quality if it occurs. Presumably, if prevention, detection, and response are practiced, a supplier will ship good-quality products.

If poor quality is produced, goes undetected, and is shipped, the costs to both supplier and customer are substantial. The longer the defective material goes undetected in the consumer's plant, the greater the cost. If defects are found during receiving inspection, the costs of inspection and raw material are involved. If the defective materials go undetected to the shop floor when they are processed, the cost of scrapping the semifinished product is much greater. If the substandard materials are shipped as finished goods to customers, the final cost of poor quality can be many, many times the cost of the original substandard materials.

There are direct and measurable costs associated with poor quality. Yet the more important and difficult-to-measure costs are those associated with the damage to a supplier's reputation, the loss of a customer's capacity, and the dissatisfaction if the customer in the field vows never again to buy the product. We could describe the costs of providing the other elements of customer dissatisfaction similarly. The balance that management seeks is between:

1. Cost of customer satisfaction—A
2. Cost of dissatisfied customer—B

QUALITY

We hear so much about quality that it may come as a surprise that even experts don't agree about how to achieve it. *Fortune* recently asked the gurus of industrial quality to define it and to assign responsibility for quality. To some, quality is a technical matter. It has to do with engineering—both the process technology and product design. To others, quality is a statistical measure that utilizes sampling to achieve process control and make certain that inferior-quality material isn't shipped from the plant. There is a third view—that quality depends upon motivation. This means making a slogan a rallying cry—"Zero Defects" or "Quality is Free." The most revered of the quality gurus, W. Edwards Deming, hammers away at management as being the culprit when quality is poor. If management doesn't properly equip workers, how can they be expected to turn out high-quality products?

Is quality technical, statistical, motivational, or managerial? The answer is all of these. What the opposing points of view forget is that different situations call for different treatments. Not all quality problems respond to the same remedies. A firm might have the very best process technology, but its people may be poorly motivated. On the other hand, motivated and experienced workers can do little to improve quality if their materials, process technology, and supervision are second-rate.

Perhaps what the gurus need is a unifying focus. Quality, we have said, is an element of *customer satisfaction*. When all is said and done, quality is what the consumer says it is. As the baseball umpire retorted when the batter asked if the pitch was a ball or a strike, "It ain't a ball or a strike until I say what it is."

Quality is neither good nor bad until consumers cast their ballots in the marketplace. Even though the technology of quality is steeped in statistics and manufacturing engineering, materials managers first need to consider quality as part of the expectations of customers, whether intermediate or final. The quality of materials is uppermost in the minds of end users. Not only should products meet the customer's expectations, they should arrive in good condition. Intermediate customers (e.g., internal) have the same expectations. Buyers of materials evaluate suppliers on the basis of quality, reliability, and price. Note that quality ranks first. Consequently, materials managers, as suppliers, are increasingly concerned about the quality of raw materials, work in process, and finished goods.

Quality is a strategic decision. What should the quality of a product or material be? How do we compete with offshore manufacturers that enjoy reputations for leadership in quality? What's the quality level of domestic producers in our industry? Top management must decide the *quality level* of materials—high, low, or in between.

All sorts of factors contribute to a customer's perception of quality. Perhaps the reputation of the supplier is important. Advertising may influence one's perception, "We are the Rolls Royce of our industry." Sometimes advertising underscores historical quality, "Made in the centuries old tradition . . .." The claim that products are handcrafted is meant to suggest high quality. Customers often believe that high-priced materials are also high in quality, "It's *worth* what you paid for it."

Quality, in large part, is what people perceive it to be. Once formed, perceptions about the quality of a supplier's materials are slow to change. Despite the subjective nature of quality, expectations about quality are conditioned by public and private organizations that test materials and publish their findings. Consumers Union, a nonprofit organization, is probably the best known. To *qualitatively* evaluate consumer products and services, Consumers Union first identifies the relevant characteristics of a product. It then tests comparable products of various manufacturers and classifies products as:

- Best buy
- Acceptable
- Not acceptable

"Best buy" implies a product with high *value*. Value, in turn, is the ratio of quality and price:

$$\text{Value} = \text{Quality/Price}$$

Suppose we have comparable products of three manufacturers. The quality ratings and prices of the three products are shown below:

Product	Quality Rating	Price	Value
A	9	$110	8.2*
B	7	137	5.1
C	7	105	6.7

*Best buy.

Quality is a value in the range of 1–10 with 10 being the highest possible rating. Product A is not the least expensive at $110, but with a quality rating of 9, its value is

$$[\text{Quality/Price}] \times 100 = [9/110] \times 100 = 8.2$$

Product A is regarded as a *best buy*. Assuredly, the quality ratings of the respective manufacturers would differ from those shown above. To each manufacturer, the quality would be high, but the manufacturers are defining quality from an engineering specifications point of view.

Quality in the above example is the degree to which a product meets customer expectations. In an issue of *Consumer Reports*, low-price lawn mowers were evaluated. The quality-defining product characteristics were:

- Evenness of cut
- Dispersal of clippings
- Freedom from clumping
- Handling

Judgments were made during field trials by experienced operators who tested a total of 30 side- and 11 rear-bagging mowers. Two of the lowest-priced mowers at $120 were judged *best buys*. The top-quality mower was priced at $250. Its performance was not sufficiently better than the $120 models to qualify as a best buy. The purchaser of a *best buy* product is able to say, "I really got my money's worth."

The quality-defining characteristics of products are those that are important to the end user of the product. Owners of lawn mowers are not primarily concerned with detailed mechanical or electrical specifications. They want a product that leaves a good-looking lawn and provides relatively trouble-free operation. Owners look first at the way a product serves the purpose for which it was acquired. I am not suggesting that design specifications and manufacturing conformance to specifications are irrelevant where product performance is concerned. I am suggesting that the perceptions of quality held by the consumer and the producer are both important.

A product designer's job is to capture (in the product's design) the expectations of the customer. It's not a matter of designing a product and then foisting it off on the customer. "But customers don't know what they want until we tell them." Arrogance of that kind is fatal in this age of upwardly spiraling expectations of better-informed buyers.

Design means setting the *specifications* for a material or product. Specifications result in the *functional* and *aesthetic* characteristics of the product. The job of the materials manager is to ensure that products are made in the least costly way so that the item qualifies as a best buy.

The Quality Level

The process technology and experience of a supplier limit the range of quality possible. We wouldn't expect a general machine shop to produce high-quality integrated circuit chips. The design of a product must "be producible" given the process capability of the supplier. Within that range, top management sets the quality level—the degree to which the product *functionally* satisfies customers. If it should turn out that the design fails to meet customer expectations (regardless of price), the firm needs to invest in better technology or forfeit the market. This intersection of process capability and expectations is shown in Figure 4.2.

Within the area of intersection, management calls for the quality level it believes to be strategically best. But what does it mean to say that a product's quality is high or low? We have repeatedly said that quality is subjective. It's what a customer says it is. On the other hand, on what basis could the mower manufacturers claim that their products are high-quality? There is an *objective* definition of quality.

FIGURE 4.2
Expectations Capability Intersection

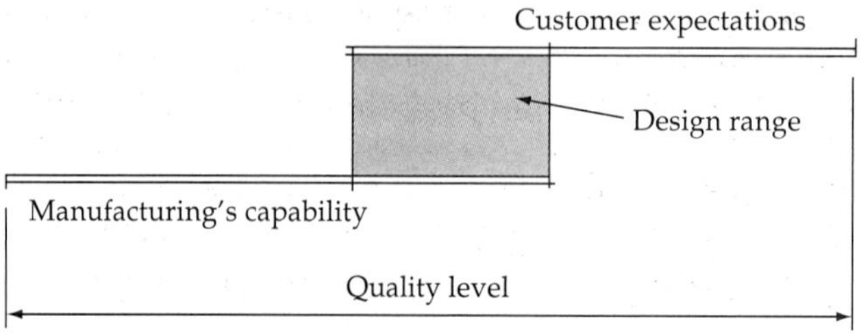

Objective Quality

This is the degree to which material *conforms* to specifications. If conformance is high, the company can claim that product quality is high. Lawn mower specifications are complex. Hundreds of parts are produced and assembled. Each part has numerous dimensions and properties. Surfaces of mating parts are finished to extremely small tolerances to ensure proper assembly. Overall product specifications are fixed—engine size, weight, blade length, and so forth.

It's quite possible to make a mower exactly to specifications, and yet that mower may function poorly—cut uneasily, leave clumps of grass, and be difficult to manipulate. When management decides the quality level, it has in mind the functional or operating characteristics of the mower—how well it cuts grass. Management identifies the market segment in which to compete—low-priced power lawn mowers. The quality–price decisions impose limits on the costs of production and distribution.

Is it possible that *objectively* a product is high quality but *subjectively* low quality? Too often the answer is yes. High quality products must both:

1. Conform closely to specifications.
2. Satisfy consumer expectations.

Can a product's quality be too high? Again, the answer is yes, but in this case we mean that *objective* quality can be too high. Tolerances are closer than need be, finishes are smoother than necessary—"the bottoms of the drawers are painted." Customers have little difficulty accepting the product, but it's much better than it needs to be, and very few customers would be willing to buy so high a quality item. It does in fact cost more to produce a Rolex watch than to produce a Timex. If accuracy, durability, and appearance are the quality-defining properties of wristwatches, the Rolex should meet the customer's expectations better. Note, however, that, objectively, *both* watches are high quality if both conform closely to their respective specifications.

We should now be able to understand that *conformance* isn't a sufficient test of quality. The design of the product must be satisfactory. We also can understand why two customers appraising the quality of the same item can have very different opinions about its quality. In Figure 4.3, only one of four outcomes results in a high-quality product. See Chapter 12 for a comprehensive discussion on quality.

SPECIFYING MATERIALS

Disagreements between supplier and customer about quality often stem from misunderstandings about material specifications. Suppliers frequently interpret specifications in ways customers never intended. Qualified suppliers, given identical

FIGURE 4.3
Objective–Subjective Quality

Quadrant	Design	Execution	Quality
1	Good	Good	High
2	Good	Poor	Low
3	Poor	Poor	Low
4	Poor	Good	Low

specifications, may come to quite different conclusions about what a customer wants. If one definition of quality is conformance to specs, the specifications must be *unambiguous*. The manner of specifying materials depends on the kinds of material ordered.

Raw Materials

These are semiprocessed materials intended for further processing—raw stock, crude oil, bituminous coal, paperboard, paper, lumber, copper, wheat, and cotton, for example. The materials listed are called **commodities.** Their specifications result from agreements on standards, as, for example, the U.S. Department of Agriculture's specifications for meat and grains.

By definition, commodities are homogeneous. The output of one producer is indistinguishable from that of another. Commodity markets are organized to facilitate the exchange (buying/selling) of commodities. The quantities available at a particular market and the prices of commodities are reported daily. Spot (current) prices, as well as future prices for commodities, are quoted by specification, for example, "#2 winter wheat/bushel" or "'choice' beef/hundred weight."

Even though specifications are known, judgment is still a factor. For example, the beef buyer for a fast-food restaurant chain may specify "USDA prime beef." The grade, *priori*, implies age, appearance, weight, and so on. Strictly speaking, there are no physical measurements for appearance, such as for "marbling," or the distribution of fat throughout the meat. Whether a side of beef is prime, choice, or good depends on one person's interpretation of the specifications (written description). Recall the umpire calling balls and strikes. The strike zone is defined for each player. It can be measured. But once play begins, umpires rely on judgment to decide the location of a ball traveling 90 miles an hour as it passes in front of a batter.

Materials such as steel are specified by *process* (e.g., "hot rolled"), physical properties (hardness, strength), and dimension. A steel buyer who orders by industry specification or *standard* incurs little risk that suppliers will misunderstand what material is required. "One-inch diameter, 1020 cold rolled steel bars, 16 feet long" means the same to everyone who makes steel. Note that while specs are unambiguous, the quality of the material produced may fail to conform to the specifications. It's the same problem we discussed earlier—poor execution of a good design.

Purchased Parts

Purchased parts include semifinished items that will be further processed and finished materials that will become components of finished end items. The usual way of specifying purchased parts in a *made-to-order environment* is with a graphic description, that is, engineering drawings. Drawings utilize standard conventions for showing dimensions, finishes, hardness, and other properties. The drawing completely and unambiguously describes the part. Exactly what processes are used to make it is decided by the supplier. It is necessary that the customer and supplier understand blueprints.

When only one or a small number of parts are made to order, the buyer may not provide the supplier with finished drawings. Instead, a prototype of the part is given to the supplier with the request to "make the part as per sample." This opens the door to misinterpretation of the exact part specification.

Many parts can be purchased off the shelf. They are like commodities in the sense that they are standardized. In effect, they are *made to stock* according to specifications established by an industry, professional association, or independent testing organization. Many small mechanical parts, for example, fasteners, are manufactured to standards established by the Society of Automotive Engineers, SAE. The specifications for parts such as fixtures and wire are concerned with the satisfaction of safety standards. The buyer is assured that the part is safe to use in a particular application and that its correct installation complies with standards, for example, building construction.

MAINTENANCE, REPAIR, AND OPERATING (MRO) SUPPLIES

MRO materials are quite diverse; they are specified in various ways. The keys are quality and uniqueness.

Maintenance

These are items that we expect to periodically replace in a piece of equipment. Over time, machine parts are subject to wear and are replaced. The original equipment manufacturer expects to resupply these parts during the life of the equipment. Not infrequently, a contract to purchase equipment includes a specified number of replacement parts. Airlines purchase aircraft and spare engines. Periodically engines are removed for overhaul. Replacement parts are specified by manufactured part number and the model number of the unit in which it is installed. Problems arise when manufacturers discontinue making equipment. Replacements will be available as long as sufficient machines are in operation in the field. After that, procurement and specifications become a problem. Some equipment owners may elect to supply themselves, in which case they must provide complete documentation (specification) of the parts required. The same is true if the parts are purchased externally. Sometimes an equipment manufacturer will produce replacement parts if a sufficient number are ordered to make their manufacture profitable. The older the model being maintained, the less current experience the supplier has, and the more difficult the task of specifying. For example, try to obtain a repair part for a 20-year-old plumbing fixture in your home.

Maintenance also means the application or renewal of materials such as lubricants and coolants. Periodic maintenance (labor and materials) ensures longevity and satisfactory machine operation. In most cases, these maintenance materials are commodity-like in nature and are specified by industry or association standards. These materials are carried in stock and managed as part of raw materials inventory by purchasing management.

Repair

The distinction between maintenance and repair materials is not always clear. In theory, if good maintenance is practiced, events requiring repair will occur infrequently. Repair suggests the unexpected, which means the need to patch up or replace equipment components that we don't expect to fail. Usually the parts are not carried as inventory by the equipment manufacturer. The repair material may have to be described in very specific ways, that is, drawings and photographs. Perhaps field engineers from the machine supplier will need to be called. The more common event is repair of equipment failure in which the services of skilled craftsmen are more important than specific materials.

Operating Supplies

These supplies, also called "indirect materials," become part of the end item and are essential for its production, but their unit value or size is too small to plan or control usage unit by unit. A good example is rivets used in airframe construction. Rivets are "counted" by weighing them. Bins of rivets are located throughout the plant and are available to anyone on a "help yourself" basis. Rivets are set, drilled out, replaced, dropped on the floor, and so on, without regard for usage. No one would suggest counting rivets or holding assembly workers accountable for them. Adhesives are another common example. These materials are supplied as needed to assemble components or provide seals between components.

Generally speaking, operating supplies are standard items and are specified by manufacturer or industry codes. Nonstandard items should be questioned by the purchasing manager. Is the special item really necessary? Can a standard material be substituted?

TOOLING

There are two kinds of tooling with respect to their specifications. The first kind is standard tooling. Various holding devices, partitioners, material cutting, and forming tools are standard with respect to their size and capacity. As with standard materials, tools are specified by the manufacturer's part or model number, or by an industry code.

The nonstandard kinds of tooling require elaborate specification. Tooling in this class is one of a kind and highly engineered. It is a make-to-order item. Detailed drawings of the tooling are necessary. Frequently the tool supplier works with the customer to design the item. The quality of this kind of tooling is especially critical. Whether the tooling is designed to position or hold material during processing, or to modify or extend the operation of processing equipment, the tooling must be built to specifications; otherwise, the quality of the material produced is unacceptable.

Summary

The purpose of this chapter was to focus on materials management in support of the transformation of raw materials and component parts into shipped goods and finished goods inventories. The basic function of inventory is to decouple the entire transformation process. The functions included in the materials management concept include (1) materials planning and control, (2) production scheduling, (3) receiving, (4) stores, (5) traffic, (6) disposal of scrap, (7) quality control, and (8) inventory control.

The scope of materials management is vast. The various subfunctions include materials planning and control, purchasing, stores, and inventory management. Specifically, the materials management scope encompasses:

- The acquisition aspects of the organization
- Inventory control and stores management
- Material logistics, movement control, and materials handling aspects
- Purchasing, supply, and transportation
- Supply management and logistics management
- Customer satisfaction and quality-related activities

The evolution of the materials management concept has resulted in firms becoming more profitable through functional integration.

Discussion Questions

1. Discuss the relationship between material requirements planning and capacity planning.
2. What is the relationship between capacity planning and inventory management?
3. What are the costs associated with quality? How does quality relate to the purchasing function?
4. Explain at least three expert views of the quality function. Which view do you agree with? Why?
5. Quality is a subset of customer satisfaction. What is meant by this statement? What is the definition of *value*?
6. What are the characteristics of a *good* supplier?
7. What is meant by *specifying materials*?
8. How are maintenance, repair, and operating (MRO) supplies different from purchased components?
9. What skills are required to be an effective materials manager?

Suggested Cases

Butler Systems
Hudson Fabricators
Temko Earthmovers

References

Benton, Jr., W. C., and L. Krajewski. "Vendor Performance and Alternative Manufacturing Environment." *Decision Sciences* 21, no. 2 (Spring 1990).

Benton, Jr., W. C., and H. J. Shin. "Manufacturing Planning and Controls: The Evolution of MRP and JIT Integration." *European Journal of Operational Research* 109 (1998), pp. 2–17.

Chapter Five

Inventory Management

Learning Objectives

1. Discuss the relationship between the purchasing function and inventory control.
2. List the primary reasons for holding inventory.
3. Explain the differences between independent and dependent demand.
4. Identify the necessary requirements for effective inventory management.
5. Describe ABC analysis.
6. Identify the cost components of the classical EOQ model.
7. Summarize the basic assumptions of the EOQ model.
8. Define quantity discounts.
9. Characterize service levels.
10. Identify the differences between fixed-order quantity and variable-order inventory systems.

INTRODUCTION

The purchasing function is taking on increasing importance in today's industrial economy. Since materials constitute the largest single percentage of their purchasing dollars, profit-oriented firms have turned to professionally operated purchasing departments to make sure they are getting full value for their outlays on materials.

In many purchasing situations, there are a number of different considerations conflicting with one another that influence the final purchasing decision. Rush orders usually cost more. Large-quantity orders lower the unit cost but may increase inventory. It is the task of the purchasing department to evaluate all of these considerations and to come up with the proper buying decision. This decision may have to be made on the basis of inadequate information and under the pressure of time. The purchasing professional must be able to make profitable buying decisions under these conditions. The focus of this chapter will be on helping the purchasing professional make profitable inventory management decisions.

Inventory is the lifeblood of any business. Most firms store thousands of different items. There are many inexpensive supply or operating type items. The type of business a firm is in will usually determine how much of the firm's assets are invested in inventories. Hospitals carry beds, surgical instruments, food, pharmaceuticals, and other miscellaneous items. On the other hand, manufacturing firms

FIGURE 5.1
Purchases as a Percent of Value of Shipments
(Selected Industries Each with Sales Exceeding $1 Billion)

Source: U.S. Bureau of the Census, Census of Manufacturers (2000).

Pharmaceutical	22.0
Photographic equipment and supplies	26.4
Book publishing	33.6
Aircraft equipment	35.0
Cement, hydraulic	36.5
Oil field machinery	38.1
Values and pipe fittings	42.1
Motors and generators	42.1
Shipbuilding and repairs	42.6
Furniture and fixtures	43.0
Miscellaneous plastic products	44.7
Fabricated rubber products	44.9
Organic chemicals	45.8
Electronic computing equipment	46.6
Electronic components	46.7
Inorganic chemicals	47.0
Tires and inner tubes	47.7
Weaving and finishing mills, wool	48.1
Automotive stampings	49.6
Construction machinery	50.1
Paperboard mills	51.8
Sheet metal work	52.2
Weaving mills, cotton	52.2
Refrigeration and heating equipment	52.4
Farm machinery	52.9
Primary aluminum	55.1
Synthetic rubber	56.0
Fabricated sheet metal	56.1
Paper bags	56.2
Sanitary paper products	58.1
Blast furnace steel mills	58.5
Metal cans	60.1
Radio and TV sets	61.1
Tufted carpets and rugs	68.0
Copper rolling and drawings	74.6
Petroleum refining	81.6
Primary cooper	82.9

carry office supplies, raw materials, component parts, finished products, and many other industry-related items. As shown in Figure 5.1, a large number of American firms spend between 40 and 80 percent of their sales dollars for materials purchased outside of the firm. These data only include raw materials and component parts. The data in Figure 5.1 show that the purchasing-inventory activity is the key factor affecting the prosperity and survival of an industry or firm. These data also suggest that sound management of the purchasing-inventory interface will give firms a significant competitive advantage in any industry.

The objective of this chapter is to provide a framework for inventory management. First, a discussion of the traditional order-point system will be presented. Second, a description of the dependent-demand concept will be presented. The general MRP lot-sizing problem for time-phased requirements will be used to illustrate the dependent-demand concept. Specifically in manufacturing, several well-known, time-phased, lot-sizing procedures will be presented to illustrate how order quantities are determined in a dependent-demand manufacturing environment.

This chapter is divided into two major sections, independent-demand inventory systems and dependent-demand inventory systems. Independent demand is demand for end items (i.e., distribution items, finished goods, spare parts, etc.).

INDEPENDENT VERSUS DEPENDENT DEMAND

In order to manage the various types of inventory, attributes of the items first must be analyzed in terms of cost, lead time, past usage, and the nature of demand. The nature of demand is perhaps the most important attribute. The nature of demand can be either independent or dependent. *Independent* demand is unrelated to the demand for other items. In other words, demand for an independent item must be forecasted independently. *Dependent* demand is directly derived from demand for a another inventoried item demand. In manufacturing firms, raw materials, component parts, and subassemblies are dependent on the final item's demand. Thus, demand for a dependent item should not be forecasted independently. As an example, a completed automobile is an independent demand item that is forecasted. However, we know that each automobile requires a chassis assembly. It would make no sense to forecast the chassis assembly independently, simply because the wheels are dependent and are derived from demand for the automobile. Inventory management for dependent items is usually managed by material requirements planning. In distribution firms, demand is usually *independent*. The order quantities for each inventory item should be forecasted separately. Stock replenishment in independent-demand systems is usually determined by statistical inventory control or order-point systems.

INVENTORY MANAGEMENT OVERVIEW

Management of inventories is a major interest of purchasing managers. In many industries, the investment in inventories comprises a substantial share of the firm's assets.

If the productivity of the inventory asset can be enhanced, the improvement will go directly to the bottom line. How does the purchasing professional know how much inventory to carry? How does the purchasing professional know when to place a replenishment order? Specifically, what guidelines should be used for making purchasing decisions? Remember, the purchasing function is directly influenced by inventory management decisions. Before inventory productivity can be improved, one must take a careful and critical look at the specific business entity. In the area of inventory management, the purchasing professional should make explicit decisions regarding the following:

1. *What to stock*. The purchasing professional, at the very minimum, must meet the requirements and needs of the manufacturer or distribution operation.
2. *How much to invest*. The purchasing professional must first review the level of capital support for inventory. This decision is usually made at the vice president level.
3. *How much service to offer*. What level of protection against stockouts is acceptable for the competitive environment? It is impossible to achieve a service level of 100 percent.

As can be seen, none of these decisions is independent of the other. Moreover, combining these decisions is complex and may be closely correlated with the industry and the type of firm within the industry. In the case of a manufacturing firm, you must consider whether the production process is make-to-order, make-to-stock, or some hybrid of the two. For instance, if the process strategy in your industry follows a make-to-stock strategy, customer service becomes a key management concern. On the other hand, if you operate a distributor or retail store, you must make managerial decisions based on the potential for profitability. The production-inventory system taxonomy is shown in Figure 5.2.

FIGURE 5.2
Production-Inventory System Taxonomy

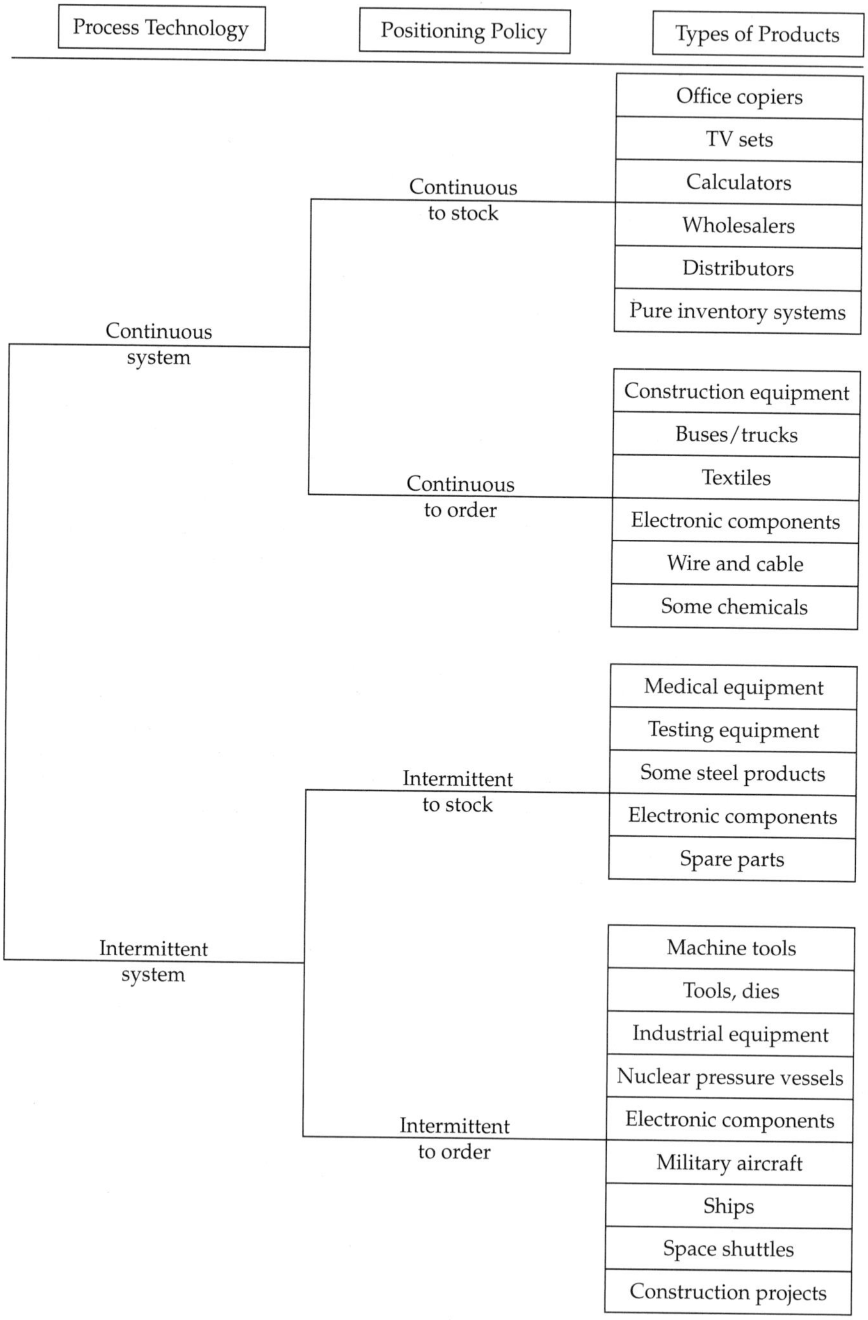

The production processing technology is divided into two categories: continuous systems and intermittent systems. The taxonomy is based on continuous systems producing standardized products through an assembly line, while intermittent systems are used to produce nonstandardized products through a job shop. Another category (not shown in the taxonomy) associated with continuous systems is pure inventory systems. Pure inventory systems are distribution stocking points, such as warehouses or distributors.

Batch operations or job shops are associated more with nonstandard products produced in discrete batches. The second-level classification of the taxonomy is the way in which goods and materials flow through productive systems, and the function of inventories in facilitating this flow. There has been an extensive literature dedicated to inventory over the past 40 years. Currently, inventories account for between 60 and 80 percent of a typical industrial firm's assets. What's more, inventory serves as the lifeblood that allows businesses to operate competitively. Their existence either in the form of finished products, work-in-process, or raw materials is the lubricant of any production system. Inventories affect costs, profits, customer service, and investments in facilities. The purchasing manager must have a clear understanding of the role of inventory in the materials management system.

ABC CLASSIFICATION OF INVENTORY ITEMS

The inventory items that are the most important for a specific industry or firm should be items that account for the greatest dollar value. In order to determine which items these are, two variables must be considered: unit cost of each item and item demand. Inventory items can be classified into "A" items, which have a high dollar usage, "B" items, which have an immediate dollar usage, and "C" items, which have a low dollar usage. In other words, those items that are the most demanded and most costly are the most important inventory items and the items that are the slowest moving and least expensive are least important. To determine the usage value of an item, multiply the unit cost by annual sales volume. If a particular item costs \$100 and 150 are sold in one year, then its usage value is \$100 × 150, or \$15,000. With only these two data points (sales and costs), you can *not only* rank all of your inventory items by importance but also take the first step toward controlling independent demand and distribution inventories. If you analyze what sells the most and what costs the most, a predictable pattern will emerge with most distribution inventories.

1. Certain items are demanded by a great many customers.
2. Most items are only demanded by certain customers.
3. Some items are demanded by few customers.

As a result of this general pattern, a small percentage of the total item usage accounts for a large proportion of total usage value. It is hypothesized that 80 percent of the total inventory cost is vested in approximately 20 percent of the items. Thus, managers should allocate 80 percent of their managerial resources to the 20 percent A classification. It may make economic sense to carry larger quantities of B and C items and apply fewer managerial resources for less

FIGURE 5.3
Typical ABC Analysis Curve

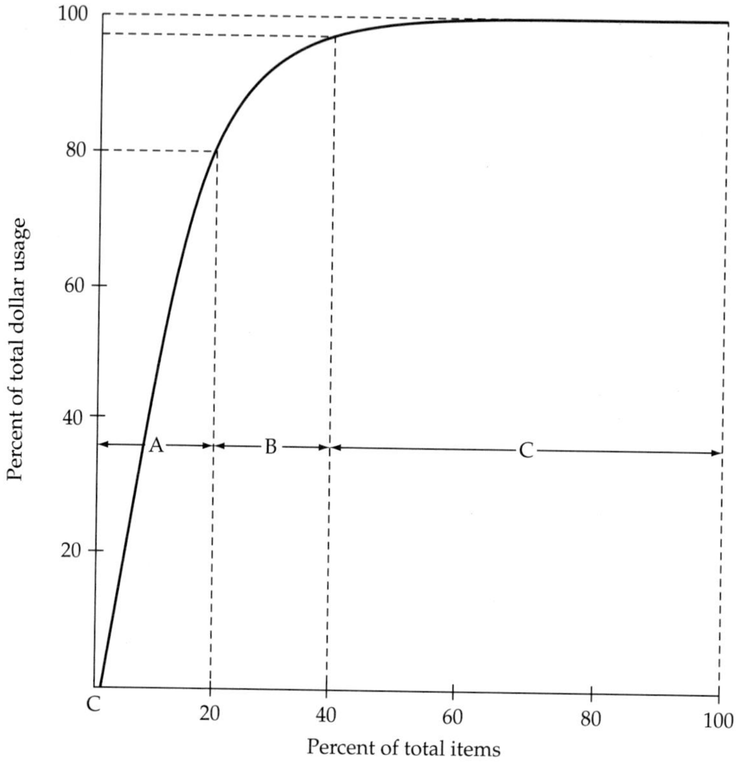

important B and C inventories. The following procedure is one way of implementing an ABC analysis:

1. Calculation of the annual usage value.
2. Sorting of the items regarding their annual usage value in decreasing order.
3. Calculation of the ratios of the annual usage per item and accumulated percentages.
4. Calculation of the ratios of the annual usage value per item and accumulated percentages.
5. Classify items into A, B and C groups.

A relationship similar to the curve shown in Figure 5.3 is a result of the ABC analysis. An illustrative example is given in Figure 5.4a and Figure 5.4b.

INDEPENDENT DEMAND

In this section, we are concerned with the control of end items. The inventory management concepts covered in this section are also applicable to retailing and distribution.

There are five primary functions of inventories:

1. *Pipeline inventory*. The supply pipelines of the entire system require a considerable investment in inventory. If the system's volume is 1,000 units per week and

FIGURE 5.4(a)
An ABC Analysis Illustration

Item	Annual Usage (units)	Cost per Unit ($)	Annual Usage Values ($)
1	10,120	$0.20	2,024
2	3,520	0.40	1,408
3	3,830	9.50	36,385
4	4,368	0.25	1,092
5	3,590	0.90	3,231
6	4,820	0.70	3,374
7	1,050	0.30	315
8	1,100	0.44	484
9	710	31.60	22,436
10	4,700	0.38	1,786

FIGURE 5.4(b)
An ABC Analysis Solution

Item	Annual Usage (units)	Cost per Unit ($)	Annual Usage Values ($)	Cumulative Ratio of Annual Usage (%)	Cumulative Ratio of Usage Value (%)	Classification
3	3,830	$9.50	$36,385	50.16%	50.16%	A
9	710	31.60	22,436	30.93%	81.09%	
6	4,820	0.70	3,374	4.65%	85.65%	B
5	3,590	0.90	3,231	4.45%	90.01%	
1	10,120	0.20	2,024	2.79%	92.89%	
10	4,700	0.38	1,786	2.46%	95.35%	C
2	3,520	0.40	1,408	1.94%	97.29%	
4	4,368	0.25	1,092	1.50%	98.79%	
8	1,100	0.44	484	0.6%	99.39%	

it takes one day to transport from the supplier to the plant, there are $\frac{1}{7} \times 1,000$, or about 143, units in transit on the average.

2. *Cycle stocks.* Assume that the average unit sales volume is five units per week or 15 units in the three week ordering period. Thus, the firm must have no fewer than 15 units of cycle stock on hand when the order is placed for an average on hand cycle stock of 15/2 = 7.5 units. During the 3 week replenishment period cycle stock is required. The concept of average inventory will be addressed in the next section.
3. *Seasonal inventories.* If demand follows a seasonal pattern, inventories can be accumulated during low-sales periods and depleted during high-usage periods to avoid problems associated with adjusting capacity.
4. *Safety stocks.* Safety stocks are designed to absorb random demand uncertainties.
5. *Decoupling stocks.* Stocks of inventories at major stocking points throughout the system make it possible to carry on each activity independently. That is, the presence of inventories allows for each work center to begin at the same starting time.

Costs in an Inventory System

The objective of an inventory system is the minimization of total operating costs. The unavoidable costs of operating pure inventory systems are ordering costs, stockout costs, and holding costs. To illustrate the cost behavior of a fixed-order-size system, let's look at the simple classical economic lot-size model (EOQ). The EOQ derives the optimal lot size for purchasing by minimizing the cost components involved (ordering costs and holding cost).

The classical inventory model assumes the idealized situation shown in Figure 5.5a and b, where Q is the order size.

Assume an annual requirement of $A = 52{,}000$ units, or an average of 1,000 units per week. If we ordered in quantities of 1,000 units, the cycle inventory, on the average, is $Q/2 = 500$ units. On the other hand, if the purchasing manager chooses to order in quantities of 500 units, the associated average inventory level falls to $500/2 = 250$ (see Figure 5.5).

Upon receipt of an order, units are assumed to be withdrawn at a constant rate from the beginning level of Q units; this is illustrated in Figure 5.5a and b. When inventory reaches the dotted line in Figure 5.5a (reorder point), a new

FIGURE 5.5 Simple Classical Inventory Model

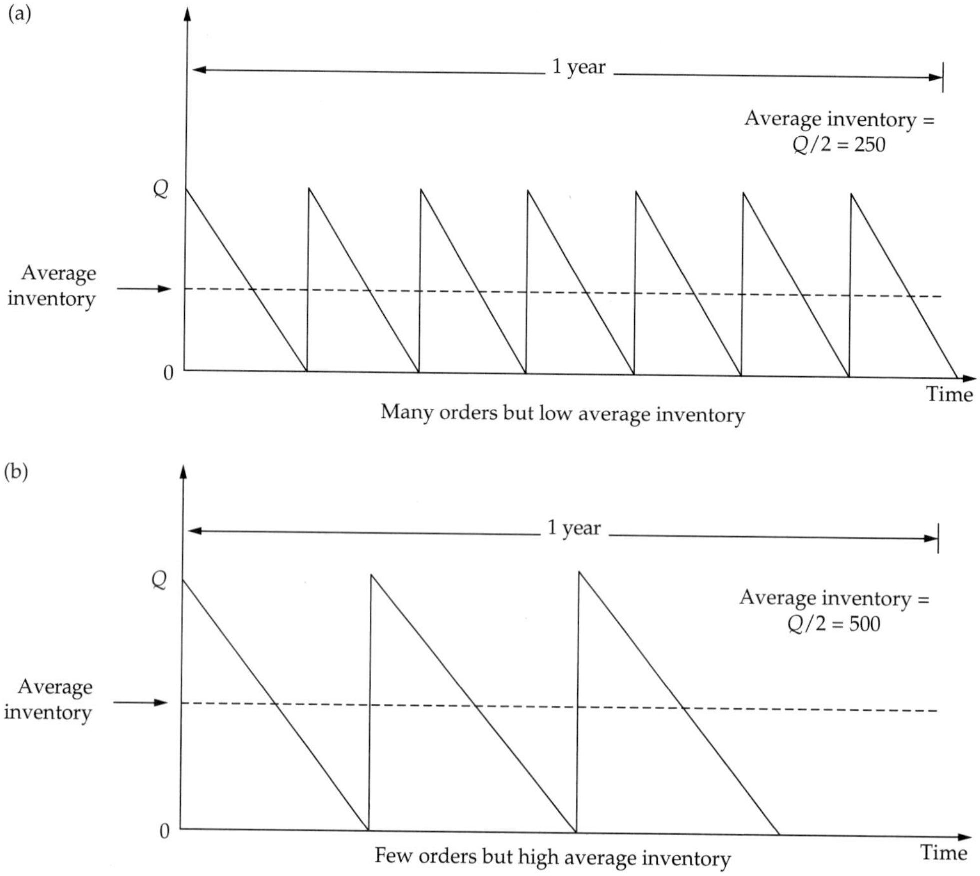

order is placed for Q units. After a fixed lead time period, the units are replenished with the entire order quantity Q. The vertical line represents the instantaneous replenishment of Q. The inventory holding cost (C_H) will be proportional to the lot size. The relationship between the holding cost and ordering cost is shown in Figure 5.6a–c.

Inventory cost C_H is defined as the cost of carrying one unit of inventory for one year. The costs include insurance, taxes, interest, and obsolescence. As Q increases, the annual holding cost increases. The ordering cost C_P is defined as the cost of preparing and following up on an order. Thus, as Q increases, the annual incremental ordering cost decreases because fewer orders need to be placed.

Figure 5.6c shows the resulting total cost by adding the annual holding and ordering costs:

$$TC = [(A/Q \times C_P) + (Q/2 \times C_H)] \quad \textbf{(1)}$$

FIGURE 5.6
Total Cost Curve

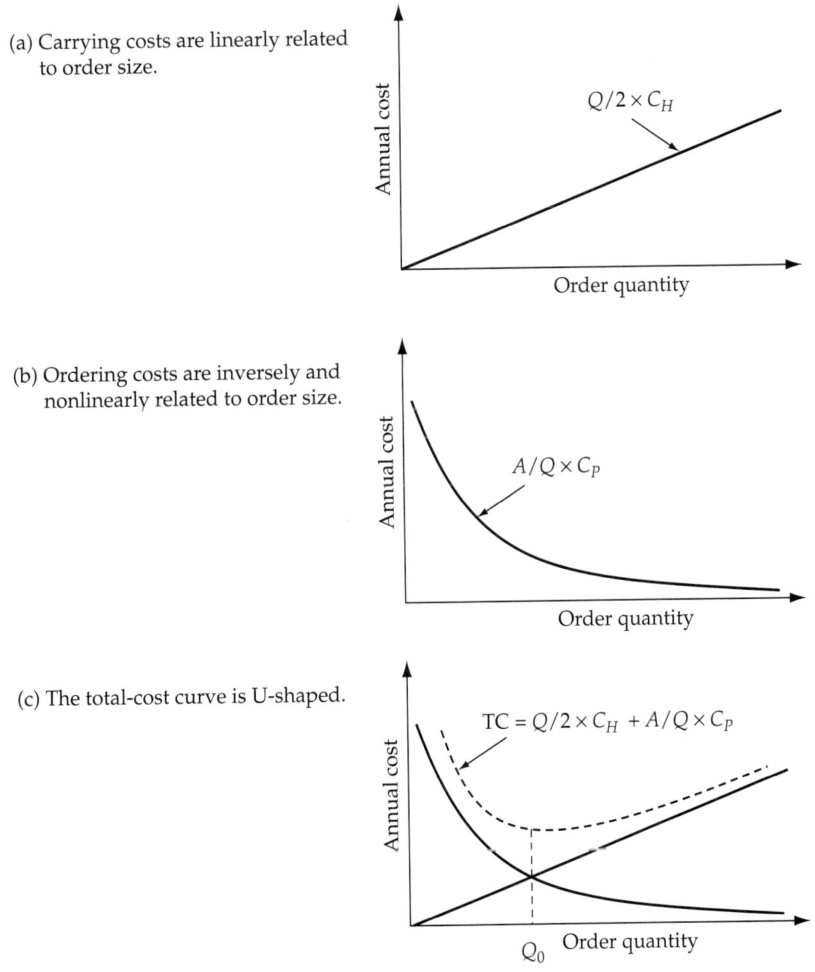

where

A/Q = Number of orders per year

C_P = Cost of an order

$Q/2$ = Average inventory

C_H = Unit inventory cost per year or item cost (P) times the annual carrying cost rate (r)

The new quantity Q is received as the inventory reaches zero, so the average inventory is $(Q + 0)/2$ or $Q/2$. Figure 5.7 shows a flow diagram for the basic EOQ model.

The sum of the two costs (ordering and holding) will be the total inventory cost per year for any purchased item. To derive the minimum-cost lot size (EOQ), take the first derivative with respect to Q and set it equal to zero. The calculus is used to determine the point of inflection on the total cost curve where it is no longer decreasing and beginning to increase.

$$\frac{\delta(TC)}{\delta Q} = -\left(\frac{A}{Q^2}\right)C_P + \frac{C_H}{2} = 0 \qquad \textbf{(2)}$$

FIGURE 5.7
Flow Diagram for Classical EOQ Inventory Systems

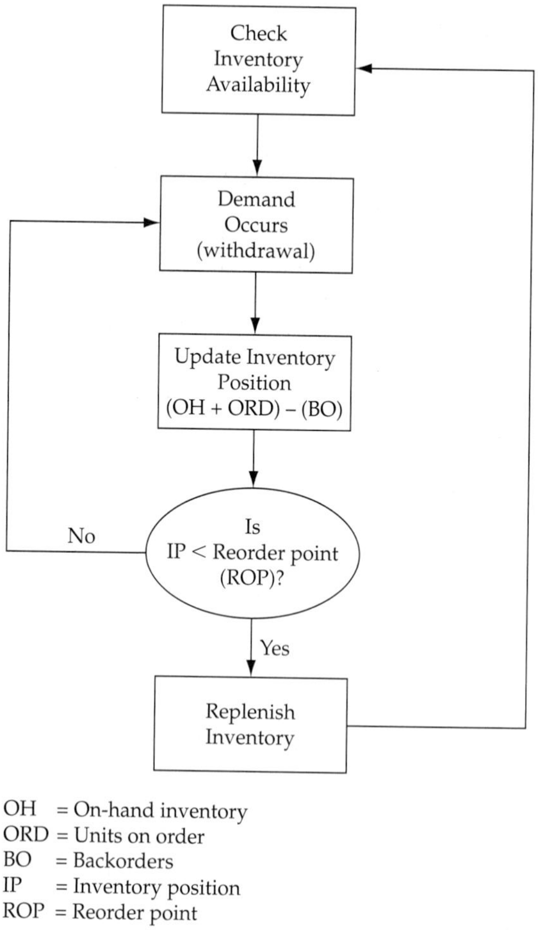

$$C_P \frac{A}{Q^2} = \frac{C_H}{2} \quad (3)$$

$$Q^2 = 2C_P \frac{A}{C_H} \quad (4)$$

The solution to Equation (2) is

$$Q^* = \sqrt{2AC_P/C_H} \quad (5)$$

As can be seen by Equation (5), expensive items will be ordered frequently and in small quantities, and inexpensive items will be ordered less frequently and in larger quantities.

Once the most economical order quantity is known, several other measures can be taken:

1. The expected number of orders during the year, $N_O = A/Q$.
2. The expected time between orders, TBO $= 1/N_O = Q/A$.
3. The reorder point, $R = (A/12) \times L$, where lead time, L, is expressed in months. If L is expressed in weeks, $R = (A/52) \times L$.

The minimum total cost per year is obtained by substituting Q^* for Q in Equation (1). The classical EOQ model assumes the following:

1. Constant demand
2. Constant lead time
3. Constant unit price
4. Fixed order cost per order
5. Fixed holding cost per unit
6. Instantaneous replenishment
7. No stockouts allowed
8. No demand uncertainty
9. Quantity discounts are not available

The Classical EOQ Model with Quantity Discounts

From time to time, buying firms receive discounted price schedules from their suppliers. This usually means that the price per unit is lower if larger orders are purchased. It may or may not be to the buyer's advantage to accept the quantity discount. The buyer must be careful not to compromise the economies of his or her firm's cost structure. Although the discount schedule may appear attractive in terms of material cost savings, higher holding costs may reduce overall profitability. At the same time, a specific discount schedule could produce economic advantages for both the buyer and seller.

The classical EOQ model assumes that the per-unit material price is fixed. The quantity discount condition invalidates the total cost curve in Figure 5.6c. Quantity discounts induce a discontinuous total cost curve. Assuming the discount applies to *all units* (and not just in *incremental* units beyond the discount point), the minimum total cost point will be either at the point of discontinuity or at the traditional EOQ point compared with the original price.

Figure 5.8 shows the new total cost curve. As can be seen, the behavior of the EOQ does not change. The effect is a constant increase in the total cost curve. Specifically, there are separate discount curves for each price break. No one curve

FIGURE 5.8
Total Cost Curve for All Units with Quantity Discounts

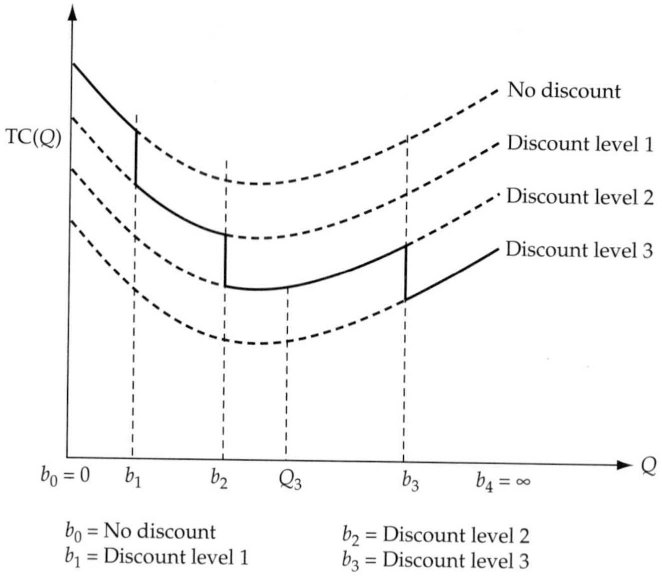

applies to the entire range of quantities; each curve applies to a portion of the curve (the solid portion).

A five-step method can easily be used for determining the minimum-cost order quantity:

1. Calculate the economic order quantity using the minimum unit prices. If this quantity falls within the range for which the vendor offers the discount price, it is a valid economic order quantity and will result in the minimum cost for the particular item.
2. If the EOQ calculated in step 1 is not valid (i.e., is less than the break quantity), find the total annual cost for each price break quantity.
3. Calculate an EOQ for each unit price.
4. Calculate the total annual cost for each valid EOQ determined in step 3.
5. The minimum-cost order quantity is that associated with the lowest cost in either step 2 or step 4.

An example of quantity discounts is given in the box on the next page (Magee and Boodman, 1971).

For a more comprehensive discussion of quantity discounts, see Benton, 1985; Rubin & Benton, 1993, 2002a & b.

Demand Uncertainty and Safety Stock

When there is uncertainty in demand, safety stock must be considered. Safety stock is extra inventory held to protect against randomness in demand or lead time. Safety stock is needed to cover the demand during the replenishment lead time in case actual demand is greater than expected demand.

Figure 5.9 illustrates the impact of safety stock. In the case below, safety stock covers demand during the replenishment cycle. If a variation in demand occurs, safety stock can be used to protect against stockouts.

As an example, consider an inventory system with an average daily demand of five units; if lead time is six days, then the expected demand during the lead time

Quantity Discount Example

The Value City Hardware Company purchases 10,000 units of product #605 each year. The supplier offers the units for sale at \$10.00 per unit for up to 799 units and \$8.75 per unit for orders of 800 units or more. What is the economic order quantity if the order cost is \$50.00 per order and the holding cost is 40 percent per unit per year? The total cost for the single price break quantity of 800 units is as follows:

1. Calculate the economic order quantity using the minimum unit prices. If this quantity falls within the range for which the vendor offers the discount price, it is a valid economic order quantity and will result in the minimum cost for the particular item.

   $Q_{\$8.75} = \sqrt{2C_P A / C_H} = \sqrt{2(50)(10{,}000)/\$8.75(.40)}$

   $= 535$ units, not valid

   The EOQ with the unit price of \$8.75 is invalid since it is not available for quantities less than 800 units (i.e., since $535 < 800$).

2. If the EOQ calculated in step 1 is not valid (i.e., is less than the break quantity), find the total annual cost for each price break quantity.

   $TC_{DQ} = AP + C_p \times (A/Q) + C_H \times Q/2$

   $TC_{8.75} = 10{,}000(8.75) + 50(10{,}000/800) + (800/2) \times (0.40)(8.75)$

   $TC_{DQ} = 87{,}500 + \$625 + \$1{,}400 = \$89{,}525$

3. Calculate an EOQ for each unit price.

   $Q_{\$10} = \sqrt{2C_p A / C_H} = \sqrt{2(50)(10{,}000)/\$10(.40)}$

   $= 500$ units

   The EOQ for the \$10 unit price is valid.

4. Calculate the total annual cost for each valid EOQ determined in step 3. The total cost of the valid EOQ with \$10 is as follows:

   $TC_{10} = 10{,}000(\$10) + 50(10{,}000/500) + 500(.40)10/2$

   $= \$102{,}000$

5. The minimum-cost order quantity is that associated with the lowest cost in either step 2 or step 4.

Comparing the total costs of the single price break quantity and the valid EOQ, the minimum cost order \$89,525 occurs at 800 units. The discount is attractive and a lot of 800 units should be ordered.

FIGURE 5.9 The Impact of Safety Stock

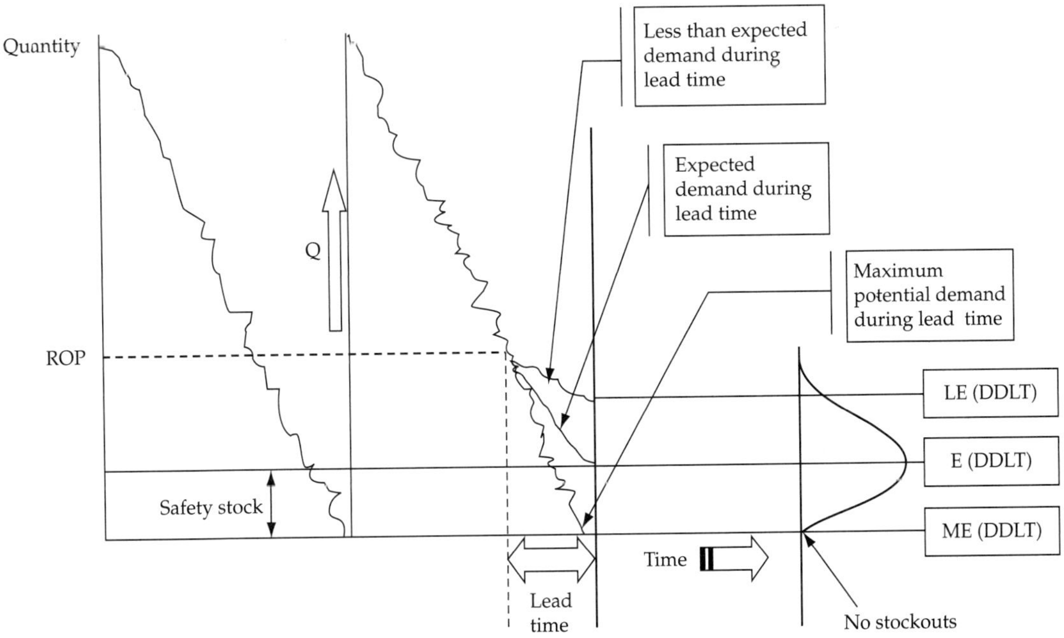

FIGURE 5.10
Normal Distribution of Demand During Lead Time (DDLT)

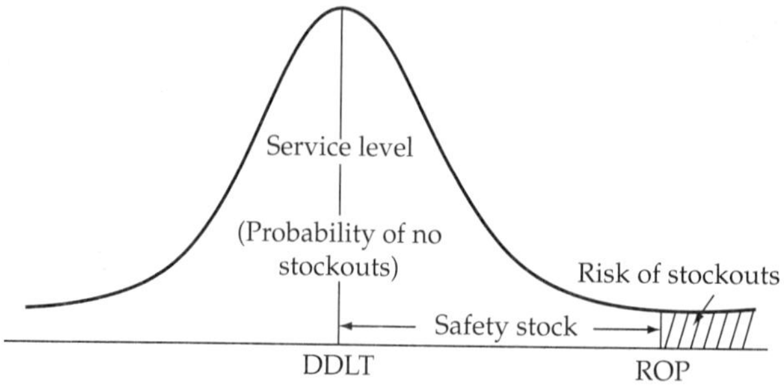

will be five units times six days, or 30 units. The distribution of demand during the lead time is assumed to follow a normal distribution, as shown in Figure 5.10.

The safety stock adjusted reorder point is

$$\text{ROP} = (\text{Average demand during lead time}) + (\text{Safety stock})$$

$$\text{Safety stock (SS)} = Z\sqrt{(\text{Lead time expressed as some multiple of forecast interval})} \times (\text{Standard deviation of demand})$$

$$= \text{DDLT} + Z\sqrt{(\text{Lead time expressed as some multiple of forecast interval})} \times (\text{Standard deviation of demand})$$

$$= \text{DDLT} + Z\sqrt{LT} \times \sigma_d \qquad \textbf{(6)}$$

Example of Fixed Order Quantity with Safety Stock

Consider a small retail outlet that has normally distributed demand during lead time, a mean of 1,000 units, and standard deviation of 20 units per week. Lead time interval is two weeks. What reorder point should be used in order to average no more than one stockout every 20 reorder cycles? Also, for safety stock = 30 determine the service level if we choose to carry 30 units of safety stock.

SOLUTION

Service level = 1/20 = .05

1 − .05 = 95%

Z = 1.645 (see Z table in Appendix A)

$$\text{Reorder point} = \text{DDLT} + Z\sqrt{LT} \times \sigma_d = 1{,}000 + 1.645 \times \sqrt{2} \times 20 = 1{,}047$$

$$\text{Safety stock} = Z\sqrt{LT} \times \sigma_d = 1.645 \times \sqrt{2} \times 20 = 47$$

$$Z = (\text{ROP} - \text{DDLT})/(\sqrt{LT} \times \sigma_d) = (1{,}030 - 1{,}000)/(1.41 \times 20) = 1.06$$

This equates to a service level of 85.54 percent (see Z table).

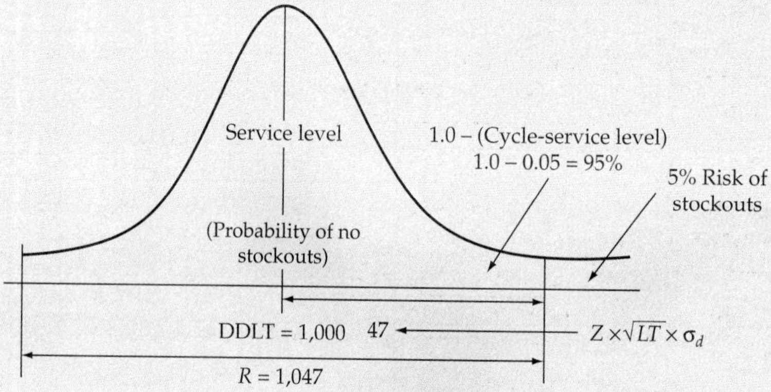

where

DDLT = Average demand during lead time

LT = Lead time expressed as some multiple of forecast interval (e.g., days, weeks)

Z = Number of standard deviations from the mean demand

σ_d = Standard deviation of demand rate

When demand is considered to be normally distributed, the reorder point can be easily determined from the following formula:

$$= \text{DDLT} + Z \times \sigma_d$$

The standard deviation also can be estimated to be 1.25 times the mean absolute deviation (MAD) of forecast errors under normality conditions (for a more comprehensive discussion, see Benton, 2013).

An example of the fixed order quantity model with demand uncertainty is given in the box on page 98. (Also see Brown, 1987)

DEPENDENT-DEMAND SYSTEMS

Order-point (statistical inventory control) techniques are based on the assumption of uniform requirements per unit time. If this assumption of the demands is unrealistic, these techniques can lead to inappropriate inventory decisions.

For components of assembled products, the demands are not usually constant per unit time, and depletion is anything but gradual. Inventory depletion for component parts tends to occur in discrete "lumps" because of lot sizing of the final product. Requirements dependent on the final product are usually discontinuous and lumpy since requirements for these components depend on when the product is built. In some periods, there may be a few or no component requirements, and in the next, a requirement for many will occur. As an example, Figure 5.11 shows a case in which customer demand is fairly uniform but, because of the build schedules, the requirements for the components are "lumpy." The build schedule shows periods of zero requirements before a requirement of 50 component parts is encountered. This requirement sequence, very common to component parts, is not handled well with traditional non-time-phased order-point techniques.

With the order-point system, the purchasing manager does not plan for future requirements but reacts to the current situation, which may require expediting to

FIGURE 5.11
Lumpy Requirements Example

On hand = 50 units
Safety stock = 5 units
Lead time = 1 period

Periods	**1**	**2**	**3**	**4**	**5**	**6**	**7**	**8**
Projected customer demand	15	15	15	10	15	10	10	10
Build schedule				50				50
Component requirements			50				50	

prevent a materials shortage. In these situations, expediting is used as a substitute for planning future requirements. An improved basis for planning to meet future needs would be to extend the requirement information throughout enough time periods to cover the entire manufacturing lead time. This provides the time-phased requirement information that is the basis for material requirements planning (MRP) systems.

MRP systems utilize substantially better information on future requirements than is possible by the traditional non-time-phased order-point system. MRP systems are helpful for companies with assembled products that have component requirements dependent on the final product. The system provides information to better determine the quantity and timing of component parts and purchase orders than is possible with the non-time-phased order-point system.

The Material Requirements Concept

The MRP concept provides the basis for projecting future inventories in a manufacturing operation. MRP can help improve the traditional non-time-phased order-point system because it allows the operating manager to plan requirements (raw material, component parts) to meet the final assembly schedule. That is, MRP provides a plan for component and subassembly availability that allows certain end products to be scheduled for final assembly in the future. Once a firm's final assembly schedule has been determined and the product bills of materials have been finalized, it is possible to precisely calculate the future materials needs for the final assembly schedule. The product bill of materials for a given finished product can be broken down, or "exploded," and extended for all component parts to obtain that product's exact requirements for each component part.

The General Lot-Sizing Problem

The general lot-sizing problem for time-phased requirements for a component part involves converting the requirements over the planning horizon (the number of periods into the future for which there are requirements) into planned orders by batching the requirements into lots. The specific method for determining the order quantities for a part is given by a lot-sizing procedure. In many cases, the lot-sizing procedure is based on the minimization of the sum of ordering and inventory carrying costs subject to meeting all requirements for each period. An ordering cost is incurred for each purchase order placed. A carrying cost is charged against the ending inventory balance in each period. The sum of these two cost components is the total inventory cost.

Lot-sizing procedures evaluate orders that cover the requirements for one or more periods. For example, from Figure 5.12, a minimum of 80 units must be ordered for period one (to meet that period's requirement), but other alternatives would include an order of 180 (two periods' requirements), 304 (three periods' requirements), and so on.

FIGURE 5.12
Net Requirements for 12 Periods

Order cost = $92
Inventory carrying cost = $0.50/period/unit

Period	1	2	3	4	5	6	7	8	9	10	11	12
Net requirements	80	100	124	50	50	100	125	125	100	100	50	100

In order not to be out of stock, there must be an order received in the first period in which there is a requirement not covered by inventory (net requirement). In order to fill the first net requirement, the firm will incur the cost of ordering (all costs associated with placing and receiving an order). It may be less expensive to combine the first net requirement with another requirement and to hold the additional units in inventory until they are needed rather than to pay for another order. Additional net requirements for periods beyond the first should be included as long as the cumulative units, times the number of periods to be held, times the cost to hold a unit for one period, are less than or equal to the order cost. When this is no longer true, another order is less costly. In general, this is the criterion used to establish the purchase order quantity for the lot-sizing procedures.

Quantity Discounts for the Variable Demand Case

It was shown in the previous section that MRP provides time-phased requirements to determine planned orders using lot-sizing procedures. The general lot-sizing problem is to batch requirements to minimize the sum of ordering and carrying costs each time an order is to be placed. Up until now, conditions for quantity discounts have not been discussed.

There are situations where the purchase price of a unit can vary extensively as different quantities are purchased. The quantity at which a price changes is called a *price break*. Price breaks occur because the suppliers provide incentives to buy in larger quantities compatible with their cost structure. In addition, similar discounts are offered by transportation companies, the price break occurring at full-carload shipments as opposed to shipping at less than truckload (LTL).

There may be a number of purchase discount contract structures available to a purchasing manager. Consider one very common possibility—a single discount purchase price that applies to "all units" ordered when the order quantity (lot size) exceeds a specified discount quantity.

Because of the quantity discount, determination of the best lot size for any particular situation can be very difficult. Under what conditions should a particular discount be taken? It is not sufficient to compare the lower purchase cost per unit at the higher volume with the higher cost per unit. It is necessary to analyze the impact on total inventory cost before deciding to order the higher quantity.

The total cost per unit must be considered when making the choice of lot sizes for a particular unit when quantity discounts are available. Various lot-sizing procedures will be compared with the objective of minimizing the total cost per unit, which equals [(Total purchase cost ÷ Total number of units purchased) + (Sum of the setup costs ÷ Number of units purchased) + (Sum of the inventory carrying costs ÷ Number of units used)].

In addition to determining the size of the order, the purchasing manager must schedule delivery so that the requirements are met. When the requirements are uncertain (subject to random variation as plans become reality), this means the purchasing manager must provide a prespecified level of "service" to manufacturing.

In an inventory system, whenever the inventory position will be insufficient to cover the requirements during the delivery lead time, a purchase order should be released. The inventory position for a particular period is the sum of the stock on hand and the stock already on order.

The purchase order should represent sufficient inventory to last through the lead time. When requirements are uncertain (as they are in most cases), it is obvious that the purchase order should be set equal to the planned requirements and the maximum reasonable requirements over the lead time. An allowance is added to the planned inventory for protection against uncertainty inherent in the planned requirements. This allowance is called *safety stock.*

The safety stock should be set to achieve a prespecified service level. Setting safety stock so as to achieve a prespecified service level enables fair comparison of the alternative lot-sizing procedures. The service level, S, is defined as

S = (The number of units required that were in inventory)/(The number of units required)

For example, a 99 percent service level means that 99 percent of the units that were required were in inventory when they were needed.

The purchase quantity discount (PQD) lot-sizing procedures evaluated here provide orders that cover one or more periods' requirements. In all of the procedures, requirements for successive periods are accumulated for an order until, at some integer number of periods of requirements, the quantity ordered is at least enough to qualify the entire order for a quantity discount. The next step is to determine if the discount qualifies by splitting the order for the period being considered. If the discount is not desirable, the order quantity is determined as though no discount existed. As an example, the least unit cost (LUC) PQD lot-sizing procedure is used to illustrate how a PQD lot-sizing procedure might work.

For the LUC PQD lot-sizing procedure, requirements are accumulated and unit costs are calculated for each period at least through the period in which the quantity discount is reached. The calculations are continued until the unit cost increases. Next, the unit cost for the exact discount quantity is calculated and compared to the lowest unit cost for a full period's requirements. The quantity purchased is that which provides the lowest unit cost.

Figure 5.13 presents an example of applying the LUC procedure using data from Figure 5.12.

FIGURE 5.13
Least Unit Cost PQD Example

Order cost = \$92
Inventory cost = \$0.50/period/unit
Base price = \$500.00
Discount price = \$447.55
Discount quantity = 368

Least Unit Cost

	Period's Supply	Requirements	Lot Size	Order Cost	Inventory Carrying Cost	Total Cost	Unit Cost
	1	80	80	\$92	\$0	\$40,092.00	\$501.15
	2	100	180	92	50	90,142.00	500.79
	3	124	304	92	174	152,266.00	500.88
yes→	4	50	354	92	249	177,341.00	500.98
	4+	14	368	92	277	165,067.40	448.55
	5	50	404	92	377	181,279.20	448.71

The total cost per unit is calculated for orders of one period's planned requirements and so on, through the period in which the discount quantity is reached. The discount quantity cost per unit is also computed. In the example above, the least unit cost occurs at the discount quantity in period 4.

$^{+}$Indicates that the discount quantity (368 units) is more than a four-period supply.

In Figure 5.13, the ordering cost of $92 is incurred once it has been determined an order must be placed. The inventory cost is accumulated at $0.50 per unit times the number of periods it will be carried until the period in which it is used. The purchase price is $500 per unit until more than 368 units are purchased. At a lot size of 368, the purchase price drops to $447.55, but 14 units (368 − 354) more than needed for four periods must be purchased. The additional inventory cost of these 14 units is 14 × $0.50 × 4 = $28, since they would not be used until period five. Total cost per unit is the total cost divided by the lot size (cumulative requirements). When the cost per unit increases (as with a five-period supply) and the discount quantity has been surpassed, the LUC procedure chooses as the lot size the quantity that provides the minimum cost per unit (i.e., $448.55, lot size = 368). This example illustrates the essentials of the PQD lot-sizing problem.

If a discount is available, there is a price differential (lower price) for ordering an increased number of units. In this chapter, the discount applies to all units provided an amount at least as big as the discount quantity is purchased. In situations where discounts are not available, the price per unit is constant regardless of the number of units ordered.

Illustration of Various Variable-Demand Lot-Sizing Models

There has been a significant amount of attention given to the variable-demand order lot-sizing problem. Both developmental and comparative literature will be discussed in this section.

Among the better-known lot-sizing methods for the single-item, nondiscount, time-phased, certain-demand models are (1) lot for lot, (2) economic order quantity, (3) periodic order quantity, (4) least unit cost, (5) McLaren's order moment, (6) Silver–Meal, and (7) the Wagner–Whitin dynamic programming algorithm. The procedures of these lot-sizing methods all determine how the period net requirements should be combined into production lots, or purchase orders. A description will be given for each lot-sizing method, along with an example problem using the data shown in Figure 5.12.

Example Calculation for the Lot-for-Lot Discount Procedure for Variable Demand

The lot-for-lot (LFL) method places an order for each period in which there is a net requirement. Thus, no inventory is carried from period to period. This method is usually used when setup costs are low or inventory carrying costs are high. Figure 5.14 shows the lot sizes of the LFL lot-sizing method for the example problem. The resulting lot sizes of the LFL method produce an order in each period in which there is a positive net requirement.

Example Calculation for the EOQ Procedure for Variable Demand

The economic order quantity (EOQ) method for determining the quantity to order was first worked out by F. W. Harris. With this method, the quantity ordered will always be greater than or equal to the economic order quantity. The objective of the method is to balance opposing costs (inventory carrying versus ordering). Figure 5.15 shows the lot sizes and costs for the example problem.

Example Calculation for the Periodic Order Quantity Procedure for Variable Demand

The periodic order quantity (POQ) lot-sizing method is based on the economic order quantity (EOQ). As shown in Figure 5.16, the EOQ method is insensitive to

FIGURE 5.14
Example of Lot-for-Lot Lot-Sizing Procedure

Required Receipts Schedule

Period	Net Requirements	Required Receipts
1	80	80
2	100	100
3	124	124
4	50	50
5	50	50
6	100	100
7	125	125
8	125	125
9	100	100
10	100	100
11	50	50
12	100	100

Total ordering cost = 12 × 92 = \$1,104
Total inventory carrying cost = 0↓ = 0
Total ordering plus inventory cost = \$1,104

FIGURE 5.15
Example of the EOQ Lot-Sizing Procedure

Ordering cost (C_P) = \$92
Inventory carrying cost (C_H) = \$0.50/unit/period
Average demand ($\bar{A}$) = 92/period

$\text{EOQ} = \sqrt{2 \times \bar{A} \times C_P/C} = \sqrt{2 \times 92 \times \$92/.5} = 184$

Required Receipts Schedule

Period	Net Requirements	Required Receipts
1	80	184
2	100	
3	124	184
4	50	
5	50	184
6	100	
7	125	184
8	125	184
9	100	
10	100	184
11	50	
12	100	

Total ordering cost = 6 × \$92 = \$552.00
Total carrying cost = 968 units × .5/period = 485.50
Total ordering plus inventory carrying costs = \$1,037.50

time-phased demand for the 12 periods of demand. The POQ method is an adjustment to the EOQ method for time-phased demand. The EOQ is converted to the equivalent number of periods of demand to be included in a lot. The EOQ is calculated and then divided by the average demand. This result is then rounded to the nearest integer value.

FIGURE 5.16
Example of Periodic Order Quantity Lot-Sizing Procedure

EOQ = 184 units
$\bar{A}$ = 92 units/period
Periodic order quantity = EOQ/$\bar{A}$ = 184/92 = 2 periods

Required Receipts Schedule

Period	Net Requirements	Required Receipts
1	80	180
2	100	
3	124	174
4	50	
5	50	150
6	100	
7	125	250
8	125	
9	100	200
10	100	
11	50	150
12	100	

Total ordering cost = 6 × \$92 = \$552.00
Total carrying cost = 575 units × .5/period = 287.50
Total ordering plus inventory carrying costs = \$839.50

Figure 5.16 shows the lot sizes and costs for the example problem. In the example problem, the POQ method performs better than the EOQ method.

Example Calculation for the Least Unit Cost Procedure for Variable Demand

The objective of the least unit cost (LUC) lot-sizing method is to determine the economic lot size on the basis of the least unit cost per item. For the LUC procedure, net requirements are accumulated and unit costs are calculated for each period.

The calculations are continued until the unit cost increases. The quantity purchased is that quantity that provides the lowest unit cost. Figure 5.17 shows the lot sizes and costs for the example problem. In the example problem, an order was coincidently scheduled every two periods.

Example Calculation for the McLaren Order Moment Procedure for Variable Demand

The McLaren order moment (MOM), in its simplest version, accumulates requirements for consecutive periods into a tentative order until the accumulated part-periods (one unit carried in inventory for one period) reach or exceed a specified part-period target. The MOM method compares the carrying cost incurred by including the requirements above the target with the cost of placing a new order. Either the requirements are included in the current lot or a new lot is started, depending on which cost is less. Figure 5.18 shows the lot sizes and costs for this example.

Example Calculation for the Silver–Meal Procedure for Variable Demand

The Silver–Meal lot-sizing method is based on minimum cost per period. As shown earlier, the fixed EOQ approach does not perform well when the demands

FIGURE 5.17 Example of Least Unit Cost Lot-Sizing Procedure

Period	Net Requirement	Cumulative Requirement	Excess Inventory	Periods Carried	Carrying Cost Unit Cum.	Setup Cost	Total Cost	Unit Cost
1	80	80	0	0	0	$92	$40,092	$501.15
2	100	180	100	1	50	92	90,142	500.79
3	124	304	124	2	174	92	152,266	500.88
3	124	124	0	0	0	92	62,092	500.74
4	50	174	50	1	25	92	87,117	500.67
5	50	224	50	2	75	92	112,167	500.75
5	50	50	0	0	0	92	25,092	501.84
6	100	150	100	1	50	92	75,142	500.95
7	125	275	125	2	175	92	137,767	500.97
7	125	125	0	0	0	92	63,592	500.74
8	125	250	125	1	67.50	92	125,159	500.64
9	100	350	100	2	167.50	92	175,259	500.74
9	100	100	0	0	0	92	50,092	500.92
10	100	200	100	1	50	92	100,142	500.71
11	50	250	50	2	100	92	125,192	500.77
11	50	50	0	0	0	92	25,092	501.84
12	100	150	100	1	50	92	75,142	500.95

Required Receipts Schedule

Period	Net Requirements	Required Receipts
1	80	184
2	100	
3	124	174
4	50	
5	50	150
6	100	
7	125	250
8	125	
9	100	200
10	100	
11	50	150
12	100	

Total ordering cost = 6 × $92 = $552.00
Total carrying cost = 968 units × .5/period = 287.50
Total ordering plus inventory carrying costs = $839.50

vary from one period to the next. The Silver–Meal method selects the order quantity so as to minimize the total relevant costs per unit of time. The basic objective of Silver–Meal is to evaluate the total cost per period for successive periods until the first time the new period's total cost exceeds the current period's total cost. Figure 5.19 shows the lot sizes for the example problem.

FIGURE 5.18
Example of McLaren's Order Moment Lot-Sizing Procedure

Target = Order moment target
EOQ = 184 units
$\bar{A}$ = Average demand/period = 92/period
TBO = Expected time between orders = 184/92 = 2 periods

$$\text{Target} = \bar{A}\left[\sum_{t=1}^{T^*-1} t + (\text{TBO} - T^*)T^*\right]$$

Where T^* is defined as the largest integer less than TBO.
Thus, the target for the example problem is

$$\text{Target} = 92\left[\sum_{t=1}^{T^*-1} 1 + (2 - 1^*)1^*\right] = 184$$

Period	Requirement	Cumulative Requirement	Part-Periods	Cumulative Part-Period
1	80	80	80 × 0 = 0	0
2	100	→180	100 × 1 = 100	100
3	124	304	124 × 2 = 248⁺	348
3	124	124	124 × 0 = 0	0
4	50	174	50 × 1 = 50	50
5	50	→224	50 × 2 = 100	150
6	100	324	100 × 3 = 300	450
6	100	100	100 × 0 = 0	0
7	125	→225	125 × 1 = 125	1250
8	125	350	125 × 2 = 250	375
8	125	125	125 × 0 = 0	0
9	100	→225	100 × 1 = 100	100
10	100	325	100 × 2 = 200	300
10	100	100	100 × 0 = 0	0
11	50	→150	50 × 1 = 50	50
12	100	250	100 × 2 = 200	250
12	100	→100	100 × 0 = 0	0

Required Receipts Schedule

Period	Net Requirements	Required Receipts
1	80	180
2	100	0
3	124	224
4	50	0
5	50	0
6	100	225
7	125	0
8	125	225
9	100	0
10	100	150
11	50	0
12	100	100

Total ordering cost = 6 × \$92 = \$552.00
Total inventory cost = 525 × .5/period = 262.50
Total ordering plus carrying costs = \$814.50

→ Indicates the lot size.
⁺ The 124 units required in period three must be carried for two periods.

FIGURE 5.19 Example of the Silver–Meal Lot-Sizing Procedure

Period	Net Requirement	Cumulative Requirement	Excess Inventory	Ordering Cost	Total Cost	Cost per Period
1	80	80	0	$92	$40,092	$40,092
2	100	180	100	92	90,142	45,071
2	100	100	0	92	90,902	90,092
3	124	224	124	92	112,159	56,079
4	50	274	174	92	137,204	45,736
5	50	324	224	92	162,284	40,571
6	100	424	324	92	212,392	42,478
6	100	100	0	92	50,092	50,092
7	125	225	125	92	112,659	56,329
7	125	125	0	92	62,592	62,592
8	125	250	125	92	125,159	62,579
9	100	350	225	92	175,192	58,397
10	100	450	325	92	225,409	75,136
10	100	100	0	92	50,092	50,092
11	50	150	50	92	75,117	37,558
12	100	250	150	92	125,167	41,722
12	100	100	0	92	50,092	50,092

Required Receipts Schedule

Period	Net Requirements	Required Receipts
1	80	80
2	100	0
3	124	324
4	50	0
5	50	0
6	100	0
7	125	100
8	125	350
9	100	0
10	100	0
11	50	150
12	100	100

Total ordering cost = 6 × $92 = $552.00

Total inventory cost = 749 × .5/period = 374.50

Total ordering plus carrying costs = $926.50

Example Calculation for the Wagner–Whitin Procedure for Variable Demand

Wagner and Whitin developed a dynamic programming-based lot-sizing method that explores all the various alternatives in setting order quantities to minimize total cost over a planning horizon. The Wagner–Whitin method guarantees optimal solutions for lot-sizing problems when requirements are known with certainty over a fixed number of periods and the carrying cost is nondecreasing over time.

The technical description of the procedure is beyond the scope of this chapter, but Figure 5.20 shows the resulting lot sizes for the example problem for comparison purposes.

FIGURE 5.20
Example for the Wagner–Whitin Lot-Sizing Procedure

Required Receipts Schedule

Period	Net Requirements	Required Receipts
1	80	180
2	100	0
3	124	224
4	50	0
5	50	0
6	100	225
7	125	0
8	125	225
9	100	0
10	100	150
11	50	0
12	100	100
Total ordering cost = 6 × $92		= $552.00
Total inventory cost = 525 × .5/period		= 262.50
Total ordering plus carrying costs		= $814.50

There have been numerous articles and papers written on the comparison of various time-phased lot-sizing methods. Under certain experimental conditions, even the EOQ procedure performed just as well as the optimizing method (the Wagner–Whitin algorithm).

The lot-sizing methods in this section have been used extensively in material requirements planning systems. The principles of the economic order quantity (EOQ), the least unit cost, and McLaren's order moment lot-sizing methods have emerged as the most effective managerial approaches to the variable-demand lot-sizing problem.

Summary

Inventory management is a key element of a well-run purchasing organization. An increasingly large number of firms are spending between 60 and 80 percent of their sales dollars for materials purchased outside of the firm. This significant shift has increased the importance and profile of purchasing professionals. This also means that the need for tight control over inventories is extremely important to profitability. The trend is to implement computerized inventory control systems. In many industries, the investment in inventories comprises a substantial share of the firm's assets. The traditional fixed-order-quantity system was compared with variable-order-quantity systems.

The purchasing professional must first ascertain the item characteristics and the operating environment before determining the appropriate inventory management system. The fixed-order-quantity system has many limitations. It is a reactive system, and reactive systems require constant demand. Variable-order-quantity systems are designed to handle lumpy demand. The MRP concept provides the basis for projecting future inventories in a manufacturing environment. The general lot-sizing problems for MRP-based systems involve converting the requirements over the planning horizon into planned orders by batching the requirements into lots. Finally, several lot-sizing procedures for variable demand were discussed and compared.

Discussion Questions

1. Why is inventory management important to the efficiency of the purchasing function?
2. What are the differences between independent and dependent demand?
3. Discuss the various inventory costs.
4. What is the relationship between purchasing and the classical EOQ model?
5. How are inventory decisions related to forecasting?
6. How are quantity discounts evaluated when using the classical EOQ model?
7. What is meant by ABC analysis?
8. How is safety stock determined in the classical EOQ model?
9. What are the differences between the classical EOQ inventory system and MRP?
10. What are the cost implications of various lot-sizing methods?

Exercises

5.1. Bell Technologies stocks and sells its own brand of laptop computers. It costs the firm $543 each time it places an order with the manufacturer for laptops. The cost of carrying one laptop in inventory for a year is $210. The store manager estimates that total annual demand for the computers will be 1,800 units with a constant demand rate throughout the year. Bell's policy is never to have stockouts of the store-brand laptop. The store is open for business seven days per week from 9 a.m. to 6 p.m. Determine the following:

a. Optimal order quantity per order
b. Minimum total annual inventory costs
c. The number of orders per year
d. The time between orders (in working days)

5.2. Bell assumed with certainty that the ordering cost is $543 per order and the inventory carrying cost is $210 per unit per year. However, the inventory model parameters are frequently only estimates that are subject to some degree of uncertainty. Consider three cases of variation in the model parameters as follows: (a) both ordering cost and carrying cost are as originally estimated; (b) both ordering cost and carrying cost are 20 percent less than originally estimated; (c) both ordering cost and carrying cost are 20 percent higher than originally estimated; (d) ordering cost is 20 percent higher and carrying cost is 20 percent lower than originally estimated. Discuss your findings.

5.3. Premier Golf Shop operates 300 days per year. The shop pays $300 for a particular beginner golf club set purchased from a local manufacturer. The annual holding cost per club set is estimated to be 25 percent of the dollar of the inventory. The shop sells an average of 20 per week. The ordering cost for each order is $50. Determine the optimal order quantity and the total minimum cost.

5.4. Mitch's body shop uses a highly flammable solvent. It must have the product delivered by special cargo trucks designed for the safe shipment of chemicals. The delivery cost for the solvent is $1,200 each time an order is placed. The solvent is packaged in one-gallon plastic containers. The cost of holding the chemical in storage is $120 per gallon per year. The annual demand for the chemical, which is constant over time, is 1,783 gallons per year. The lead time from time of order placement until receipt is 14 days. The company operates 250 working days per year. Compute the optimal order quantity, total minimum inventory cost, and reorder point.

5.5. The Buckeye Carryout store stocks Scarlet and Grey (S&G) beer mugs. Demand for S&G is 10,200 per year. It costs $120 per order of mugs, and it costs $1.35 per mug per year to keep the mugs in stock. Once an order for mugs is placed, it takes seven days to receive the order from the distributor. Determine the following:

a. Optimal order size

b. Minimum total annual inventory cost

c. Reorder point

5.6. The Apple Valley Company makes apple butter to supply to local street vendors in Monterey, California. Apple Valley can make 330 pounds of apple butter per day, and demand from the street vendors is 190 pounds per day. Each time Apple Valley makes apple butter, it costs $176 to set up the production process. The annual cost of carrying a pound of apples in a refrigerated storage area is $6.50. Determine the optimal order size and the minimum total annual inventory cost.

5.7. The Scarlet and Grey Brewery produces Buckeye Light Beer, which it stores in barrels in its warehouse and supplies to its distributors on demand. The demand for Buckeye Light is **36,000** barrels of beer per day. The brewery can produce **3,000** barrels of Buckeye Light per day. It is stored in a refrigerated warehouse at an annual cost of $80 per barrel. Determine the economic ordering quantity and the minimum total annual inventory cost.

5.8. The purchasing manager for Worthington Industries must determine a policy for ordering boring drills to operate five horizontal boring machines. Each machine requires exactly 30 boring drills per day to operate, and the firm operates 360 days per year. The purchasing manager has determined that the ordering cost is $80 per order, and the cost of holding the drills is 25 percent of the average dollar value of the inventory held. The purchasing manager has negotiated a contract to obtain boring drills for $165 per drill for the coming year.

a. Determine the optimal quantity of boring drills to receive in each order.

b. Determine the total inventory-related costs associated with the optimal ordering policy.

c. If five days' lead time is required to receive an order of drills, how many drills should be on hand when the order is placed?

5.9. The SBX Bookstore at The Ohio State University purchases from a vendor jackets emblazoned with the Ohio State logo. The vendor sells the jackets to the store for $43 dollars per jacket. The cost to the bookstore for placing an order is $150, and the annual carrying cost is 22 percent of the cost of a jacket. The bookstore manager estimates that 2,500 jackets will be sold during the year. The vendor has offered the bookstore the following all unit volume discount schedule:

Order Size	Discount
1–299	0%
300–499	2
500–799	4
800+	5

The purchasing manager wants to determine the bookstore's optimal order quantity, given this quantity discount information.

5.10. Determine the optimal order quantity of jackets and total annual cost in exercise 5.9 if the carrying cost is a constant $13 per jacket per year.

5.11. The purchasing manager for Medco Research Laboratory orders letterhead forms and stationery from an office products firm in boxes of 500 sheets. The company uses 5,000 boxes per year. Annual carrying costs are $4.50 per box, and ordering costs are $34. The following all unit discount price schedule is provided by the office supply company:

Order Quantity (boxes)	Price per Box
200–999	$13
1,000–2,999	12
3,000–4,999	11
5,000+	10

Determine the optimal order quantity and the total annual inventory cost.

5.12. Lee's Machine Shop has estimated net requirements for a particular part as follows:

Month	1	2	3	4	5	6	7	8	9	10	11	12
Requirements	200	20	30	40	140	500	500	500	500	80	0	200

Ordering cost associated with this part is $600. Estimated inventory carrying cost is $4 per unit per month calculated on average inventory. Currently, no parts are available in inventory. The company wishes to know when and how much to order over the next 12 months.

a. Apply the economic order quantity and the part-period balancing procedures to solve this problem.

b. What important assumptions are involved in each of the approaches used in part a?

5.13. The Beam Brake Company is trying to decide which of several lot-sizing procedures to use for its MRP system. The following information pertains to one of the typical component parts:

Setup cost = $50/order
Inventory cost = $0.75/unit/week
Current inventory balance = 10 units

Week	1	2	3	4	5	6	7	8
Demand Forecast	55	35	25	0	105	15	75	10

a. Apply the EOQ, POQ, and LUC lot-sizing procedures and show the total cost resulting from each procedure. Calculate inventory carrying costs on the basis of average inventory values. Assume orders are received into the beginning inventory.

b. Indicate advantages and disadvantages of using each procedure in part a.

5.14. Apply the McLaren order moment (MOM) lot-sizing procedures to the following 12 periods of requirements data, indicating order receipts' size and period. Assume order costs are $150 per order placed and $2 inventory carrying costs on the basis of *ending* inventory values. Calculate inventory carrying costs.

Period	1	2	3	4	5	6	7	8	9	10	11	12
Requirements	40	20	5	30	30	55	65	40	95	0	20	15

5.15. The following table contains figures on the annual volume and unit costs for a random sample of 10 items from a list of 2,000 inventory items at a health care facility. Please develop an ABC analysis for these items. Also, draw an ABC diagram reflecting your results. How could the purchasing manager use this information?

Item	Annual Usage	Unit Cost
1	2,400	$19.51
2	6,200	32.60
3	8,500	10.20
4	3,200	6.80
5	6,000	4.50
6	750	55.70
7	8,200	3.60
8	9,000	44.90
9	5,800	35.62
10	820	82.60

5.16. The purchasing manager for Omni Enterprises requested the following data from the accounting department:

Annual demand = 15,500

Cost of placing an order = $180

Annual inventory holding costs = 20 percent

Unit cost = $75

a. Please calculate the following:
   i. The optimal order quantity.
   ii. The average number of orders.
   iii. The total annual inventory costs.

b. Suppose that Omni has been arbitrarily ordering 50 times per year. What is the total annual inventory cost?

c. Assume that Omni incorrectly estimates the order cost to be $250 per order. What order quantity will Omni use? What actual annual inventory costs will be incurred?

5.17. Assume Omni's demand for an item during the lead time is normally distributed with a mean of 5,000 and a standard deviation of 50. What reorder point should be used in order to average no more than one stockout every 20 reorder cycles? If safety stock is 70, how often will a stockout occur during a reorder cycle?

5.18. Daltrey Systems is now offering Omni quantity discounts of 5 percent on orders over 1,500 units and 10 percent on orders over 6,000 units. Omni currently orders 1,000 units five times a year to meet annual demand. Omni's current purchase cost is $3.00 and the selling price is $4.95 per unit. The order cost is $42 per order. The annual inventory holding cost is 25 percent. Based on the new discount policy, what is the best strategy for the purchasing manager to follow?

Suggested Cases

Point Clear
Medical Laser
MARS, Inc. (O)
Two-Bucks Wine Operations

References

Benton, W. C. Supply Chain Focused Manufacturing Planning and Control, Cengage, New York, 2013, pp. 126.

Benton, W. C. "Multiple Price Breaks and Alternative Purchase Lot Sizing Procedures." *International Journal of Production Research*, 1985.

Benton, W. C. "Safety Stock and Service Levels in Periodic Review Inventory Systems." *Journal of Operations Research Society* 42, no. 12 (1991).

Brown, Robert G. *Decision Rules for Inventory Management*. New York: Holt, Rinehart and Winston, 1987.

Magee, John F. and David M. Boodman. *Production Planning and Inventory Control*. 2nd ed, New York: McGraw-Hill, 1971, pp. 76, 77.

Rubin, P. A., and W. C. Benton. "Jointly Constrained Order Quantities with All Units Discounts." *Naval Research Logistics* 40 (1993), pp. 255–78.

Rubin, P. A., and W. C. Benton. "Evaluating Jointly Constrained Order Quantity Complexities for Incremental Discounts." *European Journal of Operational Research* 147 (2002a), pp. 557–570.

Rubin, P. A., and W. C. Benton. "A Generalized Framework for Quantity Discount Pricing Schedules." *Decision Sciences* 33, no. 4 (Fall 2002b).

Appendix **A**

Areas under the Normal Curve

Area under the standard normal curve from 0 to z, shown shaded, is $A(z)$.

Examples. If Z is the standard normal random variable and $z = 1.54$, then

$$A(z) = P(0 < Z < z) = .4382,$$
$$P(Z > z) = .0618,$$
$$P(Z < z) = .9382,$$
$$P(|Z| < z) = .8764.$$

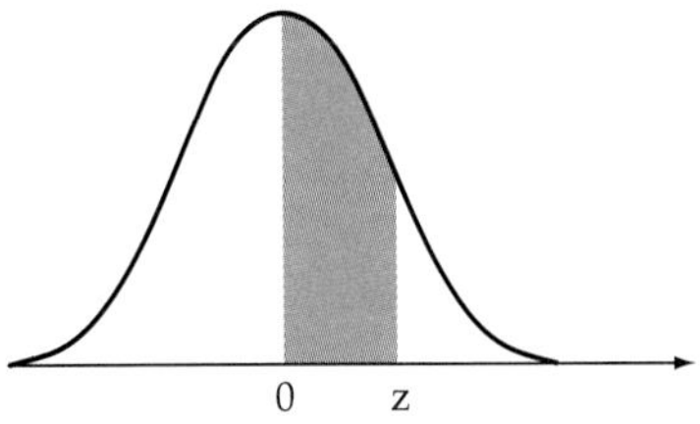

z	.00	.01	.02	.03	.04	.05	.06	.07	.08	.09
0.0	.0000	.0040	.0080	.0120	.0160	.0199	.0239	.0279	.0319	.0359
0.1	.0398	.0438	.0478	.0517	.0557	.0596	.0636	.0675	.0714	.0753
0.2	.0793	.0832	.0871	.0910	.0948	.0987	.1026	.1064	.1103	.1141
0.3	.1179	.1217	.1255	.1293	.1331	.1368	.1406	.1443	.1480	.1517
0.4	.1554	.1591	.1628	.1664	.1700	.1736	.1772	.1808	.1844	.1879
0.5	.1915	.1950	.1985	.2019	.2054	.2088	.2123	.2157	.2190	.2224
0.6	.2257	.2291	.2324	.2357	.2389	.2422	.2454	.2486	.2517	.2549
0.7	.2580	.2611	.2642	.2673	.2704	.2734	.2764	.2794	.2823	.2852
0.8	.2881	.2910	.2939	.2967	.2995	.3023	.3051	.3078	.3106	.3133
0.9	.3159	.3186	.3212	.3238	.3264	.3289	.3315	.3340	.3365	.3389
1.0	.3413	.3438	.3461	.3485	.3508	.3531	.3554	.3577	.3599	.3621
1.1	.3643	.3665	.3686	.3708	.3729	.3749	.3770	.3790	.3810	.3830
1.2	.3849	.3869	.3888	.3907	.3925	.3944	.3962	.3980	.3997	.4015
1.3	.4032	.4049	.4066	.4082	.4099	.4115	.4131	.4147	.4162	.4177
1.4	.4192	.4207	.4222	.4236	.4251	.4265	.4279	.4292	.4306	.4319
1.5	.4332	.4345	.4357	.4370	.4382	.4394	.4406	.4418	.4429	.4441
1.6	.4452	.4463	.4474	.4484	.4495	.4505	.4515	.4525	.4535	.4545
1.7	.4554	.4564	.4573	.4582	.4591	.4599	.4608	.4616	.4625	.4633
1.8	.4641	.4649	.4656	.4664	.4671	.4678	.4686	.4693	.4699	.4706
1.9	.4713	.4719	.4726	.4732	.4738	.4744	.4750	.4756	.4761	.4767
2.0	.4772	.4778	.4783	.4788	.4793	.4798	.4803	.4808	.4812	.4817
2.1	.4821	.4826	.4830	.4834	.4838	.4842	.4846	.4850	.4854	.4857
2.2	.4861	.4864	.4868	.4871	.4875	.4878	.4881	.4884	.4887	.4890
2.3	.4893	.4896	.4898	.4901	.4904	.4906	.4909	.4911	.4913	.4916
2.4	.4918	.4920	.4922	.4925	.4927	.4929	.4931	.4932	.4934	.4936
2.5	.4938	.4940	.4941	.4943	.4945	.4946	.4948	.4949	.4951	.4952
2.6	.4953	.4955	.4956	.4957	.4959	.4960	.4961	.4962	.4963	.4964
2.7	.4965	.4966	.4967	.4968	.4969	.4970	.4971	.4972	.4973	.4974
2.8	.4974	.4975	.4976	.4977	.4977	.4978	.4979	.4979	.4980	.4981
2.9	.4981	.4982	.4982	.4983	.4984	.4984	.4985	.4985	.4986	.4986
3.0	.4987	.4987	.4987	.4988	.4988	.4989	.4989	.4989	.4990	.4990

Chapter Six

Just-in-Time (Lean) Purchasing

Learning Objectives

1. Understand lean production systems.
2. Explain the differences between JIT and MRP.
3. Discuss the relationship between JIT and purchasing.
4. Name critical JIT purchasing advantages.
5. Identify the activities needed to implement JIT purchasing.
6. Determine the role of culture in the implementation of JIT purchasing.
7. Analyze the impact of JIT purchasing on a buying firm.

INTRODUCTION

There has been a shift in manufacturing business processes in practically every American industrial setting. The so-called lean thinking paradigm now includes the purchasing function. Lean concepts have had a significant effect on the profitability in almost all industrial settings. The key lean principles focus on people, postponement, efficiency, and the elimination of waste. All of these key business principles have a direct effect on the purchasing function.

Over the last couple of decades, Japan has achieved new levels of productivity and product quality. Much of the Japanese success in the global market is attributed to its people-oriented management style and innovative manufacturing techniques developed around just-in-time and total quality control concepts. The **just-in-time (JIT) system** is no longer an esoteric concept in the manufacturing world today. In the face of intense global competition, many firms in the United States are looking at improved techniques to manage their manufacturing operations. While debates continue regarding the applicability of JIT concepts outside Japan, a comprehensive survey of JIT practices in the United States found that 45 percent of the firms contacted had implemented JIT programs and another 22 percent were planning to implement JIT the following year. JIT has evolved from a novel manufacturing concept based on a philosophy of trust and commitment of the entire organization. The benefits of implementing a JIT system impact all entities involved in supply chain management.

The purchasing department plays an important role in the profitability of any manufacturing firm. To improve their on-time delivery performance, some Chinese firms have implemented the JIT philosophy in purchasing. As an example, Dongfeng Citroen Automobile Company (DCAC), a Sino-French joint venture in China, has established close relationships with several suppliers through JIT purchasing. DCAC reported that the relationship has improved the timeliness of delivery and reduced inventory costs (Zhixiang, 2004). The purpose of this chapter is to describe the potential advantages of JIT in the purchasing function and to discuss some of the common obstacles encountered in the implementation process. In doing so, a brief review of lean production systems will be given in the next section.

LEAN PRODUCTION SYSTEMS

In its simplest form, "the manufacturing process" is a composition of the material flows. JIT is designed to manage the flow of materials, components, tools, and associated information. JIT production is based on planned elimination of all waste and on continuous improvement. JIT is also referred to as *lean production*. An organization driven by a JIT philosophy can improve profits and return on investment by reducing inventory levels, reducing variability, improving product quality, reducing production and delivery lead times, and reducing setup costs. With JIT (lean) the entire manufacturing system from purchasing to shop floor management can be measured and controlled. Therefore, the JIT (lean) system is a powerful management tool that could easily determine the success or failure of the manufacturing system.

JIT applies primarily to repetitive manufacturing processes in which the same products and components are produced over and over again. The general idea is to establish flow processes (even when the facility uses a job shop or batch process layout) by linking work centers so that there is an even, balanced flow of materials throughout the entire production process similar to that found in an assembly line. To accomplish this, an attempt is made to reach the goals of driving all inventory buffers toward zero and achieving the ideal lot size of one unit.

For more than three decades, JIT and MRP production systems have followed two independent research streams. As the popularity of JIT motivated by the success of Japanese manufacturing firms has grown, numerous global practitioners initiated complete changeovers from the traditional MRP-based methods to JIT methods. For instance, Harley–Davidson and Hewlett–Packard are two of the most popular examples of JIT success testimonials.

There rarely exists a pure JIT production system in practice. Even at Toyota, the inventor of the JIT system, production smoothing is planned by the master production schedule (MPS), and the material requirement plan is followed based on the MPS, using a bill of materials (BOM). This type of manufacturing planning has been adopted by most automobile manufacturers. The integration between MRP and JIT in literature reflects the trend toward a more realistic hybrid manufacturing environment.

The current shift toward the so-called lean thinking manufacturing environment is one of the major motivations for future JIT research. There is also a strong

FIGURE 6.1 JIT Conceptual Framework

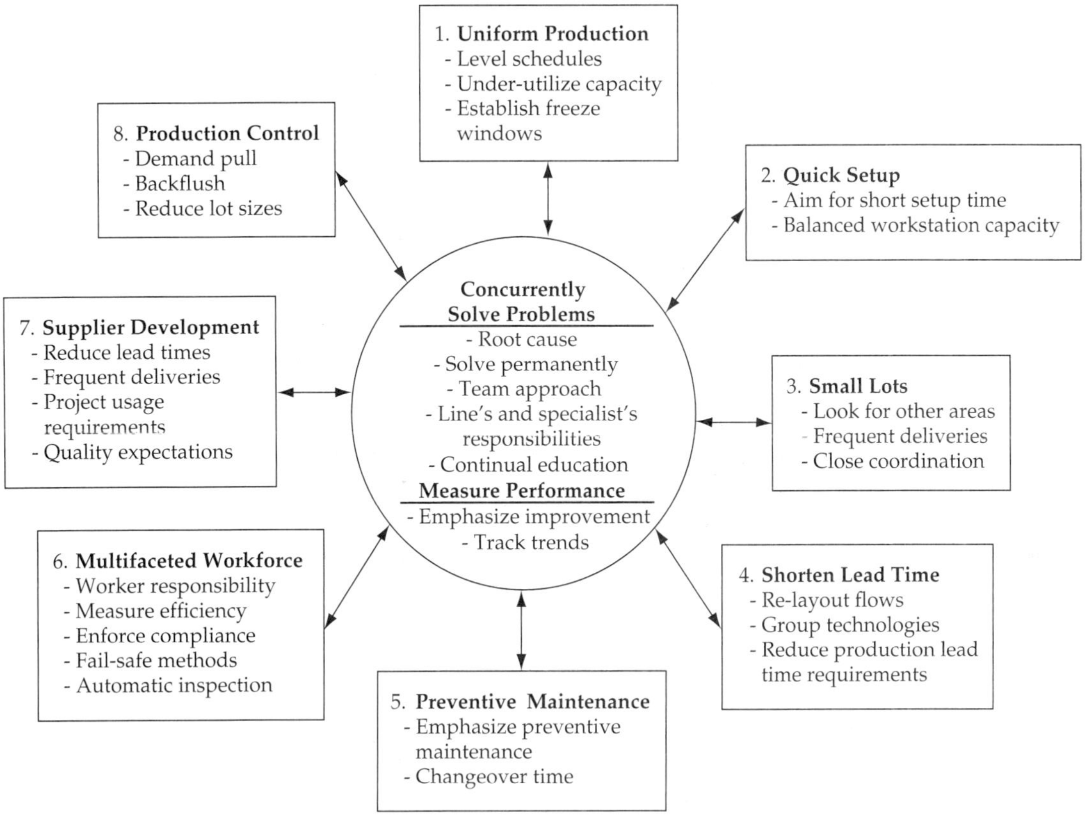

need to organize the previous JIT studies and provide directions for innovative JIT implementations and research focus. The conceptual framework for JIT is shown in Figure 6.1.

The following practices are considered essential for a comprehensive JIT implementation:

1. *Uniform production* (also known as *heijunka*). Create a uniform load on each workstation through constant daily production and producing the same mix of products each day, using a repeating sequence. Meet demand fluctuations through end-item inventory rather than through fluctuations in production level. Use of a stable production schedule also permits the use of *backflushing* to manage inventory: an end item's bill of materials is periodically exploded to calculate the usage quantities of the various components that were used to make the item, eliminating the need to collect detailed usage information on the shop floor.
2. *Quick setup times.* Aim for short setup times—this can be done through better planning, process redesign, and product redesign. A good example of the potential for improved setup times can be found in the airline industry, where Southwest Airlines can turn around 30 full-capacity flights per day between Dallas and Houston. (How long does it take American Airlines to turn around just one flight?) Southwest's efficiency is the result of a team effort using the correct aircraft (container) size and a coordinated, well-rehearsed process.

3. *Small lot sizes.* Reducing setup times allows economical production of smaller lots; close cooperation with suppliers is necessary to achieve reductions in order lot sizes for purchased raw materials and component parts since this will require more frequent deliveries.
4. *Short lead times.* Production lead times can be reduced by moving workstations closer together, applying group technology and cellular manufacturing concepts, reducing queue length, and improving the coordination and cooperation between downstream processes. Delivery lead times can be reduced through close cooperation with supplying organizations, possibly by inducing suppliers to locate closer to the factory.
5. *Preventive maintenance.* Use machine and worker idle time to maintain equipment and prevent breakdowns.
6. *Multifaceted workforce.* Workers should be trained to operate several machines, to perform maintenance tasks, and to perform quality inspections. In general, JIT requires teams of competent, empowered employees who take responsibility for their own work.
7. *Supplier development.* All defective items must be eliminated since there are no buffers of excess parts. A *quality at the source (jidoka)* program must be implemented to give workers the personal responsibility for the quality of the work they do, and the authority to stop production when something goes wrong. Techniques such as "JIT lights" (to indicate line slowdowns or stoppages) and "tally boards" (to record and analyze causes of production stoppages and slowdowns to facilitate correcting them later) may be used.
8. *Kanban production control.* Use a control system such as a *kanban* (card) system (or other signaling system) to convey parts between workstations in small quantities (ideally, one unit at a time). In a large sense, JIT is *not* the same thing as a kanban system, and a kanban system is not required to implement JIT (some companies have instituted a JIT program along with an MRP system), although JIT is required to implement a kanban system and the two concepts are frequently equated with one another.

This chapter proceeds in the following order: First, the JIT production system is discussed. Second, the kanban production control system will be presented. Third, the JIT purchasing framework will be evaluated. Next, the role of culture will be discussed. Finally, a critical analysis of the JIT philosophy will be conducted.

Just-in-Time Production System

JIT is Toyota's manufacturing philosophy to minimize waste, and the JIT production system is a subsystem controlled by kanban. The kanban-controlled JIT production system is based on the premise of minimizing work-in-process inventories (waste) by reducing or eliminating discrete batches. The reduced lot sizes not only contribute to production efficiency and product quality, but also reduce the overall costs associated with production in the JIT manufacturing environment. This proposition holds true only when certain conditions are sustained. The success of Toyota's kanban-controlled production system is supported by smoothing of production, standardization of jobs, reduction of setup times, improvement of activities, design of machine layout, and automation of processes (automation with a human touch). In fact, the JIT production system appears most suitable for repetitive manufacturing environments.

Improvements in the kanban-controlled production systems have followed a pragmatic approach-*continuous improvement*. Therefore, success of the JIT production system must be explained in conjunction with continuous improvement. Experience and commitment of the workers on the shop floor to continue to improve performance and methods are the major drivers of the JIT production system. A host of cases and evidence from the literature indicate that the JIT success has been achieved not by the predetermined scheduling technique, but by the aggressive continuous improvement effort.

The JIT production system is not a panacea. As with the MRP system, there are also operational problems with the JIT system. In fact, there is a list of reasons why the Toyota manufacturing system may not work for all firms. The reasons include cultural differences, geographical dispersion of suppliers, supplier power, different management styles, and so forth.

The Toyota manufacturing system has been viewed in different ways by a variety of researchers. The JIT production system is often called *lean production system* because it uses less of every resource compared with the conventional mass production system (Womack et al., 1990). On the other hand, the JIT system is viewed as a conventional *reorder point* system with extremely small lot sizes (Zipkin, 1991). The most common standpoint in understanding the JIT production system is that the JIT production is a *pull* system as opposed to the conventional push system. In the MRP/JIT comparison or integration literature, the pull nature of the JIT production system has been discussed extensively. Thus, it is only natural to portray the push/pull debates in conjunction with the MRP/JIT studies. Also see Benton and Shin (1998).

Kanban Production Control System

Kanban is the Japanese word for card. The kanban card contains the part number, the part description, the type of container, and various workstation information. A kanban production control system uses simple, visual signals to control the movement of materials between work centers, as well as the production of new materials to replenish those sent downstream to the next work center. The kanban card is attached to a storage and transport container. The kanban card is used to provide an easily understood, visual signal that a specific activity is required. Kanbans are similar to fixed-order inventory systems where an order for Q is placed when the inventory level falls below the reorder point. The reorder point is determined based on the demand during the lead time. The only inventory required is during the replenishment lead time.

In a dual-card kanban system, there are two main types of kanban:

1. *Production kanban* signals the need to produce more parts. Each kanban is physically attached to a container.
2. *Withdrawal kanban* signals the need to withdraw parts from one work center and deliver them to the next work center.

The kanban-controlled manufacturing system functions as a pull system. As discussed above, in a pull system, removing an end item (or a fixed lot of end items) triggers the order release, by which the flow of materials or components is initiated. In contrast, push systems allow for the production or material flow in anticipation of future demand. The second way is to examine the structure of the information flow. See Olhager and Ostlund (1990). In a pull system, the physical flow of materials is triggered by the local demand from the next server. The local demand in this system is signified by the local information, empty kanbans. In this context, the pure pull system is a decentralized control strategy in which the ultimate goal of meeting demand (orders) is disregarded in the local servers (individual stations). However, a push system uses global and centralized information. Global information of customer orders and demand forecasts is released and processed to control all the levels of production in the push system.

In some pull systems, other signaling approaches are used in place of kanban cards. For example, an empty container alone (with appropriate identification on the container) could serve as a signal for replenishment. Similarly, a labeled, pallet-sized square painted on the shop floor, if uncovered and visible, could indicate the need to go get another pallet of materials from its point of production and move it on top of the empty square at its point of use.

A kanban system is referred to as a pull system because the kanban is used to pull parts to the next production stage only when they are needed. In contrast, an MRP system (or any schedule-based system) is a push system in which a detailed production schedule for each part is used to push parts to the next production stage when scheduled. Thus, in a pull system, material movement occurs only when the workstation needing more material asks for it to be sent, while in a push system the station producing the material initiates its movement to the receiving station, assuming that it is needed because it was scheduled for production. The weakness of a push system (MRP) is that customer demand must be forecast and production lead times must be estimated. Bad guesses (forecasts or estimates) result in excess inventory and the longer the lead time, the more room for error. The weakness of a pull system (kanban) is that following the JIT production philosophy is essential, especially concerning the elements of short setup times and small lot sizes, because each station in the process must be able to respond quickly to requests for more materials. The dual-card kanban rules follow:

1. No parts are made unless there is a production kanban to authorize production. If no production kanban are in the "inbox" at a work center, the process remains idle, and workers perform other assigned activities. This rule enforces the "pull" nature of the process control.
2. There is exactly one kanban per container.
3. Containers for each specific part are standardized, and they are always filled with the same (ideally, small) quantity. (Think of an egg carton, always filled with exactly one dozen eggs.)

Decisions regarding the number of kanbans (and containers) at each stage of the process are carefully considered because this number sets an upper bound on the work-in-process inventory at that stage. For example, if 10 containers holding 12 units each are used to move materials between two work centers, the maximum inventory possible is 120 units, occurring only when all 10 containers are full. At this point, all kanbans will be attached to full containers, so no additional units will be produced (because there are no unattached production kanbans to authorize production). This feature of a dual-card kanban system enables systematic productivity improvement to take place. By deliberately removing one or more kanbans (and containers) from the system, a manager also will reduce the maximum level of work-in-process (buffer) inventory. This reduction can be done until a shortage of materials occurs. This shortage is an indication of problems (accidents, machine breakdowns, production delays, defective products) that were previously hidden by excessive inventory. Once the problem is observed

FIGURE 6.2a
Traditional Production Planning System (Push System)

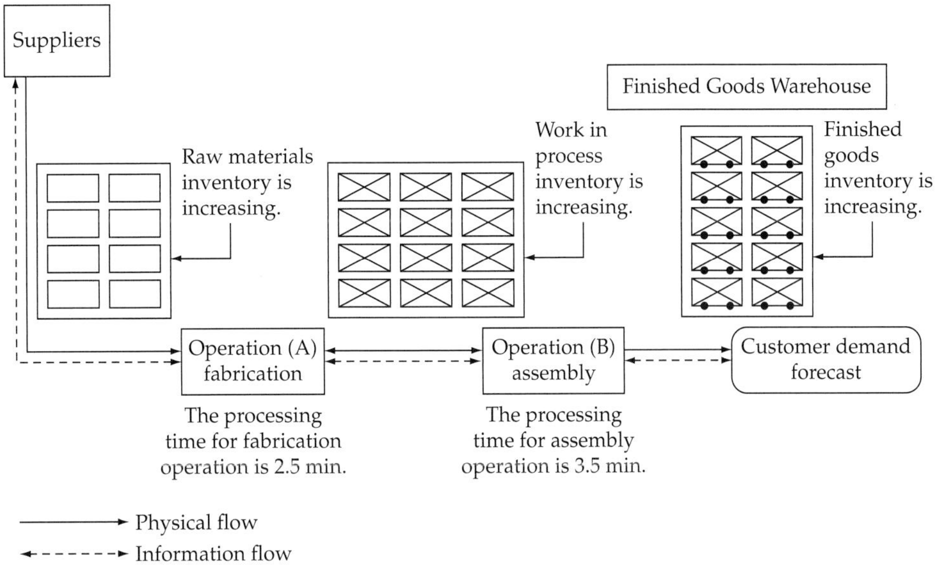

and a solution is identified, corrective action is taken so that the system can function at the lower level of buffer inventory. This simple, systematic method of inventory reduction is a key benefit of a dual-card kanban system.

A Simple Kanban Example

An illustration of the push and pull manufacturing concepts is given in this example. Traditional MRP manufacturing systems use *push* systems, where the goal is to ensure all workstations and equipment are optimally used. A result of this is that where there are a series of operations (fabrication, assembly, and finished goods), they are independently optimized. Thus, if an earlier operation is faster than a later operation, increasing levels of inventory will build at the succeeding workstation as in Figure 6.2a.

As shown in Figure 6.2a, overproduction is an element of waste. Less inventory also reduces the amount of scrap or rework required when a defect is discovered. And, since less inventory means shorter lead times, it takes up space, uses up working capital, and is liable to damage and devaluation. The ultimate inventory pile is at the end of the assembly process, where finished goods are stacked up in warehouses, waiting for customers to buy them.

The principle of pull is that control is transferred from the beginning of the line to the end. Thus, in the example above, Operation B needs to control what Operation A gives them. The secret of this is the kanban card. A kanban card is a control device that effectively says to the recipient, "Give me *N* items, and *N* items only. When you have done that, stop! Wait until you get the next kanban card." Figure 6.2b now shows the changed conversation between the suppliers, Operation A, and Operation B. Operation A now may stand idle for a while, which may seem like a cost, but it is not as great as the cost of idle inventory.

The objective of the pull systems is to see how small a number of items you can pull with a kanban. A certain number are needed to manage natural variation in the process, but no more than the minimum is needed for the natural variation. Reducing the number of items pulled, even by one, is an effective way of highlighting problems and bottlenecks in the system. For example, reducing the kanban number in the example to five may lead to Operation B being idle sometimes, but if

FIGURE 6.2b **JIT Kanban Production Phasing System (Pull System)**

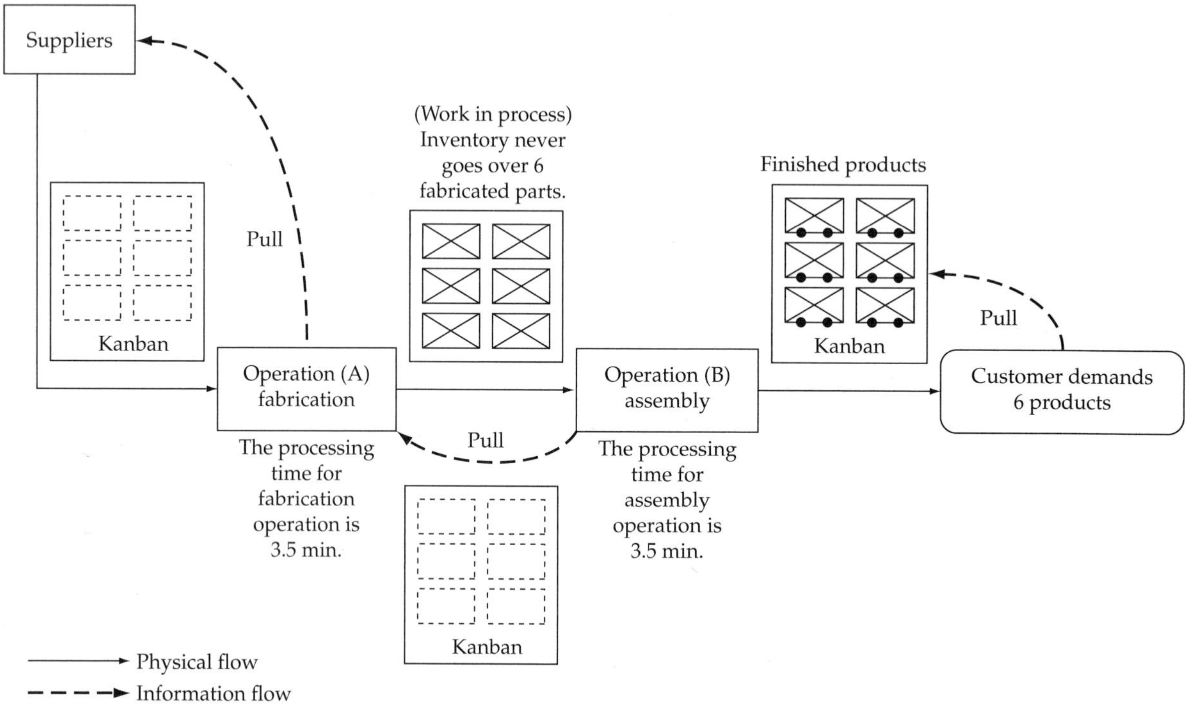

some process improvement is done on it, it may even be able to handle as low as four kanban items.

Determining the Number of Kanbans (Containers)

The formula for determining the number of kanbans needed to control the production of a particular product/component part is

$$\text{Number of kanbans} = \frac{\text{Average demand during lead time} + \text{Safety stock}}{\text{Container size}}$$

$$N = \frac{dL + S}{C}$$

where

N = Number of kanbans or containers
d = Average demand per unit of time
L = Lead time; the time it takes to replenish an order
S = Safety stock, usually given as a percentage of demand during lead time or the level of expected variance
C = Container size

To promote continuous improvement, the container size is usually set at a smaller level than the demand during lead time, say, 10 percent of daily demand. This approach will result in reducing the number of kanbans. The fewer number of kanbans causes work methods and process problems to become visible.

Example

Marcus works as an operator at Health First, a supplement manufacturer. He is asked to process an average of 90 bottles an hour through his workstation. One kanban is attached to each container, a container holds six bottles, and it takes 20 minutes to receive new bottles from the upstream workstation. The safety stock level is set at 10 percent. How many kanbans are required for the bottling process?

SOLUTION

$$N = \frac{(90 \times 0.33) + (90 \times 0.33 \times 0.10)}{6}$$

$$= \frac{29.7 + 2.97}{6} = 5.44^{*}$$

*We can round either up or down. If we round down, we would be promoting continuous improvement. If we round up, we would be allowing more inventory into the process.

SIGNIFICANCE OF PURCHASING

The cost of raw materials has traditionally been a serious concern of top management. Over the years, material cost, as a proportion of total cost of the end product, has risen sharply and is as high as 80 percent in some instances. Consequently, the role of the purchasing function in a manufacturing organization has become increasingly important. The JIT production control system focuses on reducing both raw materials and work-in-process inventories. Specifically, JIT requires that the right materials are provided to workstations at the right time. The purchasing function is heavily involved in making necessary arrangements with suppliers so that the material flows are possible in the manufacturing plant. The role of purchasing is becoming increasingly important even in nonmanufacturing environments where long cycle times from customer requests through service delivery create serious problems for such organizations.

JIT PURCHASING

The function of purchasing is to provide a firm with component parts and raw materials. Purchasing also must ensure that high-quality products are provided on time, at a reasonable price. A comparison of critical elements associated with JIT purchasing and traditional purchasing approaches follows:

1. *Reduced order quantities.* One of the most crucial elements of the just-in-time system is small lot sizes. Traditionally, long and infrequent production runs have been considered beneficial for the overall productivity of a manufacturing organization. However, long production runs usually lead to high levels of raw material and finished-goods inventories. Large setup times have been the primary motivating factor for longer production runs. The JIT concept reduces setup times and the associated costs by introducing clever changeover techniques and simpler product designs. This permits more frequent production runs and smaller lot sizes. In turn, the JIT purchasing function becomes responsible for more frequent but smaller orders compared to the traditional

FIGURE 6.3
Lean Order Cost Example

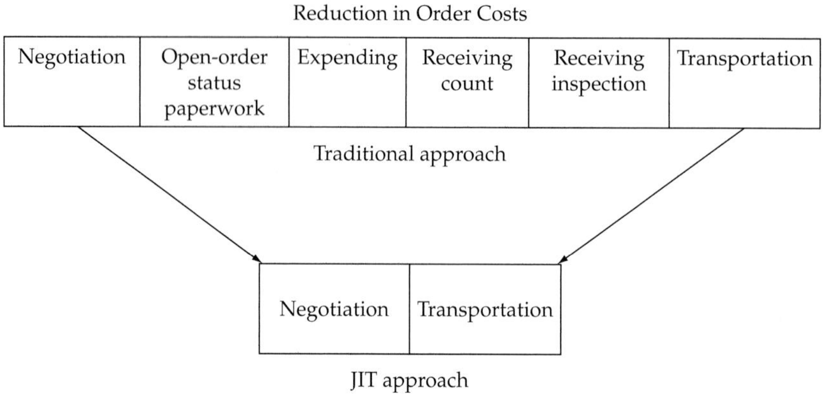

case. Under the traditional manufacturing system, suppliers, on average, ship enough materials to cover two months of production; since adopting JIT, the lot size has been trimmed to less than three weeks. If frequent purchase orders are to be a viable option, traditional inventory theory suggests that order costs be minimal for JIT purchasing to be cost-effective. Indeed, the JIT philosophy strives to drive the ordering costs down to a bare minimum. A breakdown of the ordering costs associated with conventional purchasing practices is shown in Figure 6.3. Under the JIT purchasing approach, the relationship between the supplier and buyer allows the ordering costs to be reduced to simplify the negotiation and transportation costs.

All the intermediate costs are eliminated once the supplier meets the requirements of a Class A supplier. A substantial decrease in the ordering costs permits a greater number of orders to be placed over shorter intervals.

2. *Frequent and "on-time" delivery schedules.* Supplier performance can be measured more accurately under the JIT purchasing approach compared to the traditional one. In order to obtain small lot sizes for production, the order quantity size needs to be reduced and corresponding delivery schedules need to be made more frequent. The "on-time" windows have been reducing systematically over the years. In the pre-JIT days, "on-time" meant anything arriving up to 12 days ahead of the nominal schedule, and as late as six days. On an average, today JIT buyers set the window at five days early and two days late. Yet, the surprising fact is that on-time deliveries increased from 62 percent to 79 percent in spite of the 11-day reduction in delivery window time (see Radovilsky, et al.).

3. *Reduced lead times.* To be able to maintain low inventory levels, it is critical that replenishment lead times be as short as possible. The JIT philosophy inherently attempts to reduce lead times for order completions. Under traditional purchasing practices, the lead time is made up of the following components: paperwork lead time, manufacturing time for supplier, transportation lead time, and time spent on receiving and inspection. A comparison between the JIT approach to lead time and the traditional approach is shown in Figure 6.4.

Under the JIT system, suppliers are usually associated with the company on a long-term basis. Consequently, it is possible for them to reduce paperwork significantly. Also, the supplier may be able to reduce the manufacturing time because of the guaranteed volumes. As a result of building quality into the products, the

FIGURE 6.4
Lean Lead Time Example

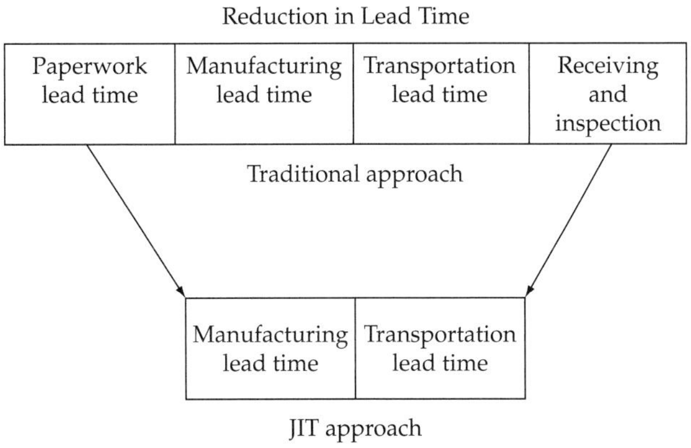

receiving and inspection time spent by the buyer usually decreases. Replenishment lead times also may be reduced by locating a supplier close to the buying firm's plant.

4. *High quality of incoming materials.* Japanese manufacturers attempt to reduce incoming material inspection as much as possible. In order to eliminate the associated receiving inspection costs, a very high emphasis is placed on the quality of incoming materials under the JIT system.

Xerox provides a good example of the unnecessary resources spent on the incoming inspection of goods in its pre-JIT days. All deliveries from suppliers had to pass through Xerox's Webster plant in upstate New York before they could be redirected to the appropriate plants around the United States. In some instances, component parts from West Coast suppliers were first shipped to the East Coast for inspection and shipped back to the West Coast manufacturing plants. The JIT approach favors material inspection at the supplier's plant. Motivation for the suppliers to furnish high-quality materials is cultivated by long-term agreements and strategic relationships between buyers and suppliers. JIT purchasing, therefore, plays a very critical role in improving product quality at the manufacturing source.

5. *Reliable suppliers.* Since the JIT system does not provide for buffer stocks, unreliable supply, in terms of delivery time and quality of incoming material, may lead to frequent problems in production. Consequently, reliability of supply is a critical consideration in the selection of JIT suppliers. Since JIT purchasing has gained popularity within the United States, the purchasing function has been preoccupied with trimming the overall supplier base in quest of so-called superior suppliers. Xerox, for example, reduced its supplier base by nearly 4,700 over a period of one year (Inman, 1992). Ford has reduced its supplier base by nearly 25 percent over the past decade. The number of superior suppliers is on the rise as JIT promotes the concept of fewer but better suppliers.

A brief summary of the comparison between the traditional and JIT purchasing approaches is shown in Table 6.1. JIT purchasing systems are much more difficult to manage. If JIT purchasing systems are not properly implemented and managed, the synergies will be lost and the system will collapse. However, significant advantages are realized if these elements are implemented successfully.

TABLE 6.1 **Comparison between Traditional and Just-in-Time (Lean) Purchasing Approaches**

	Traditional Purchasing	JIT Purchasing
Order quantities	Based on trade-offs between ordering and carrying costs	Based on small lot sizes for production
Delivery schedules	Infrequent, primarily because of high ordering costs involved	Frequent because of small lot sizes and low ordering costs
Delivery windows	Relatively wide	Very narrow
Delivery lead times	Relatively long and relaxed	Stringent and reduced significantly
Parts quality	Responsibility of the quality function in the organization	Responsibility of supplier
Supplier base	Fairly broad	Considerably smaller

PURCHASING BENEFITS

Implementation of JIT purchasing assists the purchasing function in its major objectives of improving quality of incoming materials and supplier delivery performance, along with reducing lead times and cost of materials. Some of the critical JIT purchasing advantages for the manufacturer are discussed below.

1. *Reduced inventory levels.* JIT purchasing facilitates the reduction in inventory levels and the associated inventory holding costs. Asian firms like Toyota have been able to reduce inventory levels to such an extent that their inventory turnover ratios have gone up to over 60 times per year, compared to corresponding ratios of 5–8 times per year reported by most American manufacturers. U.S. manufacturers have been trying to reduce inventory levels by using JIT purchasing techniques. NCR's Ithaca plant, for instance, has been successful in reducing its number of days of inventory from 110 to 21 within three years of implementing JIT. However, a strong debate exists as to whether or not manufacturers shift the burden of inventories to suppliers using the guise of JIT. This issue will be addressed later. Reduced inventory levels are indeed one of the benefits of the JIT system, which basically stresses continuous improvement and elimination of waste.

2. *Improved lead-time reliability.* Compared to traditional purchasing approaches, delivery lead times under the JIT system are considerably shorter. Lead-time reliability is usually much better for JIT systems. This implies higher levels of customer service and lower safety stock requirements for the company. Lower levels of safety stock contribute significantly to reduced working capital requirements for the firm.

3. *Scheduling flexibility.* JIT emphasizes scheduling flexibility by reducing purchasing lead times and setup times. Such flexibility prevents confusion in the manufacturing plant and offers unique competitive advantages to manufacturing firms since they are capable of adapting to changes in the environment more quickly.

4. *Improved quality and customer satisfaction.* JIT purchasing results in improved quality and corresponding levels of higher customer satisfaction. Since high-quality products are critical in achieving a competitive advantage in today's global business world, manufacturers gain immensely by implementing the JIT production control

system. High-quality incoming materials result in savings associated with reduced rework and scrap.

5. *Reduced costs of parts.* As cooperation and relationships between suppliers and manufacturers build up in a JIT system, so do the opportunities to conduct an extensive value analysis and focus on reducing the cost of parts purchased. A comprehensive JIT progress report indicates that supplier costs were reduced by 11 percent when they adopted the JIT system in cooperation with their customers. Long-term commitments on the part of the manufacturer allow volume purchases, development of supplier learning curves, and overall productivity increases.

6. *Constructive synergies with suppliers.* A JIT purchasing program involves close technical cooperation with suppliers. This particularly means the cooperation between manufacturing and design engineers. Because of smaller lot sizes and frequent delivery schedules, suppliers are in a position to receive quick feedback regarding any potential manufacturing or design problems. Also, manufacturing is in a position to implement engineering changes quicker because of the reduced inventory levels. The JIT progress report mentioned above indicates that supplier quality improved by 26 percent since the JIT system was adopted.

7. *Cost decreases.* It is well documented that JIT reduces physical inventory levels. Reductions in physical inventory also will have a favorable impact on

- Reduced insurance premiums associated with the storage of inventory.
- Reduced inventory holding costs.
- Reduced labor cost in storerooms and material handling costs.
- Reduced clerical and administrative costs.
- Reduced waste from the manufacturing process.
- Reduced obsolescence costs.
- Reduced depreciation of handling and storage equipment.

Each of the cost savings will result in a leaner, more profitable operation.

IMPLEMENTATION OF JIT PURCHASING

As attractive as the JIT purchasing philosophy might initially seem, it is quite difficult to implement. The switch to a JIT system presents formidable challenges. Marketing must be prepared to change its behavior when its customers are using the JIT system. Some of the common problems associated with implementing the JIT system are as follows:

1. *Lack of cooperation from suppliers.* In a detailed survey of U.S. firms involved with JIT manufacturing, 47 percent of the respondents indicated that they had serious problems with some of their suppliers. Many suppliers see little incentive in adopting the JIT approach when the primary benefits of the program go to the buyer. Also, there seems to be a lack of commitment from the buyers, who treat the suppliers as independent parties and foster intense competition among them. Moreover, many suppliers feel a considerable strain in providing the good-quality materials to the buyer in the right quantity and the right time on an ongoing basis.

These problems may be resolved to some extent by educating and training the suppliers in JIT purchasing. This may be done by conducting intensive presentations

TABLE 6.2
Expectations of JIT Suppliers

1. A long-term business agreement
2. A fair return on supplier investment
3. Adequate time for thorough planning
4. Accurate demand functions
5. Correct and firm specifications
6. Parts designed to match supplier's process capability
7. Smoothly timed order releases
8. A fair profit margin
9. Fair dealings with regard to price
10. A minimum number of change orders
11. Prompt payment of invoices

and group discussions at the suppliers' plants, supplemented with continuing in-house training with the help of selected quality-control and engineering personnel from the manufacturer's plant. Manufacturers using the JIT purchasing concept must realize that long-term materials cost reductions are possible only if supplier costs are reduced. The manufacturer, therefore, must assist the supplier in identifying possible areas where improvements can be made. Some of the important expectations of suppliers involved with JIT programs are listed in Table 6.2.

Therefore, emphasis needs to be shifted from the competitive and adversarial relationship between the manufacturer and supplier to a long-term cooperation-oriented relationship. Companies that have made JIT work smoothly at the supply end, such as Dell and Hewlett–Packard, have developed elaborate mechanisms for supplier relations, with an emphasis on partnership rather than impatient demands. One of the important secrets to JIT success is to keep no secrets from suppliers.

2. *Lack of top management support.* Implementation of the JIT philosophy requires a cultural change in the organization. Such a concept cannot be implemented successfully without total support from top management. However, another survey of U.S. manufacturing firms indicated that 48 percent of the firms did not receive total support from top management in their efforts to implement the JIT manufacturing system. Some of the lack of enthusiasm during the past decade from top management in the United States stems from the heavy focus on short-term planning, skepticism about the suitability of JIT in the American context, and frustration from the numerous problems encountered in the implementation process.

An attitudinal change is required in order to get top management involved in the implementation process. Visits to other companies that have implemented a JIT program, coupled with positive JIT results experienced by other firms, may serve to provide the necessary motivation for general managers who are initially skeptical about the program.

3. *Lack of employee readiness and support.* Many firms report lack of support from their employees as being one of the major problems encountered in the implementation of JIT. Very often, such resistance is encountered because the employees are required to change their long-standing work habits, or because they interpret the new system as being a threat to their jobs. Also, the JIT system requires most employees to assume more problem-solving responsibilities on the job, which may lead to additional frustration.

Education and training are very important to winning the support of employees. They need to have a thorough understanding of how JIT purchasing will be a major factor in the long-term growth and profitability of the firm, and that their professional future depends on the successful implementation of the JIT system.

4. *Lack of support from design engineering personnel.* Design engineering is responsible for making technical specifications for the materials a company buys. Quite often, the purchasing function in an organization does not receive adequate support from engineering functions, and, as a result, purchasing is often unable to advise suppliers on material quality design options. Thirty-nine percent of the firms surveyed using JIT practices in the United States indicated that they had serious problems regarding lack of support from engineering.

The solution to this problem is an operating climate that permits or promotes a high level of integration in all operations, including production, material control, design and process engineering, and purchasing. Such an environment is conducive to resolving problems. Suppliers also will reap benefits from the improved interaction between engineering and other personnel because they may resolve some of the quality problems with buyers more quickly and effectively.

5. *Low product quality.* If suppliers fail to provide materials of adequate quality on a regular basis, production slowdowns and stoppages will occur regularly. The study reports that 53 percent of American manufacturing firms implementing JIT cited this factor to be a major obstacle.

In order to overcome this problem, a quality management program needs to be developed by JIT buyers that would help identify critical quality characteristics during the design and manufacturing stages of the supply process. A supplier quality certification program can be implemented that would ensure that parts leaving the suppliers' plants meet all quality specifications. Nissan has implemented a supplier audit program in which six Nissan engineers regularly audit the local suppliers' plants and provide assistance on quality issues.

6. *Lack of support from carrier companies.* Table 6.3 gives an indication of the huge sums of money that the purchasing function of some major firms spends every year in order to move materials in and out of the factory. Few buying firms, however, work closely with carriers to develop long-term relationships that provide for highly structured delivery schedules that lower costs. Buyers have traditionally accepted terms offered to them by the carriers with regard to their inbound freight.

However, increased freight activity because of JIT has not entirely been an easy ride for carriers. As a result of deregulation, transportation becomes a more competitive and quality-driven business; most manufacturing firms have begun to realize that there are significant savings possible in negotiating better terms with carriers. There has been a substantial reduction in the number of carriers used over

TABLE 6.3
Annual Expenditure on Freight

Company	Dollars Spent
General Motors	$7,300,000,000
Ford	6,500,000,000
International Paper	3,200,000,000
General Electric	2,500,000,000
Chrysler	1,200,000,000

the years, which provides significant leverage to the buyers. In order to promote cooperation between buyers and carriers, computer interfaces are being used by some buyers to help carriers update the buyer's information system as materials move through the carrier's system. Specific contractual features are becoming popular to meet the unique delivery requirements of the buyer. The current fuel crisis will become an important factor in the procurement of transportation services.

7. *Lack of communication*. Effective development and implementation of the JIT system require integration of important functional areas such as purchasing, manufacturing, quality, production, and transportation. Lack of proper communication among these areas poses a major obstacle to the implementation of JIT. While there is no easy solution to this problem, the purchasing function in an organization must assume the responsibility of calling on top management regularly for leadership and support.

ROLE OF CULTURE

A crucial issue to be considered is the relevance of culture in the successful implementation of the JIT system in a country. Honda's culture and its focus on group-oriented activities are particularly suitable to the implementation of the JIT production control system. Harmony in the organizations provides for better manufacturer–supplier relationships at Toyota and Honda. Moreover, long-term relationships between supplier and manufacturer are the norm of doing business in Japan. Severance of a business relationship between manufacturer and supplier has a strong stigma associated with it, which both manufacturers and suppliers try to avoid as much as possible.

Within the United States, however, such relationships between manufacturers and suppliers are a little more difficult to cultivate. Traditionally, the business firms in the United States are so short-term oriented that they have their immediate interests in mind. Moreover, the level of employee and supplier commitment to the JIT concept is not as uniform and high as it is in Japan. This does not mean that JIT is not a viable concept in the United States. It is not advisable, however, for U.S. firms to blindly emulate the Japanese JIT approach. In fact, U.S. firms should try to tailor JIT to their needs and circumstances. Some firms in the United States have developed and implemented their own version of JIT under different names, such as ZIPS (zero inventory production systems), MAN (material-as-needed), and nick-of-time. A case study on JIT indicates how Hutchinson Technology (a publicly held company that manufactures a variety of products for computer peripheral and military markets) organized and implemented JIT manufacturing (Ray, 1990). The major difficulties encountered in the process included the inability of purchasing personnel to make the immense cultural transformation and the lack of resources to effect the change properly. Despite these difficulties, their JIT purchasing program has been successful.

Greater geographic separation between supplier and manufacturer in the United States is also a major impediment to the implementation process according to the one survey (Freeland, 1991). The survey also indicates that JIT does not imply single sourcing in the United States, as it does in Japan. This reflects the reality of the marketplace in the United States and efforts of manufacturers to adjust to JIT as best they can.

CRITICAL ANALYSIS OF THE JIT CONCEPT

Most of the testimonials published on JIT systems exalt the simplicity inherent in the system processes and procedures. However, the key issue for a firm in the United States is whether it is simple to implement JIT in an existing manufacturing environment. Does JIT really provide the solution to most manufacturing problems in the United States? It is also worth investigating whether traditional purchasing approaches have been outdated in light of JIT purchasing.

Just-in-time came under intense scrutiny when Japanese manufacturers stormed into the U.S. markets and took away a substantial share from the U.S. automobile industry. Subsequent investigations revealed, much to the relief of U.S. manufacturers, that it was not only the work culture in Japan that provided the Japanese an edge but also the JIT approach to manufacturing management. Many U.S. manufacturers have been in strong pursuit of this manufacturing revolution and manufacturing excellence that JIT was portrayed to bring. Several manufacturing firms that adopted the JIT approach early include General Motors, Hewlett-Packard, Ford, and Dell. Unfortunately, the excitement about the radically new manufacturing approach, coupled with the romantic version of JIT put forward by many, lulled quite a few manufacturers into believing that JIT would bring instantaneous results for their companies. Too many companies turned to JIT looking for a relatively painless financial cure that would yield substantial short-term benefits. Over the years, these companies have come to realize the tremendous effort and commitment required to make a JIT system run smoothly.

The radical proponents of JIT manufacturing in the United States during the 1980s and 1990s, the so-called JIT revolutionaries, are to some extent responsible for this initial misunderstanding. The practitioners painted an extremely romantic picture of JIT, emphasizing simplicity and efficiency, along with an illusion that employee morale would be high and relations between buyers and suppliers would be completely harmonious. They also called for immediate action and changeover to JIT without really considering the possible ramifications of implementation in the United States. Nor did they convey the message that driving obstacles and impediments out of the system would take serious and substantial effort, commitment, and time.

The pragmatic version of JIT put forth by Japanese authors focuses on the details of the production process. Here the emphasis is on identifying impediments to the smooth flow of materials and innovative techniques to overcome those problems. The Japanese perspective clearly stresses the need for careful and slow implementation, following thorough preparation. It takes time to change attitudes of the workforce and nurture long-term relationships with suppliers.

The transition to JIT has not necessarily been a smooth one for many companies in the United States. However, this does not imply that switching from a pure MRP system to a JIT or hybrid system was a mistake for most companies. There are two serious drawbacks with the MRP production control system. First, the master production schedule that drives MRP is based on estimated customer requirements; and second, MRP's production control system utilizes a "push" system for manufacturing goods. That is, the purchasing function places orders for materials in large lot sizes even though the material may not actually be required, and one workstation pushes materials to the next regardless of actual production requirements. Changes in demand, estimates, or forecasts may allow inventory to pile up in the plant. Very frequent adjustments to the master production schedule make the production system extremely nervous and place enormous pressures on purchasing. However, it must be admitted that MRP is an elegant technique for exploding materials requirements for production. This system has increasingly become easier to implement with the advent of sophisticated computing technology. It is not surprising to find some Western manufacturers who still utilize MRP for ordering purchased materials but require that delivery schedules be based on the kanban system.

Another critical issue for JIT manufacturers is the variability in product demand. The JIT system seems to work best when its smooth production and low inventory requirements are aimed at meeting a relatively stable product demand. However, demand patterns are not stable for all products. In order to induce a relatively stable demand, companies using JIT manufacturing often consolidate their product lines. They emphasize high quality and low cost of the product, but not variety and availability. This suggests that not all marketing strategies are compatible with the JIT system.

Does this mean that JIT, as a concept, is not particularly suited to manufacturers in the United States? Certainly not. The basic concept is as applicable in the United States as it is in Japan. The JIT system does yield substantial benefits where it has been implemented properly. Undoubtedly, proper implementation of JIT is the key to its success. There are significant benefits to other functional areas as well. However, it should be realized that JIT is not a panacea for all manufacturing problems and scenarios. A comprehensive study by Krajewski et al. revealed that selection of a production or inventory system can be of less importance than the improvement in the manufacturing environment itself (Krajewski et al., 1987). Keeping this in mind, manufacturers in the United States should evaluate the potential benefits of a JIT system from their own perspective, not from that of the romantic visionaries.

Summary

JIT has changed the role of purchasing from merely placing orders to investigating the supplier's technical and process capabilities. Value analysis, which aims at seeking cost reductions through buyer and supplier cooperation, has become an integral part of the JIT purchasing practice. Perhaps the most important realization is the fact that suppliers should become an extremely important consideration for the purchasing function, wherein they should be viewed as partners and not adversaries.

The benefits of JIT purchasing will not be realized overnight. It took Toyota Motors 25 years to develop and implement the JIT system fully, and it will take at least 10 years for those that wish to obtain satisfactory results by copying it. A lot of hard work, commitment, and communication are needed before any concrete results can be seen. However, it is important to realize that significant competitive advantages can emerge for a firm that utilizes its JIT purchasing function effectively.

Discussion Questions

1. What is meant by just-in-time (JIT) purchasing?
2. What are the elements of JIT purchasing?
3. What are problems associated with implementing JIT purchasing?
4. What are some of the expectations of the suppliers? What is the role of culture in the implementation of JIT?
5. What are some of the advantages of JIT purchasing? Please compare JIT purchasing with traditional purchasing.
6. How does JIT purchasing affect order costs and lead time?
7. Does JIT really provide the solution to most manufacturing problems in the United States?

Suggested Cases

Austin Woods
Swisher Systems
Two-Bucks Wine Operations

References

Benton, W. C., and H. Shin. "Manufacturing Planning and Control: The Evolution of MRP and JIT Integration." *European Journal of Operational Research* 110 (1998), pp. 441–44.

Freeland, J. R. "A Survey of Just-in-Time Purchasing Practices in the United States," *Production and Inventory Management* 32, no. 2 (1991), pp. 43–50.

Inman, Anthony R. "Time-Based Competition: Challenges for Industrial Purchasing." *Industrial Management* 34, no. 2 (March–April 1992), pp. 31–32.

Kavnak, Hale. "Implementing JIT Purchasing: Does the Level of Complexity in the Production Process Make a Difference?" *Journal of Managerial Issues*, Spring 2005, pp. 255–272.

Krajewski, L., B. E. King, L. P. Ritzman, and D. S. Wong. "Kanban, MRP, and Shaping the Manufacturing Environment," *Management Science* 33 (1987), pp. 39–57.

Olhager, J., and B. Ostlund, "An Integrated Push-Pull Manufacturing Strategy," *European Journal of Operational Research*, 45, 1999, pp. 135–142.

Radovilsky, Zinovy, William Grotcher, Ravy Mistry, and Rebbecca Yip. "JIT Purchasing: Analyzing Survey Results." *Industrial Management*, November–December 1996.

Ray, Steven. "Just-in-Time Purchasing: A Case Study." *Hospital Material Management Quarterly* 12, no. 1 (August 1990), pp. 7–12.

Womack, J. P., D. Jones, and D. Ross. *The Machine that Changed the World: The Story of Lean Production*. Simon & Schuster, New York, 1990.

Zhixiang, C. "Investigation of Supplier Coordination Performance in Chinese Companies," *Gestao & Producao* 11, no. 3 (2004), pp. 289–96.

Zipkin, Paul H. "Does Manufacturing Need a JIT Revolution?" *Harvard Business Review*, January–February 1991, pp. 40–50.

Part Three

Fundamentals of Purchasing and Supply Chain Management

Chapter Seven

Purchasing Procedures, E-Procurement, and Systems Contracting

Learning Objectives

1. Identify the steps in the conventional purchasing cycle.
2. Explain the differences between buying and purchasing.
3. List the main activities of a typical purchasing department.
4. Define routine versus nonroutine purchasing/buying methods.
5. Identify the technical requirements for e-procurement.
6. Know the differences between EDI and e-procurement.
7. Introduce the RFID technology.

INTRODUCTION

A typical purchasing department is responsible for the acquisition of a broad range of materials and supplies. Depending on the sales volume, the number of employees, and the functional sophistication, the purchasing activities can be either complex or simple. In most cases, large multidivisional firms like IBM, Ford, and Toyota usually establish a set of systematic policies based on the overall corporate missions.

Purchasing directives usually serve as the road map for all material (OEM) and supply (MRO) transactions. The driving force behind any purchasing corporate policy considers the following objectives:

1. Spend corporate funds wisely.
2. Operate in a professional manner.
3. Purchase the right materials in the right quantities, at the right time and price, from the right source.
4. Practice the highest level of ethical standards to ensure confidence among all parties.

FIGURE 7.1a
Purchase Order Cycle
(Procurement Cycle Standard Documentation)

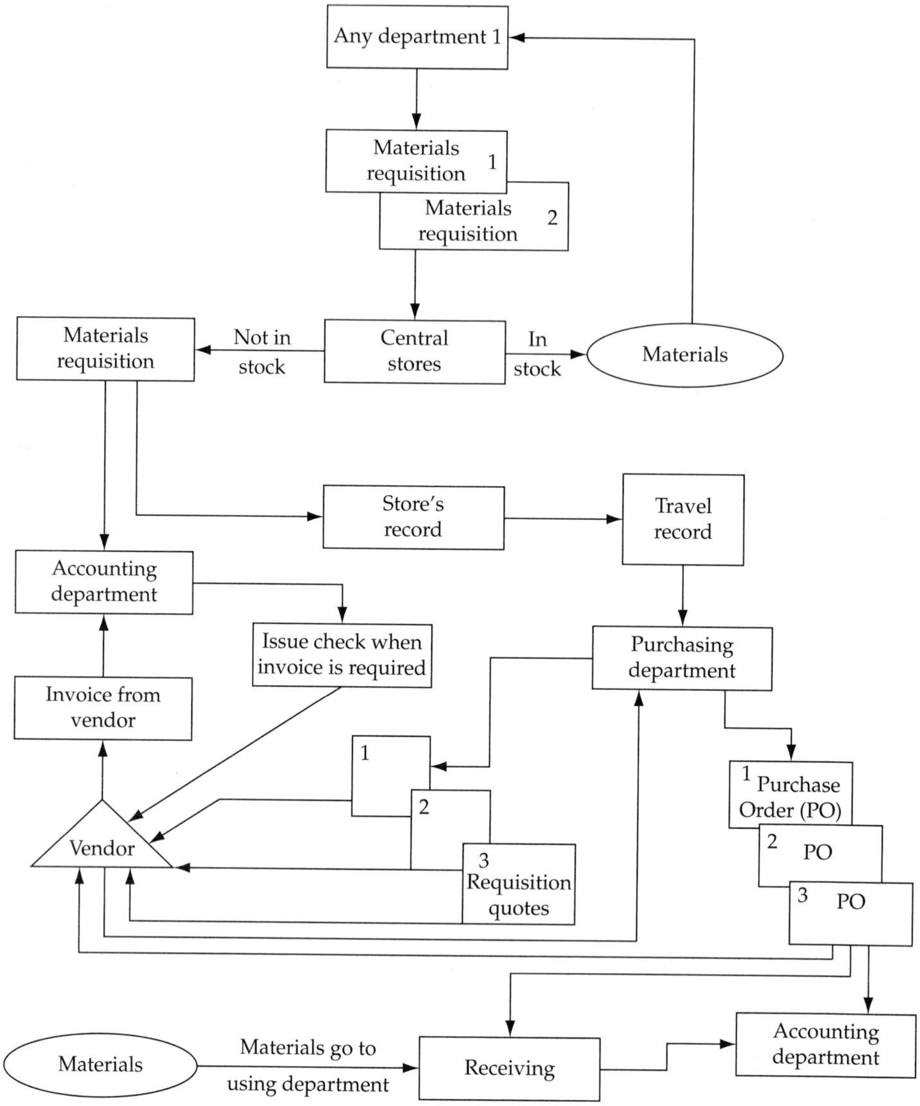

PURCHASING PROCEDURES

The standard purchase order cycle is shown in Figures 7.1a and 7.1b. Consider a simple situation in which the training department for a medium-size firm is purchasing 2,000 three-hole binders:

1. Work area involved: Training department.
2. Material required: Three-hole binders.
3. Specification: Three holes, inside pocket, company logo.
4. Point of need: Training department.
5. Procedure: Training manager determines need for binders and issues a materials requisition.

This sort of simple transaction is repeated daily in every firm. The routine practice of this type of transaction is the basic motivation for establishing system contracts.

FIGURE 7.1b
Procurement Order Cycle Standard Procedure
(Documentation)

1. Requisition material
   a. Storeroom requisition
   b. Purchase requisition
   c. Traveling requisition—eliminates separate purchase requisitions
2. Determine vendor
   a. Price card
   b. Traveling requisition—same information as on price card
   c. SAL (same as last)
   d. Inquiry of potential vendors—phone or e-mail (request for quotation)
   e. Evaluate bids and select vendor. Establish prices, quality, and delivery
3. Issue a purchase order
   a. Distribute copies (multiple)
4. Follow and expedite delivery
   a. Open and close order files
5. Document receipt of material
   a. Multiple copies required
6. Move to storeroom (or point of use)
7. Receive and handle invoice
   a. Purchasing
   b. Accounts payable
8. Issue payment

Price cards and traveling requisitions are often maintained for materials even though the items are not repetitive enough to be stocked in a storeroom.
The traveling requisitlon also may include information regarding the order point and economic order quantity for inventory control purposes.

Moreover, this example shows the significant difference between buying and purchasing. In general, the purchasing process refers to buying goods and services for use by the buying organization. Buying typically means procuring items for resale. Of course, the terms are sometimes used interchangeably. The specific documentation for the procurement cycle is given in Figure 7.1b.

Details for the third purchasing objective became evident when the material requirements arose:

1. The right material: Vinyl three-hole binder
2. The right quality: Standard
3. The right quantity: 2,000 units
4. The right place: The training area
5. The right time: Now

Thus, based on the above criteria specified by the using department manager, the main functions of the purchasing department are to:

1. Determine the supplier.
2. Negotiate the actual price.
3. Determine the delivery date.

This procedure is also systematically followed for many items other than binders. To what other items can we apply this buying/purchasing method? More than 75 percent of a firm's procurement activities are routine. Unfortunately, many firms spend more than 75 percent of the time buying low-value routine supplies. This level of commodity purchasing is increasingly automated. However, knowledge of the standard purchasing cycle must be understood by all purchasing professionals.

When the need for the binders was apparent, the supply of binders was replenished from the training materials storage area. The storeroom attendant is usually held responsible for maintaining inventory levels. Most storerooms are full of inexpensive items and 90 percent of stores' transactions are for low-value routine materials related to nonproductive requirements. Acquisition of supplies from the company storerooms in most cases is a relatively simple process. A standard three-part requisition form is usually used to initiate the transaction. The department number is used to post the requisition charge. Because of human handling of the requisitions, it is difficult to maintain record and budget accuracy. The cost of the manual requisition system also may lead to productivity losses. As an example, if 30 employees each make three round trips to the stores, we can estimate the loss in productivity. Assume that it takes each employee an average of 20 minutes (including waiting time); with a labor rate of $10 per hour, the total cost is $300 per day (30 hours × $10).

Materials and supplies are usually received by the requisitioning department in less than 24 hours. The inventory system is then updated. This process is continued until some predetermined reorder point is activated and storeroom replenishment occurs. A traveling requisition is used to request repetitive materials/supplies. Sources of supply, the previous price paid, and the order quantity are some of the information on the traveling requisition. Most purchasing departments operate as surrogate procurement operations.

From the information given above, it is easy to see that even with the most developed systems, purchase processing can be costly and inaccurate. In the next section, we will attempt to streamline the purchase process system using systems contracting.

SYSTEMS CONTRACTING

What Is Systems Contracting?

Systems contracting is a stockless inventory method for ordering and stocking MRO and related items. The use of systems contracting will aid the firm in reducing ordering and inventory costs. The systems contracting process requires the use of a negotiated agreement between buyers and sellers. The agreement includes the following terms: the type of material, scope of contract, price, billing policy, stocking policy, and delivery requirements. Systems contracting is an efficient form of purchasing that is based on reductions in processing and administrative costs.

As an example, Massachusetts General Hospital recently signed a five-year systems contract with Advanced Medical Systems. The control materials management system will replace the current system at the 900-bed hospital that has been in use since 1994. The materials management control system is a real-time contracting system that assists the materials manager in the determination of minimum and maximum levels, records receipts, suggests reorder points, and enables just-in-time distribution. This system will be used for more than 1,000 hospital items. When the pallets reach the dock at the hospital's off-site warehouse, the items are checked and the bill is paid on the spot. Massachusetts General maintains a backup system with Stuart Medical, a competitor. The savings from this system are expected to reach $1.5 million annually.

Systems contracting is a purchasing management technique that seeks overall reduction in the cost of an item from the time a need is recognized to the time that need is fulfilled. Recognizing that purchase price is but one element of the total cost picture, the scope of systems contracting goes far beyond the purchase price for any given item.

In recent years, top-level managers have made substantial commitments in time and money to improve the efficiency of all facets of their operations. Primary emphasis has been placed on improved production capacity as evidenced by the increased use of automation to reduce process overhead. Information technology has become a vital tool for tracking and controlling process operations from the raw material stage to the finished product.

To extend this commitment to increasing productivity in all departments within a given facility, many companies have adopted the concept of profit centers. As a profit center, each department makes a direct contribution to the overall success of the total organization. Regardless of whether the purchasing, maintenance, and accounting departments are formally recognized as profit centers or not, these areas represent a source of potential savings to any company. The purchasing professional, in conjunction with storeroom personnel and the accounting department, can save the organization thousands of dollars annually. The purchasing function has become an indispensable part of modern management effectiveness. Purchasing professionals are primarily charged with the responsibility for controlling the **total cost of ownership (TCO)**.

The true cost of an item is its purchase price, plus fixed, variable, and overhead costs. Beyond the direct costs are the total procurement costs. The cost of procurement includes the following steps:

1. Identify need.
2. Requisition material.
3. Inquire with potential suppliers.
4. Evaluate bids/quotes.
5. Issue purchase order.
6. Expedite order.
7. Document receipt of material.
8. Receive and handle invoice.
9. Issue payment.

A detailed example of a systems contract is given in Appendix A.

Systems contracting will be widely adopted for low-cost, high-volume commodities. New information technology will force both large and small firms to consider the competitive advantages of systems contracting. An example of savings from a systems contract is given in Figure 7.2.

E-PROCUREMENT

The commercial purchasing literature on e-procurement has suggested that significant savings for businesses and organizations can be realized by migrating to electronic procurement systems for all of their purchasing requirements. The savings include inventory and purchase costs. However, many of the *e-procurement software vendors* fail to take into account the total cost of implementing these systems, the

FIGURE 7.2
Total Cost Savings from Implementing a Systems Contract

Total Sales	Total Transactions	Total Lines
$186,250.00	541	1,712

The estimated savings to Chlorine Products on the above volume using systems contracting:

1. Issuing of purchase order to include forms, preparation, mailing, and so forth, using $25.00 per P.O. issued	$13,525.00
2. Reduction of inventory to include holding costs (taxes and insurance) estimated at 8% of volume	14,900.00
3. Expediting—for example, time to write letters and make phone calls, obtain high-cost logistics support	1,850.00
4. Receiving time, including report generation	1,000.00
5. Pilferage and obsolescence of inventory	800.00
6. Price protection—manufacturer's price increases that normally would be passed on immediately but due to 90-day protection results in savings of approximately 10%	18,625.00
Total savings	$50,700.00

Systems contracting also eliminated approximately 6,500 pieces of paper

difficulty of realizing savings during the development and deployment phases of the transition, and the cost of training employees and getting suppliers to participate in the e-procurement system.

Procurement is a very broad term. There is, in general, a broad push by e-procurement software vendors for companies to migrate all types of purchasing to e-procurement. In most cases, the best place to apply electronic procurement is in circumstances where a very close business relationship must be established and ongoing cooperation is needed with suppliers, especially when developing new products or technologies.

Online or e-procurement technology has become an important part of purchasing and supply chain management and the rate of adoption has increased significantly. An e-procurement technology is defined as any technology designed to facilitate the sourcing of goods and services by commercial or a government organization over the Internet. Table 7.1 summarizes the major e-procurement applications across the supply chain. The responses in Table 7.1 are based on a study by Sigala (2006).

Some companies are investing significant resources in e-procurement in order to gain a competitive advantage in their industry. Other companies are more selective in their investment in e-procurement. The conservative adopters are taking a follow-the-leader approach. Regardless of the nature of the adoption process, the overall concensus is that e-procurement technologies will become an integral tool in the performance of the supply management function. The four most popular e-procurement technology models are e-procurement software, market exchanges, B2B auctions, and purchasing consortia as shown in Table 7.2. Figure 7.3 shows the most frequent barriers to e-procurement technologies.

Two Broad E-Procurement Purchasing Categories

It is important to first understand the two broad purchasing categories of purchased materials, goods, and services in order to fully appreciate the role of e-purchasing.

TABLE 7.1
Respondents' Adoption and Use of E-Procurement Technology (% of Respondents)

Source: Sigala (2006).

Adoption of e-procurement types/systems	
At least one e-purchasing technology	39.6
No e-purchasing technology	64.4
E-procurement software	24.6
Internet B2B auctions	5.2
Internet market exchanges	8.2
Internet purchasing consortia	1.5
E-procurement use	
Purchasing operations	28.3
Inventory management applications	23.1
Purchase from catalogues	17.1
JIT delivery programs	9.4
Communicate with vendors	15.3
Communicate out of stock	13.9
Negotiate with vendors	2.1
Track order and ship date delays	4.2
Check vendor price quotes	18.6
Manage supplies' inventory levels	6.3
Warning damage/expiration notification	0.7
Field warehouses/depots inventory levels	0.0
Transportation applications	2.9
Emergencies affecting inventory	4.7
Pickups, regional distribution centers	1.4
Field depots on out of stock	1.4
Drop-offs, regional distribution centers	0.7
Ordering processing applications	1.4
Monitor on-time arrivals of carriers	1.4
Monitor vendors' order efforts	0.0
Manage claims and overall performance	0.7
Check vendor credit	0.0
Vendors' deliveries to depots	0.7
Obtain price quotes/bids from vendors	1.4
Vendors' raw material stock levels	0.0
Production scheduling applications	1.4
Provide vendor information from queries	0.7
Coordinate schedules with vendors/field depots	0.7
Vendor ratings on overall performance	1.4
Exchange data with vendors/field depots	0.0
Process returns/damaged products	1.4
Coordinate with JIT of vendors	0.7
Ratings of on-time carriers' performance	1.4
Coordinate schedules with affiliated units	1.4

Likert scale: 1, totally disagree; 5, totally agree. Adopters versus nonadopters: $p < 0.001$.

The two major purchasing categories are **direct** and **indirect** materials. Direct materials are directly related to the production of the finished goods, and indirect materials are any commodity or service that is not directly involved in the production of finished goods. Direct materials tend to be purchased in quantities based on complicated production planning and control systems. Some direct material purchasing situations may involve long intricate negotiations. Many high-technology

TABLE 7.2
E-Procurement Mode Definitions

Source: Devila et al. (2003).

E-Procurement Model	Description
E-procurement software	Any Internet-based software application that enables employees to purchase goods from approved electronic catalogues in accordance with company buying rules, while capturing necessary purchasing data in the process. The employee's selection of a good for purchase from a supplier catalogue is automatically routed through the necessary approval processes and protocols. E-procurement software investment may take several forms, including purchase of a software package from a third-party technology provider (e.g., Ariba, CommerceOne), use of an e-procurement system embedded in an Internet market exchange, subscription to e-procurement software hosted and supported by an application service provider (ASP), or development of a proprietary in-house system.
Internet market exchanges	Websites that bring multiple buyers and sellers together in one central virtual market space and enable them to buy and sell from each other at a dynamic price that is determined in accordance with the rules of the exchanges.
Internet B2B auctions	Events in which multiple buyers place bids to acquire goods or services at an Internet site. There are a variety of e-auction formats. The two most popular auction formats are the Dutch auction (where the sellers control the minimum bid and prices move upward from the minimum bid) and the reverse auction (where buyers post requests for quotations and sellers bid the price down). A major benefit of auctions is that they enable organizational buyers to identify the best offer from an expanded base of potential suppliers from around the world. Sellers benefit by obtaining access to bids for business on a level playing field rather than attempting to obtain business based on networks of personal relationships. Auctions also provide sellers with a ready market for the anonymous sale of excess inventory. Websites such as freemarkets.com, purchasepro.com, fastparts.com, and sorcity.com, among others, can enable the e-auction process.
Internet purchasing consortia	Internet service that gathers the purchasing power of many buyers to negotiate more aggressive discounts. Some organizations aggregate buying power for manufacturing inputs (such as FOB.com), while others perform similar functions for indirect goods (such as BizBuyer.com).

manufacturing firms purchase fully assembled component systems. Because of the long contract development and predictable high volumes, the number of transactions is relatively low compared to low-cost, high-transaction-volume indirect purchases. For many manufacturing firms, the direct materials account for between 60 and 80 percent of the spend and 10 and 20 percent of the transactions. On the other hand, indirect materials and services account for between 20 and 40 percent of the spend and 80 and 90 percent of the total number of transactions.

FIGURE 7.3
Three Most Frequently Identified Barriers to E-Procurement Technologies Utilization

Source: Devila et al. (2003).

E-Procurement Software

- Problems integrating with existing systems
- Lack of common standards for e-commerce software development
- Lack of suppliers accessible through the organization's e-procurement system and/or lack of supplier investment in catalogue development

Internet Exchanges

- Not enough suppliers to create a liquid marketplace
- Suppliers reticent to participate in selling environments where preeminent focus is on price
- Suppliers reticent to participate because control is lost over the presentation of brand name and product features

E-Auctions

- Organizational discomfort with auctions, as opposed to honoring commitments to supplier partnering and consolidation
- Downward price pressure on vendors resulting in diminished customer service or quality
- Inability to identify potential items for auction

Purchasing Consortia

- Pricing that is not significantly better than available without consortia
- Getting a sufficient number of vendors into the process
- Ensuring conformance to state laws and regulations that require a bidding process

Indirect Materials Purchasing

Indirect purchasing can be divided into two categories: operating resource management (ORM) and maintenance repair and operations (MRO). ORM purchasing is a term used for purchasing office equipment, furniture, office supplies, forms, computers, travel services, maintenance services, light bulbs, janitorial supplies, and many other relatively low-cost items. MRO purchasing is concerned with critical maintenance and replacement parts, highly engineered machine parts, and manufacturing equipment. Many e-procurement software vendors do not separate these two categories of indirect costs. It is unwise to lump ORM and MRO together. It is easy to see that critical-mission-driven machine parts are more important than office supplies and light bulbs. MRO buyers must select suppliers with high quality and technical support. A detailed comparison of ORM and MRO purchasing is given in Table 7.3. The problem with indirect purchasing is the lack of standardization, tedious paperwork, delays, and errors. Another problem is the tendency for employees to intermittently buy indirect items "off contract." This practice is referred to as maverick buying. E-procurement is an excellent platform for purchasing indirect materials.

The world of business-to-business commerce has become essential to the purchase of ORM and MRO items. E-procurement has fundamentally transformed the traditional indirect purchasing function. E procurement has lead to significant cost saving and coordinated efficiency. Online-driven indirect purchasing reduces the day-to-day waste in the manual purchasing system. Electronic purchasing for indirect materials is far more efficient than making phone calls and sending faxes. Transaction costs account for approximately 40 percent of the cost of purchasing

TABLE 7.3
Comparison of ORM and MRO Purchasing

Criteria	Noncritical (ORM)	Critical (MRO)
Number of orders	Moderate	Often hundreds of thousands
Quantity per order	Few to moderate	Varies from one to thousands
Delivery criticality	Generally low	Routine to critical to the point of work stoppage for delivery failures
Ratio of single source	Low	High percentage (up to 30% by count, more by value); may be single/very limited sources
Services/contracts	Some	Almost always required—performance is critical in many cases
Accounting tie back	Generally only to a GL account	May be multiple—to work order, equipment, GL, and other accounts; capital tie back as well
Controlled inventory	Rarely	Always
Internal item master	None	Frequently—usually critical functionality
Vendor performance measurement	Minimal—usually by contract	Almost always—variable measurement criteria

materials and managing the supply function. It is not a good idea to implement e-procurement on systems that have a high supply risk and low profit impact, especially if there are a very limited number of suppliers to choose from.

Direct Materials Purchasing

Critical items and systems are not the first place to apply a new e-procurement system. Anything that will immediately impact profits or bottleneck your operations is not a good place to experiment with a new electronic procurement system. Emerson Electric, the world's largest supplier of sophisticated computer air-conditioning and power security systems, has successfully implemented an e-procurement system for sourcing strategic direct operating materials. Emerson uses an Internet-driven e-procurement system to issue purchase orders to suppliers. They also allow each strategic supplier access to the database that contains forecast information, open orders, and usage history on the items supplied by the supplier. Each supplier also can access a report containing all of the open purchase orders that have been placed with Emerson by the supplier.

Effective E-Procurement Implementation

1. Start with noncritical items. An initial e-procurement system should slim the amount of paperwork needed for purchasing and reduce order complexity by standardizing the exchange process between supplier and buyer.
2. Bring all internal stakeholders on board with your new procurement process to establish internal customer behavior.
3. Streamline, map, test, troubleshoot, and improve the process before expanding it to external suppliers. Work with a favored supplier to test the system.

4. Leverage your system once it's running. Exploit your full purchasing power by using reverse auctions. Invite new suppliers to participate once the system has proven itself.
5. Aggregate buyers within your organization to increase your purchasing power and gain better pricing.
6. Use an incremental approach to expand your system. It is not possible to have uniform relationships with all suppliers nor are all purchasing requirements the same. Sort purchasing needs into groups that can use a similar process and a similar template.
7. Once the bumps have been ironed out of the system, move on to the manufacturing operations.

REVERSE AUCTIONS

What Are Reverse Auctions?

The Internet has revolutionized commodity purchasing. Firms routinely place orders with suppliers online and in real time, for example. Perhaps the most significant change in the purchasing process is the advent of reverse auctions. Businesses that use reverse auctions, or e-auctions, have given testimonials of savings of more than 50 percent. As an example, General Electric reported savings of more than $600 million by putting $12 billion in contracts up for bid online. The use of reverse auctions also has spread into the construction industry and governmental agencies.

The purpose of a traditional auction is to create competition between bidders. A seller offers a good or service and bidders compete with one another by increasing the current bid price. At the end of the auction, the highest bidder wins the item. With reverse auctions, conditions are somewhat different. First, the buying firm initializes the auction by submitting a description of the product or service. Sellers then place bids based on their offer to fulfill the buyer's needs. The competition between the sellers drives the price down, instead of up, so the buyer pays less at the expense of the seller. Finally, the buyer chooses the winning bidder. Although price is often the most important factor, the winner is not necessarily the highest or the lowest bidder but is selected by the buyer on the basis of a number of factors.

As technology develops, firms have been working much more closely and have recognized the need to integrate information technology with supply chain practices. One good example is Covisint, an e-commerce company founded jointly by Ford, General Motors, and DaimlerChrysler (now Chrysler). Covisint uses advanced information technology to facilitate the transactions between suppliers and manufacturers. Particularly because of some high-profile, ill-advised implementation, firms increasingly need to justify their significant supply chain information technology investment. Despite the fact that firms have made significant information technology investment on supply chain practices, firms have increasing needs to financially justify the information technology investment.

Implementing a Reverse Auction

Implementing the reverse auction process requires the steps shown in Figure 7.4.

Reverse auctions may not be the solution for all commodity buying. As an example, if there are too few sellers, reverse auctions will not yield the best price. By definition, the price in reverse auctions is driven down by competition, so if only

FIGURE 7.4
Reverse Auction Steps

1. Define market specifications
2. Identify suppliers
3. Perform preaward review
4. Approve suppliers' listing
5. Identify specific terms and conditions
6. Invite suppliers
7. Set up auction
8. Conduct auction
9. Write up contract

limited competition exists, then the price will not decrease enough to save the buyer a substantial amount of money. A more devastating downside of reverse auctions is the buyer–seller relationship damage that may result from this method of buying. The buyer runs the risk of alienating both current and potential sources for the goods or services.

Reverse auctions should be used to gain market information (new suppliers, prices, new methods, etc.) but should not be used as a routine sourcing method. To maintain trust and cooperation between buying and selling firms, reverse auctions should be used carefully. Requests for quotes (RFQs) are less traumatic and can maintain healthy relationships between buying and selling firms.

ELECTRONIC DATA INTERCHANGE (EDI) AND PURCHASING

What Is EDI?

EDI is the direct computer transmission of orders and other transaction information. In purchasing, EDI is usually used for the electronic transmission of orders, invoices, and payment between buyer and seller. The main elements of an EDI system are computer hardware, software, computer compatibility between the sender and receiver, and subscription to a common network.

There are many benefits to using EDI. For a smaller company, EDI may help keep a valued trading partner or customer or even gain new ones. For larger firms, the main benefit is generally the cost savings, or to be known as a leading-edge company.

A simple example of what EDI can do for a company follows. A buyer takes a request from someone within the organization, creates a purchase order (PO), and mails it to the supplier to fill and ship. This process speeds up when the buyer enters the purchase order on a computer screen as he or she is talking to the user and sends the order electronically to the supplier's system as soon as he or she hangs up the phone. This, of course, would only be done if the person ordering had the authorization and if the order needed to be sent that quickly. Traditionally, a company would collect the orders to a single vendor and send them all together at the end of the day. EDI software technology enables the orders to be converted into a standard format and translated either directly to the supplier's system or to an electronic mailbox on a third-party value-added network (VAN) accessed by the partners. On the supplier end, there must be a computer either to receive the communication or to go to the VAN to get the messages. Once the data are received, they must be converted back into readable information. If the format of the data is not the same or corruption occurs, the data are useless. Industry trade groups have developed standard formats that allow different systems to communicate with each other.

There are some definite benefits to utilizing EDI. The first major benefit is reduced labor. The overall reduction in document handling is one that saves time and allows more time for data analysis. Higher information quality due to a reduction in data entry errors also can be attributed to EDI. EDI capabilities can show potential customers a supplier's willingness to cooperate, which improves relations and leads to better long-term relationships.

EDI requires some additional costs that must be considered. The obvious ones are the computer hardware and software costs, as well as the monthly fee for the mailbox (VAN) usage. The largest and most important cost is the training of the users and the suppliers. The system itself is a waste of money if it is not effectively used. This means extensive training of buyers, administrators, management, suppliers, and auditors will be required. Implementing EDI also will demand new procedures that will take time to learn and use effectively, as well as for management and auditing to learn to control.

As with any major change, like implementing EDI, at least some resistance and many barriers are to be expected. Informing users of the change along with heavy training and education will support the move to EDI. This is vital to users, who need to feel comfortable with their jobs. EDI is a concept designed to support the company operations and, without proper training, it will cost a company quality and efficiency. Data integrity and legal issues are barriers that management also will encounter. Top management support also may be hard to obtain, but it is vital for a successful move to EDI operations.

There are also some risks when using EDI that should be considered. EDI is not inexpensive. The machine and training costs will add up to a large amount, and cutting corners may cost a company more than it saves. Security is also an issue. Procedural safeguards have not kept up with technology in this area. The problem is exposure to outside users, which opens up a doorway to false messages. These messages may come in the form of a person who is not a supplier sending data or the data being interrupted and/or altered. Operational procedures need to have safeguards in place in order to avoid such situations. Buyers and sellers must interactively communicate, especially if a questionable transaction is received. An obvious risk is that current trading partners may refuse to use EDI. This is a situation that must be addressed by company policy. A decision must be made whether to trade singularly through EDI or use both EDI and traditional methods.

Implementation

Introducing new technologies into organizations will almost always result in some combination of social, technical, psychological, and structural changes. When managers or employers resist the logical arguments presented in support of EDI, they may not be resisting the technical aspects of the proposed change as much as the perceived social or psychological ramifications. It is this perceived threat, some of which is real behavior, that governs the users. Workers may be laid off or job descriptions may change when incorporating EDI. Some of the consequences of the change are uncertain or even unknown. One way to overcome the resistance to change is to focus on the process itself. The Lewin–Schein theory of change is a concise description of this process and consists of the following three steps:

1. *Unfreezing*. Creating an awareness of the need for change and a climate of receptivity to change

2. *Moving*. Changing the magnitude or direction of the forces that define the initial situation; developing new methods and/or learning new attitudes
3. *Refreezing*. Reinforcing the changes that have occurred, thereby maintaining and stabilizing a new equilibrium situation

Change requires difficult planning; before implementation takes place, management should authorize use of the necessary resources to educate the people involved and obtain commitments of support from them. As much time should be spent educating people about the specifics of the change, how it affects their jobs, and how they interface with the new system as is spent in the development of the system's changes themselves.

The way in which the process of developing and implementing an EDI system is managed can greatly influence the success of implementation. Four key areas are top management support, commitment to the project, influence, and institutionalization. Top management support has long been recognized as one of the most important ingredients necessary for the introduction of any organizational change, and the same holds true for the introduction of an EDI system. Commitment to the project relates to management assurance that the problem the EDI system is designed to improve is understood and that EDI is the right solution to this problem. Less understood is the role of influence and when it should be applied by top management. People are more comfortable working with today's problems than planning for tomorrow's problems today. Therefore, it should come as no surprise that management usually exerts its influence on a system just before implementation, which is after many of the strategic design decisions have already been made.

Management usually exerts only minimum influence during the early life cycle phases and very heavy influence immediately before final implementation. Unfortunately, it is at the implementation phase of systems development that changes are most difficult and costly. If a change costs $1 when feasibility is being considered, it would cost $16 at implementation. Thus, management tends to spend most of its time at a point in the development cycle when it will have the least influence on the overall direction of the system. It is also the time when exerting influence is the most costly.

Finally, institutionalization is the process through which the system becomes incorporated as an ongoing part of the organizational activities. This can occur in several ways: diffusion of the system to other users, changing the work of employees, and changing the structure and process of the organization. All of these changes are expected to be permanent.

The Implementation Team

In order to orchestrate the various aspects of the implementation process, a steering committee guiding various project teams is recommended. The steering committee acts as the overseer of the entire project and represents the functional groups of the enterprise. Its primary concerns are setting policy, exercising control mechanisms to ensure that the desired results are achieved, and monitoring to measure the effectiveness of the EDI system. Policy setting includes setting a course of action for the project teams and setting a time schedule for the states of implementation. Other related areas within the scope of policy setting include selection of hardware and software, assignment of data responsibility and accountability, distribution of funds, use and design of the actual system, and selection of

EDI partners. The control function is concerned with budget approval, authorization of projects, and assessment of previously defined performance measures.

The project teams assume a liaison role between the steering committee and the departments, and ultimately represent the **end user**. The structures of most teams start small and gain size as the project progresses. The project teams are responsible for defining performance requirements, meeting the various objectives set by the steering committee, and, ultimately, successfully implementing the EDI system.

EDI in Practice

Possibly one of the largest users of new computer technology and EDI for purchasing purposes is Walmart. Walmart also pioneered the concept of Vendor Managed Inventory (VMI) through the use of Point of Sale (POS) information system. To help in forecasting, Walmart has developed a system called "traiting that analyzes 2,500 traits of each store's environment." By using this system, Walmart can accurately predict what products should be stocked and inventoried in each store.

Another area where Walmart is incorporating improved technology is its use of EDI itself. It currently uses EDI for ordering for many of its more than 20,000 suppliers and, in many cases, invoices the company electronically. The obvious benefits of this system are the reduction in paperwork, saving the buyers time, and an increase in vendor responsiveness.

Walmart allows suppliers representing its fast-moving items to receive sales data directly from the point of purchase. When an item is purchased, an EDI system is used to immediately trigger an automatic merchandise replenishment process. Virtually no personnel are involved with the entire purchasing sequence for these items except the supplier's distribution center, the transportation, and the receiving personnel. The savings in paperwork and manhours are immense and offer insight into how Walmart has been able to gain competitive advantage and market share in the retail market so quickly. The results of this program have been a doubling of both sales and inventory turn for the affected categories and suppliers.

The Basics of Becoming a Walmart Supplier

1. To be an approved **Walmart supplier**, you must be **EDI capable** and **AS2 communication** is required to transmit EDI transactions to and from Walmart.
2. Walmart requires their suppliers to be 100 percent synched and to provide accurate data through GDSN (Global Data Synchronization Network). Walmart offers free workshops to help their suppliers with this requirement, and most **EDI providers** can walk you through GDSN compliance as well.
3. Walmart requires security source tagging in order to reduce shrinkage. Security source tagging is the practice of incorporating disposable anti-theft labels at the manufacturing, packaging, or distribution level. According to www.walmartstores.com, "All products must be certified, prior to tagging, by an authorized Source Tagging Lab."
4. You must have a D&B risk rating of less than 7 to be considered by Walmart.

For more details on what it takes to become an approved Walmart supplier, see http://www.walmartstores.com/Suppliers/252.aspx.

The measures Walmart has taken have not come without expense. In order to accomplish all of its programs, over $1 billion has been invested in the past 10 years. It is currently planning to expand all of its programs and ultimately may require all of its suppliers to be EDI-capable. The fact that any large corporation is currently thinking about making EDI a requirement for a supplier is evidence that EDI may be an essential element of any business in the not-so-distant future.

Another large retailer, Sears, although far behind Walmart in its implementation, has realized the importance of the new technology and EDI applications. Prompted by the loss of its market share to Walmart and other competitors recently, Sears has been forced to take a hard look at how it does business. The major area it has singled out as needing improvement has been its use of new computer technology including EDI. As a much older institution than Walmart, with a long-standing company culture and tradition, Sears is faced with a more difficult situation in the implementation of EDI and increased computer reliance. Sears quickly realized that just buying the computers and EDI systems and having them in place isn't sufficient to get the desired results. Sears states, "The new plan is only 10 percent technology—and 90 percent culture." In other words, the changes it hoped for cannot be accomplished immediately. Training and corporate adjustment must be allowed to occur over what may be a significantly long period of time. To speed up the process, Sears has implemented dedicated training for 500 employees every month on the new computer systems and EDI technology. The Sears training program is scheduled to continue until all employees have participated.

Future Outlook

Walmart's use of EDI and the benefits associated with it provide a strong argument for the universal implementation of EDI and computer-run inventory/purchasing systems. Sears' experiences show that managers considering applying the new technology also must determine the effects on company culture and the training necessary to facilitate the effective use of any new system. In many cases, the total expense of implementation will be great, but the potential benefits also will be large and the possibility of getting left behind competitively often will help outweigh the initial expense.

As more and more companies shift to EDI systems, an inherent problem has been the different programs and systems that are being employed. Around the United States and the world, enclaves of users of particular EDI programs have developed. For example, differences would be expected between a company doing business in the United States and a company doing business in Japan. The different languages of the two countries themselves dictate that computer systems are going to be different. Less evident are the differences in languages that sometimes exist within industries and their EDI systems, which can be just as different as systems from two countries. As EDI really takes hold and international EDI becomes more commonplace (it is currently used by only 5 percent of firms in the marketplace), a major stumbling block will be overcoming the language barriers that now exist.

The most widespread EDI language in the United States is the ANSI X12 standard. In Europe, EDIFACT is the preferred standard, and in Japan, numerous standards are common. The European automotive industry uses a particular system called ODETTE and the U.S. auto industry is considering changing its system to match the one used in Europe. It is evident that the numerous different standards ultimately will create havoc in any attempt toward globalization of EDI capabilities. Much time and money will be required to create translating programs that will provide the necessary data exchange between existing languages.

Another problem that will require increased attention in the future is the possible security risk associated with using EDI. As businesses use more and more EDI, their dependence on the information technology involved grows even faster. The potential for damage from unauthorized access or from computer viruses that could cause

FIGURE 7.5
E-Procurement Benefits by Category

Source: Minahan and Degnan (2001, p. 5).

Indirect	Direct	Sourcing
Price reduction Improved contract compliance Shortened cycle times Reduced administrative costs Enhanced inventory management	Visibility of customer demand Visibility of supply chain capacity Accuracy of production capacity Reduced inventory costs Shortened process cycle times	Unit cost reduction Enhanced decision making Improved market intelligence

irreparable damage to the system must be minimized. Physical, electronic, and procedural safeguards must be developed to counter any potential threat.

A final element of EDI for the future would be tying in the final consumer as a final link in the EDI chain. If the end user can be incorporated into the system, it will reduce to the absolute minimum the need for any inventory buildup and the costs associated with it. What makes this future possible is that as every day passes, more and more people gain access to increasingly capable computer systems. The proliferation of PCs at home as well as in the office has created a potential purchasing revolution of unheralded proportions. For those who don't have, or can't afford, a computer, the new smart phone may fill the gap. If approached properly, nearly every commodity in the world could be sold using a network of PCs or smart phones to order products well ahead of the time they are needed. The requirements necessary for distributing a product in such a manner would be that quality of the product is expected to be high so the consumers will feel comfortable ordering in advance. They must feel comfortable that any dissatisfaction will be quickly remedied by the company supplying the product. For a company that can break ground using such a system, the potential competitive advantages would be unbeatable. A properly devised EDI network with consumers would be tied to the company's MRP system, ultimately eliminating the production, transport, or stocking of unwanted goods entirely. In essence, a product would go from raw material all the way to the consumers' possession in the minimal amount of time possible.

The potential savings are significant; however, the investment and risk will be high as well. Will the customer be a willing participant in the EDI revolution and order goods in advance, and if so, how well will the concept of fencing fit the long-established consumer's prerogative of changing his or her mind? The three e-procurement solutions given above expect to achieve the results shown in Figure 7.5.

RADIO FREQUENCY IDENTIFICATION (RFID)

What Is RFID and How Does It Work?

Radio frequency identification, or RFID, is a universal term given to any technology that uses radio waves to identify and track items. Items such as a product, a container, an automobile, an animal, or a person can all be automatically identified and tracked through RFID technology. RFID originated in the government sector during World War II but is just now gaining momentum due to drastic price reductions and availability increases.

Walmart is currently using RFID for 600 suppliers, which is roughly 3 percent of the company's 20,000-strong supplier base. A few deep-pocketed suppliers, like Procter & Gamble and Kimberly–Clark, have rallied on behalf of Walmart, sending executives to industry conferences to proclaim the future in retail is RFID. Yet it's an endorsement that's failed to calm the doubts of many small and midsize Walmart suppliers. Before this announcement, everyone questioned whether RFID technology really worked and offered competitive advantages, or whether it was all just hype. Walmart believes it has the answer, but even if RFID is appropriate for the world's largest retailer, others have to ask whether RFID is appropriate in their own unique environments, and what strategies should be used in implementing it.

The RFID technology can be constructed in many ways, but the most common procedure is to store a serial number on a microchip and attach it to a coiled antenna. Through this process, RFID, often called *inlays*, is produced. Inlays in manufacturing applications can be built directly into the product, affixed with adhesive paper to form "smart labels," or combined with packaging in a myriad of ways. Although the technical details vary with different designs, readers convert radio waves from the tags into data that are decoded and transformed into information.

Through the construction of these tags and implementation of assorted infrastructure such as readers and software for RFID technology, many of the problems associated with barcodes can be solved. As an example, one of the major drawbacks in using barcodes is that identifying items requires line of sight. This means that there has to be someone, or something, physically present to verify proper orientation to the scanner while scanning the barcode for each item. With RFID technology, this is not the case. RFID technology allows placing one tag in a container full of identical products, moving through a conveyor belt process, and then knowing exactly the type or quantity of items and where they have been and still need to go. With RFID technology, a container full of products can be placed on a conveyor and move past a reader, and information about all the individual items will be identified and recorded.

RFID systems are also distinguishable by their frequency ranges. Low-frequency (30–500 KHz) systems are often associated with having the shortest reading ranges. They are most commonly used in security access, product tracking, and inventory-level controls. High-frequency (850–950 MHz and 2.4–2.5 GHz) systems offer much longer read ranges, sometimes over 100 feet, and at high reading speeds. High-frequency systems are mainly used for railroad car tracking and automated toll collection.

Advantages of RFID

An RFID system provides many advantages for companies, suppliers, and retailers. Below is a list of some of the benefits RFID can offer:

- Reduced labor costs
- Simplified business processes
- Improved inventory control
- Increased sales
- Reduced shrinkage

Several major manufacturers and retailers expect RFID tags to aid in managing the entire supply chain, starting with inbound distribution, to manufacturing, shipping, and provision of in-store inventory and stocked shelves.

Unlike the barcode-based tracking system, an RFID system offers a no-contact, no-line-of-sight reading and tracking system. This automation provides reductions in the need for the manual scanning of products and the time required for labor-intensive duties, which, in turn, can reduce the overall labor costs for companies. Another advantage of reducing the labor required for monitoring goods movement and inventory flow is that it will free personnel who can be used to provide better customer support. RFID tags can be read through snow, fog, ice, paint, and crusted grime, unlike the barcode system. The tag also can be programmed to hold information such as the item's serial number, color, size, manufacture date, and current price, as well as a list of all distribution points the item reaches as it moves before arriving at a store. This is an advantage for cross-docking, shipping, and receiving by efficiently locating items to complete shipments.

Retailers as well as suppliers hope to benefit from RFID systems. As retailers and suppliers deal with many issues and problems when managing inventory, RFID provides effective and efficient ways to solve many obstacles. Item-level tracking with an RFID system gives each unit of inventory a unique ID number. This improves inventory accuracy and lead time and reduces shrinkage. Suppliers can then provide retailers with the right goods, in the right quantities, and in the right places. Supply chain visibility for individual items is maintained with RFID technology.

As RFID systems are implemented, manufacturers will tag goods from production so information can be provided to suppliers, manufacturers, logistics teams, and, finally, end customers. With this implementation, everyone benefits from having access to the same information, which can be used to coordinate and promote supply chain interactions. Consumers also benefit from having RFID tags inserted in their products, such as increased availability information and reduced stockouts and prices.

Disadvantages of RFID

RFID readers typically range from $1,000 on up. Companies implementing RFID might need to purchase thousands of readers to cover all their facilities, warehouses, and stores. RFID tags are also quite expensive, ranging from 50 cents or more each. Active tags, which use a battery to improve range and other capabilities, can cost far more than the aforementioned prices of the passive tags. Though it is a costlier technology (compared with barcode), RFID has become extremely necessary for a wide range of automated data collection and identification applications that would not be possible otherwise.

RFID Implementation

Companies must ask themselves many questions before implementing an RFID system, such as:

- Does the company need RFID to keep pace with its competitors?
- Will RFID offer a competitive advantage for the company?
- Will the company have the power to manage its business without accurate information about its processes and inventory that could be gained from RFID?
- Will RFID cost-effectively improve the ability of the company to serve its customers?
- Will RFID save the company money eventually (long term)?

To integrate an RFID system successfully, a company must have a strong understanding of the basic elements of the system. As with EDI, the implementation stage determines the project's success or failure.

As is the case with any new technology, change requires a strong commitment from top management before implementation takes place. There also should be extensive training in the planning stages of the implementation process.

System Requirements

To achieve success in implementation, the company needs to be concerned with a few major areas.

Item Environment

The item environment relates to the tagged item's attributes and how it is used.

- What is the item to be tagged?
- In what ways will the tag be read?
  - Will it be in groups or individually?
  - Over what distances will it need to read?
  - What is the environment to which the item is exposed?
- What about the temperature, damage potential, handling equipment, and so forth?
- What, if any, business processes need to be changed in order to work with the technology?
- What, if any, physical changes to the item or its dimensions need to be adjusted?

System Environment

System environment is the area in which the tagged items will be utilized.

- What is the configuration of the manufacturing facility, warehouse, store, shipping dock, and so on?
- What are the physical surroundings?
- Do the items sit for a long period or are they frequently moved?
- Is there machinery that can interfere with our system?
- What are the distances involved with reading this item?

Data Requirements

- Tag data storage.
- Data transmission requirements.
- Back-end data storage.
  - Tag data can be stored and edited.
  - Storage size matters.
  - Backup or copy of the data needs to be maintained.
  - High-speed transmission needs to be addressed.

Tag Structure

Tag structure refers to the physical structure of the tag.

- Size (affecting performance and antenna positions, affecting performance).
- Formats (smart label, credit card style, hard tag).
- System environment affects the antenna requirements for the tag.
- Item environment drives the requirements for the tag structure.

Tag Mounting

The tag must be affixed to the item so that it survives the system environment. It must protect the tag and provide a required angle possibly needed by the system. Both the tag and the material that attaches it must be protected and properly positioned to facilitate optimal read rates.

Reader Capabilities

- Readers may control multiple antennas.
- Multiple connectivity options must allow support needed in the company.

Antenna Selection and Placement

- Choosing placement of the right type of antenna
- Consideration of the area of coverage desired
- Balance of controlling the RF field and distance

Software

Support Functions

- Ability to handle multiple simultaneous reads of multiple items by multiple readers
- Understanding of the expected number of items in a read zone
- Coordination of timing and material flow
- User feedback features
- Event management
- Back-end systems update

RFID can become a solution that provides great benefits: cost reductions, increased accuracy, improved workforce efficiency, and improved ability to execute, but there are many issues a company needs to examine before making any decisions. An example of an RFID analysis is given in Table 7.4.

E-Sourcing and Purchasing

As we look into the future, the traditional purchasing approach will be transformed into e-sourcing. E-sourcing will be the tool that drives supply management. As the world market for goods and services becomes a key competitive advantage, e-sourcing is redefining the way companies manage their supply chains. Buyers and sellers located on different continents can meet electronically. E-sourcing also will lead to higher transactional accuracy and cost reductions

TABLE 7.4
RFID Analysis Example: Panther Machine, Inc.

Panther Machine, Inc., located in Michigan, is a manufacturer of multipiece crankshafts. It is in the lawn and garden market and produces crankshafts for items such as chainsaws. Its largest customer is Frigidaire, a European company. Panther has several suppliers of raw materials, such as raw steel, counterweights, and pins, and outsources some of these from China to cut costs. Shafts are turned in-house, although Panther is looking at possibly outsourcing this operation. The plant is divided into three cells: (1) CSI, which produces one part, the 062, for Electrolux; (2) VICI, which produces two parts, the 979 and 980, for another customer, Homelite; and (3) Lawn and Garden, which produces many different parts for both customers and includes robot lines. The 062 part in CSI and the 979 and 980 parts for VICI sell for almost $7 each, so those are the major money-making parts, compared to the other parts, which sell for an average of $1–2.

Parts are boxed and placed on skids every day and shipped daily in volumes of one thousand to tens of thousands per skid. Panther recently underwent a complete reengineering of processes and labor with a consulting firm. It implemented a new, extremely complex operating system that tracks inventory, shipments, and customer demand and integrates all the scheduling processes with a production log filled out at each machine each day to utilize capacity as efficiently as possible and give daily production reports. Panther was able to implement lean manufacturing and value stream mapping to streamline its processes and has been able to increase profits this year due to these changes. Total revenue brought in for an average month is around $2.3 million, with about $2 million of those sales coming from the customer Electrolux. So far in the year 2008, the company has brought in revenue of $21.3 million. This compares to revenue of $24.4 million for the year 2007.

Recently, the president attended an industrial conference on implementing RFID technology. In the past, Panther has relied on technology as a competitive weapon. Should Panther implement RFID technology?

Panther should not implement an RFID system. Given the company size and resource base, an RFID system would result in major disruptions. It appears that the newly implemented tracking system is working well. The current system must first be carefully evaluated before implementing any new technology. Also, since the parts that Panther manufactures and distributes are not high-value items, the company would probably not benefit from using an RFID system. As noted throughout this section, decisions made by the customers (retailers) may come into play. If Frigidaire demands that Its suppliers implement RFID systerns, Panther Machine, Inc., would have to weigh the costs of implementing such a system with the benefits of continuing to be Frigidaire's top supplier.

for the entire supply chain. As shown in Figure 7.6, e-sourcing creates value by

1. Reducing the total cost of ownership.
2. Streamlining the purchasing process.
3. Business innovation.

The purchased item's position on the value chain determines the degree of applicability of e-sourcing. The lower the value for the good or service, the more ideal for e-sourcing. E-sourcing frees up company resources for strategic options and business innovation. The e-sourcing commodity continuum is given in Figure 7.7. The generic products and services are easily specified commodities. The complexity increases as we move from left to right on the continuum.

FIGURE 7.6
Benefits of E-Sources

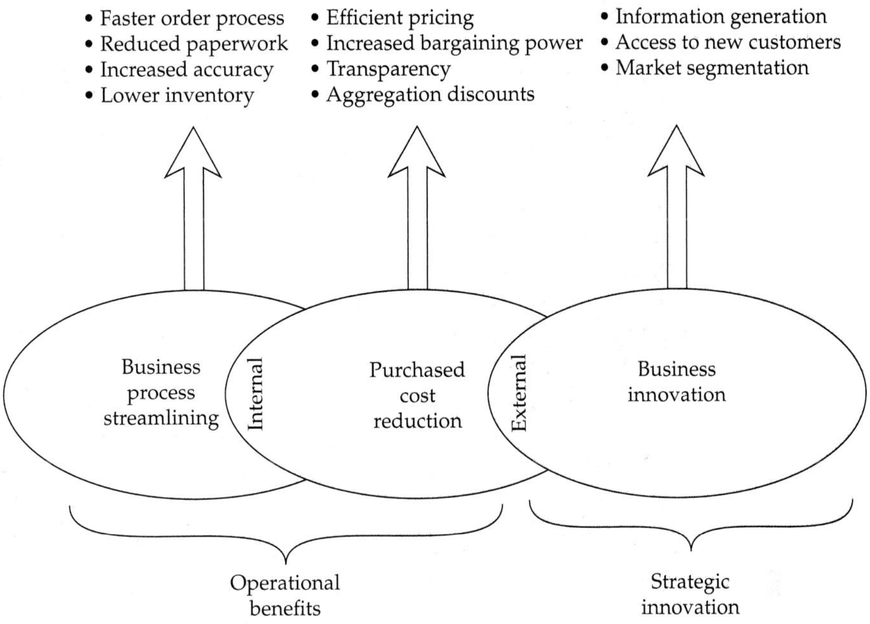

FIGURE 7.7 **E-Sourcing Commodity Continuum**

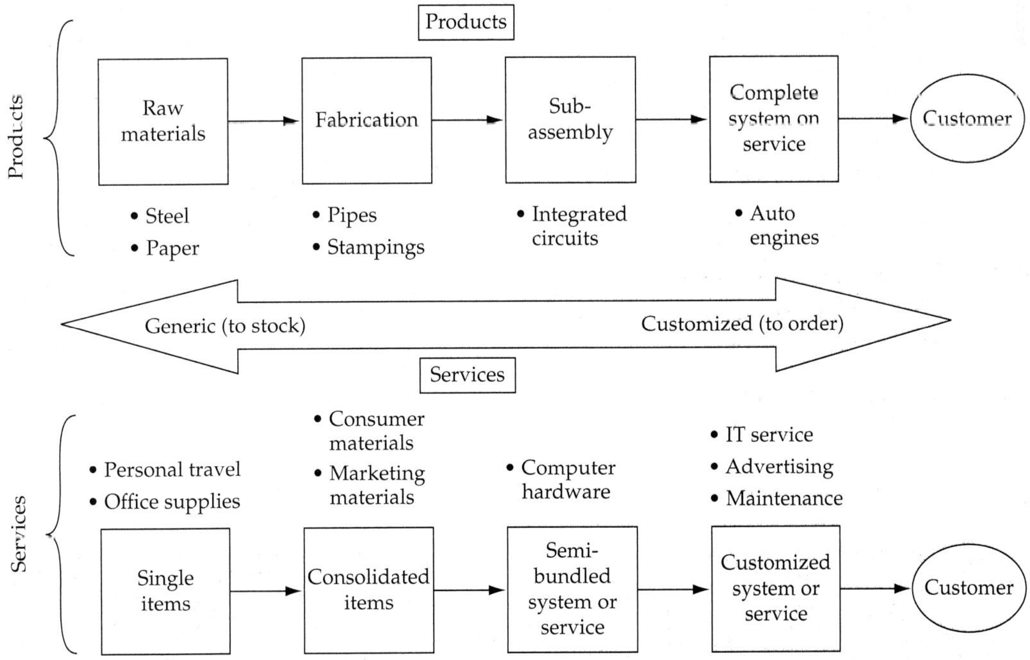

Summary

The main functions of the purchasing department are to (1) determine the supplier, (2) negotiate the actual price, and (3) determine the delivery date. Systems contracting is a modern purchasing management technique that seeks to provide an overall reduction in the cost of an item from the time a need is recognized to the time that need is fulfilled. Purchase price is one element of the total cost picture; the scope of systems contracting goes far beyond the purchase price for any given time. During the next decade, systems contracting will be widely adopted for expensive high-volume commodities. The new information age will force large, medium, and small firms to consider the competitive advantages of systems contracting.

The most significant change in the purchasing process is the advent of reverse auctions. Businesses that use reverse auctions have made testimonials of savings of more than $1 billion from online bidding.

Today, electronic data interchange (EDI) is used extensively as an integrated company operation. Low-price, high-speed, highly capable personal computers combined with modern Internet capabilities place at least rudimentary EDI capabilities within reach of even the smallest firms. Successful companies must get in line with the technological parade or else risk being left standing alongside watching the parade go by. Those who get in the procession early will undoubtedly have a competitive advantage in the future.

Radio frequency identification is a universal term given to any technology that uses radio waves to identify and track items. Items such as a product, container, automobile, animal, or person can all be automatically identified and tracked. The retail industry appears to be one of the industries with the most to gain from this technology. E-sourcing is a powerful tool that is required to transform the implementation of an effective purchasing system.

Discussion Questions

1. What are the procedural objectives for sound purchasing systems?
2. What are the main functions of a purchasing department?
3. What is systems contracting?
4. What is meant by total cost of ownership?
5. What are reverse auctions? What is EDI? How have they changed the purchasing function?
6. What are the steps in the Lewin–Schein theory of change?
7. What is RFID? How does it work? What are its advantages and disadvantages?
8. What are the advantages and disadvantages of purchasing technologies?
9. How has the Internet changed the purchasing function?

Suggested Cases

The Auction Case
Swisher Systems
The ARMS Procurement System at Tustin State University
Two-Bucks Wine Operation

References

Devila A., M. Gupta, and R. Palmer. "Moving Procurement Systems to the Internet: The Adoption and Use of E-procurement Technology Models." *European Management Journal* 21 (2003), pp. 11–23.

Minahan, T., and C. Degnan. *Best Practices in e-Procurement*. Boston: Aberdeen Group, 2001.

Schein, E. H. "How Can Organizations Learn Faster? The Challenge of Entering the Green Room." *Sloan Management Review*, Winter 1993, pp. 85–92.

Sigala, M. "E-Procurement Diffusion in the Supply Chain of Foodservice Operators: An Exploratory Study in Greece." *Journal of Information Technology & Tourism*, 8, no. 2 (2006), pp. 79–90.

Appendix A

Systems Contract Agreement

______________________________, herein designated the "Buyer," agrees to buy, and McJunkin Corporation, herein designated the "Seller," agrees to sell upon the following terms and conditions:

1. *Material:* Pipe, Valves, and Fittings (etc.) meeting the specifications set forth in Schedule A attached hereto and made a part hereof. Items not listed in Schedule A should be priced as per Schedule B.
2. *Scope:* Buyer's purchase requirements for its ______________________ Plant(s) and/or ______________________ construction site(s).
3. *Price:* Seller's prices are set forth in Schedule A and discounts as posted in Schedule B. Seller shall submit to Buyer a list of standard price sheets under Schedule B to be considered for the purpose of this provision. Changes in these price sheets or of specific items on Schedule A shall occur only on January 1, April 1, July 1, and October 1. The Seller must advise the Buyer by the end of the first working day of the previous month (December, March, June, and September) those items to be revised. Items on which no notice has been given by the above deadline will remain in effect until the next price change date. This price change pattern can only be overridden when both Buyer and Seller mutually agree to an abnormal change, affecting either party, and immediate action should be taken, that is, abnormal manufacturer price change, allocations. If any price change is unacceptable, Buyer shall have the right to terminate the items(s) so affected from the contract by giving Seller written notice thereof on or before the effective date of the proposed price adjustment.
4. *Billing:* Seller shall submit a summary invoice on the ____th of each month covering shipments made during preceding billing period. Prices shown shall be net and shall include the case discount. Buyer shall remit the total amount due no later than the ____th working day following receipt of said invoice.
5. *Stock:* The Seller agrees to maintain adequate inventories of the items contained in Schedule A (and Schedule C) to prevent backorders and to ensure prompt delivery. Buyer and Seller will mutually agree on inventory quantities until a usage level is established. Once a level has been established, the Seller will only be responsible for maintaining the agreed on quantities over a specific time period. If the Buyer's purchases exceed established inventory levels by more than ___ percent during this time period, Seller will be given a reasonable time to replenish his stock. If Buyer does not exceed inventory level and cannot accept a lesser quantity or substitute, it shall be the responsibility of the Seller to furnish the quantity and kind of item ordered.
6. *Indemnification:* Buyer agrees to indemnify Seller against any and all loss as a result of discontinuance or obsolescence of any items not considered standard by Seller and stocked at the Buyer's specific written request. All requests for the stocking of nonstandard material will be made by the Buyer in writing and shall constitute Schedule C attached hereto and made part hereof. The quantity for which the Seller shall be indemnified is the total number of a particular item stocked at Buyer's request. In the event that the actual inventory is

less than the total specified, the value of the lesser amount will be the subject of the indemnity.

7. *Contingencies:* No liability shall result to either party from delays or nonperformance caused by circumstances beyond the reasonable control of the party affected.
8. *Delivery:*
   a. *Stock Shipments:* F.O.B. delivered to the specific plant area specified by the Buyer.
   b. *Direct Shipments:* (If applicable) F.O.B. delivered with freight charges per manufacturer's terms and conditions.
9. *Insurance:* If deliveries hereunder are made in Seller's equipment, then Seller shall carry insurance of minimum limits as follows:

   Automotive Public Liability Bodily Injury (covering owned, hired, and all classes of nonowned vehicles) $100,000/$300,000 and Property Damage $25,000. Certificates indicating this insurance is in effect and a statement that the insurance companies will not cancel or reduce the coverage without giving Buyer ten days' prior written notice must be filed with Buyer before starting plant deliveries and shall be subject to Buyer's approval.

10. *Patents:* Seller warrants that the use or sale of the material delivered hereunder will not infringe any United States Patent Claim covering the material itself, but does not warrant against infringement by reason of the use thereof in combination with other materials or in the operation of any process.
11. *Fair Labor Standards Act:* Seller warrants that all goods delivered within this contract will have been produced in compliance with the requirements of the Fair Labor Standards Act of 1938, as amended.
12. *Assignment:* This contract is not assignable or transferable by either party, either in whole or in part, without the prior written consent of the other party.
13. *Entireties:* This instrument constitutes the entire contract between the parties, and no modification or supplement shall be effective unless agreed to in writing by both parties.
14. *Duration:* This agreement shall become effective on __________ for a period of ____________ years subject to the right of either Buyer or Seller to terminate said agreement by not less than 30 days' prior written notice.

Chapter Eight

Supplier Selection and Evaluation

Learning Objectives

1. Identify the qualifications of a good supplier.
2. Learn about the key elements of the make-versus-buy decision.
3. Identify appropriate supplier selection techniques.
4. Learn about supplier relationship management.
5. Discuss potential disadvantages of single sourcing.
6. Analyze how to reduce the number of suppliers.
7. Learn about strategic supplier relationship management.
8. Explain how supplier evaluation is accomplished in a variety of industrial environments.

INTRODUCTION

In today's competitive environment, progressive firms must be able to produce quality products at reasonable prices. Product quality is a direct result of the production workforce and the suppliers. Buying organizations can no longer afford to maintain a large supplier base. In today's competitive sourcing environment, buying firms select suppliers based on their capabilities and not purely on the competitive process. The current trend in sourcing is to reduce the supplier base. In order to select suppliers who continually outperform the competition, suppliers must be carefully analyzed and evaluated. (See Weber, Current and Benton (1991).)

More manufacturing firms are increasing the percentage of parts they outsource versus those that they produce internally. This has led to an increasingly important role for the purchasing function. Traditional purchasing professionals who act as little more than order placers are giving way to strategically involved analytical managers who control vital inputs to the production process. More and more power is being placed in the hands of professional purchasing managers because industry is beginning to realize the importance of defect-free parts and the value-added capabilities of suppliers.

FIGURE 8.1
The Strategic Make-versus-Buy Decision

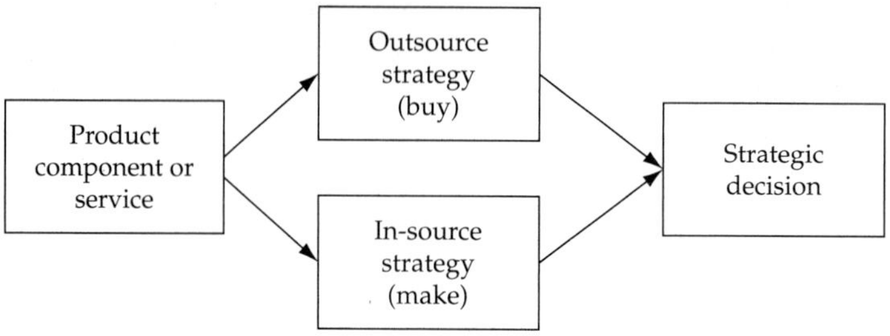

MAKE VERSUS BUY

The use of outsourcing has quickly become a competitive weapon for an increasing number of businesses. It is no easy task for management to decide to make, lease, or buy component parts and services. The decision to outsource has led to a need for strategic partnerships. The nature of the outsourcing relationship will be discussed in detail in the next chapter and the lease-versus-buy decision will be covered in Chapter 16, on capital equipment acquisition. (See Figure 8.1.)

As can be seen, the make-versus-buy decision is strategic, not merely a routine operational decision. The make-versus-buy decision actually consists of a series of interrelated decisions that evolve over time. The make-versus-buy decision must first determine what product or service is under consideration. The firm must then consider the in-house capability for producing the product or service. Following are the key issues related to the make-versus-buy decision.

Key Make-or-Buy Mistakes

- In most cases, businesses are not proficient at identifying their core capabilities. They rationalize in-house decisions based on capacity capabilities.
- They wait too late to assess the value of consultants or strategic partners.
- They do not recognize that the product or service is approaching maturity. There are always new competitors with new technology attacking the market.

Key Make-or-Buy Success Factors

- Perform a realistic assessment of the capabilities and expertise of each member of the in-house team. If the core competencies exist, what happens if a key member leaves the team? Can the member be easily replaced?
- Evaluate alternative strategic partnership arrangements and select the appropriate partner.
- Share information with all functional areas and request their input.

BENEFITS OF OUTSOURCING

Outsourcing can produce many benefits for a firm that would normally produce a part internally. Internal production of subassemblies and parts is actually a backward vertical integration policy. Vertical integration gives a firm more control over the part in question. However, the greater the percentage of internal parts an assembly firm produces, the greater its need to have competence in each of the areas involved. It is very difficult for a manufacturer such as an automobile company to have competence in areas of production of all parts that go into producing and assembling a car. Therefore, outsourcing to suppliers reduces the pressure on firms to try to do everything.

Outsourcing, which can be viewed as a delegation of production capabilities, can enable a firm to concentrate on its true core capabilities. By concentrating on its core capability, a firm can direct its energies to the true value-adding steps that make it competitive. Likewise, suppliers can then develop their own core competence in the fields that are relevant to the production of the parts they make. Many successful Japanese automakers internally produce fewer parts and outsource more than do the North American auto manufacturers. Of the total cost of materials, tools, and finished parts needed to produce a car, Toyota only produces approximately 27 percent internally while General Motors produces approximately 70 percent. By "delegating" or outsourcing, Toyota is left to concentrate on the core functional capabilities of its autos: the engine, transmission, electronics, and major body parts.

When a firm has answered the make-or-buy question with a decision to buy, the question then becomes to whom to "delegate" this responsibility. Thus, the firm must select a supplier or suppliers for the part(s) in question.

The supplier selection problem is much easier to describe than carry out. One purpose of this chapter is to shed light on selecting only the most compatible supplier for firms in specific industries.

The buying firm may be highly skilled at (1) specifying product attributes, (2) forecasting expected requirements, and (3) ensuring the right quality at a reasonable price. However, unless the buying firm selects the right supplier, the prepurchase planning is meaningless. The selection of the correct supplier is perhaps the most important purchasing activity. The buying firm must spend extensive time analyzing and carefully selecting the correct supplier. Once the correct supplier is chosen, succeeding orders will by definition meet quality, delivery, and price expectations. Of course, there should be periodic supplier evaluations to ensure continuous supplier performance achievement. In the next sections, we address the supplier sourcing process. Four specific industry examples will be presented.

SOURCES OF SUPPLIER INFORMATION

Searching for the appropriate supplier for a specific material or component part is becoming a strategic issue in itself. In the new fast-paced and volatile buying environment, the purchasing firm must know where to look for each item. Buyers should be experts on the industry and on specific raw materials or component parts. There are many sources available for the buyer to consider when seeking out potential suppliers.

The traditional buying source is the well-known Thomas Register. The Thomas Register categorizes potential suppliers as manufacturers, distributors, manufacturer representatives, or service. Trade journals are also a valuable source of information regarding potential suppliers. All of these sources can also be accessed from the Internet. Two such journals are *Purchasing World* and *Supply Management*. Salespersons are not only important resources about materials, they also can be an excellent source of free consulting information. Local chambers of commerce, the Yellow Pages, trade shows, and city libraries are excellent sources of supplier data.

STRATEGIC SELECTION

Each business unit and department should have a clear understanding of the strategy of the whole firm and have a departmental strategy that complements and aids the overall strategy execution of the firm. Purchasing, logistics, inventory management, and production control are all linked tightly together under the materials management umbrella. These functions must work as a cohesive strategic unit where each complements the other. It is from this perspective that supplier selection/reduction should take place. Also see Chapter 2.

For example, if a firm's strategy is to be differentiated, then price will be secondary. Innovation, technology, and high quality probably dominate the way the firm stays competitive. This places a need on the operation functions to be flexible and have the ability to change. Therefore, a supplier should be chosen that can adapt to the change that is needed by the operating functions of the firm. A "strategic match" is needed between buyer and supplier, as they can then work in harmony as far into the future as they are compatible. The selection of suppliers should not be based on performance of the past, but the anticipated capabilities of the future.

In order for good communication to exist between buyer and supplier, common ground should exist in management styles, control systems, quality philosophies, and technological abilities (e.g., in engineering, design, EDI, and RFID). Since outsourcing is a delegation of responsibilities, it should be viewed as an extension of the original equipment manufacturer's (OEM's) strategy. Also see Chapter 7.

SUPPLIER RELATIONSHIP MANAGEMENT

The supply chain management process is based on the idea of efficient resource coordination and teamwork. Buyer and supplier relationships have become increasingly important for a number of reasons. There is a trend toward specialization away from manufacturing an entire product and to more contract manufacturing and purchasing. In some market segments, it is estimated that 80 percent or more of total product revenue often passes directly to suppliers as payment for labor, materials, and equipment. This significant transfer of value downstream emphasizes the importance and significance of supply chain relationship management. For any buying organization to stay competitive in today's aggressive market sectors, it is essential that it maintains strong relationships with its best contract manufacturers and suppliers.

When businesses purchase a large percentage of product value, the importance of supply chain relationship management cannot be underestimated. Buying firms experience a great deal of pressure from customers and competitors to keep their edge and stay in business by reducing costs, improving product, improving service quality, and enacting continuous improvement. At the same time, many buying firms also are reducing the number of suppliers on their list of qualified suppliers. The costs of buying materials from a larger number of suppliers, while still managing a relationship with each, may be too great for a buying firm to absorb.

With the decreasing number of suppliers used by buying firms, it is more important than ever to maintain strong buyer–supplier relationships. Keeping these relationships healthy will secure a source of highly qualified supplier capabilities and materials that allow for the possibility of lower costs and higher quality as well as offer the promise of greater market share for the increasingly competitive markets. Buying firms that are shifting toward a smaller supply base cannot ignore the role that supplier relationship management (SRM) will play with the remaining supplier capabilities. Another reason that SRM is important is the increasing shortages of skilled supplier capabilities and resources. Many resources and commodity materials are becoming harder to acquire, and in turn are becoming more expensive to purchase. With rising prices and increasingly scarce materials supply, a buying firm must maintain strong relationships with the suppliers of these materials to guarantee that they are the first-priority customer of their supplier; no buying firm can survive if it is unable to have a sustainable source of supply, even for scarce items.

Four Pure Supply Management Relationships

One model that explains supply chain relationship management includes four behavioral dimensions—the four Cs: counterproductive (lose-lose), competitive (win-lose), cooperative (win-win), and collaborative (win-win) relationships (Trent, 2005).

- *Counterproductive relationships* are those in which each organization (buying and supplying) is so focused on getting what is best for it that each puts the other at a disadvantage. This type of relationship is undesirable because it does not promote a positive rapport between buying and supplying firms involved and neither organization achieves its goals. Counterproductive relationships also discourage future dealings between organizations and create instability in each organization's reputation. Counterproductive buyer–supplier relationships are not recommended.
- *Transactional* or *competetive relationships* are those relationships in which both buying and supplying firms strive to get the very best arrangement possible in their negotiations and fail to see the benefits of both organizations obtaining their goals and objectives. In transactional relationships, the buying and supplying firms will stop at nothing to make sure that they come out on top and do not care about the other organization's well-being. Typically, the organization that is able to win in a competitive relationship has much more power than the losing organization. The more powerful organization sometimes places its focus on the *present*, not concerning itself with long-term negotiations on future business encounters. This type of relationship also will discourage an ongoing relationship to the detriment of both organizations. There are certain situations in which a competitive relationship is desirable. A competitive relationship is almost always required with *transactional/tier-three* suppliers and assures that the buying firm can lower prices to help keep its competitive edge in the market (e.g., commodities are transactional purchases unless there is a monopoly or shortage). It does not matter if the relationship is not strong enough to last because, by definition, transactional suppliers can be easily replaced at any time.
- *Cooperative relationships* recognize the potential value of both organizations getting what they want and maximize the potential of having a long-term relationship. Although it is a strong relationship, a cooperative alliance lacks the teamwork that is needed between the various buying and supplying firms in order to optimize the benefits for all of the members of the supply chain. Cooperative relationships are commonly found within a buying organization's *preferred/tier-two* service providers and suppliers list.

- In comparison, collaboration or *collaborative relationships*, usually found with the buying firm's *strategic/tier-one* suppliers, include the team component that is missing in a cooperative relationship. In collaboration, the two organizations truly realize the benefits of working together to optimize outcomes for both organizations. The two firms work together to develop a strategy to deliver a high-quality product or service on time and under budget. Strategic partners frequently share resources and information. As with any business arrangement, buying firms throughout the supply chain *must* avoid any antitrust violations including any appearance of price fixing or bid rigging.

Supplier Relationship Management Programs

Many large buying firms are implementing SRM programs in their business plans to ensure that they maintain their competitive edge. There are several different ideas on the exact process that a SRM program should follow, but the general approach is the same. Consider SMS, Inc., a large vertical manufacturing organization that is in the process of developing a supplier relationship program. Most SRM programs begin with some sort of ranking or categorization of potential suppliers. The process of supplier categorization is important for a number of reasons. This process forces the buying organization to communicate cross-functionally to develop some system for ranking the suppliers. Two main items that are considered in the categorization process are the *dollar amount* of the contract with an individual supplier and the *criticality* of the supplier to the buying firms's business strategy.

Once the system is developed, it then forces the various functions in the buying firm to evaluate which suppliers truly add value. The rankings are aggregated to enable a ranking of all suppliers. The company will then categorize the suppliers into one of three categories: *strategic, preferred,* or *transactional. Strategic suppliers* are those that are most important to the buying firm. They supply the buying firm with essential materials and capabilities that are not easily replaced. The buying firm will spend most of its efforts on maintaining and strengthening these relationships.

Preferred suppliers are those that are important to the buying firm, but alternative suppliers could be found with some effort. *Transactional suppliers* are those that provide the buying firm with items that are not critical to its core business and that can be easily replaced in a short time. SMS uses the labels of strategic, preferred, and transactional interchangeably with tier-one, tier-two, and tier-three suppliers. An example of an actual Fortune 100 pharmaceutical distributor's *supplier relationship segmentation model* is shown in Figure 8.2.

There are several ways in which a buying organization can evaluate its suppliers. If suppliers do not meet quality, delivery, and scheduling standards, the buying organization may face delays and will lose money from not being able to meet critical scheduling and manufacturing demands. It is well known that good standing relationships with suppliers can increase profitability and reduce overhead expenses. Therefore, relationships with suppliers must be developed in order to meet standards and contribute to continuous improvement goals. Specific communication strategies including supplier training and education, feedback, and frequent site visits can aid in developing suppliers. The company can evaluate a supplying firm's production methods and a supplier's quality performance. By evaluating the production methods and quality process of the supplier, the capabilities can be easily assessed. Performance-based evaluations assess the company after its product or service has been delivered. There are three common performance-based evaluations systems: the categorical method, the cost-ratio method, and the

FIGURE 8.2 Supplier Segmentation Model

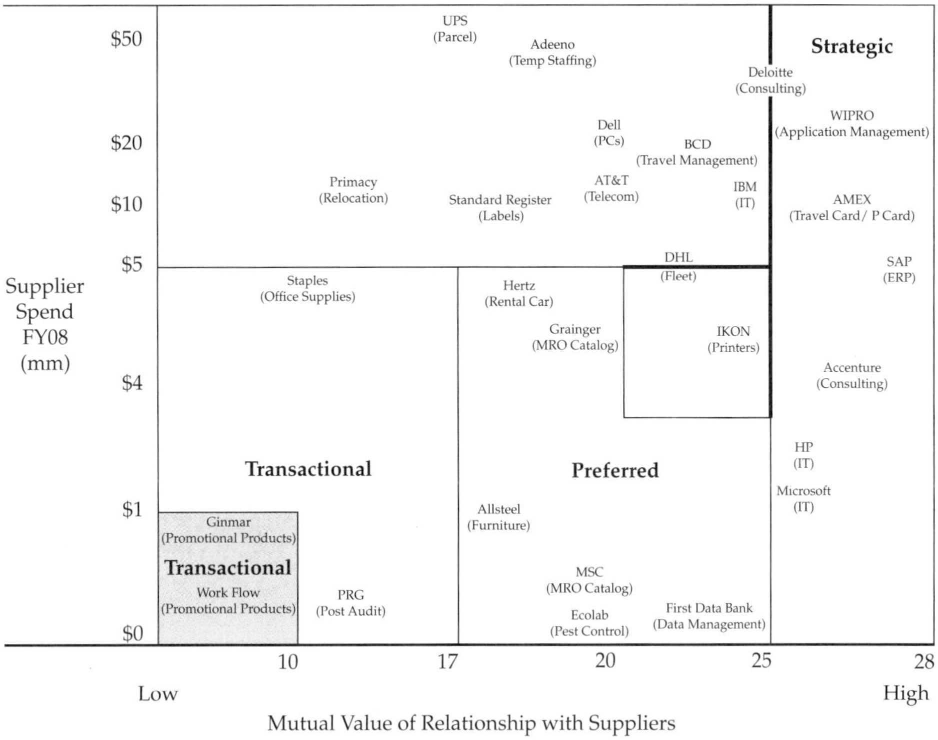

linear averaging method. In each of these evaluations, the analyses of the results are subjective and rely on the judgment of the buyer using the methods.

Criteria for Supplier Evaluation

There are two main categories of supplier evaluations: process-based evaluations and performance-based evaluations. The process-based evaluation is an assessment of the supplier's production or service process. Typically, the buyer will conduct an audit at the supplier's site to assess the level of capability in the supplier's systems. Process flow charts can be developed to identify the non-value-added activities that should be eliminated to improve the business efficiency. In addition, large buying organizations increasingly are demanding that their suppliers become certified through third-party organizations, such as ISO 9001:2008 certification or Malcolm Baldrige National Quality Awards.

Performance-based evaluation is an assessment of the supplier's actual performance on a variety of criteria, such as delivery reliability, cost, and quality defect rate. It is a more tactical assessment and measures the day-to-day performance of the supplying firm; hence, it is an after-the-fact evaluation. The performance-based evaluation is more common than the process-based evaluation, perhaps since objective data are readily available and easier to measure. Benefits of objective measurement schemes are that they reduce perceptual bias and provide a means for benchmarking a supplier's performance. Following are three common performance-based supplier evaluation systems.

Three Common Supplier Evaluation Systems

The three general types of supplier evaluation systems in use today are the categorical method, the cost-ratio method, and the linear averaging method. In general, the

TABLE 8.1 Performance Characteristics for the Categorical Method

Supplier	Cost	Product Quality	Speed	Total
A	Good (+)	Unsatisfactory (−)	Neutral (0)	(0)
B	Neutral (0)	Good (+)	Good (+)	+ +
C	Neutral (0)	Unsatisfactory (−)	Neutral (0)	−

guiding factors in determining which system is best are ease of implementation and overall reliability of the system. It must be pointed out that the interpretation of the results from any of these three systems is a matter of the buyer's judgment.

Categorical Method

The categorical method involves categorizing each supplier's performance in specific areas as defined by a list of relevant performance variables. The buyer develops a list of performance factors for each supplier and keeps track of each area by assigning a "grade" in simple terms, such as "good," "neutral," and "unsatisfactory." At frequent meetings between the buying organization and the supplier, the buyer will then inform the supplier of its performance. (See Table 8.1.)

The categorical method is a simple and informal system in the sense that detailed performance achievements or shortcomings are not measured. Instead, it is mostly used as an evaluation tool between top managers in the buying organization and the selling organization, permitting the discussion of past performance, future expectations, and long-term plans.

The advantages associated with implementing this sort of an evaluation program are that it can be implemented almost immediately and is the least expensive of the three evaluation systems discussed here. The method's major disadvantage is its dependence on the judgment of its users. The system is largely dependent on the memories of personnel to explain what "unsatisfactory" or "good" means. With this method, there are no concrete supporting data.

In the goods-producing sector, establishing performance factors and measures is a relatively simple task for management because some type of quantitative system can be developed to gauge improvement. The service area is perhaps the most difficult area to measure. When measuring service businesses, data must be collected on the quality of technical assistance, supplier attitude, supplier response time to requests for assistance, and support staff qualification. It is normal, therefore, to have a relatively simple rating scheme for services, such as outstanding, acceptable, and poor, along with explanations regarding specific incidents to explain the specific ratings.

When using any category-based evaluation system, experience is essential. As an example, a simple pass/fail approach to supplier rating will work when a company is reducing its supplier base but must be replaced after the supplier base is more manageable. In other words, the initial improvements are easier and less expensive than future evaluation methods.

Cost-Ratio Method

The cost-ratio method evaluates supplier performance by using standard cost analysis. The total cost of each purchase is calculated as its selling price plus the buyer's internal operating costs associated with the quality, delivery, and service elements of the purchase. Calculations involve a four-step approach.

TABLE 8.2
Performance Characteristics for the Cost-Ratio Method

Supplier: AA	
Elements	**Costs**
Plant visits	$200
Sample approval	25
Incoming inspection	75
Reworking costs	225
Paperwork inaccuracies	100
Lost time due to rejected parts	375
Total additional quality costs	1,000
Total value of purchase	100,000
Quality-cost ratio (Total quality cost/Total purchase)	1%

TABLE 8.3
Cost Comparison Utilizing Cost-Ratio Method of Supplier Rating

Company	Quality Cost Ratio	Delivery Cost Ratio	Service Cost Ratio	Total Penalty	Quoted Price/Unit	Net Adjusted
AA	1%	3%	−1%	3%	$86.25	$88.84
BB	2	2	3	7	83.24	89.08
CC	3	1	6	10	85.10	93.61
DD	2	1	2	5	85.00	89.25

The first step is to determine the internal costs associated with quality, delivery, and service. Next, each is converted to a cost ratio, which expresses the cost as a percentage of the value of the purchase. An example of a quality cost ratio would be as shown in Table 8.2.

The third step is to sum the three individual cost ratios (quality, delivery, and service) to obtain an overall cost ratio. Finally, the overall cost ratio is applied to the supplier's quoted unit price to obtain the net adjusted cost figures. (See Table 8.3.)

The net adjusted cost figure is used as the basis for performance comparison among other suppliers. When applying this evaluation method, all costs of conducting business with the supplier are assessed as a penalty. The best supplier is selected as the one with the lowest net adjusted cost.

The advantage associated with the cost-ratio method is that the results are cost-oriented. However, the associated costs must be known. Therefore, the cost of implementing this method may be expensive when compared to the categorical method. Moreover, this method does not take into account other aspects of supplier performance.

A hybrid of the cost-ratio method is the "total cost-of-ownership rating," developed by the director of corporate purchasing of Sun Microsystems (Ken, 1991). It includes five performance factors: quality (maximum of 30 points), delivery (25), technology (20), price (15), and service (10). A perfect supplier would receive a score of 1.00. This is calculated by deducting the number of points received (100 if perfect) from 100, dividing by 100, and adding 1. The idea is to give a simple numeric rating to the so-called hidden cost of ownership—the additional product-lifetime cost to Sun. A score of 1.20, for instance, means that for every dollar Sun spends with that supplier, it spends another 20 cents on everything from line downtime to added service costs.

Linear Averaging

The linear averaging method is the most commonly used evaluation method. Specific quantitative performance factors are used to evaluate supplier performance. The most commonly used factors in goods purchases are quality, service (delivery), and price, although any one of the factors named may be given more weight than the others. Quality is most important for a manufacturer of complex components such as electronics. Price might be given equal or greater weight in an evaluation system used by the manufacturer of highly competitive, "throwaway" items like party novelties. An example of the linear averaging method follows:

1. The first step is to assign appropriate weights to each performance factor, such that the total weights of each factor add up to 100. For example, quality might be assigned a weight of 50, service a weight of 35, and price a weight of 15. The assignment of these weights is a matter of judgment and top management preferences. These weights are subsequently used as multipliers for individual ratings on each of the three performance factors.
2. After the weights have been assigned, the individual performance factor ratings are determined. This is done by summing the scores for each factor.
3. The third step is to multiply each performance factor rating by its respective weight as a percentage. Continuing the example, a quality rating of 95 would be multiplied by .50, if quality had a weight of 50.
4. Finally, the results from step three are added to give a numerical rating for each supplier.

Example

Buyer A wishes to rate its vendors on quality, service, and price and has assigned each a weighting factor of 50, 35, and 15, respectively. For this example, quality is rated as a direct percentage of the number of acceptable lots received in relation to total lots received. The service rating is a direct percentage of the lots delivered on time in relation to total lots received. In rating price, the lowest price obtained from any supplier is used as the base price, and prices from other suppliers are rated as a ratio of this figure. Two suppliers would thus be rated as follows:

	Supplier 1	**Supplier 2**
Quality (weight = 50)		
Acceptable lots	50	35
Total lots received	58	40
Quality rating	**86.2**	**87.5**
Service (weight = 35)		
On-time deliveries	52	38
Total lots received	58	40
Service rating	**89.7**	**95.0**
Price (weight = 15)		
Lowest price	$75	$75
Price submitted	$75	$82
Price rating	**100**	**91.5**
Total performance rating	**89.8***	**90.7****

*89.8 = (.5 × 86.2) + (.35 × 89.7) + (.15 × 100).
**90.7 = (.5 × 87.5) + (.35 × 95.0) + (.15 × 91.5).

In this situation, Supplier 2 is the more satisfactory supplier. The advantage of this type of system is that it is relatively easy to implement once all the performance factors and their weights have been determined. Another advantage is that this system provides the buyer with a great deal of flexibility in determining the performance factors to be measured. The example above consists of only three factors (quality, service, and price), but any number of factors can be used. For different product classes, different factors, weights, and measures can be used to reflect the relative importance of each item to the buying organization. Finally, these types of systems produce reliable data and are relatively inexpensive to implement.

The primary objective of the buying firm's purchasing department is to provide for continuous operation of a business by ensuring the availability of goods and services. In a competitive environment, the purchasing function must ensure on-time delivery of the right goods at a reasonable price. There is a general consensus that quality, service, delivery time, and price are the key buying criteria for competitive firms. Implicit criteria such as managerial expertise, financial stability, and relative supplier location are also important in the supplier selection process.

Correct supplier selection will be an important factor in determining whether a buying firm is profitable. Firms must have a complete understanding of economic trends, innovations, and challenges in their industry.

Strategic Supplier Relationship Management

For each strategic supplier, a key contact within the buying firm must be established to ensure that the relationship is being properly managed. This person is the individual within the buying firm whom others in the buying organization should contact for information about specific strategic suppliers. It is possible that each functional manager within the buying firm will be an "owner" for a specific strategic supplier relationship.

Relationships with strategic suppliers need to be closely managed. One way to keep up on supplier relationships is for a buying organization to compile supplier profiles for each strategic supplier. These profiles should include items such as key management contacts, a company overview, SWOT (strengths, weaknesses, opportunities, threats) analysis, Porter's five key financial figures, information on current contracts, "owners" of the relationship within the firm, and an organizational chart (Porter, 1985). (See example profiles in Figures 8.3a, 8.3b, and 8.3c.) While the process of compiling these profiles should be owned by the purchasing function, the content of the profiles should be owned by all functions of the buying organization. Functional ownership of the content will ensure that all areas within the operation that deal with each of the strategic suppliers will provide input of the necessary content of the profiles. Ownership of the process by the supply manager/purchasing department makes certain that there is only one source of *strategic supplier profiles* for the entire firm. This method also ensures that the purchasing department is knowledgeable about all strategic suppliers and aware of how they are rated by each function. In addition to the strategic supplier profiles, the buying firm should clearly establish expectations for the strategic suppliers and discuss future product and supplier development plans; this is typically done with an annual review period.

FIGURE 8.3a **Strategic Supplier Profile:** BASF Corporation

Key Management Contacts

Dr. Kurt Bock
Chief Financial Officer, BASF Aktiengesellschaft
Chairman and Chief Executive Officer, BASF Corporation

- Dr. Bock joined the finance division of BASF in 1985.
- From 1987 he was staff to the company's CFO and promoted to head of technology, planning, and controlling in the engineering plastics division in 1991.
- From 1992 to 1997 was the senior vice president and managing director for Bosch Brazil.
- Rejoined BASF in 1998 as chief financial officer in Mount Olive, New Jersey.
- Appointed to the Board of Executive Directors effective January 1, 2003.
- Currently is responsible for finance, corporate controlling, global procurement and logistics, information services, and corporate audit.
- Also has responsibility for the North American regional division and the catalysts operating division.

Jurgen Hambrecht
Chairman, Board of Directors

- Hambrecht has been the chairman of the Board of Directors since 2003.
- Joined the company in 1976 and was responsible for polystyrene, styrenic copolymers, and polyphenylene ethers.
- Appointed a member of the Board of Executive Directors in 1997.
- Currently responsible for legal, taxes and insurance, strategic planning and controlling, executive management and development, Communications BASF group, and investor relations.

Contact Information

BASF Corporation
100 Campus Drive
Florham Park, New Jersey 07932
Tel: 1-800-526-1072

Company Overview

- BASF Aktiengesellchaft (BASF) was incorporated as a stock corporation in Germany in 1952. The company's original name was Badische Anilin-und Soda-Fabrik, formed in 1865.
- Headquartered in New Jersey is the North American affiliate of BASF AG, Ludwigshafen, Germany.
- BASF employs more than 15,500 in North America.
- World's leading chemical company with a portfolio ranging from chemicals, plastics, performance products, agricultural products, and fine chemicals to crude oil and natural gas.
- The agricultural products and nutrition segment is organized into two divisions: agricultural products and fine chemicals.
- The agricultural products are used by farmers to improve crop yields and crop quality and by other customers for uses in areas such as public health, structural/urban pest control, turf and ornamental plants, and vegetation management and forestry.

Strengths

- One of the world's largest chemical companies, with presence in over 200 countries and 150 production sites worldwide.
- In Ludwigshafen, the company operates the world's largest integrated chemical site.
- The concept of Verbund: BASF's innovative approach to vertical integration, using byproducts of chemical reactions, which in many cases would be disposed of.
- This concept enables BASF to have significant cost advantage and energy savings, which pushes the company's margins higher than industry averages.

Weaknesses

- Poor performance of agriculture products and nutrition division; recorded a decline of about 2 percent in 2006 of revenues and a 38.8 percent decline in operating profit.
- Sales in North America of agricultural products and nutrition segment dropped 7 percent; this segment contributed to about 9.4 percent of company's total revenues in 2009 and as a result the segment could potentially negatively impact the company's financial position.
- Profit margins also weakened in fiscal 2009; operating profit margin declined from 13.6 percent in 2008 to 12.8 percent in 2009.
- Net profit declined from 7.4 percent in 2008 to 6.6 percent in 2009.

Opportunities

- The company's large scale of operations gives it significant bargaining power to help effectively compete against regional players.
- BASF high-value products and intelligent system solutions help its customers to be more successful.
- BASF combines economic success with environmental protection and social responsibility, contributing to a better future.

Threats

- New regulations; must comply with a variety of regulatory controls on the testing, manufacturing, and marketing of its products.
- Economic slowdown in the Eurozone; Europe accounted for approximately 56 percent of BASF's net sales in 2006.
- Rising petrochemical capacity in the Middle East.

Industry Competition

- Bayer AG
- Dow Chemical Company

BASF's Primary Products
(Agricultural Division)
Herbicides
Fungicides
Insecticides

Key Figures

- Debt-equity ratio: 33.8 percent
- The company recorded revenues of €52,697.7 million during the fiscal year ended December 2006, an increase of 23.1 percent over 2005.
- BASF generates revenues through six business divisions: plastics (24.3 percent of total revenues), chemicals (22 percent), oil and gas (20.3 percent), performance products (19.3 percent), agricultural products and nutrition (9.4 percent), and others (4.8 percent).
- The agricultural products and nutrition division recorded revenues of €4,934 million in fiscal year 2006, a decrease of 1.9 percent compared to 2005.

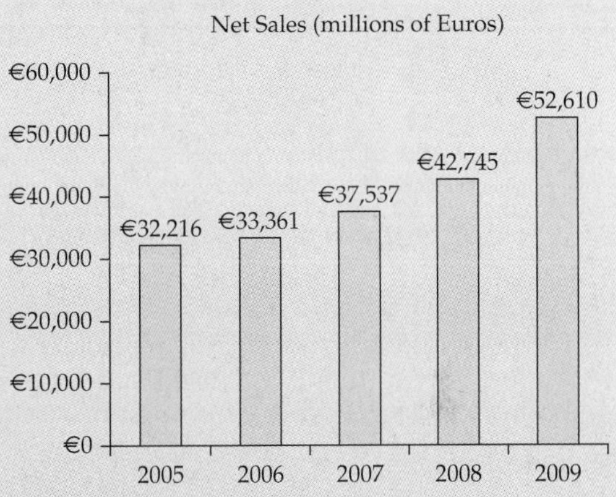

www.basf.com

Current Contracts

Supplier Performance

FIGURE 8.3b Strategic Supplier Profile: Bayer

Key Management Contacts

Werner Wenning
Chairman, Management Board (Since 2002)

- He joined Bayer in Leverkusen as a commercial trainee in 1966.
- From 1970 to 1975, he established and managed the finance and accounting department of Bayer Industrial, Peru.
- He served as the managing director and administrative head of the Peruvian company of the group from 1978 to 1983.
- He also served as the head of the staff department of the health care sector from 1983 to 1986.
- From 1992 to 1996, he was the managing director of Bayer Hispania Industrial and the senior Bayer representative for Spain.
- He was the head of corporate planning and controlling in Leverkusen in 1996.
- He joined the group's Management Board in 1997.
- He has been the chairman of the Management Board of Bayer since 2002.

Manfred Schneider
Chairman, Supervisory Board (Since 2002)

- He joined Bayer in 1966.
- He also served as the group's head of regional coordination, corporate auditing, and controlling from 1984 to 1987.
- From 1987 to 1992, he was the chairman of the Board committee for logistics and services and a member of the Board committees for research and development (R&D) and investment and technology.
- He was the chairman of the Management Board from 1992 to 2002.
- He was also the spokesman for Western Europe and the chairman of the Central Marketing Committee.
- He currently is the head of the Supervisory Board of Linde, Wiesbaden; and member of the supervisory boards of Allianz, DaimlerChrysler, Metro, TUI, and RWE.

Contact Information
Bayer House
Central A venue
Hiranandani Gardens, Powai

Mumbai 400076
Maharashtra
India
Phone: 91 22 2571 1234
Fax: 91 22 2570 8898

Company Overview

- Bayer was established in 1863 by Friedrich Bayer and Johann Friedrich Weskott as a dyeworks group.
- Bayer is a German chemical and pharmaceutical group. It primarily operates in Europe and North America. It is headquartered in Leverkusen, Germany, and employs about 106,000 people.
- Bayer is the holding company of the Bayer Group, which includes approximately 280 consolidated subsidiaries worldwide.
- The business operations of the group are organized into three divisions: health care, material science, and crop science.
- The crop science division comprises the crop protection subdivision, and environmental science and bioscience subdivision. Bayer's crop protection segment distributes chemical crop protection products for the control of insects, weeds, and fungi (plant diseases). Its major products include insecticides, fungicides, herbicides, and seed treatment.

Strengths

- Bayer has strong R&D capabilities. The group has more than 50 R&D labs.
- Bayer has a diversified business portfolio and operates in more than 100 countries, which ensures a balanced stream of revenues for the group.
- Bayer has a strong cash position. Its cash from operating activities increased.

Weaknesses

- The group has been recording a decline in its revenues generated from the crop science division.
- Bayer's average returns have been low for the three-year period 2007–2009.
- Bayer has been recording low margins in the past few years.

Opportunities

- Demand for polycarbonates in China is expected to rise sharply in the coming decades.

Threats

- Economic slowdown in Eurozone.
- Bayer is involved in a number of legal proceedings. As of February 2010, there were approximately 1,810 lawsuits pending in the United States and 60 lawsuits pending in other countries against Bayer.

Industry Competition

- BASF Aktiengesellschaft
- Syngenta AG

Significant Supplier Changes

Bayer's Primary Products
Crop science:

Fungicides
Herbicides
Insecticides
Seed treatment

Key Figures

- The group recorded revenues of €28,956 million during the fiscal year ended December 2009, an increase of 17.2 percent over 2008.
- The operating profit of the group was €2,762 million during fiscal year 2009, an increase of 9.9 percent over 2008.
- The net profit was 1,683 million in fiscal year 2009, an increase of 5.4 percent over 2005.

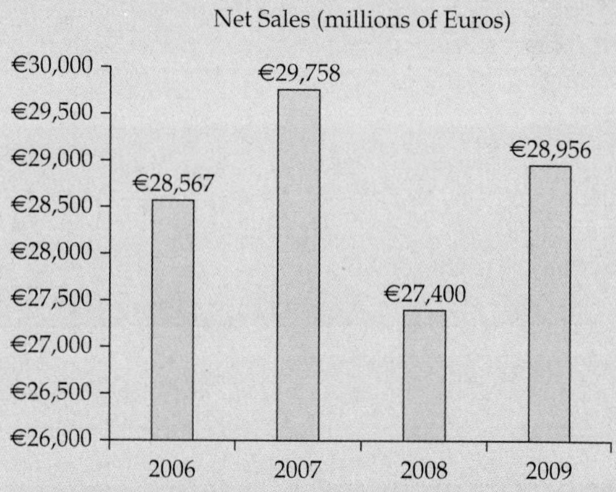

See annual report available online at www.bayer.com.

Current Contracts

Supplier Performance

FIGURE 8.3c Strategic Supplier Profile: Dow Chemical

Key Management Contacts

Andrew N. Liveris
Chairman, President and Chief Executive Officer

- He began his Dow career in 1976 in Australia. Has been with Dow for 30 years.
- He has spanned manufacturing, sales, marketing, new business development, and management.
- He has spent most of his career in Asia, where he was general manager for the company's operations in Thailand, and later head of all Asia-Pacific operations.
- He has been a member of Dow's Board of Directors since 2004 and was elected as chairman of the Board effective April 2006.
- He is an officer of the American Chemistry Council, the industry's trade association, and is a member of the following organizations: the American Australian Association, a nonprofit group dedicated to education involving both bilateral and international issues; the Business Council; the Business Roundtable; the Detroit Economic Club; the International Business Council; the National Petroleum Council; the Societe de Chimie Industrielle; the U.S.-China Business Council; and the World Business Council for Sustainable Development.

Geoffery E. Merszei
Executive Vice President and Chief Financial Officer (Since 2005)

- He is a member of Dow's Board of Directors, its Environment Health
- He has executive oversight for Dow's activities in Europe.
- He returned to the company in July 2005 after serving four years as executive vice president and chief financial officer of Alcan.
- His career with Dow has spanned 24 years.
- He joined Dow from the Royal Bank of Canada in 1977 and in 1980 moved to Hong Kong as credit manager for Dow Asia Pacific.
- He was later named credit and finance manager for the region. Mr. Merszei is chairman of Liana, Dorinco Reinsurance Company, and the Dow Credit Corporate Board.
- He is a member of the Board of Directors of Dow Corning Corporation and Chemical Financial Corporation. He is also a member of the Conference Board's Council of Financial Executives and the Corporate Executive Board Working Council for Chief Financial Officers.

Contact Information

2030 Dow Center
Midland, MI 48674, USA
Phone: 1 989 636 1000
Fax: 1 989 636 1830

Company Overview

- The Dow Chemical Company (Dow) is a science and technology company, manufacturing chemicals, specialty chemicals, and polymers. The company operates in over 170 countries. It is headquartered in Midland, Michigan.
- Dow is a global science and technology-based company that provides chemical, plastic, and agricultural products and services to various consumer markets. Dow serves customers in over 175 countries and a range of markets, including food, transportation, health and medicine, personal and home care, and building and construction, among others. The company has 156 manufacturing sites in 37 countries and supplies over 3,200 products.
- Dow operates through six divisions: performance plastics, performance chemicals, agricultural sciences, plastics, chemicals, and hydrocarbons and energy.
- The company's agricultural sciences division develops, manufactures, and markets products for crop production, weed, insect and plant disease management, and industrial and commercial pest management.

Strengths

- Dow has global operations. It is the largest chemical company in the United States and the second largest in the world after BASF in terms of sales. It has 156 manufacturing sites in 37 countries worldwide. The company markets its products in over 175 countries worldwide.
- The company has a diversified product portfolio. The company manufactures over 3,200 products.
- Dow has strong R&D capability.

Weaknesses

- The performance of the agricultural sciences division has been slow.
- The profitability of the chemicals division, despite growth in revenues, has declined.

Opportunities

- New ventures in the world's fastest growing economy would strengthen Dow's global market position.

Threats

- Dow's operations in the United States and Gulf of Mexico were affected by hurricanes in 2005.
- High feedstock prices.
- Asbestos litigation.

Industry Competition

- BASF Aktiengesellschaft
- Bayer AG
- E. I. duPont de Nemours & Company

Significant Supplier Changes

Primary Products

Agricultural sciences:

Herbicide
Fungicide
Insecticide
Gas fumigant

Key Figures

The company recorded revenues of $46,307 million during the fiscal year ended December 2008, an increase of 15.3 percent over 2007. The net profit was $4,515 million in fiscal year 2008, an increase of 61.4 percent over 2007.

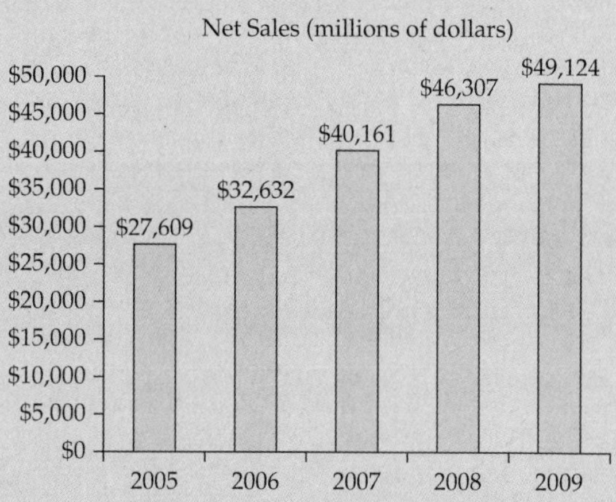

www.dow.com

Current Contracts

Supplier Performance

The buying firm should have a process for managing performance and giving feedback to the strategic suppliers. This process is typically accomplished by asking the supplying firm for a performance self-assessment and then communicating to the supplying firm exactly how the buying firm rates its performance. Most often there is some sort of reward and punishment system put in place by the buying firm to further encourage excellent performance. The feedback and performance phase is outlined in the next section.

The Strategic Supplier Performance Review Process

An overview can be beneficial in developing a clear idea of the supplier performance review process. A performance review is a set of expectations and measurements for controlling long-term relationships with existing strategic suppliers. It includes consistent measurements for establishing positive relationships with new suppliers and evaluating current performance of existing strategic suppliers according to the expectations of the buying firm. The review process must have a standard template that is used as a guideline for informing a customized review process with criteria specific to each strategic supplier. The performance review template should include a personal meeting with the functional manager. Having the functional manager in the performance review of a strategic supplier is beneficial for the buying firm and fosters cross-functional communication. By getting input from the person directly responsible for each strategic supplier, a more complete review of performance is possible.

The general review process should take approximately two workdays to complete depending on the level of complexity of the specific strategic supplier. The first step is to schedule a review process for each individual strategic supplier; the review date is usually established when the contract is signed. Approximately five days before the review date, a buyer-developed questionnaire specific to the buyer's needs and those of the strategic supplier is sent to the strategic supplier. The strategic supplier is then required to complete the questionnaire and return it to the buying firm no later than two days prior to the meeting. After an internal review is completed, a final analysis of the relationship expectations is communicated to the strategic supplier. Within the next few days, meetings are held between the buying firm and the strategic supplier where all of the action items are recorded. The final step is the distribution of the minutes from the meetings between the buying firm and the strategic supplier and the official publication of action items. See Figure 8.4.

The buying firm should have various review categories that are used in order to fully assess their strategic suppliers. Quality is a very important review category. The buying firms should require their strategic suppliers to meet or exceed their performance standards and proactively initiate quality process improvements. Customer service should be expected to be proactive and flexible, and delivery performance needs to be optimized. The most important attributes should be high quality and on-time delivery. Technology and innovation are also important in order to stay ahead of or at pace with competition and help keep the buying firm at the top of their field. It is necessary for the buying firm to have strategic suppliers who are open about their total costs. Cost reduction and continuous process improvement are necessary in order to keep costs down and create trust with strategic suppliers. The last category is the ethical characteristics of the strategic supplier. Every strategic supplier also should have formal environmental, health, operational, and safety programs. In addition, they should put forth the effort to reduce, reuse, and recycle when possible. These categories, as well as others, should be used in the development of the questionnaire for each supplier.

The SRM Scoring System

The scoring system for each strategic supplier should be done on a scale from 0.0 to 4.0, where 4.0 is the highest possible score, meaning that there are five different ratings that range from exceptional to unacceptable. The weaker the score, the more often the strategic supplier needs to be evaluated. When a supplier rates between 2.5 and 4.0 (exceptional and very good subcontractors/suppliers), there are annual evaluations. A good supplier should rate between 1.5 and 2.49 and needs to be evaluated semiannually. A marginal strategic supplier receives a rating of 1.0–1.49 and needs to be evaluated every quarter. When a supplier is unacceptable, it is given a rating between 0.0 and 0.99, which means it is necessary to develop a new source. Once an investment in developing supply chain relationships is made, buying firms must actively manage these relationships. Strategic supply chain relationships, however, do not come without risks to the buying and supplying firms.

FIGURE 8.4
Meeting Report for Strategic Suppliers

SMS, INC.
MINUTES OF MEETING REPORT

Supplier No. ______________
Supplier Name ______________
Project Location ______________
Date ______________
Page 1 of ______________
Compiled by ______________

Meeting Subject ______________

Meeting Location ______________ Date ________ Time ________

Name	Title	Representing	Comments

Item No.	Minutes/Description	Action By	Action Required Date

Remarks: ______________

Distribution: ______________

Supplier Development

As firms increasingly emphasize cooperative relationships with critical suppliers, executives of buyer firms are using supplier evaluations to ensure that their performance objectives are met. Supplier evaluations, one type of supplier development program (SDP), are an attempt to meet current and future business needs by improving supplier performance and capabilities.

When a supplier is unable to conform to the buying firm's expectations, the buying firm manager must determine the most appropriate action to resolve the issue. To maintain the working relationship, the manager must find a way to communicate the problem and motivate the supplier to change its results. The buying firm must develop a supplier evaluation, or report card, and communicate the results to its suppliers with the hope and expectation of improved performance. The supplier's perceptions of the buyer–supplier relationship and the supplier's commitment to the buying firm was tested in a study by Prahinski and Benton. Implications for business managers were drawn from this research and are given below:

1. For the buying firm manager, specific communication strategies should be designed into the SDP efforts. The program should be formalized with routine communication; incorporate supplier training, education, and site visits to aid in the learning process; and provide opportunities for feedback to clarify program objectives and improvement suggestions. The result of the SDP collaborative communication effort should enhance the supplier's perceptions of the business relationship and their commitment to the buying firm.
2. Buying firm managers should focus their SDP implementation efforts on suppliers that exhibit commitment to the buying firm. Although the buying firm's perception of the supplier's commitment is inherently biased, it represents the best proxy for the supplier's commitment.
3. As the recipient of the customer's SDP efforts, the supplier firm manager has the opportunity to improve the relationship with the customer. Improved relationships can result in increased market share, growth opportunities, and other benefits.

Finally, when SDPs are implemented, the supply firm can take advantage of the learning opportunities and improve its overall performance with the buying firm and with its other customers. Also see Prahinski & Benton (2004) and Newman (1988).

Single versus Multiple Sources

Much debate has taken place concerning the number of suppliers a firm should use. One side of the debate is the multiple-sources side. This involves the use of two or more suppliers. The other side of the debate is the **single-source** policy, in which only one supplier is used to supply a particular part.

The goal of both policies is to provide the buyer with the best value of a supplied part. Many attributes contribute to the value that the buyer receives. They include risk, quality, unit price, total cost, delivery, reliability, and service (design capabilities, productivity improvements, and R&D). See Treleven (1987).

Advantages of Multiple Sourcing

The main arguments for multiple sourcing are competition and ensured supply. It is commonly believed that competition between suppliers for a similar part will drive costs lower as suppliers compete against each other for more of the

OEM's business. This sense of competition is the very root of American thought as competition is the basis for capitalism and is the backbone of Western economic theory.

Multiple sources also can guarantee an undisrupted supply of parts. If something should go wrong with one supplier, such as a strike or a major breakdown or natural disaster, the other supplier(s) can pick up the slack to deliver all the needed parts without a disruption.

Multiple sourcing also can provide other benefits such as improved market intelligence and improved supplier appraisal effectiveness. Contact with many suppliers will allow a firm to keep abreast of new developments and new technologies as they emerge across the field. In addition, greater contact with suppliers will increase the effectiveness of evaluating a supplier's ability and progress by comparing cost and production data from supplier to supplier.

Advantages of Single Sourcing

The major arguments in favor of single sourcing are that with the certainty of large volumes the supplier can enjoy lower costs per unit and increased cooperation and communication to produce win–win relationships between buyer and seller. Naming a certain supplier as the single source and providing it with a long-term contract (three to five years) greatly reduces the uncertainty that the supplier will lose business to another competitor. With this contract guarantee, the supplier is more willing to invest in new equipment, or change its business/operating methods to accommodate the buyer.

Single sources should be able to provide lower costs per unit compared to multiple sources by reducing the duplication of operations in areas such as setup. Spreading fixed costs across a larger volume also should result in an accelerated learning curve.

Cooperation and communication can increase between buyer and seller with a single-source agreement due to the fewer number of people involved when compared to multiple sourcing. Engineers and production people from both firms can work together to improve product quality and productivity.

Advantages of Dual Sourcing

The advantages of multiple sourcing can be viewed as the disadvantages of single sourcing and vice versa. The best scenario would be one that can obtain the advantages of both. This might be done by applying significant pressure to single-source suppliers or by providing significant certainty to suppliers in a multiple-sourcing environment. This may be accomplished through the use of contract length. Short-term contracts regardless of single or multiple suppliers can be used as a source of punishment. In some instances, long-term contracts can be viewed as a reward.

Long-term contracts can provide the stability needed to produce single-source results while still using more than one supplier. Given enough volume, two suppliers may be able to achieve the economies of scale to produce a part at a per-unit price that is comparable to that of one supplier. When spreading volume over fixed costs, the per-unit savings experience diminishing returns. If the volume is great enough, two firms may eventually get the returns diminished enough so they are comparable in per-unit price to one firm. The advantage may rest in the learning curve, as a single source will be able to improve at a faster rate.

Long-Term Issues

Single-sourcing advocates may want to address the following long-term impacts. In the long run, if every firm reduces its supplier base, there will be fewer suppliers and overall supplier competition will decrease. Supplier consolidation will give suppliers more power in the long run.

Also, a supplier may be able to forward-integrate and market the very subassemblies it sells to the OEM in the aftermarket, which is a very lucrative field. This warrants using the Porter model to assess the supplier's capability to do this prior to single sourcing.[1]

Finally, many more "white collar" tasks are being done by single sources in areas such as engineering and design. So-called black-box supply contracts occur when OEMs assign a finished component to the supplier and it is the supplier's responsibility to design and produce it because all the manufacturer wants is the final product. It is these types of situations that may enable suppliers to become so specialized and obtain so much expertise that the producer cannot effectively compete with its suppliers. OEMs must be careful not to let too much of the value-added portion of their product be delegated to suppliers or the OEM's power will be reduced.

The single-source movement became popular during the 1990s. The 1980s were a period of labor stability as strikes were not a major issue. The federal government under the Reagan administration sent clear antistrike/labor signals that reduced the power of the labor movement (e.g., firing the air-traffic controllers). What is to prevent future labor unrest that could unravel single-source relationships and bring assembly lines to a halt? This was the case as strikes crippled Ford and Renault plants in Europe. Progressive and participative management style may be the answer, but management must effectively move beyond lip service to prevent labor unrest.

Japanese Reality

Many "pop" management techniques have emerged over the last 30 years by emulating the successes of the Japanese manufacturers, particularly in automobile production. Many managers believe that "if it works in Japan, it can work here." That may be true, but one of the perceptions possibly leading to the popularity of single sourcing in the United States is the belief that all Japanese firms work closely with one supplier. Therefore, the common American response has been that if Japan uses single sourcing, we should too. In fact, over 98 percent of Ford's outsourced parts are supplied by single-source suppliers.

This perception of Japanese manufacturers is true for high-tech items that require large R&D expenditures or complex parts that require major equipment investments. However, this is not the case with simpler parts. To make sure everyone tries hard (assuming they mean through competitive forces), the assemblers usually divide their parts order between two or three members of their supplier group. The assemblers don't take this step to keep prices down . . . rather, they do it to prevent anyone letting down on quality or delivery reliability. If there is a problem with one of the suppliers, volume percentages temporarily shift to others as a form of punishment.

One can therefore conclude that Japanese manufacturers provide enough stability to two or three suppliers to achieve the advantages of single sourcing. It should

[1]Michael Porter's Five Forces model.

be noted that many of the Japanese automakers use suppliers that produce many more than just one part for them. Therefore, the investment in increased communication, cooperation, and coordination with a major supplier can be spread across many parts.

Cross-Sourcing

The single-sourcing/multiple-sourcing issue does not have to be viewed as a "black or white" type of a decision. A hybrid approach that is known as cross-sourcing can be used. With this method, the supplier base is expanded without increasing the actual number of suppliers. For example, if both suppliers A and B can produce parts 1, 2, 3, 4, and 5, the advantages of both single and multiple sourcing can be achieved if supplier A produces all of parts 1, 3, and 5 and supplier B produces all of 2 and 4. If anything happens to supplier A, supplier B can pick up the slack as it has the capability to produce 1, 3, and 5 as well. Neither supplier suffers because overall volume remains the same. The reverse also can be done if a buyer wants to increase competition among the suppliers.

Supplier Reduction

Regardless of one's final analysis of the single/multiple sourcing debate, it is recommended to reduce the overall supply base. If the perceived benefits outweigh the risks, after careful analysis of both short-term and long-term needs, a single source may be appropriate. However, for operations that would be financially damaged when a supply stoppage occurs, then the use or development of a second source is wise.

Assume that it is desirable to reduce the number of suppliers. The question now is which one? The grade and hurdle methods are used to guide the supplier reduction analysis.

Grade

"Grade" methods are those that are based on a score or grade given to the supplier by the buyer for some attribute. The suppliers' performances in the past are kept on record and the suppliers receive a "report card" as to how well they are doing compared to other suppliers. The most common attributes are quality, price, and delivery, but many additional attributes can be added such as frequency of delivery; regardless, the method remains the same—for each attribute and purchase transaction, the supplier is given a grade. These attributes can be weighted equally or used to emphasize what is more important to the buyer firm.

When implementing a policy of supplier reduction, use this information, which is usually computerized, to rank the suppliers to choose the best one(s). One of the drawbacks of this method is that, many times, qualitative information cannot accurately be incorporated into the system—for example, a design change or traffic congestion may have caused a shipment to be delayed, and thus a late delivery was not the supplier's fault.

Another drawback of grade methods is that supplier performance is the only thing being used to resolve the cause of the problems.

One major problem with grade methods is that they assume that the best performance of the past will be the best performance in the future. In a way, it is by forecasting that suppliers will be able to best meet the supply needs even though the OEM's needs may be different in the future. Computerized supplier performance reports (grade methods) may be of better use if futuristic criteria are used and the criteria are very comprehensive and exhaustive.

Hurdle

The second group of methods used to reduce the number of suppliers a firm uses is what is referred to as "hurdle" methods. In this type of situation, suppliers are required to "jump" over higher and higher hurdles to win the buyer's business. Usually this is done through some sort of supplier certification program.

Certification

Supplier certification programs are very useful tools to evaluate the quality capabilities of a supplier. Since quality is one of the biggest concerns to many OEMs, this is a good way to control supplied part quality. Basically, certification involves the setting of criteria regarding quality levels as demonstrated through the use of Statistical Process Control (SPC) process capability studies of a supplier's equipment, supplier record-keeping abilities, and so forth.

If a supplier meets some but not all of the criteria, it may reach a "preferred" status and will be rewarded increased business by the manufacturer. If a supplier meets all the criteria and has demonstrated that it can sustain these levels, then it may be granted "select" status and be awarded a long-term supply contract.

By using these methods, buyers can reduce their supply base by only rewarding business to those suppliers who can become certified or by awarding the suppliers who become certified first with a bigger slice of the pie. Some of the suppliers will not be able to become certified and thus the supply base will be reduced.

The certification criteria can be changed and updated as recertification may be required. Thus, the "hurdle" can be raised higher and higher until there are only one or a few suppliers left. In combination with quality certification are the price and productivity hurdles. OEMs can add these criteria to make it more difficult to be a "select" supplier.

Ford Motor Company has used this method by creating the Q1 (quality is job one) certification program. New business is only awarded to those suppliers who have demonstrated quality and productivity improvements to obtain Q1 status. Suppliers who are awarded long-term contracts with Ford are then expected to reduce their unit price 5 percent each year. Similar programs have been developed by General Motors in its "Targets for Excellence" standards and by IBM with its six-sigma program.

Certification programs are usually only as good as their designers make them. The attributes that determine certification must be well thought out and realistic. For example, requiring a 5 percent decrease in price annually may force suppliers to look for short-term cost reductions that may hurt long-term investments, which could make a partnership with a single source stronger.

Part of the single-source philosophy is that through cooperation and input from the manufacturer, suppliers will be able to reduce their costs for a particular part. However, a Boston University survey of the major suppliers of the North American auto industry reported that assemblers had given them little assistance in reducing costs and adopting new techniques.[2]

When designing a certification program, careful attention should be paid to the selection of criteria. Good certification should include issues regarding equipment

[2]Manufacturing Roundtable Research Report Series, Boston University, 1996.

capability, quality assurance, financial health of the supplier, production scheduling methods, value analysis abilities, and cost accounting methods.

INDUSTRY EXAMPLES

Consider the apparel, chemical, electronics, and construction industries. A supplier with the lowest per-unit price may not have the best quality or delivery rating of various suppliers. A strategy seeking such suppliers may be acceptable in the apparel industry, where the highest emphasis is placed on price or price markup, but would be unacceptable in the chemical industry, where the highest priority is purity of the chemicals (i.e., quality). Each industry must analyze the various associated criteria trade-offs when selecting a supplier.

In the four sections that follow, we will take a closer look at supplier selection and evaluation criteria for the apparel, electronic, chemical, and construction industries.

Apparel Industry

Organizational buying can be broken down into two categories: retail buying and industrial buying. There are distinct differences between them. An important distinction is that the retail buyer is unique in serving as both a purchasing agent and a marketing manager. Successful retail buying depends on the ability to select suppliers who meet the perceived needs and wants of the firm and its customers.

The most important difference between industrial buying and retail buying is in the buyers' responsibility for meeting the profit objectives of the firm. While industrial buyers are responsible for controlling costs, retail buyers are responsible for both controlling costs and generating revenue through their purchases. This suggests that markup (the difference between the wholesale cost of a supplier's merchandise and the consumer's price of a supplier's merchandise) may be more appropriate than price in the study of supplier selection among retail buyers. Retail buyers need to not only consider what suppliers charge but how much profit per unit can be made in reselling the goods and in what volumes.

While industrial buyers purchase raw materials and component parts for use in production, retail buyers purchase finished goods for resale to the consumer. Consequently, the right goods for industrial buyers are those necessary to support the production process, while the right goods for retail buyers are likely to be those that the buyer expects to sell satisfactorily. Retail buyers might then be expected to use criteria such as selling history and merchandise fashionability in their supplier selection decisions.

Retail buying has always used the selection of merchandise as an important retail buying decision. However, the increasing size of retail organizations and corresponding homogenization of merchandise assortments suggest that increasingly more important retail buying decisions are supplier selection and evaluation. The most common criteria used when selecting retail vendors are delivery (usually reliabilities), quality of merchandise, and price markup (percent above plan versus percent below plan). The most important criterion is price markup, followed by delivery and final quality.

Price markup is clearly the most important criterion used when selecting a vendor in the apparel industry. Unlike industrial buying decisions, which are often made within a "buying center," retail buying decisions are usually made autonomously by the retail buyer. This, coupled with the fact that the wholesale cost of merchandise is often not negotiable, leads buyers to view sales as a profit-related variable that they can influence by choosing vendors with strong selling histories. Markup has a direct effect on gross margin and thus has implications for profit, which is the major long-range objective of many firms. The best suppliers "stand out like a sore thumb." Retailers can then pick and choose from these vendors to obtain the best price markup possible. Good relations are also a key issue at the end of a buying season when merchandise is marked down in price. The buyer and vendor must work closely together to decide on a markdown that is fair to both parties.

Ensuring the availability of goods is an essential buying function in any organization. While poor delivery on the part of vendors is a problem for all retail buyers, it is of most concern to apparel buyers because of the seasonality of fashion merchandise. As an example, the Limited sets itself apart from all other apparel buyers because it has the ability to get new fashion merchandise delivered to its stores three to four months earlier than most. This allows the company to be a leader in getting new fashions to its customers and results in increased revenues. On the other hand, Macy's Department Stores has developed a vendor matrix that allows it short lead times. Macy's does not rely on early delivery times to get the new fashions out on the showroom floor first as does the Limited but, instead, wants to see if the fashion is going to be a success. If this is the case, Macy's will then contact the appropriate vendor to manufacture the new fashion and have the merchandise in its stores within a week.

Value or quality of merchandise is an obvious choice of vendor selection criteria. Buyers must purchase goods from their suppliers that meet their customers' needs and wants. Quality is a very important factor to retail customers. It is often the case in the retail industry that various buyers obtain similar prices and delivery dates. What distinguishes one buyer from the next in this case is the quality of the merchandise. If consumers can buy a better-quality item for the same price as one of lesser quality, then they will do so. Macy's reports that it is able to obtain moderate- to high-quality merchandise 80 percent of the time. The Limited, on the other hand, requires all of its merchandise to meet its high-quality standards. The Limited's customers expect a high-quality product, and this expectation allows it to charge a higher price.

Supplier evaluation in the apparel industry is a continuing task. Each time a shipment of merchandise arrives in the stores, the goods are examined for defects and compliance with specifications (color, size, and form). If, for example, supplier X continually sends unacceptable merchandise to buyer A, then it would be customary for buyer A to stop giving supplier X orders to fill. Very often then, buyer A would "talk" about the bad experiences encountered with supplier X, and simply by word of mouth, buyers would stop using supplier X. This is the reason that "good vendors stand out like a sore thumb." Retail suppliers therefore must strive to maintain the faith of the buyers by offering acceptable-quality goods, showing very little delinquency of order deliveries, and being willing to negotiate price markup percentage.

Chemical Industry

Industrial buying in the chemical industry mostly deals with buying bulk chemicals for chemical production and synthesis. Overall, in ranking which criterion is considered most important in supplier selection, quality is number one. Reliability and dependability of the delivery ranked second, while price considerations ranked third.

Purchasing managers send requests for quotes (RFQs) to prequalified suppliers. Maintaining quality is by far the most important competitive advantage of companies in the chemical industry. During the period of time the bids are being collected, samples of the chemicals are obtained for quality testing. The chemicals must meet the buying firm's complete specifications. For example, samples of the same chemical and purity may have different tints. Even if the purity specification is met, the buying firm also must require consistency with the existing product line. Another important aspect of quality control is incoming inspection, to make sure the desired amounts are delivered. This should be done by weighing the products as they come in to the warehouse.

At Pfizer Chemicals, quality testing is considered the number one criterion. Samples are obtained from potential suppliers, and a variety of tests are done to ensure that purity and identification of unique characteristics of the specific chemical are met. Reliable quality of specific specialty chemicals is what makes a company competitive in the chemical industry. When considering the quality of the specific chemicals, historical quality performance also is evaluated in the selection process. If suppliers do not meet quality standards consistently, a firm's product may be delayed, thus leaving the buying firm in a situation where it will not be able to meet customer demand.

Delivery performance is also important in the chemical industry. The lead time for the commodity must be well established so that planning horizons for the production schedule may be made with a high degree of certainty.

Throughout the purchasing process, it is important for all of the functional areas in the corporation to work together to find a supplier that is compatible with all the needs of the firm. A trade-off of the desired qualities in a supplier must be made in order to select the best one. For the shipping and receiving department, a supplier who does not meet the delivery schedule usually causes severe operational problems. Random sampling of the raw material inventory stocked in the warehouses also should be performed to further test the quality of the chemicals.

When considering the price of chemicals, bids are evaluated and ranked according to the firms' financial strength, quality, and historical performance records. If an active bidding firm does not pass these tests, two options exist.

All of the companies lack certain fundamentals, and the buyer must work with the supplier with the best overall record to meet the desired needs of the firm. In this stage, both the supplier and the buyer should work together to meet mutual agreements. For some specialty chemicals, a very limited number of suppliers exist; therefore, these suppliers are willing to work closely with any firm that needs their products. It is also very likely that because such a small number of suppliers exist for these chemicals, sourcing for these chemicals is engaged in both international and domestic markets. This is usually not a major concern for Pfizer because the policy is to stock the warehouse and to deliver from there to the individual plants requesting raw materials for the next production run. International sourcing problems may occur due to shipping delays, customs, and the excessive amount of paperwork involved with importing raw materials.

Periodic unannounced plant visits also are performed to ensure that the suppliers are following any mutually established procedures. This is an excellent method for collecting data to evaluate the supplier performance. Usually, standardized forms consisting of standard checks to be performed in the company audit are used by the purchasing department to rate suppliers. This information is then evaluated to see if overall improvements are being made in the firm. If the variance is favorable, or if there is no variance at all, the purchasing department may favor that particular supplier. In instances where the supplier's audit does not go well, inquiries are made to determine what is being done to alleviate the problems in order to ensure better overall performance.

Electronics Industry

Industrial buying within the electronics industry is extremely competitive. Some companies place higher emphasis on pricing and delivery. The companies also vary in their methods of purchasing. For example, Dynalab prefers to deal with a single source per unit, while Tandy uses many suppliers to meet its needs for any given item.

Due to the intense competition in the electronics industry, suppliers of electronic equipment are forced to comply with standard specifications. Buyers do not have to concern themselves with checking the quality of every batch of goods because they know that suppliers understand this inherent objective. Likewise, timely delivery is not a large problem due to the massive amounts of inventory that are held in the plants. Thus, late deliveries do not severely affect the production process of the firm, as the company can simply use the surplus or buffer stock until the order is filled. Because the majority of electronic parts are small and inexpensive, large amounts of inventory may be held economically.

Supplier selection at Tandy Corporation is based solely on price. When Tandy sends out an RFQ, suppliers that lack a good reputation are ignored. Thus, the quality of the supplier chosen to bid is assumed to be high. Delivery time is not a major factor due to the fact that the firm does not operate on a just-in-time basis. Instead, electronics companies usually order large quantities of goods and then put these goods into inventory. Once the product is received, an acceptable quality level (AQL) sample check is performed before the goods are transferred to stock. On the few occasions that samples do not conform to quality standards, the entire lot is sent back to the supplier. However, the likelihood of this happening is very minimal. Supplier evaluation is therefore primarily based on previous performance criteria, not defects or delivery time.

Supplier selection also is based on price. The only instance in which delivery time is considered important is for a special project with certain time restrictions. In this unique case, the firm would purchase directly from the factory in order to bypass the extra time that is involved when dealing with a distributor. Many electronics firms attempt to single source to meet their purchasing requirements. This simply means that although the supplier might not be the lowest bidder on all of the parts, it is the lowest bidder on a total cost basis. It is easier to develop and manage one supplier than to manage four or five. The preference of most electronic firms is to deal with one supplier rather than with many suppliers. Single sourcing allows buyers to gain several advantages. First, they are able to make maximum use of their buying power. They are able to concentrate all requirements for a certain item with a single supplier and thereby get the largest possible quantity discount. Second, with single sourcing, less administrative work is required of the buyer's organization as orders, reports, and payments are issued to only one supplier. Single sourcing also allows suppliers to offer special price concessions if they can make 100 percent of a given item. Lastly, single sourcing gives suppliers the incentive to aid in methods improvement.

Selection of a supplier for a new commodity is a different process. The Thomas Register and the Gold Book trade managers are used to obtain potential suppliers for new commodities. Once a supplier is decided on, a single part is ordered and checked for quality and specifications, and then a batch is ordered and inspected for percent of defects. If the batch meets the requirements, then no further testing is done on the remaining orders. If the batch does not meet the requirements, the buying firm will usually work with the supplier to solve the problems that are causing the batches to fail the checks. Suppliers are very interested in improving their performance.

In today's market, an electronics supplier must have a quality product to survive. Thus, electronics firms do not test the quality of the electronics suppliers. Seventeen years ago, electronics firms tested each unit due to poor quality, but now, because of Chinese, Japanese, and other foreign competition, quality has become a given for each product or the supplier simply will not survive in the electronics supplier market.

Construction Industry[3]

In the construction industry, material quality, delivery dependability, and price again appear to be the most critical criteria. However, the degree of importance that construction firms place on the three criteria varies.

The supplier selection process begins by choosing potential suppliers for each material type needed for a specific project. The selection process is usually based solely on past performance. Once a pool of potential sources is formed, RFQs are sent out, negotiations are conducted, and specific suppliers are selected.

High-quality materials are expected from every potential supplier. If a supplier has shown the ability to supply a quality product in the past, it is assumed that the supplier will continue to do so. In most cases, there are no formal measures taken to ensure that high-quality materials have been delivered. Visual material inspection is used and any piece of material that is not visibly damaged is accepted and used. However, materials such as steel beams or concrete require more formal inspection to ensure that they conform to specifications. In the case of steel materials, plant visits may be made by a representative of the buying firm during testing procedures to ensure that the architect's specifications are being met. In addition, a representative of the supplier will sometimes be present at the construction site in order to ensure that the materials are being properly used. As an example, concrete samples are sometimes tested to confirm that they are of the desired consistency. Although quality is a very important aspect to the buyer, it may not play a large role in actually selecting one supplier over another. Quality is rarely a problem in the construction industry, simply because the buying firm provides the supplier with specifications and the supplier must comply. If a supplier cannot provide adequate quality, it will not receive consideration for future business from the contractor. Therefore, after the potential suppliers have been selected, considerations of delivery dependability and price may play a more important role in actually selecting one supplier over another.

Delivery dependability is obviously vital in today's fast-track construction industry, where construction is often begun before the architects' final designs are completed. If delivery deadlines are missed, the result can be costly to both the owner and the contractor. In the construction industry, time is really money. If a

[3]Also see Benton and McHenry (2009).

project is not completed by its deadline, the loss of potential profits increases with each day past the due date. In this industry, suppliers must be able to deliver materials to the contractor (buyer) when promised. If one company can supply a contractor (buyer) considerably faster than another supplier, the faster company will have an advantage. Delivery considerations are the most important criterion used in selecting suppliers for the construction industry.

Price also has a significant effect on the selection process. Price, however, cannot always overshadow all other criteria. The trick is to strike a balance between price and the other factors considered in the process. Premiums often may be required for rush deliveries. The company must weigh the desire for expected deliveries with the resulting higher prices. Through negotiation, the buyer and supplier must reach a price agreement that is satisfactory to both parties.

While quality, delivery-speed dependability, and price may play the most vital role in selecting a supplier, they are not the only considerations. Depending on the project, and the specific types of required materials, other factors may play an even more important role. As an example, a supplier must be financially stable in order to assure the buyer that it will be around to fulfill the negotiated agreement. Also, warranties may play an important role when buying roofing materials, wooden doors, and cabinets. Finally, advantages in the areas of customer service or supplier location also may sway a buyer in the direction of a particular supplier.

Summary

The selection of suppliers is a complex and demanding issue that has no real correct answer. Each firm must weigh the benefits and risks of single and multiple sourcing. If it is clear to proceed with a reduction of the supply base, numerous methods can be used. However, the author recommends that a strategic approach should be incorporated into the selection process. A strategic match between buyer and supplier can allow an easier cooperative relationship to exist and flourish. A manufacturing firm needs to investigate the strategic policies followed by the supplier and the possible ramifications of these policies to determine if a match exists.

Supplier selection is a difficult and involved process for most companies. The criterion of net price is emphasized more heavily in the apparel and the electronics industries than in the chemical and construction industries. In the electronics industry, this is due to the assumption that both quality and delivery are inherent in the product. In the apparel industry, it is very important that retail buyers not only control costs but generate revenues through their purchases. In the chemical industry, price is the least important criterion. Competition in the chemical industry is based on quality assurance and timely delivery. In the construction industry, price outweighs all aspects other than delivery. As with the electronics industry, adequate performance quality is expected. Delivery reliability and dependability are also important in the construction industry. Delays are extremely costly. If a project is not completed on time, penalty costs are incurred for each day past the deadline of the project. Therefore, in the electronics and construction industries, price is the order-winning criterion for a supplier.

Any firm making a supplier selection decision, regardless of industry, should examine its specific situation. By deciding which criteria to emphasize, firms will be able to select the suppliers from whom they will benefit the most.

Discussion Questions

1. What is meant by make or buy? What are the key make-or-buy success factors?
2. What is meant by outsourcing?
3. What are some of the sources of supplier information?
4. Discuss three common supplier evaluation systems.
5. What are the advantages of single and multiple sourcing? What is the trend?
6. What is meant by cross-sourcing?
7. Discuss the recent trend of supplier reduction.
8. Discuss how supplier selection and evaluation strategies vary across different industries.
9. What are the three common supplier evaluation systems?

Suggested Cases

Firebird Electric, U.S.
Capital State Arena
Camp Bowie Technologies Inc.

References

Benton, W. C., and Linda F. McHenry, *Construction Purchasing and Supply Chain Management*. New York: McGraw-Hill, 2009, pp. 1–22.

Ken, J. "Getting Tough with Vendors," *Electronic Business*, October 7, 1991.

Newman, R. G. "Single Source Qualification." *Journal of Purchasing and Materials Management*, Summer 1988, pp. 10–17.

Porter, M. *Competitive Advantage: Creating and Sustaining Superior Performance.* New York: Free Press, 1985.

Prahinski, C., and W. C. Benton Jr. "Supplier Development Communications Strategies." *Journal of Operations Management*, Autumn 2003, pp. 39–62.

Treleven, M. "Single Sourcing: A Management Tool for the Quality Supplier." *Journal of Purchasing and Materials Management*, Spring 1987, pp. 19–24.

Trent, R. J. "Why Relationships Matter," *Supply Chain Management Review*, November 2005, pp. 53–59.

Weber, C., J. Current, and W. C. Benton Jr. "Vendor Selection." *European Journal of Operational Research* 52 (February 1991), pp. 2–18.

Chapter Nine

Strategic Outsourcing

Learning Objectives

1. Know the precise definition of outsourcing.
2. Describe why organizations outsource manufacturing and services business processes.
3. List the benefits and pitfalls of outsourcing.
4. Discuss why the outsourcing process is not considered contracting or joint venturing.
5. Identify the hidden cost of outsourcing.
6. Discuss core and noncore competencies.
7. Identify outsourcing trends.
8. Discuss the elements of strategic outsourcing.
9. Identify the role of the outsourcing relationship manager.

INTRODUCTION

Outsourcing can be defined as *the complete transfer of a business process that has been traditionally operated and managed internally to an independently owned external service provider*. A complete transfer means that the people, facilities, equipment, technology, and other assets are no longer maintained internally once the business process is outsourced. While some have considered outsourcing decisions synonymously with make-or-buy decisions, it has been recognized that the two are not the same. Outsourcing is also sometimes thought to be similar to subcontracting, joint venturing, and contract manufacturing. Contracting is the purchasing of goods or services to facilitate a business process owned by the buyer. The outsourcing point of departure from these concepts is the complete transfer of all associated internal business process activities. When considering outsourcing, firms are evaluating whether or not to reverse a prior decision to "make." In other words, outsourcing reshapes or expands a firm's boundaries.

In a recent study, executives categorized their outsourcing activities (Handley and Benton, 2009). Table 9.1 illustrates the diverse set of outsourced activities that were reported on. Not surprisingly, information technology outsourcing (ITO) represented the largest number of responses at 25.8 percent. Approximately 35 percent of the responses represented the outsourcing of some type of manufacturing activity, with the remainder being business process outsourcing (BPO).

TABLE 9.1
Categories of Outsourced Activity Reported

Source: Handley (2008).

Category of Outsourced Activity	Frequency	Percent
Business process—information technology or systems	51	25.7%
Other—business process	38	19.2
Manufacturing of end items	33	16.7
Manufacturing of component parts	24	12.1
Other—manufacturing	13	6.6
Business process—human resources	11	5.6
Logistics services	11	5.6
Call center or customer service center	9	4.5
Business process—accounting or finance	8	4.0
Total	198	100.0%

FIGURE 9.1
Outsourcing Process

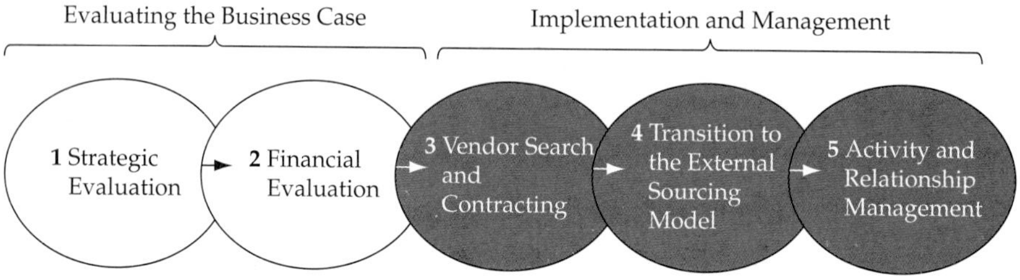

Outsourcing can be conceptualized as a process rather than simply an event. This process begins with the development of a strategic and financial business case for outsourcing. The crafting of the business case is followed by implementing the external sourcing model and, ultimately, managing the relationship with the provider. This view is summarized in Figure 9.1 and is consistent with the definition of the outsourcing process offered by the International Association of Outsourcing Professionals (IAOP, 2007).

Global business process outsourcing alone has surpassed the U.S.$6 trillion mark (Baron, 2005). A recent Booz Allen report posits the expectation that U.S. business process outsourcing will continue to grow at about 10 percent per year in the near term (Couto et al., 2006). A report by the IAOP suggests that between 25 and 34 percent of the "typical executive's budget is outsourced." There is a significant amount of attention reported by industry and the popular press. According to a recent Deloitte Consulting study, 64 percent of respondents indicated that they had brought outsourced services back in-house (Landis et al., 2005). Fifty percent of respondents identified "hidden costs" as the primary problem encountered with outsourcing, while 44 percent did not realize cost savings. Another study reported similar findings from a Bain survey of large and medium-sized firms (Gottfredson et al., 2005). They found that only 10 percent of the firms were highly satisfied with the costs they were saving, and nearly 50 percent failed to achieve cost savings expectations. Moreover, Dunn and Bradstreet found that 20–25 percent of all outsourcing relationships *fail* within two years and approximately 50 percent fail within five years. Finally, a 2005 study reported that, based on the experience of the global consulting firm Booz Allen Hamilton, they would estimate that approximately one in three outsourcing efforts fails to achieve outsourcing expectations (Disher et al., 2005). These anecdotal findings suggest that there is a troubling gap between expectations and reality; however, outsourcing is here to stay. It has become the key driver for globalization. The Internet has made outsourcing an important competitive weapon. This means that outsourcing cannot be dismissed as a passing fad. Perhaps outsourcing is one of the most important business concepts in the past 50 years.

WHY DO ORGANIZATIONS OUTSOURCE BUSINESS PROCESSES?

It is virtually impossible to generalize why organizations outsource various business processes. The final outsourcing decision depends on whether the CEO, CFO, or CIO initiates the outsourcing proposal. Whichever executive initiates the outsourcing proposal, a reduction in *direct operating costs* is usually the primary driver. The cost reduction must be significantly lower than the current *direct operating costs* in order for an outsourcing proposal to be attractive. Some of the generic strategic benefits of outsourcing are listed below:

1. *Cost minimization* is accomplished by reducing direct operating costs, eliminating overhead costs, and transforming fixed costs into variable costs.
2. *Refocusing the organization to its core competencies* is accomplished by focusing what the organization does best and/or transforming the business to focus on new products and services.
3. *Improvement in operating performance* is accomplished by increasing quality, increasing productivity, and obtaining new capabilities technologies from external sources.
4. *Increased market share and revenue* is accomplished by assessing the providers' network and accelerating expansion into new markets.

Some of the specific benefits of outsourcing are to:

1. Reduce and control operating costs.
2. Improve quality.
3. Change company focus.
4. Acquire external capabilities.
5. Refocus scarce resources for alternative uses.
6. Reduce cycle time.
7. Obtain cash infusion.
8. Reduce risks.
9. Gain flexibility.
10. Turn fixed costs into variable costs.

While a contract is required to legally protect one's interests, an extensive strategic assessment and a true commitment to a cooperative relationship with the service provider are both necessary to realize expected outsourcing benefits. These insights offer valuable guidance to outsourcing practitioners in terms of where and how sourcing resources should be applied. Outsourcing initiatives must create value. The type of management and relationship skills and capabilities must be developed through training and/or recruitment within the outsourcing organizations. The hidden costs of outsourcing are given in the next section.

THE HIDDEN COSTS OF OUTSOURCING

Quality Costs

The cost of quality is an essential consideration in sourcing decisions. The costs associated with ensuring quality are often categorized as (1) preventative, (2) appraisal, (3) internal failure, and (4) external failure. If sourcing internally, firms must estimate the costs of defect prevention (i.e., designing quality into products and processes), the costs of quality appraisal (e.g., inspections, audits, monitoring mechanisms), the costs of internal failure (e.g., scrap, rework, internal downtime), and the costs of external failure (i.e., failure as perceived by the external customer). All of these costs exist with external sourcing as well. Persistent internal quality issues at the external source will ultimately impact the buying firm. The buying firm will need to ensure that proper mechanisms are in place to make sure that they are capable of detecting quality failures by an external source. This may be more difficult than with internal sourcing because if sourcing externally, the buying firm may not have maintained sufficient internal capabilities to even appropriately assess the quality of a product or service provided by the external source.

Supplier or Vendor Relationship Management

It has long been recognized in both the strategy and operations literature that the most effective external sourcing relationships involve considerable management time and coordination (Benton and Maloni, 2005). Unfortunately, this comes at an expense. Not all external sourcing relationships are created equal, and those involving commodity products or services may not require extensive relationship building and coordination. The external sourcing of strategic products and services is on the other end of the spectrum. In these situations, relationship building and coordination activities are quite extensive. Thus, it is critical that firms considering outsourcing also evaluate the type and depth of the relationship that will be required to effectively manage the exchange. According to the Deloitte outsourcing study, 62 percent of the respondents cited requiring more management time than expected (Landis et al., 2005). It is also suggested that managing the supply relationship costs at least 3 percent and sometimes more than 10 percent of the annual contract value. On average, the IT outsourcing engagements studied resulted in an annual supplier management expense that equaled 8 percent of the contract value. Many of the costs associated with managing the external sourcing relationship are manifested in the labor expense of purchasing personnel. For instance, Toyota spends more than 7,200 man-days of face-to-face contact with suppliers each year. Other costs associated with managing the relationship include travel, IT infrastructure and management, and supplier development programs (e.g., training and performance evaluation systems).

Internal Coordination

While internal coordination costs are unique to external sourcing alternatives, they must be contrasted against the internal coordination and overhead costs associated with internally sourcing a product or service. In general, one can think of internal coordination costs as those overhead expenses incurred solely due to the decision to internally source a product or service. Presumably, sourcing internally induces higher levels of many overhead administrative functions such as payroll, benefits management, utility expenses, IT expenses, and so forth. The relationship between higher levels of vertical integration and an increase in bureaucratic costs has been noted in the extant academic literature. Some firms have cast the decision to vertically integrate (i.e., source internally) versus the decision to externally source as a comparison between the costs of bureaucracy and the cost of external coordination. However, according to the Deloitte study, 57 percent of respondents were unable to free up the anticipated level of internal resources after outsourcing. In comparing traditional internal sourcing with external sourcing options, firms need to have a thorough understanding of these marginal overhead expenses and how they would be incrementally impacted by outsourcing a particular business activity.

Implementation of External Sourcing Model

An often-underestimated expense that is incurred when switching sources (internal or external) is that associated with the transition itself. This cost category could include supplier search, evaluation and contracting, the transfer of physical assets, domestic and international travel during start-up, and training of the new source to ensure a smooth transition and seamless integration. A 2001 study of 50 IT outsourcing efforts found that supplier search, evaluation, and contracting costs alone represented an average of 3 percent of the annual contract amount (Barthélemy, 2001). This research also found that typical transitions took more than 10 months to complete. During the transition period, firms incur additional costs related to internal staff providing additional support and duplicate resources. There is usually lower efficiency and effectiveness at the beginning of the contract. Moreover, Dunn and Bradstreet found that 20 to 25 percent of all outsourcing relationships fail within two years and nearly half fail within five years (Doig et al., 2001). This implies that the likelihood of incurring these expenses again, or experiencing costs associated with reinternalizing an outsourced activity, is relatively high. Another critical financial consideration with outsourcing is the impact on the internal workforce. Some of the often "hidden costs" of outsourcing include training internal employees to become relationship managers rather than technical managers. The hidden costs also include retention bonuses, severance packages, employee turnover, and management time required to thwart labor disputes. Khosrowpour and Subramanian (1996) surveyed 146 IT professionals and found that only 19 percent would describe their perceptions toward outsourcing as "positive." Furthermore, the majority believed that their welfare was *not* a major consideration in outsourcing. In a 2004 study, 500 truck drivers were surveyed, 80 percent of whom had been transferred to an external service provider as part of a transportation outsourcing initiative. The study results indicated that employees who were highly satisfied and involved in pre-outsourcing expressed a significantly higher intent to exit the external provider (Logan et al., 2004). Another study found that 38 percent of firms who would classify their outsourcing effort as "failed" admitted to overlooking personnel issues as opposed to only 20 percent of firms who classified their efforts as "successful" (Barthélemy, 2003). These observations underscore the importance of considering the management and impact of internal staff when making outsourcing decisions.

Product/Service Design and Development

One of the most influential factors in vertical integration decisions is the coordination requirements. Perhaps nowhere is this more evident than when considering new product or service development. There appears to be a significant interplay between the architecture of the product or service and the cost of coordination. The cost of coordination has been captured in the extant literature as the number of engineering hours required to bring a new product to market. It has been suggested in the literature that tightly coupled or integrated product designs require higher levels of coordination and, therefore, may not be appropriate for external sourcing (Anderson and Parker, 2002). These findings are consistent with another set of literature that describes the difficulty and cost with which knowledge is shared between firms, particularly when this knowledge is tacit and less easily codified. Thus, it is imperative that firms develop a deep understanding of the coordination cost implications of various sourcing alternatives. This consideration may not be separable from key product and process architecture decisions.

Governmental and Political Expenses

Particularly if considering international sourcing alternatives, it is important that the decision makers develop a complete understanding of the costs involved with ensuring compliance with governmental laws, regulations, and even local business customs. Specifically, these costs could include but are not limited to legal expenses incurred to learn about a foreign location's laws and regulations, lobbying efforts, travel, taxation, tariffs, local content obligations, quota systems, and others. Tariff rates in developed countries are typically less than 10 percent but can be much higher for lesser-developed nations and for certain products such as agriculture. These environmental parameters may be highly dynamic, requiring analysts to be "on the ground" and well connected to develop a deep understanding of the evolving environment. Some multinational corporations with large international exposures have large departments dedicated to assessing and managing political risks around the globe.

Supply Chain Risk Management

A report by Cranfield University to the Department for Transport in England recognized outsourcing as one of the key factors driving increased levels of supply chain risk (Christopher, 2002). The idea of risk management should underlie all of the previously discussed cost categories. However, there are some costs that are more directly tied to the management of risk in the supply chain. Broadly, risk can be defined as a measure of the probability and severity of adverse effects. One can divide risk management into four iterative phases: (1) risk assessment, (2) risk mitigation, (3) risk monitoring, and (4) contingency planning. Each of these phases has associated costs that will vary depending on the specific sourcing decision. Risk assessment involves answering three questions: (1) What adverse events could happen? (2) What is the probability of these events happening? and (3) What is the financial impact if these events occur? Risk mitigation involves a detailed analysis of what can be done to reduce or eliminate the probability and severity of these adverse events while also considering the trade-offs involved. Managers must learn to tailor appropriate risk mitigation strategies to a particular situation. It is crucial to fully appreciate these possible financial uncertainties when considering outsourcing opportunities, for they could fundamentally impact the attractiveness of alternatives. Risk monitoring involves continuously evaluating supply chain conditions so that potential issues may be avoided or at least lessened by being more proactive. Best practices for monitoring include regular supplier financial assessments, use of supplier scorecards, use of advanced tracking technology such as RFID, increased supply chain visibility at second- and third-tier sources, as well as other practices (Elkins et al., 2005). The final phase is contingency planning. More than likely it will be impossible to eliminate all risks associated with a sourcing alternative and, thus, contingency plans need to be put into place that detail early warning detection systems, internal and external actions upon recognition, and so forth. This comprehensive risk management approach will introduce costs that are different for various sourcing alternatives because the different options will carry with them different types and sizes of risks. Some specific costs associated with risk management could include insurance, dedicated risk management personnel, financial hedging, and operations hedging.

Miscellaneous Financial Considerations

A final consideration for evaluating the costs of each sourcing alternative is learning and the appropriation of its benefits. The idea that firms tend to improve their cost position with cumulative volume and engineering time has been well established. A commonly cited source of financial benefit from outsourcing is the vendor's better economies of scale. External specialists often enjoy more efficient use of assets from being able to pool the less than perfectly correlated demands of multiple customers. Also, external suppliers can aggregate the demands of their multiple customers, which allows them to offer immediate cost benefits and to travel more quickly down the learning curve than can a firm with its individual demand alone. This is particularly true in industries with relatively standardized processes such as telecommunications equipment and consumer electronics. However, the buying firm also needs to consider what portion of the cost improvement they will be able to appropriate if they decide to outsource. This may be determined by competitive conditions in the supply market, power structures, and the overall threat of opportunistic behavior by the external supplier. These considerations have been found to have the potential to greatly impact the sourcing decision. It is critical that firms also consider their internal ability to improve, by means of innovative work, practices such as total quality management, lean production, and others. If a firm can generate nearly equal financial improvement through internal efforts as would be realized with outsourcing, then the business case may need to be called into question. According to a Deloitte study, many organizations could realize incremental savings on the order of 20–30 percent of direct labor from implementing innovative programs such as lean production (Doig et al., 2001).

This section served to develop a comprehensive overview of the multitude of factors that can materially impact the financial viability of outsourcing yet are often overlooked in developing the business case for outsourcing.

CORE COMPETENCIES

A concept very similar to the resource-based view of the firm is that of core competencies. Core competencies are the collective learning in an organization. The core competency concept is especially concerned with how to coordinate diverse production skills and integrate multiple streams of technology. Organizations continuously innovate in order to attract customers and increase revenues and market share with products and services. Core competencies are unique combinations of thought, focus, and implementation methodologies. Most organizations have numerous capabilities. The organization must have a set of *core* capabilities that ensure survival in a competitive marketplace. Core competencies are only built and learned over the long term. Alternatively, outsourcing can provide short-term competitive benefits but does not contribute significantly to developing "people-embodied" skills for a sustainable advantage. This implies that upon outsourcing, a firm is accepting a position of competitive parity for the activity in question. Organizations should concentrate on the development of a few core competencies and strategically outsource noncore activities (Quinn and Hilmer, 1994). Outsourcing core activities is the beginning of the end of the existence for any organization. Thus, the concept of core competencies along with the resource-based view of the organization provides the basis for the assertion that in considering outsourcing, the decision-making team must have a thorough understanding of *core and noncore capabilities* and how they relate to an organization's competitive advantage.

OUTSOURCING TRENDS

Outsourcing is not immune to the effects of economic volatility; however, in an economic downturn, internal and external costs will become the primary basis for considering the outsourcing business case.

At the time of this writing, things look gloomy for the global economy; however, the outsourcing market represents a dichotomy: on the downside, organizations' cost-cutting outsourcing strategies may negatively impact market growth, but the upside is that outsourcing will be adopted by more organizations to help them meet their competitive challenges. In a financially challenged economic environment, the knowledgeable buyer and provider will have a competitive advantage. The potential for outsourcing to address immediate cost pressures as well as long-term recovery goals will be unprecedented. However, only organizations that are diligent about understanding and avoiding the pitfalls of cost-focused outsourcing and that apply total business-outcome–focused outsourcing will be successful. Many outsourcing buyers must continuously reevaluate their contracts to improve efficiency and costs. This will affect provider selection and retention, how services are or will be delivered, delivery location, and contract pricing. Beyond the drivers of efficiency and cost, however, many organizations also will experience core business changes as a result of repercussions of a worldwide economic crisis.

For organizations that are outsourcing, contract terms may be altered in response to corporate change: Some will downsize, others will expand, acquisition and divestiture will impact others, and still others will cease to exist. Many organizations that are not outsourcing will consider or move aggressively to outsource their IT or business processes to focus on their *core business*. Outsourcing buyers and providers must be attentive to contract issues to ensure a certain level of flexibility, since business change is inevitable.

According to Gartner, in 2008, approximately 76 percent of announced outsourcing contracts represented new deals; the remaining percentage was a combination of contract extensions, expansions, or renewals. Almost one-quarter of these contracts were a continuation of outsourcing with an incumbent provider. Key providers are basically betting their future on forming enduring, long-lasting relationships. In uncertain economic times, outsourcing relationships can prove (and test) the durability of relationships and the outsourcing value proposition.[1]

ELEMENTS OF STRATEGIC OUTSOURCING

The following are the suggested steps to successful outsourcing:

1. Strategic evaluation
2. Financial evaluation
3. Supplier selection and contracting
4. Transition to external sourcing model
5. Managing relationships

These steps are based on the model given in Figure 9.1. These steps can and should be modified to fit the specific organization and outsourcing objectives. As can be seen from Figure 9.1, these steps are highly interrelated. The nature of the various steps is important in order to achieve continuous improvement and communication between the required outsourcing activities. Concurrent relationships also reduce the implementation cycle time. It is important to assign different team members to implement each of the steps. It is also important to assign members to more than one step in the process in order to enhance communication and information flows. Figure 9.2 illustrates the concurrency concept.

Strategic Evaluation

Outsourcing is the act of reversing a previous decision to "make" or perform a particular function internally. As outsourcing is closely related to the traditional make-or-buy decision, a discussion of the make-or-buy decision will be helpful in analyzing what may or may not be good strategic candidates for outsourcing. The first step in the make-or-buy decision is to understand the strategic importance (value) of the activity or system.

Initially, outsourcing decisions predominantly involved standardized processes, commoditized products, and activities of extremely low strategic value. However, firms are increasingly considering more strategic "capabilities" for outsourcing, making the strategic evaluation much more complex. They discourage firms from making outsourcing decisions piecemeal, but rather encourage organizations to make them as part of a comprehensive sourcing strategy.

Financial Evaluation

Along with performing a complete strategic evaluation of a potential outsourcing effort, it is also critical to ensure that outsourcing makes short- and long-term

[1] www.gartner.com.

FIGURE 9.2
The Strategic Outsourcing Process

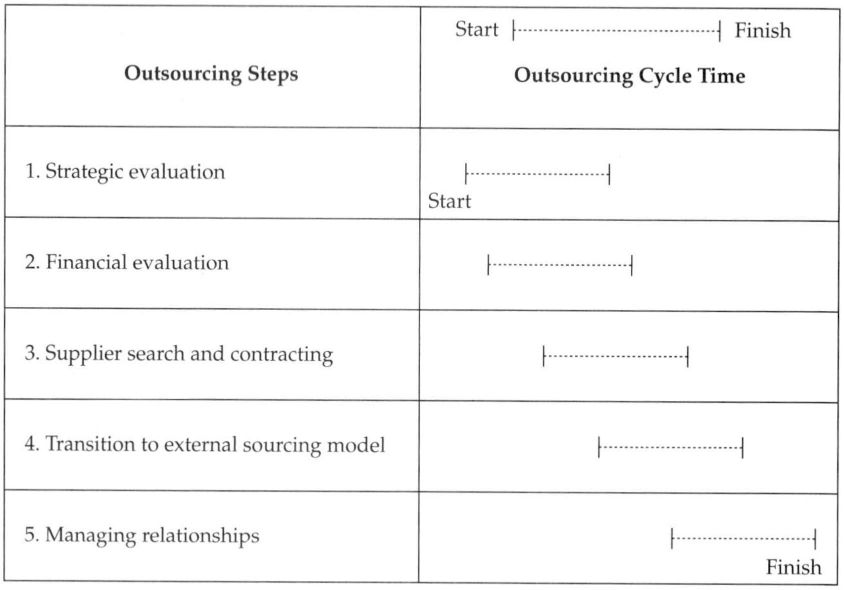

financial sense as well. In terms of the 10 financial categories discussed above, it should be noted that they are not necessarily mutually exclusive and independent constructs, but rather may be significantly interrelated. Furthermore, one may notice that some of the considerations are only pertinent in certain circumstances. For instance, many of the costs are only relevant when considering international sourcing alternatives or are only pertinent when considering the outsourcing of a manufacturing activity as opposed to a business process such as accounting, human resources, information technology, and so forth.

Supplier Selection and Contract Development

Supplier Selection

Potential outsourcing suppliers must be identified and investigated. One way to identify and investigate a potential supplier is for the buying firm to compile supplier profiles for each potential supplier. These profiles should include items such as key management contacts, a company overview, SWOT (Strengths, Weaknesses, Opportunities, Threats) analysis, Porter's five key financial figures, information on current contracts, "owners" of the relationship within the firm, and an organizational chart. (See profile examples in Figures 8.3a, 8.3b, 8.3c.) While the process of compiling these profiles should be owned by the outsourcing project team, the content of the profiles should be shared and evaluated by all related business functions within the buying firm. Functional evaluation of the content will ensure that all impacted areas within the buying firm will have input into the outsourcing process. This method also ensures that the outsourcing project team is knowledgeable about all potential suppliers and aware of how they are rated by each function within the buying firm. In addition to the supplier profiles, the buying organization should clearly establish expectations for the potential suppliers and discuss the *scope of work* and the *appropriate pricing* for the outsourcing activity.

Contract Development

The outsourcing alliance must arrive at an enforceable contract. The contract is the key to effective governance of the relationship between the two independent firms. The language of the contract must include *at a minimum* the following components:

- A clearly defined scope of work and elements of the processes to be supplied.
- An agreed-upon approximate price for each aspect of what is being supplied.
- An understanding of an acceptable level of flexibility as circumstances and requirements change.
- Consideration of a short-term contract with provisions for extensions and renegotiations.
- Ground rules that encourage relationship and alliance maintenance.
- Determination of a means for measuring performance for each aspect of the agreement.

Unfortunately, it is often observed, particularly in unpredictable environments, that it is nearly impossible, at least impractical, to construct a contract that fully addresses all possible states of nature and contingencies. When a system design is complex (many tightly coupled or technologically novel components), the ability to effectively contract with an independent provider (supplier) becomes untenable.

When a completely precise and legally binding contract is lacking, certain parties to the agreement may be enticed to act in a manner that is potentially counter to the objectives of the other party. One such risk is that of opportunistic renegotiation, especially when one party has made relationship-specific investments. The outsourcing supplier may shirk their responsibilities even if the contract is complete. This is due to incentive misalignment coupled with difficulty in *measuring* or monitoring the supplier's performance or efforts. While contractual incompleteness and misaligned interests can make maintaining a healthy relationship challenging, it has been recognized that spending the extra time to make sure the contract is precisely developed up front can save substantial costs and time down the road. The contract should be treated like a prenuptial agreement by both parties. Outsourcing arrangements form alliances, not partnerships. Thus, while having a perfectly complete contract may not be feasible, making it as inclusive as possible is critical. This often involves using a cross-functional team that includes external experts, experienced employees, and members of senior management.

Perhaps the most widely suggested means of improving goal alignment is to have clear, easy-to-understand roles and responsibilities. A critical part of this is having a contract with precise performance or service level agreements along with penalty and reward clauses. This fundamentally must begin with a clear understanding of existing performance and that which is possible, which often requires benchmarking.

It is important to make the contract as complete as possible, yet due to the uncertainty that surrounds most outsourcing efforts as well as the lack of clairvoyance by decision makers, contracts also must be flexible. In order to enhance flexibility, a shorter contract length is suggested. Further, many stipulate that contracts must clearly outline a dispute resolution process for those situations when actual operating conditions deviate significantly from contract provisions. Reversibility clauses in the contract are sometimes used to spell out the transfer of human and physical resources should the relationship come to an end. These clauses are argued to ease supplier switching or reinternalizing efforts.

A final contractual element that is posited to improve outsourcing efforts is the treatment of transferred employees. In addition to reversibility clauses, it also has been suggested that contracts should include clauses that protect transferred employees or stipulate guidelines as to their treatment. These clauses can include items such as rules for employee retention, benefits, transfer to other accounts, and so on. It is the objective of these employee-related contractual items to minimize the service impact to the organization as well as enhance the perception of procedural equity in the eyes of the impacted associates.

While hardly any contract can be airtight in its precision, following the prescriptions outlined in this section can ensure that the contract is as effective as possible. Recognizing the reality of contractual incompleteness, however, highlights the need for effective relationship management. For a more comprehensive discussion of contracts, see Chapter 3.

Transition to External Sourcing Model

The success of the outsourcing initiative depends heavily on the implementation effort beginning with the contract execution to the transfer of the agreed-upon activities and resources. The buying and selling organizations must follow the specific roles outlined in the contract. The buying organization also must appoint a relationship manager. The relationship manager and the suppliers must merge their independent plans into one consensus plan. The consensus transition plan must include, at a minimum, the following:

- Communication criteria: How should the external initiatives be communicated to the affected and unaffected employees?
- Personnel criteria: What packages will be offered to affected and unaffected employees?
- Transition criteria: When will the activities and resources be moved to the supplying organization?

Communication Criteria

The goal of effective communication is to avoid misinformation and to control the rumor mill. Prior to developing the outsourcing project team, the CEO should explain the outsourcing decision to all employees. The initial announcement to the employees should be thorough and convincing. After the contract has been signed, the CEO should meet with the affected employees. The announcement to the affected employees should

- State that the contract has been signed and awarded to the supplying firm.
- Discuss how severance packages will be offered to affected employees.
- Conduct an extensive question-and-answer session.

Personnel Criteria

Outsourcing often has a profound effect on employees. A recent study found that 38 percent of firms that would classify their outsourcing effort as "failed" admitted to overlooking personnel issues as opposed to only 20 percent of firms who classified their efforts as "successful" (Barthélemy, 2001). This observation underscores the importance of considering the management and impact to internal staff when making outsourcing decisions. Effective management of employee-related concerns is crucial when outsourcing, particularly considering the often negative perceptions that many employees have about outsourcing. Being laid off as a result of outsourcing has clear economic and emotional implications for victims and the organizations that must manage these situations. However, being transferred to the service provider also has consequences that must be addressed. Transferring employees increases the level of uncertainty that surrounds their career prospects with their new employer. Transferring employees to the supplier can have an adverse impact on transferred employee morale, productivity, and turnover. This not only has direct cost implications but also can negatively affect the provider's ability to provide high-quality service. In 2004, 500 truck drivers were surveyed, 80 percent of whom had been transferred to an external service provider as part of a transportation outsourcing initiative (Logan et al., 2004). The results indicated that employees who were highly satisfied and involved (perception that one's job represents a portion of who one is) pre-outsourcing expressed a statistically significant decrease in satisfaction after being transferred to the external provider. Additionally, those who were highly involved pre-outsourcing expressed a significantly higher intent to exit the external provider. This could manifest itself in higher turnover at the external service provider and perhaps difficulty in providing efficient and effective services.

By observing their peers being transferred or laid off, remaining employees may call into question the organization's commitment to them and their risk of being impacted in a similar manner in the future. Employees perceive that their existing psychological contract with their employer has been fundamentally altered, which can lead to a drop in their commitment to the organization, a reduction in job satisfaction, and lower productivity.

While it is clear that there are significant personnel implications of outsourcing given the frequent occurrence of downsizing (i.e., layoffs) and employee transfer, this direct relationship has been relatively neglected in the business literature.

A fundamental element of creating the perception of procedural and interpersonal justice is communication. Specifically, organizations need to communicate early and clearly to employees about why the decision has been made. This aspect of procedural and interpersonal justice has received wide empirical support as it relates to layoffs or downsizing decisions.

A second element that impacts the perceived equity of a decision is the involvement or "voice" of all interested parties. It is important to make sure that all stakeholders feel as though their interests were represented and considered in making the decision.

It is crucial to treat employees (both survivors and those directly impacted) with respect and dignity during the decision-making and implementation process. Some have noted that smooth outsourcing efforts have made explicit attempts to assist impacted employees and to protect those who are transferred to the provider or supplier.

Finally, it has been recognized that providing the retained team with new skills so they may be effective in their new role is important. Retained employees need to be trained to enhance their "lateral" skills such as relationship management, negotiation, and consensus building. Failing to appreciate these concerns and proactively manage them will have an adverse impact on the outsourcing engagement.

Transition Criteria

The relationship managers for both entities should revisit the list of activities outlined in the project management schedule. The activities are implemented either sequentially or concurrently. Some of the highlights for implementation follow:

1. An organization meeting should be conducted for employees moving from the buying firm to the supplier's organization.
2. A meeting with the buying firm's manager whose activities are being outsourced should be conducted onsite at the new location.
3. A plan should be generated to address the issues involved in transferring significant physical assets. There should be a specific third-party agreement in the contract to accomplish the physical movement and acquisition of the equipment.

The transition process will never be flawless. A high level of professionalism is required for a successful relationship between the alliance parties.

Relationship Management

In order to effectively cultivate the relationship, the buying organization should be active in monitoring and evaluating performance and solving problems. The original contract establishes the performance measures, deliverables, due dates, and expected supplier requirements. Performance measurement is the cornerstone of the buyer–supplier relationship. Without measurement, there is no control. Without control, there can be no relationship to manage. The buyer and supplier relationship managers should develop and execute the reporting system established in the contract. The performance report should be designed to compare the actual performance to the contractual standards. An example report is given in Table 9.2.

Knight 1965 [1921] defined the difference between risk and uncertainty: Risk is measurable, but uncertainty cannot be measured. Therefore, buyers outsourcing risks can be defined as BOR = PA × NC, where BOR = buyers outsourcing risks, PA = the probability that an adverse event will occur, and NC = negative consequences if the adverse event occurs, assuming that each of the adverse events is independent.

Outsourcing risks include breaches in intellectual property, provider shirking, and opportunistic renegotiation. The combination of contractual incompleteness, asset specificity, and uncertainty gives rise to these risks when firms pursue external sourcing. Outsourcing organizations must have a clear understanding of true supplier intentions.

TABLE 9.2
Sample Performance Report, September 25, 2012

Performance Measures	Weight	Performance Standard	2009 Actual	2009 Variance	2008 Actual	2008 Variance	2007 Actual	2007 Variance
Number of outputs	0.1	10000	10000	0.00%	9910	−0.09%	9820	−0.18%
Number of errors	0.4	10	45	−140.00%	15	−20.00%	70	−240.00%
Number of on-time deliveries	0.2	50	49	−0.40%	43	−2.80%	39	−4.40%
Number of days-cycle time	0.2	5	4	4.00%	6	−4.00%	8	−12.00%
Number of outputs per employee	0.1	100	105	0.50%	93	−0.70%	82	−1.80%

Traditional thinking about the most appropriate form of governance has cast the decision as somewhat of a dichotomous choice between hierarchy (i.e., internal sourcing) and market (i.e., external sources). Prior works have developed the image of market governance as an arm's length relationship between the customer and the supplier organization. However, in the past few decades, due largely to the observation of Japanese-style supply chain relationships, we have come to see that many organizations effectively pursue a governance form that is neither purely hierarchical nor a purely arm's-length market mechanism. This hybrid governance form recognizes the inherent limitations, as well as the advantages, of both of these extreme forms. It seeks to realize the control, goal alignment, and improved coordination associated with retaining an activity internally, while also benefiting from the potentially superior skills and cost position of specialized, external organizations. In this environment, the relationship is more of a long-term, collaborative partnership rather than a short-term, focused opportunistic arrangement. In an evaluation of the automotive industry, trust and goodwill over a prolonged period and the investment in *co*-specialized assets led to a reduction in transaction costs (Prahinski and Benton, 2004). Further, the greater social capital leads to improved dissemination of information and reduced motivation for opportunistic behavior. Social capital is the sum of the actual and potential resources embedded within, available through, and derived from the network of relationships possessed by an individual or social unit. Collaborative relationships can improve learning and control opportunism. See Handley and Benton (2013).

Thus, it appears that through the development of mutually beneficial long-term relationships with service providers, firms can, to a large extent, mitigate many of the traditional concerns with external sourcing while still realizing many of the proclaimed benefits.

For these long-term relationships to work, it initially requires a strong commitment from both parties. Although these longer-term relationships can bear significant benefits for the customer and service provider, the road will not always be a smooth one. Without commitment from both leadership teams, it would be easy to regress into traditional adversarial thinking. The sharing of timely, rich, and often proprietary information is required for building trust between the organizations. Information sharing also allows for more effective planning and execution. Information exchange in these deep relationships goes beyond simple transactional information exchange to include sharing demand forecasts, detailed cost information, new product plans, strategic changes, and other information.

Closely related to rich information exchange is the idea that true buyer–supplier partnerships work collaboratively in many areas. While the idea of information sharing may connote one party providing information to the other, collaboration entails joint effort by the organizations. Ultimately, people and organizations tend to act in their own best interests. Thus, it is imperative for the outsourcing alliances that the parties tie their destinies together. Equitable distribution of pain and gain will ultimately lead to enhanced partnership performance. Along with having a contract that defines performance incentives by means of penalty and reward structures, the relationship also must be able to work through unforeseen conditions in a productive manner. Put differently, it is necessary for the outsourcing alliances to have a constructive and flexible change management and dispute resolution process (Benton and Maloni, 2005).

A final key element of an effective buyer–supplier relationship is the performance evaluation. There is a strong statistical relationship between a collaborative communication strategy for supplier performance evaluations and the strength of the buyer–supplier relationship, which subsequently influences the supplier's commitment and performance (Prahinski and Benton, 2004). In the Prahinski and Benton study, collaborative communication was characterized as being formal, providing opportunities for feedback and indirect influence (evaluation, certification, recognition, training, etc.). It appears clear that effective buyer–supplier relationships should include a formalized procedure for communicating the buyer's expectations and evaluating the supplier's performance.

Summary

Outsourcing is the complete transfer of a business process that has been traditionally operated and managed internally to an independently owned external service provider. A complete transfer means that the people, facilities, equipment, technology, and other assets are no longer maintained once the business process is outsourced. Strategic outsourcing has rapidly become the building block for globalization. Fueled by the Internet, outsourcing has evolved into the most pervasive business paradigm in the past 50 years.

The anticipated economic implications of outsourcing initiatives are complex. There are significant hidden outsourcing costs that are sometimes not accounted for. The motivation for outsourcing is commonly driven by the savings in direct labor and other tangible operating costs. Yet, significant hidden costs are often overlooked when preparing a financial business case for outsourcing. Hidden costs include relationship management costs, quality costs, implementation- or transition-related expenses, and internal coordination costs among others. If not considered, these financial implications can eat away at the anticipated gains from outsourcing.

Despite the popularity of outsourcing in practice, several studies have noted that outsourcing organizations underestimate the costs and complexities associated with managing the inter-firm relationship. These difficulties result in a relatively large proportion of firms expressing disappointment with the financial outcomes of their outsourcing initiatives.

Discussion Questions

1. What is outsourcing?
2. Why do firms outsource business processes?
3. How is outsourcing similar to, or different from, contracting, make versus buy, and joint venturing?
4. List eight benefits of outsourcing.
5. What are some of the strategic benefits of outsourcing?
6. Discuss in detail three "hidden costs" of outsourcing.
7. How does supply chain risk management relate to outsourcing?
8. Discuss in detail what is meant by "core competence."
9. What are the elements of strategic outsourcing?

Suggested Cases

Microfuse, Inc.
Eastern Waves, Inc.
Great Lakes University

References

Alexander, M., and D. Young. "Outsourcing: Where's the Value?" *Long Range Planning* 29, no. 5 (1996), pp. 728–30.

Anderson, E. G., and G. G. Parker. "The Effect of Learning on the Make/Buy Decision." *Production & Operations Management* 11, no. 3 (2002), pp. 313–39.

Baron, A. "The People Impact of Outsourcing." *Strategic Communication Management* 9, no. 1 (2005), p. 13.

Barthélemy, J. "The Hidden Costs of IT Outsourcing." *Sloan Management Review* 42, no. 3 (2001), pp. 60–69.

Barthélemy, J. "The Seven Deadly Sins of Outsourcing." *Academy of Management Executive* 17, no. 2 (2003), pp. 87–98.

Benton, W. C., and M. Maloni. "The Influence of Power Driven Buyer/Seller Relationships on Supply Chain Satisfaction." *Journal of Operations Management* 23, no. 1 (2005), pp. 1–22.

Christopher, M. "Supply Chain Vulnerability." *Executive Report on Behalf of: Department for Transport, Local Government and the Regions*, pp. 1–7. Bedford, UK: Cranfield University, School of Management, 2002.

Couto, V., K. Dehoff, V. Sehgal, and J. Weinberg. "The Five Fallacies of Automotive Offshoring: Overcoming the Lingering Obstacles to Offshore BPO and Engineering Services." Booz Allen Hamilton report, 2006.

Disher, C., D. Prosko, and E. Trombetti. "Next Generation Outsourcing: Ensuring Success after Signing the Deal." Booz Allen Hamilton report, 2005.

Doig, S. J., R. C. Ritter, K. Speckhals, and D. Woolson. "Has Outsourcing Gone Too Far?" *McKinsey Quarterly* (2001), pp. 24–37.

Elkins, D., R. B. Handfield, J. Blackhurst, and C. W. Craighead. "18 Ways to Guard against Disruption." *Supply Chain Management Review* 9, no. 1 (2005), pp. 46–53.

Gottfredson, M., R. Puryear, and S. Phillips. "Strategic Sourcing from Periphery to the Core." *Harvard Business Review* 83, no. 2 (2005), pp. 132–39.

Handley, S. M., and W. C. Benton Jr. "Unlocking the Business Outsourcing Process Model." *Journal of Operations Management* 27, no. 5 (2009), pp. 344–61.

Handley, S. M., and W. C. Benton. "The Influence of Task- and Location-Specific Complexity of the Control and Coordination Costs in Global Outsourcing Relationships." *Journal of Operations Management* (online) (2013).

International Association of Outsourcing Professionals (IAOP). www.outsourcingprofessional.org/firmbulder/articles/34/184/928 (2007).

Kakabadse, A., and N. Kakabadse. "Outsourcing: Current and Future Trends." *Thunderbird International Business Review* 47, no. 2 (2005), pp. 183–204.

Khosrowpour, M., and G. H. Subramanian. "Managing Information Technology with Outsourcing: An Assessment of Employee Perceptions." *Journal of Applied Business Research* 12, no. 3 (1996), pp. 85–96.

Knight. *Risk, Uncertainty and Profit*. New York: Harper and Row, 1965 [1921].

Landis, K. M., S. Mishra, and K. Porrello. "Calling a Change in the Outsourcing Market: The Realities for the World's Largest Organizations." Deloitte Consulting report, 2005.

Logan, M. S., K. Faught, and D. C. Ganster. "Outsourcing a Satisfied and Committed Workforce: A Trucking Industry Case Study." *International Journal of Human Resource Management* 15, no. 1 (2004), pp. 147–62.

Masten, S. E., J. W. Meehan, and E. A. Snyder. "Vertical Integration in the U.S. Auto Industry." *Journal of Economic Behavior and Organization* 12 (1989), pp. 265–73.

Prahinski, C., and W. C. Benton. "Supplier Evaluations: Communication Strategies to Improve Supplier Performance." *Journal of Operations Management* 22, no. 1 (2004), pp. 39–62.

Quinn, J. B., and F. G. Hilmer. "Strategic Outsourcing." *Sloan Management Review* 35, no. 4 (1994), pp. 43–55.

Chapter Ten

Global Sourcing

Learning Objectives

1. Identify what factors/forces increase foreign trade.
2. Know the basics of global sourcing.
3. Describe how total costs are determined.
4. Understand the hidden costs of global sourcing.
5. List the quantitative and qualitative aspects of global sourcing.
6. Describe how to critically analyze various global sourcing alternatives.
7. Describe how to effectively use foreign trade zones.
8. Know how to negotiate in different countries.

INTRODUCTION

The total level of global purchases has increased significantly for the top 20 U.S. trading partners. Recent foreign purchases of manufactured goods and services are shown in Tables 10.1a and 10.1b.

The largest exporter to the United States is China. In 2011, the United States imported $399,362 billion in goods from China. Many large manufacturing and retail companies have set up purchasing centers in China to drive their global supply chains. Walmart, Microsoft, Motorola, and General Electric are some of the largest companies that have established purchasing centers in China. If a company is competitive in the furniture, toy, appliances, and consumer electronics industries, there is a high probability that the products were made in China. Chinese price quotes are also used as leverage to create lower prices against price quotes from domestic suppliers.

Purchasing departments play a major role in keeping material costs down. Many firms rely on global sourcing to remain competitive and survive in today's competitive markets. Often this strategy is taken as an initiative by a firm in order to achieve an advantage over its competition or else it is a reaction to other firms who already use global sourcing.

As an example, outsourcing is currently perceived as key to automotive suppliers' survival and is being driven by consumers in the price-pressured global market. Even as different buying organizations take different positions on the overall merit of global outsourcing, the reports and discussions nevertheless have one theme in common. The focus has been on a single aspect of outsourcing: the migration of jobs and, in particular, the outsourcing of *white-collar jobs*. A few countries, notably

TABLE 10.1a Top U.S. Trade Partners

Ranked by 2011 U.S. Total Export Value for Goods (in millions of U.S. dollars)

		Exports						Imports					
Rank	Country	2010	2011	% Change	May 2011	May 2012	% Change	2010	2011	% Change	May 2011	May 2012	% Change
1	Canada	249,105	280,890	12.8%	115,046	121,692	5.8%	277,647	315,347	13.6%	129,216	137,888	6.7%
2	Mexico	163,473	198,378	21.4%	79,062	88,925	12.5%	229,908	262,864	14.3%	106,259	116,913	10.0%
3	China	91,881	103,939	13.1%	41,808	44,318	6.0%	364,944	399,362	9.4%	148,590	161,974	9.0%
4	Japan	60,486	65,706	8.6%	27,014	28,684	6.2%	120,545	128,925	7.0%	49,405	61,771	25.0%
5	United Kingdom	48,414	55,881	15.4%	22,599	24,371	7.8%	49,775	51,236	2.9%	20,590	22,900	11.2%
6	Germany	48,161	49,156	2.1%	20,203	20,924	3.6%	82,429	98,663	19.7%	38,981	43,670	12.0%
7	Korea	38,846	43,415	11.8%	18,030	18,576	3.0%	48,875	56,661	15.9%	22,849	24,692	8.1%
8	Brazil	35,425	42,944	21.2%	16,751	17,269	3.1%	23,958	31,736	32.5%	11,649	14,326	23.0%
9	Netherlands	34,939	42,351	21.2%	17,289	16,564	−4.2%	19,055	23,451	23.1%	9,560	9,605	0.5%
10	Hong Kong	26,570	36,449	37.2%	13,759	16,226	17.9%	4,296	4,401	2.4%	1,815	1,893	4.3%
11	Singapore	29,017	31,223	7.6%	12,308	12,412	0.8%	17,427	19,113	9.7%	7,892	8,379	6.2%
12	Belgium	25,456	29,899	17.5%	12,082	12,590	4.2%	15,552	17,431	12.1%	7,647	7,239	−5.3%
13	France	26,969	27,803	3.1%	12,141	13,106	7.9%	38,355	40,040	4.4%	16,197	16,989	4.9%
14	Australia	21,798	27,542	26.4%	9,977	12,547	25.8%	8,583	10,241	19.3%	3,923	3,914	−0.2%
15	Taiwan	26,043	25,889	−0.6%	11,452	10,008	−12.6%	35,846	41,405	15.5%	16,721	15,537	−7.1%
16	Switzerland	20,687	24,425	18.1%	9,422	11,769	24.9%	19,136	24,357	27.3%	10,047	11,185	11.3%
17	India	19,250	21,501	11.7%	8,401	8,369	−0.4%	29,533	36,153	22.4%	14,641	16,409	12.1%
18	Italy	14,219	16,007	12.6%	6,791	7,164	5.5%	28,505	33,950	19.1%	13,630	14,865	9.1%
19	Chile	10,905	15,986	46.6%	6,231	7,586	21.7%	7,009	9,074	29.5%	4,435	4,197	−5.4%
20	United Arab Emirates	11,673	15,900	36.2%	5,538	8,726	57.6%	1,145	2,440	113.0%	896	1,021	13.9%
21	Turkey	10,546	14,657	39.0%	6,496	5,601	−13.8%	4,207	5,220	24.1%	2,195	2,735	24.6%
22	Colombia	12,069	14,320	18.7%	5,799	6,372	9.9%	15,659	23,113	47.6%	9,214	10,918	18.5%
23	Malaysia	14,080	14,246	1.2%	6,244	5,225	−16.3%	25,900	25,777	−0.5%	10,522	10,447	−0.7%
24	Israel	11,294	13,936	23.4%	5,839	5,751	−1.5%	20,982	23,039	9.8%	9,692	9,221	−4.9%
25	Saudi Arabia	11,556	13,830	19.7%	5,393	7,199	33.5%	31,413	47,476	51.1%	16,719	25,601	53.1%
26	Venezuela	10,649	12,343	15.9%	4,531	6,436	42.1%	32,707	43,256	32.3%	18,269	16,809	−8.0%
27	Thailand	8,977	10,899	21.4%	4,589	4,302	−6.3%	22,693	24,830	9.4%	10,079	10,549	4.7%
28	Spain	10,178	10,849	6.6%	4,602	4,101	−10.9%	8,553	11,017	28.8%	4,583	4,736	3.3%
29	Argentina	7,395	9,917	34.1%	3,659	4,260	16.4%	3,803	4,502	18.4%	1,797	1,781	−0.9%
30	Peru	6,754	8,336	23.4%	3,424	3,744	9.4%	5,057	6,605	30.6%	2,509	2,465	−1.8%
-	EU-27	239,583	268,474	12.1%	110,676	113,945	3.0%	319,195	368,355	15.4%	149,282	157,396	5.4%
-	TPP	89,207	105,398	18.2%	41,415	44,639	7.8%	81,618	91,483	12.1%	37,156	38,660	4.0%
Top 30 total		1,106,816	1,278,617	15.5%	516,481	554,814	7.4%	1,593,498	1,821,685	14.3%	720,521	790,625	9.7%
World merchandise total		1,278,263	1,480,432	15.8%	599,620	640,521	6.8%	1,913,160	2,207,824	15.4%	876,583	940,663	7.3%
Top 30% share		86.6%	86.4%	—	86.1%	86.6%	—	83.3%	82.5%	—	82.2%	84.0%	—
U.S. services trade		553,603	605,961	9.5%	248,733	258,829	4.1%	403,216	427,428	6.0%	174,231	185,945	6.7%
U.S. total trade*		1,842,485	2,103,367	14.2%	860,146	908,746	5.7%	2,337,222	2,663,247	13.9%	1,088,598	1,159,024	6.5%

*U.S. total trade is calculated on a seasonally adjusted balance of payments (BOP) basis; merchandise trade is calculated on a non-seasonally adjusted Census basis. Export figures are for total exports on a free alongside ship basis. Import figures are the customs value of U.S. general imports. Percent changes calculated using dollars.

Source: U.S. Department of Commerce, Census Bureau, Foreign Trade Division.

TABLE 10.1b **Top U.S. Trade Partners**

Ranked by 2011 U.S. Total Import Value for Goods (in millions of U.S. dollars)

		Imports						Exports					
Rank	Country	2010	2011	% Change	May 2011	May 2012	% Change	2010	2011	% Change	May 2011	May 2012	% Change
1	China	364,944	399,362	9.4%	148,590	161,974	9.0%	91,881	103,939	13.1%	41,808	44,318	6.0%
2	Canada	277,647	315,347	13.6%	129,216	137,888	6.7%	249,105	280,890	12.8%	115,046	121,692	5.8%
3	Mexico	229,908	262,864	14.3%	106,259	116,913	10.0%	163,473	198,378	21.4%	79,062	88,925	12.5%
4	Japan	120,545	128,925	7.0%	49,405	61,771	25.0%	60,486	65,706	8.6%	27,014	28,684	6.2%
5	Germany	82,429	98,663	19.7%	38,981	43,670	12.0%	48,161	49,156	2.1%	20,203	20,924	3.6%
6	Korea	48,875	56,661	15.9%	22,849	24,692	8.1%	38,846	43,415	11.8%	18,030	18,576	3.0%
7	United Kingdom	49,775	51,236	2.9%	20,590	22,900	11.2%	48,414	55,881	15.4%	22,599	24,371	7.8%
8	Saudi Arabia	31,413	47,476	51.1%	16,719	25,601	53.1%	11,556	13,830	19.7%	5,393	7,199	33.5%
9	Venezuela	32,707	43,256	32.3%	18,269	16,809	−8.0%	10,649	12,343	15.9%	4,531	6,436	42.1%
10	Taiwan	35,846	41,405	15.5%	16,721	15,537	−7.1%	26,043	25,889	−0.6%	11,452	10,008	−12.6%
11	France	38,355	40,040	4.4%	16,197	16,989	4.9%	26,969	27,803	3.1%	12,141	13,106	7.9%
12	Ireland	33,848	39,370	16.3%	15,989	14,528	−9.1%	7,276	7,644	5.1%	3,434	3,324	−3.2%
13	India	29,533	36,153	22.4%	14,641	16,409	12.1%	19,250	21,501	11.7%	8,401	8,369	−0.4%
14	Russia	25,691	34,619	34.8%	13,585	11,615	−14.5%	6,006	8,286	38.0%	3,219	4,290	33.3%
15	Italy	28,505	33,950	19.1%	13,630	14,865	9.1%	14,219	16,007	12.6%	6,791	7,164	5.5%
16	Nigeria	30,516	33,854	10.9%	14,723	8,287	−43.7%	4,068	4,912	20.8%	2,078	2,049	−1.4%
17	Brazil	23,958	31,736	32.5%	11,649	14,326	23.0%	35,425	42,944	21.2%	16,751	17,269	3.1%
18	Malaysia	25,900	25,777	−0.5%	10,522	10,447	−0.7%	14,080	14,246	1.2%	6,244	5,225	−16.3%
19	Thailand	22,693	24,830	9.4%	10,079	10,549	4.7%	8,977	10,899	21.4%	4,589	4,302	−6.3%
20	Switzerland	19,136	24,357	27.3%	10,047	11,185	11.3%	20,687	24,425	18.1%	9,422	11,769	24.9%
21	Netherlands	19,055	23,451	23.1%	9,560	9,605	0.5%	34,939	42,351	21.2%	17,289	16,564	−4.2%
22	Colombia	15,659	23,113	47.6%	9,214	10,918	18.5%	12,069	14,320	18.7%	5,799	6,372	9.9%
23	Israel	20,982	23,039	9.8%	9,692	9,221	−4.9%	11,294	13,936	23.4%	5,839	5,751	−1.5%
24	Singapore	17,427	19,113	9.7%	7,892	8,379	6.2%	29,017	31,223	7.6%	12,308	12,412	0.8%
25	Indonesia	16,478	19,111	16.0%	8,033	7,533	−6.2%	6,946	7,414	6.7%	3,074	3,415	11.1%
26	Vietnam	14,868	17,487	17.6%	6,492	7,746	19.3%	3,709	4,309	16.2%	1,781	1,764	−0.9%
27	Belgium	15,552	17,431	12.1%	7,647	7,239	−5.3%	25,456	29,899	17.5%	12,082	12,590	4.2%
28	Iraq	12,143	16,960	39.7%	5,776	7,060	22.2%	1,642	2,411	46.8%	1,170	805	−31.2%
29	Algeria	14,518	14,609	0.6%	7,587	5,132	−32.4%	1,195	1,595	33.5%	707	652	−7.8%
30	Angola	11,940	13,597	13.9%	4,705	4,615	−1.9%	1,294	1,502	16.1%	463	658	42.0%
-	EU-27	319,195	368,355	15.4%	149,282	157,396	5.4%	239.583	268,474	12.1%	110,676	113,945	3.0%
-	TPP	81,618	91,483	12.1%	37,156	38,660	4.0%	89.207	105,398	18.2%	41,415	44,639	7.8%
Top 30 total		1,710,846	1,957,793	14.4%	775,257	834,401	7.6%	1,033.131	1,177,054	13.9%	478,721	508,979	6.3%
World merchandise total		1,913,160	2,207,824	15.4%	876,583	940,663	7.3%	1,278,263	1,480,432	15.8%	599,620	640,521	6.8%
Top 30% share		89.4%	88.7%	—	88.4%	88.7%	—	80.8%	79.5%	—	79.8%	79.5%	—
U.S. services trade		403,216	427,428	6.0%	174,231	185,945	6.7%	553,603	605,961	9.5%	248,733	258,829	4.1%
U.S. total trade*		2,337,222	2,663,247	13.9%	1,088,598	1,159,024	6.5%	1,842,485	2,103,367	14.2%	860,146	908,746	5.7%

*U.S. total trade is calculated on a non-seasonally adjusted balance of payments (BOP) basis; merchandise trade is calculated on a non-seasonally adjusted Census basis. Export figures are for total exports on a free alongside ship basis. Import figures are the customs value of U.S. general imports. Percent changes calculated using dollars.

Source: U.S. Department of Commerce, Census Bureau, Foreign Trade Division.

India and China, are often targeted as the ones that are displacing American workers by offering cheap labor. The intense attention on the outflow of work to overseas locations has generated fear about which jobs or professions will be outsourced next.

COSTS OF GLOBAL SOURCING

The costs of global sourcing include some of the same costs found in domestic sourcing; there are also costs that are different. It is easiest to group these costs into the following categories: administrative, foreign, and common.

Administrative costs of foreign sourcing include identification, qualification, program development, travel, broker fees, and others that are not directly involved with the product. Some of these costs are common to both the domestic and international aspects of sourcing.

Exclusively foreign costs are those that would not be incurred if a domestic source were found. Examples of these costs are duty charges, customs fees, import fees, and currency exchange costs. Ocean and air freight could be mentioned, but these are part of the transportation costs of a good that would be incurred from any source. Many of these exclusively foreign costs are established by governments and are very difficult to avoid.

Finally, there are those costs that are common to both global and domestic sourcing. Direct labor and materials costs, lead-time costs, transportation costs, and inventory costs are a part of both domestic and offshore sourcing. Transportation costs, inventory costs, and lead-time costs tend to be higher when sourcing globally. On the other hand, labor and materials costs are often lower for firms in developing countries.

These costs must be covered when making sourcing decisions. Direct costs (labor and materials) are what make foreign products attractive. Exclusive foreign costs and administrative costs tend to be fixed in nature and are more often absorbed in the final sale of the product.

CURRENCY EXCHANGE RATES

One of the most important variables to consider is the exchange rate of currencies. Since predicting the fluctuation in currency markets is extremely difficult, foreign purchases may actually cost more or less than expected depending on the length of the contract. Depending on the performance and strength of the dollar, goods can cost American firms different amounts from what is expected. When the dollar is weak, the final cost of goods tends to be relatively more than originally agreed upon. When the dollar has a strong performance over the life of a contract, a firm can realize savings through the exchange rates. The effective exchange rate index composite for July 31, 2012, is presented in Table 10.2. The indicators are based on the relative normalized unit labor costs, relative value-added deflators, relative wholesale prices, and relative export unit values for the manufacturing segment.

Agreeing to terms of payments in U.S. dollars can eliminate risks for American firms. A second way is to use a risk-sharing contract, where payment fluctuates with exchange rates. This is usually a win-win situation for both firms.

TABLE 10.2 Exchange Rate Indexes

XE Quick Cross Rates — Add a currency ...

Auto-refresh 15x — 0 : 47

	USD	EUR	GBP	INR	AUD	CAD	ZAR	NZD	JPY
1 USD	1.00000	0.81289	0.63786	55.5551	0.95093	1.00205	8.25343	1.23373	78.1575
Inverse:	1.00000	1.23019	1.56773	0.01800	1.05160	0.99795	0.12116	0.81055	0.01279
1 EUR	1.23019	1.00000	0.78469	68.3431	1.16982	1.23271	10.1532	1.51772	96.1482
Inverse:	0.81289	1.00000	1.27439	0.01463	0.85483	0.81122	0.09849	0.65888	0.01040
1 GBP	1.56773	1.27439	1.00000	87.0954	1.49080	1.57095	12.9391	1.93416	122.529
Inverse:	0.63786	0.78469	1.00000	0.01148	0.67078	0.63656	0.07728	0.51702	0.00816

Mid-market rates: 2012-07-31 18:33 UTC

ORGANIZATIONAL AND BEHAVIORAL ISSUES

Firms can run into problems when global sourcing is introduced into their organizations. The resistance of the firm's buyers to learn to evaluate global sources is the reason for most of the problems. An attitude of "if it can't be bought here in the U.S.A., it can't be bought anywhere" can be seen with some purchasing departments. Many buyers simply do not want to learn about the other countries with whom they will be dealing. There are many ethical considerations that you must learn in order to be successful. This is one reason that many companies hire brokers to do their sourcing.

Lead times and delivery times can create problems also. Longer times can increase inventory needs and drive up carrying costs. The extended lead time also might push back the date at which a firm is able to introduce new products to the market.

A third problem companies face in global sourcing is communication. Many times there are delays and confusion in translations. Sending documents via couriers or the postal service is often time consuming and creates problems of obsolescence, more confusion, and late or even lost deliveries. However, there has been an increase in the use of the Internet to eliminate the time delay and confusion.

GLOBAL SOURCING AS A STRATEGIC SOURCING OPTION

Global sourcing is the trend of the future. Supply management is becoming very important to the survival of both American and offshore firms. In certain industries, using foreign suppliers can reduce costs, thus making a company more competitive. Firms in the apparel and electronics industries that do not use global sourcing could find themselves out of business when competing with firms that source globally. Global sourcing is in no way meant to completely replace domestic sources; however, it is a way to meet a competitor's challenge and achieve better value for goods all over the world.

Global sourcing is extremely complicated from a quantitative and qualitative viewpoint. The total cost of sourcing is perhaps the most important variable. Of course, the costs vary from firm to firm since the appropriate qualitative components of offshore sourcing must be considered. For instance, the associated qualitative risk profiles of (1) the impact of national interest, (2) the ethical

TABLE 10.3 Attributes of Sourcing

	Options Faced by a Typical Buying Firm			
	Offshore Option 1	**Offshore Option 2**	**Domestic Option**	**Mexico Maquiladora Option**
Positive attributes	• Politically stable • Pro-business government • Proven supplier • Ease of continuing sourcing supply • No tooling charges • Overall cost lower than domestic option	• Politically stable • Pro-business government • Good quality • Lowest-cost source	• Politically stable • Direct management control • Proven in-house ability • No exchange rate fluctuation • Lower transport costs • No duty • Shorter level time • Less pipeline inventory	• Lower labor costs • Increasingly favorable exchange rate • Lower transport costs than Taiwan • Low duty costs • Less pipeline inventories
Negative attributes	• Threat of trade retaliation from United States • Uneven-quality supplier • Less favorable exchange rate • Higher pipeline levels • Longer lead times than domestic option • Transaction costs • Duty costs • Impact on U.S. economy	• Threat of trade retaliation from United States • Unknown supplier reliability • Tooling costs necessary • Less favorable exchange rate • High transport costs • Transaction costs • Duty costs • Impact on U.S. economy	• High labor and tooling costs • Higher costs than foreign sources	• Unknown political stability • Variable government stance toward business • High tooling costs • Unknown reliability • Inexperienced workforce • Transaction costs • Impact on U.S. economy

consequences of "sweat shop" labor, and (3) hazardous working conditions in some foreign countries must be evaluated. The quantitative costs are (1) exchange rate uncertainties, (2) direct costs of importation (transportation costs, transaction costs), and (3) indirect importation costs (utilization of fixed assets, pipeline inventories, managerial time, engineering support). Moreover, the general uncertainty associated with the business cycle makes offshore sourcing a risky proposition.

The purchase risk perception (PRP) is based on the perceived associated risk with alternative countries. Buying professionals who evaluate the offshore sourcing option must ultimately rely on their best judgment in estimating the risk/reward that is associated with various offshore suppliers. Table 10.3 is an example of the attributes of sourcing options for an electrical appliance manufacturer.

The advantages of sourcing offshore must be weighed against the associated risk. This may seem easy enough to accomplish, but there are some not-so-obvious costs that must be considered. The decision process is further complicated by additional uncertainty associated with offshore sourcing. The buying professional who is considering offshore sourcing must be prepared to fully analyze both the qualitative and quantitative factors. In this section, an example quotation will be evaluated.

The first step in the evaluation process is the determination of accurate freight and duty costs. The actual transportation costs can be as high as 25 percent of the item value. Some products require specialized packing and expensive air

TABLE 10.4
Quote Evaluation

Component X		
Current price	$2,000	per unit
Annual usage	1,000	units
Offshore quote	$1,500	per item
Analysis		
Estimated annual purchase cost	$1,500,000	
Estimated freight additions	150,000	10% increase
Estimated duty	75,000	5%
Total costs	$1,725,000	
Actual cost reduction	13.75%	

transportation. The duty fee for various products may vary from country to country. As an example, the duty for importation of electronic components into the United States is 5.3 percent. Consider the situation where the foreign supplier offers you component X at a 25-percent cost reduction. Further assume that your competitors are currently buying high-quality products from similar suppliers in the same country. (See Table 10.4.)

While a 13.75 percent cost reduction is significant, it may not be large enough to offset other direct and indirect costs associated with offshore sourcing. The additional freight and duties are the first of many hurdles that must be overcome. Moreover, there are a number of other qualitative and quantitative issues that must be resolved. Some of these issues are distance, communication, time value of money, quality issues, pipeline inventory problems, staffing issues, and competition.

1. *Distance.* The distance between the buying and selling firm is significant in terms of time zones and physical location. Internet capabilities usually provide a partial solution. However, face-to-face contact is preferred for some sensitive issues. IBM requires the buyer to visit each supplier on a routine basis. Trips offshore are more expensive and time consuming.
2. *Communication.* Communication can be described as the glue that holds together a sourcing relationship. Without effective communication, global transactions between buying and selling firms would be futile. In addition to being absolutely necessary for the completion of the transaction, communication may also reduce or eliminate uncertainty within the relationship.
3. *Time value of money.* Since most offshore deals require the use of a "letter of credit," the buying firm loses the use of funds when the letter is established. Suppose the shipments arrive two weeks after the letter of credit is established. For a $1.5 million purchase, the buying firm bears a $30,000 (0.01 [opportunity cost %] × 1.5 million × 2 weeks) opportunity cost expense.
4. *Quality issues.* The buying firm must spend the necessary time to correctly specify and articulate quality expectations. Then evaluation makes sure that the sample is from a legitimate production run. Prototypes/lab samples should not be analyzed. Remember, the buying firm is interested in the actual production on the entire batch. In some cases, the buying firm should inspect statistical process control charts to assess projected defect rates and the inspection methods. The buyer should renegotiate the agreement ultimately if the production *process* is out of control. These quality issues can easily increase costs of offshore sourcing.

5. *Pipeline inventory.* Pipeline inventory issues will always occur when a third party (the shipper) is involved. The problems become pronounced when offshore sourcing is used. Consequently, pipeline inventory problems can sometimes be next to impossible to resolve. It is almost impossible to put specific costs on problems associated with pipeline inventory. The pipeline inventory costs are truly a hidden cost that must be considered when evaluating offshore quotes.
6. *Staffing.* If a buying firm is to be effective with an offshore sourcing strategy, it must either hire experts or develop specialists that are assigned to offshore suppliers. Ideally, these individuals must have experience in purchasing management, quality control, and basic accounting. This cost also must be considered in the evaluation process.
7. *The impact of increased competition.* The above direct and indirect costs tend to add unexpected costs to purchased items. However, the significant benefits associated with offshore sourcing enable the buying firm to gain leverage over domestic suppliers. Domestic firms are well aware that some firms are considering offshore firms in their long-term strategies. By merely evaluating the potential of offshore sourcing, domestic suppliers will be motivated to provide better-quality products at lower costs.

In general, the costs and benefits presented above are by no means exhaustive. The purpose here is to illustrate the need for careful analysis of offshore sourcing decisions. The discussion is validated by the empirical evidence given in the paragraphs that follow.

Businesses that expect to reap huge savings from outsourcing will be disappointed, according to a recent survey of more than 5,000 corporate executives around the globe. The 2005 Offshore Outsourcing Research Report, produced by Ventoro LLC, an outsourcing consulting and market research company, found that only 9 percent of any cost savings from offshore outsourcing was the result of lower overseas labor costs.

Overall, the report found that the cost savings from offshore outsourcing was not the 35–40 percent that many corporations assumed they would gain when they decided to go overseas, said Phillip Hatch, Ventoro president. Hatch stated that one of the key reasons why outsourcing programs fail is because customers have unrealistic expectations about cost savings. Savings averaged slightly less than 10 percent for all the offshore outsourcing projects that were reviewed.

Contrary to the promise of massive labor savings, the survey found that 46 percent of the cost saving was generated from process improvement that resulted from the outsourcing project and 45 percent from the quality of the system or service provided.

An example of a global sourcing policy is given in Appendix A. Also see Chapter 9 for a more comprehensive discussion of strategic outsourcing.

GLOBAL SOURCING

In today's competitive supply-chain–driven world, the ability to find a sustainable and economically viable source of goods and services is essential to every going concern. Many countries and territories around the world are actively striving for the role as a world source for goods and services. The level of protectionism and negotiation styles will be addressed for selected countries.

Protectionism in the United States

Most of us like to think of the United States as free and open, unlike our stingy neighbors across the Atlantic with their walls of protectionism. However, in a survey of U.S. port operators and carriers, 77 percent said they favored a reduction in U.S. protectionist legislation. The United States is making progress though; Figure 10.1 shows a distinct trend of decreasing tariff rates for goods coming into this country. The average U.S. tariff rate in 2002 was 4.2 percent.

In general average tariff rates are less than 20 percent in most countries, although they are often quite a bit higher for agricultural commodities (see Table 10.5). In the G-20 countries, average tariffs are less than 10 percent. On average, less-developed countries maintain higher tariff barriers, but for many countries that have recently joined the WTO, tariffs have recently been reduced substantially to gain entry.

In the United States, average tariff rates have fluctuated, sometimes significantly, during the past 175 years. In part, this reflects shifting attitudes regarding the appropriateness of free trade versus protectionist policies. Tariff rates also were usually raised when the country was at war since additional tariff revenue would be needed to finance wartime expenses.

FIGURE 10.1
Average U.S. Tariff Rate, 1821–1985

Source: U.S. Department of Commerce, Bureau of Economic Analysis, Industry Economic Accounts, March 1989; *American Economic Review*, March 1989.

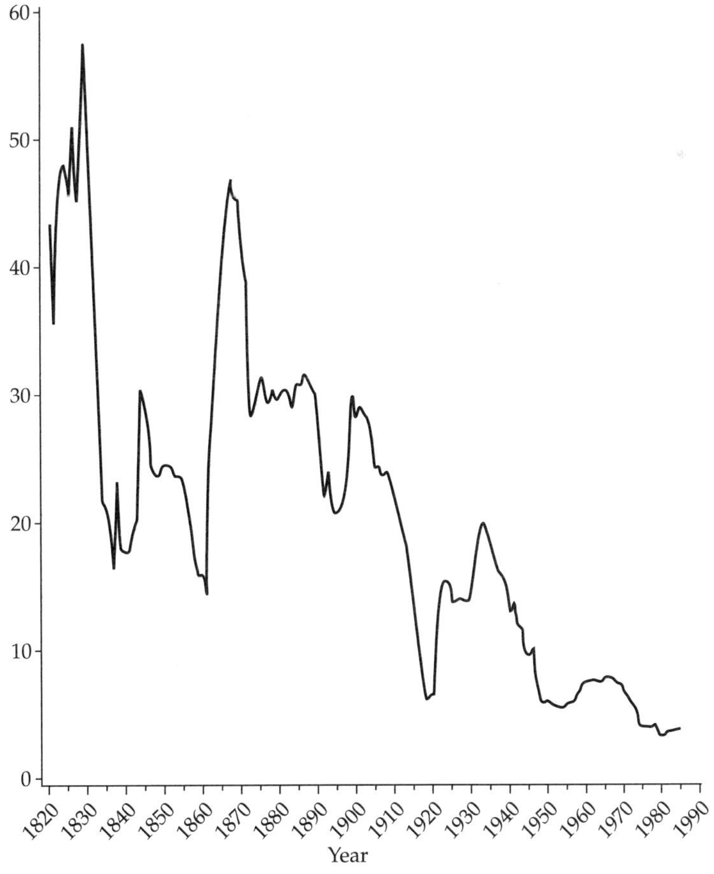

TABLE 10.5
Average Tariff Rates for the G-20 Countries and Selected Threshold Countries (2007)

Country/Territory	Average Tariff Rate (%)	Country/Territory	Average Tariff Rate (%)
Argentina	12.0	Malawi	13.5
Australia	3.5	Mexico	12.6
Brazil	12.2	Morocco	23.0
Canada	5.5	Norway	8.1
Chile	6.0	Pakistan	14.7
China	9.9	Russian Federation	11.0
European Union	5.2	Saudi Arabia	5.0
Indonesia	6.9	Singapore	0.0
India	14.5	South Africa	7.8
Japan	5.1	United States	3.5
Turkey	10.0	United Arab Emirates	5.0
Republic of Korea	12.2	Vietnam	16.8

There are many industries and products that are currently protected by such legislation. Although the legal aspects of international sourcing are beyond the scope of this chapter, two examples are given below:

1. The EU (European Union) has been limited to a market share of 7 percent of U.S. steel consumption until just recently when 10 years of protectionist legislation expired. The U.S. government also has set certain limits on machine tool imports to protect that industry. In the past three years, we have seen increased outcry for further protectionism legislation from within the United States. The first Bush administration had remained fairly firm in limiting this practice.
2. According to the 1991 Trade Policy Review of the EU, export controls and restrictions may be imposed for a range of specific purposes including national security; protection of life, health, and the environment; and the preservation of national treasures. The community also readily regulates the importation and exportation of dangerous chemicals. The governing regulation is CR Number 1734/88. Authorizations for the import and export of chemicals are still administered by the individual member states.

Importance of Negotiations

When negotiating a purchase agreement, there are certain general attributes in dealing with various offshore suppliers. We will attempt to explain the nuances of negotiating with the people of various EU countries and China.

United Kingdom

The United Kingdom's GNP is $2.78 trillion. Its monetary unit is the pound sterling. Typical trading partners include the United States, Germany, and other countries in the European Union (EU). Exports include machinery, transportation equipment, petroleum, and other manufactured goods. As the exchange rate (unit per U.S. dollar) increases, the more attractive international purchasing becomes. In a survey of international purchasing agents, the United Kingdom was ranked fourth in quality of product, third in service, and seventh in average price in the world. The United States received $58.6 billion in imports from the United Kingdom in 2008. The trend of imports from the United Kingdom is increasing. The United Kingdom has the infrastructure and experience to be a viable trading partner.

Negotiations It can't be assumed that English and American businesses operate in the same manner. English executives may appear polite and friendly, but they can be tough and ruthless when appropriate.

The English are motivated by other things besides money, such as free time, status of their work, and other intangibles. English businesspeople tend to be deliberate, yet oftentimes less prepared than the people with whom they are negotiating. At the same time, they are open and forthright. They tend not to play games. However, they will scrutinize the terms and conditions of the agreement. This trait can be attributed to their risk averseness.

In some instances, English businesspersons sometimes patronize people with whom they negotiate. However, they are often impressed by education and degrees. If you've got it, flaunt it.

Firms in the United Kingdom tend to be overstaffed, which can to delay the decision-making process. Some American buyers have been successful in developing a final package proposal in advance and presenting it to an English businessperson on a "take it or leave it" basis. This usually speeds up negotiations significantly.

The Federal Republic of Germany

Germany's GDP stands at $3.57 trillion for 2011. Its monetary unit is the euro. Typical trading partners include the United States, the United Kingdom, and other countries in the European Union. Exports include machinery, motor vehicles, chemicals, iron, and steel products. The United States received $97.5 billion in imports from Germany in 2008.

Unified Germany will continue to be a world-class purchasing source and by most experts' predictions will grow substantially stronger as a result of reunification with East Germany.

Negotiations Most of the executives you encounter will have attended a university, and 50 percent hold doctorates. The title "Dr." commands instant respect. Germans tend to be specialists in one industry with multiple company experiences. Due to technical expertise, German negotiators are extremely cautious. The opponent should be well prepared on technical details.

The German negotiator will always have an ultimate goal in mind, but he or she will be slow in revealing it. Once it is revealed, the negotiations should move forward quickly. Germans are very concerned about the precision of written contracts. It's not that they do not trust the opponent; it is that they are precise and know the cost of mistakes and misunderstandings. In general, German business executives are honest and straightforward.

Avoid being humorous at the negotiating table. In general, Germans are usually serious about business. They are serious and honest in business dealings. If you are fluent in the German language, you are ahead of the game. Germans have a habit of talking strategy and caucusing in German right in the negotiating room, even when they know the opponent understands the language. Decisions are made by committees and thus are slow to be made. Breaks in the negotiating proceedings will probably be required so that German negotiating teams can gain approval for some proposal.

Managers in Germany are more like Americans than most other European managers, evidenced by their desire to clear things up before the weekend or the end of the day. They do not leave things hanging. With this in mind, you can see why it is productive to introduce new important issues near the deadline. Germans tend to be risk averse. This behavior makes them quite willing to seek a compromise rather than risk having a confrontation or controversy.

France

The French GDP is $2.77 trillion for 2011. France's monetary unit is the euro. Typical trading partners are the other EU members, the United States, and Africa. Exports include machinery, transportation equipment, and food. The United States received $43 billion in imports in 2008 from France. In 2008, French exports to the United States increased 6.5 percent from the previous year.

The French score lower than Germans and English in the survey of U.S. purchasing agents. France scored sixth in quality, eleventh in service, and eleventh in average price. The rankings included 16 countries.

Negotiations When doing business in France, you will often go through an intermediary contact whose credentials are impeccable. Your choice of intermediary is important. The best contacts are French people who have ties with the person you want to contact—through family status, money, or schooling. Schooling is the most important aspect because the elite of French management are linked by having attended prestigious schools.

The pace of negotiating in France is slower than we are used to here in the United States. The French do not like to be rushed, and any attempt to rush them or showing impatience can be problematic. Decision making in French organizations is centralized and concentrated within a small number of top executives. If you are not dealing with the top two or three people in the firm, it will take time for your lower contacts to pass on information and receive appropriate feedback or approval. The French are fond of debate and argument. They will not be convinced of anything immediately; instead, they will spend time debating every point. You should be well versed, logical, and focused in your dealings with French people.

In general, the French have a low opinion of the act of selling. French executives are not impressed with extravagant and emotional presentations but respond to presentations that deal in logic and fact. In major negotiations, you will find it beneficial to have at least one piece, if not all of your technical material, translated into perfect French. This will elicit respect from your French counterparts.

China

China is now a major player in the world economy and accounts for more than 6 percent of world trade. This is remarkable for a developing economy. There has been strong import growth, both for processing trade and for domestic consumption. During the years 2002–2004, when the global economy was rather weak, China accounted for approximately 24 percent of world growth in purchasing-power-parity terms. China's influence on the world economy is clearly very important and rising over time.

China's GDP is $9.82 trillion. Its monetary unit is the yuan (CNY). Additional GDP statistics about the Chinese economy are given in Table 10.6. The United States received $399.62 billion in imports from China in 2008. Typical trading partners include the United States, Germany, EU countries, and other countries throughout the world. Exports include machinery, transportation equipment, construction equipment, and other manufactured goods.

TABLE 10.6
China's GDP

Source: *CIA World Fact Book*, accessed 2011.

China's GDP 2010–2011
GDP (purchasing power parity): US$9.872 trillion (2010 est.)
GDP global rank: #3 (behind the European Union and the U.S.)
GDP, real growth rate: 10.3% (2010 est.)
GDP, per capita: US$7,400 (2010 est.)
Labor force: 819.5 million (2010 est.), #1 global ranking
Population below the poverty line: 2.8%

Ford Motor Co. announced in July 2009 that it will be purchasing as much as $3 billion worth of China-made components to boost its aim to cut production costs. Bill Ford explained, "We are only scratching the surface in China. China is very key to our global sourcing strategy, particularly as the quality of the local suppliers ramps up."

In 2002, Walmart, the world's largest chain store retailer, moved its global purchasing center from Hong Kong to Shenzhen, a city in south China's Guangdong Province. In 2004, Walmart had 44 branches throughout China. In 2003, Walmart purchased U.S.$20 billion worth of Chinese-made products to sell in its outlets around the world. Today, Walmart has established partnerships with nearly 20,000 suppliers in China. Walmart operates over 10,000 units in 27 countries under 69 different banners and serves more than 200 million customers per week. Walmart recorded $419 billion in annual net sales in fiscal year 2011 (FYE10, February 1, 2010 to January 31, 2011), an increase of 3.4 percent over fiscal year 2010.

Negotiations The major problems when doing business in China are the language barrier, business practices, and a fluid and diverse legal system. A well-specified procurement strategy is a basic requirement when buying from China.

On the payment side, buying firms must learn to manage risk. There must be letters of credit (LCs). Buying firms should never pay upfront. As the trustee of documents between buyer and supplier, banks ensure that payment only occurs after the supplier meets all LC terms. Banks in China and other parts of Asia do not make preproduction loans to manufacturers based on inventory.

GLOBAL PROVIDER OPPORTUNISM

There are two germane forms of opportunism associated with outsourcing: shirking and poaching. *Shirking* represents the extent to which the service provider is inclined to deliberately underperform or withhold resources should the customer be unable to detect such action. Shirking is often associated with the problem of moral hazard and is frequently cited as a typical form of passive, yet intentional opportunism. *Poaching* is the extent to which the service provider is inclined to utilize information gained through its relationship with the customer for its own, perhaps unauthorized, benefit should the customer be unable to detect such action.

Shirking and poaching are specific forms of provider opportunism that can play a value-destroying role in global outsourcing relationships. Handley and Benton (2012) found in a recent study that service provider shirking and poaching are in fact significant risks of global outsourcing. Statistical evidence from a large-scale empirical study indicated that buyer relationship–specific investments and the use of mediated power are associated with an increased risk of outsourcing provider shirking. Conversely, provider relationship–specific investments and buyer non-mediated power had a negative influence on the risk of provider shirking. Outsourcing firm reliance on non-mediated power was also found to be related to a decreased tendency for provider poaching, while mediated power increased this risk. In sum, these results suggest that outsourcing engagements characterized by higher levels of provider relationship–specific investments and buyer influence derived from non-mediated rather than mediated power bases face a lower risk of provider opportunism. These conditions not only diminish the risks of outsourcing, but also demand lower investments in monitoring and formal control mechanisms. All else equal, this results in a more favorable risk-reward relationship for the outsourcing organization. The analysis demonstrated the value of looking at specific forms of opportunism rather than simply opportunism in general. Only by distinguishing between shirking and poaching were we able to see the differing effects of relationship-specific investments. Relationship-specific investments have a significant association with provider shirking, but not with poaching. Had we only considered the broader concept of opportunism in general, these insights would not have been fleshed out. Exchange hazards and the basis of outsourcing firm power were found to have a meaningful impact on service provider opportunism. However, it is tenable that other environmental conditions and outsourcing firm practices can instigate or mitigate provider opportunism. If one assumes that some service providers act opportunistically, then a similar assumption regarding buyer behavior seems reasonable. This would certainly be of concern to outsourcing service providers.

U.S. EXPORT ADMINISTRATION REGULATIONS

Any business or individual wanting to import goods into the United States will have to work with the Export Administration (EA) of the U.S. Department of Commerce. For complete details, consult the U.S. Export Administration Regulations (EAR). Several steps that you will need to be aware of follow:

1. Determine whether the item(s) in question is subject to the exclusive jurisdiction of another federal agency.
2. Determine if the technology or software is publicly available.
3. For an item in a foreign country, determine the origin of the item.
4. For items made in a foreign country, determine whether it is a controlled item in the United States.
5. Determine whether the foreign-made item is subject to general prohibition.

Imported items are classified as a commodity with respect to the commodity control list (CCL); the Export Control Commodity Number (ECCN) must be identified for the commodities you are planning to import. You can request the EA to verify the ECCN of commodities you wish to officially classify. Write to Export Administration, P.O. Box 273, Washington, DC 20044, for further information on this process or refer to the EAR.

Each of the four countries under our review participates in the import certificate/ delivery verification (IC/DV) procedures. Most industrialized countries participate in the IC/DV. If the importer is an individual or business in the United States that is purchasing and/or expects to receive commodities from these countries, the importer is required to furnish an International Import Certificate (IIC). The form required can be obtained by contacting a local district office of the Department of Commerce. Once the form is reviewed and approved, the transaction is approved (bringing the commodities into the United States) and a validated letter of approval and the IIC will be sent to the importer. Once approved, the IIC is valid for six months from the time it was certified by the Department of Commerce.

The importer also may need to contact additional agencies, particularly if it is buying guns, missiles, ammunition, or atomic and nuclear substances.

FOREIGN TRADE ZONES

The FTC Act of 1934 created trade zones to encourage exports from foreign countries. The act allowed for the storage of goods within the U.S. boundaries without payment until the goods passed to the buying company. The foreign trade zones (FTZs) are operated by the U.S. Customs Service. When goods enter an FTZ, the goods are classified, inspected, and placed in storage. The classification categories are given in Table 10.7. A list of the major FTZ offices in the United States is shown in Table 10.8. A receipt is then given to the owner. The Customs Service is notified when the goods are transferred to the ultimate buyer. The appraisal value of the goods is set by the transaction value.

TABLE 10.7
Classification of Merchandise in a Foreign Trade Zone

Source: Ferguson (1985).

Privileged foreign merchandise	Import duty is assessed at the most favorable class 1 duty rate. This rate is usually reserved for imported materials from countries that have "most favored nation" status. Materials on the U.S. government priority list may be awarded this classification without regard to the point of origin.
Privileged domestic merchandise	Merchandise of domestic origin can reenter the U.S. customs territory duty-free. The classification also is applied to imported merchandise on which duty and taxes have been paid or merchandise that has been previously admitted duty-free.
Nonprivileged foreign merchandise	Import duty is assessed at the less-favorable class 2 duty rate. This category includes all merchandise that does not have a privileged or zone-restricted status.
Nonprivileged domestic merchandise	This classification is never sought; it is the result of privileged domestic merchandise being reclassified because it loses its identity in the zone.
Zone-restricted merchandise	This classification includes merchandise that is admitted to the zone from the U.S. customs territory for storage, export, or destruction. "Restricted" here means that manipulation, manufacture, or return to the U.S. customs territory is not allowed.

TABLE 10.8 Foreign Trade Zone Offices in the United States

Alabama	
FTZ No. 82	Mobile
FTZ No. 83	Huntsville
Arizona	
FTZ No. 48	Pima County (Tucson)
FTZ No. 60	Nogales
FTZ No. 75	Phoenix
Arkansas	
FTZ No. 14	Little Rock
California	
FTZ No. 3	San Francisco
FTZ No. 18	San Jose (San Francisco)
FTZ No. 50	Long Beach
FTZ No. 56	Oakland
Connecticut	
FTZ No. 71	Windsor Locks (Hartford)
FTZ No. 76	Bridgeport
Florida	
FTZ No. 25	Broward County (Port Everglades)
FTZ No. 32	Miami
FTZ No. 42	Orlando
FTZ No. 64	Jacksonville
FTZ No. 65	Panama City
FTZ No. 79	Tampa
Georgia	
FTZ No. 26	Coweta County (Atlanta)
Hawaii	
FTZ No. 9	Honolulu
Illinois	
FTZ No. 22	Chicago
FTZ No. 31	Granite City (St. Louis)
Indiana	
FTZ No. 72	Indianapolis
Kansas	
FTZ No. 17	Kansas City
Kentucky	
FTZ No. 29	Jefferson City (Louisville)
FTZ No. 47	Campbell County (Cincinnati)
Louisiana	
FTZ No. 2	New Orleans
Maine	
FTZ No. 58	Bangor
Maryland	
FTZ No. 63	Prince George's County (Washington, DC)
FTZ No. 73	BWI Airport (Baltimore)
FTZ No. 74	Baltimore
Massachusetts	
FTZ No. 27	Boston
FTZ No. 28	New Bedford
Michigan	
FTZ No. 16	Sault Ste. Marie
FTZ No. 43	Battle Creek
FTZ No. 70	Detroit
Minnesota	
FTZ No. 51	Duluth
Missouri	
FTZ No. 15	Kansas City
Nebraska	
FTZ No. 19	Omaha
FTZ No. 59	Lincoln (Omaha)
New Hampshire	
FTZ No. 81	Portsmouth
New Jersey	
FTZ No. 44	Morris County (New York City)
FTZ No. 49	Newark/Elizabeth (New York City)
New York	
FTZ No. 1	New York City
FTZ No. 23	Buffalo (Buffalo–Niagara Falls)
FTZ No. 34	Niagara County
FTZ No. 37	Orange County (New York City)
FTZ No. 52	Suffolk County (New York City)
FTZ No. 54	Clinton County (Champlain–Rouses Point)
North Carolina	
FTZ No. 57	Mecklenburg County (Charlotte)
FTZ No. 66	Wilmington
FTZ No. 67	Morehead City (Beaufort–Morehead City)
Ohio	
FTZ No. 8	Toledo
FTZ No. 40	Cleveland
FTZ No. 46	Butler County (Cincinnati)
Oklahoma	
FTZ No. 53	Rogers County (Tulsa)
Oregon	
FTZ No. 45	Portland
Pennsylvania	
FTZ No. 24	Pittston (Wilkes-Barre–Scranton)
FTZ No. 33	Allegheny County (Pittsburgh)
FTZ No. 35	Philadelphia
South Carolina	
FTZ No. 21	Dorchester County (Charleston)
FTZ No. 38	Spartanburg County (Greenville-Spartanburg)
Tennessee	
FTZ No. 77	Memphis
FTZ No. 78	Nashville
Texas	
FTZ No. 12	McAllen (Hidalgo)
FTZ No. 36	Galveston
FTZ No. 39	Dallas/Ft. Worth
FTZ No. 62	Brownsville
FTZ No. 68	El Paso
FTZ No. 80	San Antonio
Utah	
FTZ No. 30	Salt Lake City
Vermont	
FTZ No. 55	Burlington
Virginia	
FTZ No. 20	Suffolk (Norfolk–Newport News)
Washington	
FTZ No. 5	Seattle
Wisconsin	
FTZ No. 41	Milwaukee

THE EUROPEAN UNION (EU): OVERVIEW AND WHAT IT MEANS TO PURCHASING

The information provided in this chapter should help the purchasing professional understand the advantages and disadvantages of sourcing from foreign countries, particularly the EU. Today the EU consists of 27 member countries. Since the Single European Act (SEA) in 1987, 279 proposals have been brought forth to eliminate most trade barriers; approximately 90 percent of the 279 proposals are now law.

Although the majority of proposals are aimed at eliminating trade restrictions within the EU itself, these laws affect the way firms within the EU do business and thus affect the competitiveness and efficiency of several large industries. The primary purpose of the EU is to protect markets such as automobiles and agriculture. In the past, under protectionism policies, certain countries were able to sell products and components at any price accepted by the consumer since foreign competition from neighboring countries was nonexistent. The breakup of cartels and blocks of industries has fostered competition between these countries. The more competition among EU countries, the more likely you are to get several competitive bids from which to choose.

This idea of competition is new to many of the members of the EU, so it will take several years for all of them to become competitive. As these trade barriers fall and an open market in the EU is established, those firms that can no longer compete due to inefficiencies are turning to other industries in which they can be profitable. This allows countries to specialize in producing and exporting those goods they make most efficiently, while importing other goods that they previously produced themselves. Prices will eventually be lower on components and items produced in Europe, which will foster greater competition worldwide as other companies realize that another power is emerging overseas. Although a foreign purchaser will benefit in the long run, most European countries will be severely hurt in the short run due to the jobs lost as firms try to "trim the fat" to become more competitive. Also, the abandonment of inefficient industries and their replacement with imported goods will result in large-scale unemployment for some time. With the lifting of border restrictions, however, those workers who have a specialized field will be able to go where the industry is. The expected benefit from the removal of protectionism will be the growth of competition.

The formation of the European Union has led to the elimination of custom formalities between countries. There are also tariff reductions in 4,000 categories of manufactured goods as well as other schedules for reducing trade barriers. In the past, a great deal of cost was added to products and components sourced in Europe to cover these multiple custom costs and tariff fees. The lowering of these costs will once again result in lower prices offered to purchasers. The formation of one EU has resulted in a single standard for buying goods. This single market also has resulted in a single value-added tax (VAT), not a different one for each country in which the part is produced. Currently, these VAT taxes fluctuate from a low level of 12 percent to some as high as 25 percent.

The main objective of Europe '92 was the formation of a single European currency and a European Central Bank. This has been accomplished and it has turned out to be a fairly strong world currency. Not only is capital able to move freely between borders in the EU, but American firms are able to cut administrative costs since fewer multiple-currency bank accounts and foreign exchange traders are necessary. The success of consolidated European currency will continue to depend on the strength of the European Central Bank. A weak bank would result in a high-inflation currency that would devalue against other currencies, thus lowering its acceptability outside Europe. This high inflation could hurt industries within the EU, thus hindering them from becoming fully efficient. A strong bank could hurt a foreign purchaser since it could erode the dollar's exchange rate, resulting in more expensive imported goods and components. The main advantage of the single currency is the ease of doing business with a larger number of countries overseas; how large of an advantage will depend on how well the new European Central Bank is managed.

Another problem resolved by the EU is doing business with other countries that are concerned as to where a product's components come from. Certain countries during times of turmoil are unwilling to purchase finished goods whose parts are produced in countries whose interests conflict with theirs. The advantage of purchasing from an EU country is that with it comes a sense of ambiguity; the selling firm will not know exactly where the parts come from, but reports can list the components as coming from the EU since differences in taxes, tariffs, and currencies are no longer present.

Now that the formulation of the EU has been completed, it is up to American businesses to respond quickly and get the first advantage over their competitors, both in the United States and abroad. The formation of the EU is a step forward in competitiveness and cooperation within Europe and around the world.

Companies buy and trade over greater and greater distances without having to move operations to the location where they wish to do business. One of the advances in the business world is the ability to purchase goods from anywhere in the world. The improved communication devices and transportation methods have allowed companies to get an edge on the competition by buying goods from countries whose costs are cheaper or quality is more reliable.

Countertrade

Countertrade is the exchange of goods for goods in full or partial payment of a sales transaction. Progressive companies must participate in countertrade or risk losing market share. The big countertraders are Lockheed Martin, Boeing Ventures, and British Aerospace. Countertrade appears to be flourishing in the current climate, largely because of the recent changes that have occurred in the international arms market since the end of the Cold War. These changes have affected both the volume of the trade and also the means through which it is financed. There are a number of countertrade arrangements. Some of the more popular forms of countertrade are given below:

1. *Offset:* Offsets are commercial compensation practices required as a condition of purchase of goods and services. Offsets would include specific forms such as co-production, licensed production, subcontractor production, and overseas investment or technology transfer. Offsets can be direct or indirect. Examples of direct offsets include the manufacture of German-designed naval patrol vessels in South Korea.

2. *Indirect offset:* Indirect offsets occur where products or services transferred in an offset arrangement are unrelated to the specific products referred to in the export agreement. In many developing countries where the industrial base and infrastructure are poorly developed, offsets are more likely to be of an indirect nature, for

example, selling military aircraft to a developing country and making arrangements to provide aerospace education for some of the citizens of the developing country.

3. *Coproduction:* This form of agreement involves the purchaser being given a share in the manufacture of a foreign-designed product. Coproduction is encouraged by recipients because of the employment and technology transfer implications. An example would be the coproduction of the British Harrier aircraft by McDonnell Douglas in the United States. Tier I suppliers gain commercial advantages under this form of arrangement when there is a high degree of technology transfer.

4. *Licensed production:* Licensed production occurs when the recipient obtains a share of the production work for its own order. The agreement may cover the assembly of an entire product or service. The agreement may be phased so that the local share of production rises over time. As an example, by the terms of the 1991 South Korean $5.2 billion purchase of F-16 fighter aircraft from General Dynamics, 12 aircraft were to be bought from the U.S. plant and a further 36 were to be assembled in South Korea before, in the final phase, South Korea was to produce parts and sub-systems for a further 72 aircraft.[1]

5. *Subcontractor production:* In this case, a prime contractor substitutes an existing supplier with one located in the buying country. As an example, Boeing placed subcontracts with several British firms in order to sell the E-3 AWACS aircraft to the United Kingdom. In some cases, this led to the elimination of U.S. subcontractors from Boeing's network of suppliers.

6. *Technology transfer:* Technology transfers are commitments for foreign direct investment made by the selling firm in order to establish joint ventures in the buying country.

7. *Barter:* Barter is the nonmonetary exchange of goods for goods. As an example, the so-called oil for food program between Iraq and the EU was designed as a barter program. However, some of the actual deals involved illegal cash transactions between some United Nations and Iraqi officials.

8. *Counterpurchase:* In a counterpurchase, the seller exchanges products for compensatory amounts of commodities. In the context of developing countries, this normally involves primary commodities. Chrysler, General Motors, and Toyota use countertrade as the method of payment in Argentina. They established programs that sell their products in exchange for grain. The grain is then traded through an intermediary for dollars and not in the heavily devalued peso. Furthermore, the car companies have to negotiate with the intermediaries and the purchaser over not only the quantity of grain but also its quality, availability, and optimum market price on the day of the sale.

9. *Buyback:* Under a buyback agreement, the original exporter agrees to accept as full or part payment products derived from the original exported product. As an example, if the exporter establishes a production facility for machine tools, the exporter agrees to accept a portion of the facility's output as payment.

Summary

In the coming decade, more and more firms will be expanding their operations into international markets. As firms' competition heats up, firms will become more global minded. To be a global firm, management must be able to critically evaluate foreign markets.

[1]http://www.cianet.org/wps/wis01/.

In the current business environment, firms are beginning to develop global procurement strategies. The electronics, chemical, and metal industries are leading the global procurement charge. The North American Free Trade Agreement and the European Union will fuel global sourcing in the next decade. In this chapter, a detailed total cost analysis also was presented to show the hidden costs associated with global sourcing. As part of global purchasing, the buyer must understand how free trade zones are used. The buying firm also must know how to negotiate in foreign countries. A brief description of the sourcing environment in the United Kingdom, Germany, France, and China was presented.

The primary purpose of the 1934 free trade zone FTC legislation was to encourage the conversion of foreign materials with domestic materials and exporting an improved final product; while goods reside in a zone they can be transformed to conform to the importing countries' requirements.

FTZs also are used to import goods into the United States for consumption. Import duties are delayed until the product is sold to the ultimate user. The importer can move goods into a zone and store them until a buyer is located. The buyer will then pay the total cost of the product, including the duty.

The FTZ cannot be used to avoid import quota restrictions. The long-term impact of FTZs is uncertain given the current changes in Western Europe. However, if the current trend continues, firms involved in global sourcing will more than likely relocate their operation into a designated FTZ or apply for FTZ status. The chapter concluded with a discussion on countertrade sales transactions.

Discussion Questions

1. How should purchasing managers train buyers for global sourcing?
2. What are some of the advantages of global sourcing?
3. Discuss the total cost of global sourcing. Does it make sense for smaller firms to buy internationally?
4. How do exchange rates impact global sourcing?
5. Discuss some of the behavioral issues associated with global sourcing.
6. What are some of the attributes associated with global sourcing?
7. Discuss how offshore quotas should be evaluated. Consider both qualitative and quantitative implications.
8. Discuss the differences and similarities of negotiating strategies for France, the United Kingdom, Germany, and China.
9. What is meant by a foreign trade zone?

Suggested Cases

Eastern Wave, Inc.
The Tank Case
Microfuse, Inc.

References

Ferguson, Wade. "Foreign Trade Zones: A Resource for Materials Managers." *Journal of Purchasing and Materials Management*, Winter 1985, pp. 22–27.

Handley, S. M., and W. C. Benton. "The Influence of Exchange Hazards and Power on Opportunism in Outsourcing Relationships." *Journal of Operations Management* (available online November 2011) 30, no. 1–2 (2012), pp. 55–68.

Appendix A

Outsourcing Policy Example

Our Global Sourcing and Operating Guidelines help us to select business partners who follow workplace standards and business practices that are consistent with our company's values. These requirements are applied to every contractor who manufactures or finishes products for Levi Strauss & Co. Trained inspectors closely audit and monitor compliance among approximately 600 cutting, sewing, and finishing contractors in more than 60 countries.

The Levi Strauss & Co. Global Sourcing and Operating Guidelines include two parts:

I. **The Country Assessment Guidelines**, which address large external issues beyond the control of Levi Strauss & Co.'s individual business partners. These help us assess the opportunities and risks of doing business in a particular country.

II. **The Business Partner Terms of Engagement**, which deal with issues that are substantially controllable by individual business partners. These Terms of Engagement are an integral part of our business relationships. Our employees and our business partners understand that complying with our Terms of Engagement is no less important than meeting our quality standards or delivery times.

COUNTRY ASSESSMENT GUIDELINES

The numerous countries where Levi Strauss & Co. has existing or future business interests present a variety of cultural, political, social, and economic circumstances.

The Country Assessment Guidelines help us assess any issue that might present concern in light of the ethical principles we have set for ourselves. The Guidelines assist us in making practical and principled business decisions as we balance the potential risks and opportunities associated with conducting business in specific countries. Specifically, we assess whether the:

- **Health and Safety Conditions** would meet the expectations we have for employees and their families or our company representatives;
- **Human Rights Environment** would allow us to conduct business activities in a manner that is consistent with our Global Sourcing and Operating Guidelines and other company policies;
- **Legal System** would provide the necessary support to adequately protect our trademarks, investments, or other commercial interests, or to implement the Global Sourcing and Operating Guidelines and other company policies; and
- **Political, Economic, and Social Environment** would protect the company's commercial interests and brand/corporate image. We will not conduct business in countries prohibited by U.S. laws.

TERMS OF ENGAGEMENT

- **Ethical Standards.** We will seek to identify and utilize business partners who aspire as individuals and in the conduct of all their businesses to a set of ethical standards not incompatible with our own.

- **Legal Requirements.** We expect our business partners to be law abiding as individuals and to comply with legal requirements relevant to the conduct of all their businesses.
- **Environmental Requirements.** We will only do business with partners who share our commitment to the environment and who conduct their business in a way that is consistent with Levi Strauss & Co.'s Environmental Philosophy and Guiding Principles.
- **Community Involvement.** We will favor business partners who share our commitment to improving community conditions.
- **Employment Standards.** We will only do business with partners who adhere to the following guidelines:

  Child Labor: Use of child labor is not permissible. Workers can be no less than 15 years of age and not younger than the compulsory age to be in school. We will not utilize partners who use child labor in any of their facilities. We support the development of legitimate workplace apprenticeship programs for the educational benefit of younger people.

  Prison Labor/Forced Labor: We will not utilize prison or forced labor in contracting relationships in the manufacture and finishing of our products. We will not utilize or purchase materials from a business partner utilizing prison or forced labor.

  Disciplinary Practices: We will not utilize business partners who use corporal punishment or other forms of mental or physical coercion.

  Working Hours: While permitting flexibility in scheduling, we will identify local legal limits on work hours and seek business partners who do not exceed them except for appropriately compensated overtime. While we favor partners who utilize less than 60 hour workweeks, we will not use contractors who, on a regular basis, require in excess of a sixty-hour week. Employees should be allowed at least one day off in seven.

  Wages and Benefits: We will only do business with partners who provide wages and benefits that comply with any applicable law and match the prevailing local manufacturing or finishing industry practices.

  Freedom of Association: We respect workers' rights to form and join organizations of their choice and to bargain collectively. We expect our suppliers to respect the right to free association and the right to organize and bargain collectively without unlawful interference. Business partners should ensure that workers who make such decisions or participate in such organizations are not the object of discrimination or punitive disciplinary actions and that the representatives of such organizations have access to their members under conditions established either by local laws or mutual agreement between the employer and the worker organizations.

  Discrimination: While we recognize and respect cultural differences, we believe that workers should be employed on the basis of their ability to do the job, rather than on the basis of personal characteristics or beliefs. We will favor business partners who share this value.

  Health and Safety: We will only utilize business partners who provide workers with a safe and healthy work environment. Business partners who provide residential facilities for their workers must provide safe and healthy facilities.

Chapter Eleven

Supply Partnerships and Supply Chain Power[1]

Learning Objectives

1. Understand the relationship between purchasing, supply partnerships, and supply chain power.
2. Describe the elements of supply chain partnerships.
3. Illustrate the continuum of interfirm relationships.
4. Discuss the potential benefits of supplier partnerships.
5. Understand the nature of supply chain power.
6. Describe the different sources of power.
7. Examine how supply partnerships work in the automotive industry.

INTRODUCTION

Critical to the implementation of purchasing and supply management techniques is the development of *supply chain partnerships*. Also termed a *strategic alliance*, a supply chain partnership is a relationship formed between two independent entities in supply channels to achieve specific objectives and benefits, and it is these partnerships that form the essential building blocks of supply chain management. The high levels of information flow and subsequent coordination of error-free deliveries by supply chain management require manufacturers to build tighter bonds with relatively few suppliers. Once traditionally driven by competition, the supplier relationships for many manufacturing firms have thus matured from an adversarial nature to one of supply chain partnerships.

Within the win-win partnership dyad, buyer and supplier share goals as well as inherent risks through joint planning and control, seeking to create a supply chain with increased information flow and enhanced loyalty. Like the overall goal of supply chain management, such coordination allows for improved service, technological innovation, and product design with decreased cost. Ideally, the end result for both firms should be decreased uncertainty, yielding greater control of costs, cycle times, inventory, quality, and, ultimately, customer satisfaction.

[1]This chapter is the result of supply chain power research conducted by W. C. Benton and Michael Maloni.

BENCHMARK SUPPLIER PARTNERSHIPS: CHRYSLER CORPORATION

As an example of supply chain partnerships, the Chrysler (formerly DaimlerChrysler) Corporation is a leader in developing intimate relationships with its suppliers. When Chrysler's team designed its LH line (Dodge Intrepid, Eagle Vision, Chrysler Concorde) and compact sedans (Neon), Chrysler outsourced more than 70 percent of its parts to a limited number of suppliers. In order to achieve this supply chain partnership arrangement, Chrysler invited several key suppliers into the early stages of the development process and actually presourced 95 percent of the component parts for its new sedan by choosing vendors prior to the design stage. In doing so, it eliminated the competitive bidding process. Several of Chrysler's domestic supply chain partners, like its Pacific Rim competitors, have full responsibility for developing the components themselves and coordinating with other subcontractors to carry out the component development process. In the end, the LH line was developed from scratch in 39 months versus the usual five to six years, and the Neon line was developed in only 31 months.

Furthermore, Chrysler's Supplier Cost Reduction Effort (SCORE) has led to 10,000 new ideas since 1993 and has resulted in $2.3 billion in supply chain savings, one-third of which the suppliers retain. Chrysler also has utilized supplier involvement to become a virtual vehicle manufacturer as its suppliers accept more responsibility and do more assembly. While Chrysler takes a role in part design, it leaves a significant portion of the assembly to suppliers, cutting its own costs and increasing overall production efficiency in the process. Each Chrysler plant once carried between $25 million and $27 million of inventory, but the number has dropped to below $8 million as supplier personnel work directly with plant purchasing personnel.

IMPORTANCE OF SUPPLY CHAIN PARTNERSHIP AWARENESS

Like supply chain management, the frequency of partnering is increasing in industry, but implementation still remains a difficult process. And like supply chain management, buyer–supplier partnering extends beyond a simple interfirm relationship to involve integration of confidential and vital processes such as strategy formation, planning, information flow, and operations. Thus, both researchers and industry practitioners must clearly comprehend when, why, and how effective partnerships are formed as well as when, why, and how these partnerships are maintained. This chapter seeks to contribute to such an understanding through an analysis of buyer–supplier relationships.

PARTNERSHIPS: DEFINITION AND OVERVIEW

Though partnering has received abundant recognition over the last few decades from both researchers and practitioners alike, the concept of a partnership is perhaps as old as, or even older than, business itself. Although many firms engage in partnering activities, the specific interpretation of a strategic alliance or partnership (the terms *partnership* and *alliance* will be used interchangeably in this chapter) is at best vague. To understand the context of a partnership, it is helpful

FIGURE 11.1 Continuum of Interfirm Relationships

Discrete arm's-length transaction	Special influence transaction	Partnership I	Partnership II	Partnership III	Joint venture	Vertical integration

→ Relationship intensity

to consider the continuum of interfirm relationships shown in Figure 11.1. A basic interaction between two firms involves a discrete arm's-length relationship equivalent to the length of time it takes to complete the single transaction. Other interactions may involve significantly more attention by one or both firms and involve what is deemed as a special influence transaction. An example of such may be found in the national account groups of firms in which specific resources, both human and nonhuman, are devoted to handling larger, more important buyers.

RELATIONSHIP INTENSITY

Partnerships move beyond special influence transactions by involving efforts of both firms to coordinate functional activities. Figure 11.1 shows how partnerships can be segmented into three tiers based on the intensity and duration of the leadership. Tier I partnerships entail short-term, single-function/division coordination. Tier II partnerships extend coordination to integration and encompass multiple activities over a longer time span. Finally, tier III partnerships dilate into "significant levels of operational integration." Independent tier III firms view their partners as difficult-to-replace extensions of themselves. Beyond a partnership, firms may want to eventually involve themselves financially in significantly large, capital-intensive projects with their partners (joint ventures) or even go so far as to outright purchase or be purchased by the partner (vertical integration). Although the concepts of joint ventures and vertical integration expand beyond the scope of this book, a primary argument for implementation of strategic partnerships involves receiving benefits of joint ventures and vertical integration without the ownership commitment.

To narrow the above discussion, Lambert and associates formally defined a partnership as "a tailored business relationship based on mutual trust, openness, shared risk, and shared reward that yields a competitive advantage, resulting in business performance greater than would be achieved by the firms individually" (Lambert et al., 1996, p. 2).

Several key concepts are critical to the essence of the above definition, with the first of these being interdependence. Partnering involves an *interdependent* relationship of coordinated planning and strategy. Ultimately, the partners work toward a mutual goal that benefits all parties. The second significant component of the above definition is the notion of *synergy* within the partnership. The two firms create a whole that functions better than the sum of its parts. Interdependence and synergy are two guiding concepts within a partnership, but significantly more elements exist as necessary pieces of the alliance.

Despite a formal definition of partnering, the orientation of partnership activities in practice is often vague. *When do firms officially move into the realm of partnerships?*

When can two firms officially call themselves partners? What if one firm considers the other its partner, but the title is not reciprocated? This obscurity complicates the buyer–seller relationship.

This chapter will continue by applying the partnering concepts specifically to the supply chain. To do so, it is first necessary to present the evolutionary background of supply chain strategy, as that is a primary driver for the intensified focus of supply chain partnerships.

TRADITIONAL SOURCING

Firms have taken bold steps to break down both intra- and interfirm barriers to smooth uncertainty and enhance control of supply and distribution channels (see Figure 11.2). The evolution of intrafirm functional integration has occurred for

FIGURE 11.2
Stages in Intra- and Interfirm Integration

Source: Stevens (1989).

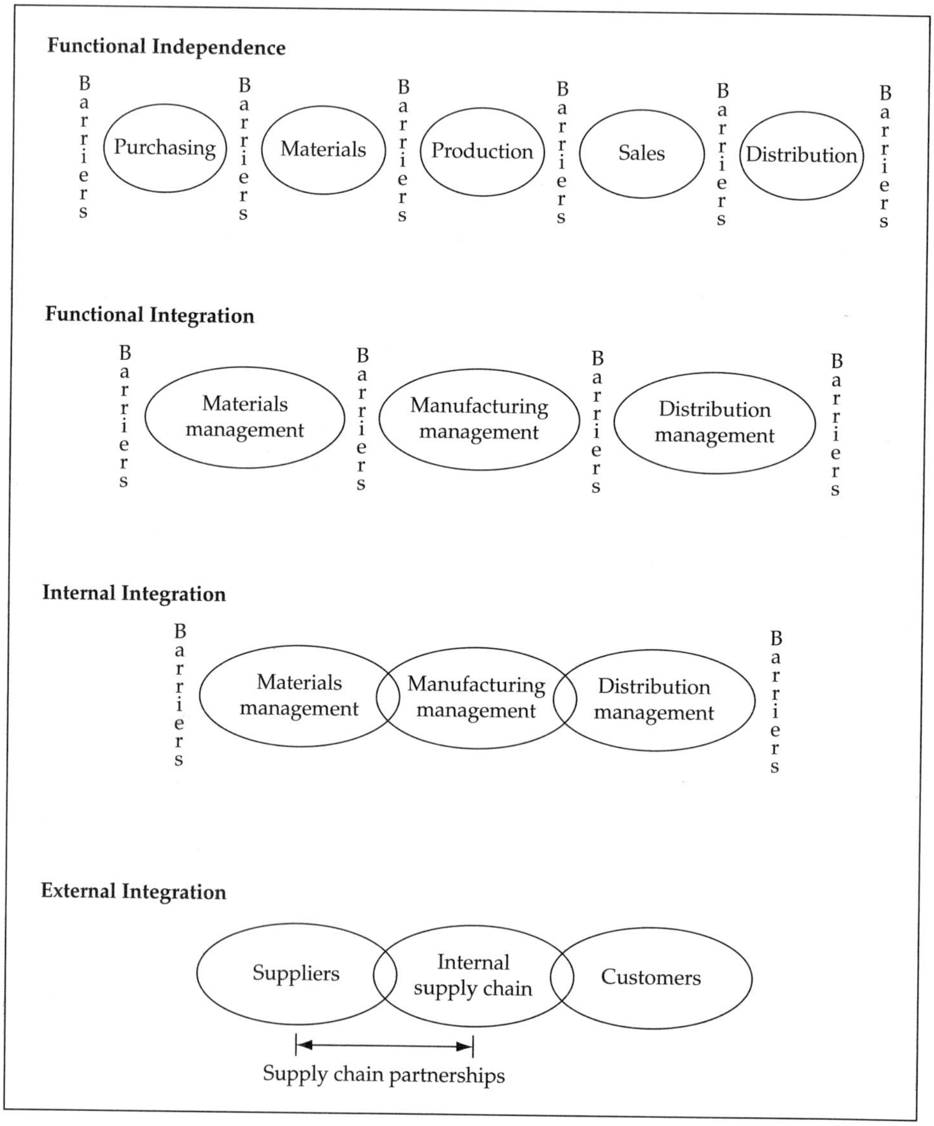

most firms over the last few decades, and the current push is toward external integration with both suppliers and customers. Supply chain partnerships bridge the barrier between buyer and seller, leading manufacturers to ally with a reduced supplier base.

Historically, American manufacturers have formulated supply strategy around the transparent benefits of a large competitive supplier base. An abundant collection of suppliers encourages competition, which the manufacturer can exploit to negotiate lower costs, higher quality, reasonable delivery times, and special exigencies. Such a strategy enhances ultimate manufacturer bargaining power as well as shelters against interruptions in supply due to strikes and other unforeseen problems. In contrast, many Asian and American firms have recognized the benefits of the opposite concept of single sourcing, which leads to an abatement of adversarial attitudes, lower switching costs, and decreased shipping errors. The association with the single source also can lead to quantity and relationship-based discounts as well as a decreased cost of quality.

REDUCED SUPPLIER BASES

Some supply managers argue that implementation of many new manufacturing techniques necessitates a reduction in the number of suppliers. The two primary factors of Asian production techniques are reduced supplier lot sizes and single sourcing. Other supply managers proclaim that single sourcing is not as widespread in Japan as believed and that many Pacific Rim manufacturers actually exercise a single/dual hybrid approach. As an example, Chrysler Corporation single-sources an individual product (such as tires for a particular car line) but will have two or three suppliers for the commodity (tires in general) in case of problems. Likewise, most supply managers promote dual over single sourcing to reduce the potential for power influence.

Despite the differences in opinions about the size of the supplier base, the major issue remains that a closer relationship with suppliers facilitates a reduced number of suppliers. There is an increased tendency toward a smaller supplier base in the United States. With regard to the automobile industry, component part sales have increased while the number of suppliers has drastically decreased. In 1983, the automobile industry relied upon approximately 10,000 suppliers to purchase $103 billion in component parts from tier I suppliers. Twenty-five years later, such purchases rose to $300 billion while the number of tier I suppliers fell to just 375. As an example of a reduced supplier base, Chrysler has been able to reduce its total (all tiers) supplier base from 3,200 vendors in 1985 to approximately 525 in 2009, and 90 percent of its purchases actually come from just 80 tier I suppliers. Furthermore, Chrysler was able to develop its LH line with approximately 200 suppliers, versus the typical 600–700.

The objective of a drastically reduced supplier base precludes an acceptance of supplier partnerships because a firm must accept dependence upon fewer suppliers before it can internalize legitimate forms of supply chain management and supplier partnerships. Although voluminous knowledge exists to examine a reduced supplier base, one key problem that is often overlooked, power asymmetry, may potentially inhibit the implementation of such a strategy in Western cultures. Asian suppliers are not "suppliers" in the Western sense of the word, and, in most instances, single sourcing will not mechanically work in the United States, as the power imbalance will lead to opportunism and exploitation. Thus, relying on a reduced supplier base requires a transformation of ingrained Western supply chain practices, and such a change may not be completely possible due to behavioral and cultural considerations. Efforts to investigate the implementation of reduced supplier bases have neglected the role of power asymmetry and thus have not realistically challenged the reality of single sourcing.

SUPPLY CHAIN PARTNERSHIPS

A Harvard Business School study concluded that a key driver in the decline of U.S. competitiveness in the international marketplace has originated from investing less in intangible benefits such as supplier relations. It is impossible to operate as a discrete entity, but while virtually no firm engages in completely discrete engagements, conventional Western and American business practices have been more oriented toward the discrete than the relational. Traditionally, U.S. firms have based their drive for success on autonomy and have viewed competition as a Darwinistic keeper of American superiority. Long-run U.S. firm planning has been independent, and considerable efforts are made to ensure privacy of corporate information.

Over recent decades, however, firms within the supply chain have begun to realize the advantages enjoyed from sharing of technology, information, and planning with other firms, even competitors, and many modern business thinkers will claim that a more open and relational attitude is not only advantageous but actually essential to maintaining a competitive advantage. As shown in Figure 11.3, the idea of relationalism between firms seeks to move away from the concept of discrete transactions, breaking down traditional interfirm barriers. Firms unite to share information and planning efforts, thus reducing uncertainty as well as increasing control. In the end, the partners reap the benefits of the joint effort.

Recognizing partnerships between buyer and supplier as a fundamental driver for the success of the Pacific Rim supply chain processes, American firms have begun to emulate these supplier alliances. Asian firms are not completely responsible for the move to supplier partnerships; many supplier alliances were due to raw materials shortages, oil crises, government price controls, and general changes in attitudes. However, the primary root of the success of the concept lies with the Pacific Rim. Modern manufacturing improvements, such as just-in-time, require the tighter control evaluated by the supply chain partnership, and there is growing evidence that Western firms have begun to implement such relational strategies.

FIGURE 11.3
Discrete versus Relational Business Strategies

Source: Maloni and Benton (1997).

Contractual Element	Discrete Orientation →	Relational Orientation
Duration	One time	Long term
Transferability (switching parties)	Completely transferable	Extremely difficult to transfer
Attitude	Independent, suspicious	Open, trusting, cooperative
Communication	Very little	Complex
Information	Proprietary	Shared
Planning and goals	Individual, short term	Joint, long term
Benefits and risks	Individual	Shared
Problem solving	Power driven	Mutual, judicious

FIGURE 11.4
Traditional versus Partnership Supply Strategies

Traditional Supply Relationships	Supply Chain Partnerships
• Price emphasis for supplier selection • Short-term contracts for suppliers • Bid evaluation • Large supplier base • Proprietary information • Power-driven problem solving • Coercive relationships	• Multiple criteria for supplier selection • Long-term contracts for suppliers • Intensive evaluation of supplier value added • Few suppliers • Shared information • Mutual problem solving • Improvement • Success sharing

Source: Adapted from Stuart (1993).

Initial efforts to involve suppliers began with their inclusion of suppliers in cross-functional sourcing teams. There must be establishment of such teams in order to improve supply chain effectiveness. Supply alliances, however, extend well beyond this notion to an even more relational level of exchange in which partners create an intensive, interdependent relationship from which both can mutually benefit. Supply partnerships emphasize direct, long-term association, encouraging mutual planning and problem-solving efforts. Figure 11.4 displays the critical elements of a supply partnership in comparison to traditional thinking.

Benefits of Supplier Partnerships

While many firms have sought vertical integration through acquisition to harness supplier expertise, some argue that partnerships can provide similar benefits without the necessity of ownership and arduous exit barriers. Buyers can gain from higher quality, and transaction costs may be reduced through economies of scale, decreased administrative and switching efforts, process integration, coordination of processes, and quantity discounts. Furthermore, the relationship will be enhanced by market stability for both the supplier and buyer. Several further benefits specific to manufacturing processes, including setup time reduction, improved process-oriented layout, better product design, and enhanced data capture, also have been proposed. Less-tangible benefits from which both firms can benefit are increased communication and goal congruence, leading to enhanced conflict resolution, less probability of opportunism, and decreased risk from externalities.

A detailed list of possible advantages of supply chain relationships composed from several sources is summarized in Figure 11.5.

Some supply professionals believe that supplier partnerships lead to improved quality of supplier operations, improved quality products, decreased supplier costs, and improved reaction to buyer changes to delivery date. However, such profit improvements tend not to be recognizable before several years of the alliance.

Risks of Supplier Partnerships

With its many benefits, supply chain partnerships retain several inherent risks that can be potentially damaging to participants. First and foremost, heavy reliance on one partner can be disastrous if the partner does not meet expectations. Also, firms risk decreased competitiveness due to loss of partnership control, complacency, and overspecialization with an affirmed partner. Furthermore, firms may overestimate partnership benefits while ignoring potential shortcomings. There is a need for more research examining direct comparisons of the

FIGURE 11.5
Potential Benefits of Supplier Partnerships

Source: Maloni and Benton (2000).

Reduced uncertainty for buyers in
- Material costs
- Quality
- Timing
- Reduced supplier base, which is easier to manage

Reduced uncertainty for suppliers in
- Market
- Understanding customer needs
- Product specifications

Reduced uncertainty for both buyers and suppliers in
- Convergent expectation and goals
- Reduced effects from externalities
- Reduced opportunism
- Increased communication and feedback

Joint product and process development
- Faster product development
- Increased shared technology
- Greater joint involvement of product design

Greater flexibility

Cost savings
- Economies of scale in ordering, production, and transaction
- Decreased administrative costs
- Fewer switching costs
- Enhanced process integration
  - Technical or physical integration
  - Improved asset utilization

Time management
- Faster product development
- Faster to market for new products
- Improved cycle time

Shared risks and rewards
- Joint investments
- Joint research and development
- Market shifts
- Increased profitability

Stability
- Lead times
- Priorities and attention

conventional and partnership strategies. There are beneficial insights from both conventional and partnership perspectives. Partnerships may actually open the weaker party up to negative influence potential, and research suggests that competition may abate power.

Partnership Implementation and Critical Success Factors

Before firms can enjoy the benefits of a buyer–supplier partnership, they must first endure the complicated and intricate partnership implementation process. A supplier partnership involves a significant attitudinal as well as structural change from traditional supply arrangements, so the allying firms must be meticulous to ensure that a true win–win partnership is developed. Guides to the implementation process are summarized in Figure 11.6.

The first step in the supplier partnership implementation process includes the strategic verification of the need for a supplier partnership. Here, the firm must evaluate the potential risks and benefits of a partnership in comparison to traditional processes. Next, criteria for potential partners are developed, and candidates are assessed. Once a partner is selected, the establishment of the actual relationship provides the next critical step in which the partners must create a complete sense

FIGURE 11.6
Supplier Partnership Implementation Steps

Supplier Partnership Implementation Steps
1. Establish strategic need for partnership.
2. Develop partner criteria, evaluate suppliers, and select partner.
3. Formally establish partnership.
4. Maintain and refine partnership (possible reduction or dissolvement).

FIGURE 11.7
Supplier Partnership Critical Success Factors

Source: Adapted from Ellram (1995).

Supplier Partnership Critical Success Factors in the Phases of Implementation

Throughout
- Top management support
- Communication
- Central coordination

Initial Strategic Analysis Phase
- Social and attitudinal barriers
- Procedural and structural barriers

Supplier Evaluation and Selection Phase
- Total cost and profit benefit
- Partner capabilities
- Cultural compatibility
- Financial stability
- Location

Partnership Establishment Phase
- Perception and needs analysis
- Intense interaction
- Documentation

Maintenance Phase
- Trust
- Goodwill
- Flexibility
- Conflict management skills
- Social exchange
- Boundary personnel
- Performance measurement

of awareness about the needs and participation of all involved parties. The final step in the partnering process includes the maintenance of the relationship to either enhance its development or bring about its dissolution.

The entire partnership implementation process holds many elements critical to the success of the relationship that are given in Figure 11.7. One rudiment that must be established immediately is top management advocacy. This requires overcoming social and attitudinal barriers as well as managerial, procedural, and structural obstacles associated with corporate change. In practice, overcoming the social and attitudinal barriers and managerial practices may prove to be extremely difficult if not impossible.

In the supplier selection/evaluation step, the chance of choosing the wrong supplier presents a severe problem in partnering. An additional list of selection criteria for supply chain partners including such elements as cultural compatibility, long-term strategic plans, financial stability, technology/design capability, management compatibility, and location also must be considered.

As shown in Figure 11.7, the final steps for establishing and maintaining the relationship necessitate several factors. Overall, the most important attitudinal factors involve cooperation, trust, and goodwill, as well as the ability for both parties to be flexible and to handle conflicts. Furthermore, attitude, communication, and shared goals are described as success factors. Other critical success factors will include effective performance measurement, as well as proper establishment of boundary personnel and procedures.

Ultimate dissolution of the partnership may be necessary if the firms are unable to successfully work through the critical steps of partnership formation or if synergies cannot be recognized. Abandonment of partners may lead to suspicion, making future partners difficult to attract. Ultimately, "little is known about disengagement," so dissolution may offer a pessimistic, yet rich, source of research. A "rule of thumb" must be developed that can be used to decide whether or not a partnership has sufficient potential.

The notion of interfirm power holds its roots in the social science (psychology, social psychology, and political science) literature and has been extensively developed by marketing channel researchers. The power component of partnerships will begin with the definition of power. As defined by Maloni and Benton (2000):

> . . . the power of a supply chain member [is] the ability to control the decision variables in the supply strategy of another member in a given chain at a different level of the supply chain. It should be different from the influenced member's original level of control over their own supply strategy.
>
> With a supply-side orientation, an appropriate definition of power in the supply chain is the ability of one channel member (the source) to influence the actions and intentions of another supply chain member (the target).

POWER INFLUENCES ON SUPPLY CHAIN RELATIONSHIPS

Extremely complex in nature, power serves as a composite relationship–oriented variable, affecting both the target and the source in many transparent as well as concealed ways. The following section will examine the effects of influence strategies on critical relationship factors including dependence, commitment, trust, compliance, cooperation, conflict, satisfaction, performance, and profitability. Exploration of the effects of power on factors of the supplier–buyer alliance provides the key to understanding the concept of the power-partnership link that is under investigation.

Power and Dependence

The notion of power in an interfirm relationship implies target dependence on the source; otherwise the target would not need to subject itself to the unbalanced relationship. Power is a direct result of dependence, and the extent of dependence is directly induced by perceptions of power. However, in situations with exercised power-dependence relationships in the presence of high commitment, no correlation has been found between power and dependence. An explanation is that power sources and dependence are inseparable, and, thus, dependence measurement will not add insight to the presence of power since they essentially measure the same concept.

With the subordinate relationship caused by dependence, one might logically conclude that the target–source relationship would be fairly strong (due to necessity) since the target would be forced to abide by the will of the source. The greater dependence is more than likely associated with greater cooperation in the relationship. Moreover, economic dependence increases compliance.

Dependence created by power could possibly yield a closer relationship, but the presence of dependence does not invite a relationship like that of the simple conceptual partnership. Critical elements of supplier partnerships include trust, goodwill, shared goals, and social exchange. A state of dependence would indicate compliance due to necessity rather than cooperation on the part of the target out of trust and goodwill. Thus, critical dependence questions that should be addressed when establishing a supply relationship are as follows:

- Does a state of dependence negate the possibility for critical supply chain partnership success factors such as goodwill, trust, and shared goals?
- Does a state of dependence create a relationship that differs from a true, mutually beneficial supply chain partnership?

Power, Commitment, and Trust

Two factors driven by power and critical to the partnership dyad are commitment and trust. Commitment may be defined as the feeling of being emotionally impelled. The relationship between power and commitment is dependent upon the origins of the commitment. Commitment is nothing more than a form of compliance (instrumental) as well as identification and involvement (normative).

> One popular dichotomization is mediated/nonmediated. Mediated power sources that include reward, coercive, and legal legitimate involve influence strategies that the source specifically administers to the target with the direct intention of bringing about some action. Such mediated bases represent the competitive, negative uses of power traditionally associated with organizational theory. Nonmediated power sources, which are more relational and positive in orientation, include expert, referent, and traditional legitimate. These power bases occur as a natural part of business transactions and do not necessitate intention from the source. In fact, the source may not even be aware that some mediated power bases may exist. (Brown et al., 1995)

Power sources tend to use noncoercive influence strategies, which are logically supported by the idea that use of coercion may risk the power advantage. In contrast, it also can be argued that the power source will tend to utilize mediated power strategies since such forms require less time to implement.

Mediated power forces the target to be committed to maintain the relationship for its sustenance, but genuine psychological commitment is lower due to the resentment over the subordinate situation. On the other hand, nonmediated power sources can increase true commitment. Ultimately, normative commitment in the form of attitude and goodwill is implied as a critical success factor for supply chain partnerships. Thus, power used positively by the source may enhance a partnering relationship.

Recent findings also imply, however, that it may be possible to increase trust through relational (nonmediated, noncoercive) power efforts. The subsequent key commitment and trust questions significant to supply chain partnerships are as follows:

- Are true trust and normative commitment possible in an interfirm environment of power asymmetry?
- Can a target in an unbalanced power relationship experience normative commitment or is such commitment merely instrumental?

- How do relational and competitive power strategies affect normative trust and commitment?
- Can a power source use relational power strategies to enhance normative commitment and trust?

Power, Cooperation, and Compliance

Power essentially attempts to force a target to comply with the source's desires, and, like commitment, the levels of compliance and, more importantly, cooperation are critical to the relationship tenure as well as profitability. Compliance is action without inherent desire, and, thus, compliance remains a relatively easy factor to measure since it implies action, not feeling. These findings point to the idea that power yields compliance regardless of the power strategy.

Cooperation, however, endures as a more difficult idea to measure due to the fact that it implies internal agreement with the actions. A target acting as the source reveals compliance, but true cooperation may not be determined without an assessment of the target's internal reasons for compliance. Thus, there can be compliance without cooperation.

In a supply chain partnership, cooperation needs to be the key driver of strategy, and the presence of compliance would essentially void a true partnership. The use of coercive power will cause compliance and eradicate a partnership. Thus, the major compliance and cooperation questions addressed when establishing supply chain partnerships are as follows:

- Can cooperation exist in a mediated power-driven supply chain partnership relationship?
- Do relational power strategies actually enhance cooperation and strengthen a supply chain partnership?

Power and Conflict

Conflict can be defined as "tension between two or more social entities . . . which arises from incompatibility of actual or desired responses" (Maloni and Benton, 2000). Conflict is present in the supply chain when one supply chain member hinders goal attainment and performance of another. Conflict is an omnipresent factor in any supply chain relationship.

Conflict will obviously be harmful if not extending to supply chain partnerships. Recent supply chain studies show that competitive power sources will increase conflict, but positive use of power can reduce conflict (Benton and Maloni, 2005; Maloni and Benton, 2000). Subsequently, the critical issues for establishing supply chain partnerships are the following:

- Does a power imbalance in a supply relationship create a level of conflict that will harm and subsequently destroy a supply chain partnership?
- Does use of relational power strategies decrease conflict and promote a supply chain partnership?
- How does power affect conflict resolution?

Power and Satisfaction

Satisfaction in the supply chain can be defined as the extent of contentment with the relationship (Benton and Maloni, 2005). Ultimate supply chain partner satisfaction remains the overriding factor in determining the future of a supply chain partnership. Drivers of satisfaction within supply chain partnerships include relationship-oriented factors such as planning, mutuality, interdependence, and operational information exchange. Without satisfaction, supply chain members will be unable to generate the psychological factors such as trust, commitment, and goodwill that are necessary for the partnership to be sustained. Subsequently, the critical issues for establishing supply chain partnerships are the following:

- How does power influence satisfaction within the supply chain?
- Within a power imbalance, can the target firm experience sufficient levels of satisfaction to retain commitment to the supply chain relationship?
- Within a power imbalance, can the source firm retain sufficient levels of satisfaction to retain commitment to the supply chain relationship?

Power, Performance, and Profitability

A final point on the effects of power concerns the ultimate performance and subsequent profitability of the supply chain members, as well as the supply chain itself. Performance may be defined as the ability to execute intentions and goals. Supply chain member performance can be affected by power, as well as countervailing power. The use of mediated power sometimes erodes performance of the target, while use of nonmediated power will improve the target's opinion of the source's performance. Furthermore, studies by Benton and Maloni found that the target's opinion of source performance was positively related to the amount of target normative commitment and negatively related to instrumental commitment (Benton and Maloni, 2005; Maloni and Benton, 2000).

Two implications for supply chain partnerships, one negative and one positive, evolve from the literature. First, it appears that a power source can benefit from increased profitability and performance through utilization of such power, suggesting that a partnership may not be necessary for the source's own success. On the other hand, the literature also suggests that nonmediated forms of power can actually help performance, supporting the notion of a true win–win partnership. Thus, important issues for establishing supply chain partnerships are the following:

- How does power influence source performance and profitability in a power-asymmetric supply chain relationship?
- How does power influence target performance and profitability in a power-asymmetric supply chain relationship?
- How does power influence supply chain performance and profitability in the supply chain?

Automobile Industry Example of Power Asymmetry

The automobile industry in the United States represents a breeding ground for power research. The industry consists of five manufacturers that account for 85 percent of market share and these manufacturers source from a supplier base of thousands. Such an oligopolistic buying structure has created a power-asymmetric environment. With a few manufacturers comprising a large percentage of the suppliers' sales, the supplier must bow to the authority of the buyers or risk financial collapse. This power imbalance is delineated in the demographics of the survey respondents from research (Maloni and Benton, 1997), as the five manufacturers accounted for an average of 23.52 percent of respondent business.

To compound the problems created by the power imbalance, firms in the automobile industry face intense competition. Each year, the manufacturers are pressed to build higher-quality, more technologically advanced cars while maintaining competitive prices. Such pressure directly affects the supplier base. The industry power imbalance has allowed the manufacturers to relinquish many of the responsibilities for product and process improvement to the suppliers. These first-tier suppliers are the key to maintaining the competitive capacities of the manufacturers, and those suppliers that cannot perform are systematically exiled to financial ruin.

To recognize the synergy from coordination between manufacturer and suppliers as well as among the suppliers themselves, there has been an industrywide inclination toward integration of the supply chain. The members of the supply chain synthesize processes and strategies, allowing the entire chain to work together to attack pressures from cost reduction, faster cycle times, and increased quality benchmarks. Supply chain management grants the supply chain a potential source of competitive advantage and will become an increasingly important part of the industry strategy.

Manufacturers in the automobile industry have been aware of their power advantage, and suppliers have long suffered from competitive, coercive power influences from these manufacturers. The use of such coercive strategy is best exemplified by General Motors. As the largest manufacturer in the industry, General Motors purchases over $90 billion of components and materials from suppliers annually. General Motors has capitalized on its buying power, maintaining a demanding attitude in its supplier relations. It is the power source that must enact the change in the relationship but needs some motivation to change its opportunistic tendencies.

Summary

The intense coordination necessary for effective supply chain integration necessitates a reduced supplier base; where manufacturers were once producing products with thousands of suppliers, successful firms are now manufacturing better products with fewer suppliers. The large pie of purchased parts and materials thus gets divided among fewer players, and more is at stake for the suppliers. The suppliers must strive to develop best practice in order to gain the critical preferred status with the manufacturers, and these preferred suppliers must maintain best practice or face effortless replacement from the large base of competitors. This intensifies the power imbalance within an industry sector. The manufacturers can maintain the attitude that the suppliers must keep pace with the industry or lose a potentially significant amount of their business.

Interfirm power may be defined as the ability of one firm (the source) to influence the actions and intentions of another firm (the target). Several sources of power, both positive and negative, exist to affect the operational strategies and processes of both the power target and the source. The influences of power affect critical interfirm relationship elements as well as firm performance and satisfaction. Despite such effects, most firms may not be completely aware of the broad scope of power dimensions and thus may not actively manage their power.

One paradigm in the corporate world that has emerged over the last few decades involves a shift to a more relational way of doing business. Firms are breaking down their own corporate barriers to recognize the synergy generated from shared strategy and processes. The move to relational business transactions has found significant potential in the supply chain. A recent flow of operations and logistics literature has promoted coordination of supply chain activities as a source of competitive advantage through reduced uncertainty, shared risk, enhanced responsiveness, faster cycle times, more effective product development, reduced costs, and higher quality.

A relational orientation, though, complicates the role of power within interfirm interactions. For instance, power may interfere with the mutuality and sincerity of interfirm alliances, inducing the power source to more directly use its power. On the other hand, allying firms may expose themselves to further opportunistic behavior by conniving partners, thus increasing the prominence of power within the relationship. Little research exists, however, to challenge the role of power with such supply chain integration. The existence of power directly challenges the effectiveness and utility of current supply chain management research.

Perhaps the most valuable contribution from recent research is that it offers evidence for incentives to avoid the use of competitive power. Recent research also has shown that relational uses of power through expert, referent, and reward sources can be used to strengthen the nature of the relationships between buying and selling firms. Thus, power may be utilized as an approach to promote effective integration of the supply chain. It also has been indicated that these enhanced supply chain relationships can yield performance benefits to all members of the supply chain, including the power source. Hence, the power source should manage its own power influences for its own good.

This discussion highlights the importance of power awareness, as well as recognition of power as a valuable approach for increasing the competitive positioning of the entire supply chain. Thus, practitioners need to take a long, hard look at their own awareness of power within the supply chain. They must understand power influences as well as the prevalent existing power bases. The power source must become conscious of its available power bases and subsequently promote the positive bases while carefully controlling the harmful, coercive bases. Furthermore, it may not simply be enough to effectively manage power, as the mere ability to exercise power may not be enough to bring about desired action. The power holder must create an environment of trust to assure the target that competitive power sources will not be exercised in any fashion.

The role of supply chain management in industry will only intensify, and power management must become a prominent part of supply chain strategy. If power source firms choose not to manage their power advantage effectively, they risk harm to the rest of the supply chain as well as to themselves. Thus, it is predicted that these firms will be unable to sustain supply chain management as a competitive advantage and will be surpassed by those that are able to develop a more relationally oriented supply chain.

Beyond its valuable contributions to the inspiration of supply chain management, this chapter only provides an initial glance at power influences within the supply chain. A more comprehensive discussion on power is given in Appendix A. More research is needed to examine the effects of power management on supply chain strategy. The direction of this chapter will hopefully enrich the evolution of supply chain management and allow buying firms to be better positioned as an effective source of competitive advantage.

Discussion Questions

1. What is the definition of a supply partnership?
2. What are some of the benefits of supplier partnerships?
3. What are the critical implementation factors?
4. What are some of the risks associated with supplier partnerships?
5. What is the definition of supply chain power?
6. What are the critical success factors for supply chain partnerships?
7. What is meant by the "bases of power"?
8. How is supply chain power associated with the purchasing function?

Suggested Cases

Butler Systems
Trip 7 Printing
TEMKO Earthmovers

References

Benton, W. C., and Michael J. Maloni. "The Influence of Power Driven Buyer/Seller Relationships on Supply Chain Satisfaction." *Journal of Operations Management* 23, no. 1 (2005).

Brown, James R., Jean L. Johnson, and Harold F. Koenig. "Measuring the Sources of Marketing Channel Power: A Comparison of Alternative Approaches," *International Journal of Research in Marketing* 12, no. 4 (1995), pp. 333–54.

Ellram, Lisa M. "Partnering Pitfalls and Success Factors." *International Journal of Purchasing & Materials Management* 31, no. 2 (1995), pp. 36–44.

Lambert, Douglas M., Margaret A. Emmelhainz, and John T. Gardner. "Developing and Implementing Supply Chain Partnerships." *International Journal of Logistics Management* 7, no. 2 (1996), pp. 1–17.

Maloni, Michael J., and W. C. Benton Jr. "Power Influences in the Supply Chain." *Journal of Business Logistics* 21, no. 1 (2000), pp. 42–73.

Maloni, Michael J., and W. C. Benton Jr. "Supply Chain Partnerships: Opportunities for Operations Research." *European Journal of Operational Research* 101, no. 3 (1997), pp. 419–29.

Stevens, Graham C. "Integrating the Supply Chain." *International Journal of Physical Distribution & Materials Management* 19, no. 8 (1989), pp. 3–8.

Stuart, F. Ian. "Supplier Partnerships: Influencing Factors and Strategic Benefits." *International Journal of Purchasing & Materials Management* 29, no. 4 (1993), pp. 22–28.

Appendix A

Channel and Supply Chain Power[1]

DEFINITION OF POWER

A comprehension of power starts with its basic definition. Gaski (1984) provides a collection of several similar definitions of power taken from the social sciences literature:

> A has the power over B to the extent that A can get B to do something that B would not otherwise do. (Dahl, 1957)
> When an agent, O, performs an act resulting in some change in another agent, P, we say that O influences P. If O has the capability of influencing P, we say that O has power over P. (Cartwright, 1965)

Maloni and Benton (2000) apply the notion of power to supply chain management:

> ". . . the power of a supply chain member [is] the ability to control the decision variables in the supply strategy of another member in a given chain at a different level of the supply chain. It should be different from the influenced member's original level of control over their own supply strategy."
>
> With a supply-side orientation, an appropriate definition of power in the supply chain is *the ability of one channel member (the source) to influence the actions and intentions of another supply chain member (the target).*

THE BASES OF POWER

Power can originate from many different sources and can be exercised via a multitude of strategies. A vast amount of power orientation is oriented toward "bases" or "sources" of power, which primarily addresses the orientation of why a firm holds the ability to influence. The first offering of bases of power comes from French and Raven (1959). (See Figure A.1.) A multitude of further research has offered extensions and new concepts to power sources, but most analyses remain closely related to the French and Raven classification.

[1]The appendix was abstracted from a working paper, "Channel and Supply Chain Power" by Michael J. Maloni and W. C. Benton (2006).

FIGURE A.1
Bases of Power

Source: French and Raven (1959).

Reward	The source has the ability to mediate rewards to the target.
Punishment	The source has the ability to mediate punishment to the target. Also termed as **coercive.**
Legitimate	The source has the legitimate right to influence behavior over the target. This is based primarily on acceptance of roles **(traditional legitimate)** as well as judiciary restraints **(legal legitimate).**
Identification	The target will allow influence by the source to maintain identification with the source. Also termed as **referent.**
Expertise	The source holds distinctive knowledge, information, and skills that are valuable to the target. Also termed as **information.**

Reward power refers to the ability of one partner in the relationship to control valued resources whether such resources are tangible or intangible. With a supply chain notion, a customer might have the ability to offer more business or long-term contracts while a supplier might be able to offer lower prices, better service, or improved technology. *Punishment power*, which is also termed as *coercive power*, involves the ability to take disciplinary action over partners. In the supply chain, customers may attempt to withdraw business or cancel contracts, and suppliers may attempt to raise prices or offer poorer service. Reward and punishment powers are closely related since withholding an expected reward may be considered a form of punishment.

Legitimate power refers to recognition of the right to hold authority over others. Legitimate power originates from perceived standing or status and thus is only present if the power target believes the power source retains the natural privilege to such power. Suppliers may believe that their customers have the right to authority within the supply chain or customers may hold such beliefs about their suppliers. *Identification* or *referent power* refers to a partner's desire to be associated with another out of admiration for him or her. Such power originates from affection or respect. Within the supply chain, partners may respect the business practices or position of a chain member and feel they are obligated to respond to the firm out of allegiance. Finally, *expert* (or *information*) *power* refers to the ability of a member of a relationship to control knowledge. With expert power, power targets believe the source has knowledge and competencies that will lead them to take proper action and, thus, it is in the target's best interest to respond to the source. In the supply chain, supply chain members may hold market, technology, or process knowledge, and, subsequently, the other channel members may yield control, believing such knowledge will lead to the best decisions.

INFLUENCE STRATEGIES

Directly related to the bases of power is the concept of influence strategy, which describes the method by which power may be mediated. Firms may choose to exert power in many different ways, and a summary of such methods is given in Figure A.2. Influence strategies range from simple control and exchange of information to issuing of rewards and punishments. Often, multiple influence strategies may be used in a single attempt.

It is of interest to note that other potential power influences exist that are not listed above due to the fact those strategies are not specifically mediated to the target. Examples of such include traditional legitimate and identification power as well as expert power. One must be careful to recognize the difference between expert power and information control. Expert power is held naturally by a source, but the intended mediation or control of the information involves more of a reward/punishment power source.

PROBLEMS WITH ANALYSES OF POWER BASES

The notion of each power base as well as strategy is relatively elementary, but several issues create potential problems for researchers. For one, there exist no defined boundaries for the different bases and strategies. Because of the ambiguity of the notion of power, perception plays a critical role in the power struggle, affecting both the intention and the communication of the power type utilized. A source may communicate a strategy that is misperceived by the target. As an example, a

FIGURE A.2
Attitudes, Behavior Influences, and Communication Strategies

Source: Adapted from Frazier and Sheth (1985).

Information exchange	Supplied information and knowledge
Information control	Withheld or manipulated information
Modeling	Examples of desired attitude or behavior
Positive normative	Statement of what a "good" channel member would do
Negative normative	Statement of what a "poor" channel member would do
Recommendation	Suggestion or endorsement
Warning	Cautionary statement
Request	Solicitation for proposed behavior
Command	Mandate
Promise	Pledged returned response
Threat	Returned sanctionary response
Legalistic reference	Reminder or threat of legal bindings
Economic reward	Monetary-based compensation
Noneconomic reward	Nonmonetary-based compensation
Economic punishment	Monetary-based discipline
Noneconomic punishment	Nonmonetary-based discipline

recommendation might be interpreted as a request or threat, creating the potential for misinterpretation and subsequent discord. Supply managers also have disagreed about the significance of certain power strategies. For example, a promise, which is typically thought of as a positive strategy, may actually be viewed negatively. Overall, the haze surrounding the power bases and strategies compounds research difficulty and creates the potential to lead to vague and deceptive results. The ambiguity with the challenge of whether or not power remains too abstract of a concept to be measurable must be considered.

A second obstacle with power source and strategy categorization lies with its inherent a priori orientation that has the potential to not only bias the research but cause it to miss the true power relationship as well.

Another problem with power classification exists with longitudinal factors in that the nature and orientation of relationships change over time, affecting types and amounts of power employed. The effects of power historically in supply chain relationships should be considered. In a final problem with power bases, much of the research that attempts to model power fails to incorporate the effects of power sources on one another, potentially biasing research results. For instance, the use of reward power sources has a positive impact upon expert, referent, and legitimate power sources. On the other hand, punishment yields a negative impact. Thus, reward and punishment may be complex, interacting power relationships.

DICHOTOMIZATION OF POWER SOURCES

Prominent dichotomizations include coercive/noncoercive, economic/noneconomic, direct/indirect, contingent/noncontingent, altered/unaltered perceptions, and mediated/nonmediated. A taxonomy of power source dichotomization and power bases is shown in Figure A.3.

One popular dichotomization is mediated/nonmediated. Mediated power sources, which include reward, coercive, and legal legitimate, involve influence strategies that the source specifically administers to the target with the direct intention of

FIGURE A.3 Dichotomizations of Power Sources and Strategies

Coercive versus (Punishment) Noncoercive (Reward, expertise, legitimate, referent)	Skinner et al. (1992) Frazier and Rody (1991) Schul and Babakus (1988) (examined reward versus coercion) Richardson and Robicheaux (1992) Gaski and Nevin (1985) Lusch (1976) Gundlach and Cadotte (1994) Hunt and Nevin (1974)
Economic versus (Reward, punishment) Noneconomic (Expert, legitimate, referent)	Etgar (1978) Brown et al. (1983) Lusch and Brown (1982)
Direct versus (Reward, punishment, legal legitimate) Indirect (Information, traditional legitimate, referent)	Kasulis et al. (1979)
Contingent versus (Reward, punishment) Noncontingent (Expert, legitimate, referent)	John (1984)
Perceptions altered versus (Information, recommendation) Perceptions unaltered (Reward, threats, legalistic, requests)	Frazier and Summers (1984)
Mediated versus (Reward, coercion, legal legitimate) Nonmediated (Referent, expert, traditional legitimate, information)	Brown et al. (1995)

bringing about some action. Such mediated bases represent the competitive, negative uses of power traditionally associated with organizational theory. Mediated power sources that are more relational and positive in orientation include expert, referent, and traditional legitimate. These power bases occur as a natural part of business transactions and do not necessitate intention from the source. In fact, the source may not even be aware that some mediated power bases may exist.

Despite these research findings for distribution channels, ambiguity (as in the case of power bases) creates a problem with power dichotomization. The boundaries between dichotomies are often hazy, and influence types may span both categories. For instance, a reward may not be directly linked to economic resources, and information from expert and referent sources can lead to economic gain. Perception also plays a role in complicating the boundaries between power source dichotomies. For example, a reward that is viewed as noncoercive by the source may be perceived as a coercive punishment. In general, researchers must be cautious not to blindly follow previous dichotomizations of power bases and should carefully validate proposed classifications for each individual study.

EXERCISED AND UNEXERCISED POWER

Beyond the aforementioned dichotomies of power sources, one more arrangement, exercised versus unexercised power, deserves analysis. Indicating a complex relationship between exercised and unexercised power legitimately warns that power holders need not necessarily exercise their power to obtain the desired response from the target. Indeed, the presence and potential of power may be enough to create a situation of perceived dependence and/or bring about some desired behavior. In many cases, exercise of power has stronger effects than power that is not exercised.

Because of the potential interaction as well as the ambiguity involved, with exercised and unexercised power in a relationship, it is critical to consider both simultaneously in research. Concentrating on exercised power could cause the underestimation of the strength of the power relationship. In fact, the stronger the amount of held power, the less likely that power needs to be exercised. Furthermore, previous exercise of power may alleviate the need to exercise it in the future, so the power history between a source and a target firm can affect the need for the actual exercise of power. Also see Maloni & Benton (1997).

RECIPROCITY AND COUNTERVAILING POWER

To understand the complete potential of power influences, it remains critical to understand how a target firm will react in the form of both reciprocity (returning power influences) and countervailing power (attempting to stop use of the other's power). In first considering reciprocity, the nature of a power relationship dictates that a source holds authority over a target, hinting that only the source will be able to exercise power bases.

Directly related to the idea of reciprocity of power is the notion of countervailing power, which target firms may utilize to avoid the effects of power exercised by the source. Gaski (1984, p. 25) defines countervailing power as "channel member B's ability to inhibit channel member A's power over B's decision variables." In other words, countervailing power is the ability of the target to stop the source from exercising power. Countervailing power implies the presence of nonpervasive power. If a firm had complete power control over another, it is unlikely that the target firm would be able to countervail any power efforts. However, if a firm's power was nonpervasive, the target firm may be able to threaten reciprocity in another area in which it might hold a power advantage. Lusch and Ross (1985) found that power among food brokers and wholesalers was issue-specific as opposed to pervasive, but, overall, the pervasiveness of power no doubt varies greatly due to industry- and firm-specific factors.

Countervailing power clouds the power relationship since the existence of power in such a situation does not imply that it may be utilized. The result would seemingly be a stalemate. The existence of countervailing power may increase supply chain conflict and decrease satisfaction to the holder, but others may argue that countervailing power would increase satisfaction to the holder in that he/she would avoid power exercised upon him/her. Reciprocity, by definition, is usually formally or informally used in most buyer–seller transactions.

REFERENCES

Brown, James R., Jean L. Johnson, and Harold F. Koenig. "Measuring the Sources of Marketing Channel Power: A Comparison of Alternative Approaches." *International Journal of Research in Marketing* 12, no. 4 (1995), pp. 333–54.

Brown, James R., Robert Lusch, and Darrel D. Muehling. "Conflict and Power-Dependence Relations in Retailer-Supplier Channels." *Journal of Retailing* 59, no. 4 (1983), pp. 53–80.

Cartwright, Dorwin. "Influence, Leadership, Control." In *Handbook of Organizations*, ed. James G. March, pp. 1–47. Chicago: Rand McNally, 1965.

Dahl, Robert A. "The Concept of Power." *Behavioral Science* 2 (July 1957), pp. 201–18.

Etgar, Michael. "Selection of an Effective Control Mix." *Journal of Marketing* 42, no. 3 (1978), pp. 53–58.

Frazier, Gary L., and Raymond C. Rody. "The Use of Influence Strategies in Interfirm Relationships in Industrial Product Channels." *Journal of Marketing* 55, no. 1 (1991), pp. 52–69.

Frazier, Gary L., and Jagdish N. Sheth. "An Attitude-Behavior Framework for Distribution Channel Management." *Journal of Marketing* 49 (Summer 1985), pp. 38–48.

Frazier, Gary L., and John O. Summers. "Interfirm Influence Strategies and Their Application with Distribution Channels." *Journal of Marketing* 48, no. 3 (1984), pp. 43–55.

French, John R., and Bertram Raven. "The Bases of Social Power." In *Studies in Social Power*, ed. Dorwin Cartwright. Ann Arbor: University of Michigan Press, 1959.

Gaski, John F. "The Theory of Power and Conflict in Channels of Distribution." *Journal of Marketing* 48, no. 3 (1984), pp. 9–29.

Gaski, John F., and John R. Nevin. "The Differential Effects of Exercised and Unexercised Power Sources in a Marketing Channel." *Journal of Marketing Research* 22, no. 2 (1985), pp. 130–42.

Gundlach, Gregory T., and Ernest R. Cadotte. "Exchange Interdependence and Interfirm Interaction: Research in a Simulated Channel Setting." *Journal of Marketing Research* 31, no. 4 (1994), pp. 516–32.

Hunt, Shelby D., and John R. Nevin. "Power in a Channel of Distribution." *Journal of Marketing Research* 11 (1974), pp. 196–93.

John, George. "An Empirical Investigation of Some Antecedents of Opportunism in a Marketing Channel." *Journal of Marketing Research* 21, no. 3 (1984), pp. 278–89.

Kasulis, Jack J., Robert E. Spekman, and Richard P. Bagozzi. "A Taxonomy of Channel Influences: A Theoretical Framework." In *Future Directions of Marketing: Proceedings of the Two European Colloquia*, ed. George Fisk et al., pp. 164–84. Cambridge, MA: Marketing Science Institute, 1979.

Lusch, Robert F. "Sources of Power—Their Impact on Intrachannel Conflict." *Journal of Marketing Research* 13, no. 4 (1976), pp. 382–90.

Lusch, Robert F., and James R. Brown. "A Modified Model of Power in the Marketing Channel." *Journal of Marketing Research* 19, no. 3 (1982), pp. 312–23.

Lusch, Robert F., and Robert H. Ross. "The Nature of Power in the Marketing Channel." *Journal of the Academy of Marketing Science* 13, no. 3 (1985), pp. 39–56.

Maloni, Michael J., and W. C. Benton Jr. "Power Influences in the Supply Chain." *Journal of Business Logistics* 21, no. 1 (2000), pp. 42–73.

Maloni, Michael J., and W. C. Benton Jr. "Supply Chain Partnerships: Opportunities for Operations Research." *European Journal of Operational Research* 101, no. 3 (1997), pp. 419–29.

Naumann, Earl, and Ross Reck. "A Buyer's Bases of Power." *Journal of Purchasing and Materials Management* 18, no. 4 (1982), pp. 8–82.

Richardson, Lynne D., and Robert A. Robicheaux. "Supplier's Desire to Influence Related to Perceived Use of Power and Performance." *Journal of Business Research* 25, no. 3 (1992), pp. 243–50.

Schul, Patrick L., and Emin Babakus. "An Examination of the Interfirm Power-Conflict Relationship: The Intervening Role of the Channel Decision Structure." *Journal of Retailing* 64, no. 4 (1988), pp. 381–404.

Skinner, Steven J., Jule B. Gassenheimer, and Scott W. Kelley. "Cooperation in Supplier-Dealer Relations." *Journal of Retailing* 68, no. 2 (1992), pp. 174–93.

Stern, Louis W., and Ronald Gorman. "Conflict in Distribution Channels: An Exploration." In *Distribution Channels: Behavioral Dimensions*, ed. Louis Stern, pp. 156–75. New York: Houghton Mifflin Company, 1969.

Chapter Twelve

Total Quality Management (TQM) and Purchasing

Learning Objectives

1. Identify purchasing's functional role in a firm within an overall quality assurance program.
2. Determine the various costs associated with quality and why it is difficult to measure these costs.
3. Define what is meant by total quality management (TQM).
4. Describe how quality specifications and targets are determined.
5. Identify the advantages of statistical process control (SPC).
6. Discuss the advantages of six-sigma implementation.
7. Identify the advantages of the Taguchi method.
8. Know the mechanics of acceptance sampling for commodity purchasing.

INTRODUCTION

Total quality management (TQM) expands beyond the traditional view of quality. The Japanese have captured almost 30 percent of the American automobile and electronics markets by offering high-value products. In response to the boom in competition, many American firms have implemented a variety of progressive quality programs. Effective TQM requires the integration of production planning, marketing, engineering, distribution, and field service. TQM is a continuous improvement process. It reaches much wider than the traditional quality view of incoming inspection and process control—it means that the entire organization is working as a team, including top management and each and every employee. TQM is an innovative way of thinking that affects the culture, the strategy, and the technology of a company. Implementing TQM requires the following:

- Defining the mission
- Identifying systems output
- Identifying customers
- Negotiating customer requirements

- Developing a "supplier specification" that details customer requirements and expectations
- Determining the necessary activities required to fulfill those requirements and expectations

Purchasing is a critical process that total quality management should focus on. Without high-quality raw materials or component parts from suppliers, a quality management program will not be successful. Therefore, any firm that wishes to achieve a high level of total quality management must carefully examine its purchasing process.

Traditionally, U.S. firms have preferred to use an arm's-length purchasing strategy; today, the best bid usually gets the business. Recently, firms are moving toward establishing long-term strategic relationships with their suppliers, especially key suppliers. In order to compete in today's competitive markets, firms have to involve their suppliers in the early stages of their product design and development. Firms need to provide suppliers with long-run demand forecasts and give suppliers performance feedback and suggestions. A healthy long-term relationship between suppliers and manufacturers is becoming more and more important and can result in reduced transaction costs. For example, Honda does not inspect the incoming materials from its suppliers; it works closely with its suppliers to improve the quality of incoming materials and holds suppliers responsible for any defects that eventually affect Honda's production.

One of the potential problems in establishing long-term relationships with a few key suppliers is that a supplier may have increasing power in the supply chain and may ask for more than the market price. In order to solve this problem, a firm usually has one key supplier for each item and a few other backup suppliers. The firm usually works closely with the key supplier and gives more than half of the order volume to the key supplier in order to gain the economies of scale. The key suppliers usually get the long-run demand forecast and are involved in the manufacturer's product development. The backup suppliers usually get a small volume of business and do not have a close working relationship with the manufacturer. Also see Crosby (1979).

TOTAL QUALITY MANAGEMENT AND SUPPLY CHAIN MANAGEMENT

Today successful organizations rely on their suppliers more than ever before. In general, supplying organizations are extensions of the buying organization. The product quality and manufacturing processes of the supplying organizations have a significant effect on the acceptance of the buying organization's final product. The incentive for the supplier is a long-term contract. In other words, the entire supply chain must practice TQM. TQM expands the traditional view of quality—looking only at the quality of the final product or services–to *looking at the quality of every aspect of the process* that produces the product or service. TQM systems are intended to prevent poor quality from occurring. Table 12.1 illustrates the differences between cultures of a TQM organization and a more traditional organization. Practicing TQM throughout the supply chain will lead to a competitive advantage for the supply chain as well as the members. In some cases, the procurement specifications released by buying organizations are flawed, and the supplying organizations often remain silent. This practice will not produce the best outcomes for the supply chain buyer–seller relationship. The

TABLE 12.1
Traditional vs. TQM Organizations

Aspect	Traditional	Total Quality Management
Overall mission	Maximize return on investment	Meet or exceed customer expectations
Objectives	Emphasis on short term	Balance of long term and short term
Management	Not always open; sometimes inconsistent objectives	Open; encourages employee input; consistent objectives
Role of manager	Issue orders; enforce	Coach; remove barriers; build trust
Customer requirements	Not highest priority; may be unclear	Highest priority; important to identify and understand
Problems	Assign blame; punish	Identity and resolve
Problem solving	Not systematic; individuals	Systematic; teams
Improvement	Erratic	Continuous
Suppliers	Adversarial	Partners
Jobs	Narrow, specialized; much individual effort	Broad, more general; much team effort
Focus	Product oriented	Process oriented

needs and expectations of the ultimate customer must be considered throughout the supply chain. Supply chain TQM effectiveness will become a competitive weapon for future buyer–seller relationships. Buying organizations must realize the following activities:

- Select supplying organizations that have a TQM supply chain philosophy.
- Replace suppliers that ignore the TQM supply chain philosophy concept.
- Investigate customer requirements and include supplying organizations in the new product development process.

TQM IMPLEMENTATION PROBLEMS

The implementation of the TQM philosophy is not easy. There have been varying levels of success. Among the factors cited in the literature are the following:

- Lack of a quality focus throughout the supply chain: There are no measurable implementation goals.
- There is no sense of urgency for change throughout the buying organization: There is no strategic plan for change.
- There is no customer or supplier focus: Without customer and supplier focus, there is a risk of customer and supplier dissatisfaction.
- There is minimal positive communications throughout the buying organization: The lack of communications leads to confusion throughout both the company and the supply chain.
- The buying organization's employees are not integrated and involved in the TQM philosophy: This lack of employee involvement will lead to serious trust problems internally and externally.
- Lack of long-term view throughout the buying and supplying organizations.
- Lack of long-term view throughout the supply chain.
- Lack of leadership internally and externally.

QUALITY REQUIREMENTS FOR SUPPLIERS

Quality Assurance Expectations

The suppliers' quality assurance systems must be consistent with the in-house quality requirements of the customer. Thus, the stated targets and expectations of the customer must meet the minimum level of performance. In cases where the quality target expectations are not achieved, the system must be programmed to rapidly respond in order to return to the agreed-upon quality targets. The typical life cycle of key component parts in a manufacturing setting are *preventive quality management* (design/development), *part approval for production* (component part approval), and *production quality management* (process control).

Quality Target Commitment

Each buying firm must specify in detail the agreed-upon quality targets. As an example, at a minimum, the following four issues should be addressed in any purchasing contract:

1. *PPM (parts per million) target agreement.* The PPM value is determined by the number of rejected parts divided by those delivered, and then multiplied by 1,000,000 (PPM = 1,000,000 × Number of rejects/Total quantity delivered).
2. *Field failure and reliability requirements.* Field failures can be devastating for most firms. It is difficult to precisely quantify a field failure. Thus, there should be zero defects in the field.
3. *Warranty agreement.* In the unlikely case of a field failure, there should be a warranty agreement that covers the reimbursement of all of the cost (i.e., parts, repair, and handling costs) related to the field failure.
4. *Urgency to solve problems.* The speed to solution of any quality variance is vital. Customer satisfaction is usually directly related to the speed with which the solution was achieved.

Preventive Quality

Strategic Components

Strategic components are the most critical parts in a project or platform and require more extensive quality assurance requirements. Strategic components generally meet one or more of the following criteria:

- Supplier participation in the designing of the component part
- A high level of systems integration required for a complex component part
- An expensive component part
- Long lead time for the component part
- Component parts that require extensive testing
- Parts with critical characteristics
- Component parts with complex legal implications

All strategic components should be required to go through a rigorous parts quality assurance (PQA) process. The PQA process validates the quality supplied to the buying firm and is a formal process that requires documentation. The general steps of a PQA process are given below:

1. Review the technical specifications.
2. Validate the reliability of the design characteristics.

3. Develop and document a quality assurance plan.
4. Identify the need for a tooling plan.
5. Perform a preprocess audit.
6. Perform a legal and governmental conformity audit.
7. Perform a packaging analysis and plan.
8. Project the effect of a process mode failure.
9. Develop a statistical process control plan.
10. Perform a production test run.
11. Perform a process audit.
12. Develop a part-handling plan.

The new or modified part agreement between the buying and the selling firm is complete after an acceptable final test sample has been generated and verified.

Statistical Process Control, Six Sigma, and the Taguchi Method

The traditional approach to manufacturing process control is to select production samples and compare the attributes/variables of the sample to the specifications. If the product does not meet specifications, the product is either reworked or scrapped. This method of process control is reactive and expensive. The goal should be to prevent process errors before they occur. Statistical process control (SPC) can resolve this manufacturing process control issue. SPC normally uses two control charts to ensure quality in manufacturing: the sample mean (X-bar) chart and the sample range (*R*) chart. The specification limits are established for X-bar and *R* charts based upon tolerances set during the design stage of the product. Samples of purchased and in-process parts are taken and measured to check if they lie within control limits. The sample mean is plotted on an X-bar chart, and the range of the sample is plotted on an *R* chart. Over time, the trends of samples are analyzed to detect trends that may predict the disposition of the process. In most cases, problems are diagnosed and resolved before any substandard parts are produced, thus reducing scrap and rework (see Figure 12.1). Also see Kackar (1985).

The specification is a description of the required output, including specific characteristics such as weights and measurements that enable the product to work in a manner acceptable to the consumer. There is always flexibility in specifications, no matter the level of design precision. As an example, if a can of motor oil should have 32 ounces of liquid, it is unlikely that the customer would mind (or would notice) if some cans contained 32.1 ounces or 31.9 ounces instead of precisely 32 ounces all the time.

The upper control limit (UCL) is the highest fill level (expected based on the sample distribution) without causing an error and the lower control limit (LCL) is the lowest fill level (expected based on the sample distribution) without causing an error. Consider that for the motor oil example, the UCL is 32.3 ounces and the LCL is 31.7 ounces. Thus, if a can of motor oil exceeded 32.3 or was less than 31.7, that can would fall outside of the acceptable product specification limits and would be rejected by the customer, as can be seen in Figure 12.2. The control limits of a process control chart refer to the sample. Characteristics (e.g., means and ranges) are used to identify whether the process is in control or not, as an example, to detect assignable cause (as opposed to common or random cause) variation, which may lead to more-than-expected defects. It would be possible to have a unit outside of the product specifications, but the sample measurement could still be within the process control limits. The UCL/LCL process control limits and the upper/lower product specifications are related but different.

FIGURE 12.1
Basic Quality Control Charts

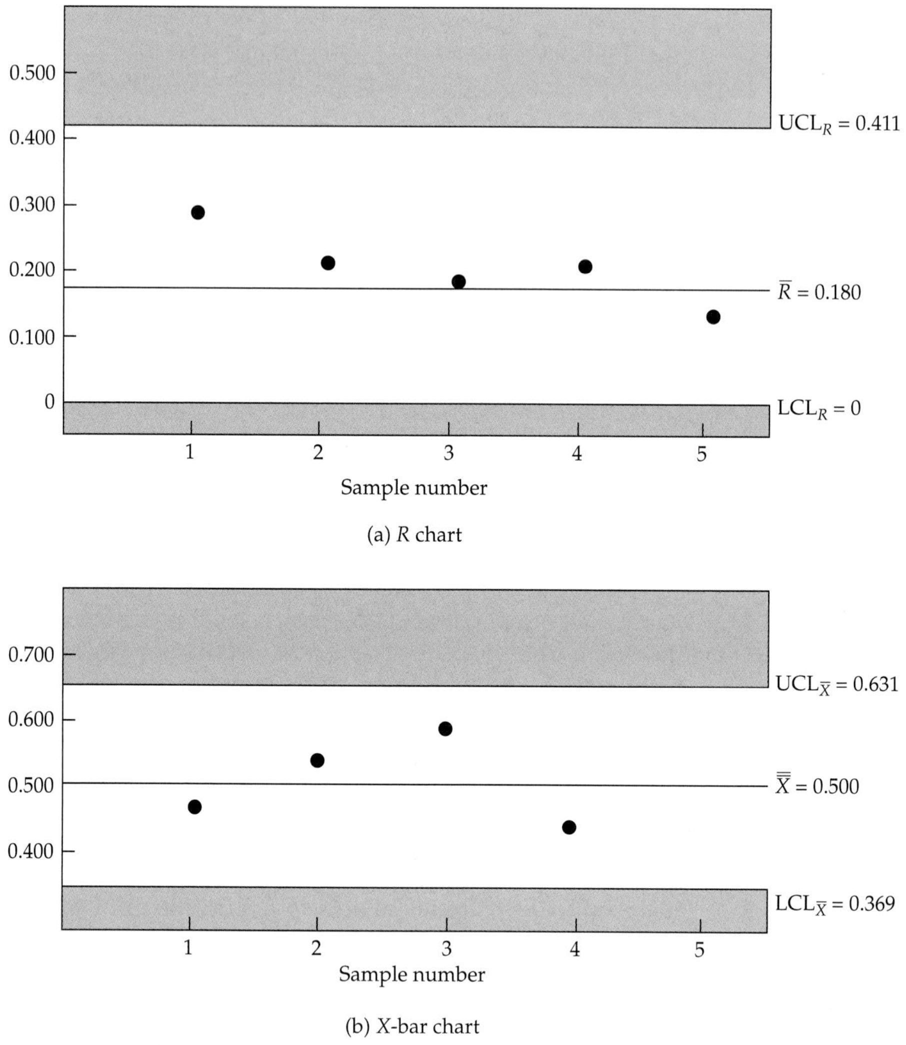

FIGURE 12.2
Control Limits Chart

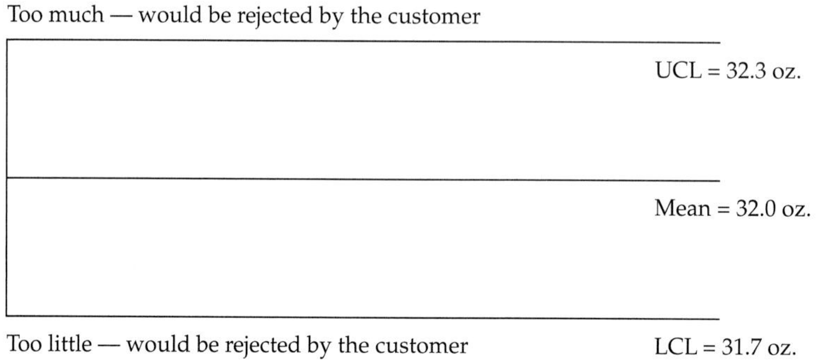

FIGURE 12.3
SPC Chart

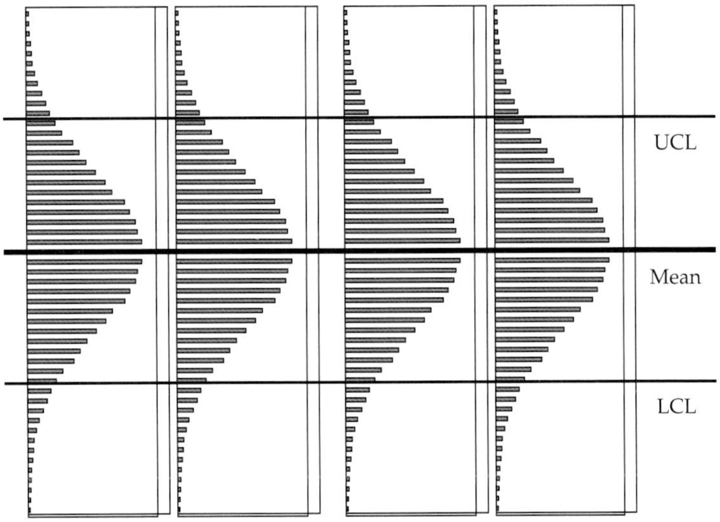

The dividing line between the UCL and the LCL is the mean. In most cases, the products produced should fall close to the mean. Of course, the normal distribution is assumed when implementing traditional SPC. The central limit theorem provides the justification for the normality assumption. In other words, the SPC chart represents a normal distribution turned on its side, as shown in Figure 12.3. As seen in Figure 12.3, most of the units fall close to the mean, but production process variances result in several observations falling outside the specifications. Product variance is synonymous with production errors. As we know from basic statistics, variance is defined as the average of the squared deviations from the mean, and the standard deviation (sigma) is defined as the square root of the variance. The standard deviation is actually the average distance a normal point is from the mean. Thus, the standard deviation represents a more tractable measure of the variance. Given the normal curve, 68 percent of the values fall between plus and minus one standard deviation, which alternatively means that 32 percent of the production process output would be rejected. On the other hand, a process control system where 95 percent of the production values fall between plus and minus two standard deviations (two sigma) represents a production process where only 5 percent of the output would be rejected. A process control system that is set at three sigma results in a false rejection rate of 0.3 percent. It is important to note that increasing sigma does not widen the acceptable specification limits. The control limits are actually set by customer specifications, and the specifications remain constant. In order to increase the sigma level, the production process variance must be reduced. Please refer to Figure 12.4. *SPC is then used to detect when the process is (becoming) out of control.*

As can be seen from the examples, six sigma requires a near elimination of production process variance. Six sigma will result in variances of 3.4 defects out of every one million parts produced. Six sigma is impressive as it represents a variance reduction of approximately 1,800 times greater than the case of four sigma.

If the buying firm has implemented six sigma, the strategic suppliers also should apply six sigma. Six-sigma standards can be applied to both manufacturing and service firms using the same methodology. SPC provides input to the six-sigma approach. However, if a firm is not currently using SPC, it is not necessary for the implementation of six-sigma standards. In most instances when a firm is

FIGURE 12.4
SPC Chart Indicating Out-of-Control Process

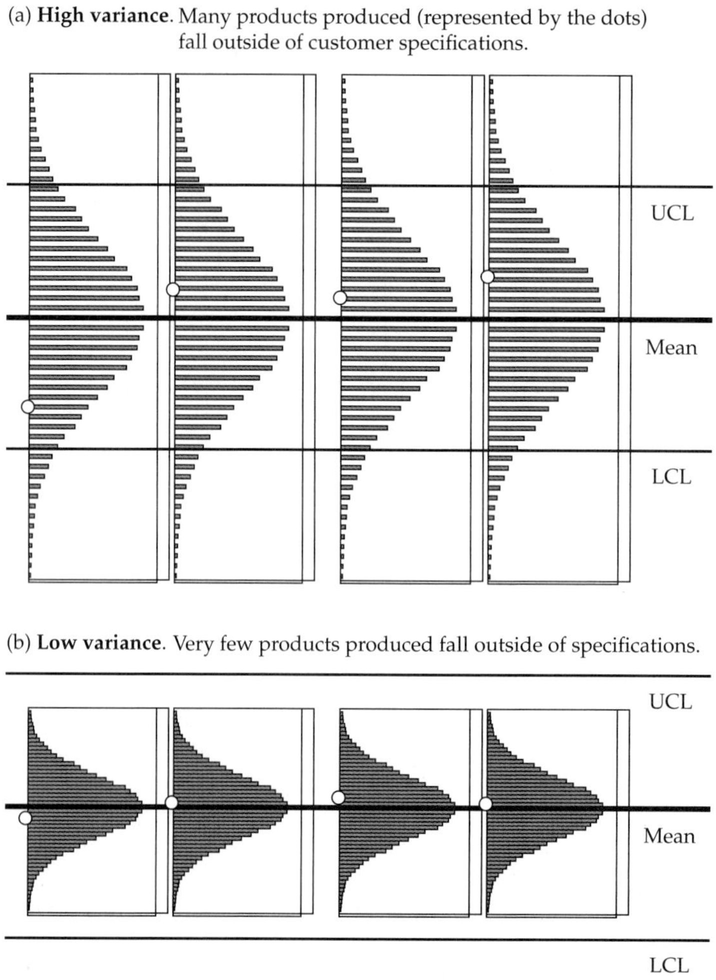

able to reduce variation, it is also able to identify the potential problems before they occur. As an example, if there is a systematic trend inconsistent with the normal distribution, in most cases the firm would be able to correct whatever was causing the variation before the problem forced production outside of the control limits. The ability to identify errors before they occur reduces scrap material, eliminates downstream inspections, and will increase profitability.

Six Sigma and the Supplier

Six sigma is a way to measure supplier quality. Supplying firms that follow the core philosophy of six sigma will make excellent strategic partners. Six-sigma suppliers focus on (1) defects per million as a standard metric, (2) extensive employee training, and (3) the reduction of non-value-added activities. If there is a pattern not consistent with the normal distribution, corrective action could be taken, as shown in Figure 12.5. There are a number of six-sigma implementation approaches. Two of the most successful six-sigma implementations are those of Motorola and General Electric. The well-known General Electric approach to six-sigma problem solving is shown in Figure 12.6.

FIGURE 12.5
Inconsistent Distribution Pattern

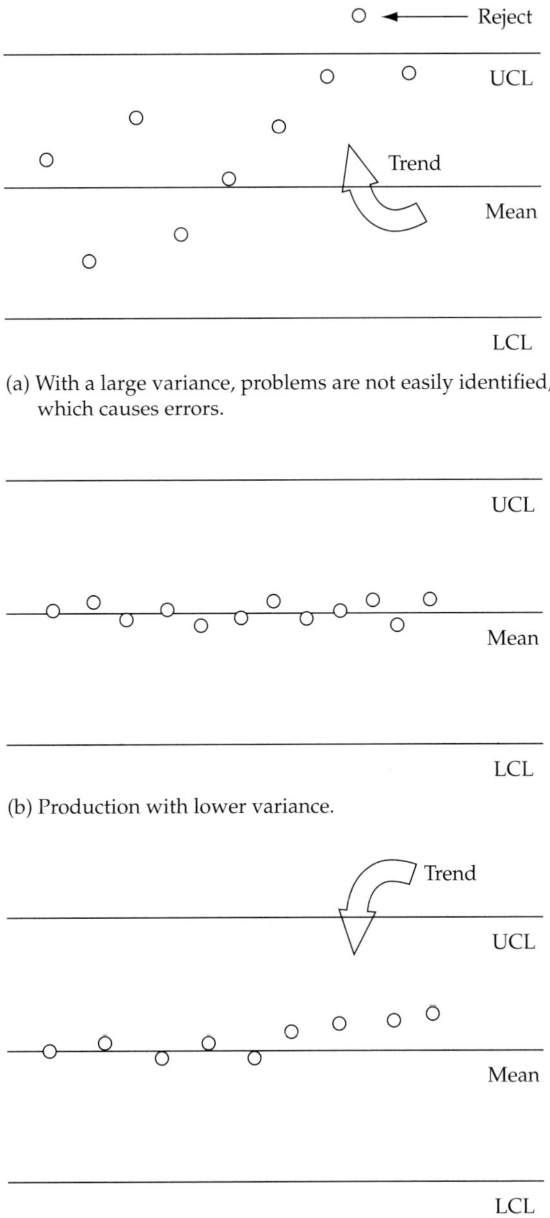

(a) With a large variance, problems are not easily identified, which causes errors.

(b) Production with lower variance.

(c) With lower variance, problems can be identified before any rejects are produced.

Taguchi Method

While it is apparent that SPC does improve quality, the improvements tend to be incremental. Next we will attempt to address some of the shortcomings of the SPC method by reviewing the Taguchi method. See Appendix A for a tutorial on the Taguchi method (TM). Also see Benton (1991); Gunter (1987); Ross (1988); Ryan (1988); and Taguchi (1989).

The TM nicely complements many of the advantages of SPC. Nevertheless, TM has some problems. First, although the basic ideas of TM are simple, the statistical

FIGURE 12.6 Six-Sigma Problem-Solving Approach
Six-Sigma Project DMAIC Cycle Questions*

* DMAIC = define, measure, analyze, improve, and control

procedures are complex and can be difficult to implement. Many managers and engineers do not have the basic statistical tools essential for the understanding of TM procedures. Even with high-speed computers and statistical techniques for simplifying analysis, testing the interactions for off-target parameters can be time consuming and costly in systems with hundreds of interactions.

Second, unlike SPC, quantifying quality losses in terms of "losses to society" is almost impossible. Thus, many American manufacturing firms have only implemented SPC alone because of its statistical simplicity and its reliance on measurable costs of poor quality. Typically, TM increases overhead without offering benefits that can immediately be quantified. As a result, from a financial standpoint, full implementation of TM cannot be easily cost justified, even though the Japanese have demonstrated the desirability of the method. On a long-term basis,

TM gives the firm strong competitive advantage, which results from increased customer acceptance of superior products. If quality were considered as a line function instead of an overhead expense, its costs could be managed, not merely accounted for. Under this scenario, implementing TM would encounter less resistance since it would not drive up overhead.

Finally, some of the methods that Taguchi employs have been challenged by mainstream statisticians. There is now literature documenting the formal statistical shortcomings of TM. If industry can critically evaluate the statistical shortcomings of TM, it may result in a viable alternative to conventional quality assurance methods.

Acceptance Sampling and Commodity Components

Commodity-based components are those components not defined as strategic components. Intensive price competition and information technology have led to the implementation of a reverse auction procurement approach for commodity components. However, prequalification of suppliers and incoming inspection have become more important.

Acceptance sampling is a methodology used to determine whether to accept or reject a batch of nonstrategic components or items. In most cases, incoming purchased parts are inspected before placing the parts into inventory. Sampling is usually used to decide whether to accept or reject a batch. (See Appendix B for an illustration of the acceptance sampling process.)

QUALITY AWARDS

There are major quality awards that ensure that suppliers are TQM effective. The most universally known quality awards are the Deming Award and the Malcolm Baldrige National Quality Award. Also see Deming (1987).

The Deming Award

Dr. W. Edwards Deming is known as the father of the Japanese postwar industrial revival and was regarded by many as the leading quality guru in the United States. He passed on in 1993. Trained as a statistician, his expertise was used during World War II to assist the United States in its effort to improve the quality of war materials. The Japanese Union of Scientists and Engineers (JUSE) created the first major management award for "contributions to quality and product dependability."

The JUSE's Deming Prize Committee administers two types of awards honoring Deming: the Deming Prize and the Deming Application Prize. The Deming Prize is given to a person or group of people who have advanced the practice and furthered awareness of TQC. The Deming Application Prize, in turn, goes only to companies based on successes attributable to implementing TQC.

Interestingly, this most significant of Japan's business awards honors the American, Deming. Many Japanese government and academic leaders credit Deming with revolutionizing Japanese postwar industry through his advocacy in Japan of quality control and managerial efficiency.

Dr. Deming is best known for his contributions in the area of statistical process control. He also suggests a 14-point system for successful quality management. These points are:

1. Create consistency of purpose with a plan.
2. Adopt the new philosophy of quality.

3. Cease dependence on mass inspection.
4. End the practice of choosing suppliers based on price.
5. Find problems and work continuously on the system.
6. Use modern methods of training on the job.
7. Change from production numbers to quality.
8. Drive out fear.
9. Break down barriers between departments.
10. Stop asking for productivity improvement without providing methods.
11. Eliminate work standards that prescribe numerical quotas.
12. Remove barriers to pride of workmanship.
13. Institute vigorous education and retraining.
14. Create a structure in top management that will push every day on the above 13 points.

The Malcolm Baldrige National Quality Award

In 1987, Congress established the Malcolm Baldrige National Quality Award. It was initiated as a result of foreign firms increasingly dominating American markets. The Malcolm Baldrige Award is much more than an award; it is equivalent to a mini revolution in the business world. As a result of this award, all major firms in America have established continuous improvement quality programs. Also see Juran (1980).

The Malcolm Baldrige Award has led to a national quality campaign, and hundreds of major U.S. firms have enlisted in this total quality management competitive weapon. In order to qualify for the award, applicants must address the following categories:

1. *Leadership*. This includes senior executives' personal leadership and involvement in creating and sustaining customer focus and clean and visible quality values. Also examined is how the quality values are integrated into the company's management system and reflected in the manner in which the company addresses its public responsibilities.
2. *Information and analysis*. This includes the scope, validity, analysis, management, and use of data and information to drive quality excellence and improve competition performance. Also addressed is the adequacy of the company's data, information, and analysis system to support improvement of the company's product, services, and internal operations.
3. *Strategic quality planning*. This includes the company's planning process and how all key quality requirements are integrated into overall business planning. Also examined are the company's short- and long-term plans and how quality and performance requirements are deployed to all work units.
4. *Human resource development and management*. This includes the key element of how the company develops and realizes the full potential of the workforce to pursue the company's quality and performance objectives. Also examined are the company's efforts to build and maintain an environment for quality excellence conducive to full participation and personal organizational growth.
5. *Management of process quality*. This includes the systematic processes used to pursue even higher quality and company performance. The key elements of

process management are design, management of process quality for all work units and suppliers, systemic quality improvement, and quality assessment.

6. *Quality and operational results*. This includes the quality levels and improvement trends of quality, company operational performance, and supplier quality. Also examined are the current quality and performance levels of competitors.
7. *Customer focus and satisfaction*. Relationships with customers and the knowledge of customer requirements are the key quality factors that determine marketplace competitiveness. This includes methods to determine customer satisfaction, current trends and levels of satisfaction, and competition.

Continuous Improvement and the Supplier

In most industrial settings, there is aggressive competition for market share. In order to successfully achieve a zero defect target, buying and supplying organizations must continuously improve their processes.

The objective of the continuous improvement process is to incrementally improve processes. Continuous improvement teams are established to accomplish process improvements. The continuous improvement teams are focused on the expectations and requirements of internal and external customers. Top management must implement the continuous process. The employees must be trained and motivated by top management. An actual continuous improvement program between a buying and supplying organization is given in Figure 12.7.

ISO 9000

The ISO standards originated in manufacturing. They are now used to certify a variety of organizations and business concerns. ISO 9001 is a set of standards that document the implementation of a quality program. Most companies require their suppliers to provide a certification that proves they have complied with all ISO 9001 requirements. In order to be certified, suppliers need to provide documentation to an external examiner that they meet the ISO 9001 requirements. Once a firm is certified, it will be listed in a directory so that all of its potential customers can know which firms have been certified and to what level.

The primary requirements for ISO 9001 include:

- Establishing a set of procedures that cover all key processes in the business;
- Monitoring processes to ensure they are effective;
- Keeping adequate records;
- Checking output for defects, with appropriate and corrective action where necessary;
- Regularly reviewing individual processes and the quality system itself for effectiveness; and
- Facilitating continual improvement.

A firm that has been independently audited and certified to be in conformance with ISO 9001 may publicly state that it is "ISO 9001 certified" or "ISO 9001 registered." Certification to an ISO 9000 standard does not guarantee any quality of end products and services; rather, it certifies that formalized business processes are being applied. Some companies enter the ISO 9001 certification as a marketing tool.

FIGURE 12.7
Continuous Improvement Example

JOHNSON CONTROLS

Continuous Improvement

WW-POS-ST-06-01-01 Rev 01 Page 1 of 2

Rev Level	Revision Date	Description of Changes
01	30-Oct-05	

Continuous improvement (CI) in all areas of business is fundamental to remaining competitive in the automobile industry. We expect each supplier to embrace the CI concept at all levels of the organization and in all areas of its business. Although the actual details will vary from supplier to supplier, the following list details the basic elements of a CI system:

- Supplier leadership commitment to continuous improvement
- Cross-functional continuous improvement teams
- Data-driven improvement based on key measures (using a QOS/MOS format)
- Regularly scheduled reviews
- A quality system in place that allows improvements to be embodied in the normal operating procedures of the business

It is essential that key business measures (defined by you and your customers' expectations) are established and tracked. We expect that quantifiable improvement will be pursued in these areas, even if there is currently no perceived problem. *Examples* of key areas for improvement are

- Unscheduled machine downtime
- Machine setup, die change, and machine changeover times
- Excessive cycle time
- Scrap, rework, and repair
- Non-value-added use of floor space
- Less than 100 percent first-run capability
- Test requirements not justified by results
- Waste of labor and materials
- Excessive cost of nonconforming product
- Difficult assembly or installation of the product
- Excessive handling and storage
- New target values to optimize customer processes
- Marginal measurement system capability

Johnson Controls has a Supplier Continuous Improvement Group dedicated to working with our suppliers to improve efficiency and eliminate waste. As part of our commitment to our suppliers, we will work to create an environment that promotes continuous improvement and train their employees how to continue the process on their own with the support of Johnson Controls materials.

Quality Function Deployment (QFD)

Quality Function Deployment (QFD) focuses on how businesses develop high-quality products for their customers. QFD is driven by cross-functional market research. This is the process of understanding customer expectations, and how well providers of products address these expectations. Customer expectations include (1) function, (2) appearance, (3) maintainability, and (4) reliability. It is impossible to consistently design products that will attract customers unless businesses understand what customers want. The customer information is then processed by marketing. Quality Function Deployment (QFD) is a methodology for collecting information on customer expectations to drive product development.

Supplier Evaluations

The buyer's evaluation of the supplier's performance is a catalyst for the supplier development activities. There are two main categories for the supplier evaluation: process-based evaluations and performance-based evaluations.

The process-based evaluation is an assessment of the supplier's production or service process. Typically, the buyer will conduct an audit at the supplier's site to assess the level of capability in the supplier organization's systems for costing, quality, technology, and other specific factors. Process flowcharts can be developed to identify the non-value-added activities that should be eliminated to improve the business efficiency. Increasingly, large buying organizations are demanding that their suppliers should become certified through a third-party organization, such as ISO 9000 certification or Malcolm Baldrige National Quality Awards.

The performance-based evaluation is an assessment of the supplier's actual performance on a variety of criteria, such as delivery reliability, cost, quality defect rate, and so on. It is a more tactical assessment and measures the day-to-day actual performance of the supplying firm; hence it is an after-the-fact evaluation. The performance-based evaluation is more common than the process-based evaluation, perhaps because it is reactive and easily measured.

Once completed, the evaluation can be either compared to the buying firm's stated goals or benchmarked to the performance evaluations of the supplier's competitors. The buying firm chooses whether to communicate the evaluation to the supplier.

ENGINEERING AND DESIGN

Although engineering and design account for less than 5 percent of the cost of a product, decisions made in the design phase of product development account for more than 75 percent of the production cost. When engineering and design are complete, 75 percent of the cost of production is yet to come, and quality control can impact less than 30 percent of the product cost.

Preliminary studies indicate that assembly time is roughly proportional to the number of parts assembled. It has been shown that the number of parts in a design can be decreased by 20–40 percent when engineers are told to design the product to minimize the number of parts. One caveat to this is that, in some instances, simply minimizing parts can increase the complexity of manufacture, or require retooling, which increases cost. In general, though, material costs per unit are reduced by cutting the number of parts.

When material costs are reduced, so are the carrying costs. The systems cost of carrying a part in inventory for one year ranges from $500 to $2,500 for a typical manufacturing firm. Obviously, reducing the number of parts that are ordered and held in inventory will reduce these costs significantly. Finally, in a manufacturing facility of more than 500 employees, the cost to modify a design once it has been released for manufacture ranges from $5,000 to $10,000 per change.

In considering these facts, the question is, how can most firms afford not to use the Taguchi method? Even if a complete TM system is not implemented, the introduction of the TM ideas for manufacturing and design engineers would be invaluable. If followed, two simple programs can allow a firm to reap the benefits of TM. First, at least one manufacturing engineer should be assigned to each design team from the start of projects. A manufacturing engineer who is familiar with the precision of machines (process capability) would be invaluable in the parameter and tolerance design phases. The design team should proceed by using QFD techniques. Design and manufacturing engineers must have the means to evaluate and improve the manufacturability of a product during the design phase. This would prevent many of the problems created by "over-the-wall" designs for manufacturing.

Second, after the design team program has been established, all engineers should be educated in the Taguchi philosophy for quality, and in the technical tools necessary to implement the philosophy. An awareness of the Taguchi philosophy, with a program to integrate design and manufacturing, is the ingredient many manufacturers need to produce high-quality, low-cost products. SPC alone will only facilitate conformance to design. It will not produce designs that enable firms to compete effectively in the world market in the millennium.

Summary

Total quality management (TQM) is an innovative way to compete in the marketplace. The purchasing function is one of the key elements of TQM. A quality management initiative will not succeed without highly qualified suppliers that ship acceptable raw materials and component parts. Statistical process control (SPC) and the Taguchi method (TM) are used to prevent process control errors.

Six sigma is a way to measure supplier quality. Supplying firms that follow the core philosophy of six sigma will make excellent strategic partners. Six-sigma suppliers focus on (1) defects per million as a standard metric, (2) provision of extensive employee training, and (3) the reduction of non–value-added activities. Finally, the Deming and Malcolm Baldrige awards provide formal recognition of supplier capability.

Discussion Questions

1. Why should the purchasing department be concerned with a firm's overall quality assurance program?
2. What are the quality requirements for suppliers?
3. What is six sigma? What are the differences between statistical process control and six sigma?
4. Describe how unethical supplier behavior can affect TQM.
5. What is ISO 9000 and why is it important to a purchasing professional?
6. What is the difference between the Malcolm Baldrige Award and the ISO certification? Which one is the most important certification if the organization is sourcing globally?
7. Go to the Malcolm Baldrige website at www.quality.nist.gov and write a two-page report on one of the most recent award winners.

8. What are the key requirements for TQM?
9. Who needs to be involved in setting TQM standards for suppliers?
10. An aircraft manufacturer is producing landing gear struts that conform to the military specification. However, the manufacturer is experiencing significant quality-related costs. Speculate on the source of the increased quality-related costs.
11. Explain the Japanese approach to TQM. Are there differences between the Japanese and the American approaches to TQM?
12. Discuss how TQM affects productivity.
13. What are the advantages of using the Taguchi method?
14. How does the Taguchi philosophy affect the purchasing department?
15. What are the costs associated with implementing a world-class quality assurance program?
16. What is a loss function?
17. What is AQL?
18. What is an OC curve? How is it used?

Suggested Cases

Eastern Waves Inc.
The Tank Case
Carter Systems Canada
Temko

References

Benton, W. C. "SPC and the Taguchi Method." *International Journal of Production Research* 29, no. 9 (1991), pp. 1761–70.

Crosby, P. *Quality Is Free*. New York: McGraw-Hill, 1979.

Deming, W. E. *Out of the Crisis*. Boston: MIT, 1987.

Gunter, B. "A Perspective on the Taguchi Methods." *Quality Process* 20, no. 6 (1987), pp. 44–52.

Juran, Joe, and Frank Grynan. *Quality Planning and Analysis*. 2nd ed. New York: McGraw-Hill, 1980.

Kackar, R. "Off Line Quality Control, Parameter Design, and the Taguchi Method." *Journal of Quality Technology* 17, no. 4 (1985), pp. 176–209.

Ross, P. J. "The Role of Taguchi Methods and Design of Experiments in QFD." *Quality Progress* 21, no. 6 (1988), pp. 41–47.

Ryan, T. P. "Taguchi's Approach to Experimental Design: Some Concerns." *Quality Progress* 21, no. 5 (1988), pp. 34–36.

Taguchi, G. *Quality Engineering in Production Systems*. New York: McGraw-Hill, 1989.

Appendix A

Taguchi Method

The Taguchi method (TM) addresses design and engineering (offline), as well as manufacturing (online), quality. This fundamentally differentiates TM from SPC, which is purely an online quality control method.

Taguchi's ideas can be broken down into two fundamental principles. First, quality losses increase as deviation from target occurs, instead of showing zero losses until the arbitrary control limits are exceeded, as with SPC. The loss function quantifies these "losses to society."

The second principle, the achievement of high system quality through *design* of the manufacturing process, also sets TM apart from SPC. As described above, quality is primarily designed and not manufactured into the product.

Conventional SPC-based methodologies consider only manufacturing processes that follow predetermined specifications. Manufacturing firms operating in this manner only consider manufacturing and purchasing functions located below the dashed line in Figure A.1. These firms have clearly disregarded the quality assurance of the design processes as shown above the dashed line in Figure A.1. Compared with conventional SPC methods, quality assurance at the design stage will greatly reduce the defect level of the design. Testing for manufacturability should be used by the engineers as a means for correcting the initial design. The same testing and correcting actions used at the manufacturing processing stage can be used at the design stage.

LOSS FUNCTION

The heart of the Taguchi philosophy is the quality *loss function*. Taguchi defines the cost of poor quality as the losses a product imparts to society from the time a product is shipped. This definition sets the Taguchi method apart from the traditional SPC approach to quality, which defines the cost of poor quality chiefly as the cost of scrap, rework, and warranty repair. Taguchi states that any deviation from target reduces the value of the product to society.

FIGURE A.1
Two Quality Assurance Approaches

Source: Benton, W. C. "SPC and the Taguchi Method." *International Journal of Production Research*, 29, no. 9 (1991), pp. 1761–70.

SPC and the Taguchi Method

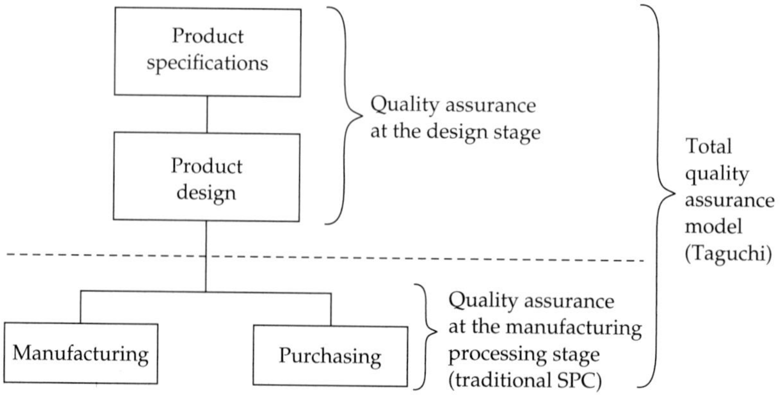

FIGURE A.2
The Traditional SPC versus the Taguchi Loss Function

Source: Benton, W. C. "SPC and the Taguchi Method," *International Journal of Production Research*, 29, no. 9 (1991), pp. 1761–70.

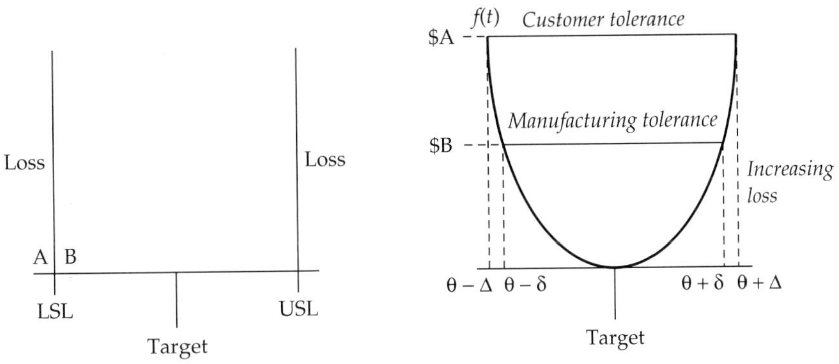

(a) Traditional SPC (b) Taguchi loss function

Figure A.2(a) demonstrates the difference between the SPC "goalpost" approach and the loss function of the Taguchi method. As shown in Figure A.2(a), there is very little difference to the customer between products A and B on the specification scale. The lower specification level (LSL) and upper specification level (USL) are the customer's tolerance intervals. This incongruity between manufacturing and the customer's view of the world is a result of the goalpost approach.

On the other hand, consider the loss function in Figure A.2(b). With the Taguchi method, a very small monetary loss occurs between A and B. This brings TM's view of the world in line with the view of the consumer. Since the loss function of the Taguchi method results in losses to society when any deviation from the nominal value occurs, reductions in variability are sought. Under the Taguchi philosophy, even though A is within the tolerance limits, further improvements in the production process would be sought. Refer back to Figure 12.1. Under the Taguchi philosophy, even though supplier 1 is within tolerance limits, further improvements in the process should be sought. The value of the loss function can deviate from the target both during the product's life span and across each unit of the product. Specifically, the loss function is a random variable with an associated probability distribution. The larger the variation in the loss function, the larger the loss is to the end user (customer). In practice, it is difficult to determine the actual form of the loss function.

As an example of the quality loss function, a few years ago, Ford partially outsourced a major subassembly to a Japanese firm. Ford and the Japanese firm were producing an identical subassembly to the same specification. However, over time it became apparent that warranty complaints were much higher for the American-made Ford product than for the Japanese product. The former was much noisier and less reliable than the latter.[1]

Ford collected samples of the Ford- and Japanese-made subassemblies. Upon investigating, they found that the Japanese parts were always on target. That is, the variability in the Japanese-made subassembly parts was significantly less than for the Ford-built subassembly parts. The Ford parts merely conformed to specification, as depicted by supplier 1 in Figure A.3. Gears and bearings fit better in the Japanese subassembly and thus worked more smoothly than did the Ford subassembly. The result was fewer complaints, repairs, and replacements even though both subassemblies had "zero defects."

[1]Gunter, B. "A Perspective on the Taguchi Methods." *Quality Process* 20, no. 6 (1987), pp. 44–52.

FIGURE A.3
Zero Defects versus Low Variability

Source: Benton, W. C. "SPC and the Taguchi Method," *International Journal of Production Research*, 29, no. 9 (1991), pp. 1761–70.

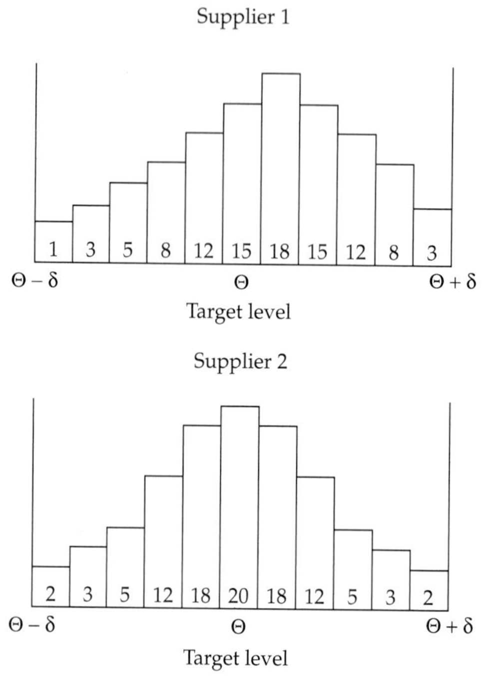

Additionally, Ford found that since the Japanese had worked to reduce variability and not just to eliminate scrap and rework, they could carry less inventory, resulting in lower costs and more consistent quality performance. In short, the Japanese had imparted fewer losses to society (and themselves) than Ford because of the use of the Taguchi philosophy.

QUALITY BY DESIGN

Taguchi calls for a robust design to handle variability in purchasing, manufacturing, production, and end use. Instead of tightening SPC control limits (which increases the cost of production) to ensure nominal performance, Taguchi and Deming advocate *designing* the product so that nominal performance is achieved, even when variability in production and end-use conditions exist.

Taguchi breaks the design process into two distinct phases:

1. The system design, where the engineering concept is set. System design is primarily concerned with achieving quality at a reasonable cost to be competitive in the marketplace. In this phase, TM offers little help.
2. The parameter design, where the design nominals are set. Allowance design is the setting of design tolerances for production. In parameter and allowance design, TM provides suggestions to help design quality into the product.

The phases of design blend together, thus creating simultaneous engineering of the design and production process.

Parameter Design

As an example, consider the performance of a hypothetical product with parameter settings ranging from a high setting (A) to a low setting (B). Suppose that, for consistent performance of the product, the parameter setting is set at B. At this point, wide variability in the parameter results in little change in performance. If the higher performance is critical, then the variability around A must be limited, thus driving up the manufacturing cost. The design engineer must ask if the higher performance is critical.

If the performance at parameter setting B is insufficient, all is not lost. Taguchi contends that there is often duality among parameters affecting design performance. Namely, there are signal variables and control variables that can be internal (design parameter) or external (environmental) in affecting performance. The example above demonstrates a control variable—a variable where performance behaves nonlinearly as the parameter varies. A control variable setting therefore can be used to control the performance when variability in parameters occurs. Signal variables, on the other hand, linearly affect the performance of the product. By strategically setting signal variables and using the appropriate settings for control variables, the design of the product can become robust. Its performance is relatively unaffected by internal and external variability. Recognizing the effect each variable has on product performance gives the design engineer a powerful tool to create a robust design.

A second consideration is the interaction of variables; in this case, a high parameter setting for B results in little variation in performance even when A changes drastically. At low levels of B, the nominal performance would be greater, but the variability in performance would be dramatic if parameter setting A is difficult to control. If B is easily controllable and A is not and peak performance is not required, then B should have a high setting.[2]

Allowance Design

Once the parameter design phase is completed, tolerances around the nominal must be set for production. At this point, TM asserts that, in setting the tolerances, the effect of parameter interaction must be considered. As was shown earlier, the design must be created such that variations in parameters do not affect nominal performance.

In addressing this issue, TM advocates the use of advanced statistical techniques.[3] The basic idea is that simply varying one parameter at a time to find its effect on product performance (a naive approach) does nothing to predict effects of interactions when several parameters are off target. Complex system interactions are important and must be investigated through experimental design. Alternatively, systems can be simulated to determine the effect of design and parameter changes. The use of high-speed computers has facilitated simulation of complex systems.

By identifying critical interactions prior to the manufacturing process, further parameter design can be used to decrease the sensitivity of performance to parameter variation. For this reason, parameter and allowance design tend to blend together into one function under TM. The result is simultaneous engineering of the product design and manufacturing process. That is, TM's focus is on design for manufacturability. This is in sharp contrast to the technique of traditional product development processes (see Figure A.2).[4]

[2]*ibid.*

[3]See G. Taguchi, *Quality Engineering in Production Systems* (New York: McGraw-Hill, 1989), for a more detailed discussion.

[4]Gunter, B. "A Perspective on the Taguchi Methods." *Quality Process* 20, no. 6 (1987), pp. 44–52.

Appendix B

Acceptance Sampling

One of the key techniques in purchasing is acceptance sampling. Competitive firms today are all concerned with the quality of their outputs. Acceptance sampling is a methodology used to determine whether to accept or reject a batch of components or items. Customers must never be dissatisfied with the expected quality of products or services. The most severe penalty for poor quality expectations is the loss of sales. If the quality of the inputs to the productive system is inferior, the final product will be inferior. Acceptance plans must be developed to determine the disposition of a lot of raw materials on component parts. If a batch of parts is inferior, it should be rejected and returned to the supplier. Setting the acceptance criteria is usually based on either predetermined standards or basic statistics. Examples of predetermined attributes are government standards for oil, gasoline, and so forth.

When sampling a batch or lot, there is a danger of making two kinds of errors based on the results. First, a buying firm could reject a batch of products that are in fact acceptable based on a predetermined maximum defect level (set by management). This type of error is a Type I error (α). On the other hand, the probability of accepting a bad batch is known as a Type II error (β). Type I errors are referred to as the *producer's risk* and Type II errors are referred to as the *consumer's risk.*

The second approach is based on the acceptance quality levels (AQL) curve. The operating characteristic (OC) curve is an important tool when using AQL. There are four things that can happen when applying acceptance plans, and two of them are not good. The buyer can (1) accept good lots, (2) reject bad lots, (3) accept bad lots, or (4) reject good lots. Consider the OC curve in Figure B.1. The OC curve shows how well an acceptance plan discriminates between good and bad lots.

OPERATING CHARACTERISTIC (OC) CURVE

An OC curve is used to reflect how well various sampling plans discriminate. A single sampling plan is shown in Figure B.1. The curve shows the probability that the sampling plan will result in accepting a bad batch. As can be seen in the figure, a lot with 1 percent of defects would have a probability of about .90 of being

FIGURE B.1
Single Sampling Plan

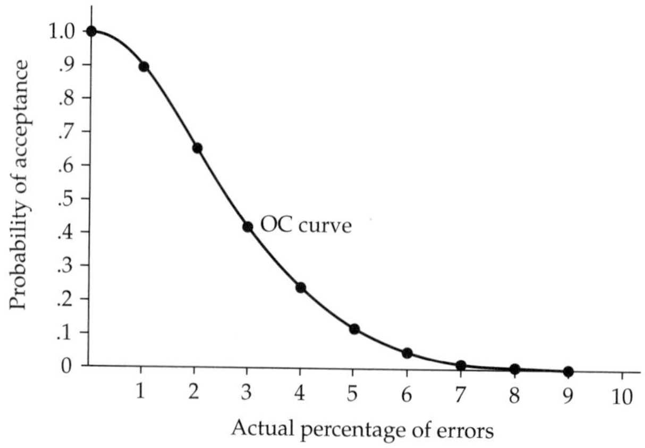

FIGURE B.2
The Effect of the Sample Size on the OC Curve

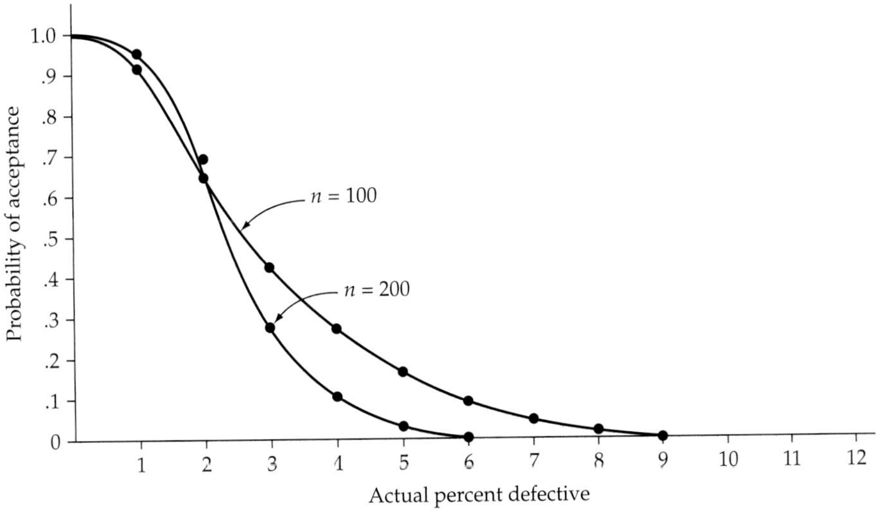

accepted or .10 (1.00 − .90 = .10) chance of being rejected. The .10 probability is the producer's risk. At the same time, if a lot contains 6 percent defects, the probability of acceptance drops to .10. The .10 is the consumer's risk.

The shape of the curve determines the discriminating power of the OC curve. The steeper the curve, the more discriminating the sampling plan. As an example, Figure B.2 shows the effect of doubling the sample size. When the number of defective units in a shipment is no larger than 1 percent, the shipment is acceptable. The acceptance number is defined as the maximum number of defective units a shipment is allowed to have. Comparing the two curves in Figure B.2, it is easy to see that the probability of rejecting an acceptable shipment is .10 (1 − .90) for $n = 100$, and .03 for $n = 200$. In addition, the error or *consumer's risk* decreases as sample size increases. If the actual percentage error was 2 percent, the probability of accepting the shipment has decreased from .877 to .829 with a doubling of sample size. Figure B.3 shows the effect of changes in the OC curve if the acceptance number were changed.

FIGURE B.3
The Effect of the Acceptance Number on the OC Curve

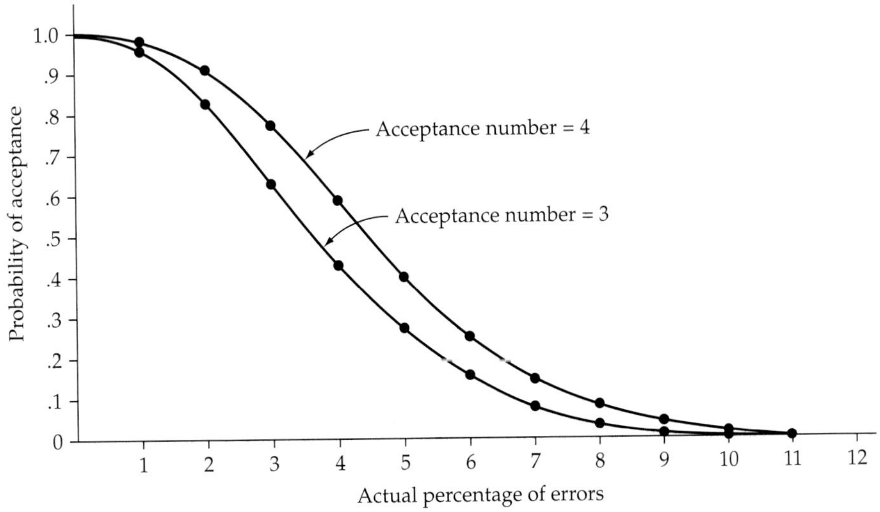

FIGURE B.4
Acceptance Sampling Decision Model
Deciding whether to accept or reject a batch is the purpose of sampling.

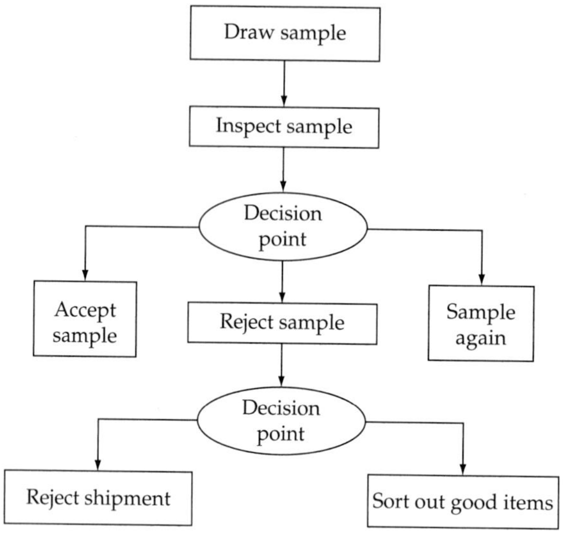

From this analysis, it is clear that the only way to reduce both the producer's risk and the consumer's risk is to increase the sample size or reduce the acceptance number.

In most cases, incoming purchased parts are inspected before they are placed into inventory. Sampling is usually used to decide whether to accept or reject a batch. As shown in Figure B.4, a decision can be made to accept the sample, reject the sample, or take another sample.

Acceptance sampling plans can be classified as single, double, or multiple. With multiple samples, if a clear-cut decision cannot be made after the first sample, additional samples are taken until the choice is clear. The single sampling plan requires the inspector to compare the number of defective items from a single sample with an acceptance number. Double sampling is similar to multiple sampling, except that no more than two samples are taken.

The total cost of the alternative sampling plans determines which is most appropriate. The trade-off is between the number of samples needed and the total number of observations. Single samples usually require a larger sample size than a multiple-sampling plan. In cases where the cost of inspection is expensive, a single-sampling plan should probably be used.

Part Four

Price/Cost Analysis and Negotiation Strategies

Chapter Thirteen

Price Determination

Learning Objectives

1. Understand the relationship between cost and price.
2. Discuss how learning curve analysis relates to materials purchase price.
3. Acquire a working knowledge of the various pricing methods.
4. Understand the competitive bidding trap.
5. Learn how price/cost analysis is used for the negotiation process.
6. Illustrate the price/cost analysis process.
7. Show the difference between gross margin and markup.

INTRODUCTION

One of the most important and complex decisions a firm has to make is how much to pay for its items and services. The buying professional should be able to easily detect prices that are too high. Thus, pricing decisions must be given careful consideration when buying industrial products and services.

The price of a product or service should be expected to cover cost of production, promotion, and distribution, plus a reasonable profit. Pricing is usually based on variation of cost.

Determining price is the ultimate responsibility of the purchasing professional. In order to obtain the most efficient and acceptable price, the purchasing professional must make sure that she or he is aware of market conditions and prices associated with quality levels required for the buying organization's needs. The effective buyer must become an expert for the item she or he purchases. Some purchasing managers believe in buying at the lowest possible price without consideration for delivery time, acceptable quality levels, or the appropriate quantities.

The effective buyer in a competitive environment will more than likely obtain purchased goods and services at a market price given that quality, delivery, and proper quantities are appropriate. If you buy items for one-half the market price without obtaining appropriate quality, delivery, or quantity standards, your firm will be rendered noncompetitive. Price is important; however, one must remember it is only one of many variables that go into purchasing decisions.

THE PURCHASING DECISION

The objective of the purchasing department is to buy the *right materials* from the *right supplier* at the *right time* and at the *right price*. At first glance, this sounds like a straightforward purchasing objective. Even though the objective appears simple, it fails to consider the interaction between the various variables. Perhaps the most important factor associated with the purchasing decision is the business environment and the power imbalance between the buying and supplying firms. There are some instances where the supplier will employ short-term strategic pricing in order to gain market share or dump unwanted items. In these cases, buying below the competitive market price is a good business decision, if there is a need. However, if the supplier is cutting costs in order to keep the doors open, it may result in poor services and even affect the buying firm's ability to meet market demand.

Given the complexity of the buying decision, the purchasing professional must be prepared to analyze each significant buying situation on the basis of the conceptual and the economic impacts of various buying decisions. The analysis phase requires the decision maker to investigate at least two potential sources of supply. The purchasing process requires constant monitoring and adjusting to the changing operations environment. In order for the purchasing professional to survive as an effective buyer, she or he must have an adequate understanding of economics and psychology. In addition, the federal, state, and local laws that affect price also must be followed. Each of the concepts mentioned above will be examined in detail in the following pages.

PRICE-SETTING STRATEGY (ECONOMIC)

There is no grand formula for setting prices for goods and services. Price setting in the chemical industry appears to be precise and firm. However, price setting in the personal computer industry appears to be completely random. The chemical industry apparently bases its pricing strategy on cost analysis, and the computer industry probably uses a more responsive market-based approach. The price/cost approach will be investigated later in this chapter. In the short term, a firm can sell its products below its total cost; however, at some point, the firm will be required to make a profit or quit the business. In other words, a cost-based approach cannot succeed in a competitive market if the product does not remain acceptable to the buying firm. In most cases, the intelligent buyer will do a **price/cost analysis** by comparing the costs and prices from two or more suppliers.

The market approach to pricing is more erratic simply because the supplier, through the use of market research, collects information on its competitors and from their customers to determine where the price should be pegged. The customer perception of quality and service is also important when determining market prices.

In today's competitive environment in which customers are demanding more service and quality, market pricing is perhaps the most popular approach. Market pricing is in the interests of both the selling firm and the buying firm. With market pricing, the buyer is able to exercise its full range of competitive priorities based on its true needs. In the end, the buying firm must determine whether the purchase price fits its competitive cost structure. This is called *target pricing*. If the target price is too low to generate interest from suppliers, it may be necessary for the buyer to consider applying a value analysis approach to the product in question.

PRICE-MAKING STRATEGY (PSYCHOLOGICAL)

In order to become an effective buyer, the purchasing professional must attempt to predict changes in the industry. The major psychological influence in a buyer–supplier relationship is power. It is conceivable that a powerful buyer could force a supplier to eliminate its overhead from the ultimate price. The danger for the buyer is that this so-called good buy may drive the supplier out of business, and that this reduction in competition may result in massive price increases in the long run. The buying firm, no matter how powerful, should attempt to obtain a fair price and good consensus. Remember, if the buyer drives all of the suppliers from the market, it will be forced to enter a new business.

DISCOUNTS

The first question a purchasing professional should ask a supplier is, "How much of a discount can I receive if I buy from you?" Some of the more popular discounts are cash, trade, and quantity discounts.

Cash Discounts

In today's business environment, when sound money management is so important, selling firms will offer cash discounts if payments for goods and services are promptly remitted. The amount of the cash discount depends on the industry and item purchased. If a buying firm is offered a cash discount of 3/10, net 30, it means that if the buyer pays for the items within 10 days of the shipment date of the invoice, it may deduct 3 percent from the invoice price. As an example, $300 savings can be deducted from a $10,000 invoice if it is paid in 10 days. Thus, $300 is even more impressive if you assume that a similar purchase is made 12 times per year. The savings would then be $3,600 (12 × $300). Thus, if the buying firm is given a 3-percent discount for anticipating payment by 20 days, this is equivalent to a rate of 3 percent multiplied by 18 periods, or 54 percent annually, since there are approximately 18 periods of 20 days each in a year.

The buyer should consider the cash discount when comparing competing suppliers. Cash discounts can be easily viewed as a reduction in item costs.

Trade Discounts

A trade discount represents the compensation for the buyer who eliminates a distributor or other middlemen from the transaction.

Trade discounts are usually used by the manufacturer to protect a unique selling opportunity. This is accomplished by providing the buying firm an incentive to buy directly from the manufacturer. In other words, the manufacturing or buying firm splits the wholesaler profit margin.

Quantity Discounts

Quantity discounts are discounts granted to the buyer for buying larger quantities. The supplier can easily justify quantity discounts on the basis of increased revenues received from selling larger quantities. There also may be a savings in production planning and scheduling associated with longer production runs.

The buying firm must consider its total cost of accepting a quantity discount. Specifically, the holding costs associated with carrying larger quantities must be compared to the expected benefit of the discounts.

In other words, quantity discounts must be tied to the buying firm's cost structure (see Chapter 5 for a more comprehensive discussion). The supplier must not discriminate with product pricing. The legal issues related to pricing will be discussed in the next section.

PRICE AND THE LAW

The Robinson–Patman Act states that it is illegal to offer a quantity discount for commodities of like grade and quality that is not based on differences in the cost of manufacturer sales, or delivery resulting from the differing methods or quantities in which such commodities are sold or delivered. Justifying a quantity discount is the responsibility of the selling firm. The seller must be able to document the actual cost savings. The following actions from the U.S. Department of Commerce describe the courses of action that can be taken to enforce the Robinson–Patman Act.

1. *Informing the seller.* The fact that you are charged more than somebody else for an item is not in itself proof of illegal discrimination. You may be able to get your supplier to eliminate discrimination or to show why she or he is not discriminating illegally if you inform her or him when you believe she or he is discriminating against your organization.
2. *Reporting to the Federal Trade Commission (FTC).* The FTC carries the major burden for enforcing the Robinson–Patman Act. Its normal procedures include investigation, complaint, hearing, and—if the facts seem to warrant—a cease-and-desist order. Orders may be appealed to the circuit court of appeals and finally to the Supreme Court. The procedure is normally slow since the seller does not have to change his or her pricing practice until an order against him or her becomes final.
3. *Reporting to the Department of Justice.* The antidiscrimination section of the Robinson–Patman Act is a part of the Clayton Act.
4. *Bringing private suit.* You may ask the courts for injunctive relief against threatened damage from illegal price discrimination. You also can bring suit for triple damages for losses you have sustained because of a discriminatory high price.

Given the complexity of the Robinson–Patman ban, it makes more business sense to discuss the incident directly with the seller. Both parties can then reach a business solution to the problem. If this approach fails, the legal solution could result in both sides suffering the consequences of a lawsuit. (See Appendix A for price discrimination examples.)

PRICE

Price determination is becoming the most important competitive weapon necessary to ensure survival in today's competitive environment. Companies are spending an increasingly larger percentage of their revenue dollars for the acquisition of goods and services. Ten years ago, manufacturing firms fabricated more than 60 percent of component parts in-house. Today more than 70 percent of component parts and services are purchased from outside suppliers. Moreover, in the past, the vice president of manufacturing was responsible for making sure that fabrication or in-house service costs were kept under control. As resource shifts occur from fabrication to outsourcing companies, managerial responsibility must

FIGURE 13.1
Competitive Pressure

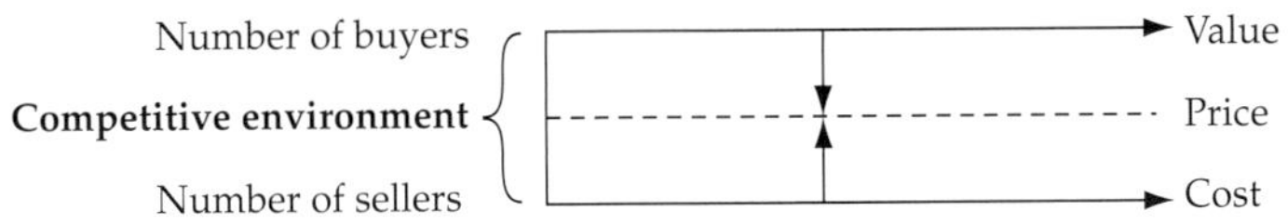

change to adapt to the new assemble-to-order manufacturing environment. Later in this chapter, we will consider price/cost as a key competitive advantage in the new environment.

Price reflects more than cost and profit; pricing decisions also must be based on the degrees of competition and buyer–seller relationships. As can be seen in Figure 13.1, the competitive pressures of price also must consider the number of sellers in the market, the number of buyers in the market, and the general economic environment.

The dynamics of simultaneous shifts in the number of sellers, the number of buyers, and the general economic conditions will ensure a better measure of price determination for buying firms. As an example, consider the business cycle in Figure 13.2. The buying firm operating in this environment must plan for critical materials/components/service requirements at points A and B. If critical requirements are not planned between points A and B, the buyer will forgo an important window of opportunity. The interval between A and B ensures reasonable contract prices and short lead times due to low utilization in the industry. This is especially true for the computer/microprocessor industry.

The firms that enter into contracts after point B will pay premium prices and experience extended lead times. This planning approach sounds like a good strategy; however, it is naive to assume that the buying firm has the financial strength to lock in economical long-term blanket orders or systems contracts during a necessary period. In the case of both financially healthy and not-so-healthy firms, strategic planning must be incorporated into the overall business strategy. Consider Z, a healthy Fortune 500 company, and Y, a five-year-old threshold firm. Both companies are in the personal computer business. Firm Z, which can easily afford to set up long-term blanket orders, misses the window of opportunity and pays premium prices for component parts. On the other hand, a well-managed lean firm purchased component parts by negotiating a partnership agreement where both buyer and seller agreed to share in the savings.

FIGURE 13.2
Business Cycle

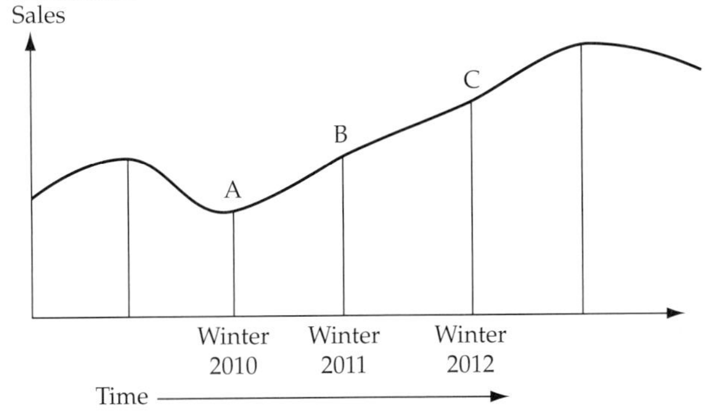

The general sources of price information are (1) published price lists, (2) quotations, (3) other buyers in the market, (4) trade journals, (5) negotiations, (6) competitive bidding, and (7) distribution. Perhaps the specific supplier is the best source of price information. Although there are no written rules that require the supplier to furnish cost information, the buyer should always be able to obtain a cost breakdown.

COSTS

The cost components of price determination can be divided into *direct* and *indirect* costs. **Direct costs** relate to the actual units of production. Direct labor and direct materials costs are classified as direct costs. If the unit is not produced, direct costs are not incurred. **Indirect costs** are associated with non–manufacturing-related costs. Insurance, managerial salaries, property taxes, and depreciation expenses are examples of indirect costs.

A facility that is operating at a high utilization level is incurring significant operating costs. At the same time, if a facility is operating at low utilization levels, there are still costs associated with operating the facility. Facility overhead costs can be very complicated since this cost category is associated with salaried workers and various operating supplies. In some cases, supplies are treated as expense items.

Finally, one of the most important costs from the suppliers' viewpoint is profit. A firm cannot afford to operate without a realized profit. Profit is essentially an economic *cost* of doing business. The learning curve concept and its usefulness in the prediction of variable cost (direct labor hours/direct material) will be discussed next.

THE LEARNING CURVE

The purchasing professional must understand the dynamic nature of variable cost. Improvements are possible in the way most tasks are performed. The improvement process may have a significant effect on the buyer's total purchase price. It would be a mistake to assume that the supplier's costs remain constant as volumes increase. The learning curve is a well-known method used to measure and predict the efficiencies of increasing outputs. The underlying behavior of the improvement curve reflects a systematic improvement (percentage reduction) of labor per unit as a function of cumulative units produced. Figure 13.3a shows an 80-percent learning curve.

The earliest use of the learning curve was in the airframes industry. It was observed that as aircraft production increased, the direct labor cost per airplane decreased. This observation was the result of the labor force learning how to do their jobs better as they produce more and more units. As major defense contractors use the learning curve to evaluate subcontractors, they estimate cost and report progress to the buyer. The characteristic learning curve is exponential and depicts a constant percentage reduction of labor as a function of cumulative units produced. Learning curves are especially important in various assembly operations.

Learning curves have been applied and misapplied to a variety of problem situations. The learning curve techniques have been used extensively in cost

FIGURE 13.3a
Eighty-Percent Learning Curve

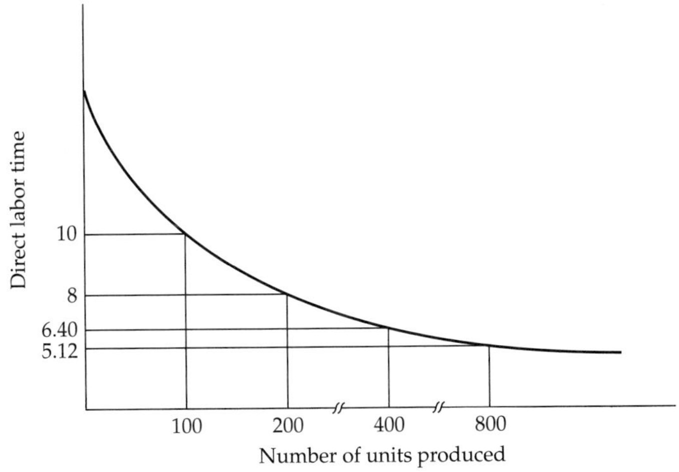

estimating, pricing, negotiating contracts, and estimating the major implications of changes in design. Also see Cochran (1969); Conway and Schultz (1959); and Hirschman (1964).

The Model

As stated previously, the learning curve model is based on a constant percentage reduction in required inputs as output increases. These reductions are most typically expressed in terms of the effect of output doubling. As can be seen in Figure 13.3a, when output doubles, a 20-percent reduction in cost occurs. The curve represents an 80-percent learning curve; if the 100th unit requires 10 direct labor hours, then the 200th unit requires (10 × .80) = 8 direct labor hours, the 400th unit requires (8 × .80) = 6.40 direct labor hours, the 800th unit requires (6.40 × .80) = 5.12 direct labor hours, and so on. This relationship can be expressed mathematically in the following way:

$$y_i = y_1 - i^{-b}$$

where

y_i = Direct labor hours required for the ith unit

y_1 = Direct labor hours for the first unit

i = Count of cumulative units produced

b = Slope of the learning curve

Figure 13.3b shows the relationship between unit cost and cumulative average time. As can be seen, the time for the curves intersects at the first unit. In other words the unit cost and the cumulative average costs are the same for the first unit. The cumulative cost curve is observed to be log linear over the entire unit production range. The unit cost curve is asymptotically parallel to the cumulative cost curve.

If any two values of i are stated so that $i_2 \div i_1 = 2$, we know the power to which 2 must be raised in order to achieve the desired learning percentage. Thus, $2^{-.3219} =$ .80, and a curve for which $b = .3219$ is an 80-percent learning curve and $2^{-.2345} =$ 85-percent learning curve.

FIGURE 13.3b
Unit Cost Curve and the Cumulative Cost Curve Relationship

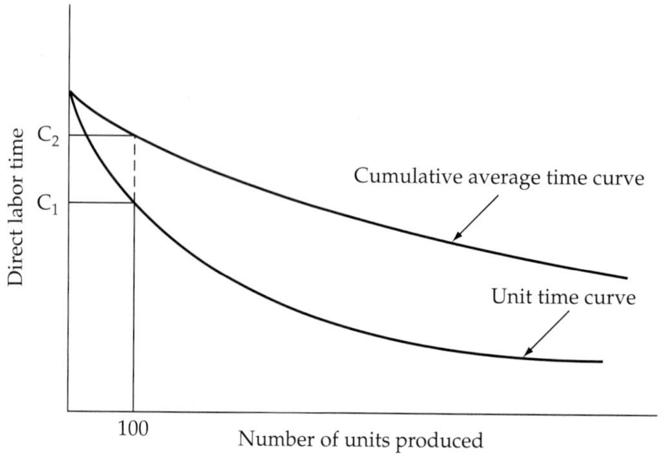

To use the table in Appendix B, we are given information (direct labor time or direct labor cost) for some base unit (BU). As an example, using an 84-percent learning curve, it takes five direct labor hours to build the tenth unit. Thus, BU equals the tenth unit.

This base unit is then used to estimate the required inputs (hours, money, or whatever) for any unit, regardless of whether it is made before or after the base unit. The pivot percentage is the unit in question divided by the base unit:

$$\text{Pivot percentage (PP)} = \text{Unit in question (UIQ)/Base unit (BU)}$$
$$\text{PP} = \text{UIQ/BU} \quad \textbf{(1)}$$

For the example:

$$12/10 = 120\%$$

We now know two data points:

1. Pivot percentage (PP) = 120%
2. Percent learning curve (PLC) = 84%

We are now ready to find the *F* factor. To do this, we look in Appendix B for table values of *F*. The row entry is PP, here 120 percent. The column entry is PLC, here 84 percent. The table value for this problem is 0.9552.

$$\text{Estimated time or cost} = F \times \text{Time or cost for BU}$$
$$= 0.9552 \times 5 = 4.77 \text{ hours} \quad \textbf{(2)}$$

Next consider a company that estimates that it will take 20 direct labor hours to construct the 50th unit and that an 80-percent learning curve will be experienced. What is the expected average time for the first four units?

Using Equations (1) and (2), we find

$$\text{PP} = 5/50 = 10\%$$
$$\text{Estimated time} = 2.0986 \times 20 = 42 \text{ hours (see Figure 13.4)}$$

FIGURE 13.4
Cumulative Average Cost Example

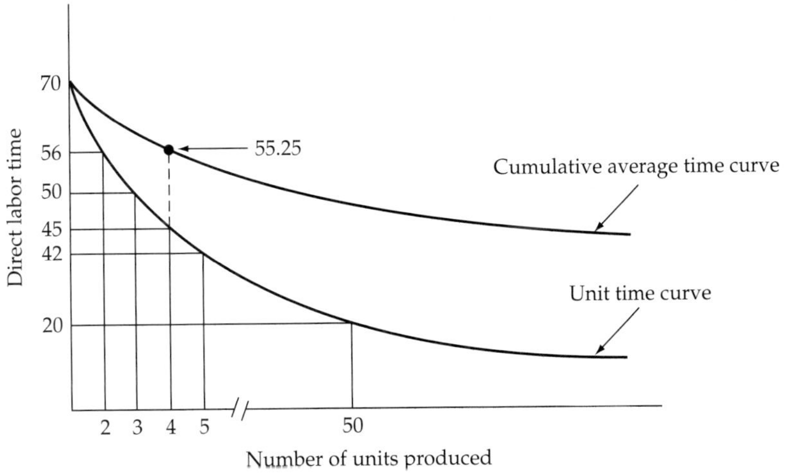

Easy, right? Try using the first unit. Run into trouble?

$$PP = 1/50 = 2\%$$

There is no 2-percent value in Appendix B. We must figure out a way around this inconsistency. For example, assume that we shift from BU = 50 to BU = 5. Why did we choose 5? The reason is that unit 5 is the only other unit about which we have information. Making the shift from BU = 50 to BU = 5 enables us to work the problem, as shown below using Equation (1):

PP = 1/5 = 20% by formula 1 shown on page 294

Thus, a PP of 20 percent and a PLC = 80 percent yield a table value for *F* of 1.6789. Then, using Equation (2), we have

$$\text{Estimated time} = 1.6789 \times 42 = 70 \text{ hours}$$

Stated differently, it takes 70 hours to make the first unit and 42 hours to make the fifth unit. Now try your luck for units two, three, and four.

Your answers should be:

56 hours for unit two
50 hours for unit three
45 hours for unit four
The average time for the first four units is [(70 + 56 + 50 + 45)/4] = 55.25 hours

In summary:

1. Identify BU and the input required for BU.
2. Identify the unit in question.
3. Get the value of PP by Equation (1).
4. Solve the problem by Equation (2) *if possible*, that is, if the computed value of PP appears in the *F* table.
5. If PP is not listed, shift to another value of BU that enables you to solve the problem.

Example

Now consider a purchasing contract in which the buyer is purchasing a hand-held assembly for a power tool. The pricing strategy is based on bidding a contract for 500 hand-held assemblies built in-house last year. Production control has produced the following data:

Unit	Time (minutes)	Find Percent Learning Curve*
1	65.6	20/10→30.2/36.5 = 82.73
10	36.5	40/20→26.3/30.2 = 87.08
20	30.2	60/30→23/27.4 = 83.94
30	27.4	84.5%
40	26.3	or approximately 85%
50	23.9	See the pivot point in
60	23.0	Appendix B.

* Each time ouput doubles, calculate a ratio using the associated information for the doubling effect. Next, sum all ratios and divide by the number of ratios.

Note: The percent learning curve is based on the double-declining method. Each time the number of units doubles, a ratio is calculated. All of the ratios are summed and divided by the number of ratios.

SOLUTION

Since we only have unit times for the units, we must estimate an average time for 500 units. Let the first five units be the pivot point.

Unit in Question	Pivot Percentage	$F \times$ BU (time)	Time (minutes)
1			= 65.6
2	2/1 = 200%	.8500 × 65.6	= 55.68
3	3/1 = 300%	.7729 × 65.6	= 50.62
4	4/1 = 400%	.7225 × 65.6	= 47.32
5	5/1 = 500%	.6857 × 65.6	= 44.91
Average time			= 52.80*

*The average time for the first five units will be used to pivot to the 500th unit. This is an estimation approach. By definition we should pivot unit by unit until we reach the 500th unit.

To calculate average labor time for the first five units, use this.

50/5 = 1,000%

F = 0.5604

Estimated time = 0.5604 × 52.80 = 29.58

500/50 = 1,000%

F = 0.5604

Estimated time = 0.5604 × 29.58
= 16.58 (average time per unit)

Therefore, the total time for 500 units is

500 × 16.58 = 8,292 minutes = 138.20 hours

Total labor costs = 138.20 hours × $10 per hour
= $1,382

Profit margin = $138.20 (1,382 × .10)

Thus, the total contract cost is $1,520.20 ($1,382 + $138.20)

Estimate

Labor Costs = $1,382
Profit Margin= 138.20
$1,520.20

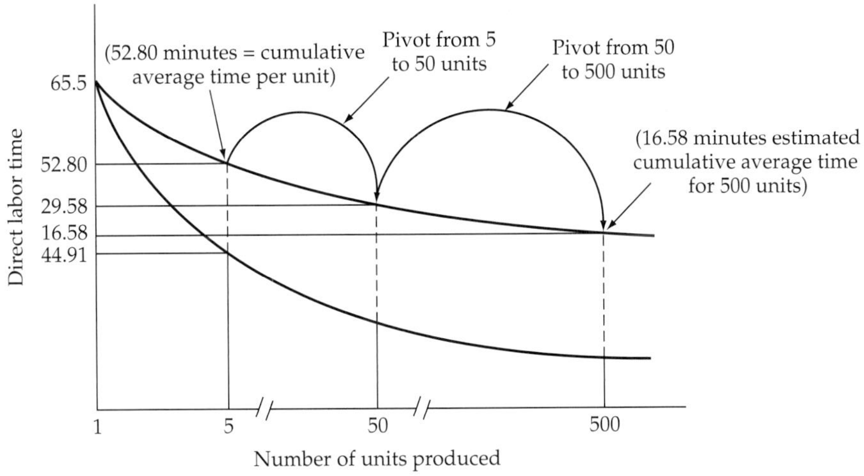

FIGURE 13.5 Graphical Illustration for the Example Problem

An illustration of the pivot solution steps is shown in Figure 13.5.

PRICING STRATEGY

A competitive firm's purchasing objectives must include the following:

1. The right material (quality)
2. The right quantity
3. The right source
4. The right timing
5. The right price

The first four objectives must be considered as given if a firm is operating in a profit-maximizing mode in today's global markets. The fifth objective must follow the correct pricing method in order to achieve a competitive advantage. The most utilized pricing methods are standard price lists, competitive bidding, and negotiations.

Standard Price List

Standard price lists are usually prices generated based on the seller's total cost structure. The selling firm usually offers quantity discount schedules in order to influence the behavior of the buying firm. This pricing method also is used when selling commodities.

Competitive Bidding

The competitive bidding process must begin with an assessment sizing up the suppliers' pricing strategies on competitive positions. The buyer can determine the selling firms' pricing strategies. If the suppliers are selling their products in target markets other than the buying firm's market, the pricing will more than likely be higher. On the other hand, when the buying firm is buying from sellers that service firms similar to the buying firm's markets, the prices will more than likely decrease.

The supplier's competitive advantage is critical when the formal competitive bidding process is used. In most government competitively bid contracts (sealed bids), the lowest bid is the winning bid. In the case of sealed bids, each certified bidder submits a written bid that is opened at a prespecified date. The sealed-bid method is excellent when the bid is for specified construction contracts, standardized capital equipment, janitorial services, and so forth. In cases where highly specialized or professional services are procured, negotiated bidding should be employed. In these cases, the winning criterion is based on much more than price. After the winning bid has been selected, the contracting officer may negotiate several cost components, quality upgrades, and delivery objectives. The competitive bidding process should be employed when the following conditions prevail:

1. The dollar value of the spend must be large enough to justify the expense of the competitive bidding process.
2. The specifications of the product or service must be precise enough for both the buying and selling firms to accurately estimate.
3. There are enough selling firms in the market.
4. There is adequate time to use this form of bidding. The competitive process usually takes from four to eight weeks for most industrial firms.

After the decision to use the competitive bidding process, a buying strategy must be designed. Most well-managed selling firms that use the competitive bidding process usually use a probabilistic bidding strategy. The probabilistic bidding strategy is based on the profit-maximization strategy. The probabilistic strategy also assumes that the buying firm will select the firm with the lowest bid.

The buying firm must develop an estimate of a reasonable bid amount. The buying firm's estimate should be based on market data, including the following:

- The dollar value of previous bids.
- The expected profit from previous bids.

The data set is used to estimate the probability of different bid scenarios. The scenario should include mock bids with low, moderate, and high profit margins. The expected profit equation is given as

$$E(\pi_A) = P(A) \times y(A)$$

where

A = Dollar amount of bid

$P(A)$ = Probability of accepting bid price

$y(A)$ = Profit if bid A is accepted

$E(\pi_A)$ = Expected profit at this bid

Consider a mock competitive bidding process by the buying firm in which we have data on 10 bids, cost, and profit combinations. These data will enable the buyer to estimate various expected bid prices given that we set $E(\pi_A)$ *a priori*. The purchasing manager can easily assess the historical bidding on similar buys. Suppose the purchasing director tabulates the data in Table 13.1.

The buying analysis in Table 13.1 indicates that the highest bid should not exceed \$410,000. Thus, the bidding range should be between \$360,000 and \$410,000 depending on the economic environment. Sixty percent of the bidders should fall within this range. Finally, as with another pricing strategy, competitive bidding,

TABLE 13.1
Historical Bid Tabs

Bid Price (A)	Actual Cost	Cumulative Probability of Winning at the Bid, $P(A)$	Profit, $y(A)$	Expected Profit, $E(\pi A)$
$480,000	360,000	0.00	120,000	$ 0
460,000	360,000	0.03	100,000	$ 3,000
450,000	360,000	0.10	90,000	9,000
440,000	360,000	0.20	80,000	16,000
420,000	360,000	0.38	60,000	22,800
410,000	360,000	0.54	50,000	27,000
380,000	360,000	0.73	20,000	14,600
360,000	360,000	0.92	—	—
350,000	360,000	0.98	−10,000	−9,800
340,000	360,000	1.00	−20,000	−20,000

the final price is determined by the number of sellers/buyers and the economic environment.

Negotiations

Negotiations should include discussions and each of the five purchasing objectives. Negotiations should be used exclusively when there are time constraints, the specifications are not clearly stated, there are not enough sellers, and the dollar value is too low to consider using the competitive bidding process. Negotiation should be used any time the buyer does not have confidence in the standard price lists and competitive bidding seems unreasonable. This topic will be covered extensively in the next chapter.

PROJECT PRICING

Markups versus Margins

In today's competitive construction market, markup and margin are sometimes used interchangeably. However, gross margin and markup are not the same. A clear understanding of markup versus gross margin is an important concept when estimating and bidding jobs in the construction industry. Using gross margins in the construction industry involves complicated calculations and can lead to erroneous competitive bidding results.

Specifically, gross margin is defined as the difference between the price of the job and the costs to build a job. By definition, the gross margin is the included overhead and profit for the specific job. As an example, a 30-percent gross margin on a job that sells for $100,000 generates $30,000 to cover overhead and profit. Net margin refers to profit alone. Consider that an 8-percent net margin on a $100,000 sale yields $8,000.

On the other hand, markup is job costs times a factor that covers direct costs, overhead cost, and profit. The difference between gross margin and markup is illustrated in the example below:

Forecasted annual dollar volume − *Annual job cost* = *Gross margin*

$150,000 − $100,500 = $49,500

$49,500 is the projected gross margin for the year.

The gross margin percentage is

Gross margin/Forecasted annual dollar volume = Gross margin percentage

$49,500/$150,000 = 33%

The markup factor is

Forecasted annual dollar volume/Forecasted annual job

$150,000/100,500 = 1.49

If a contractor projects a 33-percent annual gross margin for the business, the markup must be set to a factor of 1.49 times the job cost. This illustrative example clearly shows that a 33-percent gross margin is not equivalent to a 1.33 markup. Mathematically, markup will always be a larger result compared to the gross margin. Consequently, contractors who do not understand the differences between margin and markup will overstate their profitability. Consider another example, a margin of 30 percent for a $100,000 job is $30,000. A 30-percent gross margin leaves $70,000 contribution for the job cost. Now calculate the total selling price for the project using a 1.30 markup (1.30 × $70,000). As can be seen, the selling price for the job is $91,000, which is $9,000 less than the $100,000 expected job selling price. Thus, in order to achieve a 30-percent gross margin for the job, the markup is 1.43 ($100,000/70,000).

In practice, the inexperienced building contractor who focuses on the so-called "big margins" may not understand markup. If the business generates annual sales of $1,000,000, a 30-percent gross margin appears to be a reasonable return for the business. On the other hand, if annual sales are $150,000, there is only $45,000 generated to pay all of the company's bills (including salaries, profit, and overhead costs). This pricing scenario is not unique to the construction industry. The markup for each firm is based on the firm's cost structure (specific management salaries, expected profit margins, and overhead costs).

Successful construction-related businesses use the markup pricing approach. A margin versus markup conversion chart is given in Table 13.2.

Breakeven

The breakeven point is that point in time when total income from all jobs sold, built, and collected equals the total expenses. The breakeven point is an important measure for any business simply because management can determine whether the company is ahead of schedule or behind schedule in terms of its goals.

TABLE 13.2
Margin versus Markup Conversion Chart*

15% Markup	= 13.0% Gross Profit
20% Markup	= 16.7% Gross Profit
25% Markup	= 20.0% Gross Profit
30% Markup	= 23.0% Gross Profit
33.3% Markup	= 25.0% Gross Profit
40% Markup	= 28.6% Gross Profit
43% Markup	= 30.0% Gross Profit
50% Markup	= 33.0% Gross Profit
75% Markup	= 42.9% Gross Profit
100% Markup	= 50.0% Gross Profit

*(Formula: Markup = Cost/(1 − Desired GP (decimal)). For example, if you want a GP of 25%, the markup should be Cost/(1 − .25) = 1.33 times the cost, or 33% of the cost.

The breakeven point is calculated on the total projected annual sales for a company each year. The breakeven point should be calculated after the company decides on the annual goals.

A breakeven example is given below:

$$\text{Breakeven} = \text{Total overhead} \div \frac{(\text{Total sales} - \text{Total job costs})}{\text{Total sales}}$$

- Total sales = \$150,000
- Total overhead = \$37,500
- Total job costs = \$100,500

$$\begin{aligned}\text{Breakeven} &= \$37{,}500 \div \frac{(\$150{,}000 - \$100{,}500)}{\$150{,}000}\\ &= \$37{,}500 \div \frac{\$49{,}500}{\$150{,}000}\\ &= \$37{,}500 \div 0.33\\ &= \$113{,}636\end{aligned}$$

Thus, the breakeven point for the year is \$113,636. Once the firm has sold and built jobs equal to \$113,636 of the forecasted \$150,000, the total projected overhead and job costs for the year will have been covered. The breakeven analysis provides an effective monitoring mechanism for the construction-related business. As an example, if the breakeven is expected in July and is actually achieved in May, the company is ahead of schedule in terms of performance to the goal. On the other hand, if the breakeven point is reached in September, the profitability goal is lagging behind schedule.

THE PRICE/COST ANALYSIS PROCESS

A buying firm must consider the price variation that is inherent in buying high-priced components in order to understand various design specifications and associated costs. Moreover, the buyer must obtain reasonable cost comparisons based on historical data of similar equipment and from his or her own experience with conditions in the specific industry. In other words, the buyer must become an expert in the associated industry. It is a good practice to make a careful estimate of the probable cost. After performing research and analyzing the production process/materials, a per-unit cost estimate must be made.

At the same time, several requests for proposals (RFPs) should be sent out. Ideally, the usable RFPs will have cost estimates that are lower than the in-house production cost estimate. Example proposals from two feasible bidding firms are given in Table 13.3.

The adjustments are made for each of the firms in Table 13.4. Using the appropriate standard cost components, firm A is encouraged to reduce direct labor costs from \$5 per hour to \$4.50 per hour, and, alternatively, firm B is encouraged to reduce the labor hours from 7 DLH (direct labor hours) to 6 DLH. Similar comparisons between firms A and B and subsequent adjustments were made for the remaining cost components in Table 13.4.

As can be seen from Table 13.3, the following observations should be discussed with respect to firms A and B.

TABLE 13.3 Price/Cost Analysis Example Problem

	Firm A	Firm B
Direct labor hours (DLH) (average)	6 hours	7 hours
Hourly rate	$5/hour	$4.50/hour
Direct labor cost (DLC)	6 × $5 = $30.00	7 × $4.50 = $31.50
Direct material cost (DMC)	$10.00	$10.00
Tooling cost (TC)	$2.00	$3.00
Manufacturing overhead (MO)	50% × DLC = $15.00	75% × DLC = $23.62
General and administration expense	5% × (DLC + DMC + TC + MO) = $2.85	7% × (DLC + DMC + TC + MO) = $4.78
Total cost	$59.85	$72.90
Profit	7% × Total cost = $4.19	5% × Total cost = $3.64
Selling price	$64.03	$76.54

1. Direct labor for firm A is probably too high, and measures should be made to reconcile firm A's labor costs. Maybe the average hours needed to produce each unit are overstated. Alternatively, the learning curve may be a source of the inconsistency in the variance in labor hours between firms A and B. We show the proposed negotiated adjustments in Table 13.3.
2. The tooling cost for firm B is too high. Why does the tooling cost exceed industry norms? This should be investigated. The buyer should negotiate an adjustment.
3. The manufacturing overhead for firm B is significantly higher than firm A's overhead costs. This issue should be addressed. If the selling firm insists on this rate, the buyer should ask for exact data to support the claim. The supplier will probably make adjustments before agreeing to an audit. Please see the adjustments in Table 13.3.

Finally, consider buyers who buy on impulse. If a buying firm fails to negotiate, there will be an immediate competitive disadvantage [((64.03 − 58.97)/58.97) × 100 = 8.5%] (ceteris paribus).

Price/cost analysis is a natural input into the negotiation process. The negotiation process is a learned behavior. In order to effectively negotiate for industrial firms, both the buyer and the seller must win. Because of dynamic business cycles and loosely defined cost components, each and every aspect of a business transaction

TABLE 13.4 Price/Cost Analysis Solution

	Firm A	Firm B
Direct labor hours (DLH) (average)	6 hours	6 hours (B1)
Rate	$4.50/hour (A1)	$4.50 per hour
Direct labor cost (DLC)	6 × $4.5 = $27.00	6 × $4.5 = $27.00
Direct material cost (DMC)	$10.00	$10.00
Tooling cost (TC)	$2.00	$2.50 (B2)
Manufacturing overhead (MO)	50% × DLC = $13.50	50% × DLC = $13.50 (B3)
General and administration expense	5% × (DLC + DMC + TC + MO) = $2.62	7% × (DLC + DMC + TC + MO) = $3.71
Total cost	$55.12	$56.71
Profit	7% × Total cost = $3.86	5% × Total cost = $2.84
Selling price	$58.97	$59.54

is negotiable. Direct labor, overhead, and administrative costs are all excellent candidates for negotiations. To the extent that these costs are pegged, there exists a possibility for negotiation.

One key negotiating issue is setup cost. Setup and tooling costs usually occur during the early stages of the initial production run. Setup cost must be explicitly accounted for. If setup cost and learning rates are ignored, a buying firm will more than likely fall into a *competitive bidding trap*. Large setup and tooling costs can easily be amortized by the selling firm. If the buying firm fails to give explicit specifications and/or prices for alternative quantities of the item, what appears to be a good buy may result in an excessive price. A selling firm may include in the contract price various setup and tooling costs each time the item is purchased. Setup and tooling costs should be amortized over several quantity levels and completely applied in the first purchase order. As an example, consider a buying firm that is expected to need 10,000 barrels of a chemical X. The entire 10,000 barrels will be consumed in the first year. The best way to price the component parts assemblies is to ask for quotes on quantities of 10,000; 20,000; 30,000; 40,000; and 50,000. This approach will force the supplier to amortize the setup and tooling costs. The buying firm has implicitly forced the supplier into a quantity discount schedule. Thus, the buyer will avoid a competitive bidding trap. By investigating alternative quantities, the buying firm can predict the expected learning rate. An illustrative example of an actual price/cost analysis is given in Appendix C.

Summary

Price determination is one of the most important decisions that a successful firm makes. The purchasing professional must become an expert on the product or services for which he or she is responsible. Given the complexity of the buying decision, the purchasing professional must be prepared to analyze each significant buying situation on the basis of the conceptual and the economic impact of various buying decisions. The foundations for price determination are rooted in the *economics* and *psychology* disciplines. From an economics point of view, the effective buyer will conduct a price/cost analysis by comparing the costs and prices from two or more suppliers. The major *psychological* influence in a buyer–supplier relationship is power. It is conceivable that a powerful buyer could force a supplier to eliminate its overhead from the ultimate price.

Selling firms will offer cash discounts if payments for goods and services are promptly remitted. The amount of the cash discount depends on the industry and item purchased. Price determination is becoming the most important competitive weapon necessary to ensure survival in today's competitive environment. Companies are spending an increasingly larger percentage of their revenue dollars for the acquisition of goods and services. Price reflects more than cost and profit; pricing decisions also must be based on the degree of competition and buyer–seller relationships. The general sources of price information are (1) published price lists, (2) quotations, (3) other buyers in the market, (4) trade journals, (5) negotiations, and (6) competitive bidding.

The purchasing professional must understand the dynamic nature of variable cost. Improvements are possible in the way most tasks are performed. The improvement process may have a significant effect on the total purchase price. It would be a mistake to assume that direct labor costs remain constant. The learning curve is a well-known phenomenon used to measure and predict the efficiencies of increasing outputs.

Discussion Questions

1. What are the components of pricing? What are the psychological aspects of pricing?
2. How is pricing included in the negotiation process?
3. Explain why price/cost analysis is frequently slighted by purchasing managers.
4. What is the difference between cost and value? Why is this important for the negotiation process?
5. What is meant by competitive bidding?
6. How does profit fit into the cost equation?
7. What is meant by a cost breakdown? How should a buyer go about convincing a seller to disclose its various cost elements?
8. What are the elements of price/cost analysis?
9. What is a learning curve? Why should a buying firm be concerned about the effect of the learning curve?
10. How much profit is socially acceptable for a selling firm?
11. How is price/cost analysis related to the negotiation process?
12. What is meant by the learning curve phenomenon?
13. What are the assumptions that drive learning curve theory?

Exercises

13.1 The Bureau of Disability Services (BDS) has a large pool of clerical employees who process level one disability claim forms on networked computers. When BDS hires a new clerical employee, it takes that person about 56 minutes to process a form. The learning curve for this job is 82 percent, but no additional learning will take place after the 50th form is processed. DBS has recently acquired a smaller competitor that will add 800 new forms per week to its clerical pool. If an employee works six hours per day per five-day week, how many employees would be hired to complete 1,000 forms per week?

13.2 Professor Davis teaches a course in supply chain management at North Texas State University. She is scheduled to give her class of 32 students a final exam on the last day of exam week, and she is leaving town the same day. She is concerned about her ability to finish grading her exams. From past experience, she knows the first exam will take her about 20 minutes to grade. She estimates her learning curve to be about 88 percent. What is the expected grading time for the 16th exam? What is your estimate of her total grading time? What is the average grading time for the entire batch of exams?

13.3 Medco, Inc. manufactures microsurgical instruments used in products such as minimally invasive surgical procedures. The primary customers for these products are hospitals. Hospitals require that the learning curves be employed in the bid process for awarding contracts. Medco is planning to bid on a 350-unit contract offered by Ohio State Medical Center. Medco estimates that the first unit will require 126 hours of direct labor to produce. The industry learning curve for this particular type of product is 78 percent. Determine the average number of labor hours required to produce the first 100 units. How many hours are required to produce 350 units?

13.4 The Fly High Aircraft Company produces avionics testing equipment for the U.S. military. The company is planning to bid on a new digital radome specially equipped for desert military action. The company has experienced an 84-percent learning curve in the past for producing similar radomes. Based on a prototype model, it estimates the first radome produced will require 10,000 hours of direct labor. The order is for 200 digital radomes. Determine the time that will be required for the 30th and 60th units. If the direct labor cost is $25 per direct labor hour, determine the total contract value, including a 10-percent profit margin.

13.5 Fly High also is considering making a bid for a drone intercepter for the U.S. military. However, the company has almost no experience in producing this type of weapons system. Although Fly High could not obtain direct learning curve rates, they did learn from one contact that for a system with similar features, the first unit required 7,290 hours of direct labor to produce and the 50th and final unit required 2,256 hours to produce. Determine the learning curve rate for the drone interceptor.

13.6 Laptops-R-US has received an order for 450 specially configured personal computers for a large construction company. The small four-person operation has so many orders that they can no longer perform the work themselves, and they must hire extra labor to assemble the units for this new order. They have hired six students from Cal State University to work part time, 20 hours per week, to assemble the computers. The prototype unit required 45 hours of direct labor; from experience, the owners know that their computer assembly operation has an 86-percent learning curve. How long will it take Laptops-R-US to deliver the completed order? If the six students are paid $10 per hour, how much should Laptops-R-US charge the customer. (Assume that Laptops-R-US's overhead rate is 145 percent of direct labor cost and the expected profit margin is 10 percent.)

13.7 The Fort Worth Weapons Company was asked to bid on the barrel assembly for the 30 mm recoilless rifle. The company estimates that it will take 10 hours to complete the 25th unit, and, based on historical data on similar barrel assemblies, an 85-percent learning curve is expected.

a. What is the expected average time for the first two units?

b. What is the approximate *estimated* time for the 100th unit?

c. Repeat parts *a* and *b* above with a learning rate of 76 percent and 90 percent and compare the results. What can be concluded from the exercise?

13.8 Kalle Houston has kept careful records of the time required to build her company's new automated leaf mulching machine.

Unit Number	Unit Time (hours)
50	120.8
100	102.5
200	92.2
300	90.1
400	87.2
600	86.2

a. Estimate the rate of improvement.

b. What is the average time for the first five units?

c. What is the estimated cumulative average time for 1,000 units? Assuming the total cost is $18.90 per direct labor hour, what is the estimated labor cost to produce 1,000 mulching units. Make all assumptions explicit.

13.9 Given an expected learning curve of 80 percent and 943 direct labor hours required for the first unit, how many direct labor hours do you expect in total for the first 10 units? How much time do you expect the 100th unit to require?

13.10 Jan Edwards, the purchasing manager at Highland Hills Manufacturing, Inc., was quoted an estimated time of 47 labor hours to produce the prototype for a new product. The supplier also estimated the learning rate to fall between 82 and 85 percent.

a. What percentage decrease should Jan expect in required manufacturing time by the fifth unit?

b. Suppose an *expected* decrease of approximately 37 percent over the first units was 30 percent. What should Jan infer about the supplier's efficiency?

13.11 Captain Michael Houston is a fighter pilot on the *USS Coral Sea* aircraft carrier. He has prepared the following chart on his landing performance. An excellent grade is a score of 70.

Landings (touch and go)	Expected Score	Actual Score
25	88.5	88
50	84.1	83
75	81.6	84
100	79.9	80
125	78.6	81
150	77.6	79
175	76.7	80
200	75.9	78
225	75.2	
250	74.7	
275	74.2	
300	73.6	

a. What is Captain Houston's expected learning rate? What is his actual learning rate?

b. What is Houston's progress rate based on his first 200 landings?

c. What will his grade be after 500 landings?

d. How many landings will he need to make in order to reach a score of 70?

Suggested Cases

The Auction Case Corp
CBT
McGruder Power, Inc.
The Allen & Gary Show
Sage Imaging Center, Inc.

References

Cochran, E. B. "Learning: New Dimension in Labor Standards." *Industrial Engineering*, January 1969, pp. 28–31.

Conway, R. W., and Andrew Schultz. "The Manufacturing Progress Function." *Journal of Industrial Engineering* 10, no. 1 (January–February 1959).

Hirschman, W. B. "Profit from the Learning Curve." *Harvard Business Review*, January–February 1964, pp. 125–139.

Appendix A

The Robinson–Patman Act: General Price Discrimination

INTRODUCTION

The Robinson–Patman Act of 1936 is an amendment to Section 2 of the Clayton Act of 1914. Therefore, technically, it should be referred to as the Robinson–Patman Amendment to Section 2 of the Clayton Act. However, everyone, including lawyers, simply refers to it as the Robinson–Patman Act. The act prohibits discrimination in price as well as discrimination in services and allowances. It applies to buyers as well as sellers, though, as will be seen, buyers are shielded to some extent by judicial interpretation of the act as applied to buyers. The main thrust of the act is to prevent a seller from selling the same kind of goods ("goods of like grade and quality") to two or more different buyers at different prices. The neophyte will immediately react by saying, "But what about quantity discounts?" Just because the seller supplies larger quantities to one buyer versus another buyer does not permit the seller to charge the large-volume buyer a lower price. This aspect of the act as well as the many other problems related to it will be discussed. The purchasing agent (PA) must be aware of all of the implications of the Robinson–Patman Act. While the PA may feel concerned only in relation to the liability of the buyer under the act (for inducing a discriminatory price), the buyer also must be aware of the act in relation to the seller's problems in complying with it so that, among other things, the buyer can negotiate intelligently with the seller when the subject of Robinson–Patman enters the negotiations. As usual, we warn the buyer not to be his or her own lawyer in dealing with Robinson–Patman. The focus of this appendix is to alert the PA to legal problems that he or she might encounter in his or her job. The alert PA will know when to contact an attorney for assistance if he or she is aware of the fundamental legal pitfalls that may confront him or her on a regular basis.

THE BACKGROUND OF THE ROBINSON–PATMAN ACT

Prior to the enactment of Robinson–Patman in 1936, there were a number of highly publicized hearings and reports in relation to large buyers such as chain stores and mail-order houses that were allegedly receiving discriminatory (lower) prices than their smaller rivals. Using their tremendous purchasing power, the large buyers were placing undue pressure on suppliers with inferior bargaining power to induce discriminatory price concessions. Not only were the smaller buyers paying higher prices, but their sellers, the wholesalers, were seriously affected by the practices of the big buyers. Many wholesalers felt threatened because it appeared that the traditional channel of distribution—manufacturer–wholesaler–retailer—was itself threatened. Therefore, wholesaler groups were extremely active in pursuing a price discrimination amendment that would stop the practices of the large buyers. There is little question that the act was aimed at the elimination of chain stores or, at least, the diminishing of their power. The fact that chain stores and other large buyers have prospered notwithstanding the Robinson–Patman Act does not, in any way, remove the difficulties spawned by the act.

THE ELEMENTS OF A ROBINSON–PATMAN VIOLATION

Section 2 of the original Clayton Act was divided into six subsections by the Robinson–Patman amendment. Each subsection will be surveyed to determine its essential ingredients.

Section 2(a). Price; selection of customers

Section 2(a) is the heart of the act. It requires at least two sales (at least one of which must be in interstate commerce) to be made to two different buyers at different prices. Moreover, the goods sold must be virtually identical goods, that is, "goods of like grade and quality." The price discrimination must cause a reasonable possibility of injury to competition. If these elements are found in a given fact situation, there is a *prima facie* violation of section 2(a) and, unless the respondent (the alleged violator) can justify the price discrimination in one of three ways (to be discussed below), there is an absolute violation of the act. The elements just listed—two or more sales of goods of like grade and quality, at least one of which is in interstate commerce, at different prices, to two or more customers, which may injure competition—are often called the "jurisdictional criteria" of the Robinson–Patman Act. If any one of these is missing, *the act does not apply*. Each of these criteria may raise difficult problems. We now explore a few examples to illustrate such problems.

Example 1

The PA enters into a contract to purchase three items for his company: (a) television advertising time, (b) a lease of property for a period of three years, and (c) a construction contract involving labor and materials. As to each, the PA subsequently learns that his company was charged a higher price than were other customers who bought under almost identical terms. Does the buyer have a Robinson–Patman complaint?

Analysis: The answer is no. The "goods of like grade and quality" under the Robinson–Patman Act are called "commodities of like grade and quality" and "commodities" include goods, "wares, merchandise and other commodities." Basically, the act applies only to tangible, movable property. Therefore, in the example, (a) is not a commodity since it is intangible; (b) is real (immovable) property and, therefore, not a commodity; and (c) involves tangible movable property (which lawyers call "personal property"), but it is, essentially, a contract for services. The act does not apply.

Example 2

The PA purchases industrial drills for his company that are sold under the brand label of a famous industrial drill maker. After the drills are purchased, the PA learns that the identical drills under identical circumstances except for the brand name were sold to a competing buyer at 20 percent less than the price the PA agreed to pay. When the PA complained, the supplier explained that it always charges 20 percent less for drills marketed under a nonbrand (private) label. Is there a Robinson–Patman violation?

Analysis: The problem involves whether a difference in brand names (one well-known, highly advertised brand versus an unknown, unadvertised brand) is sufficient to suggest that the goods are *not* "goods of like grade and quality." Of course, if they are not of like grade and quality, the act does not apply. In a famous Supreme Court case, the Court held that differences in brand names do not prevent the goods from being of like grade and quality. The act applies and unless the supplier can justify the price discrimination in ways that will be discussed below, there is a violation.

Note: Insignificant (nonfunctional) physical differences in products sold by the supplier at different prices will not take the transactions out of the "like grade and quality" category. In order for the goods to be *not* of like grade and quality, their physical differences must be more than fanciful.

Example 3

An interstate dairy company, W, processed milk in Ohio. It discriminated in price among certain retailers, but all of the discriminatory prices were charged in Ohio, the same state where the processing occurred. Is this a Robinson–Patman violation?

Analysis: The answer is no. All of the discriminatory sales were made within Ohio—that is, they were all *intrastate*—therefore, the interstate commerce requirement of the act was not met. At least one of the sales involved in the price discrimination must "cross a state line."

Example 4

Dairy Q transported milk from Colorado to New Mexico, where it was processed. It then engaged in discriminatory sales of the milk, all within New Mexico. Does the act apply?

Analysis: Yes. Under the "stream of commerce" doctrine, a court held that milk produced in one state and processed in another does not lose its interstate commerce character. Thus, if a transaction is part of a larger transaction in which there has been interstate activity (crossing state lines), the transaction will be "in commerce" for the purposes of the act.

Note: There are other technical problems with the Robinson–Patman Act's interstate commerce requirement. In general, the Robinson–Patman interstate commerce requirement is narrower (therefore, more difficult to prove) than the "commerce" requirement under the Sherman Act.

Exemptions: Sales to governments and their institutions (U.S. government, state governments, and municipalities) are exempted from the Robinson–Patman Act. The same is true of nonprofit institutions (such as hospitals). However, resales for profit by the institution will bring the transaction within the act.

Example 5

The X, Y, and Z Corporations were manufacturers of frozen dessert pies that were sold through retail stores such as supermarket chains. All three corporations were interstate sellers of goods that sold their frozen pies throughout the country. P was a small pie company in Salt Lake City, Utah, that decided to enter the frozen pie business in competition with X, Y, and Z. P sold its pies at lower prices than the three competitors and sometimes sold at different prices. X, Y, and Z began to engage in a price war with P by undercutting P's price. The price war continued for a few years. At the end, P was in a very strong market position (45 percent of the Salt Lake City market). P brings a private treble-damage action against X, Y, and Z, charging its competitors with a violation of section 2(a) of the Robinson–Patman Act. What was the result?

Analysis: The U.S. Supreme Court held that P wins. Even though P was undercutting the prices of its competitors, P sold exclusively in intrastate commerce. Moreover, there was a reasonable possibility of injury to competition under the act (one of the requirements is "injury to competition") because X, Y, and Z had been charging higher prices in other states while lowering their prices in Utah, which resulted in an "erosion of the price structure" in Utah. This may have caused P to lose considerable profits, which made it a less-effective competitor with X, Y, and Z. Though P ended up with a substantial market share, this is no defense to price discrimination such as that practiced by the three competitors. What may appear to be a state of healthy price competition on its face may really be, upon further analysis, a situation that creates a reasonable possibility of substantial competitive injury.

Note: The cost-justification defense. One of the three affirmative defenses under the Robinson–Patman Act is the cost-justification defense. This allows the seller to show that its price discrimination is based on *actual cost savings* in dealing with the lower-priced customer as compared with the customer who paid the higher price. Such cost savings must be based (normally) upon distribution and not manufacturing costs—such as the cost of transportation, warehousing, selling expense, advertising, and any other distribution costs. Moreover, the cost defense can be established only by a refined study of distribution costs, and those costs must be allocated over the particular products and customers involved in the price discrimination. Customer groupings can be used in such cost analyses so long as the customers in the group are homogeneous (i.e., they receive the same distribution services). The cost defense is tricky and difficult to establish. *Moreover, it will not work if the distribution costs are simply not in existence.* There is no magic in this defense. If the costs exist to justify the price discrimination, they can be found. However, an expensive cost analysis is doomed to failure if the costs simply do not exist.

Note: The changing-market-conditions defense. The second of three affirmative defenses under Robinson–Patman is called "changing market conditions." This defense is little used but does allow different prices to be charged based upon seasonal price variations, distress goods sales, and the like. The seller can change its price from time to time, but it must change its price for all buyers. It cannot "get cute" and have a "special sale" for a large buyer, only to immediately hike its prices to all other buyers.

Section 2(b). Burden of rebutting prima-facie case of discrimination

Section 2(b) of the Robinson–Patman Act is well known because it establishes the third affirmative defense, "meeting competition in good faith." Essentially, this defense permits the seller to lower its price to one buyer while maintaining higher prices to its other buyers (a price discrimination) if it does so merely to meet the competition of another seller who is threatening to take that buyer away. Some examples follow.

Example 6

An old customer of the seller informs the seller that the buyer can procure goods for 10 percent less from another supplier. The seller reasonably believes the old customer and grants the customer a similar discount while maintaining its prices to its other buyers. A new customer informs the seller that it can procure the goods from another supplier at a 10-percent discount. Again, the seller believes the customer and grants a 10-percent discount to the new customer while charging other buyers the regular (higher) price. Is the seller violating the Robinson–Patman Act in either or both situations?

Analysis: The seller will use the "meeting competition in good faith" defense and, as to the old customer, assuming the seller had reasonable grounds to believe that the lower price was offered by one of his competitors, will prevail. This is known as "defensive" meeting competition in good faith to *retain* an old customer. Whether the seller can use the same defense as to the new customer, even though it is reasonable to believe the new customer, is questionable. This is called "offensive" meeting competition in good faith to gain a new customer. The courts are currently split on this issue, but the better view seems to be that offensive as well as defensive use of the defense is sound.

Note: How does the seller know that the buyer who wants a lower price is telling the truth in asserting the buyer can get it cheaper elsewhere? In fact, the seller does not know for certain. However, the test generally stated is that the seller must operate in a reasonably prudent fashion in believing or not believing the buyer. The seller should make discreet inquiries, particularly of its own salespeople, in determining the state of the market and whether a competitor (or competitors) is offering similar goods at lower prices. If this careful investigation reveals that such lower prices are being offered, the seller may use the defense. An attorney should be consulted in this area to ascertain that a proper record has been established before the lower prices are offered to certain customers.

Note: Other aspects of the "meeting competition in good faith" defense. There may be many other complexities in using the defense that require the skill of an attorney. One of the troublesome areas is whether the defense may be used to meet an entire pricing schedule (quantity discount schedule) as contrasted with merely meeting one price in an individual sale situation. There is recent case law indicating that, under certain conditions, the defense may be used to meet the prices charged under a discount schedule of competitors. Again, an attorney's advice is essential before any seller should attempt such action. The buyer should be aware of these problems confronting the seller.

Section 2(c). Payment or acceptance of commission, brokerage, or other compensation

Section 2(c) of the act deals with brokerage payments. It was established to avoid a basic evil known as "phantom brokerage." A genuine, independent broker performs services and is entitled to a legitimate brokerage commission. However, if either the buyer or seller employs a party, calling that party a broker, and that "phantom broker" receives a brokerage commission that he or she merely pays over to his or her employer, this is a violation of section 2(c) of the act.

Section (d). Payment for services or facilities for processing or sale

> It shall be unlawful for any person engaged in commerce to pay or contract for the payment of anything of value to or for the benefit of a customer of such person in the course of such commerce as compensation or in consideration for any services or facilities furnished by or through such customer in connection with the processing, handling, sale, or offering for sale of any products or commodities manufactured, sold, or offered for sale by such person, unless such payment or consideration is available on proportionally equal terms to all other customers competing in the distribution of such products or commodities.

Section (e). Furnishing services or facilities for processing, handling, etc.

> It shall be unlawful for any person to discriminate in favor of one purchaser against another purchaser or purchasers of a commodity bought for resale, with or without processing, by contracting to furnish or furnishing, or by contributing to the furnishing of, any services or facilities connected with the processing, handling, sale, or offering for sale of such commodity so purchased upon terms not accorded to all purchasers on proportionally equal terms.

Example 7

A manufacturer sells to some retailers directly and to others through distributors. Retailer X purchases the manufacturer's product from a distributor and resells some of it to Retailer Y. Retailer X is a customer of the manufacturer. Retailer Y is not a customer unless the fact that it purchases the manufacturer's product is known to the manufacturer.

Analysis: A genuine, independent broker performs services and is entitled to a legitimate brokerage commission. However, if either the buyer or seller employs a party, calling that party a broker, and that "phantom broker" receives a brokerage commission that he merely pays over to his employer, this is a violation of section 2(c) of the act; the FTC will not be able to successfully prosecute B under section 2(d) or 2(e) because those sections may be interpreted to apply only to sellers and not to buyers. However, though sections 2(d) and 2(e) are technically not available, the FTC may proceed under its very general statute, section 5 of the FTC Act, since the activities of B constitute an "unfair method of competition." Therefore, B will be liable under that act.

Section (f). Knowingly inducing or receiving discriminatory price

Section 2(f) of the Robinson–Patman Act is the most important section of the act for the buyer as it applies to *buyer liability*. It is somewhat ironic that the act was designed to deal with the unfair pressures exerted by large buyers in extracting price concessions from suppliers with inferior bargaining power; yet most of the act [sections 2(a) through 2(e)] says nothing about buyers, at least directly. Section 2(f) is the only section dealing directly with buyers. In essence, section 2(f) states that a buyer that *knowingly* induces a discriminatory price from a seller violates the act in the same way that a price-discriminating seller violates the act under section 2(a). The magic word in this statement is *knowingly*, which requires some explanation.

The most important case interpreting section 2(f) was decided in 1953, *Automatic Canteen Co. of America v. FTC*. In that case, the U.S. Supreme Court suggested a test for buyer liability under section 2(f) that could be interpreted to make the burden of proving a violation of that section extremely difficult. This, of course, is good for buyers. The language of the Court in the *Canteen* case suggested to some observers, including the FTC, that the party bringing the action against a buyer under this section will have to prove that the seller's price discrimination was not cost-justified. This meant that the FTC (or private party) would have to prove negative cost justification, which is next to impossible. For many years, this interpretation of the Supreme Court's *Canteen* decision was very popular. However, recently, the FTC has suggested another, easier-to-prove test:

(i) The buyer induced or received a more favorable (discriminatory) price than other buyers.

(ii) The buyer knew or should have known that the prices it received were discriminatory.

The second element, (ii), takes care of the "knowingly" requirement in section 2(f). In essence, it suggests that a buyer who knows the industry in which he or she buys should reasonably know whether he or she is getting a better price than competitors are getting or could procure from the supplier. If these two elements are the only two that the FTC or a private plaintiff in a treble-damage action must show, section 2(f) violations are not that difficult to prove, and there will be much more activity under this section than heretofore. However, at the moment, the federal courts of appeal are split as to the proper test to be applied. While some courts take the position that the two elements just listed are sufficient, other courts (in other circuits) have required these two elements *plus a third element:* (iii) the buyer knew or should have known that the price discrimination could not be cost-justified or that it was granted to meet competition. Now, for the complaining party to prove that the buyer *knew or should have known* that the price discrimination could not be cost-justified or that it was granted to meet competition is practically impossible. If this third element is added to the necessary proof for a section 2(f) violation, the buyer, again, is quite safe. However, the buyer should not rely upon this stiff test being applied.

Caution: Buyers, particularly buyers with bargaining power superior to their suppliers, should never induce a lower price that they know (or should know) is a better price than the price that the seller is charging or will charge other customers. If the buyer engages in such a practice, it is more than possible that the buyer will face a Robinson–Patman charge by the FTC or a private plaintiff (such as a competitor of the buyer who paid a higher price). The FTC has recently indicated that it will look hard at buyers who receive low prices to determine whether any section 2(f) violations are evident.

Example 8

The PA knowingly induces a discriminatory price with supplier 1 (S-1). Having been offered this price by S-1, the PA then goes to supplier 2 (S-2), informing S-2 that S-1 has offered the lower price and showing S-2 a copy of the offer. S-2 reasonably believes the PA and, to meet competition in good faith, offers the PA the same low price that S-1 has offered. The PA makes the deal with S-2. Is either S-2 or the buyer liable under the act?

Analysis: The answer is that the buyer is liable and the seller is not, at least according to one FTC case. The S-2 has met competition in good faith, but the buyer (who started the whole process) is not entitled to use that defense. This seems fair, though some language of Supreme Court opinions does not necessarily allow for this result. Yet, any buyer who engages in this practice may well find itself without the defense even though the defense will be available to its supplier under the facts of the example.

FUNCTIONAL DISCOUNTS

There is one additional defense available under the Robinson–Patman Act. It is often referred to as an "unwritten" defense since there is nothing in the act specifically dealing with it. If a seller charges a wholesaler-buyer a lower price than the seller charges direct-buying retailers, there is price discrimination. However, this "functional discount" is permitted because of the position occupied by the wholesaler in the chain of distribution. The wholesaler does not compete with retailers and, therefore, there is no possible injury to competition granting the wholesaler a better (discriminatory) price than the price charged retailers.

Caution: If a wholesaler is not a "pure" wholesaler, that is, if it engages in some retailing operations as well as wholesaling operations, the seller may not grant a functional discount to the wholesaler. Since many wholesalers today engage in operations as retailers, sellers must be careful in deciding whether to grant a functional discount to such a buyer. The functional discount concept is *not* based on cost savings. It is often suggested that the reason for permitting such discounts is that the wholesaler (or other middleman) performs valuable functions that save the seller money in dealing with the wholesaler as contrasted with retailers. But that is not the correct analysis. If a wholesaler is a pure wholesaler and receives a lower price than retailers to whom the supplier sells the same goods of like grade and quality, the wholesaler is entitled to the lower price because he or she is a wholesaler, not because of any cost savings to him or her that can be used to cost-justify the price discrimination. The wholesaler does not compete with retailers and, therefore, there is no injury to competition.

ENFORCEMENT OF THE ACT AND SECTION 3 OF THE ACT

By informal agreement between the Federal Trade Commission and the Department of Justice, Antitrust Division, the FTC enforces the Robinson–Patman Act except for section 3, which has not yet been discussed. The Antitrust Division could enforce all of the Robinson–Patman Act since it is really an amendment to the Clayton Act. Both the FTC and the Justice Department can enforce Clayton Act violations. Only the Justice Department can enforce Sherman Act violations. Only the FTC can enforce its own act, the Federal Trade Commission Act. Finally, there is another section of the Robinson–Patman Act, section 3, that prohibits blatant kinds of price discrimination such as sales below cost or other predatory discriminatory sales. Violations of section 3 may result in fines of $5,000 or up to one year imprisonment or both. Corporations and individuals are subject to this section. Since section 3 is a criminal section, only the Department of Justice can enforce it.

When the Federal Trade Commission finds a violation of the act, it issues a cease-and-desist order. These orders can be difficult to live with, and each violation of a final FTC order is subject to a civil penalty of up to $5,000, with *each day* of a continuing failure to obey the order constituting a separate offense. The penalty for violating such an order is recoverable by the Department of Justice in a federal court. Of course, the party violating the Robinson–Patman Act (like the other antitrust laws) must be concerned about that terrible calamity—the private treble-damage action. Finally, it should be noted that private parties have a great advantage when they sue for treble damages after the government has won its case against the antitrust violator. The private party is entitled to use the government's case (already won) as its case and only has to prove its damages, which, if successfully proven, are then tripled plus reasonable attorney fees and costs. There is only one stark exception to this favorable effect for private plaintiffs: Section 3 of the Robinson–Patman Act has been interpreted, for various reasons, *not* to be an antitrust law. Therefore, if the government wins a case under section 3, this will not help the private party in his or her treble-damage action. However, as to any other part of the Robinson–Patman Act or the other antitrust laws, the private party (plaintiff) does have this great advantage. The advantage can be removed by the defendant pleading *nolo contendere* in a criminal action (under the Sherman Act) or taking a *consent decree* in a civil antitrust action brought by the government. Since these cases do not proceed to trial, the government has really not established a case that a private party could later use. This is why there are so many pleas of *nolo contendere* or the taking of consent judgments.

Appendix **B**

Unit Factors for Progress Functions

F Values

% Pivot	70%	72%	74%	76%	78%	80%	81%	82%	83%	84%	
5	4.6717	4.1362	3.6743	3.2743	2.9266	2.6232	2.4861	2.3577	2.2374	2.1245	5
10	3.2702	2.9780	2.7190	2.4804	2.2827	2.0986	2.0133	1.9333	1.8570	1.7546	10
15	2.6544	2.4574	2.2799	2.1194	1.9739	1.8418	1.7801	1.7214	1.6653	1.6116	15
20	2.2891	2.1442	2.0120	1.6912	1.7805	1.6789	1.6311	1.5853	1.5413	1.4991	20
25	2.0401	1.9290	1.8262	1.7313	1.6437	1.5625	1.5242	1.4872	1.4516	1.4172	25
30	1.8561	1.7693	1.6871	1.6107	1.5397	1.4734	1.4028	1.4116	1.3822	1.3537	30
35	1.7164	1.6447	1.5778	1.5154	1.4569	1.4021	1.3768	1.3506	1.3261	1.3022	35
40	1.6024	1.5438	1.4889	1.4373	1.3888	1.3431	1.3212	1.3000	1.2793	1.2592	40
45	1.5082	1.4600	1.4146	1.3718	1.3314	1.2731	1.2747	1.2549	1.2394	1.2224	45
50	1.4286	1.3889	1.3514	1.3198	1.2020	1.2500	1.2348	1.2195	1.2048	1.1905	50
55	1.3602	1.3275	1.2965	1.2671	1.2390	1.2122	1.1993	1.1867	1.1743	1.1623	55
60	1.3006	1.2709	1.2464	1.2242	1.2009	1.1787	1.1889	1.1575	1.1472	1.1371	60
65	1.2482	1.2265	1.2058	1.1860	1.1670	1.1488	1.1399	1.1313	1.1228	1.1144	65
70	1.2015	1.1842	1.1676	1.1517	1.1364	1.1217	1.1149	1.1073	1.1006	1.0939	70
75	1.1595	1.1461	1.1331	1.1206	1.1086	1.0970	1.0914	1.0859	1.0804	1.0750	75
80	1.1217	1.1115	1.1018	1.0924	1.0833	1.0749	1.0708	1.0660	1.0618	1.0577	80
85	1.0872	1.0801	1.0731	1.0665	1.0600	1.0537	1.0908	1.0476	1.0447	1.0417	85
90	1.0557	1.0512	1.0468	1.0426	1.0385	1.0345	1.0325	1.0306	1.0287	1.0269	90
95	1.0267	1.0246	1.0225	1.0205	1.0186	1.0167	1.0157	1.0148	1.0139	1.0130	95
100	1.0000	1.0000	1.0000	1.0000	1.0000	1.0000	1.0000	1.0000	1.0000	1.0000	100
105	0.9752	0.9771	0.9790	0.9809	0.9827	0.9844	0.9853	0.9861	0.9870	0.9878	105
110	0.9521	0.9558	0.9594	0.9630	0.9664	0.9698	0.9714	0.9731	0.9747	0.9763	110
115	0.9306	0.9359	0.9411	0.9462	0.9511	0.9560	0.9582	0.9608	0.9631	0.9655	115
120	0.9105	0.9172	0.9239	0.9304	0.9367	0.9430	0.9461	0.9491	0.9522	0.9552	120
125	0.8915	0.8997	0.9076	0.9154	0.9231	0.9307	0.9564	0.9381	0.9418	0.9454	125
130	0.8737	0.8831	0.8923	0.9013	0.9103	0.9190	0.9233	0.9276	0.9319	0.9361	130
135	0.8569	0.8674	0.8778	0.8880	0.8980	0.9079	0.9128	0.9177	0.9225	0.9273	135
140	0.8410	0.8526	0.8040	0.8753	0.8864	0.8974	0.9028	0.9082	0.9135	0.9189	140
145	0.8260	0.8386	0.8510	0.8632	0.8753	0.8873	0.8932	0.8991	0.9050	0.9108	145
150	0.8117	0.8252	0.8385	0.8517	0.8647	0.8776	0.8849	0.8904	0.8967	0.9030	150
155	0.7981	0.8125	0.8267	0.8407	0.8546	0.8684	0.8755	0.8821	0.8889	0.8956	155
160	0.7852	0.8000	0.8153	0.8302	0.8450	0.8596	0.8869	0.8741	0.8813	0.8885	160
165	0.7729	0.7888	0.8045	0.8202	0.8357	0.8511	0.8588	0.8664	0.8741	0.8817	165
170	0.7611	0.7777	0.7942	0.8105	0.8268	0.8430	0.8910	0.8591	0.8071	0.8751	170
175	0.7498	0.7871	0.7842	0.8013	0.8183	0.8352	0.8438	0.8520	0.8603	0.8687	175
180	0.7390	0.7569	0.7747	0.7924	0.8100	0.8276	0.8304	0.8451	0.8539	0.8626	180
185	0.7287	0.7471	0.7655	0.7839	0.8021	0.8204	0.8294	0.8385	0.8476	0.8567	185
190	0.7188	0.7378	0.7567	0.7756	0.7945	0.8133	0.8228	0.8322	0.8415	0.8509	190
195	0.7092	0.7287	0.7482	0.7677	0.7871	0.8066	0.8168	0.8260	0.8357	0.8454	195

% Pivot	85%	86%	87%	88%	89%	90%	92%	94%	96%	98%	
5	2.0186	1.9191	1.8256	1.7376	1.6548	1.5767	1.4339	1.3066	1.1929	1.0912	5
10	1.7158	1.6904	1.5882	1.5291	1.4727	1.4191	1.3191	1.2282	1.1452	1.0694	10
15	1.5602	1.5110	1.4640	1.4189	1.3757	1.3342	1.2564	1.1845	1.1182	1.0569	15
20	1.4584	1.4194	1.3818	1.3456	1.3107	1.2772	1.2138	1.1545	1.0994	1.0480	20
25	1.3841	1.3921	1.3212	1.2913	1.2625	1.2346	1.8119	1.1317	1.0851	1.0412	25
30	1.3262	1.2995	1.2737	1.2486	1.2244	1.2008	1.1558	1.1135	1.0735	1.0357	30
35	1.2791	1.2566	1.2348	1.2136	1.1930	1.1730	1.1346	1.0982	1.0638	1.8311	35
40	1.2397	1.2206	1.2021	1.1541	1.1669	1.1494	1.1148	1.0852	1.0554	1.0271	40
45	1.2059	1.1898	1.1740	1.1587	1.1437	1.1290	1.1008	1.0739	1.0482	1.0235	45
50	1.1745	1.1628	1.1494	1.1344	1.1236	1.1111	1.0878	1.0638	1.0417	1.0204	50
55	1.1505	1.1389	1.1276	1.1166	1.1057	1.0951	1.0744	1.0548	1.0358	1.0176	55
60	1.1272	1.1176	1.1081	1.0988	1.0897	1.0807	1.0638	1.0467	1.0305	1.0150	60
65	1.1063	1.0983	1.0904	1.0827	1.0751	1.0677	1.0532	1.0392	1.0257	1.0126	65
70	1.0872	1.0807	1.0743	1.0680	1.0618	1.0557	1.0438	1.0324	1.0212	1.0105	70
75	1.0698	1.0646	1.0595	1.0545	1.0496	1.0447	1.0321	1.0260	1.0171	1.0084	75
80	1.0537	1.0498	1.0459	1.0420	1.0392	1.0345	1.0272	1.0201	1.0132	1.0065	80
85	1.0388	1.0360	1.0332	1.0304	1.0277	1.0250	1.0197	1.0146	1.0096	1.0047	85
90	1.0250	1.0232	1.0214	1.0198	1.0179	1.0101	1.0128	1.0095	1.0062	1.0031	90
95	1.0121	1.0112	1.0104	1.0095	1.0087	1.0078	1.0062	1.0046	1.0030	1.0015	95
100	1.0000	1.0000	1.0000	1.0000	1.0000	1.0000	1.0000	1.0000	1.0000	1.0000	100
105	0.9886	0.9894	0.9902	0.9918	0.9918	0.9926	0.9942	0.9957	0.9971	0.9986	105
110	0.9779	0.9795	0.9810	0.9826	0.9841	0.9856	0.9586	0.9915	0.9944	0.9972	110
115	0.9678	0.9701	0.9723	0.9746	0.9768	0.9790	0.9832	0.9876	0.9918	0.9959	115
120	0.9582	0.9611	0.9640	0.9669	0.9698	0.9727	0.9788	0.9839	0.9893	0.9947	120
125	0.9490	0.9526	0.9562	0.9597	0.9632	0.9667	0.9738	0.9803	0.9869	0.9935	125
130	0.9403	0.9445	0.9487	0.9520	0.9569	0.9009	0.9689	0.9769	0.9847	0.9924	130
135	0.9321	0.9368	0.9415	0.9462	0.9508	0.9554	0.9648	0.9736	0.9825	0.9913	135
140	0.9241	0.9294	0.9346	0.9398	0.9450	0.9501	0.9608	0.9704	0.9804	0.9902	140
145	0.9166	0.9223	0.9281	0.9338	0.9394	0.9451	0.9568	0.9674	0.9784	0.9892	145
150	0.9093	0.9156	0.9218	0.9280	0.9341	0.9402	0.9524	0.9645	0.9764	0.9883	150
155	0.9024	0.9091	0.9157	0.9224	0.9290	0.0356	0.9487	0.9616	0.9745	0.9873	155
160	0.8957	0.9028	0.9099	0.9170	0.9240	0.9311	0.9450	0.9389	0.9727	0.9864	160
165	0.8892	0.8968	0.9043	0.9118	0.9193	0.9267	0.9415	0.9563	0.9709	0.9855	165
170	0.8830	0.8910	0.8989	0.9068	0.9147	0.9225	0.9301	0.9537	0.9692	0.9847	170
175	0.8770	0.8854	0.8937	0.9020	0.9102	0.9185	0.9340	0.9513	0.9676	0.9838	175
180	0.8713	0.8000	0.8886	0.8973	0.9059	0.9145	0.9317	0.9489	0.9660	0.9830	180
185	0.8657	0.8747	0.8937	0.8928	0.9018	0.9107	0.9287	0.9466	0.9644	0.9822	185
190	0.8603	0.8697	0.8790	0.8884	0.8977	0.9071	0.9257	0.9443	0.9429	0.9815	190
195	0.8551	0.8648	0.8744	0.8841	0.8938	0.9035	0.9228	0.9421	0.9614	0.9807	195
200	0.8500	0.8600	0.8700	0.8800	0.8900	0.9000	0.9200	0.9400	0.9600	0.9800	200
210	0.8403	0.8509	0.8615	0.8721	0.8827	0.8934	0.9146	0.9359	0.9573	0.9786	210

% Pivot	70%	72%	74%	76%	78%	80%	81%	82%	83%	84%	
200	0.7000	0.7200	0.7400	0.7600	0.7800	0.8008	0.8100	0.8200	0.8300	0.8400	200
210	0.6826	0.7035	0.7245	0.7455	0.7665	0.7876	0.7981	0.8086	0.8192	0.8298	210
220	0.6665	0.6802	0.7100	0.7319	0.7532	0.7759	0.7869	0.7980	0.8090	0.8201	220
230	0.6514	0.6739	0.6964	0.7191	0.7419	0.7648	0.7768	0.7879	0.7994	0.8110	230
240	0.6373	0.6604	0.6837	0.7071	0.7307	0.7544	0.7664	0.7783	0.7903	0.8024	240
250	0.6241	0.6477	0.6716	0.6957	0.7201	0.7446	0.7569	0.7693	0.7817	0.7942	250
260	0.6116	0.6358	0.6603	0.6850	0.7100	0.7352	0.7479	0.7607	0.7735	0.7864	260
270	0.5995	0.6245	0.6496	0.6749	0.7004	0.7264	0.7306	0.7525	0.7657	0.7790	270
280	0.5887	0.6139	0.6394	0.6652	0.6914	0.7179	0.7313	0.7447	0.7583	0.7719	280
290	0.5782	0.6037	0.6297	0.6560	0.6827	0.7099	0.7239	0.7373	0.7511	0.7651	290
300	0.5682	0.5941	0.6205	0.6473	0.6745	0.7021	0.7161	0.7302	0.7443	0.7586	300
310	0.5587	0.5850	0.6117	0.6389	0.6666	0.6947	0.7098	0.7234	0.7378	0.7524	310
320	0.5496	0.5742	0.6033	0.6310	0.6591	0.6877	0.7022	0.7160	0.7315	0.7464	320
330	0.5410	0.5679	0.5953	0.6233	0.6518	0.6809	0.6953	0.7105	0.7255	0.7406	330
340	0.5327	0.5399	0.5877	0.6160	0.6449	0.6744	0.6998	0.7044	0.7197	0.7351	340
350	0.5249	0.5523	0.5803	0.6090	0.6382	0.6681	0.6838	0.6986	0.7141	0.7297	350
360	0.5173	0.5449	0.5732	0.6022	0.6318	0.6621	0.6773	0.6930	0.7087	0.7246	360
370	0.5101	0.5379	0.5665	0.5957	0.6256	0.6563	0.6718	0.6876	0.7035	0.7196	370
380	0.5031	0.5312	0.5599	0.5894	0.6197	0.6507	0.6664	0.6823	0.6985	0.7148	380
390	0.4964	0.5247	0.5537	0.5834	0.6139	0.6458	0.6618	0.6773	0.6936	0.7102	390
400	0.4900	0.5184	0.5476	0.5776	0.6084	0.6400	0.6501	0.6724	0.6889	0.7056	400
410	0.4838	0.5124	0.5416	0.5720	0.6030	0.6349	0.6512	0.6677	0.6843	0.7012	410
420	0.4779	0.5066	0.5361	0.5665	0.5079	0.6300	0.6464	0.6631	0.6799	0.6970	420
430	0.4721	0.5009	0.5307	0.5613	0.5928	0.6253	0.6418	0.6586	0.6756	0.6929	430
440	0.4665	0.4955	0.5254	0.5562	0.5880	0.6207	0.6374	0.6543	0.6715	0.6889	440
450	0.4612	0.4903	0.5203	0.5913	0.5832	0.6162	0.6338	0.6501	0.6674	0.6850	450
460	0.4560	0.4852	0.5153	0.5465	0.5787	0.6118	0.6288	0.6460	0.6635	0.6812	460
470	0.4510	0.4803	0.5106	0.5419	0.5742	0.6076	0.6247	0.6421	0.6597	0.6775	470
480	0.4461	0.4755	0.5059	0.5374	0.5699	0.6035	0.6207	0.6382	0.6559	0.6740	480
490	0.4414	0.4709	0.5014	0.5330	0.5657	0.5995	0.6169	0.6344	0.6523	0.4705	490
500	0.4368	0.4664	0.4970	0.5200	0.5616	0.5956	0.6131	0.6308	0.6488	0.6671	500
550	0.4159	0.4458	0.4769	0.5092	0.5428	0.5776	0.5958	0.6138	0.6324	0.6513	550
600	0.3977	0.4278	0.4592	0.4919	0.5261	0.5617	0.5801	0.5987	0.6178	0.6372	600
650	0.3817	0.4118	0.4435	0.4766	0.5112	0.5474	0.5661	0.5851	0.6046	0.6245	650
700	0.3674	0.3976	0.4294	0.4628	0.4978	0.5345	0.5531	0.5729	0.5927	0.6129	700
750	0.3546	0.3848	0.4167	0.4503	0.4857	0.5227	0.5421	0.5616	0.5818	0.6024	750
800	0.3430	0.3732	0.4052	0.4390	0.4746	0.5120	0.5314	0.5514	0.5718	0.5927	800
850	0.3325	0.3627	0.3947	0.4286	0.4644	0.5021	0.5217	0.5419	0.5625	0.5837	850
900	0.3228	0.3530	0.3850	0.4190	0.4549	0.4929	0.5127	0.5331	0.5540	0.5754	900
950	0.3140	0.3441	0.3761	0.4101	0.4467	0.4844	0.5044	0.5249	0.5460	0.5676	950
1000	0.3058	0.3398	0.3678	0.4019	0.4381	0.4765	0.4966	0.5172	0.5385	0.5604	1000

% Pivot	85%	86%	87%	88%	89%	90%	92%	94%	96%	98%	
220	0.8312	0.8424	0.8535	0.8647	0.8759	0.8871	0.9095	0.9320	0.9546	0.9773	220
230	0.8226	0.8343	0.8459	0.8576	0.8693	0.8811	0.9047	0.9234	0.9521	0.9760	230
240	0.8145	0.8266	0.8387	0.8509	0.8631	0.8754	0.9001	0.9248	0.9498	0.9748	240
250	0.8067	0.8193	0.8319	0.8465	0.8572	0.8700	0.8956	0.9215	0.9475	0.9737	250
260	0.7993	0.8183	0.8253	0.8385	0.8516	0.8648	0.8914	0.9182	0.9453	0.9725	260
270	07923	0.8097	0.8191	0.8326	0.8442	0.8599	0.8874	0.9152	0.9432	0.9715	270
280	0.7855	0.7993	0.8132	0.8271	0.8411	0.8551	0.8835	0.9122	0.9412	0.9704	280
290	0.7791	0.7932	0.8074	0.8217	0.8361	0.8506	0.8708	0.9093	0.9392	0.9694	290
300	0.7729	0.7874	0.8020	0.8166	0.8314	0.8462	0.8762	0.9066	0.9374	0.9685	300
310	0.7670	0.7818	0.7967	0.8117	0.8268	0.8420	0.8720	0.9039	0.9355	0.9676	310
320	0.7613	0.7764	0.7916	0.8070	0.8224	0.8380	0.8694	0.9014	0.9338	0.9667	320
330	0.7559	0.7712	0.7868	0.8024	0.8182	0.8341	0.8662	0.8989	0.9321	0.9658	330
340	0.7506	0.7653	0.7821	0.7980	0.8141	0.8303	0.8631	0.8965	0.9305	0.9650	340
350	0.7455	0.7616	0.7775	0.7937	0.8101	0.8266	0.8601	0.8942	0.9289	0.9641	350
360	0.7406	0.7568	0.7731	0.7896	0.8043	0.8231	0.8572	0.8920	0.9273	0.9634	360
370	0.7359	0.7523	0.7689	0.7856	0.8026	0.8197	0.8544	0.8898	0.9258	0.9626	370
380	0.7313	0.7479	0.7648	0.7818	0.7990	0.8164	0.8517	0.8877	0.9244	0.9618	380
390	0.7268	0.7437	0.7608	0.7781	0.7955	0.8131	0.8490	0.8856	0.9230	0.9611	390
400	0.7225	0.7396	0.7569	0.7744	0.7921	0.8100	0.8464	0.8836	0.9216	0.9604	400
410	0.7184	0.7357	0.7532	0.7709	0.7888	0.8070	0.8439	0.8817	0.9203	0.9587	410
420	0.7143	0.7318	0.7496	0.7675	0.7857	0.8040	0.8415	0.8798	0.9190	0.9590	420
430	0.7104	0.7281	0.7460	0.7642	0.7826	0.8012	0.8391	0.8779	0.9177	0.9584	430
440	0.7065	0.7245	0.7426	0.7609	0.7795	0.7984	0.8368	0.8761	0.9164	0.9577	440
450	0.7028	0.7209	0.7392	0.7578	0.7766	0.7957	0.8345	0.8744	0.9152	0.9571	450
460	0.6992	0.7175	0.7360	0.7547	0.7737	0.7930	0.8323	0.8727	0.9141	0.9565	460
470	0.6957	0.7141	0.7328	0.7517	0.7709	0.7904	0.8302	0.8710	0.9129	0.9539	470
480	0.6923	0.7109	0.7287	0.7488	0.7682	0.7879	0.8281	0.8693	0.9118	0.9553	480
490	0.6889	0.7077	0.7267	0.7460	0.7656	0.7854	0.8263	0.8678	0.9107	0.9547	490
500	0.6857	0.7045	0.7238	0.7432	0.7630	0.7830	0.8240	0.8662	0.9096	0.9542	500
550	0.6705	0.6901	0.7100	0.7303	0.7508	0.7718	0.8146	0.8589	0.9045	0.9513	550
600	0.6570	0.6771	0.6977	0.7187	0.7399	0.7616	0.8061	0.8522	0.8999	0.9491	600
650	0.6448	0.6655	0.6866	0.7081	0.7301	0.7524	0.7984	0.8461	0.8956	0.9469	650
700	0.6337	0.6548	0.6764	0.6985	0.7210	0.7440	0.7918	0.8406	0.8917	0.9449	700
750	0.6235	0.6451	0.6671	0.6896	0.7127	0.7362	0.7848	0.8354	0.8881	0.9430	750
800	0.6141	0.6361	0.6585	0.6815	0.7050	0.7290	0.7787	0.8306	0.8847	0.9412	800
850	0.6055	0.6277	0.6505	0.6739	0.6978	0.7224	0.7731	0.8261	0.8816	0.9395	850
900	0.5974	0.6200	0.6431	0.6668	0.6911	0.7161	0.7678	0.8219	0.8786	0.9380	900
950	0.5899	0.6127	0.6362	0.6602	0.6849	0.7103	0.7628	0.8180	0.8758	0.9345	950
1000	0.5828	0.6059	0.6296	0.6540	0.6790	0.7047	0.7581	0.8142	0.8732	0.9351	1000

Appendix C

Estrada Systems[1]

Estrada Systems, located in Bridgeport, California, is a divisional headquarters of the Estrada Corporation. Estrada is a leading tier-one automotive supplier of climate control systems. Formerly a part of Ford Motors, Estrada's Ford sales account for nearly 72 percent of its sales revenue. The assembly plant produces a variety of products, including accumulator dehydrators, compressors, condensers, HVAC modules, evaporators, and heater cores. The Estrada Corporation uses the hybrid purchasing approach to manage its various business units. Buyers are located at each of the Ford divisions, along with purchasing managers and one purchasing director. Located at the firm's headquarters in Michigan are commodity specialists and high-level purchasing executives.

The commodity team has already prequalified and received quotes from four suppliers: Vortex Group Automotive Systems; Hong Kong Automobile Air-Conditioner Accessories Co., Ltd.; Prahinski Corporation; and Hozak-Zhou.

Vortex Automotive is a U.K.-based private limited company. Almost all facilities are QS/ISO 9000 certified; it is Vortex Automotive's goal to achieve ISO 14001 certification on a global basis. Vortex supplies fluid storage, transfer, and delivery systems including brake, fuel, and air-conditioning applications. Vortex employs over 20,000 people in more than 100 facilities and has operations in 29 countries on six continents.

With annual sales exceeding $6 billion, Prahinski Corporation is the world's leading diversified manufacturer of motion and control technologies, providing systematic, precision-engineered solutions for a wide variety of commercial, mobile, industrial, and aerospace markets. The company's products are vital to virtually everything that moves or requires control. This includes the manufacture and processing of raw materials, durable goods, infrastructure development, and all forms of transport. Prahinski is strategically diversified, value-driven, and well positioned for global growth as the industry consolidator and supplier of choice.

In 2001, Hozak-Zhou merged Hozak North America and Zhou Corporation to form Hozak-Zhou North America. The company is well poised to meet the challenges of its domestic and global customers. Worldwide design and production facilities, as well as subsidiaries and joint ventures, deliver common platform modules, with customization as needed. Engineers listen to what consumers want—increased comfort and safety, advanced display and information technology, less noise, improved fuel economy, reduced emissions, durability, recyclables, and more—and provide either an individual component or a complete integrated system or module to meet performance and design expectations.

Hong Kong Automobile Air-Conditioner Accessories Co., Ltd., is the first joint venture that specializes in designing and producing all kinds of modern automobile refrigerant hose assemblies to form a relationship with Estrada Automobile Air Conditioner Systems Co., Ltd., Hong Kong AAA supplies, Hong Kong Volkswagen GOL, Jetta from FAW-VW, HONG KONG GM Buick, Sail, Beijing Cherokee, Shenyang Golden Cup, Chongqing Alto, Chang'an Station Wagon Plant, and others.

[1]The author expresses appreciation to Jacob Estrada and Jasman Lee for their contributions to this case. Names and data have been disguised.

PROBLEM STATEMENT

Currently, the metallic buyer at Estrada is looking to contract for a tube line and fitting assembly, part #36648622. The tubing is used to hook up the HVAC module to the vehicle. For example, one of these assemblies would hook up the compressor to the condenser, or the transmission to the oil cooler. Annual volume for this part is 95,000 units. There does not seem to be any predetermined market price, possibly due to the high number of parts making up the assembly. The base price is determined only by the lowest bid received, granted there is no suspicion of missing or erroneous information.

The auto industry has felt the effects of the economy's large recession. Before the terrorist attacks, the U.S. economy was already showing signs of stagnation, but the effects of these attacks on consumer confidence was profound and immediate. To bolster sales, the U.S. automotive industry (with Ford leading the charge) began a campaign of heavy discounting in the form of zero-percent financing and huge cash-back incentive programs. At the same time, the industry began cutting capacity to bring supply in line with decreased demand. But the combination of price war incentives and production cuts was a dangerous duo. Incentives ceased to be effective when the loss in revenue per vehicle was not made up for in volume; thus, volume was difficult to attain if production was significantly reduced. Recently, the Japanese have become an even bigger threat as Toyota is poised to replace DaimlerChrysler (now Chrysler) as one of the Big Three automakers. Now more than ever, strategic purchasing and price/cost analysis are necessary components in choosing quality products at a competitive price.

The purchasing manager from zero-percent four quotes from the 15 RFQs that were disseminated. Estrada's selection alternatives are as follows: perform a price/cost analysis, award the contract to the previous supplier, or award the contract to the lowest bidder.

Assumptions

A_1: All suppliers are prequalified. Criteria for this include:

- Financial health.
- Management expertise.
- Manufacturing capacity.

A_2: Prices don't change with capacity: the first part costs the same as the millionth part.

A_3: Cost is composed of two components: variable and fixed costs.

A_4: Prices are good for one year.

Alternatives

- Estrada Thermal Systems has the option of using cost management through the price/cost analysis method; this will help to improve the suppliers' prices and the ability to choose suppliers.
- Stay with the current supplier, Hozak-Zhou.
- Choose the supplier on the basis of cost, no price/cost analysis.

Economic Alternatives

The auto industry is currently facing an all-time-low market. In this instance, it would be reasonable for the buyer at Estrada to choose the lowest-cost bid.

FIGURE C.1
Hong Kong AAA

	Initial		After Negotiations		Savings	Standard
Material	$7.09		$7.09		$ —	
Labor	$0.40		$0.40		$ —	
Burden	$0.84		$0.84		$ —	
SG&A	$0.83	10%	$0.75	9%	$0.08	PH
Profit	$0.46	5%	$0.45	5%	$0.01	
Selling price	$9.62		$9.53		$0.09	
Annual volume	95,000		95,000			
Annual cost	$913,900		$905,700		$8,199.92	
Setup cost	$100,000		$100,000			
Total cost	**$1,013,900**		**$1,005,700**		**$8,199.92**	

Choosing the supplier based on these criteria alone would help the buyer save time; however, this may not always be the best alternative. For total costs, refer to Figures C.1 through C.4.

ANALYSIS

The first option is to utilize the price/cost analysis. The cost standard concept is the idea of creating baseline, idealized "best-of-the-best" values across an industry of the lowest-cost values for each cost component. There must be an attempt to develop and use such a standard to choose suppliers who fit that standard the most closely, and to also use that standard to help the suppliers to achieve better costs. Furthermore, the cost standard can be used in price negotiations to identify the best possible price or for planning purposes where suppliers are involved in decreasing costs to baseline levels.

Primary to the cost of the part is TMC, or the total manufacturing cost, which is made up of three distinct elements: direct material cost, direct labor cost, and burden (overhead). Burden can be broken down further into fixed and variable costs.

Examining Figures C.1 and C.2, it becomes clear that leading the pack in overall low selling cost is Hong Kong AAA, with $9.62. Next is Vortex Automotive with $10.48, third is Prahinski with $11.15, and finally the highest price is Hozak-Zhou

FIGURE C.2
Vortex Automotive

	Initial		After Negotiations		Savings	Standard
Material	$5.67		$5.67		$ —	
Labor	$1.60		$1.60		$ —	
Burden	$1.26		$1.26		$ —	
SG&A	$1.05	12.30%	$0.77	9.00%	$0.28	PH
Profit	$0.90	9.40%	$0.46	5.02%	$0.43	Hong Kong
Selling price	$10.48		$9.76		$0.72	
Annual volume	95,000		95,000			
Annual cost	$995,600.00		$927,663.03		$67,936.97	
Setup cost	$500,000.00		$500,000.00			
Total cost	**$1,495,600.00**		**$1,427,663.03**		**$67,936.97**	

FIGURE C.3
Prahinski

	Initial		After Negotiations		Savings	Standard
Material	$5.08		$5.08		$ —	
Labor	$0.16		$0.16		$ —	
Burden	$4.46		$1.26		$3.20	TI
SG&A	$0.87	9%	$0.59	9%	$0.29	
Profit	$0.58	5.50%	$0.39	5.50%	$0.19	
Selling price	$11.15		$7.48		$3.68	
Annual volume	95,000		95,000			
Annual cost	$1,059,601.50		$710,389.09		$349,212.41	
Setup cost	$ —		$ —		$ —	
Total cost	**$1,059,601.50**		**$710,389.09**		**$349,212.41**	

with $13.53. These prices represent a wide range, with the base price from Hong Kong AAA being only 71 percent of Hozak-Zhou's price.

The breakdowns of the total manufacturing costs are then evaluated. The material costs for each supplier are shown first (see, e.g., Figures C.1 and C.2). Hozak-Zhou's material costs are by far the highest, at $7.27. Although it is the incumbent supplier, Hozak-Zhou is asking for a $2 increase from last year's price due to an increase in its material purchases. Close behind is Hong Kong AAA at $7.09. Coming in much lower, Vortex Automotive's costs are $5.69 and, finally, Prahinski is at $5.08. Prahinski's cost is 70 percent of Hozak-Zhou's cost.

Next, the labor cost is considered. Here, the geographical location of the plants plays a big part in the direct labor costs that go into making the HVAC hose assembly. The two North American suppliers, Hozak-Zhou and Vortex Automotive, have $2.09 and $1.60 direct labor costs, respectively. This comprises 16 and 18 percent, respectively, of their overall selling price. By comparison, the two offshore suppliers, Hong Kong AAA and Prahinski, have labor costs of $0.40 and $0.15. Hong Kong AAA's and Prahinski's labor percentages are only 1 and 3 percent, respectively, of the overall part price.

The burden component is the final element of the total manufacturing cost. Burden represents nondirect costs such as taxes, depreciation, rent, utilities, maintenance, repair, and other things that keep the manufacturing process running but aren't directly used in making the product. There are two parts of burden—variable and fixed—that relate to each product made.

FIGURE C.4
Hozak-Zhou

	Initial		After Negotiations		Savings	Standard
Material	$7.27		$7.27		$ —	
Labor	$2.09		$2.09		$ —	
Burden	$2.10		$1.26		$0.84	TI
SG&A	$1.41	12.30%	$0.96	9%	$0.45	PH
Profit	$0.66	5.10%	$0.59	5.10%	$0.07	
Selling price	$13.53		$12.17		$1.36	
Annual volume	95,000		95,000			
Annual cost	$1,285,350		$1,156,221		$129,128.92	
Setup cost	$ —		$ —			
Total cost	**$1,285,350**		**$1,156,221**		**$129,128.92**	

With variable cost, Vortex Automotive keeps cost down at $0.10. The other manufacturers are much higher. For example, Hong Kong AAA is at $0.75, Hozak-Zhou is at $1.75, and Prahinski is at a very high $2.90.

As far as fixed costs go, Hozak-Zhou had the lowest costs, with $0.06. Hong Kong AAA is very close with $0.09. The other two suppliers, Vortex Automotive and Prahinski, are much higher, by orders of magnitude. The fixed costs for Vortex Automotive are $0.86, with Prahinski at $1.56.

To summarize, Hong Kong AAA's total burden is $0.84, Vortex Automotive's is $0.96, and Hozak-Zhou's burden is $1.81, while Prahinski's total burden is $4.46. Some of the information that supports these data can help explain the widely differing burden costs. One reason why Hong Kong AAA's burden is so low is because the company is based in China, and the Chinese government subsidizes tooling and machinery costs. In addition, the company has easy access to cheap labor resources. As for Hozak-Zhou, part #36648622 is constructed on machinery that is used to create other parts, meaning it already has a capital investment not directly related to the HVAC hose assembly. For Prahinski, the company has a large investment in automated equipment, capital investments, and perishable tooling. Moreover, Vortex Automotive has some of the same costs as Prahinski, but not to the same degree.

A high difference in burden cost is attributed to two additional components. For example, each company may have different procedures for filling out the same forms and may attribute different costs to burden. Second, suppliers may try to hide additional costs within the burden figures to elevate their selling price.

Other remaining costs to consider outside of total manufacturing costs are sales, general, and administrative (SG&A) costs and profit, where "pure profit" is made from the sale of each part. The Hong Kong AAA has the lowest SG&A costs with $0.83. Next is Prahinski with $0.87. Following up are Vortex Automotive at $1.05 and Hozak-Zhou at $1.41. In terms of profit, Hong Kong AAA was again the lowest, with a profit of $0.46. This was about 5 percent of its total price. Prahinski was second with $0.58; this was 5.13 percent of its total item price. Hozak-Zhou was at $0.66, which totaled 5.5 percent of its final price. Last was Vortex Automotive, which earned $0.90 of profit on each sale, which reflected 9.35 percent of its total item price.

After analyzing the data, we developed a cost standard that Estrada can use for this particular product. The lowest overall materials cost is $5.08. The lowest labor cost is $0.15, while the baseline burden is made up of a fixed cost of $0.06 and a variable cost of $0.10, for a total baseline burden of $0.16. Finally, the lowest SG&A cost in the industry was $0.83, while the lowest profit per sale was $0.46.

The second option would be to award the contract to Hozak-Zhou, the company that supplied the parts in the past.

One option that Estrada has is to pick the supplier that could provide the lowest cost per unit. A supplier should never be chosen based solely on price. Contracts awarded only on this basis place the supplier in control; this could lead to bad deals and supplier advantages in the long run. Furthermore, the buyer loses the option of negotiation and therefore loses the power of leveraging a buy to its lowest possible cost.

Benefits for choosing this alternative include improving the suppliers' competitive position, while Estrada increases profitability and cost flow, reduces total cost, and develops commodity expertise.

The goal for Estrada should be to focus on cost management. Cost management is a way of evaluating the supplier's material, labor, and burden (overhead) costs.

Cost management allows buyers to work with the suppliers to identify different areas needing for improvement. One issue of importance is to have the supplier produce its respective product as efficiently as possible. Estrada customers expect the company to deliver top-quality parts on time, every time; customers assume that the quality is there and that Estrada ensures continuous improvement.

The concept of meeting quality, continuous improvement, and customer expectation is limited by choosing the supplier on the basis of cost alone. The end may result in high risk for the company as customers show dissatisfaction and the image of the company is portrayed negatively. A buyer risks this when all aspects of a supplier are not assessed.

RECOMMENDATIONS

The cost standard approach versus the other two alternatives would provide the overall best solution for Estrada. Now that the supplier cost elements have been analyzed, Estrada needs to use these cost standards in future negotiations. This is an essential step for an assembly with such a large annual purchase value (APV). It is apparent that all the suppliers have both competitive and noncompetitive cost elements. The cost standard approach must be used to negotiate costs using the other suppliers as benchmark comparisons. Negotiable elements include SG&A, burden, and profit. The two lowest-quoted suppliers should be used as the baseline for negotiating the various cost components. The best cost components for negotiation are SG&A, overhead burden, and profit. Direct labor and direct material costs are less likely to be significantly different. However, in the current outsourcing environment, labor may be significantly lower for offshore suppliers. The analysis must consist of a comparison between the upper bound of the quoted prices and a realistic lower bound that may be achieved through the negotiation process. The setup costs involved in switching suppliers also must be accounted for. The price/cost analysis is given in the next section.

IMPLEMENTATION

Hong Kong, although the lowest initial bid, had very little room for possible negotiations. The material costs between the suppliers should have very little variation. Unless Hong Kong can buy the materials at a competitive price, it will never be able to compete in the market. However, labor and burden costs were very competitive and provide a good base for comparisons with the three remaining suppliers.

Vortex Automotive, our second-lowest bidder, had a couple of areas that could be leveraged during negotiations. Unfortunately, these were not areas that contained high costs. Vortex was competitive in the regions of material, labor, and burden. We believe Vortex had margin for negotiation in the areas of SG&A and profit. Its 12.3 percent was among the highest markups and was most likely an area where Vortex was hiding profits. Here, we used Prahinski as the standard for SG&A at 9 percent. Vortex, by far, had the highest profit margin among the four suppliers. Therefore, it was not unreasonable to use Hong Kong as the benchmark at 5.02 percent. This process yielded a $0.72 per-unit savings, moderately impressive considering the annual volume. But where Vortex throws itself out of competition was its extremely high setup cost of $500,000. Obviously, it needed a complete restructuring of its operations in order to handle this. Although annual savings opportunities of about $68,000 were discovered, its total cost was not close to being competitive.

Prahinski, by far, was identified as having the greatest negotiation opportunities. Prahinski appeared to be very competitive in materials, labor, SG&A, and profit. The company was the cost standard for three of the five cost elements, but it was easy to see where Prahinski was hiding profits from the initial quote. Its burden cost of $4.46 was almost double that of the next-lowest competitor. The standard chosen for burden costs was $1.26 from Vortex Automotive. The reasoning behind this is because of the similarity in automation capabilities of the two suppliers. Prahinski understands how to compete and leverage in many areas. It seems as though the company was hoping to hide additional profits in burden costs.

We see great potential in negotiations with Prahinski because it required no setup costs. We have found that Prahinski built this part on the equipment it used for another part, which gave it great advantage. We discovered almost $350,000 in opportunities based on its original quote. Also, Prahinski's total cost of $710,389 per year was the lowest of the four.

Hozak-Zhou was the incumbent supplier for this part. Unfortunately, it was asking for around a $2 increase from its previously contracted price. Most of these costs stemmed from an increase in material costs. Hozak-Zhou quoted the highest material costs of any competing supplier. Despite the price increase, there were still opportunities to bring down the price through burden and SG&A. Burden could possibly be benchmarked by Vortex's initial quote of $1.26. Hozak-Zhou's SG&A markup was the highest of the four at 12.3 percent. We believed a more competitive number of 9 percent would put Hozak-Zhou at Prahinski's standard. A potential reduction of $1.36 was discovered through our analysis. In addition, Hozak-Zhou had an advantage because it was the previous supplier of the part and would not incur future setup costs if awarded the contract. Total savings of $129,128 have been identified.

Figure C.5 shows the extrapolated cost and potential savings over the four-year life of the program.

As stated previously, the analysis above should be done before going into negotiations. This analysis would help to find the two suppliers with the lowest potential price. Although we suggest pursuing only two suppliers for negotiations, we believe it would be highly beneficial to use all four suppliers as sources of

FIGURE C.5
The Program's Costs and Savings

(a) Costs

Year	Hong Kong	Vortex	Prahinski	Hozak-Zhou
1	$1,005,700	$1,427,663.03	$710,389.09	$1,156,221
2	$905,700	$927,663.03	$710,389.09	$1,156,221
3	$905,700	$927,663.03	$710,389.09	$1,156,221
4	$905,700	$927,663.03	$710,389.09	$1,156,221
Total cost	**$3,722,800**	**$4,210,652**	**$2,841,556**	**$4,624,884**

(b) Savings

Year	Hong Kong	Vortex	Prahinski	Hozak-Zhou
1	$8,199.92	$67,936.97	$349,212.41	$129,128.92
2	$8,199.92	$67,936.97	$349,212.41	$129,128.92
3	$8,199.92	$67,936.97	$349,212.41	$129,128.92
4	$8,199.92	$67,936.97	$349,212.41	$129,128.92
Total savings	**$32,799**	**$271,747**	**$1,396,849**	**$516,515**

benchmark comparisons. With a high APV item such as this, it is important to utilize every piece of leverage available.

It is recommended that Estrada select Hong Kong Automobile and Prahinski as the two suppliers with which it should enter negotiations. Their total costs are $3,722,800 and $2,841,556, respectively. We would first approach Hong Kong at the negotiations table since it is the lowest original bidder. Hong Kong, despite its high material costs, is very competitive. The area of concern that needs to be addressed is SG&A. Hong Kong quoted 10 percent; however, Prahinski set the standard at 9 percent. If there was resistance, Estrada should simply ask to see the people involved to prove the quote. Hong Kong's high material costs are basically nonnegotiable. Although the standard for material is $5.08, there was not much that could be negotiated because Hong Kong does not buy at high volumes or have the purchasing power to command those prices. It would be to Estrada's advantage to investigate deeper into the supplier's material purchases to help it stay competitive.

Estrada should approach Prahinski next. The area that must be addressed at the negotiations table is burden costs. Prahinski, like Hong Kong, is very competitive in most cost elements. Prahinski is aware of how efficient it is, and it can easily hide profits in its burden cost. Although we know it cannot compete with a lowly automated Hong Kong, we believe it would not be unreasonable to negotiate Prahinski down to Vortex's standard of $1.26. Prahinski most likely will defend its burden quote. If this situation were to arise, Estrada can respond in two ways. First, Estrada should tell Prahinski it is very uncompetitive based on an industry standard, in this case Vortex's. Then Estrada should ask to see the machines that would be used for production. These tactics should be enough to help bring down the burden costs.

Chapter **Fourteen**

Bargaining and Negotiations

Learning Objectives

1. Understand the difference between bargaining and negotiations.
2. Identify the differences between distributive and integrative bargaining.
3. Identify the differences between the psychological and the economic aspects of bargaining.
4. Learn the six psychological factors that affect bargaining.
5. Learn the factors related to the payoff system.
6. Implement bargaining strategies.
7. Identify the elements of negotiation.

INTRODUCTION

This chapter examines the important human interactions called *bargaining* and *negotiation*. Economics and psychology provide important concepts and variables that, when combined, produce favorable insights into bargaining and negotiations. Whenever the terms of a sales transaction are determined, or a business deal is settled, bargaining is likely to have occurred. In a sense, everyone becomes a bargainer at one time or another. Bargaining occurs between all forms of human groupings including individuals, groups, organizations, and countries. The condition under which "bargaining" takes place is that two or more parties have divergent interests or goals and communication between the parties is possible. Three additional conditions also must exist in order for bargaining to occur (Chertkoff and Esser, 1976): (1) Mutual compromise must be possible. If one of the parties must choose between total victory and complete loss, no bargaining occurs. Bargaining situations require intermediate solutions for the parties involved. (2) The possibility must exist for provisional offers to be made by those involved in the situation. (3) The provisional offers must not determine the outcome of the situation until the terms are accepted by all parties. A bargaining situation can then be defined as an interaction where parties with certain disagreements confer and exchange ideas about a possible solution until a compromise is reached or the bargaining is terminated. This definition of bargaining is referred to as explicit bargaining.

In this chapter, we will only consider the kind of bargaining that occurs between two parties who possess resources the other desires. While bargaining often occurs in what has been referred to as multi-opponent bargaining situations—where a consumer visits several dealerships when shopping for a new automobile or where an industrial buyer negotiates a new purchase with several alternative suppliers—this will not be the main focus of this chapter. Instead, the emphasis will be on bargaining in a "bilateral monopoly" system. This does not rule out the influence of others on the two bargainers such as their constituencies, but it does limit the bargaining to only two parties.

Two-party bargaining can be divided into two types: distributive and integrative. The parties in distributive bargaining are in basic conflict and competition because of a clash of goals: The more one party gets, the less the other gets. That is, the total gains from the situation must be "distributed" between the two parties involved, and each party usually wants as much as it can get. However, if either party is too greedy, an agreement will not be reached. In dealing with distributive bargaining, the influence of both parties must be considered. Discussion, understanding, and agreements are vital to distributive bargaining. By the very nature of the situation, cooperation is important. Without some degree of cooperation, either party can block trading and reduce individual gain to zero. Distributive bargaining can therefore be modeled and examined by using "game theory." A two-party, varying-sum, or zero-sum schedule is suitable depending upon the payoff schedule involved. In a varying-sum schedule bargaining situation, the profits (and/or losses) of the respective bargainers, when added together, need not always equal the same fixed amount, thus the term *varying sum*. While the payoff schedules are usually inversely related—if one gains, the other must lose—there can be some situations where both parties realize a gain (or loss) not in direct proportion to what happens to the other bargainer.

In the zero-sum bargaining situation, the profits (and/or losses) of the respective bargainers always sum to the same fixed amount. The term *zero sum* stands for the fact that what one bargainer gains, the other loses and the gains (and/or losses) net out to be zero. Both of these situations readily exist in the business environment. The varying-sum schedule is often found in customer service situations where the supplier is at or above the 90-percent service level. To go from the 90-percent level to the 95-percent level, a gain of only 5-percent improvement for the customer often can mean a doubling of the costs to the supplier to attain that increased level. The zero-sum schedule is usually found in retail situations where the merchant's costs are relatively fixed. The less the consumer pays for a product, the less profit there is for the retailer almost on a dollar-for-dollar basis.

Integrative bargaining exists where there are areas of mutual concern and complementary interests. The situation is a varying-sum schedule such that, by working together, both parties can increase the total profits available to be divided between them. This is often the case between manufacturers and distributors because of the existence of an ultimate consumer. If the ultimate consumer can be persuaded to pay more for a product, there is more to be divided between the manufacturer and the distributor. At this point, we are tempted to generalize that integrative bargaining is more common to industrial markets and interactions while distributive bargaining is more common to consumer markets and interactions.

In most bargaining situations, there is usually a preliminary discussion, called *negotiation*. The word *negotiation* is derived from Latin and in civil law means "trading on deliberations leading to an agreement." The modeling approach to bargaining is to determine what contract, that is, agreed joint strategy, might or should be reached. The bargaining model offers an agreement (solution). Others (Rubin & Brown, 1975), however, have felt the similarities of definition are so strong that the terms *bargaining* and *negotiation* can be used interchangeably, even though occasional distinction is made between the terms.

A model of a bargaining problem calls for an asymmetric form of analysis and both a normative focus on one's own behavior and a predictive view of one's opponent. The bargainer needs to determine how he or she as a decision maker *ought* to behave in light of his or her analysis of how his or her opponent *might* behave. And, of course, as the decision maker analyzes the problem, he or she should bear in mind that the opponent is also thinking how the decision maker is thinking, and so on. The minimum necessary variables for a model of the overall bargaining process include both the decision maker's and the opponent's initial offers, desired outcomes, maximum level of concession (zero profit level), and rate of concession.

Two parties can bargain over price; the seller usually wants the price to be high, while the buyer wants the price to be low. The seller is often working under a profit-maximization strategy and the buyer is more interested in minimizing cost. Sometimes the resource in contention may be time. The building contractor wants more time; the future owner wants the building completed in less time.

The distributive bargaining situation has been most fully explored by psychologists. The results of this research are a myriad of small laboratory studies that have not generated a general theory of bargaining or a comprehensive model to incorporate the many isolated findings. Economists, on the other hand, have seen distributive bargaining as a problem that only involves two parties dividing fixed resources with no opportunity for any outside influence of third parties. Economists, therefore, have seen the solution to distributive bargaining as indeterminable and left its exploration to others. Economists have spent most of their efforts in examining bargaining in integrative bargaining situations.

PSYCHOLOGICAL BARGAINING FRAMEWORK

The findings by psychologists can be categorized under six areas, each representing a major factor assumed to affect bargaining. These six factors are explained below and examples of each are provided:

1. *General bargaining predispositions*. Individual differences in bargaining predispositions may affect bargaining behavior. For example, bargainers may have a cooperative or a competitive general orientation.
2. *Payoff system*. Payoffs result from various aspects of the negotiated agreement. For example, certain terms may yield a specific amount of profit, or there may be a bonus for attaining a specified agreement, or the time spent in bargaining may involve certain costs.
3. *Social relationship with the opponent*. This factor refers to the social relationship existing between the bargainers. Examples are degree of friendship or differences in status or power.
4. *Social relationship with significant others*. This factor refers to the relationships of the bargainers to significant others not participating directly in the bargaining. Examples of significant others are the bargaining constituents or a mediator.
5. *Situational factors*. The physical and social setting of the bargaining may have an effect. Is the bargaining being conducted in the home territory of one of the bargainers or on neutral ground? What, if any, is the seating arrangement?

6. *Bargaining strategy*. This factor includes the specific actions of the bargainer during bargaining. How extreme is his or her opening? Does he or she concede frequently or infrequently?

Payoff system and bargaining strategy are highly relevant at this point in the chapter and worth exploring further at this time. Later, using a conceptual model, the other four areas will be brought together and applied to buyer–seller negotiations and bargaining. (See Bonoma and Johnson (1978).)

Payoff System

The actual payoff system that bargainers face in an interaction must certainly be a major determinant of bargaining behavior. Several different factors related to the payoff system have been studied. They include:

1. The amount that has to be exceeded if the bargainer is to realize a profit.
2. The cost of time spent in bargaining.
3. The cost of failure to reach agreement.
4. Added benefits achieved by obtaining a specific threshold value.
5. Qualitative or quantitative variations in the general level of payoff values.
6. Whether payoffs are based solely on one's own profit schedule or are based, in whole or in part, on the degree to which one's profits exceed those of others.
7. Whether conflict is constant-sum or varying-sum.
8. Penalties the bargaining opponent (or perhaps a third party) is likely to impose for failure to yield.

A discussion of these factors and the research findings follows. Only directly pertinent findings will be presented. There is a voluminous amount of research on bargaining, a great deal of which is only tangential to this discussion.

Breakeven Point

Various names have been used to describe the amount that must be exceeded in the bargaining interaction in order to obtain a profit: maximum concession point, breakeven point, zero-profit point, minimum necessary share, resistance point, or minimum disposition (Chertkoff and Esser, 1976). However, it has been argued that the value in natural settings, including business, is frequently uncertain. The bargaining that takes place is often an attempt to convince the other person that he or she can profitably accept a lower value than the one he or she maintains is necessary. This is true in most business situations where future profits are being negotiated. Without knowledge of future costs and revenues, the breakeven point would remain uncertain.

A bargainer's resistance to making concessions is positively correlated to both the time required to make a further concession and the probability of withdrawing from the negotiations. The level of resistance also is assumed to be related to the minimum necessary share. As a bargainer concedes toward his or her minimum necessary share, the bargainer's resistance should increase. It also can be predicted that for a given offer, the higher the minimum necessary share, the greater the resistance.

Time Pressure

The amount of time left before bargaining must be concluded also is believed to have a significant impact on bargaining behavior. Consider the situation in many labor–management negotiations. If the contract is not successfully renegotiated prior to the expiration of the existing contract, a labor walkout may occur. In cases of buyer–seller negotiating, time pressure may be created by the buyer's imminent need for the product or service, the length of delivery time possibly being extended by long negotiations. Sellers may realize time pressure by quotas for sales that must be accomplished in set time periods. The greater the time pressure, the faster the concession making. Time pressure in psychological experiments has been exerted in various ways:

1. High or low probability that the present round of offers would be the last.
2. Warning that time was almost up.
3. Number of offers remaining before penalties for additional offers.
4. Cost of each of the trial offers.

More rapid yielding under greater time pressure may reflect the desire of bargainers to avoid either the undesirable costs associated with making offers or zero profit (which results from no agreement).

Cost of No Agreement

In most of the psychological research, the majority of experiments have been structured so that the alternatives of reaching an agreement and its possible terms are usually preferable to no agreement. Warning the subjects that the end of negotiations is imminent often produces extremely rapid concession making, so uniformly rapid, in fact, that any differences in levels of toughness prior to the warning may be obliterated (Benton, Kelley, and Liebling, 1972). This is not necessarily true in buyer–seller negotiations as they can usually be resumed in some future time period and other buyers or sellers exist for future interactions.

Multiple Bargaining Interactions

In most psychological research, participants are given the goal of maximizing their own gain; however, they also may be interested in outperforming the other bargainers. In personal selling situations where the same salesperson often negotiates with the same buyer, this may be an important issue. The question is, "What is the effect of being bested on a previous bargaining encounter?" How will this translate into bargaining strategy on subsequent interactions with the same opponent? It appears that in the second encounter, those who had failed on the first encounter bargain in a tougher manner than those who had succeeded.

In conclusion, any theoretical mode of bargaining must include assumptions about the payoff system under which the bargainers are operating. The breakeven point, the cost of time spent in bargaining, the cost of failure to reach an agreement, time pressure, the effect of previous bargaining outcomes, and other factors all have an effect on bargaining behavior and need to be incorporated into the bargaining process. A large amount of psychological research has examined the effect of the payoff system on bargaining. Some of this research has direct implications for buyer–seller interactions. When buyers and sellers are negotiating over future profits, outcomes may have a wider variance than when the payoff is known with certainty. Resistance to making concessions is related to time pressure, breakeven point, the cost of no agreement, and perhaps previous bargaining outcomes.

Bargaining Strategy

Usually a tougher bargaining strategy—one using a more extreme opening position, fewer concessions, and/or smaller concessions—will result in failure to reach an agreement (Bartos, 1966, 1970). There appear to be exceptions to such a conclusion, however. Never making a concession may be responded to by the other side in a similar fashion, leading to little or no convergence in the bargaining interaction. When time allotted to bargaining (or that which is left) is very short and when not reaching an agreement is clearly disadvantageous, toughness may be a poor strategy because it could result in no agreement (Benton et al., 1970, 1972). Also, when bargaining is deadlocked, toughness is counterproductive. Excessive toughness in bargaining could be a particularly bad strategy in buyer–seller interactions where future interactions are expected. If one party always chooses a very tough stance, the other party will develop a similar approach to the bargaining interaction. This could result in high transaction costs, lack of future agreements, and, where possible, replacement of the bargaining opponent.

The best strategy is to give the other side the impression that one is tough but fair. A strategy of always reciprocating both the frequency and the magnitude of the other bargainer's concessions was found to be more effective in obtaining concessions from the other bargainer than strategies involving less reciprocation. Conceding only in response to a concession by the other side gives the impression that one is strong, while always reciprocating a concession gives the impression that one is fair. Dispositions attributed to the other party in a bargaining situation are crucial in mediating yielding. If you give a little, I will give a little and vice versa. Concession begets concession and reciprocal concessions can lead to reaching agreement. This leads to the general conclusion that every agreement ought to lie somewhere between the two starting points of the bargainers. Obviously, some agreements are closer to one bargainer's starting position than the other's because of tough or skillful bargaining tactics. A problem, however, is what the other party thinks of his or her opponent's reasons for tough negotiation, particularly if there are to be other instances of bargaining between the two parties.

In conclusion, giving a bargaining opponent the impression that tough bargaining is because of one's payoff system and that one is firm but fair is the best strategy. This will lead to greater yielding on the part of the other party in the bargaining interaction. Another important aspect of the perceived bargaining strategy deals with whether the opponent attributes the need for the level of toughness in bargaining to the opponent or to the opponent's constituency. If the level of toughness is because of the opponent's constituency, it may be beneficial for the bargainer to directly contact members of the constituency and deal with their expectations before returning to the negotiations. An example of this in an industrial setting occurs when a salesperson must contact other members of the "buying center" before continuing negotiations with a purchasing manager who is under pressure from his or her constituency to obtain a "very low price."

ECONOMIC BARGAINING FRAMEWORK

While most of the empirical research to date has been in distributive bargaining and done by psychologists, most of the work done on integrative bargaining has been of the theoretical nature and accomplished by economists.

In the Nash solution, the bargaining problem is conceived in the usual game theoretic terms (Nash, 1950). He considers as relevant data only the utilities that each alternative point of agreement provides to the players.

FIGURE 14.1
Pareto Optimal

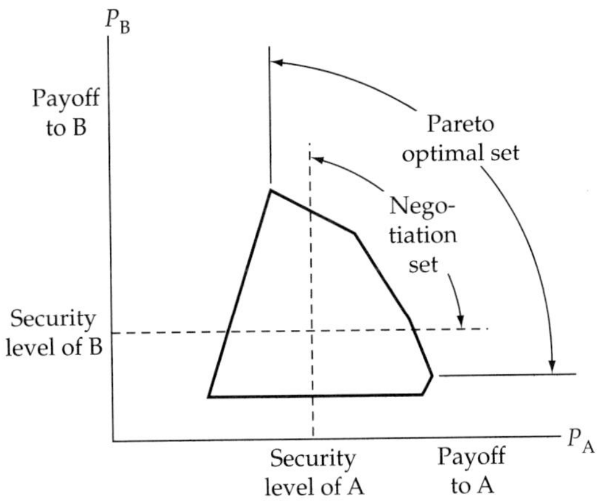

Nash originally took the position that his model constituted a positive theory and that it would describe actual bargaining outcomes, but it is now much more common to give a normative interpretation to the analysis and to treat the Nash solution as a "desirable" outcome of the bargaining process.

The actual result of any bilateral bargain will only be a single imputation, but the economic assumptions made are usually not strong enough to enable the economist to forecast the specific imputation that will be chosen. Often all that he or she can do is to indicate a range in which the outcome must fall (the contract curve). In that case, the specification of this range constitutes the solution in the sense that it fully utilizes the available economic information. In order to single out an imputation within this range, dynamic sociological and psychological information may be needed.

The Nash solution assumes individual utilities are not comparable. It is of a normative nature and assumes away such features as bargaining ability. The Nash solution to the bargaining problem suggests a method of *fair division*. It suggests a way of dividing joint profits that is "fair" in the sense that a referee or judge "should" follow it, if called upon to settle a division between two corporations.

The contract should be Pareto optimal (see Figure 14.1). However, some points on the Pareto optimal joint strategy curve leave a player worse off than if he or she had not made an agreement. The subset of Pareto optimal joint strategies offering each player at least his or her security level is called the *negotiation set* (contract curve).

A Pareto optimal solution requires a contract with a specific quantity of goods, calculable from the economic model. This quantity maximizes joint profit. Assuming both players agree on the Pareto optimal quantity of goods, there remains the division of the joint profit between the players. This is determined by the price the distributor agrees to pay the manufacturer and the manufacturer accepts. The unit price in a Pareto optimal contract can vary anywhere between the two limiting prices, the higher of which would give all the joint profit to the manufacturer and the lower of which would give all the joint profit to the distributor.

The actual subset of contract quantities varies around the Pareto optimum; the more complete the information each had about the other, the less the variability of different pairs of bargainers around the Pareto optimum.

The tendency in this situation is to split the joint profit evenly between the buyer and the seller. This seems to agree with all proposed theories yielding a specific Pareto optimal strategy (when utility is linear with money). For example, the only reasonable status quo point seems to be no-deal, in which case the Nash solution requires a 50-50 split of the profits. Neither player can enforce a relative advantage over the other; this also leads to an even split.

One problem here is that the subjects are not in direct contact with each other; therefore, psychological aspects are not a part of the process.

Experimentation with the Nash model has proven to be useful in predicting the actual outcomes of buyer–seller negotiations (Neslin and Greenhalgh, 1983). The experimental results suggest that an understanding of any conflict present prior to the actual bargaining is key for predicting the actual outcome. It also was found that management must accurately communicate its preferences to the negotiators because the negotiators' preferences strongly affect the outcome. Weakness in bargaining skills also has an effect on the outcome of bargaining situations according to their findings. While the outcomes of the bargaining situations were distributed around the Nash solution, other psychological variables or individual differences affected the actual outcome.

In general, economic theory can help predict the approximate outcome of bargaining situations, but psychological conditions will cause the true solution to vary around the predicted outcome point. A combined economic/psychological approach will help provide the truest solution and best approach to understanding bargaining and negotiation situations and their outcomes.

AN EXPERIMENT IN DISTRIBUTIVE BARGAINING

To better illustrate the effects of both economic and psychological aspects on the outcome of bargaining situations, it is necessary to turn to a field experiment in distributive bargaining. The experiment examines the effect of contingency compensation on both buyers and sellers. It also allows speculation about the difference in the power systems of buyers and sellers and how they affect the outcome of bargaining situations.

Consider the following sales situation where an agreement has to be reached on the specifications of the product to be bought and the money to be paid. Both the seller and the buyer can make concessions. To simplify matters, also assume the following bargaining conditions:

1. Only one deal is being negotiated.
2. The bargainers are honorable people.
3. The decisions made are binding.
4. No arbitration or third party is available to assist bargainers.
5. Any party can break off the negotiation and continue as before.
6. The setting and language are not important.

Sellers and buyers tend to have conflicting bargaining goals. The aim of a selling organization is to instill in its salespeople the objective of influencing the buyer's actions to the advantage of the seller. This goal is effectively communicated and reinforced by the seller's compensation system. Salespeople are often compensated on the basis of salary plus commission, making their earnings directly contingent upon some measure of selling effectiveness. Logic dictates a similar objective for the buying organization. Since purchases represent costs to the buyers, professional buyers are encouraged to reduce costs. The seller's reservation price (R_S) is usually his or her minimum selling price for any final deal, δ^*. This price includes the total costs plus an expected profit margin. The buyer's

FIGURE 14.2
Distributive Bargaining Model

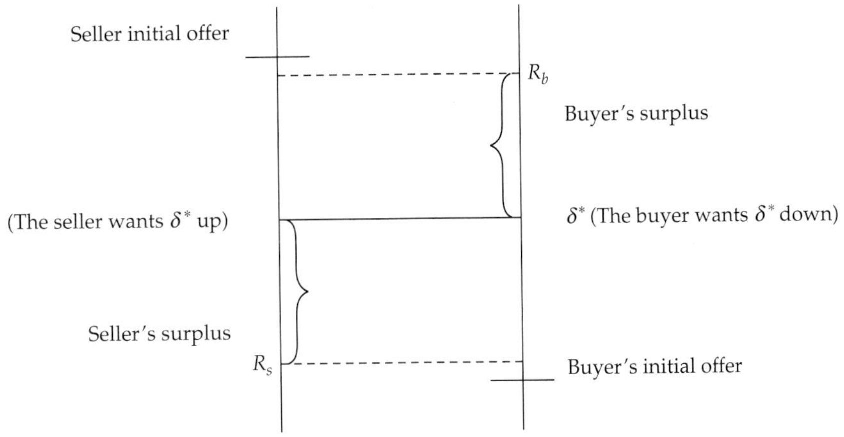

Note: If $R_b < R_s$, there is no bargaining zone.

reservation price (R_b) represents the maximum amount that he or she is willing to pay for any final deal, δ^*. To pay more than the reservation price. R_b, the buyer would be better off with no agreement (see Figure 14.2).

If $R_s < R_b$, the bargaining zone is the interval from R_s to R_b. Suppose that the final deal is some value of δ^* where δ^* is between R_s and R_b. The buyer's marginal gain in value is $R_b - \delta^*$ and the seller's marginal dollar gain is $\delta^* - R_s$. At first glance, it appears that a final deal is easily obtained if a bargaining zone exists. This is not really the case simply because the buyer and seller might not agree to settle for an even division of the bargaining zone value. The bargainers generally do not know the exact size of the bargaining zone, $R_b - R_s$. Each party usually knows his or her reservation price but has only probabilistic information on the other party's reservation price. Each party must assess the other party's reservation price. The negotiation process is used to uncover the other party's (buyer's) reservation price. At the same time, the seller may often lead the buyer to think that his or her reservation price is higher than it really is.

A simple bargaining example will be presented to illustrate concession behavior for distributive bargaining. The instructions for the example follow: A bargaining experiment run at The Ohio State University informed the sellers that they had been hired to represent an individual who wished to sell an office building (McFillen et al., 1983). Because of the owner's financial situation, the building could be sold for no less than $100,000, R_s. The buyers were told that they had been hired to represent a person who wished to purchase an office building, but that the potential buyer could afford to pay no more than $150,000, R_b. A bargaining zone exists because $R_s < R_b$. The bargaining game was designed such that no party had a relative advantage over the other due to either the urgency of settlement or the possession of more complete information. The time limit for the game was 25 minutes. Half of the sellers were told that they would be contingently compensated and they would be rewarded in cash in proportion to the final negotiated price of the building. In their instructions, they were told that they would receive one dollar for each $5,000 by which the final price exceeded the $100,000 minimum required by the owner, up to a maximum of $10. The participants in this study would actually be allowed to keep this money as an incentive to make the bargaining more extrinsically involving. If no agreement was reached, the contingently compensated sellers would receive no commission. The remaining half of the sellers were told that they would be paid $10 for having represented the owner during the negotiations, regardless of whether or not a sale was negotiated. Similarly, half of the buyers were told that they actually would be compensated according to the final agreed-upon price. They were informed that they would receive one dollar in cash for each $5,000 by which the final price was lower than the $150,000 maximum that the potential purchasers could pay, up to a maximum of $10. No agreement therefore meant no money for the contingently compensated buyer. The remaining half of the buyers were told that they would receive $10 for having represented the potential purchaser in the negotiations, regardless of the outcome of the negotiations. These instructions constituted the contingent and noncontingent reward conditions. No buyer or seller knew whether the opposing negotiator was or was not being contingently rewarded.

The results yielded a number of interesting findings. First, the initial offer from the buyer was always consistently above the seller's reservation price. This case will result in an agreement favorable to the seller in each situation.

Second, the results suggest that the way a negotiator is paid will affect significantly the process and outcome of the negotiations. As shown in Figure 14.3a–d, the effects of contingent rewards are to shift the seller's marginal surplus upward and the buyer's marginal value downward. When only one party is contingently rewarded, the effect is to shift the settlement in that party's favor. When both

FIGURE 14.3
Distributive Bargaining Example

(a) Seller contingent/buyer contingent

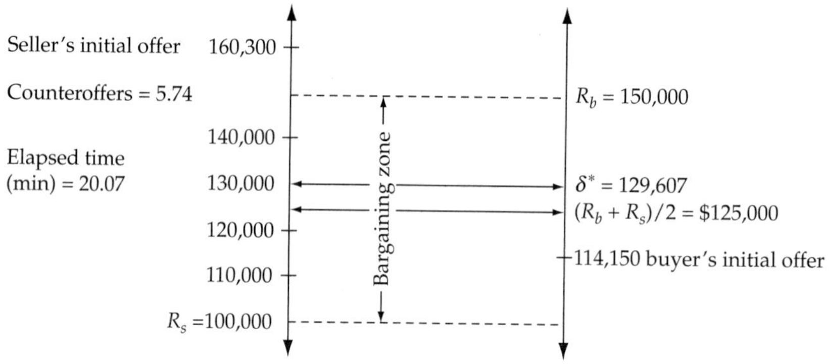

(b) Seller contingent/buyer noncontingent

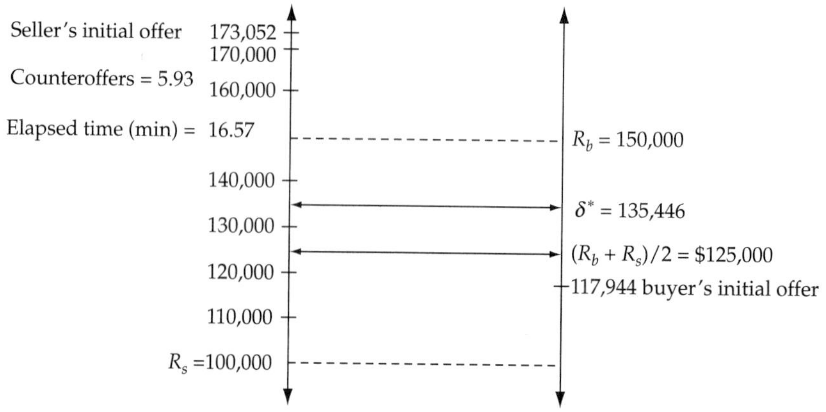

(c) Seller noncontingent/buyer contingent

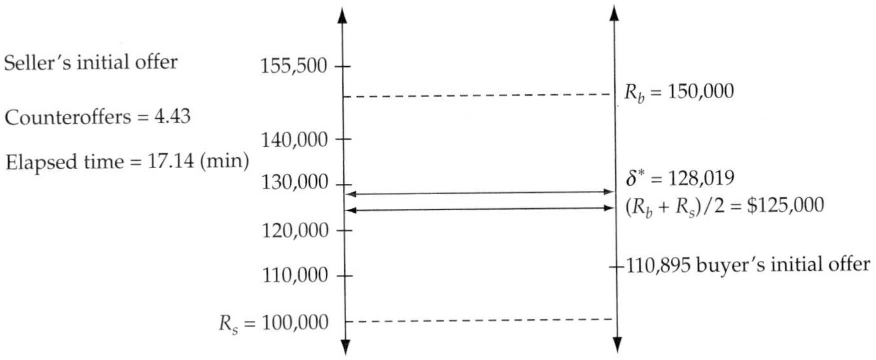

(d) Seller noncontingent/buyer noncontingent

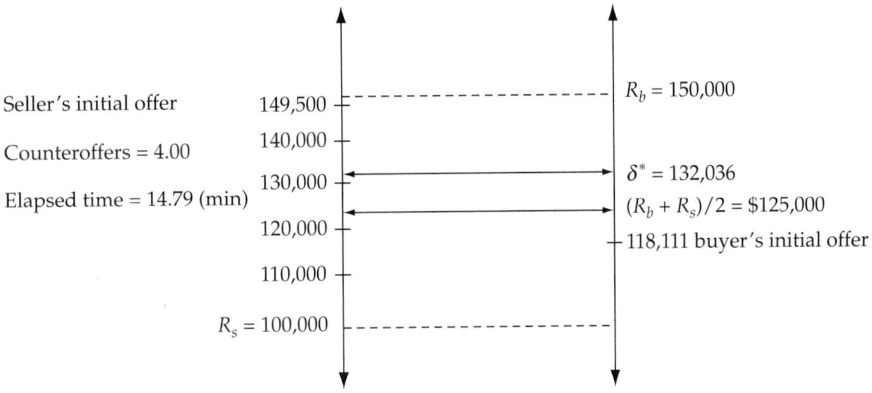

parties are contingently rewarded, the result is a much longer and more difficult negotiation process.

This study, like much of the bargaining research, focused exclusively on price as the relevant criterion. While this is not always true of bargaining situations, the results of this study have three specific implications for understanding bargaining and negotiations and help to merge economic considerations with psychological variables. First, contingent rewards make a difference in negotiation outcomes. The reward practices that exist today in purchasing put the buying organization at a distinct disadvantage. Although the sales activity is essentially a mirror image of the buying activity, sales organizations have developed reward systems that motivate their personnel through compensation; purchasing organizations, for the most part, have not.

Second, purchasing organizations need to be aware of the salesperson's reward system. By knowing about the contingencies created for sellers, the buying organization can develop competing contingencies for its personnel where the efforts would have the greatest benefit. A purchasing representative also can take advantage of the seller's own motivation to maximize some element of the negotiation by seeking important concessions on other elements of the negotiation.

The third implication is that management must develop stronger contingencies to encourage purchasing effectiveness. This can be done by concentrating on the areas of purchasing that are most critical, recognizing the most important variables involved in the negotiations for any given purchase, and improving performance appraisal processes to reflect purchasing effectiveness in relation to the reward system.

PLANNING FOR A FORMAL NEGOTIATION

Planning (Seller's Perspective)

The most important planning activity for a seller is to submit the most responsive request for proposal (RFP) or request for quote (RFQ). The seller's proposal should be based on a thorough conceptual and economic analysis. If this phase in the planning process is nonresponsive, the negotiations will not be conducted. The seller cannot alter the proposal after it is submitted. On the other hand, until an agreement is signed, the buyer can change his or her mind. There is always a chance of rejection no matter how strong the seller's initial RFP. At the same time, no matter how weak a competing proposal, it still has a probability of acceptance no matter how remote. As an example, Custer-Battle, a security firm contracted by the U.S. government to provide security for commercial aviation at the Baghdad Airport, arrived in Iraq immediately after the ground war looking for work. According to published reports, Custer-Battle scribbled a contract on a sheet of notebook paper and was given $15 million as a down payment on the same day.

There are standard procedures for processing RFPs. After receipt of the initial proposals, the proposals should be screened for responsiveness in terms of technical quality, if requested; managerial capability; financial stability; experience on similar projects; and other relevant criteria. If the buyer chooses to negotiate with multiple bidders, the buyer should not reveal a supplier's prices to the competing firms. It is, however, allowable for the buyer to inform the supplier if the supplier's prices are too high. The buyer should maintain strict confidentiality after the proposals are received. No information regarding the identification of the participating bidders or the number of proposals should be disseminated to anyone not officially involved in the selection process. In most significant governmental RFPs, a mandatory prebid meeting is required. At this meeting, each bidder has the opportunity to ask clarification questions and size up the competition. In cases where a seller is the sole source, the seller is assured, in most cases, that negotiations will eventually occur. When there is more than one bidder, the seller is not assured an opportunity to negotiate. The seller should use creative ways to determine if his or her proposal is being considered. The manner in which the buyer acknowledges the seller is a strong indication of the seller's chances for success.

If the seller believes that the proposal is not being considered, immediate troubleshooting steps should begin. If the problem is the technical approach, there is very little he or she can do to reverse the situation. But if the proposal is technically sound, the differences may be the cost proposal. Whether or not the seller should reduce the cost should be based solely on the selling firm's cost structure. Finally, if both the technical approach and the cost proposal are acceptable, the problem is probably political.

The negotiation planning activities should be driven by the proposal. The proposal is never complete in terms of various cost components. Questions on overhead rates should be anticipated. The negotiating team should analyze the competitor's strengths and weaknesses. The selling team should also analyze their proposal from the buyer's point of view. The seller should then evaluate his or her own strengths and weaknesses. The seller's bargaining strengths depend on the following:

1. The seller's current capacity
2. The probability of being the successful bidder
3. The seller's deadline
4. The status of the seller

The buyer's bargaining strengths are the following:

1. The number of bidders
2. The urgency of the buyer needs
3. The length of time before agreement
4. The status of the buyer

Price is not always the major selection criterion. The quality of the technical proposal and the seller's managerial team can easily become the controlling criteria. The seller also should determine the buyer's pricing behavior in terms of fixed price versus cost-plus contracts.

The first step in the seller's plan is to determine the objectives of the negotiations. Each of the components of the negotiations should be evaluated for the best-case scenario and alternative courses of action. The seller should make an opening statement using effective visual aids. PowerPoint presentations and handouts should be used for formal negotiations. The seller should conduct several mock presentations for complex high-dollar proposals. The author was involved in a mock presentation involving a public relations coach that lasted more than three weeks.

Planning (Buyer's Perspective)

The planning process for the buyer is consistent with the seller's planning process. The buyer's strengths are driven by the number of sellers in the market, the number of buyers in the market, knowledge of the item or service, the cost breakdown (if applicable), and the level of preparation. The buyer must carefully analyze all of the information submitted by the seller. The buyer also can select specific items from the seller's proposal to negotiate. The buyer also must evaluate the seller's strengths and weaknesses. The buyer must be thoroughly prepared for each and every negotiation. Data collection is the first step in the preparation process. The next step involves establishing the negotiations' objectives, strategies, and tactics.

Time is clearly the most important shortcoming in the preparation process for the buyer. The seller has prepared numerous proposals for a variety of customers. On the other hand, buyers must spend many hours studying numerous proposals. Buyers usually have heavy workloads and sometimes they are unprepared for negotiation sessions.

Once the buyer has a complete understanding of what he or she is buying, a thorough price/cost analysis should be performed using the seller's cost data. The buyer cannot be an effective negotiator without the price analysis. The only reasonable way to reduce the price proposal is convincing the seller through data analysis. It is not reasonable to ask for price reductions without a price/cost analysis. For detailed information on pricing, price/cost analysis, and learning curves, see Chapter 13.

Prior to the negotiations, the negotiations' objectives should be established. The buyer should establish specific direct cost dollar amounts and profit limits. It is not enough to set as an objective to negotiate a percentage improvement from the

TABLE 14.1 Minimum and Maximum Strategies

	Objective	Minimum	Maximum
Direct labor hours	80	75	100
Labor rates	$10.00	$ 8.95	$11.00
Direct material costs	$40.00	$32.00	$45.00
Material costs per unit	$ 4.00	$ 3.20	$ 4.50

seller's original price proposal. The buyer should never reveal its objectives to the seller. The ultimate objective of the buyer should be to develop a reasonable contract price. The buyer also must be flexible in selecting the type of contract (fixed cost or cost-plus) that will be appropriate for a specific spend. The negotiations' objectives also should use a data-driven approach to determine minimum and maximum pricing strategies. Of course, the buyer's minimum and maximum strategies should be listed, as shown in Tables 14.1 and 14.2.

The buyer must determine the points of difference between the seller's proposal and the buyer's difference objective (base). For a more detailed example, see Appendix C of Chapter 13.

There are many surprises in the business world. One way to minimize these surprises is to gain more systematic knowledge through the negotiations process. In today's competitive business environment, pricing is usually the biggest factor in the negotiations process. Industrial purchasing uses the negotiations process extensively for capital equipment purchases, annual blanket orders, system contracts, change orders, penalties, price changes, and many other situations. As stated earlier, price is usually the major negotiating factor simply because delivery, quality, and adequate quantities should be the minimum expectation from the supply source. The procedure for a formal negotiation is given below.

Procedure

1. *Team.* Select team, if needed. You may need the cost accountant and certain engineers. Select the chief negotiator.

TABLE 14.2 List of Objectives

	Objective	Minimum	Maximum	Seller's Proposal	Comments
Direct labor cost (DLC)	$2.88	$2.50	$4.00	$3.44	Higher than base
Direct material cost (DMC)	4.24	4.24	4.08	4.48	Higher than base
Tooling cost (TC)	1.04	1.04	2.32	1.92	Higher than base
Manufacturing overhead (MO)	2.96 (103% of DLC)	2.57 (103% of DLC)	3.04 (76% of DLC)	5.16 (150% of DLC)	Higher than base
General and administration expense	.64 (6% of TC)	0.621 (6% of TC)	.26 (2% of TC)	.752 (5% of TC)	Higher than base
Total cost	11.76	10.35	13.44	15.752	Higher than base
Profit	.56 (5% of TC)	.518 (5% of TC)	1.20 (9% of TC)	1.58 (10% of TC)	Higher than base
Selling price	$12.32	$11.48	$14.90	$17.33	Higher than base

2. *Objectives*. Determine objectives, such as a win–win outcome for both parties.
3. *Preparation*. Prepare a price/cost analysis look at comparative bids; perform a vendor visit; look at vendor rating-evaluation records; perform a value analysis; look at contract terms, industry price trends, new product ideas, survey data, and test reports. Prepare a proposal analysis: determine questions, get input from ultimate users, establish criteria, and get information on past purchase volume from the supplier.
4. *Bargaining strength*. Determine bargaining strength—be honest.
5. *Plan*. Develop the plan: the agenda, place, time, min–max positions. Is this a reorder? Establish your authority.
6. *Strategy*. Set your strategy based on a list of obtainable objectives—goals.
7. *Tactics on how to achieve the strategy*. Start with the easy issues. Set the tone; establish rapport; prepare questions and decide who asks; determine when to recess or ask for a new proposal; have several responses. Establish rules such as "never reveal your maximum on items such as price," no games, no dishonesty, no psychological tricks (this is business, not a card game). Give when it is proper, reasonable, and so forth. Determine roles for each team member. Use a cost analysis to check labor rate and time; have the facts at hand.
8. *Follow-up*. Conduct a postnegotiation review and follow-up. Develop the action plan based on your agreement. Critique team member performance.

Hints

1. Read, study, and tear apart the supplier's proposal.
2. Be persuasive, not conceited.
3. Stress tact for all team members.
4. Stress listening.
5. Prepare questions in writing on 3 × 5 cards, and so on.
6. Record—take notes.
7. Assign roles and practice.
8. Write down the plan.
9. Have reasonable objectives, positions.
10. Be firm but fair; give when you make a mistake.
11. Have expert assistance on the team.
12. Admit when you make a mistake or "don't know." Recess and find out.
13. Be honest. Do *not* give competitor prices. Do *not* guess about volume requirements.
14. Develop *patience*.
15. Recess and review; change your position?
16. Don't play psychologist or "big man" or "big woman."
17. Background data are the key to cost and production methods. You must know how the product is made to be a good negotiator. You must know the terms. Visit the supplier's plant, other users.
18. Learn from your mistakes.
19. Learn the personalities of the supplier's team. Use the knowledge to establish rapport. Capitalize on their weakness such as lack of cost data.

20. Try to stay on the offensive yet get them to talk—then *listen*!
21. Remember you are *not* negotiating with the cold-war Russians. You want the supplier to win also for a long-term, mutually rewarding relationship.

A RICHER MODEL OF THE BUYER–SELLER INTERACTION

What should be clear by now in the chapter is that, while both economics and psychology offer useful insight into bargaining and negotiation, a richer conceptual model of the buyer–seller interaction is necessary. This model needs to capture both the economic and psychological aspects of the bargaining situation. To this end, an exchange model of buyer–seller interactions is proposed.

The buyer–seller interactions exchange model given in Figure 14.4 captures both the economic aspects and the surrounding psychological variables of the bargaining situation. It allows for the effects of constituents for both the buyer and seller and permits contingency compensation for either side of the bargaining dyad. The model is built on the relationships inherent in a bargaining situation and illustrates at least five major types of relations that can be affected by any bargaining interaction:

1. The buyer–seller relationship might be an exchange of information and help in problem solving on the part of the seller for credit for the specific "sale" given by the buyer. Cooperation, trust, and mutual liking are variables that can develop in a

FIGURE 14.4
Exchanges in Buyer–Seller Interactions

Source: Johnson and Benton (1988).

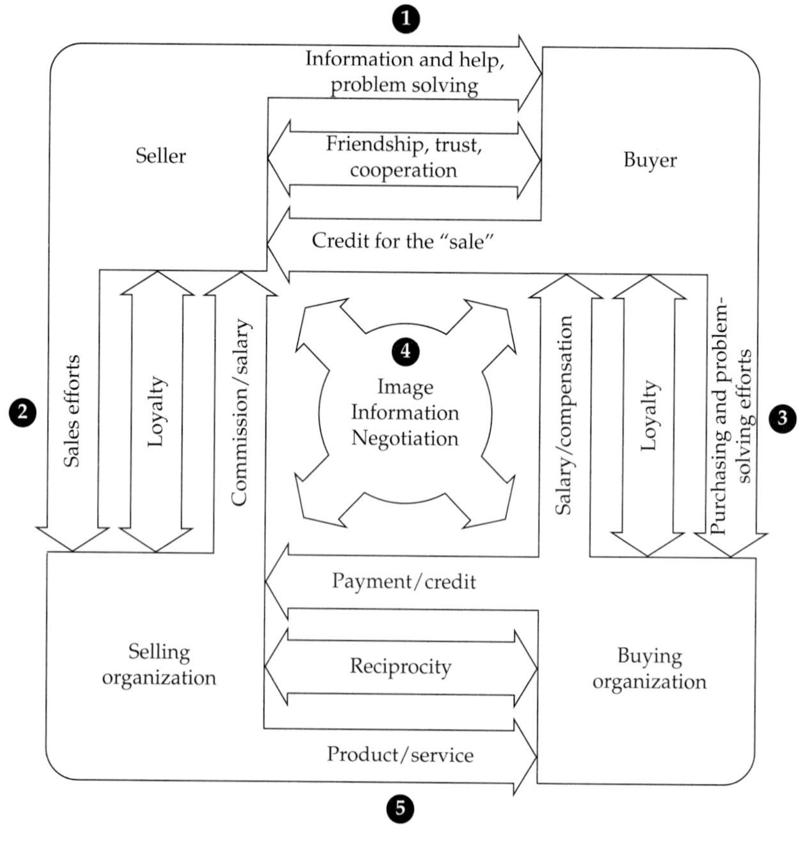

positive interaction between buyer and seller. The parties in the sales/purchasing relationship usually share some values and have mutual interests. Each may want something the other has and can give or in some way be dependent. This mutuality of interests can take the form of strategic alliances, coalitions, contract purchasing agreements, partnerships, or other relationships.

Conflict between the buyer and seller also may be a common variable. Just how conflict or disagreement over issues is resolved is a key issue for continued investigation. In situations where a long-term relationship between parties is desired, mutual problem solving may be the appropriate conflict resolution mode. In other situations of a deteriorated nature or where a "one time only" sale is sought, fraud and chicanery may be exchanged for future distrust.

The dyadic relationship will invariably exhibit social influence attempts by the seller and the buyer. These social influence attempts can involve a number of strategies including the use of promises, threats, warnings, recommendations, and/or the control of information or other cues.

2. The seller exchanges sales efforts with the selling organization for money in the form of a commission or salary. Often there are side payments such as a trip to the Bahamas for meeting a special sales quota. Recognition and praise also often are exchanged for loyalty. This dyadic relationship has received a considerable amount of research effort. Sales territory allocation, compensation systems, sales force motivation, and sales force selection and management are all aspects of this particular dyad in the model.

3. The buyer exchanges his or her talents and abilities at buying and problem-solving within his or her organization for money, usually a salary. However, buyers are sometimes rewarded in the form of a percentage of the volume of purchases, or from a cost-savings perspective. The status that an organization awards the buyer and that buyer's efforts and feelings of loyalty toward the organization are further examples of exchanges that take place between the buyer/buying organization dyad. If the rewards that the buying organization is willing to exchange with the buyer seem insufficient to the buyer, he or she may look elsewhere for more rewarding exchanges, such as by moving to another organization, or seek to increase the rewards that accrue by accepting benefits from interested sellers.

4. Images of the buying organization are held by the seller while the buyer harbors feelings and images about the selling organization. The images held by the buyer and other members of the buying organization have been examined frequently in the literature. However, the images held by the seller have received little attention. It would make sense to examine these perceptions because they determine what type of marketing approach or product characteristics the seller will emphasize to the buyer. Dyadic relations depend upon the individual actions and purposive behavior of the parties involved. The seller and the buyer both have plans, goals, set ways of behaving, and intentions they hope to satisfy. Sometimes these are the subject of negotiation. Invariably, they set restrictions on what is acceptable or not in an exchange and serve as the starting point for the interaction process. Clearly each one's image of the other helps to establish these boundaries of the purchasing interaction.

5. The primary economic exchange occurs between the buying and selling organizations where the product service is exchanged for money or credit. Reciprocal trade relations or some form of agreement may develop between the two organizations. The supply and demand parameters of each individual bargaining

situation dictate what type of interaction develops between buying and selling organizations.

Under this conceptual approach, most purchases are better viewed as negotiated settlements between all those individuals involved internally in the buying organization and those external to it (i.e., intermediate marketers, competing sellers, the government, and the general public). These interactions lead to a purchase decision that is truly some social result of those interactive forces rather than any individual response. The outcome of these interactions also has economic and psychological consequences.

Summary

This chapter examines the important human interactions called *bargaining* and *negotiation* in a setting. Bargaining occurs between individuals, groups, organizations, and countries. In this chapter, we considered bargaining between two parties, each possessing resources the other side desires. Distributed bargaining is a situation where the two parties involved are in basic conflict and competition because of a clash of goals: The more one party gets, the less the other gets. Integrative bargaining is a situation where some areas of mutual concern and complementary interest exist. The situation is a varying-sum schedule such that, by working together, both parties can increase the total profits available to be divided between them.

The distributive bargaining situation has been fully explored by psychologists. Economists, on the other hand, have spent most of their efforts examining bargaining in integrative bargaining situations.

Next, an experiment in distributive bargaining was presented to better illustrate effects of both economic and psychological aspects on the outcome of bargaining situations. The experiment examines the effect of contingency compensation on both buyers and sellers. It also allows speculation about the differences in the power system of buyers and sellers and how they affect the outcome of bargaining situations. Preparation guidelines for the negotiations process were presented.

The chapter ended with the introduction of an exchange model of buyer–seller interactions. The exchange model of buyer–seller interactions captured both the economic aspects and the surrounding psychological variables of the bargaining situation.

Discussion Questions

1. Explain how learning curve analysis is used in the negotiation process.
2. When and how is negotiation used, and what can be negotiated?
3. How do you prepare for negotiation?
4. What is meant by distributive bargaining? What is meant by integrative bargaining?
5. What is meant by psychological bargaining? What are the psychological bargaining factors?
6. Discuss the various payoff systems.
7. Discuss the characteristics of economic bargaining.

8. Discuss the rationale for the outcome of the purchasing experiment given on page 334.
9. Discuss several negotiation tactics and strategies.

Suggested Cases

AMD Construction Company: Negotiating the Old-Fashioned Way
Hoosier Pride Construction, Inc.
Pendleton Construction
The Capital State Arena
NEP: The Art and Science of Purchasing Coal

References

Bartos, O. J. "Concession Making in Experimental Negotiations." In *Sociological Theories in Progress*, vol. 1, eds. J. Berger, M. Zelditch, and B. Anderson. Boston: Houghton-Mifflin, 1966.

Bartos, O. J. "Determinants and Consequences of Toughness." In *The Structure of Conflict*, ed. P. Swingle. New York: Academic Press, 1970.

Benton, A. A. "Accountability and Negotiations between Group Representatives." *Proceedings of the 80th Annual Convention of the American Psychological Association*, 1972, pp. 227, 228.

Benton, A. A., H. H. Kelley, and B. Liebling. "Effects of Extremity of Offers and Concession Rate on the Outcomes of Bargaining." *Journal of Personality and Social Psychology* 24 (1972), pp. 73–83.

Bonoma, T. V., and W. J. Johnson. "The Social Psychology of Industrial Buying." *Industrial Marketing Management* 17 (1978), pp. 213–24.

Chertkoff, J. M., and J. K. Esser. "A Review of Experiments in Explicit Bargaining." *Journal of Experimental Social Psychology* 12 (1976), pp. 464–86.

Johnson, W., and W. C. Benton Jr., "Bargaining and Negotiations." In *The Handbook of Economic Psychology*, eds. W. F. van Raij, G. M. van Veldhoven, and K.-E. Wärneryd. Boston: Kluwer Academic Publishers, 1988.

McFillen, J., R. Reck, and W. C. Benton Jr. "An Experiment in Purchasing Negotiations." *Journal of Purchasing and Materials Management* 19 (1983), pp. 2–9.

Nash, John F. "The Bargaining Problem." *Econometrica* 18 (1950), pp. 155–62.

Neslin, Scott A., and L. Greenhalgh. "Nash's Theory of Co-operative Games as a Predictor of the Outcomes of Buyer-Seller Negotiations: An Experiment in Media Purchasing." *Journal of Marketing Research* 20 (1983), pp. 368–79.

Rubin, J. Z., and B. R. Brown. *The Social Psychology of Bargaining and Negotiation*. New York: Academic Press, 1975.

Part **Five**

Special Purchasing Applications

Chapter Fifteen

Purchasing Transportation Services

Learning Objectives

1. Understand how to purchase transportation services.
2. Discuss the changes in the transportation sector.
3. Identify the advantages and disadvantages of various transportation modes.
4. Describe how to select and evaluate the most appropriate transportation mode for specific products.
5. Know how to determine the appropriate price determination strategy for alternative transportation modes.
6. Explain how "third-party relationships" work.
7. Summarize the terms and conditions of transportation of merchandise.
8. Understand what F.O.B. means.

INTRODUCTION

Supply managers usually manage the flows of information and physical supply from the supplier to the ultimate customer. As illustrated in the purchasing transportation network of a typical manufacturing firm shown in Figure 15.1, the systems flows are impressive. In traditional systems, inventory management is a manufacturing activity. However, many Fortune 500 firms have moved to just-in-time (JIT) manufacturing, which involves scheduling receipts from suppliers so that deliveries occur just as the supplies are needed in the manufacturing process. They then produce the end product by the customer's ship date. The transportation activity associated with the traditional manufacturing process is one of the most expensive components of most manufacturing firms. With JIT systems, the transportation costs are magnified. Some of the transportation costs include such activities as selecting the mode of transportation to be used in moving a particular shipment.

Freight and transportation costs are significant for manufacturers. The frequency, product type, and size of shipments can have a significant impact on these costs. The freight and transportation services category typically includes larger volume and

FIGURE 15.1
Purchasing Transportation Network

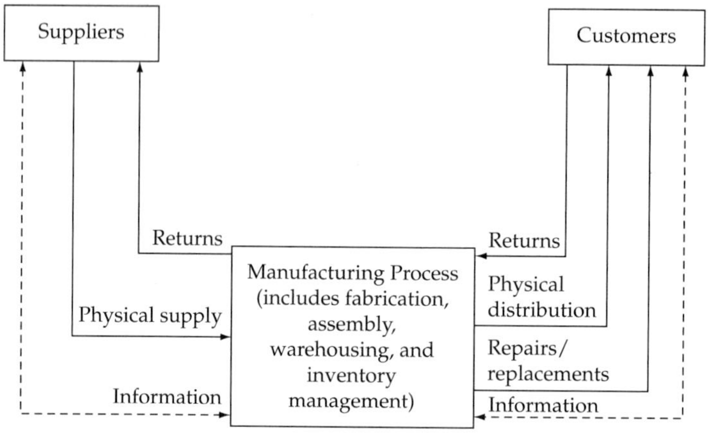

more frequent shipments, not suitable for UPS or FedEx. Service providers in this business offer the following shipping service and modes:

- Inbound/outbound freight
- LTL (less than load) shipments
- TL (truckload) shipments
- Rail
- Air
- Truck
- Ocean cargo
- Inter-modal transportation (ocean, rail, truck)

Inbound freight costs are usually a component of materials costs (e.g., F.O.B. delivered). Freight movement buying is complex, simply because there are so many alternatives. Many buying arrangements are brokered through many levels of unknown middlemen. Most of the brokers have no risk. Loads are often quoted before assets are acquired. Therefore, the markup is as high as 30–40 percent. There are many opportunities for purchasing professionals to leverage inbound and outbound freight costs by developing expertise in-house or partnering with a freight management service provider.

In 2009, transportation revenues were approximately $1.1 trillion. As can be seen in Table 15.1, the U.S. Gross Domestic Product (GDP) attributed to transportation revenue is 8.7 percent. Over-the-road transportation accounted for approximately 80 percent of the total transportation costs. In other words, a large share of the expenditures was associated with moving products from the manufacturing facility to the ultimate consumer. There are more than 50,000 private trucking fleets in the United States.

THE IMPACT OF THE NORTH AMERICAN FREE TRADE AGREEMENT (NAFTA) ON DOMESTIC TRANSPORTATION

Canada and Mexico are second and third behind China in terms of trade with the United States. The surface transportation impact between the two countries and the United States has been significant. Surface transportation between the United States and its North American Free Trade Agreement (NAFTA) partners, Canada

FIGURE 15.2
North American Freight by Mode, July 2012

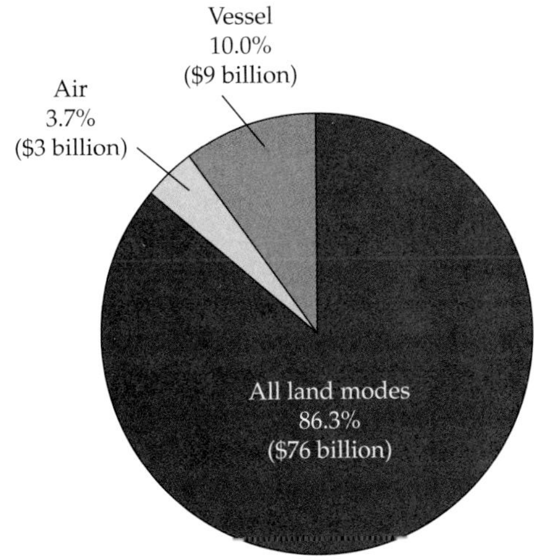

and Mexico, was 4.6 percent higher in July 2012 than in July 2011, totaling $75.7 billion. Surface transportation includes freight movements by truck, rail, pipeline, mail, Foreign Trade Zones, and other modes of transport. In July 2012, 86.3 percent of U.S. trade by value with Canada and Mexico moved via land, 10.0 percent moved by vessel, and 3.7 percent moved by air (see Figure 15.2).

U.S. trade by surface transportation with Mexico has increased at a faster pace than trade with Canada. U.S.–Canada and U.S.–Mexico surface transportation trade in July 2012 both increased compared to July 2011 with U.S.–Canada trade reaching $42.9 billion, a 1.0 percent increase, and U.S.–Mexico trade reaching $32.7 billion, a 9.7 percent increase. For trade statistics by mode, see Table 15.1 for Canada and Table 15.2 for Mexico.

The top commodity category transported between the United States and Canada by surface modes of transportation in July was oil and gas, valued at $7.9 billion (Table 15.3). Oil and gas displaced vehicles as the top commodity in July, due to auto plant retooling in July. The top commodity category transported

TABLE 15.1
U.S. Surface Transportation Trade with Canada (millions of current U.S. dollars)

Mode		July 2011	June 2012	July 2012	Percent Change June 2012–July 2012	Percent Change July 2011–July 2012
All surface modes	Imports	22,374	24,764	22,155	−10.5	−1.0
	Exports	20,138	23,630	20,792	−12.0	3.2
	Total	42,512	48,394	42,946	−11.3	1.0
Truck	Imports	10,422	12,049	10,625	−11.8	1.9
	Exports	15,304	18,080	15,558	−13.9	1.7
Rail	Imports	4,806	6,039	4,967	−17.8	3.3
	Exports	2,335	3,008	2,728	−9.3	16.8
Pipeline	Imports	6,318	5,523	5,430	−1.7	−14.0
	Exports	563	455	510	12.1	−9.3

Source: BTS TransBorder Freight Data.

TABLE 15.2
U.S. Surface Transportation Trade with Mexico (millions of current U.S. dollars)

Mode		July 2011	June 2012	July 2012	Percent Change June 2012–July 2012	Percent Change July 2011–July 2012
All surface modes	Imports	16,413	19,314	17,971	−7.0	9.5
	Exports	13,438	14,893	14,777	−0.8	10.0
	Total	29,851	34,207	32,748	−4.3	9.7
Truck	Imports	13,273	15,641	14,478	−7.4	9.1
	Exports	10,568	11,773	11,734	−0.3	11.0
Rail	Imports	2,838	3,317	3,215	−3.1	13.3
	Exports	2,053	2,274	2,083	−8.4	1.4
Pipeline	Imports	31	27	16	−41.5	−50.6
	Exports	233	220	240	8.9	3.0

Source: BTS TransBorder Freight Data.

TABLE 15.3
Top Five Commodities Transported between the United States and Canada by All Surface Modes of Transportation, July 2012 (millions of current U.S. dollars)

Commodities	Exports	Imports	Total
Oil and gas	1,091	6,869	7,960
Vehicles other than railway	3,367	3,374	6,741
Computer-related machinery and parts	3,522	1,435	4,956
Electrical machinery; equipment and parts	1,704	498	2,202
Plastics	1,112	833	1,946

Source: U.S. Department of Transportation, Research and Innovative Technology Administration, Bureau of Transportation Statistics, based on TransBorder Freight Data, as of July 20, 2012.

TABLE 15.4
Top Five Commodities Transported between the United States and Mexico by All Surface Modes of Transportation, July 2012 (millions of current U.S. dollars)

Commodities	Exports	Imports	Total
Electrical machinery; equipment and parts	2,575	4,093	6,668
Computer-related machinery and parts	2,822	3,564	6,386
Vehicles other than railway	1,606	4,309	5,915
Plastics	1,151	313	1,464
Measuring and testing instruments	385	839	1,225

Source: U.S. Department of Transportation, Research and Innovative Technology Administration, Bureau of Transportation Statistics, based on TransBorder Freight Data, as of July 13, 2012.

between the United States and Mexico by surface modes of transportation in July was electrical machinery with $6.7 billion in trade (Table 15.4).

TRANSPORTATION'S ROLE IN PURCHASING

Transportation is often the most costly and time-consuming component of purchasing management. Its planning is also critical in meeting manufacturing and customer delivery scheduling requirements. Transportation involves facilitating the movements of raw materials and component parts from suppliers through the firm's manufacturing process to the ultimate customers.

The management of the purchasing/transportation interface is complex and requires the buying organization to gain knowledge of basic transportation decision-making activities. The major activities will be presented further in this section.

Mode Selection

The initial decision requires the buying firm to select the appropriate shipment mode. Each of the modes has specific operating and cost characteristics, and the buying professional must weigh them in selecting the most appropriate transportation mode. The most basic selection decision is the trade-off between cost, reliability, and speed. The cost of shipment is usually tied to the speed of the mode. In certain situations when speed is critical, the cost of shipment becomes less important. However, under more normal operating conditions, the mode's record of on-time deliveries and service quality are more important measures of effectiveness.

In many cases, most Fortune 500 firms use a variety of transportation modes depending on their aggregate transportation needs. The "model split" is usually determined by time pressures, the product mix, the final shipment destination, and competitive market forces. The various courier choice characteristics are given in Table 15.5. The most recent statistical data for modal freight activity in the United States are presented in Table 15.7. As can be seen in Tables 15.6a, b and 15.7, freight activity for all modes increased significantly in value, tons, and ton-miles between 1993 and 2007.

Rail

The railroads provide service over an extensive physical network that includes more than 113,000 miles of rail lines and 190,500 miles of track. As can be seen in

TABLE 15.5 Characteristics of Transportation Modes

	Motor	Rail	Air	Water	Pipeline
Economics Characteristics					
Cost	Moderate	Low	High	Low	Low
Market coverage	Point-to-point	Terminal-to-terminal	Terminal-to-terminal	Terminal-to-terminal	Terminal-to-terminal
Degree of competition	Many	Few	Moderate	Few	Few
Predominant traffic	All types	Low to moderate value, moderate to high density	High value, low to moderate density	Low value, high density	Low value, high density
Average length of haul (in miles)	515	617	885	376–1,367	276–343
Equipment capacity (tons)	10–25	50–12,000	5–125	1,000–60,000	30,000–2,500,000
Service Characteristics					
Speed (time in transit)	Moderate to fast	Moderate	Fast	Slow	Slow
Availability	High	Moderate	Moderate	Low	Low
Consistency	High	Moderate	High	Low to moderate	High
Loss and damage	Low	Moderate	Low	Low to moderate	Low
Flexibility	High	Moderate	Moderate to high	Low to moderate	Low

TABLE 15.6a Shipment Characteristics by Mode of Transportation for the United States: 2007 and 2002

[Estimates are based on data from the 2007 and 2002 Commodity Flow Surveys. Because of rounding, estimates may not be additive.]

	Value			Tons			Ton-miles[1]			Average miles per shipment		
Mode of transportation	2007 (million dollars)	2002 (million dollars)	Per-centage change)	2007 (thousands)	2002 (thousands)	Per-centage change	2007 (millions)	2002 (millions)	Per-centage change	2007	2002	Per-centage change
Total	**11,684,872**	**8,397,210**	**39.2**	**12,543,425**	**11,667,919**	**7.5**	**3,344,658**	**3,137,898**	**6.6**	**619**	**546**	**13.5**
Single modes	**9,539,037**	**7,049,383**	**35.3**	**11,698,128**	**11,086,660**	**5.5**	**2,894,251**	**2,867,938**	**0.9**	**234**	**240**	**2.4**
Truck[2]	8,335,789	6,235,001	33.7	8,778,713	7,842,836	11.9	1,342,104	1,255,908	6.9	206	173	19.4
For-hire truck	4,955,700	3,757,114	31.9	4,075,136	3,657,333	11.4	1,055,646	959,610	10.0	599	523	14.6
Private truck	3,380,090	2,445,288	38.2	4,703,576	4,149,658	13.3	286,457	291,114	−1.6	57	64	−10.5
Rail	436,420	310,884	40.4	1,861,307	1,873,884	−0.7	1,344,040	1,261,612	6.5	728	807	−9.9
Water	114,905	89,344	28.6	403,639	681,227	−40.7	157,314	282,659	−44.3	520	568	−8.5
Shallow draft	91,004	57,467	58.4	343,307	458,577	−25.1	117,473	211,501	−44.5	144	450	−67.9
Great lakes	(S)	843	(S)	17,792	38,041	−53.2	6,887	13,808	−50.1	657	339	93.9
Deep draft	23,058	31,034	−25.7	42,540	184,610	−77.0	32,954	57,350	−42.5	923	664	38.9
Air (includes truck and air)	252,276	264,959	−4.8	3,611	3,760	−4.0	4,510	5,835	−22.7	1,304	1,919	−32.0
Pipeline[3]	399,646	149,195	(S)	650,859	684,953	(S)	(S)	(S)	(S)	(S)	(S)	(S)
Multiple modes	**1,866,723**	**1,079,185**	**73.0**	**573,729**	**216,686**	**164.8**	**416,642**	**225,715**	**84.6**	**975**	**895**	**8.9**
Parcel. U.S. Postal Service or courier	1,561,874	987,746	58.1	33,900	25,513	32.9	27,961	19,004	47.1	975	894	9.0
Truck and rail	187,248	69,929	167.8	225,589	42,984	424.8	196,772	45,525	332.2	1.007	1,413	−28.8
Truck and water	58,389	14,359	306.6	145,521	23,299	524.6	98,396	32,413	203.6	1.429	1,950	−26.7
Rail and water	13,892	3,329	317.3	54,878	105,107	−47.8	47,111	114,986	−59.0	1.928	957	101.5
Other multiple modes	45,320	3,822	1,085.8	113,841	19,782	475.5	46,402	13,788	236.5	1,182	(S)	(S)
Other and unknown modes	**279,113**	**268,642**	**3.9**	**271,567**	**364,573**	**−25.5**	**33,764**	**44,245**	**−23.7**	**116**	**130**	**−10.7**

(S) Estimate did not meet publication standards.

[1] Ton-miles estimates are based on estimated distances traveled along a modeled transportation network.

[2] "Truck" as a single mode includes shipments that were made by only private truck, only for-hire truck, or a combination of private truck and for-hire truck.

[3] J Estimates for pipeline exclude shipments of crude petroleum (SCTG 16).

Note: Value-of-shipments estimates have not been adjusted for price changes. Appendix B tables provide estimated measures of sampling variability. The Introduction and appendixes give information on confidentiality protection, sampling error, nonsampling error, sample design, and definitions. Links to this information on the Internet may be found at www.census.gov/cfs.

TABLE 15.6b Shipment Characteristics by Mode of Transportation for the United States: 2007

[Estimates are based on data from the 2007 Commodity Flow Survey. Because of rounding, estimates may not be additive.]

Mode of transportation	Value		Tons		Ton-miles[1]		Average miles per shipment
	2007 (million dollars)	Percentage of total	2007 (thousands)	Percentage of total	2007 (millions)	Percentage of total	
Total	**11,684,872**	**100.0**	**12,543,425**	**100.0**	**3,344,658**	**100.0**	**619**
Single modes	**9,539,037**	**81.6**	**11,698,128**	**93.3**	**2,894,251**	**86.5**	**234**
Truck[2]	8,335,789	71.3	8,778,713	70.0	1,342,104	40.1	206
For-hire truck	4,955,700	42.4	4,075,136	32.5	1,055,646	31.6	599
Private truck	3,380,090	28.9	4,703,576	37.5	286,457	8.6	57
Rail	436,420	3.7	1,861,307	14.8	1,344,040	40.2	728
Water	114,905	1.0	403,639	3.2	157,314	4.7	520
Shallow draft	91,004	0.8	343,307	2.7	117,473	3.5	144
Great Lakes	(S)	(S)	17,792	0.1	6,887	0.2	657
Deep draft	23,058	0.2	42,540	0.3	32,954	1.0	923
Air (includes truck and air)	252,276	2.2	3,611	(Z)	4,510	0.1	1,304
Pipeline[3]	399,646	3.4	650,859	5.2	(S)	(S)	(S)
Multiple modes	**1,866,723**	**16.0**	**573,729**	**4.6**	**416,642**	**12.5**	**975**
Parcel, U.S. Postal Service or courier	1,561,874	13.4	33,900	0.3	27,961	0.8	975
Truck and rail	187,248	1.6	225,589	1.8	196,772	5.9	1,007
Truck and water	58,389	0.5	145,521	1.2	98,396	2.9	1,429
Rail and water	13,892	0.1	54,878	0.4	47,111	1.4	1,928
Other multiple modes	45,320	0.4	113,841	0.9	46,402	1.4	1,182
Other and unknown modes	**279,113**	**2.4**	**271,567**	**2.2**	**33,764**	**1.0**	**116**

(S) Estimate did not meet publication standards.

(Z) Estimate is between zero and half the unit shown, thus rounded to zero.

[1] Ton-miles estimates are based on estimated distances traveled along a modeled transportation network.

[2] "Truck" as a single mode includes shipments that were made by only private truck, only for-hire truck, or a combination of private truck and for-hire truck.

[3] J Estimates for pipeline exclude shipments of crude petroleum (SCTG 16).

Note: Value-of-shipments estimates have not been adjusted for price changes. Appendix B tables provide estimated measures of sampling variability. The Introduction and appendixes give information on confidentiality protection, sampling error, nonsampling error, sample design, and definitions. Links to this information on the Internet may be found at www.census.gov/cfs.

TABLE 15.7
Transportation Shipping Modes (2007)

Mode of Transportation	2007 Value ($ millions)	2007 Tons (thousands)	2007 Ton-miles[c] (millions)
TOTAL, all modes	**11,831,503**	**13,016,610**	**3,490,806**
Single modes, total	**9,554,880**	**12,087,756**	**2,953,076**
Truck[a]	8,363,657	8,957,687	1,390,102
For-hire truck	4,764,442	4,029,016	1,011,018
Private truck	3,599,215	4,928,670	379,084
Rail	387,567	1,928,530	1,294,921
Water	106,905	423,282	175,973
Shallow draft	95,420	381,566	163,571
Great Lakes	705	13,261	4,830
Deep draft	10,779	28,455	S
Air (includes truck and air)	209,611	3,525	4,014
Pipeline[b]	487,140	774,732	S
Multiple modes, total	**1,938,884**	**626,539**	**489,767**
Parcel, U.S. Postal Service or courier	1,597,931	36,029	29,535
Truck and rail	197,748	213,411	188,547
Truck and water	31,112	74,421	48,870
Rail and water	7,744	44,979	30,444
Other multiple modes	104,350	257,698	192,372
Other/unknown modes, total	**337,739**	**302,315**	**47,964**

Key: P = preliminary; S = data are not published because of high sampling variability or other reasons.
[a]"Truck" as a single mode includes shipments that went by private truck only, for-hire truck only, or a combination of both.
[b]Excludes most shipments of crude oil.
[c]Ton-miles estimates are based on estimated distances traveled along a modeled transportation network.

Source: U.S. Department of Transportation, Statistics, and U.S. Department of Commerce Census Bureau, *2008 Commodity Flow Survey:* United States (Washington DC: December 2008).

Tables 15.6a, b and 15.7, the rail mode ranks second in terms of ton-miles. The rail service also includes more than 23,000 locomotives and 1.2 million freight cars. The Class I railroads are systems that generated more than $387.5 billion in total revenues in 2007. The Class I freight systems are shown in Table 15.8.

Burlington Northern, CSX, the Norfolk Southern, and the Southern Pacific generate 80 percent of the total railroad operating revenues in a typical year. There are also more than 520 regional and local railroads. The majority of the regional railroads have limited operations. The Class I railroads in the United States also account for approximately 75 percent of the total ton-mileage operated, and 90 percent of railroad employment and 90 percent of the operating revenues.

TABLE 15.8
Class I Freight

Source: Association of American Railroads, Policy & Economics Department. Copyright © 2008, Association of American Railroads, January 15, 2008.

- BNSF Railway
- CN Canadian National Railway
- CP Canadian Pacific Railway
- CSX Transportation
- FXE Ferrocarril Mexicano (Ferromex)
- KCS Kansas City Southern Railway
- NS Norfolk Southern
- KCSM Kansas City Southern de México (formerly TFM)
- UP Union Pacific Railroad

Deregulation has allowed the railroad carriers to integrate into other modes of transportation. CSX–Sea Land Corporation, Union Pacific–Overnite (trucking), and Norfolk Southern–North American Van Lines (trucking) are the most significant intermodal firms.

It is not unusual for several railroads serving different regions to enter into interchange agreements that allow the shipper to contract only with the originating carrier. However, the interchange process itself is time-consuming and tends to slow service.

The TTX Company, which is jointly owned by 14 railroads, operates a pool of more than 80,000 specifically equipped railroad flat cars that are used for transporting highway trailers and containers and for hauling new automobiles. The total cost structure of the railroad industry is characterized by high fixed costs. However, nearly two-thirds of the railroads' fixed costs are unrelated to volume. The railroad industry possesses a *theoretical* pricing advantage over alternative competitive modes.

The rail mode has the largest share of the ton-miles in the United States. Most bulk commodities are initially shipped by rail and later shifted to motor carriers. Rail transportation is generally less expensive than air and truck modes. Rail cargo is usually shipped from terminal to terminal; therefore, flexibility is not an attribute. The primary products shipped via rail are lumber, iron, steel, coal, automobiles, grains, and chemicals.

Truck

Federal deregulation of the trucking industry has dramatically changed not only the outcome of the trucking industry, but also how it operates. The industry is composed of a large number of for-hire and private carriers. The for-hire category includes both regulated carriers and nonregulated carriers. Approximately two-thirds of intercity truck ton-mileage is carried by private and exempt carriers. The total trucking industry revenues for 2007 were estimated to be $836.3 billion (American Trucking Association, Inc., 2008). The products carried by trucks are different from those carried by other modes. Approximately 85 percent of the tonnage originated by Class I motor carriers is manufactured goods. On the other hand, more than 80 percent of the rail tonnage consists of products of mines, forests, and agriculture. In other words, the trucking industry controls the majority of high-valued commodity movements. The trucking industry also controls the delivery of the largest portion of fresh fruit and minerals.

Class I carriers are those that generate annual operating revenues of more than $5 million; motor carriers generating between $1 and $5 million in annual operating revenue are considered Class II carriers, and those with annual operating revenues of less than $1 million are categorized as Class III carriers. There are approximately 850 Class I carriers. United Parcel Service is currently the largest Class I carrier with revenues in excess of $150 billion. The categories of products transported by Class I carriers include household goods, heavy machinery, petroleum products, motor vehicles, building materials, and hazardous materials.

General commodity carriers usually specialize in either truckload (TL) or less-than-truckload (LTL) operations. TL shipments are defined as loads in excess of 10,000 pounds. Currently, there are more than 40,000 small TL carriers. These companies have been typically low-cost and nonunion. The three largest carriers in this industry sector are Schneider National, J.B. Hunt Transport, and Werner Enterprises. The 10 largest TL carriers control approximately 30 percent of the TL market. The average TL shipment distance is 228 miles.

In comparison, the LTL business handles small shipments below 10,000 pounds. Because of the flow pattern of these shipments, each shipment is handled several times and labor costs are high. The average shipment for LTL carriers is 589 miles. There has been an increased concentration of business in the LTL sector, with approximately 150 carriers currently. The largest LTL carriers are Consolidated Freightways, Roadway Express, and Yellow Freight System. These three carriers account for two-thirds of the revenue in this sector.

UPS is the largest parcel delivery carrier. It has approximately 250,000 employees in more than 48 states. In 2007, UPS delivered more than 10.6 billion parcels and documents. To an insignificant extent, UPS has three competitors: the U.S. Postal Service, FedEx, and Roadway Package System.

Finally, there are more than 50,000 private trucking fleets in the United States. Most of the privately owned trucking companies handle local and intercity truck tonnage. A recent study revealed that one-third of all manufacturers, 75 percent of producers of construction materials, and 55 percent of food processors own private fleets.

The truck mode is used to transport a variety of perishable consumer goods, such as fresh meats, frozen meats, dairy products, baked goods, and beverages. The primary advantages of this mode are flexibility and versatility. The truck mode is the only transportation mode that can be used to ship from point to point. The competition in the trucking industry is fierce, so in order to be successful, a carrier must provide the shipper with high service and low costs.

Motor Carrier Rates and Price Competition

The average revenue per intercity ton-mile realized by motor carriers was $6 in 2007. The average rail revenue was 29.9 cents per ton-mile. These average prices are misleading when selecting one mode over another. However, it is safe to suggest that, in general, truck rates are lower than rail rates on small shipments and on high-valued commodities. In contrast, in long-haul volume movements of bulk commodities, motor carriers are typically unable to quote rail-competitive rates. The rate difference is only one dimension of a complex selection problem. For the most part, most of the rate competition is *within* the TL markets, but there is also rate competition *within* the LTL market.

There is also strong rate competition between owner-operators engaged in exempt commodity movements and railroads. Most of the owner-operators compete on a cost basis. The various levels of competition between owner-operators clearly show that they do not understand their cost structure. Irrational owner-operators will eventually go bankrupt.

Motor Carrier Services

Realizing that most shippers are interested in more than transportation, some carriers have formed third-party logistics enterprises. UPS, Yellow Freight, and Roadway Express have expanded into this market.

Just-in-time manufacturing also has resulted in a significant operating change in the general commodity carriers. Many of the firms have invested in new technology in order to foster better coordination with their customers. In addition, several of America's largest motor carriers have diversified into international operations.

Air

The domestic air cargo market in 2009 was approximately $252.2 billion, based on 4.5 billion tons carried over 40.1 billion miles. The average shipment was 10.8 pounds.

TABLE 15.9
U.S. Domestic Air Freight and Express Revenue in 2009 ($ millions)

Source: ACMG's U.S. Domestic Air Freight & Express Industry Performance Analysis, 2010.

US Domestic Air Freight and Express Revenue in 2009 ($ millions)			
Express	FedEx (including USPS support)	$ 11,520	45.5%
	UPS	$ 8,820	34.8%
	DHL	$ 120	0.5%
	USPS Express Mail	$ 850	3.4%
	Schenker/BAX Global	$ 590	2.3%
	Express subtotal	*$ 21,900*	*86.5%*
Freight	Combination carrier freight	$ 1,020	4.0%
	All-cargo carrier freight	$ 1,200	4.7%
	Freight forwarders	$ 953	3.8%
	Freight subtotal	*$ 3,173*	*12.50%*
Mail	Combination carrier mail	$ 187	0.7%
	All cargo carrier mail	$ 69	0.3%
	Mail subtotal	*$ 256*	*1.0%*
Grand total		*$ 25,329*	*100.0%*

Among the major categories moving as air freight are computer components, electronics, and fashion goods.

Integrated air cargo companies have air service–related support and handle air cargo from origin to destination. The companies with a significant presence in the market are FedEx, UPS, Airborne, DHL, and the U.S. Postal Service. As can be seen in Table 15.9, FedEx accounts for more than 45.5 percent of this market and UPS more than 34.8 percent. Only premium and emergency goods are shipped via air because air is clearly the highest-cost shipping mode. See Table 15.6b.

Air Cargo Rates and Competition

With the movement toward high customer service, air cargo has become an integral strategic weapon for firms that compete on a fast-delivery, low-inventory strategy. The average revenues per ton-mile of air cargo carriers in 2009 were $55.93 versus $6.21 for trucking and 33 cents for rail. The difference is even more impressive for the small package traffic handled by FedEx or UPS. The revenues per ton-mile for FedEx and UPS are approximately $1.11. For the most part, the competition in this mode is between UPS and FedEx.

Water Carriers

Water carriers are classified into several categories: (1) inland (such as rivers and canals), (2) lakes, (3) coastal and intercoastals, and (4) international deep sea.

American water carriers compete directly with rail and pipelines. In 2009, water carriers accounted for approximately $114.9 billion in revenues. The revenue per ton mile is 73 cents. The majority of commodities shipped via water carriers are semi-processed materials, fuel, oil, coal, chemicals, minerals, and petroleum products. Water carriers are an excellent transportation shipping mode for low-valued bulk commodities in large quantities. Speed is not a critical criterion for those raw materials.

Pipelines

Pipelines are used to transport low-valued, nonperishable products such as oil, diesel fuel, jet fuel, kerosene, and natural gas. In 2009, pipelines accounted for

$399.6 billion in revenues. A comparison of each of the transportation modes is shown in Table 15.7.

Relative Prices for Transportation Goods and Services

The United States had relatively lower prices for transportation goods and services in 2002 than did 15 out of 25 Organization for Economic Cooperation and Development (OECD) countries. (See Table 15.10.) However, the nation's top two overall merchandise trade partners, Canada and Mexico, had lower relative prices in 2002 than did the United States. Prices in Japan and the United Kingdom—both major U.S. trade partners—were much higher than in the United States. Half of the OECD countries that had less-expensive transportation goods and services than the United States are developing and transitional economies.

Carrier Selection

The choice of transportation mode is the most important element in distribution management. Selecting the incorrect transportation mode can easily jeopardize a firm's operational efficiency because it may lead to higher costs and lower service levels. Carrier selection requires careful research and numerous economic trade-offs. Transportation costs consist of all direct costs associated with the movement of a product from one location to another. In order to identify the significance of

TABLE 15.10
Relative Prices for Transportation Goods and Services for the United States and Selected Major Trade Partners: 2002

Sources: U.S. Department of Transportation, Research and Innovative Technology Administration, Bureau of Transportation Statistics; calculations based on data from Organization for Economic Cooperation and Development (OECD), *Purchasing Power Parities and Real Expenditures, Benchmark Year 2002* (Paris: OECD, 2005), table 1.11.

Country	2002
Turkey	0.82
Poland	0.95
Mexico	0.98
Greece	1.00
United States	1.00
New Zealand	1.05
Australia	1.06
Hungary	1.06
Canada	1.07
Spain	1.16
Italy	1.24
Belgium	1.25
France	1.26
Portugal	1.28
Germany	1.43
Austria	1.44
Netherlands	1.45
Japan	1.47
Ireland	1.53
Switzerland	1.55
Sweden	1.60
United Kingdom	1.61
Denmark	1.94
Norway	2.24

Note: 2002 was the most recent year for which these data were available by country at the time this report was prepared. Data are not available for goods and services separately. Relative prices are based on purchasing power parity for transportation-related goods and services.

the mode choice, it is necessary to determine the total supply costs. Total supply chain costs can vary from 1 percent (for heavy equipment) to approximately 35 percent (for perishable food products) of the recommended selling price for the specific item or product.

The most important criteria to consider for carrier selection are competitive rates, customer service, transit time reliability, pickup and delivery service, availability of equipment, loss and damage claims, electronic data interchange (EDI), geographic coverage, problem resolution, insurance coverage, and billing accuracy.

The most recent trend in the selection process is to reduce the number of carriers. The shipper gains a competitive advantage over the carrier that usually results in lower costs and higher service levels.

After the appropriate transportation mode is selected, the specific carrier within the mode must be determined. In specific markets, there may be a large variety of carriers to choose from. There also may be variation in the prices and the quality of service. Depending on the shipper's needs, the type of shipment, and the quantities, the shipper may choose to use one shipper or multiple shippers. Using multiple shippers is perhaps better than using a single shipper. By diversifying the shipments, the shipper will achieve better prices and higher service quality. When more than one carrier is used, evaluation of the carrier is easier.

Carrier Evaluation

Once a specific carrier selection is made, the buyer must routinely evaluate the performance in terms of consistency and quality of service. Some of the performance measures should include on-time deliveries, loss and damage claims, and billing accuracy. Remember, the primary objective of the buying/shipping firm is to provide for cost-effective continuous operation of the business by ensuring the availability of goods and services. In a competitive environment, the transportation function must provide delivery of undamaged goods on time and at a reasonable price. The general consensus is that on-time delivery and price are the key competitive criteria.

Rate Determination

The Rate Quotation Process

Submitting rate quotations to shippers involves a complex process. The complexity is the result of the millions of different commodities that are shipped, but also the numerous origins and destinations over which these commodities might move, as well as alternative routes that might be used in moving between any two specific origin-destination combinations.

Factors Considered in Rating Freight

There are numerous factors that are included in rate determination for a particular commodity. These factors include the following:

1. Shipping weight per cubic foot
2. Liability for damage
3. Perishability
4. Liability for damage to other commodities being transported
5. Liability for spontaneous combustion or explosion
6. Susceptibility to theft

7. Value per pound in comparison with other articles
8. Ease or difficulty in loading and unloading
9. Excessive weight
10. Excessive length
11. Care or attention necessary in loading and transporting
12. Trade conditions
13. Value of service
14. Competition with other commodities transported
15. Quantity offered as a single consignment

This list of the factors is compounded by the specific commodity that is being shipped. The basic steps involved in the determination of the applicable rates are as follows: (1) use the classification to look up the commodity being shipped and determine its rating, (2) select the appropriate tariff and determine the rate basis number that applies to the origin-destination combination of the shipment, and (3) cross-reference the rating and the rate base number in the section of the tariff that gives class rates in cents per 100 pounds shipped.

Rate Negotiation[1]

Deregulation has given carriers more pricing freedom; negotiating skills have become very important for both carriers and shippers. The carriers must become more aware of their costs and their resulting pricing strategy. Shippers also must become experts at buying transportation services. Deregulation requires that both the carrier and the shipper become better managers.

In many instances, the negotiation process in transportation has become more formalized. The larger shippers usually send out a formal request for proposals for how carriers would handle the company's traffic in specific markets. The negotiation process should be based on a win–win strategy.

Negotiation is a management process that involves planning, analysis, and reviewing. Negotiation activities are influenced by the characteristics of the current business environment, the organization, and the individuals. The environmental factors include competition, technology, and legislation. Of all the environmental factors, competition is the most important factor that the shipper controls. Competition influences the relationship between carriers and shippers. At the carrier level, there is direct competition between various carriers within a specific transportation mode. On the other hand, as competition increases in the shippers' market, increases or decreases of demand influence the level and costs of transportation services. Depending on the competitive environmental factors, the negotiators gain or lose power.

The business climate between shippers and carriers offers an *a priori* assessment of the power dependence relationship. Bargaining activities involve face-to-face meetings between the shipper and the carrier. The shipper's negotiator usually prefers meeting at the shipper's office. A day is set aside to handle all of the bidders one after another in rapid-fire fashion. This method allows the shipper to control the surroundings of the bargaining activities and gives it the ability to use power ploys as manipulative tools.

Technology also influences the transportation negotiation process. Computer technology offers shippers real-time information related to shipment tracking,

[1] For a more detailed discussion on negotiations, see Chapter 14.

equipment availability in various locations, and the ability to compare base pricing.

Shippers and carriers also must observe antitrust restrictions. They must consider the implications of legal constraints on each movement under the final contractual agreement. Moreover, most carriers demand fuel increase allowances within the terms of the contractual agreement. For a more detailed discussion on contracts, see Chapter 3.

Third-Party Relationships

There are several challenges that buyers face in order to transfer logistics activities to a third party. The decision must include all of the parties that will be affected by the third-party relationship. In some cases, the third-party logistics decision is made in the finance department and not at the operations and logistics level in the shippers' firm. Third parties are traditionally approached by either the transportation manager or the purchasing department. Because of the complexity of third-party relationships, many firms have organized transportation councils composed of individuals representing the transportation function across several sites or operating divisions. These councils combine their freight to simplify the negotiations process with third parties as well as attempt to lower freight costs. This systemwide negotiation approach has resulted in firms using fewer third parties and spending less on transportation.

In developing a negotiation strategy, the shipper must identify the type of relationship desired with the third party. As with any other buying situation, the shipper must establish a set of desires (costs) and demands (services) expected from the carrier. The first step is to prequalify a set of carriers that will be offered an opportunity to be considered as a third-party provider. Only those third parties that can meet certain minimum service levels will be offered an opportunity to negotiate.

If the shipper only requires standard third-party service but desires a longer-term relationship, the bidding process is appropriate. The shipper must carefully identify and communicate to the third-party base all data needed to describe the shipper's business and service requirements. Data must be accurate, complete, and timely because they will be used by the third party as a base for its proposal. To properly evaluate bids from several third-party providers, it is important that the bids be presented in a common format. Once a relationship between a shipper and a third party is established, an agreement, the third-party contract, should be executed by the shipper and the third party.

The scope of the operation section of the contract must be detailed and specific. Activities such as vehicle spotting, loading, and unloading should be assigned as the responsibility of one of the parties. The performance measures should be part of the agreement. Specific performance measures are transit time, pickup/delivery reliability, damage and rates, and billing accuracy. Many firms require certain indemnification clauses to be included with any third-party agreement with suppliers. The indemnification clause protects the shipper from liability caused by the action or lack of action by the third party on issues not under the control of the supplier.

Freight Consolidation

As the size of a shipment increases, the transportation charge per unit of weight will fall. To take advantage of these rate economies, the shipper should attempt to consolidate shipments. Instead of shipping each day, the shipments are accumulated for several days and then shipped.

Documentation/Tracing/Claims

Shipping documentation such as the "bill of lading," defined below, must be prepared. This serves as the basic contract between the carrier and the shipper and specifies the commodities and quantities shipped, routing, rates, and carrier liability.

Sometimes shipments must be traced with the carrier. Bar coding is usually used to track down a shipment. Loss and damage claims are a reality of life, even when dealing with highly efficient carriers. This process is time-consuming and frustrating.

Terms and Conditions of Transportation Purchasing

Freight Terms

The freight terms associated with the payment arrangements between shippers and carriers are usually misunderstood. Freight terms outline the responsibilities of the shipper and the carrier. The following definitions must be understood before entering into an agreement:

1. *Prepaid* means that the shipper owns the freight.
2. *Collect* means that the consignee owns the freight.
3. *Prepaid/collect beyond* means that there is a shipper's prepayment portion of the freight and the consignee is responsible for the balance of the payment.
4. *Third party* establishes that neither the consignor nor the consignee owns the payment process function. The legal payment function may or may not belong to the third party. The obligation is determined from the parties indicated on the bill of lading contract. Unless the payment party is a party to the bill of lading contract, it has no responsibility for payment and no legal obligation.
5. *Prepay and add* means that the shipper advances the charges to the carrier and then bills the beneficiary an amount that approximates or equals the actual freight charges.

Terms of Sale/Purchase

The terms of sale or purchase are used to identify the passage of title and are usually expressed by an **F.O.B.** designation: F.O.B. origin or F.O.B. destination.

1. **F.O.B. origin** means that the title to the merchandise passes at the time and place of pickup.
2. **F.O.B. destination** means that the title to the merchandise passes at the time and place of delivery.

Bills of Lading

Bills of lading convey the freight terms and act as both a contract for carriage and a receipt for delivery.

1. Order notify bills of lading are negotiable and are similar to letters of credit.
2. Sales/purchase orders convey the passage of title and are legal documents.

THREE TRANSPORTATION PURCHASING EXAMPLES[2]

To see how three unique segments of the economy accomplish the purchasing of transportation services, three company transportation executives were surveyed, at Ross Labs, Consolidated Stores, and Copeland Inc.

Ross Laboratories

Background

Ross Product Division was founded in 1903 by Harry Moores and Stanley Ross under the name of Moores and Ross Milk Company in Columbus, Ohio. They were the first to operate the old stand-and-drive milk truck. They were also the first to deliver milk in glass bottles to homes. In 1924 the partners made an innovative move by producing and marketing milk-based infant formula, and in 1959 the company introduced Similac with Iron infant formula.

In 1964, the company was renamed Ross Laboratories and merged with the world's largest health care company, Abbott Laboratories. Today the Ross Labs Product Division has its headquarters in Columbus, Ohio, with facilities in Ohio, Arizona, Michigan, and Virginia.

Transportation Purchasing at Ross Labs

The core carriers for Ross's transportation needs are KLLM, Martin, ROCOR, FWC, Gasel, Consolidated Freightways, UPS, and FedEx. Ross's carrier selection criteria consist of the following:

1. Service level
2. Equipment base
3. Systems capabilities
4. Cost containment and reduction programs
5. Financial stability
6. Nature of client base
7. Organizational structure
8. Regional versus national focus
9. Rates
10. Accessories
11. Accident record
12. Driver turnover

The Ross Pricing Process

The executive in charge of purchasing transportation services stated that in order for Ross to negotiate effectively, it must understand the cost drivers associated with each potential transportation mode. The carriers' proposals cannot be analyzed effectively if the carriers' cost drivers are unknown. The competitive bidding process is used exclusively for third-party carrier relationships.

Ideally, the competitive bidding process is usually more objective and will lead to lower prices. A detailed agreement is executed following the competitive bidding process.

[2] Since the time of the interviews, each of the firms has also experimented with reverse auctions.

Consolidated Stores

Background

Consolidated Stores is the nation's largest broadline closeout retailer with annual sales over $3 billion and more than 1,300 stores nationwide. In 2004, all of the store names were changed to Big Lots, Inc. The company has more than 45,000 employees. Annual sales have increased by at least 11 percent since 1991. The company opened 83 new stores and 105 new furniture departments. The company has stores in 46 states. Distribution centers are located in Columbus, Ohio; Montgomery, Alabama; Rancho Cucamonga, California; and Tremont, Pennsylvania.

Transportation Purchasing at Consolidated Stores

The core carriers for the distribution centers' needs are UPS, BNSF, CSX, NS, and KCS rail lines along with stack train operators such as Mitsui, Pacer, and K-line. The stack train operators utilize the railroad tracks, ramps, and trains. The core trucking companies are J. B. Hunt and Warner. The core drayage carriers are Total Express, BTT, We R Drayage, Golden Eagle, and Pacer Cartage. Finally, the core steamship carriers are Trailer Bridge, Crowley, Navieras, Sea Star, CSX Lines, Maesk Seal, Mitsui, Yang Ming, Hanjin, Hyundai, and P&O Nedloyd.

According to the executive in charge of purchasing transportation services, Consolidated's carrier selection criteria consist of the following:

1. Prequalification of the carrier
2. Service (transit and schedule)
3. Capacity (equipment and power availability)
4. Rate (price plus accessories)
5. Relationship (integrity, trust, and problem resolution process)

The Consolidated Pricing Process

Both electronic and conventional competitive systems are used at Consolidated. Electronic bidding is conducted via the Internet. The manual bids are conducted via requests for proposals. The bidders are required to fill in a standard spreadsheet and e-mail it to Consolidated before the deadline. The negotiation process is different for each of the transportation modes.

Consolidated attempts to secure all negotiated contracts during the lowest point in the business cycle prior to the heavy cycle. Motor carrier (drayage and highway) agreements are the easiest to negotiate because Consolidated knows their costs and the responsibilities are simplistic. Rail carriers are usually firm with their pricing structure and are not usually interested in long-term relationships. The pricing variance between competitors is insignificant. The steamline carriers are the most difficult carriers with which to negotiate. They take the attitude that if you did not need them, then why are you talking to them? Most of Consolidated's contracts range between one and five years.

Copeland Inc.

Background

Copeland was founded in 1921 by Edmund Copeland in Detroit, Michigan. Copeland manufactures scroll compressors for commercial air conditioning. The company has more than 8,000 employees and gross sales of $15.5 billion. Copeland manufactures its products in 11 countries throughout North America, Europe, and Asia.

Transportation Purchasing at Copeland

Copeland currently maintains contracts with 4 major steamship lines, 18 LTL motor carriers, 4 TL carriers, and 3 multimode carriers.

According to the executive in charge of purchasing transportation services, Copeland's carrier selection criteria consist of the following priorities:

1. Service standards
2. Geographic coverage
3. Experience
4. Price
5. Financial stability
6. Nature of client base
7. Relationship with management

The Copeland Pricing Process

The basic contract is the same for both LTL and TL carriers. However, the specific negotiating techniques are different. In the case of TL traffic, price is negotiated on lines for which the carrier is strongest. The result is usually lower cost and higher service. On the other hand, LTL traffic is negotiated based on frequency and size of shipment organized locally or regionally. The competitive quoting process at Copeland is as follows:

1. Set service criteria and expectations
2. Prequalify eligible bidders
3. Communicate with qualified bidders (expectations, values, and objectives)
4. Set the rules of engagement
5. Analyze the RFQ responses
6. Select the best service provider
7. Award contract
8. Implement program

The carriers are cautioned to submit their best pricing package first. Copeland does not like to bargain. It seeks quick win–win solutions. Carriers who do not follow the appropriate guidelines are quickly eliminated from the selection process.

Summary

The transportation activities associated with the traditional manufacturing process are one of the most expensive components of most manufacturing firms. With JIT systems, the transportation costs are magnified. Some of the transportation costs include such activities as selecting the mode of transportation to be used in moving a particular shipment.

In 2007, transportation costs were about $1.1 trillion. Over-the-road transportation accounted for approximately 80 percent of total transportation costs. In other words, a large share of the expenditures was associated with moving products from the manufacturing facility to the ultimate consumer. There are more than 50,000 private trucking fleets in the United States. Most of the privately owned trucking fleets handled both local and intercity truck tonnage.

The truck mode is used to transport a variety of perishable consumer goods, such as fresh meats, frozen meats, dairy products, baked goods, and beverages. The primary advantages of this mode are flexibility and versatility. The truck mode is the only transportation mode that can be used to ship from point to point. The competition in the trucking industry is fierce, so in order to be successful, a carrier must provide the shipper with high service and low costs.

The U.S. railroad system is extensive and generates more than $387.5 billion in annual revenues. The domestic air cargo market in 2007 was approximately $209.6 billion, based on 3.5 billion shipments. The average shipment was 10.8 pounds. Among the major categories handled by air freight are computer components, electronics, and fashion goods.

The American water carrier shipment revenues were approximately $106.9 billion in 2007. The majority of commodities shipped via water carriers are semi-processed materials, fuel, oil, coal, chemicals, minerals, and petroleum products. In 2007, pipelines accounted for $487.1 billion in revenues.

Once a specific carrier selection is made, the buyer must routinely evaluate the performance in terms of consistency and quality of service. Some of the performance measures should include on-time deliveries, loss and damage claims, and billing accuracy. In a competitive environment, the transportation function must provide delivery of undamaged goods on time and at a reasonable price. The general consensus is that on-time delivery and price are the key competitive criteria. The chapter concluded with interviews with three Fortune 500 purchasing executives.

Discussion Questions

1. What is transportation's role in purchasing? What has been the impact of deregulation?
2. List the alternative transportation modes. Give examples of each mode.
3. What transportation mode is most appropriate for shipping furniture from North Carolina to Texas? What is the most appropriate mode for shipping pharmaceuticals from Columbus, Ohio, to Los Angeles?
4. What are the important carrier selection criteria? What factors should be considered?
5. What is meant by the term *Class I freight carrier*?
6. What factors are considered when rating freight? How are rate negotiations conducted?
7. Why is the negotiation process critical to purchasing transportation services?
8. What is meant by the term *third-party relationship*?
9. What is meant by freight terms?
10. What is a bill of lading?
11. What does F.O.B. mean?

Suggested Cases

The Auction Case

Firebird Electric

Pendleton Construction, Inc.

References

American Independent Trucking Association (ATA). http://www.aitaonline.com/.

American Trucking Association. 2004 Trucking Trends. http://www.truckline.com/publicaffairs/newsreleases/archive.

American Trucking Association, Inc. *American Trucking Trends*. Arlington, VA: American Trucking Association, 2008.

Ballou, Ronald H. *Business Logistics Management*. 5th ed. Upper Saddle River, NJ: Prentice Hall, 2004.

Eno Transportation Foundation, Inc. *Transportation in America*. 11th ed. Lansdowne, VA: The Eno Transportation Foundation, 1993.

Chapter Sixteen

Equipment Acquisition and Disposal

Learning Objectives

1. Identify the issues in the capital equipment acquisition process.
2. Know the various steps in the capital equipment acquisition process.
3. Learn the three criteria applied to a cash flow analysis for equipment acquisition.
4. Describe how an economic evaluation is accomplished.
5. Discuss the role purchasing plays in capital equipment acquisitions.
6. Explain the evaluation criteria for selection.
7. Know about life cycle costing.
8. Understand how to evaluate lease-versus-buy decisions.

INTRODUCTION

The acquisition of capital equipment is a major decision in most firms. The capital acquisition decision has a significant effect on numerous aspects of the firm's financial health. The tax-planning process is also a significant component of this decision. Most high-value capital equipment purchases are usually processed at the vice president level and above. However, the purchasing professional serves a critical role in the acquisition process. In most large firms, there is usually an expert equipment buyer with expertise in a particular industry. Most of the equipment costs are pegged to industry norms. Sometimes it is more cost-effective to buy the equipment at an auction than some of the more traditional sources. The purchasing department should be familiar with these sources and continuously look for opportunities.

The acquisition of capital equipment involves the allocation and commitment of funds. These investments usually require significant expenditures and are made with the expectation that the returns will be extended over several years. The timing of these capital acquisition decisions is critical to the financial health of a firm. However, once capital investment decisions are made, they are not easily reversible.

THE CAPITAL EQUIPMENT ACQUISITION PROCESS

In Figure 16.1, a generic capital equipment acquisition process is presented. Depending on the industrial and economic environments, the process may be slightly altered. Long-term investment decisions are usually driven by the tax effect of acquiring equipment now rather than later. There are numerous steps in the acquisition process. Each cross-functional step is a subsystem of the entire process, which is closely related to a variety of other subsystems. A Department of Defense information technology example is given in Appendix A.

Department Requisition

The capital acquisition process is initiated with a department requesting equipment replacements and expansions. An example of a requisition is shown in Figure 16.2. The request is then measured against *the organization's goals.*

This step requires the authorization of the plant manager, the superintendent, or the executive in charge of the department.

The requisition process is sometimes initiated by a "wish list," low-cost projection, or special appropriation for major acquisitions. Sometimes firms place a monetary limit upon acquisition that can be made without special approval. As an example, IBM places a limit of $25,000 for general acquisitions. Capital purchases in excess of $25,000 require the plant manager's or superintendent's approval. Typical policies might allow a department to purchase computer equipment or a compressor in the regular course of business whereas a request for an automobile or tractor would have to first be recommended by the plant manager or superintendent. This process has a built-in control mechanism.

Company Goals And Objectives

The next step in the process is to compare the acquisition request with the overall long-run objectives of the firm. These objectives will be the basis for evaluating proposals for new equipment and making selections. The objectives of the company are important because the purchase of any major equipment will probably affect the capacity and the methods of the company for many years in the future. Company goals may be slightly different across organizations, but all *for-profit* organizations must eventually maximize profitability.

New Project Ideas

In any progressive firm, the various departments usually provide a continuous stream of attractive capital equipment opportunities. Each manager for the requesting department must spend many hours brainstorming, analyzing, and carefully planning for equipment needs. The classification of the various capital equipment requests must be based on certain common characteristics. Although equipment classification varies from company to company, capital projects are frequently grouped according to the following categories:

- Replacements
- Expansion (new products)
- Expansion (existing products)
- Other (heating system for plant)
- Other (new construction)
- Other (renovation)

FIGURE 16.1
The Equipment Acquisition Process

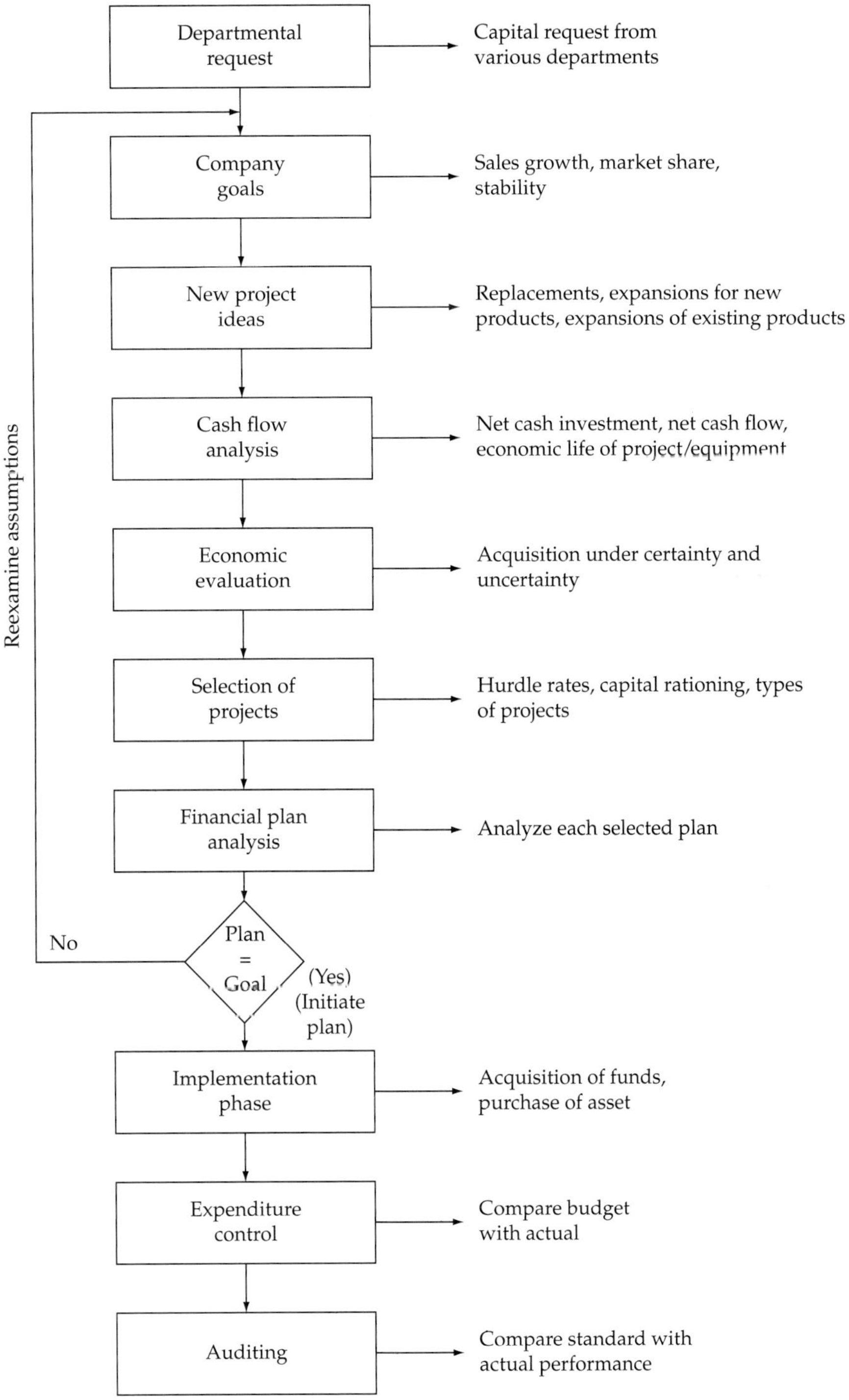

FIGURE 16.2 DOD Industrial Plant Equipment Requisition Form

DOD INDUSTRIAL PLANT EQUIPMENT REQUISITION	REQUISITION NUMBER	*Form Approved OMB No. 0704-0246 Expires Feb 28, 2006*

The public reporting burden for this collection of information is estimated to average 1.5 hours per response, including the time for reviewing instructions, searching existing data sources, gathering and maintaining the data needed, and completing and reviewing the collection of information. Send comments regarding this burden estimate or any other aspect of this collection of information, including suggestions for reducing the burden, to Department of Defense, Washington Headquarters Services, Directorate for Information Operations and Reports (0704-0246), 1215 Jefferson Davis Highway, Suite 1204, Arlington, VA 22202-4302. Respondents should be aware that notwithstanding any other provision of law, no person shall be subject to any penalty for failing to comply with a collection of information if it does not display a currently valid OMB control number.

PLEASE DO NOT RETURN YOUR FORM TO THIS ADDRESS. RETURN COMPLETED FORM TO
DEFENSE SUPPLY CENTER RICHMOND, ATTN: JH, 8000 JEFFERSON DAVIS HIGHWAY, RICHMOND, VA 28297-5100

SECTION 1 - ITEM DESCRIPTION

1. COMMODITY CODE	2. MANUFACTURER	3. MODEL NUMBER

4. STOCK NUMBER	5. POWER CODE	6. ESTIMATED COST	7. PHYSICAL INSPECTION REQUIRED *(X one)* ☐ YES ☐ NO	8. PROCUREMENT SPECIFICATION ATTACHED *(X one)* ☐ YES ☐ NO

9. DESCRIPTION

CONTINUED UNDER REMARKS SECTION ☐ YES ☐ NO

SECTION II - ROUTING AGENCY/FACILITY/CONTRACTOR

10. NAME AND ADDRESS *(Include ZIP Code)*	11. CONTRACT NUMBER	12. DATE *(YYYYMMDD)*	13. COMMAND CODE
	14. PROGRAM *(X one)* ☐ MILITARY ☐ CONTRACTOR		

15. INTENDED USE	16. DATE ITEM REQUIRED AT DESTINATION *(YYYYMMDD)*	17. DATE CERT. N/A REQUIRED *(YYYYMMDD)*	18. PRIORITY

19. BASIS FOR AUTHORIZATION *(X one)* ☐ PRODUCTION ☐ MOBILIZATION ☐ REPLACEMENT	20. PROCUREMENT PLANNED *(X one)* ☐ YES ☐ NO *(if "YES," cite Appropriation)*	21. REBUILD/OVERHAUL CANDIDATE ☐ YES
22. TYPED NAME AND TITLE OF REQUESTING OFFICIAL	23. SIGNATURE OF REQUESTING OFFICIAL	24. DATE *(YYYYMMDD)*

25. CERTIFICATION OF NEED BY ADMINISTERING ACTIVITY	a. ADMINISTERING OFFICE CODE	
b. NAME AND ADDRESS *(Include ZIP Code)*	c. TYPED NAME AND SIGNATURE OF PRODUCTION REPRESENTATIVE	d. DATE *(YYYYMMDD)*
	e. SIGNATURE OF ADMIN. CONTRACTING OFFICER	f. DATE *(YYYYMMDD)*

SECTION III - APPROVAL AUTHORITY

26. NAME AND ADDRESS *(Include ZIP Code)*	27. TITLE, SYMBOL AND TELEPHONE NO. OF APPROVING OFFICIAL	
	28. TYPED NAME & SIGNATURE OF APPROVING OFFICIAL	29. DATE *(YYYYMMDD)*

SECTION IV - ALLOCATION AND AUTHORITY TO INSPECT *(To be completed by DSCR)*

30. COMMODITY CODE	31. I.D./GOVERNMENT TAG NUMBER	32. DESCRIPTION *(See attached copy of DD Form 1342, dated)*

33. PRESENT LOCATION *(Name, address and ZIP Code)*	34. SHIPPED TO *(Name, address and ZIP Code)*

35. ESTIMATED TIME REQUIRED FOR SHIPMENT FROM DATE OF ACCEPTANCE *(Enter number of days)*

a. AS IS CONDITION	b. TEST REQUIRED	c. REPAIR REQUIRED	d. REPAIR/OVERHAUL REQUIRED	e. STANDARD ATTACHMENTS REQUIRED

36. TYPED NAME AND SIGNATURE OF ALLOCATING OFFICIAL	37. DATE *(YYYYMMDD)*	38. DATE OFFER EXPIRES *(YYYYMMDD)*

SECTION V - NON-AVAILABILITY CERTIFICATE *(To be completed by DSCR)*

39. The item described in Section 1 of this form has been screened by DSCR against the idle inventory of the Department of Defense and it is hereby certified as not available or cannot be delivered on or before the date specified in Section II *(Item 16)*. Procurement action resulting from this Certification of Non-Availability must be initiated within 45 calendar days of the date included in this Section *(Item 42)* or complete rescreening is required. Equipment offered by DSCR in Section IV must be considered if the supplier cannot deliver new equipment before expiration of the period specified in Section IV (Item 35).

40. TYPED NAME AND SIGNATURE OF CERTIFYING OFFICIAL	41. DATE CERTIFICATE ISSUED *(YYYYMMDD)*	42. DATE CERTIFICATE EXPIRES *(YYYYMMDD)*	43. CERTIFICATE NUMBER

DD FORM 1419, JUN 2003 PREVIOUS EDITION IS OBSOLETE.

SECTION VI - CERTIFICATE OF ACCEPTANCE							
44. THE ITEM ALLOCATED IN SECTION IV OF THIS FORM *(X as applicable)*							
	a. HAS BEEN PHYSICALLY INSPECTED AND IS ACCEPTABLE				b. IS ACCEPTABLE WITHOUT PHYSICAL INSPECTION		
	c. IS ACCEPTED UNDER ONE OF THESE CONDITIONS:						
	(1) AS IS CONDITION		(2) REPAIR REQUIRED		(3) TEST REQUIRED		(4) REBUILD/OVERHAUL REQUIRED
	(5) OTHER						
	d. IS NOT ACCEPTABLE *(A complete description of conditions making item unacceptable must be stated under REMARKS below)*						
45. TYPED NAME TITLE OF CERTIFYING OFFICIAL				46. SIGNATURE OF CERTIFYING OFFICIAL		47. DATE *(YYYYMMDD)*	

SECTION VII - SPECIAL SHIPPING INSTRUCTIONS		
48. SHIP TO *(Include ZIP Code)*		49. FOR TRANSSHIPMENT TO *(Include ZIP Code)*
50. MARK FOR		
51. APPROPRIATION CHARGEABLE FOR		d. PAYING OFFICE/ACTIVITY NAME AND ADDRESS *(Include ZIP Code)*
a. PACKING/CRATING/HANDLING		
b. TRANSPORTATION		
c. OTHER		
52. SPECIAL DISTRIBUTION OF SHIPPING DOCUMENTS AND OTHER INSTRUCTIONS		

SECTION VIII - REMARKS
53. REMARKS

DD FORM 1419 (BACK), JUN 2003

The *replacement* of old equipment is usually motivated by a need to increase quality, reduce operating expense, and provide more efficiency. The company can easily do an in-depth cost savings and efficiency study. Companies on a growth pattern fueled by technology acquire new equipment to expand into a *newly introduced product line*. Investment in capital equipment for expansion purposes should increase incremental revenue. Sometimes firms are interested in expanding the output of *existing product* lines, which is usually an alternative to replacing the current equipment. Expanding existing equipment is also a way to increase output. The other categories of capital investment revolve around the plant, facilities, and construction. As an example, the capital acquisition process for construction projects must follow a well-designed process of specification, construction bid process, contractor selection, and the actual construction phase. This process is guided by well-defined planning and scheduling methods. The construction acquisition team usually includes personnel from engineering, finance, management, and purchasing. As can be seen, this is an excellent example of a cross-functional purchasing strategy.

Cash-Flow Analysis

If a capital equipment request survives the new project ideas step, cash-flow estimates must be considered for each capital investment idea. The after-tax cash inflows and outflows of each capital project alternative must be evaluated on an incremental cash-flow basis. Three criteria should apply to the cash-flow analysis:

- The net cash investment
- The net cash flow
- The economic life of the project

In other words, we must consider net cash outlays and the total implementation costs. Net cash flows are net economic benefits generated by an investment project. The net incremental cash flows should be measured. The economic life of the project versus the physical life of the project also must be considered.

The U.S. Department of Defense uses a concept called "life cycle costing." Life cycle costing is an evaluation method used to evaluate alternative capital acquisitions based on the total cost of the equipment over the expected life of the product. The total cost components are given below:

1. Research
2. Development
3. Production
4. Operation
5. Maintenance

There are numerous testimonials regarding the use of life cycle costing for both capital equipment and systems acquisition. Consider a trucking firm that currently spends an average of $363 per month to maintain each vehicle. Recently the firm purchased 10 trucks by competitive bidding using the life cycle costing concept. The average monthly maintenance cost for the new trucks is $195 per unit for the life of the vehicles. The total operating costs also will have a significant effect on the capital acquisition. Productivity, dependability, and durability are the principal operating variables that must be investigated.

Economic Evaluation

With cash-flow data in hand, the company can begin the formal process of evaluating capital equipment or projects. The five most commonly used methods for an economic evaluation of individual projects are payback, average rate of return, net present value, internal rate of return, and profitability index. Each of these methods measures the financial performance of each of the capital projects. There should be a predetermined required rate of return. To illustrate the concept of economic evaluation, consider the following example.

Suppose a hospital considering investing in a new heart pump assumes that the complete stream of estimated after-tax cash flows (EATCF) is as follows:

Year	0	1	2	3	4
EATCF ($)	−100,000	40,000	40,000	30,000	30,000

These data will be used to illustrate the five economic evaluation criteria.

Payback

Payback is the best-known investment criterion. Payback is the number of years it takes to repay the initial investment. Using the example above

$$\text{Payback} = 40{,}000 \text{ (year 1)} + 40{,}000 \text{ (year 2)} + 20{,}000 \text{ (.67 of year 3)} = 2.67 \text{ years}$$

given that the cash flows are constant and positive. Suppose the maximum payback period is set equal to three years. Then, in the example problem, the project is a candidate for acceptance. On the other hand, if the standard payback period was two years, the project would be rejected.

Average Rate of Return

The average rate of return is the average cash flow after tax divided by the initial investment:

$$\text{Average rate of return} = \text{ARR} = (\Sigma \text{ EATCF/Economic life})/\text{Initial investment}$$

$$\begin{aligned}\text{ARR} &= [(40{,}000 + 40{,}000 + 30{,}000 + 30{,}000)/4]/100{,}000 \\ &= 35\%\end{aligned}$$

If ARR > the required ARR, accept project.

If ARR < the required ARR, reject project.

This method ignores timing of the cash flows. What if most of the $140,000 in the example problem was all lumped into one year? The ARR would still be 35 percent. The ARR is the most popular evaluation criterion used today.

Net Present Value

The net present value recognizes that a dollar today is worth more than a dollar tomorrow, simply because the dollar today can be invested to start earning interest immediately. Net present value (NPV) is concerned with netting the initial investment, which is negative, and the present value of the subsequent EATCF, most of which are usually positive.

$$\text{NPV} = \sum_{t=0}^{n} \frac{\text{EATCF}}{(1 + k)^t}$$

where

k = Project's required rate of return

m = Number of periods

For the example problem

$$\text{NPV} = \sum -100{,}000 + \frac{40{,}000}{1+k} + \frac{40{,}000}{(1+k)^2} + \frac{30{,}000}{(1+k)^3} + \frac{30{,}000}{(1+k)^4}$$

Year	0	1	2	3	4
EATCF	<100,000	40,000	40,000	30,000	30,000
Discount factor	1,000	0.909	0.826	0.751	0.683
Present value	−100,000	36,360	33,040	22,530	20,490

$k = 10\%$

$$\text{NPV} = -100{,}000 + 36{,}360 + 33{,}040 + 22{,}530 + 20{,}490 = 12{,}420$$

The investment decision is as follows:

If NPV > 0, accept project.

If NPV < 0, reject project.

Notice that the difference between the ARR and NPV methods is the timing of the various EATCF cash flows. In other words, if the EATCF increases, the project becomes increasingly more attractive.

Internal Rate of Return

The internal rate of return rule (IRR) is to accept the investment project if the opportunity cost of capital is less than the internal rate of return. If the cost of capital is equal to the IRR, the project has zero NPV. On the other hand, if the cost of capital is greater than the IRR, the project has a negative NPV. The IRR will give the same answer as the NPV. The IRR is defined as the discount rate that will make the NPV of the project equal zero.

$$\sum_{t=0}^{m} \frac{\text{EATCF}}{(1+\text{IRR})^t} = 0$$

As an example, find

$$\sum -100{,}000 + \frac{40{,}000}{(1+\text{IRR})^1} + \frac{40{,}000}{(1+\text{IRR})^2} + \frac{30{,}000}{(1+\text{IRR})^3} + \frac{30{,}000}{(1+\text{IRR})^4} = 0$$

For a discount rate of 20 percent, the NPV= –$7,060.

Using a trial-and-error approach, the IRR can be determined. If the EATCF was $40,000 for each of the four years, the IRR would be approximately 22 percent. Since the EATCF for the last two years is $30,000 per year, the discount rate should be decreased. We calculated a negative NPV of −$7,060 at a 20-percent discount rate; thus, we must lower the discount rate, say to 16-percent. At a 16-percent discount rate the NPV = $138.9. Thus, the IRR is approximately 16 percent.

If IRR > k, accept project.

If IRR < k, reject project.

where

k = Required rate of return

m = Number of periods

If it is assumed that the cost of capital is 10 percent, the project will be accepted.

Profitability Index

The profitability index (PI) is defined as the present value of future flows divided by the initial investment:

$$PI = \left[\sum_{t=1}^{m} \frac{EATCF_t}{(1+k)^t}\right] / \text{Initial investment}$$

Since the future cash flows are typically positive,

$$PI = \left[\frac{40{,}000}{1.10} + \frac{40{,}000}{(1.10)^2} + \frac{30{,}000}{(1.10)^3} + \frac{30{,}000}{(1.10)^4}\right] / 100{,}000$$

$$= (36{,}360 + 33{,}040 + 22{,}530 + 20{,}490)/100{,}000$$

$$= 110{,}243/100{,}000 = 1.12$$

The decision rule is as follows:

If PI > 1, accept project (*ceteris paribus*).

If PI < 1, reject the project (*ceteris paribus*).

Like the NPV and IRR methods, the PI method accounts for timing.

Selection

The final selection is usually based on the accept–reject decision. The hurdle rate may be based on the cost of capital, the opportunity cost, and other conceptual standards. As in any case, each proposal must compete for limited funds. The evaluations discussed above are summarized in Figure 16.3.

FIGURE 16.3 Capital Acquisition Evaluation Methods

Method	Good Features	Bad Features
Payback	Easily understood Easy to calculate Provides a crude risk screen	Doesn't account for the time value of money of prepayback cash flows Completely ignores past-payback cash flows
ARR	Easily understood Easy to calculate Considers past-payback cash flows	Doesn't account for the time value of money of any of the cash flows
NPV	Relatively easy to calculate Best method for mutually exclusive ranking problems Tied for best method for accept–reject decision problems (with PI)	Hard to understand May not work well in capital rationing problems
IRR	Easily understood Has intuitive economic meaning Works okay on simple accept–reject problems, which are most common investment problems	Can be tedious to calculate May not work well on nonsimple accept–reject problems (multiple rates), mutually exclusive choices, or capital rationing problems
PI	Relatively easy to calculate Best method for one-period capital rationing problems Tied for best method for accept–reject decision problems (with NPV)	Hard to understand May not work well in some mutually exclusive choice situations

Financial Plan Analysis

At this stage, a comprehensive comparison of the selected alternatives is performed. The planned project selections are then measured against the initial company goals and objectives. Capital equipment acquisitions can be financed in a variety of ways. For the purpose of the purchasing professional, two methods will be considered: traditional loans and leases. The leasing method has become very popular in the last 20 years and can be used to finance nearly any kind of fixed asset. The lease-versus-purchase decision usually requires many considerations. Some of these considerations are listed below:

- *Tax effect*. Lease payments are expenses that can be written off against income immediately. Loans are depreciated over a longer period of time. One major advantage of leases over loans is the impact leases have on land use. When a firm leases land for its operations, it can easily deduct the lease expense for the income burden. Purchased land, on the other hand, cannot be deducted from tax obligations.
- *Effects on future financing*. Leasing versus purchasing also can free up cash needed for other purposes or alternative projects. There is also a positive balance sheet effect of leasing simply because the lease is not considered a debt or an asset. A leasing arrangement can actually increase a firm's borrowing capacity. Most loans require the borrower to place a reasonable down payment. Leases generally do not require an initial down payment, beyond the first and last monthly payments.
- *Risk of obsolescence*. In the case of fast-moving technology, it is possible for the lessee to shift the risk level to the lessor. Computer technology is a good example of the risk of obsolescence.
- *Salvage value*. The lessor is responsible for the salvage value of the leased assets. If expected salvage value is high for leased equipment, the cost of ownership to the lessee may be lower. In this case, the lessee should write a contract that will enable it to buy the fixed asset at the end of the lease term.
- *Maintenance*. In most lease agreements, the responsibilities and risks for each party are spelled out in detail. If the lessor assumes the costs of maintenance, insurance, and taxes, it will usually pass the expense to the lessee in the form of increased lease payments.
- *Discount rate*. The after-tax borrowing rate is commonly known as the discount rate. Both leasing and buying involve cash outflow over an extended period. Since the lease payment is fixed and other costs associated with the lease (salvage value, operating expenses, and interest rates) are highly uncertain, it is important to evaluate the implicit interest rate for a lease-versus-buy decision.

Equipment Leasing

The lessor (owner) receives a series of monthly, semi-annual, or annual payments from a lessee who promises to pay for the use of a specific piece of capital equipment. When the lease period ends, the leased equipment goes back to the lessor. However, the lease agreement does in most cases give the lessee (equipment user) the option to purchase the equipment for or initiate a new lease. *Operating leases* are short-term leases that can be cancelled during the contract period. Operating leases make it possible for a company to use assets such as computers, company vehicles, and furniture. The lease term is usually shorter than the life of the asset.

On the other hand, capital leases cannot be cancelled during the lease period without a significant penalty. *Financial leases* represent a source of financing for companies that require positive cash flows during the lease period. It is like borrowing money from the bank. The lessee is legally bound to making the payments specified in the lease agreement. Thus, the equipment acquisition is to lease, borrow, or buy the equipment in question.

Lease versus Borrow and Purchase

The lease-versus-buy decision can be made quickly for some companies. There is a tax advantage if the leasing company has a high tax liability; thus, buying equipment and leasing it to contractors is a profitable business. Since the equipment still must be used on construction projects, the company leases the equipment it owns to contractors. A detailed tutorial on the lease-versus-purchase decision is presented in Appendix B.

Implementation

The implementation stage is the process in which companies encumber funds for accepted projects. The approval process usually ends with the board of trustees. This stage in the process is basically a rubber stamp.

Expenditure Control

The time between approval of the capital and completion of the acquisition is the critical scheduling stage. At this stage, the project should stay within budget, and corrective action should be taken if the budget is violated.

Auditing

The capital acquisition process is complex and leads to many assumptions and estimates. The entire project should be audited to analyze the differences. The audit stage also will identify mismanagement and flaws in the process. If the process has been unsatisfactory, it should be revised or replaced.

Disposal of Capital Equipment

The disposal of capital equipment is becoming more complicated. The Environmental Protection Agency has developed specific guidelines for disposing of specific types of obsolete equipment. The purchasing function is usually charged with the task of scrapping or selling retired equipment. In some cases, the business is able to trade in the obsolete equipment for new purchases. This clearly transfers the burden to the vendor. If the equipment is usable, there may be an active dealer that may purchase the used equipment. In general, most firms have not yet designed a clean process for the disposal of used equipment.

PURCHASING NEW VERSUS USED CAPITAL EQUIPMENT

Despite today's competitive markets, it may not be cost-effective to procure new equipment. Depending on the purpose and expected use of the purchased equipment, it may be more cost-effective to buy used equipment. In this section, the guidelines for purchasing new versus used equipment will be established.

New Equipment Purchases

When a company buys new equipment, there is no uncertainty regarding the conformance to stated specifications. The buying firm must first determine the number of hours per year the equipment will be employed. The buyer must be careful to pay close attention to the theoretical usage levels of certain equipment. As an example, the life expectancy of construction equipment is easy to predict given the normal operating conditions. Most construction equipment is usually purchased new. In cases where significant demand or uses already exist for a particular piece of equipment, the purchase of new equipment is appropriate. The technological advantages of new equipment also may increase productivity in these situations. In the case of computers, copiers, and other high-tech products, it may be more cost-effective to purchase new equipment. However, if an older model is adequate for the expected use, significant savings could occur.

Remember, new equipment requires less maintenance than used equipment. This is perhaps the strongest argument for considering only new equipment. As an example, after a backhoe is used for more than 10,000 hours, a new $10,000 bucket is usually required. The maintenance record must be considered when deciding to buy used equipment.

Specifications must be carefully considered when purchasing major equipment. It is an easy task to compare new equipment. It is next to impossible to compare different models of used equipment. Sometimes low equipment prices may lead to purchasing equipment that is ready to be scrapped. However, if the used equipment dealer is willing to give you a reasonable warranty and other guarantees, purchasing a specified piece of equipment may be justified.

Used Equipment Purchases

Low cost is usually the only reason to buy used equipment. The determination of the true value of used equipment is extremely difficult. A review of the historical maintenance record should be the first step in the acquisition of used equipment. In some cases, used equipment may provide a good short-term solution to a company's production problems. The buying company also must consider the trade-off between long-term financing costs and short-term maintenance costs. In this case, financial efficiency is more important than maintenance costs. Thorough inspection *must* be performed when buying used equipment. As we all know, used car dealers are experts when it comes to cleaning and painting severely damaged vehicles. Some used equipment dealers will do whatever it takes to mislead an unsuspecting buyer. The selling terms are usually "as is" and net cash with no warranty.

Summary

In most companies, the acquisition of capital equipment is a major decision that requires the attention of high-level executives. However, capital equipment acquisition is a specialized function for the purchasing department.

A step-by-step capital acquisition process is given. The steps are based on (1) requisition, (2) company objectives, (3) new product ideas, (4) cash-flow analysis, (5) an economic evaluation, (6) a financial plan analysis, and (7) expenditure control. Next, an extensive lease-versus-buy decision was discussed and illustrated.

When does it make more sense to buy capital equipment? When does it make more sense to lease? A detailed tutorial of a construction industry lease-versus-buy decision is given in Appendix B. The chapter concluded with a discussion of used versus new equipment purchases.

Discussion Questions

1. What role does purchasing play in capital equipment purchasing?
2. Discuss the various steps in the capital equipment acquisition process.
3. Explain the concepts underlying (a) payback analysis, (b) average rate of return, (c) net present value, (d) internal rate of return, and (e) profitability indexes.
4. Discuss the reasons why a company may want to invest in new equipment instead of used equipment.
5. What are the advantages and disadvantages of leasing as a financing option?
6. What are the evaluation criteria for the lease-versus-buy decision?

Exercises

16.1 The SBX Construction Company is considering an investment of $50,000 for a horizontal boring machine. There is no increase in working capital requirements and no tax credits. Depreciation is straight line and the salvage value is zero. The tax rate is 40 percent and the required IRR is 15 percent. Cash operating costs are $10,000 a year. Cash operating revenues are $30,000 per year. The estimated life of the boring machine is five years.

a. Determine the EATCF stream.

b. Determine NPV at 10 percent for the equipment investment.

c. Determine the IRR for the investment.

d. Is the boring machine a desirable investment? Explain your answer in a memo to the project manager.

16.2 *a.* What is the payback period on each of the following projects?

	Cash Flows ($)				
Project	**C0**	**C1**	**C2**	**C3**	**C4**
A	−50,000	+10,000	+10,000	+30,000	0
B	−10,000	0	+10,000	+20,000	+30,000
C	−50,000	+10,000	+10,000	+30,000	+50,000

b. Given that you wish to use the payback rule with a cutoff period of two years, which projects would you accept?

c. If the opportunity cost of capital is 10 percent, which projects have positive NPVs?

16.3 *a.* Calculate the net present value of the following project for discount rates of 0, 50, and 100 percent.

Cash Flow($)		
Year 1	**Year 2**	**Year 3**
−7,645	4,670	19,302

b. What is the IRR of the project?

16.4 The Morningside Hospital has the following investment opportunities, but only $100,000 available for investment. Which projects should it take?

Project	NPV	Investment
1	10,000	20,000
2	15,000	15,000
3	20,000	100,000
4	25,000	70,000
5	25,000	85,000
6	13,000	25,000

16.5 The Tremont Company has received a proposal for a four-year financial lease. The cash flows are given in the table below:

Year	0	1	2	3
Lease cash flow	+62,000	−26,800	−22,200	−17,600

These flows reflect the cost of the machine, depreciation tax shield, and the after-tax lease payments. Ignore salvage value. Assume the firm could borrow at 10 percent and faces a 35-percent marginal tax rate.

a. What is value of the equivalent loan?

b. What is the value of the lease?

c. Suppose the machine's NPV under normal financing is $5000. Should Tremont invest? Should Tremont sign the lease?

Suggested Cases

AMD Construction: Negotiating the Old-Fashioned Way
Firebird Electric, U.S.
Sage Imaging Center, Inc.
Tom and Jerry Construction

Appendix A

Federal Acquisition Regulation; Electronic and Information Technology[1]

DEPARTMENT OF DEFENSE
GENERAL SERVICES ADMINISTRATION
NATIONAL AERONAUTICS AND SPACE ADMINISTRATION
48 CFR Parts 2, 7, 10, 11, 12, and 39
[FAC 97-27; FAR Case 1999-607]
RIN 9000-AI69

Federal Acquisition Regulation; Electronic and Information Technology Accessibility

AGENCIES: Department of Defense (DoD), General Services Administration (GSA), and National Aeronautics and Space Administration (NASA).

ACTION: Final rule.

SUMMARY: The Civilian Agency Acquisition Council and the Defense Acquisition Regulations Council (Councils) have agreed on a final rule amending the Federal Acquisition Regulation (FAR) to implement Section 508 of the Rehabilitation Act of 1973. Subsection 508(a)(3) requires the FAR to be revised to incorporate standards developed by the Architectural and Transportation Barriers Compliance Board (also referred to as the "Access Board").

DATES: *Effective Date:* June 25, 2001.

Applicability Date: For other than indefinite-quantity contracts, this amendment applies to contracts awarded on or after the effective date. For indefinite-quantity contracts, it is applicable to delivery orders or task orders issued on or after the effective date.

FOR FURTHER INFORMATION CONTACT: The FAR Secretariat, Room 4035, GS Building, Washington, DC 20405, (202) 501-4755, for information pertaining to status or publication schedules. For clarification of content, contact Ms. Linda Nelson, Procurement Analyst, at (202) 501-1900. Please cite FAC 97-27, FAR case 1999-607.

SUPPLEMENTARY INFORMATION

A. Background

The Workforce Investment Act of 1998, Public Law 105-220, was enacted on August 7, 1998. Title IV of the Act is the Rehabilitation Act Amendments of 1998. Subsection 408(b) amended section 508 of the Rehabilitation Act of 1973 (29 U.S.C. 794d). Subsection 508(a)(1) requires that when Federal departments or agencies develop, procure, maintain, or use Electronic and Information Technology (EIT), they must ensure that the EIT allows Federal employees with disabilities to have access to and use of information and data that is comparable to the access to and use of

[1] As published at *Federal Register* 66, no. 80 (April 25, 2001), pp. 20894-96.

information and data by other Federal employees. Section 508 also requires that individuals with disabilities, who are members of the public seeking information or services from a Federal department or agency, have access to and use of information and data that is comparable to that provided to the public without disabilities. Comparable access is not required if it would impose an undue burden.

Subsection 508(a)(2)(A) required the Access Board to publish standards setting forth a definition of BIT and the technical and functional performance criteria necessary for accessibility for such technology by February 7, 2000. Subsection 508(a)(3) required the Federal Acquisition Regulatory Council to revise the FAR to incorporate the Access Board's standards not later than 6 months after the Access Board regulations were published. The Access Board published the final standards in the *Federal Register* at 65 FR 80500, December 21, 2000.

A proposed rule to amend the FAR was published in the *Federal Register* at 66 FR 7166, January 22, 2001. The 60-day comment period ended March 23, 2001.

This final rule implements the Access Board's regulations by—

- Including the definition of the term "electronic and information technology," a term created by the statute;
- Incorporating the EIT Standards in acquisition planning, market research, and when describing agency needs; and
- Adding a new Subpart 39.2.

Applicability

The proposed rule did not address the issue of whether the new rule would apply to contracts already in existence. A number of public commentors asked for clarification about the applicability of the rule.

For other than indefinite-quantity contracts, this amendment applies to contracts awarded on or after the effective date. For indefinite-quantity contracts, it is applicable to delivery orders or task orders issued on or after the effective date. Indefinite quantity contracts may include Federal Supply Schedule contracts, governmentwide acquisition contracts (GWACs), multi-agency contracts (MACs), and other interagency acquisitions. Exception determinations are not required for award of the underlying indefinite-quantity contracts, except for requirements that are to be satisfied by initial award. Indefinite-quantity contracts may include noncompliant items, provided that any task or delivery order issued for noncompliant EIT meets an applicable exception. Accordingly, requiring activities must ensure compliance with the EIT accessibility standards at 36 CFR part 1194 (or that an exception applies) at time of issuance of task or delivery orders.

Contracting offices that award indefinite-quantity contracts must indicate to ordering offices which supplies and services the contractor indicates as compliant, and show where full details of compliance can be found (e.g., vendor's or other exact web page location).

The Access Board's EIT standards at 36 CFR part 1194 do not apply to—

- Taking delivery for items ordered prior to the effective date of this rule;
- Within-scope modifications of contracts awarded before the effective date of this rule;
- Exercising unilateral options for contracts awarded before the effective date of this rule; or
- Multiyear contracts awarded before the effective date of this rule.

Exceptions

Unless an exception at FAR 39.204 applies, acquisitions of EIT supplies and services must meet the applicable accessibility standards at 36 CFR part 1194. The exceptions in 39.204 include—

- Micro-purchases, prior to January 1, 2003. However, for micro-purchases, contracting officers and other individuals designated in accordance with 1.603-3 are strongly encouraged to comply with the applicable accessibility standards to the maximum extent practicable;
- EIT for a national security system;
- EIT acquired by a contractor incidental to a contract;
- EIT located in spaces frequented only by service personnel for maintenance, repair or occasional monitoring of equipment; and
- EIT that would impose an undue burden on the agency.

Micro-purchases

The exception for micro-purchases was in the proposed rule. It was made in recognition of the fact that almost all micro-purchases are made using the government-wide commercial purchase card. Government personnel, who are not warranted contracting officers, use the purchase card to purchase commercial-off-the-shelf items. Use of the purchase card makes it generally impractical to comply with the EIT accessibility standards unless commercial-off-the-shelf products are labeled for standards compliance. Manufacturers are continuing to develop products that comply with the EIT accessibility standards. It is expected that almost all products will comply with the standards within the next two years, and be labeled by the manufacturer accordingly. Therefore, we have established a sunset date of January 1, 2003, for the micro-purchase exemption. Prior to that date, the Government will revisit the state of technology and the pace at which manufacturers have conformed to the required standards.

The micro-purchase exception does not exempt all products that cost under $2,500. Some commentors were confused about this. The exception is for a one-time purchase that totals $2,500 or less, made on the open market rather than under an existing contract. A software package that costs $1,800 is not a micro-purchase if it is part of a $3,000 purchase, or part of a $3,000,000 purchase. Regardless of purchase price, there still is an agency requirement to give reasonable accommodation for the disabled under section 504 of the Rehabilitation Act of 1973. The current micro-purchase limit is $2,500, set by statute. If the threshold is increased by a statutory change, the FAR Council will consider keeping the FAR Subpart 39.2 limit at $2,500.

In addition, GSA will recommend that agencies modify cardholder training to remind purchase cardholders of EIT accessibility requirements.

Undue Burden

Another set of comments wanted the FAR to elaborate on undue burden. The Access Board discussed undue burden in its final rule preamble (at 65 FR 80506 of the *Federal Register*). Substantial case law exists on this term, which comes from disability law. The Access Board chose not to disturb the existing understanding of the term by trying to define it. The FAR Council agrees with this approach. Agencies are required by statute to document the basis for an undue burden. Requiring officials should be aware that when there is an undue burden, the statute requires an alternative means of access to be provided to individuals with disabilities.

Clauses

Some commentors asked for a clause, pointing out that unless the FAR prescribes a clause, agencies may produce different clauses, resulting in inconsistent coverage across the Government. Some procurement offices want a clause to help address their lack of experience with the Access Board standards. No clauses were in the January proposed rule. The FAR Council is carefully considering whether clauses are needed and welcomes comments on this issue that would inform a potential rulemaking.

Other Issues

A topic of concern to commentors was the play between the definition of EIT and a contractor's incidental use of EIT. The rule was not intended to automatically apply to a contractor's internal workplaces. For example, EIT neither used nor accessed by Federal employees or members of the public is not subject to the Access Board's standards (contractor employees in their professional capacity are not members of the public for purposes of section 508).

Commentors asked for further information on section 508 product compliance. There is a website at http://www.section508.gov, providing information from manufacturers and vendors on how they meet Access Board standards. The website reference has been added to the FAR language at Subpart 39.2.

Commentors asked whether the Committee for Purchase from People Who Are Blind or Severely Disabled, and Federal Prison Industries (UNICOR) were covered. These are required sources for certain items. Agencies must consider noncompliant EIT items from these sources the same way that they would consider items from commercial sources, i.e., whether purchasing the item would come under an exception. As a matter of policy, purchases from the Committee for Purchase from People Who Are Blind or Severely Disabled, and Federal Prison Industries are to be treated as procurements.

The current status of compliance testing also was discussed in comments. Currently there is no uniform testing. However, there is an industry-led, Government-sponsored, program in the works, Accessibility for People with Disabilities through Standards Interoperability and Testing (ADIT). See the Section 508 website for information.

Questions arose on draft rule section 39.X03, Applicability, on the interpretation of standards available in the marketplace. The rule intended to recognize that initially there will be many products that do not meet all the Access Board's technical standards. Agencies may need to acquire these products. When acquiring commercial items, an agency must comply with those accessibility standards that can be met with supplies and services available in the commercial marketplace in time to meet the agency's delivery requirements. Individual standards that cannot be met would be documented by the requiring official, with a copy to the contract file. If products are available that meet some, but not all applicable standards, agencies cannot claim a product as a whole is nonavailable just because it does not meet all of the standards.

Requirements Development, Market Research, and Solicitations

The requiring official must identify which standards apply to the procurement, using the Access Board's EIT Accessibility Standards at 36 CFR part 1194. Then the requiring official must perform market research to determine the availability of compliant products and services; vendor websites and the section 508 website would be helpful here. The requiring official must then identify which standards, if any, would not apply in this procurement because of, for example, nonavailability (FAR 39.203) or undue burden (FAR 39.204(e)). Technical specifications and minimum requirements would be developed based on the market research results and agency needs. This information would be submitted with the purchase request. The solicitation would then be drafted, or a task order or delivery order would be placed. Proposal evaluation may yield additional information that could require reconsideration of the need for an exception.

B. Executive Order 12866

The Access Board determined that their December 21, 2000, final rule was an economically significant regulatory action under E.O. 12866, and was a major rule under 5 U.S.C. 804. An economic assessment was accomplished and was placed on the Access Board's website at http://www.access-board.gov/sec508/assessment.htm. A copy can be obtained from the Access Board. The FAR Council has determined that the assessment conducted by the Access Board provides an adequate economic assessment of both the Access Board rule and this change to the FAR. Accordingly, the Access Board's regulatory assessment meets the requirement of performing a regulatory assessment for this change to the FAR and no further assessment is necessary.

This is an economically significant regulatory action and was subject to review under section 6(b) of Executive Order 12866, Regulatory Planning and Review, dated September 30, 1993. This rule is a major rule under 5 U.S.C. 804.

C. Regulatory Flexibility Act

This rule has a significant economic impact on a substantial number of small entities within the meaning of the Regulatory Flexibility Act, 5 U.S.C. 601, *et seq.*, because small businesses that choose to market their products to the Federal Government must ensure that their electronic and information technology supplies or services meet the substantive requirements of the Access Board's standards. Since this may result in increased costs of producing and selling their products, a Final Regulatory Flexibility Analysis (FRFA) has been performed and the analysis is summarized as follows:

> The objective of this rule is to revise the FAR to improve the accessibility of electronic and information technology used by the Federal Government. The standards developed by the Access Board affect Federal employees with disabilities as well as members of the public with disabilities who seek to use Federal electronic and information technologies to access information. This increased access reduces barriers to employment in the Federal Government for individuals with disabilities and reduces the probability that Federal employees with disabilities will be underemployed. The EIT standards developed for the Federal Government may result in benefiting people outside the Federal workforce, both with and without disabilities. The accessible technology from the Federal Government may spill over to the rest of society.
>
> Section 508 uses the Federal procurement process to ensure that technology acquired by the Federal Government is accessible. Failure of an agency to purchase electronic and information technology that complies with the standards promulgated at 36 CFR part 1194, may result in an individual with a disability filing a complaint alleging that a Federal agency has not complied with the standards. Individuals may also file a civil action against an agency. The enforcement provision of section 508 takes effect June 21, 2001.

> This rule establishes that contractors must manufacture, sell, or lease electronic and information technology supplies or services that comply with standards promulgated at 36 CFR part 1194. For many contractors, this may simply involve a review of the supply or service with the standards to confirm compliance. For other contractors, these standards could require redesign of a supply or service before it can be sold to the Federal Government. According to the Federal Procurement Data System in fiscal year 2000, we estimate that there are approximately 17,550 contractors to which the rule will apply. Approximately, 58 percent, or 10,150, of these contractors are small businesses.
>
> Small businesses will have to analyze whether the electronic and information technology they or their customers plan to sell to the Federal Government complies with the standards. Manufacturers may want to redesign to make their supplies and services compliant to have a better chance for their items to be purchased by the Government. Retailers will need to coordinate with the manufacturers. The statute will decrease demand for some supplies and services that are not compliant, leading to decreased sales for small entities manufacturing or selling those items. Conversely, the statute will increase demand for some supplies and services that are compliant, leading to increased sales for small entities manufacturing or selling those items.
>
> Since the statute imposes private enforcement, where individuals with disabilities can file civil rights lawsuits, the Government has little flexibility for alternatives in writing this regulation. To meet the requirements of the law, we cannot exempt small businesses from any part of the rule.

The FAR Secretariat has submitted a copy of the FRFA to the Chief Counsel for Advocacy of the Small Business Administration. A copy of the FRFA may be obtained from the FAR Secretariat. The Councils will consider comments from small entities concerning the affected FAR parts in accordance with 5 U.S.C. 610. Comments must be submitted separately and should cite 5 U.S.C. 601, *et seq.* (FAR case 1999-607), in correspondence.

Appendix B

Lease versus Borrow and Purchase Example

When does it make more sense to buy equipment? When does it make more sense to lease? As an example, in the construction industry, the rent/lease-or-own decision is a routine decision when acquiring new and used equipment.

The lease-versus-buy decision can be made quickly for some companies. There is a tax advantage if the leasing company has a high tax liability; thus, buying equipment and leasing it to contractors is a profitable business. Since the equipment still must be used in the construction industry, the company leases the equipment it owns to contractors.

On the other hand, many contractors have higher after-tax costs for buying capital equipment than those faced by the leasing company, allowing the leasing company to pass some of its savings on to contractors and still make a profit. The contractor must then decide whether the savings from leasing are economically attractive. The following lease-versus-buy method can be used to compare (1) the purchase price and lease payments, (2) income tax effects, and (3) present values.

The following example shows how to use these steps. A trucking contractor has two choices: (1) buy a new tri-axle dump truck or (2) lease it for three years. The dump truck has a useful life of five years and costs $100,000. The Helpful Bank is willing to loan the contractor $88,000 at 6-percent interest and requires a down payment of $12,000 and annual payments of $20,891, which are due at the end of each of the next five years. Since the contractor does not have the proper facilities, the bank will require the contractor to sign a maintenance contract with ACME Mack Trucks. The contract, good for five years of maintenance, requires annual payments of $5,000. ACME made the contractor a proposal that competes with the bank's offer. ACME is willing to lease the contractor the same dump truck for three years. Since the contractor's cash situation is very tight, ACME structured the lease with the $30,917 payment due at the end of each year. In addition, ACME agreed to

- Perform all of the maintenance during the lease period.
- Give the contractor the right to purchase the dump truck at the end of three years for the prevailing market price (estimated to be $35,000).
- Allow the contractor to buy a maintenance contract for two years on the dump truck for $6,000 annually, paid at the end of years four and five.

STEP 1: COMPARING PURCHASE PRICE AND LEASE PAYMENTS

The first step in a lease-versus-buy analysis is listing the purchase price and lease payments.

	Buy	Lease
Today	$12,000	
1 year from today	20,891	$30,917
2 years from today	20,891	30,917
3 years from today	20,891	30,917
4 years from today	20,891	—
5 years from today	20,891	—

The Today row in the example shows that purchased equipment must be paid for upon delivery. This payment may be from cash reserves or from money borrowed from a lending agency, but it must be paid to the bank upfront. The first lease payment, at least in this example, also is shown as one year from today. The purchase option must include interest payments, depreciation, and maintenance expense that also must be paid by the contractor. ACME assumes these costs for the first three years of the lease option. At the end of year 3, a final payment of $35,000 is made to ACME.

STEP 2: COMPARING INCOME TAX EFFECT

One of the most important economic differences between leasing and buying equipment is the way each is treated for income tax purposes. Since the value of these tax benefits varies greatly among individuals and corporations, it is important to calculate potential tax benefits on an individual basis.

How much will a tax deduction reduce taxes owed? That depends on the marginal tax rate. The marginal tax rate is how much of each additional dollar earned must be paid as income taxes. Individuals or corporations with high incomes may have marginal tax rates of 35 percent or more, while those losing money will have tax rates of 0 percent.

The higher the marginal tax rate, the more a tax deduction is worth. The value of a tax deduction is determined by multiplying it by the tax rate. Using this rule, a $10,000 tax deduction is worth nothing if the tax rate is 0 percent, $1,500 at 15 percent, and $2,800 at 28 percent.

The situation is relatively simple with leases. Each lease payment is a tax deduction for the company leasing the equipment. Its value can be determined by multiplying the marginal tax rate by the lease payment.

If the buy option is chosen, depreciation on a tractor must be taken over a five-year period. Both straight-line and accelerated methods are possible, and either can have its advantages depending on the contractor's tax situation. In this example, straight-line depreciation of $20,000 for each of five years will be used. The example contractor has a 40-percent tax rate, so the tax savings will be

$$\text{Tax savings} = 40 \text{ percent} \times (\text{Interest payment} + \text{Depreciation} + \text{Maintenance})$$

If the lease option is chosen, the tax savings would be calculated as follows:

$$\begin{aligned} \text{Tax savings (years 1–3)} &= 40 \text{ percent} \times \text{Lease payment} \\ \text{Tax savings (years 4 and 5)} &= 40 \text{ percent} \times (\text{Lease payment} \\ &\quad + \text{Depreciation} + \text{Maintenance}) \end{aligned}$$

The table from step 1 can now be rewritten to include taxes, as shown below.

	Tax Deduction Expense	
	Buying Option	**Leasing Option**
Today		
1 year from today	$30,280	$30,917
2 years from today	29,343	30,917
3 years from today	28,350	30,917
4 years from today	27,298	23,500
5 years from today	26,183	23,500

STEP 3: COMPARING PRESENT VALUES

The after-tax values of the leasing and buying costs have been considered, but the time at which these costs are incurred has not been taken into account. Ignoring their timing can lead to an incorrect decision because money has a time value. Time value is evident every time money is invested for a period of time to earn interest or borrowed for a period of time in exchange for interest payments.

The time value of money affects leasing or buying because the farther into the future a cost comes due, the less of today's dollars it will take to repay it. How many of today's dollars it will take to pay a cost due in the future depends on the level of interest rates. Interest rates are used to choose present value factors, which are, in turn, used to convert future costs into today's dollars. A future cost, expressed in terms of today's dollars, is called a present value. The interest rate chosen is either that at which money can be borrowed or that at which money can be invested.

In the case of the contractor, a 6-percent rate is used. The present value factor table is used to find the *present value* factors for today through five years from today. The contractor must now multiply the present value factors (PV = $1/(1 + k)^t$) by the net cash outflows. See Figure B.1.

	Net Cash Outflows for Buying Option		Factor*	Present Value
Today	$12,000	×	1.0000	= $12,000
1 year from today	13,779	×	0.9434	= 12,999
2 years from today	14,154	×	0.8900	= 12,597
3 years from today	14,551	×	0.8396	= 12,217
4 years from today	14,972	×	0.7921	= 11,859
5 years from today	15,418	×	0.7473	= 11,521
Total present value cost				$73,193

* The discount factors for a 6-percent interest rate per year are given in Appendix C.

The contractor then uses the same discount factors to find the present value of the after-tax costs of leasing.

	Net Cash Flows for Leasing Option		Factor	Present Value
Today	0	×	1.0000	= 0
1 year from today	$18,550	×	0.9434	= $17,500
2 years from today	18,550	×	0.8900	= 16,510
3 years from today	18,550	×	0.8396	= 15,575
3E years from today	35,000	×	0.8396	= 29,387
4 years from today	(3,400)	×	0.7921	= (2,693)
5 years from today	(3,400)	×	0.7473	= (2,541)
Total present value cost				$73,738

The completed dump truck analysis is given in Figure B.1.

CONCLUSION

The borrow purchase option is slightly better than the lease option. However, it is easy to see that both options are not significantly different. The three-step method will remain valid, but legal and accounting advice must be added to any economic analysis before making a decision on leasing or buying capital equipment.

FIGURE B.1 Solution for Lease versus Borrow and Purchase Example

Tax rate (TR) = 0.4
Discount rate = 0.06
Interest rate = 0.06
Lease rate = 0.06

Borrow and Purchase

Year	Payment (1)	Interest (2)	Reduction (3)	Principal (4)	Depreciation (5)	Maintenance (6)	Tax-Deductible Expense (7 = 2 + 5 + 6)	Savings (8 = 7 × TR)	Net Cash Outflow (9 = 1 + 6 − 8)	PV Factor (10)	PV of Purchase (11 = 9 × 10)
				$100,000							
Beg.	$ 12,000		$ 12,000	88,000					$(12,000)	1	$(12,000)
1	20,891	$ 5,280	15,611	72,389	$ 20,000	$ 5,000	$ 30,280	$12,112	(13,779)	0.9434	(12,999)
2	20,891	4,343	16,548	55,842	20,000	5,000	29,343	11,737	(14,154)	0.8900	(12,597)
3	20,891	3,350	17,540	38,301	20,000	5,000	28,350	11,340	(14,551)	0.8396	(12,217)
4	20,891	2,298	18,593	19,708	20,000	5,000	27,298	10,919	(14,972)	0.7921	(11,859)
5	20,891	1,183	19,708	0	20,000	5,000	26,183	10,473	(15,418)	0.7473	(11,521)
	$116,454	$16,454	$100,000		$100,000	$25,000	$141,454				$(73,193)

Lease

Year	Payment (1)	Depreciation (5)	Maintenance (6)	Tax-Deductible Expense (7 = 1 + 5 + 6)	Savings (8 = 7 × TR)	Net Cash Outflow (9 = 1 + 6 − 8)	PV Factor (10)	PV of a Lease (11 = 9 × 10)
1	$ 30,917			$ 30,917	$12,367	$(18,550)	0.9434	$(17,500)
2	30,917			30,917	12,367	(18,550)	0.8900	(16,510)
3	30,917			30,917	12,367	(18,550)	0.8396	(15,575)
3E	35,000					(35,000)	0.8396	(29,387)
4	0	$17,500	$ 6,000	23,500	9,400	3,400	0.7921	2,693
5	0	17,500	6,000	23,500	9,400	3,400	0.7473	2,541
	$127,751	$35,000	$12,000	$139,751				$(73,738)

Appendix C

Present Value Table

Discount factors: Present value of $1 to be received after t years = $1/(1 + r)^t$.

Number of Years	Interest Rate per Year														
	1%	2%	3%	4%	5%	6%	7%	8%	9%	10%	11%	12%	13%	14%	15%
1	.990	.980	.971	.962	.952	.943	.935	.926	.917	.909	.901	.893	.885	.877	.870
2	.980	.961	.943	.925	.907	.890	.873	.857	.842	.826	.812	.797	.783	.769	.756
3	.971	.942	.915	.889	.864	.840	.816	.794	.772	.751	.731	.712	.693	.675	.658
4	.961	.924	.888	.855	.823	.792	.763	.735	.708	.683	.659	.636	.613	.592	.572
5	.951	.906	.863	.822	.784	.747	.713	.681	.650	.621	.593	.567	.543	.519	.497
6	.942	.888	.837	.790	.746	.705	.666	.630	.596	.564	.535	.507	.480	.456	.432
7	.933	.871	.813	.760	.711	.665	.623	.583	.547	.513	.482	.452	.425	.400	.376
8	.923	.853	.789	.731	.677	.627	.582	.540	.502	.467	.434	.404	.376	.351	.327
9	.914	.837	.766	.703	.645	.592	.544	.500	.460	.424	.391	.361	.333	.308	.284
10	.905	.820	.744	.676	.614	.558	.508	.463	.422	.386	.352	.322	.295	.270	.247
11	.896	.804	.722	.650	.585	.527	.475	.429	.388	.350	.317	.287	.261	.237	.215
12	.887	.788	.701	.625	.557	.497	.444	.397	.356	.319	.286	.257	.231	.208	.187
13	.879	.773	.681	.601	.530	.469	.415	.368	.326	.290	.258	.229	.204	.182	.163
14	.870	.758	.661	.577	.505	.442	.388	.340	.299	.263	.232	.205	.181	.160	.141
15	.861	.743	.642	.555	.481	.417	.362	.315	.275	.239	.209	.183	.160	.140	.123
16	.853	.728	.623	.534	.458	.394	.339	.292	.252	.218	.188	.163	.141	.123	.107
17	.844	.714	.605	.513	.436	.371	.317	.270	.231	.198	.170	.146	.125	.108	.093
18	.836	.700	.587	.494	.416	.350	.296	.250	.212	.180	.153	.130	.111	.095	.081
19	.828	.686	.570	.475	.396	.331	.277	.232	.194	.164	.138	.116	.098	.083	.070
20	.820	.673	.554	.456	.377	.312	.258	.215	.178	.149	.124	.104	.087	.073	.061

Number of Years	Interest Rate per Year														
	16%	17%	18%	19%	20%	21%	22%	23%	24%	25%	26%	27%	28%	29%	30%
1	.862	.855	.847	.840	.833	.826	.820	.813	.806	.800	.794	.787	.781	.775	.769
2	.743	.731	.718	.706	.694	.683	.672	.661	.650	.640	.630	.620	.610	.601	.592
3	.641	.624	.609	.593	.579	.564	.551	.537	.524	.512	.500	.488	.477	.466	.455
4	.552	.534	.516	.499	.482	.467	.451	.437	.423	.410	.397	.384	.373	.361	.350
5	.476	.456	.437	.419	.402	.386	.370	.355	.341	.328	.315	.303	.291	.280	.269
6	.410	.390	.370	.352	.335	.319	.303	.289	.275	.262	.250	.238	.227	.217	.207
7	.354	.333	.314	.296	.279	.263	.249	.235	.222	.210	.198	.188	.178	.168	.159
8	.305	.285	.266	.249	.233	.218	.204	.191	.179	.168	.157	.148	.139	.130	.123
9	.263	.243	.225	.209	.194	.180	.167	.155	.144	.134	.125	.116	.108	.101	.094
10	.227	.208	.191	.176	.162	.149	.137	.126	.116	.107	.099	.092	.085	.078	.073
11	.195	.178	.162	.148	.135	.123	.112	.103	.094	.086	.079	.072	.066	.061	.056
12	.168	.152	.137	.124	.112	.102	.092	.083	.076	.069	.062	.057	.052	.047	.043
13	.145	.130	.116	.104	.093	.084	.075	.068	.061	.055	.050	.045	.040	.037	.033
14	.125	.111	.099	.088	.078	.069	.062	.055	.049	.044	.039	.035	.032	.028	.025
15	.108	.095	.084	.074	.065	.057	.051	.045	.040	.035	.031	.028	.025	.022	.020
16	.093	.081	.071	.062	.054	.047	.042	.036	.032	.028	.025	.022	.019	.017	.015
17	.080	.069	.060	.052	.045	.039	.034	.030	.026	.023	.020	.017	.015	.013	.012
18	.069	.059	.051	.044	.038	.032	.028	.024	.021	.018	.016	.014	.012	.010	.009
19	.060	.051	.043	.037	.031	.027	.023	.020	.017	.014	.012	.011	.009	.008	.007
20	.051	.043	.037	.031	.026	.022	.019	.016	.014	.012	.010	.008	.007	.006	.005

Note: For example, if the interest rate is 10 percent per year, the present value of $1 received at year 5 is $.621.

Chapter Seventeen

Health Care Purchasing and Supply Management

Learning Objectives

1. Understand how purchasing in the health care field is carried out.
2. Learn about the various supply management methods in the health care field.
3. Explain how inventory control is accomplished in the health care field.
4. Learn about group purchasing organizations.
5. Identify the current trends in health care purchasing.
6. Illustrate the capital equipment acquisition process.
7. Show how various health care plans are evaluated.

INTRODUCTION

The health care industry is expected to grow and consume an even greater share of GNP in the next few years. At the same time, many health care organizations will be driven from the market because of uncontrollable nonsalary costs and declining profits. This radical shift is the result of increased price competition and the regulatory environment. This is good news for health care providers who have planned for the forthcoming changes.

The focus of this chapter will be on purchasing day-to-day supplies and capital equipment acquisition. In the next section, we will show how supplies are bought and controlled. The third section will consider the acquisition of specialized capital equipment.

Hospitals are complex organizations providing a multitude of services to patients, physicians, and staff. These services include dietary, housekeeping, physical plant engineering, pharmacy, laboratory, inpatient treatment (nursing units), surgery, radiology, administration, and others. See Li & Benton, 2003, 2006; Siferd and Benton, 1992. Each area has specific and often unique materials and supply needs, creating a requirement in these facilities for a supply management system that can provide the necessary supplies when needed. In the current climate of increasing health care costs, systems inventory must be optimized without sacrificing the level of service provided. The functions of inventory in the hospital setting, methods of inventory management utilized, factors that are unique to the health care setting, and current trends in hospital inventory management will be examined.

PURCHASING, SUPPLIES, AND SERVICES

As in any business concern, the functions of all departments must be consistent with the overall mission and purpose of the business. In hospitals, the primary objective is to provide patient care; the supply management function is in place to support this objective. Inventory control is an important *component of supply management*; there are many other functions that are also critical to a successful supply management system, and some of these functions will be addressed indirectly in this discussion.

There are two primary functions of inventory in the hospital setting: "to maximize supply service consistent with maximum efficiency and optimum inventory investment and to provide a cushion between the forecasted and actual demand." The service levels required by the departments will vary depending on the degree of the cost of a stockout. An illustration of the difference is the cost of a stockout of laser printer toner for the administrative offices as opposed to a stockout of an item such as a diagnostic coronary catheter, which may be critical in an emergency situation. The items in this example may cost the same to purchase and hold in inventory, but the allowable risks of stocking out are very different. This phenomenon also will affect the optimal level of "inventory cushion" from a service perspective. The criticality of an item may depend on the restocking lead time, the shelf life, or the special conditions under which the item must be held as well as the effect on hospital operations of a shortage of the item.

Many of the items necessary in the operation of hospitals are *independent-demand purchased items*. However, there are items that are produced in the hospital setting for which the supplies follow a dependent-demand pattern and the inventories supporting these functions are essentially raw materials used in production. Departments that produce supplies include the print shop (e.g., forms), dietary production (food items), and the pharmacy (unit dosage packaging, IV mixtures, etc.). Make-or-buy decisions here are key, and the corresponding inventory issues must be addressed. In addition, the demand for certain items may be derived in advance from the surgical schedule. For example, a certain number of units of blood plasma of specific types may need to be held at the ready on certain days when open-heart or other complex surgeries are being performed.

Even with only these few examples, it is clear that the supply management functions and inventory control issues in a hospital are complex. Functions of a management system include purchasing, storage space utilization, inventory management, supply distribution, supply chain management, linen service, printing, and often mail, patient transportation, and courier/messenger services. Effective management of materials requires tremendous time and energy in the constant monitoring of changes in usage, ordering practices within the facility, and pricing. The control and management systems used depend on the size of the institution, degree of automation, and the competitive environment. The hospital administrator's measurement criterion is the highest level of customer satisfaction at the lowest cost, but this satisfaction must be achieved under severe cost constraints.

Operating cost in hospitals has become extremely important as the reimbursement system is no longer based solely on cost. In the mid-1980s, a system of reimbursement based on specific diagnosis-related groups (DRG) was instituted. Under the DRG system, the hospital is reimbursed a flat rate based on a patient's diagnosis regardless of the associated costs. Before the DRG system was instituted, there was little incentive to operate hospitals efficiently or cost-effectively. Today, cost containment is critical to an institution's financial health. Better supply management practices must be implemented in order to ensure appropriate service levels in the new cost containment environment.

SUPPLY (MATERIALS) MANAGEMENT SURVEY[1]

In 1993 a survey was mailed to 2,376 hospital CEOs. Approximately 523 usable questionnaires were returned. Forty questionnaires were received from Canadian hospitals. The balance of 483 were from the United States. The same survey was mailed to an identical sample in 1987. Approximately 85 percent of the hospitals sampled reported that they had a supply management program. The results of the two samples are given in Figure 17.1.

As can be seen in Figure 17.1, the primary objective of a supply management program is to ensure systems are adequate to keep departments supplied without stockouts. However, it appears that *training* and *education* are also becoming a key priority for supply managers. The reduction in inventory levels is becoming less important since the purchase price and adequate supply levels will implicitly resolve the inventory problem. All of the other priorities show very little change. Another important finding is the reporting structure for the supply manager. Approximately one-third of the supply managers report to the chief financial officer and another one-third report to a vice president.

This study is the most comprehensive hospital CEO study to date. However, based on an in-depth analysis of the New Albany Surgical Hospital (NASH) located in Columbus, Ohio, the results are shown to continue to be relevant. Some of the results also were confirmed by findings in a recent study by Li and Benton (2006). The most significant departure from the 1993 study is the inclusion of the physicians in the materials acquisition process. NASH is a doctor-owned specialty hospital. In most hospitals, there are supplies from a wide number of suppliers. As an example, there are at least 25 kinds of different knee replacement kits, but NASH only uses five of them. The doctors were informed that five out of the 25 would be sourced and they would be involved in the selection process. This approach was adopted for all of the surgical equipment as well as in other areas. The cost savings were significant. In the next section, specific supply management methods will be presented. Texas Health Resources reports another supply management success story.[2] Texas Health Resources' annual supply volume reaches upward of $275 million. Texas Health Resources is a 13-hospital health care system headquartered in the Dallas–Fort Worth metro area. The health care organization has established a corporate supply chain management department that has aggressively reduced annual inventory costs by approximately $30 million over the past three years. The supply management system is driven by eliminating nonmoving supplies and by implementing a stockless distribution service for most of the hospitals in the system and changing the attitudes and behavior of the nursing staff and physicians. The financial impact of health care supply management will be discussed in the next section.

[1] The original study was called a *Materials Management Survey*. The term has been updated to *supply management* for consistency. To date, this study is the most comprehensive longitudinal study of hospital CEO attitude opinions.

[2] *The Health Care Purchasing News*, June 2002.

FIGURE 17.1 An Abstract of CEO Attitude Opinion Survey Results

Source: *Hospital Management,* January 1994.

1. What should be the highest priority of a supply manager? 1 = Highest priority	1993	1987
• Reduce purchase prices	2	2
• Reduce inventory levels	6	3
• Ensure systems are adequate to keep department supplied without stockouts	1	1
• Train, educate, and motivate department to reduce nonsalary expenses	3	7
• Maximize use of group purchasing order (GPO) contracts	7	4
• Eliminate unnecessary expenditures resulting from waste and abuse	4	5
• Prevent the introduction of more costly new products or services where less expensive alternatives exist	8	8
• Research current products or services to determine if there are less costly alternatives	5	6

2. Which attributes does your supply manager lack?	1993	1987
• Communication skills	3	3
• Ability to manage personnel	4	5
• Knowledge of purchasing principles	8	7
• Ability to negotiate with vendors	7	8
• Knowledge of products	6	6
• Ability to negotiate with department manager to create win-win situations	2	2
• Ability to keep inventory levels at lowest possible level without interruption to service levels	5	4
• Ability to establish a leadership role to reduce hospitalwide nonsalary expenses	1	1

3. What is the title of the person to whom the material/supply manager reports?	1993	1987
• CEO	4%	16%
• COO	13%	19%
• CFO	34%	19%
• VP/Asst. Admin.	30%	10%

4. Has your opinion of the importance of material/supply management changed?	1993	1987
• Less important	1%	0%
• Slightly more important	11%	13%
• Much more important	33%	35%
• Much more important and more so in the future	55%	52%

HEALTH CARE SUPPLY CHAIN MANAGEMENT

There are critical differences between the health care supply chain and industrial supply chains such as the automotive supply chain. One difference is the manner in which revenue is generated. In traditional industrial supply chains, hospitals have been compensated through cost-based reimbursement systems, leading to little incentive to focus on cost or efficiency. The prolonged cost-based reimbursement systems have had lasting effects on internal operations at hospitals, compared to operations at traditional cost-conscientious industrial firms. A second key difference between the health care supply chain and traditional industrial supply chains is the number of suppliers relative to the number of buyers. Industrial buyers have access to a multitude of suppliers, and these suppliers are dependent on the volumes requested by the buying organization. Hospitals, on the other hand, have access to only a limited number of suppliers, in the case of most product groups, and these suppliers are much less dependent on the volume requested by an individual hospital. Simply put, while most well-defined traditional industries often times have few buyers and more possible suppliers, the health care industry is one of the unique industries with many buyers and few suppliers. The number of suppliers in an industry represents the number of alternative sources for buyers, which in turn affects a buyer's switching cost and dependence on a supplier.

A third key difference between traditional industrial supply chains and the health care supply chain is in the performance criteria. Members of the health care supply chain should put forth a coordinated effort to deliver the greatest patient value at the lowest cost. Therefore, the hospital purchasing system must contribute to value for patients.

A fourth important difference between traditional industrial supply chains and the health care supply chain concerns the fact that many hospital supply chain managers have relationships with a variety of organizations that bridge the gap between suppliers and the hospital buying organizations, including distributors/wholesalers and the group purchasing organization (GPO). In a recent GAO report (GAO-323R, 2010), it was revealed that participation in GPOs may lead to increases in product prices for hospitals buying products on nationwide contracts and through the establishment of price ceilings in their agreements with GPOs.

Another key difference between the health care supply chain and traditional industrial supply chains considers the nature of the relationships between the different members of the supply chains. In a traditional industrial supply chain, firms typically develop close relationships with their suppliers (i.e., strategic suppliers and some of their preferred suppliers) based on the value that they provide to the organization. More traditional relationships are maintained with transactional suppliers (see Chapter 7). The presence of purchasing partners, or middlemen, such as GPOs in the health care supply chain is a distinctive characteristic. While over 600 GPOs are active in the United States, a relatively small number of GPOs dominate the market. In 2007, the six largest GPOs accounted for nearly 90 percent of the GPO market (GAO-12-399R, 2012). Since Premier Inc., Novation LLC, and MedAssets, the three largest GPOs, account for approximately 75 percent of the purchasing volume, the health care supply chain is an oligopolistic environment. GPOs develop long-term purchasing contracts with suppliers such as original equipment manufacturers (OEMs) that its members, the hospitals, can access. These exclusive contracts may last as long as three to five years, and GPOs typically limit the supplier competition by narrowing the number of suppliers to two or three per product or product category (Burns, 2002). GPOs attempt to increase their hospital members' adherence to these negotiated agreements by having the members agree to use a specific contracted supplier for a contracted product, services, and equipment. The primary source of GPO revenues is the contract administration fee (CAF), paid by the product supplier, which is typically 2–3 percent of the contracted purchase price. GPOs may then distribute a portion of these fees to their customers, the health care organizations (HCOs) (GAO-10-738, 2010). As hospitals outsource part of their procurement process on a large scale to GPOs, they will save money by not having to employ the necessary support staff to test, research, negotiate, and purchase items on their own (Schneller and Smeltzer, 2006). However, a smaller purchasing staff and consequently less purchasing expertise increase the hospitals' dependence on a GPO. The pool of possible suppliers narrows from the total number of available suppliers to those that are under contract with the GPO for a given product. Consequently, hospitals' use of GPO services directly increases its dependence on the GPO for purchasing support and expertise. It also increases indirectly the dependence on the supplier since purchasing through the GPO reduces the number of available suppliers for the hospital. This double dependence of an HCO may have significant effects on the relationships between a hospital and a supplier and between the hospital and the GPO, through the phenomenon of interfirm power. The role of power has received significant research attention in the marketing channel literature. Also see De Jong and Benton (2013).

Opportunities in Health Care Supply Management

Purchasing and supply management in the health care supply chain has received wide attention because of its significance in determining hospital financial performance. The cost of supply management can exceed 40 percent of a hospital's operating budget, with nearly 25–30 percent attributable to materials cost directly. The health care supply chain is different from and more complex than supply chains in other more stable traditional industrial environments. In contrast to the health care supply chain, supply chains in many industries have gone through significant transitions over the last few decades.

Historically, the health care supply chain has consistently lagged behind traditional industrial supply chain efficiencies. As an example, health care investment in information technology for all processes (i.e., not just supply chain) occurred at only 3.9 percent of revenue in 2009, which is significantly less than other industries. Recently, clinical process improvement has been aggressively pursued in many hospitals and medical centers. The basic process has included flowcharting the current systems, eliminating wastes, and redesigning the health care delivery processes. The same level of attention is needed for the health care supply chain.

Hospital systems are finding it challenging to maintain profitability. See Table 17.1. Lack of investment in information technology and declining Medicare reimbursements are negatively impacting profitability. Hospitals need to refocus some of their attention to the low-hanging fruit related to supply management. Successful hospitals must consider the following areas for increasing profitability and improving operations:

- Supply chain planning
- Product management
- Sourcing and contracting
- Distribution and inventory management
- Technology enablement

Although the supply chain accounts for the second largest spending area in a hospital, executive leadership typically does not emphasize supply chain management or materials management operations as an area of opportunity. Supply management must be elevated to an integral component of the hospital executive management team. Supply chain leadership influence disparity is needed. Specifically,

TABLE 17.1 Industry Profitability Comparison of Honor Roll Hospitals with Other Industrial Sectors

Profitability Measures (Median %)	2008 U.S. Honor Roll Hospitals	General Medical and Surgical Hospitals	Electro-medical Equipment	National Commercial Banks	Department Stores	Construction Machinery	Semiconductor and Related Services	Cold Finishing of Steel Shapes
Profit margin	3.66%	2.1%	−2.8%	9.9%	1.6%	3.7%	0.2%	6.8%
Return on equity	14.9%	11.4%	5.4%	8.3%	10.5%	11.0%	5.6%	16.1%
Return on assets	9.1%	2.7%	−3.8%	0.4%	2.8%	3.9%	0.2%	8.4%
Example Organization (Actual %)	**The Cleveland Clinic**	**Tenet Healthcare**	**Medtronic**	**Bank of America**	**Target**	**Caterpillar**	**Intel**	**Worthington Industries**
Profit margin	3.23%	2.2%	16.5%	8.7%	4.4%	7.8%	17.3%	3.10%
Return on equity	13.10%	196.0%	19.8%	7.5%	18.6%	43.7%	17.4%	10.5%
Return on assets	5.5%	2.4%	10.7%	0.7%	6.0%	6.6%	13.3%	4.9%

producing a supply chain strategy showing how the organization plans to source, distribute, and replenish supplies will enable hospital personnel to properly manage human and capital resources. These are costly investments, and hospitals must prioritize between clinical and supply management investments.

Examples of Health Care Savings Opportunities

1. Crozer-Chester Healthcare System had operating and storage facilities at four hospitals and four nursing homes. The health care system consolidated the four facilities into a centralized off-site distribution center and saved approximately $1.5 million annually. At the same time, inventory was reduced by more than $300,000. Contract consolidation also generated $400,000 in savings while item standardization accounted for another $500,000 in savings (Hospitalconnect.com, 2002).
2. Connecting PeopleSoft's Purchasing Module to inventory applications enabled Dartmouth-Hitchcock Medical Center (DHMC) to replenish inventory as supplies were depleting. The inventory cost decreased by almost 50 percent. As can be seen, the implementation of technology helped DHMC integrate its business processes to obtain reduced costs and better visibility into supplies and replenishment (Danish, 2003).
3. A hospital health care system located in the Southeast identified approximately $3 million in savings in the clinical and support services areas. Supply management had identified the need to standardize clinical and nonclinical items. Clinical focus areas included high-dollar physician preference items, such as orthopaedic implants, where savings of over $300,000 was achieved by reducing the number of suppliers and pursuing demand matching. Similarly, another $200,000 could be realized through reducing the number of suppliers and more aggressively negotiating with the reduced supplier base.

METHODS OF SUPPLY MANAGEMENT

Traditional inventory control methods used in manufacturing are not common in the hospital setting. Modifications are necessary to fit the health care industry, but the fundamental theories are used. Three of these approaches will be discussed individually in this section.

Fixed Order Quantity System[3]

This system is referred to as a fixed order quantity (FOQ) system in which inventory is checked (theoretically) on a perpetual basis after each inventory transaction. When the inventory is withdrawn to a point at which there is just sufficient material to cover the demand during the replenishment lead time, an order is initiated for a fixed quantity. It is also sometimes called an order point system. Determination of the optimum order quantity is influenced by at least two factors: inventory carrying costs and ordering costs. The trade-offs in this instance are obvious. If we order frequently, thus incurring high order costs, we do not have to carry so much in inventory. If we order less frequently, the carrying costs will be higher. Often, the cost to backorder an item and the cost of stocking out are considered as well. Although these costs may be harder to determine, they may be critical, as a patient may not survive if some items are stocked out.

Economic order quantity (EOQ) calculations may be used in the determination of the optimum order size. However, the EOQ is usually based on inappropriate assumptions for the situation and can lead to erroneous decisions. For instance, the assumptions of constant uniform demand and the instantaneous replenishment of stock at the zero level may not reflect clearly the inventory situation faced by most hospitals. Modifications to the basic formula are necessary. Quantity discounts are not considered in the basic EOQ. Some of these assumptions may be relaxed, although standard EOQ decisions are fairly robust. The order quantity decision is easily implemented, involving a series of calculations that arrive at an order quantity that is most advantageous in a given situation. Reorder points, safety stock (as a function of service level), and total cost of the plan must then be determined. Simple-to-program spreadsheets may be utilized to determine close-to-optimal order quantities and reorder points.

Fixed Order Interval

In the fixed order interval (FOI) method, users or buyers review quantities periodically at fixed intervals of time, and an order is placed for a quantity sufficient to replenish the stock to a predetermined maximum level. This level also is calculated to minimize the combined costs of holding and managing inventories. The FOI method was developed primarily for use in mass production schedules in industry and has not been widely used in health care. However, there are several instances in which hospitals may be interested in this method: (1) when there is frequent ordering, calling for stringent control; (2) when it is convenient to order many items from one supplier; (3) when serving the needs of discrete or irregular usage; (4) when there are large-volume orders that represent a large portion of the supplier's capacity; and (5) when storeroom balances are calculated only periodically. This will be a particularly important method for hospitals that move increasingly into assembly and "production" of their supplies. Purchasing agents often

[3] For a detailed discussion on inventory management, see Chapter 5.

encourage the use of FOI methods, since the review period often can be coordinated with a supplier representative's visit to the hospital.

Stockless Inventory Systems

Just-in-time (JIT) inventory control is a common name for this concept, which has been used in industry since the 1950s when it was developed by Toyota. Increasingly, hospitals are finding uses and methods for this concept in their own materials management systems. The stockless inventory system is the process where a hospital's prime suppliers manage product purchasing, storage, delivery, and inventory control of medical/surgical supplies used in the hospital. Stockless inventory systems have the potential to reduce redundant activities in the system, the investment by the hospital in inventory, the storage space required, and the handling functions. To ensure successful implementation, several criteria must be met, including the existence of a prime supplier contract and excellent communication and cooperation within the hospital departments, as well as between the hospital and its supplier. Specialized departments such as the laboratory and radiology are particularly suited to a stockless inventory system, but implementation in the entire hospital is an idea that is gaining popularity.

When a supplier can manage stockless inventory systems for several hospitals, both the buyer and supplier can take advantage of the economies of scale in warehousing and in transportation inherent in such a situation. The supplier may act as the buyer's central warehouse, and less inventory will be needed to meet the same needs for several locations. The reason for this phenomenon is that variances are pooled, with a lower variance in total than the sum of the variances over all locations.

In addition, transportation may be routed quite efficiently because the supplier will be making many small deliveries weekly or even multiple times a day to a number of hospitals. The central supplier is also able to take advantage of quantity discounts in purchasing materials, and in having full truckloads delivered from large hospital supply houses and from pharmaceutical companies.

The Best Method

It is true that there is no one system that is the best overall. Certainly the size, purchasing power, and level of control that the supply management department has within the hospital are all factors that must be evaluated. The degree to which the hospital is automated and to which computer systems are integrated is also a factor in the decision in terms of the complexity of the systems models and in the level of calculations required. Clearly, cost/benefit analyses must be performed and systems developed that perform and provide the desired service level. There is little doubt that the system that would be most useful may not be one of the pure systems discussed but a combination of all of them. This is particularly true because of the complex and various needs of the different departments of the hospital.

Group Purchasing Organizations

Group purchasing organizations (GPOs) are intermediaries that help health care providers such as hospitals, nursing homes, and home health agencies realize savings and efficiencies by aggregating purchasing volume and using that leverage to negotiate discounts with manufacturers, distributors, and other vendors. Nearly every hospital in the United States (approximately 96–98 percent) chooses to utilize GPO contracts for their purchasing functions. Additionally, estimates are that hospitals across the United States use, on average, at least two and as many as four GPOs per facility. The U.S. health care industry spends $250+ billion annually in medical and nonmedical products with more than 70 percent allocated through a GPO. GPOs save hospitals and free-standing nursing homes between 10 and 15 percent off their purchasing costs. There are more than 600 organizations in the United States that participate in some form of group purchasing. Knowledge Source's annual Group Purchasing Organizations (GPOs) Market Overview provides the information you need to gain an understanding of the GPO market and trends. Some of the typical GPO characteristics are listed below:

- GPOs negotiate contracts with vendors (e.g., manufacturers) on behalf of members (e.g., hospitals).
- Vendors pay GPOs administrative fees based on sales.
  - Fees finance operations.
  - Surplus fees are distributed to owners or used to finance new ventures.
- GPOs vary by size, scope of service, and ownership type.

FIGURE 17.2
Money Flows Related to Hospital Purchases Using a GPO

Source: GAO, 2003.

Money Flows Related to Novation VHA and VHAHF

Source: GAO, 2003.

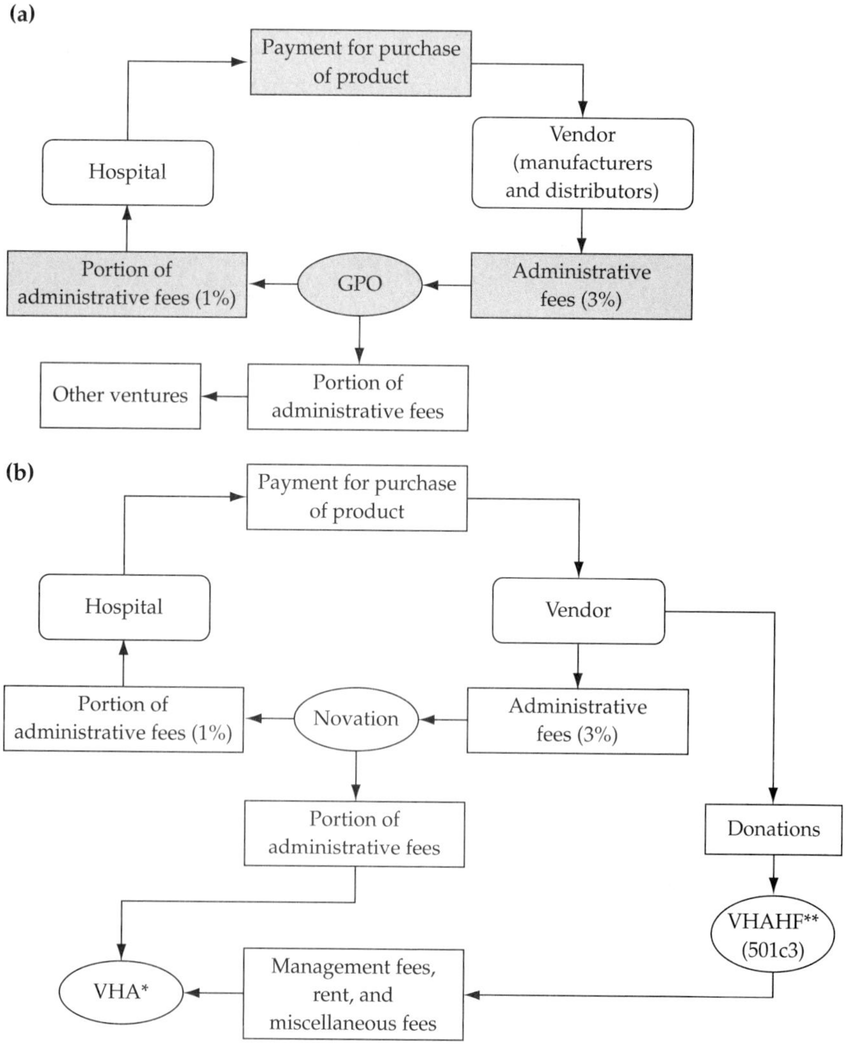

*VHA—Novations nationwide (for profit) network of community-owned health care system and their physicians.

**VHAHF—Novations (nonprofit) health care foundation.

TABLE 17.2
Hospital Purchase Model Through GPOs That Engage in Exclusionary Purchasing

Source: Elhauge (2003).

GPO	Share	Exclusionary Purchasing
Novation	29–30%	Yes
Premier	24%	Yes
Amerinet	9%	Yes
Managed Health Care	6%	Not reported
HSCA	5%	Yes
Consorta	4%	Yes
National Purchasing Alliance	1.50%	Yes
All Health	1.50%	Yes
Innovatix	1.50%	Yes

- GPOs do not maintain inventories or engage in other aspects of supply chain management.
- In 2008 GPO-contracted purchases amounted to $500 billion.

The money flows related to hospital purchases using a GPO are shown in Figure 17.2. The market share for exclusionary purchasing by GPO is listed in Table 17.2.

Antikickback Issues

In 1986, the safe harbor exemption allowed these fees, otherwise considered as "kickbacks" or illegal payments, to be paid to GPOs. To each participating member, a GPO must disclose

- That fees are to be 3 percent or less of the *purchase price*, or the amount or maximum amount that each vendor will pay.
- At least annually, the amount received from each vendor with respect to purchases made by or on behalf of the member.

COMPLICATING FACTORS UNIQUE TO HEALTH CARE FOR INVENTORY CONTROL

Two factors that are used in the application of all methods of inventory management are problematic for the health care system: inaccurate demand estimations or forecasts and safety stock.

Demand Problems

With the availability of computers in all areas of health care today, forecasting demand using past data and statistical techniques is a far more realistic possibility than it was in the past. Forecasts are never perfect, but they can assist the supply manager to better control inventory to the best economic advantage of the hospital.

Demand, however, is impacted by several unique factors in health care. For instance, the length of stay and patient mix (types of patients and diagnoses) patterns are fundamental to the assessment of the types of supplies required in any given time frame. This is particularly influential to inventory use in a hospital of 400 beds or less. Changes in medical staff and the possible related changes in treatment as a result will have a direct impact on the kind of supplies that are needed. Overall changes in treatment practices also will have an effect. If short-term forecasts for materials could be tied to the demand forecasts of certain types of DRG for patients admitted, then better material forecasts might be possible. Similarly, some hospitals now have critical path plans (CPPs) for patients, where a plan is made for each new admission to a unit. These plans are outcome-driven, where certain outcomes are expected at certain points of time during the patient's stay. If these CPPs could be linked by computer programs to supply management, forecasting for material needs would be more accurate.

Communication between the practitioners (medical staff) and the supply management function is vital, and this is inevitably the area in which the system breaks down. Several situations exist in the hospital that make communication a difficult task. First, practitioners historically give little thought to the evaluation of supply usage, or to the prediction of future needs.

The assumption in the past has been that what is needed will be made available, regardless of the cost or inconvenience of obtaining it. Further, hospitals have traditionally functioned as a set of "little fiefdoms," which fosters competition and difficult communication. This is changing by necessity, as the once unlimited resources are now increasingly limited and everyone in the hospital must concern himself or herself with the efficient and cost-effective utilization of those resources. Attention to the issue of supply utilization and communication between practitioners and supply management is crucial. Incorporating responsibility for supplies in the formal budgeting process of individual departments has been suggested as a way to encourage practitioners to take a serious look at supply needs and utilization.

Product-line organizational structures incorporating the supplies issue into the profitability of the product line is another approach to encourage middle- and first-line supervisors to increase their concern for supply management. By holding a product-line manager accountable for profit, attention to the efficient and cost-effective utilization of resources and supplies will result. The product-line manager approach has the potential to work quite well with the critical path plan for patient care because one individual, usually a registered nurse, is in charge of the team of individuals administering a patient's CPP. In addition, patients with similar CPPs are likely to have similar diagnoses. These patients are likely to be in the same DRG and therefore in the same nursing units during the course of their hospital stay. Thus, the nursing unit managers would be a natural choice for product-line managers of selected DRG- or CPP-related products. Careful planning and communication are paramount to the success of such a plan. Extensive audits and interviews using feedback and constant monitoring are the fundamental elements if supply master planning should be implemented. Again, communication is the key. By whatever innovative method, cooperation and communication must be improved so that higher throughput and lower cost will result.

In the case of dependent demand in which the hospital is producing an item, an explosion-type approach can be taken. This approach resembles a classic material requirements plan, based upon a master production schedule. These concepts can be applied to the production of supplies in the hospital setting, and the resulting materials and inventory demands can be derived. The master production schedule is a counterpart to the master surgery schedule and short-term (three- to six-week) forecast for other expected patient care. Material requirements can be derived from the surgery schedule and forecast, and "exploded" backward to determine when to begin the production of certain supplies assembled or within the hospital. Similarly, continued backward explosion to the lowest levels of raw materials will indicate when and how much raw material to purchase.

Safety Stock

Unique to health care is a classification of the stockout tolerances of a hospital, categorized by Reisman as urgency requirements (Holmgren and Wentz, 1982). They are as follows:

1. *Use-location urgency*. No stockout is allowed at a use location. These are the most urgent items and must be available to the materials users at all times.
2. *Facility-location urgency*. No stockout is allowed at a facility. Interdepartmental transfers can be used to satisfy these local stockouts. However, the item must be available in the facility as a whole.
3. *Regional-location urgency*. No stockout is allowed for the region. Interdepartmental and interfacility transfer can be used to satisfy the stockouts, but the item must be available in the region as a whole.
4. *No urgency*. Items for which stockouts are allowed at all levels.

Service levels and the corresponding safety stock levels can be derived for many items using this categorization. As discussed earlier, if demand from several locations can be pooled, the overall variance of demand is reduced so that safety stock required to provide the same level of customer service is lowered. Thus, in each situation of lowered urgency, fewer total units of inventory are needed.

Costs of stockouts are influenced by many factors in the health care arena. These factors include the costs of extra materials, personnel inconvenience, personnel and transportation costs, costs of expedited or emergency orders, lost sales as well as a myriad of intangibles ranging from mild dissatisfaction of the practitioner staff to the serious impact that a shortage might have on the treatment and health of a patient. It is difficult to quantify the results. Further, there is little correlation between the cost of the item and the costs associated with its stockout. Careful evaluation is required; the urgency component must be incorporated into all models and plans. ABC analyses are frequently used to identify the items of supply that are most costly to manage (also including the urgency requirements) and therefore require the most attention.

Stockouts can be prevented on a temporary basis with substitutable products. The substitutability issue is one of great concern to the supply manager and often a difficult one to reconcile with practitioners. A current listing of one- and two-way substitutability of products must be maintained and updated.

CURRENT TRENDS

The health care industry is increasingly looking to proven business techniques to improve performance in many functional areas. This desire to adapt more businesslike approaches is a direct result of the DRG system of reimbursement and increased competition. As indicated throughout this discussion, the most significant trend in the area of supply management in hospital settings is simply the magnitude of the importance and resulting attention to efficiency and cost-effectiveness.

Two trends are emerging: inventory management and control by a primary source or supplier and use of automation technology.

Primary Supplier

Primary sources assume most of the functions of the supply management department, much the same as the stockless inventory method described earlier. There are many advantages to this arrangement in that manpower costs for the hospital are reduced and redundancy of activities as well as stock is reduced. Perhaps the critical element of the success of such an arrangement is the level of communication and coordination between hospital departments and the supplier. An outside entity may facilitate and optimize these behavioral issues by being objective as well as being interested in the provision of a high level of service.

Automation Technology

There is no doubt that high technology is a main component of health care today. However, the advanced technology associated with hospitals is in the areas of diagnosis and treatment of illness. Using automation technology and sophisticated information systems in the operation of a hospital is becoming more common but is significantly behind the advances in the manufacturing sector. Its time has come, as evidenced in several studies of the implementation of bar coding in pharmacy inventory management (Chester and Zilz, 1989). Results of this application have been reported to be increased efficiency, decreased total inventory costs, improved storage space utilizations, and reductions in inventory values. Automated technology has been implemented for all aspects of hospital supply management.

ACQUISITION OF CAPITAL EQUIPMENT PROCESS OVERVIEW

Capital equipment acquisitions require health facilities to go through an internally defined process. Differing corporate policies and preferred methods of financing will impact this process. As an example, the dollar value for an item to be classified as a capital item is $500 at one Columbus, Ohio, area hospital and $1,000 at another comparable hospital. Commonalities exist in the capital budgeting/acquisition process among health facilities. A sample of the common appropriations process used at Grant Hospital in Columbus, Ohio, is shown in Figure 17.3.

A capital item request initiates the process. The requesting departments are required to provide information on utilization statistics. It is important that this information be as accurate and precise as possible. An example of an item request form is shown in Figure 17.4. The requests are then reviewed by one or more of the following: a capital item committee, the supply management department, facilities management/plant operations, and the finance department. The approved request is then compared to the overall expected budget. The most appropriate requests are then recommended for funding. It should be noted that even if an item does not "make the cut," contingency funds are established in most hospitals for the emergency replacement of items. This contingency will generally be 10–25 percent of the total budget. Also see Chapter 16.

FIGURE 17.3
Capital Appropriation Request (CAR) Process

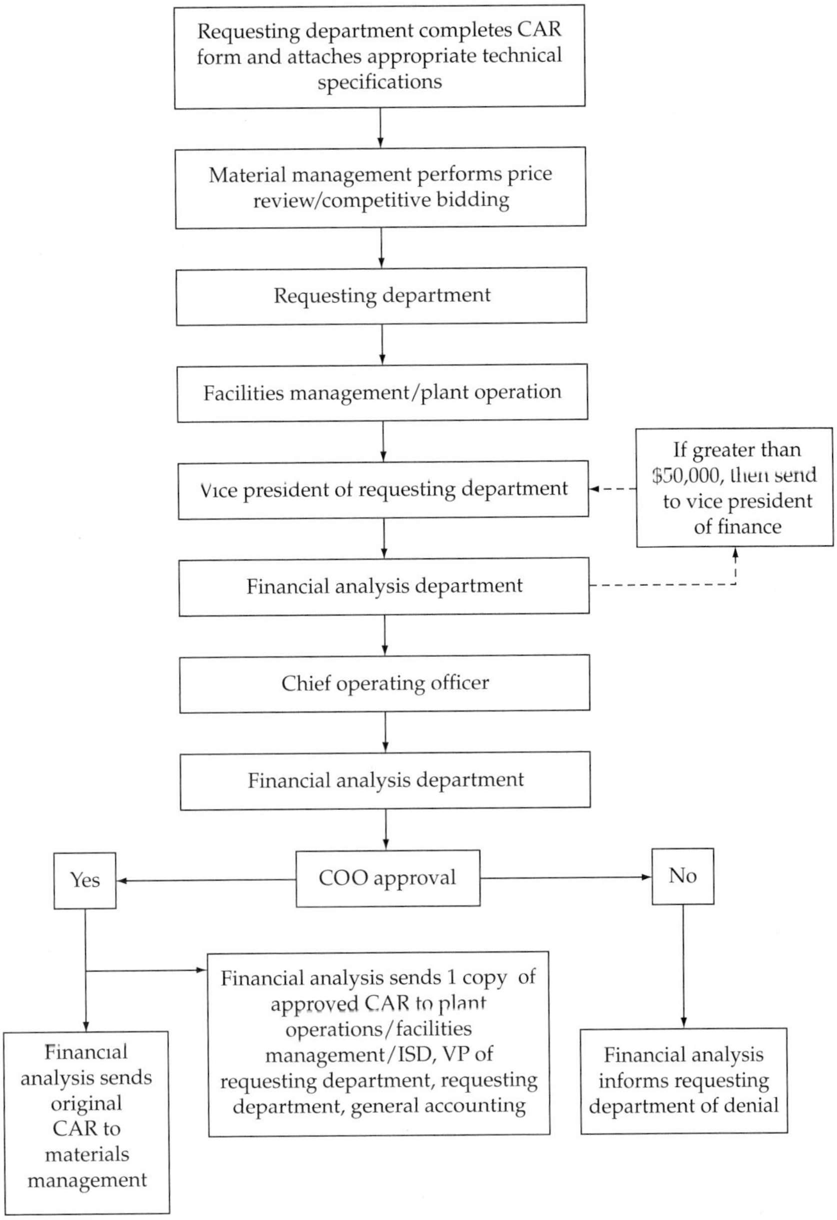

Overview of the Process

This capital item requisition (CIR) form is divided into two primary sections. The first section is to be completed by the department requesting the item. This section calls for details concerning the type of request, a summary of the requested item's capabilities, how the item contributes to the hospital's goals (specifically those relating to patient care), and the anticipated changes in operating costs.

The second section is for the actual financial review of the requested item. This section will be completed by the purchasing department.

FIGURE 17.4
Capital Item Requisition Instructions

Section I. (To be completed by Requesting Department.)

Facility: DN DW Other **Department:** ________ **Cost Center:** ________
Priority: ____________________
Location of proposed project: ________________________________

Type of Request (As a manner of verifying the request, please include documentation of the regulation requiring the requested item, maintenance records of current unit, or utilization data, whichever is appropriate.): Required by Regulation of Accreditation __________
Replacement of Current Unit ________ Expansion of Existing Service __________
Addition of a New Service ________ Other: (Please Explain) ____________________

Date Needed: ______________

Summary Description of the Requested Item, including quantity, components, options, etc.

____
____
____
____

Will additional space be required for the item? Yes ________ No ________

Will physical plant changes (e.g., plumbing, electrical, heating, ventilation, remodeling, safety codes, etc.) be required?
If yes, provide a brief description of the required physical plant changes and estimated cost for the modifications:

____
____
____

Brief Description of the Use and Capabilities of the Requested Item:

____
____
____
____

Please describe how the new item will contribute to hospital goals, specifically those relating to the quality and cost of patient care:

____
____
____
____

Additional Comments (Please describe the present system used to accomplish the same or similar function; why this system is inadequate; what will be done with the existing equipment; and other areas that will be affected or will be needed to support the new item):

____
____
____
____

Appropriate signatures are required for both sections. It is important not only that the appropriate signatures be obtained but also that the form be completed in its entirety. It is in everyone's best interest that the form is complete and concise since the request must be prioritized.

Upon completion of both sections, the CIR should be forwarded to the director of materials management.

FIGURE 17.4
(concluded)

Suggested Vendor____________________

Increase or (Decrease) in Annual Operating Cost:

Personnel/Payroll	$ ________
Personnel/Benefits	$ ________
Materials and Supplies	$ ________
Maintenance/Service Agreements	$ ________
Insurance	$ ________
Other	$ ________
Total Change in Operating Cost	$ ________

Who is responsible for:
Installation: ____________ Maintenance: ____________

Is a Trial Period Required? Yes _____ No _____

Is Medical Staff Review Required? Yes _____ No _____

Signature of Department Head: ________________ Date Signed: ________

Signature of Vice President: ________________ Date Signed: ________

- -

Section II. (To be completed by Purchasing Department)

Cost Information:

Cost per Unit	$ ________	× Number of Units	________ =
Total Equipment Cost			$ ________
Installation Cost			$ ________
Physical Plant Modification Cost			$ ________
Transportation Cost			$ ________
Total Acquisition Cost	$ ________	/ useful life (yrs)	________
Equipment Cost per Year			$ ________

Cost to Purchase:

Cash Expenditures	Cost Reimbursement	Net Cash	Present Value
________	________	________	________
________	________	________	________

Total Present Value: ____________
Less Salvage Value of Replaced Item: ____________
Total Cost to Purchase: ____________

Signature of Materials Management Director: ________________ Date: ________

Signature of Capital Improvements Chair: ________________ Date: ________

Signature of President: ________________ Date: ________

The approved proposals are then submitted to the appropriate governing board committee (e.g., Finance Committee, Planning Committee). The final step is the approval process.

Factors and Decision Rules

The financial merits of the various proposals are then considered. That is, if two projects are judged to be of equal financial worth, the preference for expenditure would be for the project serving the larger number of people, the one that prevents disease rather than simply preventing fatality, or the one serving children versus the aged. Several qualitative factors are also of utmost importance in identifying capital expenditure projects in health care, namely, community need, marketability of the project, urgency for the capital item, competition, and technological need.

1. *Community need* must be given the utmost consideration for capital expenditure project selection. The hospital must be dedicated to serving the needs of the community, and its purchasing practices should reflect this practice.
2. *Marketability* is a concept affecting both the internal and external audience of the facility. In conjunction with the community needs assessment, a hospital should consider how marketable a new piece of equipment will be to the community. Internally, the hospital must "sell" the new item and its virtues to the medical staff. If the administration seeks to purchase a machine that is a "money-maker" for the facility or that is to be used to attract new physicians to the facility, the item must be marketable to the current staff. They must see its worth. This will lead to their usage of the machine when appropriate.
3. *Hospital business objectives* relate to whether or not the capital item is for the replacement of current equipment, expansion of current technology, or expansion into a new technological field. From a business perspective, new technology usually is less urgent and more difficult to justify than updating or replacing current technology.
4. *New technology* coupled with external marketability suggests another factor to be considered, *competition*. Hospitals are businesses and must compete. The hospital management, again, should not be *telling* the community what it needs but must be aware of what is needed and seek to provide for that need on a competitive basis.

The more difficult factor for a hospital to consider when ranking requests is to assess the technology involved. In an often "politically sensitive" arena, the most pressing capital needs must be determined and satisfied by individuals who lack technological as well as medical expertise. Technological assessment can help alleviate this problem.

Technological assessment can be defined as a method of evaluating current and requested capital equipment by considering the results of published clinical investigations and of physical assessment of the equipment in the decision-making process. Three key areas are addressed in technological assessment, namely, what the needs of the department are, what the abilities of the current equipment are, and what the abilities of new/replacement equipment would be. The technological assessment is then integrated into the capital item request process.

For technological assessment to occur correctly, priorities must be set beforehand. That is, not all requests will need to undergo as thorough an assessment as will most of the costlier items. Subcommittees are then formed that should include medical personnel who use the equipment as well as physicians. The committee must tour the facility and become familiar with the equipment on hand. Interviews of the personnel who use the equipment should be undertaken. The information gained should be entered into a database. Examples of what the database should contain are as follows: type of equipment, year purchased, condition, useful life, and whether it will need replacing in the near future (i.e., within five years).

When comparing the findings to the predetermined criteria, the committee should be able to rank the needs within and among the departments. The committee members may be aware of ways to upgrade current equipment that would suffice until another capital budgeting year or until a more advanced piece of equipment is released to the market. The suggestions should be brought forth. The committee must consider the strategic goals of the hospital and what equipment (as well as acquisition timing) will be needed to fulfill these goals. This leads to the development of a more comprehensive, multiyear plan. This entire technological process is to promote the efficient allocation of the hospital's resources. Its main points are a comprehensive database, physician involvement, and interdepartmental planning (Watts et al., 1993).

A final factor to be considered with capital expenditures is the need in some states for governmental permission to purchase. If the certificate of need (CON) is not granted by the state, all the above key factors are meaningless. The goals of a CON law are to protect the consumers, generate benefits for them, and prevent the acquisition of unneeded equipment (i.e., ensure access to quality service at a reasonable cost). Those state officials reviewing CON applications try to determine the need for such a project by looking at the current utilization of like services and their specific locations. CONs are required in about half of the states, each with varying stipulations for dollar limits and types of purchases. For example, in Ohio a CON is needed for purchases over $1 million for medical equipment, for expenditures over $2 million for capital improvements, or for a project that will entail greater than $450,000 worth of operating cost per year.

Selecting the Right Supplier

Following appropriate justification and formal approval for the acquisition of a new piece of capital equipment, the actual purchasing process begins. The objective of this process and subsequent supplier evaluation is to fulfill a hospital's need with the best equipment for its intended function at the lowest possible total cost. Inherent in the process is the requirement that all segments of the management team be involved in the decision-making process. It must be emphasized that buying the best equipment for a function requires planning several months in advance to enable access to a wide range of vendors and ensure that no opportunities for functional enhancement or cost savings have been overlooked.

Functional Specifications

Before developing an initial base of qualified suppliers, the purchasing and requesting user departments must develop a list of functional specifications that are as detailed as possible. Each specification is to be categorized as a necessary feature, a desirable feature, or a characteristic that is irrelevant or even undesirable. This list of generic specifications will be presented to all prospective bidders and provide a foundation for price competition. It is important that each item specified can be provided by more than one supplier and reflect criteria that can be applied to each seller fairly.

Preference Point System

The preference point system is one useful method of specification. It is not the only one, nor should it be used for all capital equipment purchases. It has proven to be valuable in the purchases of radiology and nuclear medicine equipment and computer systems, but it is certainly not limited to these areas. The system assumes that no two suppliers can offer identical equipment, the requesting department has identified minimal requirements and preferred characteristics, and it is unlikely that in any fair competitive quotation process a supplier would be able to meet all of the preferences.

Once the functional specifications are detailed as either absolute requirements or preferences, a framework for financial comparisons is provided for the buyer. Degrees of preference are allocated to each characteristic, and usually a point scale of 1–10 is sufficient to identify to vendors the magnitude of a given preference. For example, an option that has 10 points means the buyer is willing to pay 10 times as much for it as for a one-point option. The hospital will establish a specified dollar amount for each point; however, suppliers will not be informed of this amount. They will only be aware of the relative value placed upon each preference.

The assignment of dollar-per-point can pose a problem. In an ideal situation, this would be decided on the basis of the *return on investment* that each specification would contribute, but this is usually almost impossible to determine. The most feasible approach is to survey the market for the expense of an option by analyzing suppliers informally to determine the expected cost. Whatever method is used, dollar amounts should be determined and agreed upon internally before the detailed specifications are put out as requests for bids.

Establishing a Bid List

The initial base of suppliers from which to solicit bids will be a subjective list of those already known to the user department. Purchasing can then supplement the list with its own recommendations. Instructions for bidding vary depending on project size and complexity needed for quick delivery, installation, type of institution, and other factors.

Past suppliers' performance can aid in refining a bid list. For instance, suppliers who have failed to provide adequate service or have defaulted on a bid bond may immediately be eliminated. Submitting a preliminary evaluation form to prospective vendors also can help shrink the list by identifying differences among suppliers that may need clarification.

Once a final list is established, a prebid conference should be arranged. This meeting involves representatives from all potential vendors and all relevant hospital departments in order to discuss general perceived requirements of the equipment. It also provides an opportunity to solicit advice and exchange new ideas. Most importantly, the conference ensures that all vendors have heard the same information from the institution.

Evaluation of Bids

After bids have been returned, the first step is to review their compliance with the stated specification requirements. In some situations, even though some have been characterized as absolute requirements, deviations will be accepted. This initial appraisal decides immediately if a proposal will be further considered.

When the number of bids has been narrowed down, preference points are then totaled among the different alternatives. The dollar amount of this total is discounted from the total quoted price. This process will sometimes yield a situation in which the highest quoted price turns out to be lower than others when weighted for the enhancements. The example below compares two price quotes that are weighted for enhancements. The main objective is to award the contract based on the highest overall value rather than comparing initial bottom lines.

Bids Evaluation Example	System A	System B
Total bid price	$145,000	$160,000
Preference point	14	76
Dollar value per point	× 250	× 250
Enhancement value	$ 3,500	$ 19,000
	145,000	160,000
Adjustment	− 3,500	− 19,000
Comparison	$141,500	$141,000
Decision: Buy System B		

Final Step

The final step in choosing the right supplier is to derive the total cost of the equipment over its expected life by weighting for service and installation. Installation fees should be known for each vendor, but maintenance and service expenses may not be known. If this is the case, an average weight may be assigned. When all calculations have been completed, the institution should have a price comparison basis that enables it to choose the best equipment for its dollars.

Health Care Costs

Businesses spend hundreds of millions of dollars on group health plans every year, and premiums keep increasing. In 2004, health care costs accounted for approximately 14 percent of GNP. According to the Kaiser Family Foundation Employer Health Benefits 2008 Annual Survey, the costs for providing health insurance increased by an average of 15.1 percent in 2008, the fourth straight year of double-digit premium increases. Health care benefit costs have clearly dominated overhead expenditures. Employers are responding to the increased health care benefit costs by moving away from traditional employer-sponsored insurance plans to consumer-driven health care plans. It is unclear how the new consumer-driven plans will factor into the hospital cost structure. For a detailed discussion, see Appendix A.

Summary

The cost of health care is expected to increase at an accelerating rate. Many businesses and health care organizations will be driven from the market because of uncontrollable nonsalary costs and declining profits. This radical shift is the result of increased price competition and the regulatory environment.

The focus of this chapter was on purchasing day-to-day supplies and capital equipment acquisition. The day-to-day services include dietary, linen, housekeeping, physical plant engineering, pharmacy, laboratory, inpatient treatment (nursing units), surgery, radiology, administration, and others. Each area has specific and often unique materials and supply needs, creating a requirement in these facilities for a supply management system that can provide the necessary supplies when needed. In the current climate of increasing health care costs, systems inventory must be optimized without sacrificing the level of service provided.

The Kaiser Family Foundation's 2008 Health Care Benefits Survey shows that health care insurance costs increased by an average of 15.1 percent in 2008. Health care benefits costs represent the largest component of overhead expenditures. Businesses have responded to increased health care costs by moving away from traditional employer-sponsored insurance plans to consumer-driven health care plans.

Discussion Questions

1. Discuss the purchasing process for supplies and services in the health care field.
2. Discuss the purchasing process for capital acquisition in the health care field.
3. How does supply management work in the health care industry?
4. Define cooperative or group purchasing in the health care field.
5. What are the various health care plans available to employers and employees? What is the trend for purchasing health plans? (See Appendix A.)
6. What percentage of the GNP is accounted for by the health care sector?

Suggested Cases

Hoosier Pride Construction
Medical Laser Equipment

References

Burns, L. *The Health Care Value Chain*. San Francisco, CA: Jossey-Bass, 2002.

Burns, L. R., and J. A. Lee. "Hospital Purchasing Alliances: Utilization, Services, and Performance." *Health Care Management Review* 33, (2008), pp. 203–215.

Chester, M. I. S., and D. A. Zilz. "Effects of Bar Coding on Pharmacy Stock Replenishment." *Journal of Hospital Pharmacy* 46, no. 7 (July 1989), pp. 1380–85.

Danish, Scott A. "Dartmouth-Hitchcock Medical Center Reduces Inventory Management Costs with PeopleSoft." *HCT Project*, 1, July 1, 2003.

De Jong, J. L., and W. C. Benton. "GPO Dependence and Power in the Healthcare Supply Chain." *Working Paper,* The Ohio State University 2013.

Elhauge, E. "The Exclusion of Competition for Hospital Sales Through Group Purchasing Organizations." Statement for DOJ-FTC Hearing on GPOs. September 26, 2003.

GAO. *Group Purchasing Organizations: Research on Their Pricing Impact on Healthcare Providers*, pp. 1–4. United States Government Accountability Office, GAO-323R, 2010a.

GAO. *Group Purchasing Organizations: Services Provided to Customers and Initiatives Regarding Their Business Practices*, pp. 1–20. United States Government Accountability Office, GAO-10-738, 2010b.

GAO. *Group Purchasing Organizations: Federal Oversight and Self-regulation*, pp. 1–16. United States Government Accountability Office, GAO-12-399R, 2012.

Holmgren, J. H., and W. J. Wentz. *Material Management and Purchasing for the Health Care Facility*. Ann Arbor, MI: AUPHA Press, 1982.

Hospitalconnect.com. "Do Off-Site Consolidated Warehouses Make Sense?" *Hospitalconnect.com*, July 1, 2002.

Li, L., and W. C. Benton. "Strategic Hospital Capacity Management Decision: Emphasis on Cost Control and Quality Enhancement." *European Journal of Operational Research* 146, no. 3 (2003), pp. 596–614.

Li, L., and W. C. Benton. "Hospital Technology and Nurse Staffing Management Decisions." *Journal of Operations Management* 24, no. 5 (2006), pp. 676–91.

Schneller, E. S., and L. R. Smeltzer. *Strategic Management of the Health Care Supply Chain.* San Francisco, CA: Jossey-Bass, 2006.

Siferd, S. P., and W. C. Benton. "Workforce Staffing and Scheduling Hospital Nursing Models." *European Journal of Operational Research* 60, no. 3 (August 10, 1992).

Watts, D., D. L. Finney, and B. Louie. "Integrating Technology Assessment into the Capital Budgeting Process." *Healthcare Financial Management*, February 1993, pp. 21–29.

Appendix A

Purchasing Health Care Plans

U.S. businesses spend hundreds of billions of dollars on group health plans every year. Premiums are increasing at an accelerating rate. Table A.1 shows the percentage of covered workers in the United States for each of the main types of group medical insurance. In 2004, health care costs accounted for approximately 14 percent of GNP. According to the Kaiser Family Foundation Employer Health Benefits 2004 Annual Survey, the costs for providing health insurance increased by an average of 11.2 percent in 2004, the fourth straight year of double-digit premium increases. For the first time, the average cost of a family PPO plan went above $10,000 a year. Most public and private organizations tend to reevaluate their health care options every year. Health care benefit costs have clearly dominated overhead expenditures. Employers are responding to the increased health care benefit costs by moving away from traditional employer-sponsored insurance plans to the following plans:

1. *Traditional plan.* A major advantage of traditional group medical insurance is the flexibility. Under this plan, employees can go to any specialist without a referral, and the insurance company has no say as to whether or not the visit is necessary. Unfortunately, for people who prefer this flexibility, few employers offer traditional group medical insurance any more. Traditional plans have become too expensive for most private and public organizations to maintain.
2. *Health maintenance organizations (HMOs).* HMOs control costs by creating a network of doctors and hospitals to provide services based on negotiated rates. The employees are restricted to the doctors and hospitals that are participating in the network. Employees must switch doctors to participate.
3. *Preferred provider organizations (PPOs).* A PPO operates similarly to HMOs. PPOs control costs by creating a network of doctors and hospitals to provide services based on negotiated rates without the restrictions.
4. *Point of service (POS).* A POS plan is a hybrid plan between the HMO and PPO plans. As with an HMO, members choose a primary care physician who will provide referrals when needed. Participants are free to visit out-of-network providers if they desire, with or without a referral—and the plan will still cover a portion of the expense, which is usually higher.

Finally, a new type of health plan that is rapidly gaining popularity is the consumer-driven health plan.

The first step in purchasing health insurance for a private or public organization is to engage an experienced broker. The broker must be licensed by the state to sell and service contracts of multiple health plans or insurers.

TABLE A.1
Percentage of Covered Workers in the United States for Each of the Main Types of Group Medical Insurance

	Traditional	HMO	PPO	POS
1988	73%	16%	11%	(na)
1998	14%	27%	35%	24%
2003	5%	24%	54%	17%

Source: Kaiser Family Foundation/Health Research and Educational Trust, Employer Health Benefits, 2004 Annual Survey.

Chapter Eighteen

Sourcing Professional Services

Learning Objectives

1. Understand the service sector characteristics and strategies.
2. Identify the activities involved in procuring professional services.
3. Describe why governmental agencies and private firms are moving toward outsourcing professional services more often.
4. Know the differences between procuring professional services in the public sector versus the private sector.
5. Discuss what is meant by scope of work.
6. Understand how professional service contracts are priced.
7. Describe how to measure project process.
8. Discuss how the critical path method is used to plan, schedule, and control complex projects.

INTRODUCTION

Over the past 60 years, the service sector has taken on an increasingly important role in the world economy. In the United States, jobs in the service sector have increased from just fewer than 50 percent of the total jobs in the U.S. economy to more than 85 percent of the total jobs. One-third of this growth has taken place in the last 20 years as organizations offering financial services, health care, communications, food, insurance, transportation, utilities, hospitality, entertainment, and virtually every other kind of service have proliferated. Many organizations in the service sector, especially those offering transportation, financial, and communication services, have encountered changes in their regulatory environment and in their technological structure. These changes have opened up new global markets but at the same time forced service industries to determine ways in which to remain competitive, or they would cease to exist.

Expanding competition, emerging technologies, and improved communications have altered most of the customers' tolerance for less than full satisfaction with the products and services they receive. In recent years, many manufacturing and service firms have been challenged to increase their focus on customer satisfaction and quality of service. These organizations also have had to increase productivity and quality and decrease cost of service while dealing with the demands of changing technology. For service sector firms, the responses to these challenges often have resulted in making their operations more "manufacturing-like." For example, service sector firms have adapted bar-coding and RFID procedures from manufacturing, using them not only for scanners at checkout counters but also for such diverse applications as tracking auto rentals and identifying hospital patients. At the same time, manufacturing firms have been increasing the emphasis on the "services" they provide to external and internal customers. Remaining in the service sector are many operations for which direct personal contact between customers and service providers must occur. Direct customer contact is increasing in the manufacturing sector as manufacturing flexibility allows more customized design. The need for employees in all types of organizations to recognize and be able to provide high-quality, efficient service to customers has become essential. The importance of a responsive workforce, able to execute procurement activities in keeping with organizational objectives, cannot be overstated.

One purpose of this chapter is to review characteristics and strategies of service-producing organizations. The characteristics are related to various strategies available to service organizations for achieving productivity; managing capacity, growth, and change; and differentiating services in order to be competitive. This chapter also addresses the procurement of professional services. Recently, the sourcing of professional services has received exceptional attention. Two real-world professional service sourcing examples are given in Appendixes A and B.

SERVICE SECTOR CHARACTERISTICS AND STRATEGIES

In the last 45 years, researchers and writers in the field of operations management have noted the differences and similarities between characteristics of operations in the service sector and in manufacturing. Some of the generally agreed-upon characteristics are shown in Table 18.1. Table 18.1 gives the extreme characteristics most often associated with "pure services" or "pure manufacturing." These characteristics have been divided into those describing operations, the product or service, employees, response time, quality, location, facilities, and capacity. Most of the characteristics of manufacturing and service operations fall along a continuum between the two extremes given in the table. In categorizing the operations of any given organization, a complicating factor is that individual operations of different segments of a service or goods-producing organization may fall on entirely different parts of the continuum from other segments in the same organization.

OUTSOURCING AND THE SERVICE SECTOR

The service sector has become the engine of growth for the American economy, fundamental to the health and prosperity of U.S. businesses, large, medium, or small. Service companies engaged in every type of commercial activity—manufacturing, transportation, energy and utilities, retail and wholesale trade, finance and government—rely on the edge that service firms offer to be integral to their business success. Just as service firms have found a sustainable niche in the

TABLE 18.1 **Service Sector Characteristics versus Manufacturing Characteristics**

Source: Siferd, Benton, and Ritzman (1992).

Focal Point	Service Sector Characteristic	Manufacturing Characteristic
Operations	Humanistic	Technocratic
	Volatile, uncertain	Stable, predictable
	Labor intensive	Capital intensive
	Decentralized	Centralized
	System malfunction directly affects the customer	System malfunction affects the customer only indirectly if at all
	Difficult-to-balance resources available with demand	Easy-to-balance resources available with demand
	Customer is part of the process	Customer is isolated from the process
Product or service	Simultaneous production and consumption	May be produced ahead of time
	Performed on an individual basis, customized	Mass-produced, standardized
	Intangible, perishable	Physical, durable
	Demand is time-dependent; in general, no backorders	Can have backorders
	Cannot be inventoried	Can be inventoried
	Cannot be transported	Can be transported
	Cannot be mass-produced	Can be mass-produced
Employees	Loosely supervised	Closely supervised
	Must be able to interact with public	Need technical skills only
	High personal judgment required	Low personal judgment required
	High contact with customers	Low or no contact with customers
	Wages may be based on hours worked	Wages may be based on output
Response time	Short	Long
Location	In local markets	National or international markets
	Near customer	Near supply, labor, or transportation

United States, many of these companies have expanded to the global arena. Today, U.S. service companies are disseminating knowledge and technology throughout the world. The U.S. government led the effort to complete the North American Free Trade Agreement (NAFTA) between the United States, Canada, and Mexico, and also encompasses trade in service industries. See Chapter 15 for NAFTA Statistics. Service providers bring hundreds of billions of dollars and thousands of high-wage jobs to the U.S. economy through global transactions. The two fastest growing outsourced service industries are information services and professional services.

Increasingly, American firms are outsourcing their information technology and services globally. Information services and information technology products have become fundamental to the overall growth and development of the U.S. economy and others around the world. With the development and growth of the Internet, virtually every sector of the economy employs information technology and services in its operations.

The professional business services sector is also becoming a major outsourced business sector. Through innovation and improvements in information technology, U.S. businesses are outsourcing many of their non-core professional services domestically and globally.

MANAGING COMPLEX GLOBAL OUTSOURCING SERVICES

Service sector businesses attribute two-thirds of U.S. gross domestic product and non-farm private-sector employment (U.S. Department of Commerce, 2012). The service sector accounts for about 80 percent of U.S. economic growth. Notwithstanding the prevalent role that the service sector now plays in nearly every industry, many firms struggle to realize the performance benefits they sought when deciding to outsource. Indeed, numerous industry sources (e.g., Bain & Co., Booz Allen Hamilton, and Dun & Bradstreet) have estimated that 30–50 percent of outsourcing organizations fail to realize their performance expectations. Many buying organizations ignore the significant expense related to managing the relationship. A Deloitte Consulting report found that 62 percent of outsourcing firms indicated that they required more management resources than initially estimated (Landis et al., 2005). These additional expenses are referred to as the "hidden costs" of outsourcing. Given the number of studies identifying these costs, it is not apparent that they are actually "hidden." Yet, it is clear that firms experience difficulty in accurately estimating the costs of outsourcing beyond simply supplier cost and profit. The provider relationship management costs become even more impressive in the complex globalized context.

In 2006, the Commonwealth of Virginia entered into a 10-year, $2.3 billion information technology service contract with Northrop Grumman Corporation (Towns, 2009). This disappointing relationship sheds light on many of the challenges for the buying organization. In 2009, the Joint Legislative Audit and Review Commission (JLARC) released a scathing assessment of the initiative's progress and impact on the 72 in-scope agencies (JLARC, 2009). The report outlines several performance shortfalls, including severely missed milestones, operational disruptions at multiple agencies, and unsatisfactory network reliability. Among the causes cited for this disappointing performance are inadequately understanding the *complexity* of the engagement, poor communication and coordination between internal and external stakeholders, inadequate contractual provisions, and an ill-defined and incomplete performance measurement system (PMS). This non-anomalous example illustrates two common challenges firms face in managing interorganizational relationships: control and coordination.

Several prior studies have identified control and coordination as two necessities for managing interorganizational relationships effectively (Dibbern et al., 2008). The successful buying organization must align the service provider's behaviors with the buying firm's interests. Aside from these behavioral concerns, the performance of the service provider relationship also depends on effectively integrating processes, resources, and information across firm boundaries (i.e., coordination). The time, effort, and resources associated with achieving adequate levels of provider control (i.e., *control costs*) and interfirm coordination (i.e., *coordination costs*) are prominently noted "hidden costs" with outsourcing. Given the difficulties firms experience in estimating these extra costs, few buying organizations understand the importance of control and coordination.

The Virginia JLARC report identified complexity as a root cause of the control and coordination difficulties experienced in the Commonwealth's relationship with Northrop Grumman by asserting "Complexity of the State's IT environment was not understood." This industry observation is consistent with two prominent theoretical perspectives that emphasize the salient role of complexity in causing interfirm control and coordination difficulties. Transaction cost theory asserts that complexity enhances the risk of opportunism and the need for more costly formal control mechanisms. Likewise, information processing theory contends that greater complexity is associated with the need for more expansive coordination mechanisms (Tanriverdi et al., 2007). Thus, these established theoretical perspectives as well as observations from practice suggest that an important point of departure for understanding factors contributing to greater control and coordination costs is the complexity of the outsourcing engagement. Complexity is a multifaceted construct examined in an array of fields. The two broad categories of factors that contribute to the overall complexity of the outsourcing engagement are task-specific complexity factors (i.e., scale, breadth, and customization) and location-specific complexity factors (i.e., geographic dispersion, geographic distance, and cultural distance). The decision to focus on task- and location-specific complexity and no other complexity dimensions was motivated by three considerations. The extant literature recognizes task- and location-specific factors as important outsourcing considerations that contribute to complexity and the often underestimated control and coordination costs in interorganizational relationships. Accordingly, buying organizations must address the following question when assessing the merits of service providers' performance:

> How does the task- and location-specific complexity of the outsourcing service influence the extent to which our (the customer) organization incurs control and coordination costs?

The primary managerial concern is the examination of how salient decisions are made regarding the scope and location of the outsourced work. Task- and location-related decisions may have an influence on the extent to which control and coordination costs are incurred. This deficiency is especially true with respect to coordination costs as there is scant empirical research linking *either* task- or location-specific complexity factors to interfirm coordination costs. Buying organizations must deploy effective control mechanisms to manage control and coordination tasks.

Control and coordination complexity make it more difficult to develop and maintain a completely specified contract. They also make it more difficult to deploy monitoring mechanisms to reduce information asymmetry. The combined effect translates into a greater concern for provider opportunism and the need for more elaborate (and costly) formal controls. The scale of the service, and to a lesser degree the breadth of activities, is also associated with uncertainty. This elevated uncertainty corresponds to greater information processing and coordination requirements.

Larger and more broadly defined outsourcing operations require more extensive interorganizational management resources. These additional expenses may include (but are not limited to) a larger retained management team, developing and maintaining a more complex formal contract, establishing a more elaborate performance monitoring and evaluation program, and more extensive information systems integration, among others. Many outsourcing organizations acknowledge the need for more managerial resources than originally planned (Handley and Benton, 2011). In some cases, it may be that the resources needed to control and coordinate effectively with the provider will largely nullify the benefits of lower labor rates, provider economies of scale, and so forth. Hence, outsourcing organizations must be especially cautious about establishing large, task-diverse arrangements. Outsourcing firms should consider establishing more narrowly scoped relationships. From a managerial perspective, exhaustively evaluating outsourcing opportunities from a strategic perspective allows firms to enter the arrangement with more realistic financial expectations and allows them to focus on critical management factors to mitigate potential strategic risks.

Service customization may be associated with specialized provider investments that in turn increase the commitment for the service provider, not the buyer. This diminishes the service provider's proclivity to act opportunistically (Handley and Benton, forthcoming). This reasoning is consistent with evidence that greater provider relationship-specific investments are associated with a lower risk of opportunism. Customized services require greater information exchange and open lines of communication early in the outsourcing process. This may enhance the relationship quality from the outset, which mitigates the need for costly formal controls.

As the relationship involves more countries, it becomes characterized by greater diversity in the legal and regulatory regimes, as well as more dispersed operational responsibility. These factors serve as obstacles to managing fully specified contracts and monitoring provider behavior and outcomes. Uncertainty also increases with the number of geographic locations. This enhanced uncertainty may contribute to greater information processing and coordination requirements. Greater geographic separation complicates monitoring of the service provider's activities and exacerbates information asymmetry. This will lead to a more amplified risk of opportunism and the need for more elaborate and costly formal control mechanisms. Geographic proximity is also noted to facilitate communication and knowledge transfer, which are central to effective coordination. Thus, all else equal, as the geographic distance between customer and provider locations increases, the costs associated with achieving adequate interfirm coordination also increases.

In some cases, geographic coverage may be a service requirement that the customer has stipulated. In such situations, the outsourcing firm needs to be prepared to have the proper resources in place and their cost accounted for. This may include the expenses associated with developing a more complex contract, ensuring that the various legal and regulatory frameworks are being followed, deploying more elaborate monitoring mechanisms, investing in integrated information systems, accounting for the need for more extensive travel to the provider's operations, and retaining a larger management team. Depending on the competitiveness of the supply market, the customer may be able to ask the service provider to bear some of these expenses. In other cases, the outsourcing customer may bear the entire cost. Either way, these insights should assist outsourcing organizations in developing a more realistic business case. In other cases, these geographic and cultural characteristics may simply be a result of the chosen service provider's existing global footprint and not a customer requirement.

If this is the case, buying organizations should factor in the impact on control and coordination costs when comparing the relative attractiveness of potential service providers.

PROFESSIONAL SERVICES

The purchasing of professional services is gaining exceptional attention. Thomas discussed growth strategies for service operations and how these strategies were different from those for manufacturing operations (Thomas, 1978; Wessel, 1989). He based his discussion on a classification scheme that separates service into equipment-based and people-based. The spectrum of types of service business is given in Table 18.2. IBM has evolved into a solutions provider. As a solutions provider, IBM delivers its hardware and integrates the hardware with software in order to produce business solutions. On the other hand, CISCO Systems is a product provider that focuses on product innovation. Perhaps the largest growth has come from the governmental sector. Federal, state, and city governments are hiring fewer people and outsourcing their tasks. As an example, the Federal Highway Administration (FHWA) and state departments of transportation (DOTs) outsource the design, construction, and inspection of new highways and bridges. Unlike manufacturing, it is more difficult to measure the performance of design consultants, contractors, and inspectors.

The statement of work or scope of work (SOW) is the most important component of highway and bridge design contracts. The SOW is an *agreement* between the project owner (the FHWA and a specific state DOT) and the contractor. The first step in the sourcing of a bridge design professional services contract for the governmental owner is a request for a *letter of interest* from *prequalified* bidders. The letter of interest includes company financial information, reputation, qualifications of key personnel, history on similar projects, and the proposed project approach. The letter of interest is usually limited to not more than 12 pages. Predetermined criteria are used to determine the successful bidder. Some of the criteria include capacity, reputation, performance on past projects, the project approach, and financial health. The formal

TABLE 18.2
Types of Service Organizations

Source: Adapted from Thomas (1978).

Service Basis	Dominant Labor Force	Examples
Equipment	Automation	Vending machine Automatic car wash
	Relatively unskilled operators	Motion picture theaters Dry cleaners
	Skilled operators	Airlines Excavation
People	Unskilled labor	Lawn care
	Skilled labor	Appliance repair Catering
	Professionals	Lawyers Professional engineers Accountants Business solutions

negotiations process follows the SOW. To illustrate the level of complexity, the SOW for an actual FHWA project is given in Appendix A.

PROJECT MANAGEMENT

The management of the project is the last line of defense. If the SOW is adequate, the right contractor is selected, and the ultimate price is reasonable, then a good management effort will secure the project. A poor management effort will undo all three pre-execution achievements. On the other hand, if the project is in trouble when the execution starts, a good project management effort can bail it out, and, conversely, a poor effort will put the final nail in the coffin. In order to be successful, the project must come in meeting the SOW specifications, on time and within budget.

The duties and responsibilities of the project or contract manager are diversified. The precise duties depend on the owner's organization. The skill and experience of the contractor are the ultimate determinants of a successful project.

Two Important Factors

1. Adequacy of site management
2. Relationship between the owner and the contractor

Costs are often divided into two categories, direct and indirect costs, defined as follows:

1. Direct costs include materials, labor, and subcontract expenditures associated with the actual implementation (subdivided into various accounting codes to reflect the actual work, the work breakdown structure (WBS)).
2. Indirect costs are all other expenditures, sometimes referred to as hidden costs.

The tasks involved in a typical complex project are given below:

1. Establish a reasonable budget.
2. Know where expenditures are being made.
3. Forecast final expenditures.
4. Identify problem areas by comparing expenditures and budgets.
5. Apprise contractors and managers of the information early so that actions can be taken to achieve enhanced economies.
6. Determine total cost of each labor classification.
7. Labor crew productivity must be maximized.
8. The field manager must properly balance the indirect costs to achieve the maximum level of efficiency.
9. Contractors/managers must be assigned indirect cost center responsibility early.
10. Joint reviews of indirect cost must take place on a scheduled basis.
11. Tracking curves or lists must be used to monitor budgeted versus actual costs.
12. Work hours must be controlled.
13. At least a 20-percent productivity improvement over previously established norms for the type of work in question must be established.
14. Labor budgets must be available to the owner early in the project.
15. Measures of actual performance against budgeted performance must be collected accurately. The data must be reliable.
16. The data should then be used for decision making.

17. Labor productivity, or effectiveness, should be tracked for each of the direct labor accounts.

$$\text{Labor productivity} = \frac{\text{Percent complete}}{\text{Percent of budget labor hours}}$$

    Historical plots are useful for tracking labor productivity.
18. Subcontracts should be issued to cover both direct and indirect work activities.
    - Direct activities—well-defined scope of work
    - Indirect activities—work only on necessary activities
19. Changes to the contracts must be strictly controlled and documented. If not documented, what are the possible outcomes?
20. See the change order form shown in Figure 18.1.
21. Schedule control is essential to the success of any complex project.
22. Major projects are a complex effort to mobilize and coordinate large numbers of personnel, materials, and equipment.
23. Good schedule control is to develop a plan, implement the plan, monitor execution of the plan, and make changes to the plan when necessary in order to meet the target.
24. The master schedule is generally a logical network-type schedule that reflects perfect execution plans, the strategy, equipment delivery estimates, and engineering plans. Project milestones must be reviewed and assessed.
25. Gantt charts or CPM should be used to assess progress.

PROJECT PLANNING AND SCHEDULING PROCESSES

Planning must be done before perfoming any function. A schedule is a time-phased plan. The principal use of schedules in the implementation process is discussed below:

Before Starting Project

1. Provides an estimate of the time required for each portion of the project as well as for the total project
2. Establishes the planned rate of progress
3. Forms the basis for management to issue instructions to subordinates
4. Establishes the planned sequence for the use of manpower, materials, machines, and money

During Project

1. Enables the contractor and the administrator to prepare a checklist of key dates, activities, resources, and so on.
2. Provides a means for evaluating the effects of changes and delays.
3. Serves as a basis for evaluating progress.
4. Aids in the coordination of resources.

After Completion of Project

1. Permits a review and analysis of the project as actually carried out.
2. Provides historical data for improving future planning and estimating.

FIGURE 18.1 Change Order Example

AMENDMENT OF SOLICITATION/MODIFICATION OF CONTRACT

1. CONTRACT ID CODE

PAGE OF PAGES: 1 | 2

2. AMENDMENT/MODIFICATION NO.: A0002

3. EFFECTIVE DATE: 05/11/2004

4. REQUISITION/PURCHASE REQ. NO.

5. PROJECT NO. *(If applicable)*

6. ISSUED BY — CODE: DTS-852

U.S. DOT/RSPA/Volpe Center
55 Broadway
Cambridge MA 02142

7. ADMINISTERED BY *(If other than item 6)* — CODE: DTS-852

U.S. DOT/RSPA/Volpe Center
55 Broadway
Cambridge MA 02142

8. NAME AND ADDRESS OF CONTRACTOR *(No., street, county, State and ZIP Code)*

CODE

FACILITY CODE

(x) 9A. AMENDMENT OF SOLICITATION NO.: DTRS57-04-R-20020

× 9B. DATED *(SEE ITEM 11)*: 04/27/2004

10A. MODIFICATION OF CONTRACT/ORDER NO.

10B. DATED *(SEE ITEM 13)*

11. THIS ITEM ONLY APPLIES TO AMENDMENTS OF SOLICITATIONS

☒ The above numbered solicitation is amanded as set forth in Item 14. The hour and date specified for receipt of Offers ☐ is extended. ☒ is not extended.
Offers must acknowledge receipt of this amendment prior to the hour and date specified in the solicitation or as amended, by one of the following methods: (a) By completing Items 8 and 15, and returning ______copies of the amendment; (b) By acknowledging receipt of this amendment on each copy of the offer submitted; or (c) By separate letter or telegram which includes a reference to the solicitation and amendment number. FAILURE OF YOUR ACKNOWLEDGEMENT TO BE RECEIVED AT THE PLACE DESIGNATED FOR THE RECEIPT OF OFFERS PRIOR TO THE HOUR AND DATE SPECIFIED MAY RESULT IN REJECTION OF YOUR OFFER. If by virtue of this amendment you desire to change an offer already submitted, such change may be made by telegram or letter, provided each telegram or letter makes reference to the solicitation and this amendment, and is received prior to the opening hour and date specified.

12. ACCOUNTING AND APPROPRIATION DATA *(If required.)*

13. THIS ITEM APPLIES ONLY TO MODIFICATIONS OF CONTRACTS/ORDERS. IT MODIFIES THE CONTRACT/ORDER NO. AS DESCRIBED IN ITEM 14.

(x)	
	A. THIS CHANGE ORDER IS ISSUED PURSUANT TO: *(Specify authority)* THE CHANGES SET FORTH IN ITEM 14 ARE MADE IN THE CONTRACT ORDER NO. IN ITEM 10A.
	B. THE ABOVE NUMBERED CONTRACT/ORDER IS MODIFIED TO REFLECT THE ADMINISTRATIVE CHANGES *(such as changes in paying office, appropriation date, etc.)* SET FORTH IN ITEM 14, PURSUANT TO THE AUTHORITY OF FAR 43. 103(b).
	C. THIS SUPPLEMENTAL AGREEMENT IS ENTERED INTO PURSUANT TO THE AUTHORITY OF:
	D. OTHER *(Specify type of modification and authority)*

E. IMPORTANT: Contractor ☐ is not. ☐ is required to sign this document and return__________copies to the issuing office.

14. DESCRIPTION OF AMENDMENT/MODIFICATION *(Organized by UCF section headings, Including solicitation/contract subject metter where feasible.)*

The Purpose of this Amendment is to incorporate the following changes:

Page 55 L4A Paragraph 1 Change From: The offeror must develop fixed fee, and profit an Schedule 5,
Change To : The Offeror must develop fixed fee, and profit on Schedule 4.
See continuation sheets for questions and answers

Except as provided herein, all terms and conditions of the document referenced in item 9A or 10A, as heretofore changed, remains unchanged and in full force and effect.

15A. NAME AND TITLE OF SIGNER *(Type or print)*

16A. NAME AND TITLE OF CONTRACTING OFFICER *(Type or print)*

15B. CONTRACTOR/OFFEROR

(Signature of person authorized to sign)

15C. DATE SIGNED

16B. UNITED STATES OF AMERICA

(Signature of Contracting Officer)

16C. DATE SIGNED

NSN 7540-01-152-8070
Previous edition unusable

STANDARD FORM 30 (REV. 10-83)
Prescribed by GSA
FAR (48 CFR) 53.243

(continued)

(concluded)

DTRS57-04-R-20020 Amendment A0002

Question 1: Does this submittal require that the cost proposal be submitted in BOTH CPFF and FFP format?
Answer 1: See H9

Question 2: Schedule 1 — Proposal Cover Sheet — page 60: Assuming this submission requires fees to be presented in both CPFF and FFP formats, do we complete a separate schedule 1 for each cost proposal type, i.e. one for CPFF format and another for FFP, or use columns in item 6 to represent the total price for each type of contract?
Answer 2: See H9

Question 3: Schedule 2 — Summary of Proposed Costs and Fixed Fee — page 61: Is an ODC Burden a fixed fee/profit on the ODC amount? If not, what is it?
Answer 3: See page 56 Other Direct Cost (ODC's)

Question 4: Schedule 3 — Summary of Proposed Costs and Profit — page 62: Is an ODC Burden a fixed fee/profit on the ODC amount/ If not, what is it?
Answer 4: See page 56 Other Direct Cost (ODC's)

Question 5: Schedule 5 — Labor Cost Realism Information — page 64: Should Labor Rate descriptions in column 3 be consistent with the Labor Category titles?
Answer 5: See page 64 Labor Cost Realism Information

Question 6: Are the labor rates requested from Schedule 6 based upon category averages?
Answer 6: Schedule 6 is Allocation of Labor Hours

Question 7: Schedule 6 — Allocation of Labor Hours — page 66: It appears that the Junior Engineer category was omitted from this form. Will there be a new Schedule 6 to replace it?
Answer 7: See page 65 schedule 5 (continued)

Question 8: Indirect Rates: Page 57 indicates that offerors are required to provide a schedule of indirect rates which a Government audit agency has approved for forward pricing or if not approved state basis of proposed rate. However, this paragraph also states that if an offeror is submitting on the basis of a proposed rate, the offeror must provide actual expense pool amounts, allocation bases, and rates which have been submitted to the DCAA or other cognizant agency. This appears to conflict with the statement that the offeror is not required to be audited or submit an audit prior to award. Can you clarify?
Answer 8: See page 57 Indirect Rates paragraph 2

Question 9: Should the 3 copies of the "Cost/Business Proposal" and 8 copies of the "Technical Proposal" be presented in individual loose-leaf binders as is required with the original Volumes?
Answer 9: See Page 53 4. Binding

Gantt Chart (or Bar Chart) Method

Gantt charts are useful tools for planning and scheduling projects. Gantt charts

- Allow you to assess how long a project should take.
- Lay out the order in which tasks need to be carried out.
- Help manage the dependencies between tasks.
- Determine the resources needed.

Progress Curves

Progress curves are useful tools when a project is under way. Progress curves

- Monitor progress. You can immediately see what should have been achieved at a point in time.
- Allow you to see how remedial action may bring the project back on course.

The Critical Path Method

The critical path method (CPM) is a robust logical system for planning and scheduling using bar charts. CPM is a graphical representation of the interrelationships of the various project activities. With CPM, the contract administrator can assess the status of the project at any time, and it enables the contract administrator to monitor and revise scheduling during the project to meet the desired completion date. Specifically, the CPM establishes

- The quantity of work for each activity.
- The start-up and sequence or order in which the work or the activity is to be done.
- The rate at which the work will be performed to reach completion.

FIGURE 18.2
Simple Network Diagram

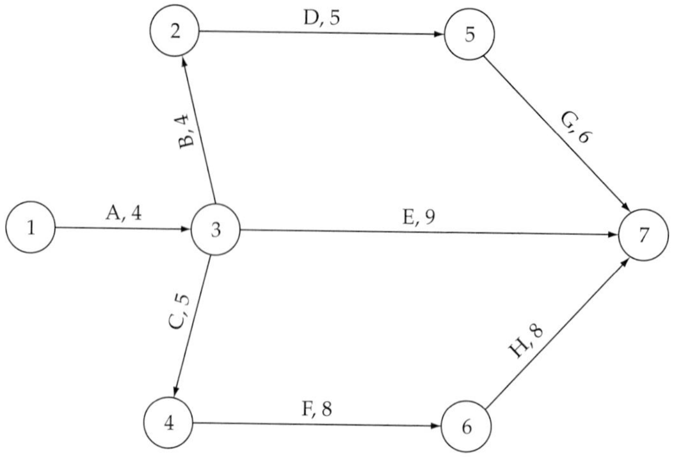

The CPM network consists of arcs and nodes. The arcs represent the actual activities while the nodes (events) represent when the activity starts and finishes. Each node (event) combination between two nodes is unique. The end of one activity is the start of a succeeding activity. The times on the activities (arcs) represent the duration for the specific activity. Each activity is identified by letters on the arcs. In general, the network diagram represents logical relationships between the activities to complete the project. Unlike a tabular list of project activities, the network diagram can be manipulated mathematically.

In Figure 18.2, A is the beginning of the project and must be completed before B, E, and C can start. B, E, and C can then start at the same time. D must be completed before G can begin and F must be completed before H can start. G, E, and H must be completed before the project can finish.

The critical path is represented by the longest path through the network from node 1 to node 7. Thus, *the critical path* for Figure 18.2 is A–C–F–H, which totals 25 days. There could be more than 100 activities in a typical project. In most large, complex projects, CPM-related computer software is implemented. This discussion of CPM is not meant to be exhaustive; 16-week courses are sometimes dedicated to the topic.

Steps in CPM Project Planning

1. Specify each individual activity.
2. Sequence the activities.
3. Draw a network diagram.
4. Estimate the completion time for each activity.
5. Identify the critical path (longest path through the network).
6. Update the CPM diagram as the project progresses.
7. CPM crashing.

1. Specify Each Individual Activity

From the WBS, a listing can be made of all the activities in the project. This listing can be used as the basis for adding sequence and duration information in later steps.

2. Sequence the Activities

Some activities are concurrent with other activities. A listing of the immediate predecessors of each activity is useful for constructing the CPM network diagram.

3. *Draw the Network Diagram*

Once the activities and their sequencing have been defined, the CPM diagram can be drawn.

4. *Estimate Activity Completion Time*

CPM is usually used for projects with predictable task times. CPM is a deterministic model that does not take into account variation in the completion time, so only one number is used for an activity's time estimate.

5. *Identify the Critical Path*

The critical path is the longest-duration path through the network. Activities located on the critical path cannot be delayed. Because of its impact on the entire project, critical path analysis is an important aspect of project planning.

The critical path can be identified by determining the following four parameters for each activity:

- ES—earliest start time: the earliest time at which the activity can start given that its precedent activities must be completed first
- EF—earliest finish time, equal to the earliest start time for the activity plus the time required to complete the activity
- LF—latest finish time, equal to the latest start time for the activity plus the time required to complete the activity
- LS—latest start time, equal to the latest finish time minus the time required to complete the activity

The *slack time* for an activity is the time between its earliest and latest start time, or between its earliest and latest finish time. Slack is the amount of time that an activity can be delayed past its earliest start or earliest finish without delaying the project.

The critical path is the path through the project network in which none of the activities have slack, that is, the path for which ES = LS and EF = LF for all activities in the path. A delay in the critical path delays the project. Similarly, to accelerate the project it is necessary to reduce the total time required for the activities in the critical path.

6. *Update CPM Diagram*

As the project rolls through time, the actual task completion times will be known and the network diagram can be updated to include updated information. A new or multiple critical paths may emerge, and the project requirements must be updated.

7. *CPM Crashing*

Speeding up the project is referred to as crashing. As an example, an activity must be located on the critical path. There is a crash cost associated with any feasible activity on the critical path.

Summary

The service sector has taken on an increasingly important role in the world economy. In the United States, jobs in the service sector have increased from just under 50 percent to 85 percent of the total jobs. Thus, the purchasing of professional services is gaining exceptional attention. The largest growth has come from the governmental sector. Unlike manufacturing, it is more difficult to measure the performance of design consultants, contractors, and inspectors. The chapter ends with two appendixes, one dedicated to an extensive example of the scope of work for an FHWA project.

Discussion Questions

1. Why are organizations buying more professional services?
2. What are some of the key differences between buying services and buying OEM goods?
3. How are governmental megaprojects procured?
4. How are megaprojects managed? What is meant by contract administration?
5. What are global sourcing trends? Give at least three real-world examples from the Internet.
6. Discuss some of the complexities of global outsourcing? Give specific examples.
7. As a buying organization, what questions do you suggest asking each of the following potential service providers? You must be specific.
   - Construction management
   - Underground construction
   - Above ground construction
   - Engineering design
   - Health and safety
   - Environment
   - Printing and promotions
   - Legal services
   - Facilities maintenance
   - Information technology

Suggested Cases

KACI Products, Inc.
The ARMS Procurement System at Tustin State University
Camp Bowie Technologies, Inc.
Hoosier Pride Construction, Inc.

References

Dibbern, J., J. Winkler, and A. Heinzl. "Explaining Variations in Client Extra Costs between Software Projects Offshored to India." *MIS Quarterly* 32, no. 2 (2008), pp. 333–66.

Handley, S., and W. Benton, Jr. "The Influence of Exchange Hazards and Power on Opportunism in Outsourcing Relationships." *Journal of Operations Management* 30, no. 1–2 (2011), pp. 55–68.

Handley, S. M., and W. C. Benton. "The Influence of Task- and Location-Specific Complexity of the Control and Coordination Costs in Global Outsourcing Relationships." *Journal of Operations Management* (forthcoming).

Joint Legislative Audit and Review Commission (JLARC). "Review of Information Technology Services in Virginia: Commission Briefing." Joint Legislative Audit and Review Commission, October 13, 2009. Retrieved from http://jlarc.state.va.us/meetings/October09/VITA.pdf (accessed on February 6, 2012).

Landis, K. M., S. Mishra, and K. Porrello. "Calling a Change in the Outsourcing Market: The Realities for the World's Largest Organizations." Deloitte Consulting Report.

Siferd, S. P., W. C. Benton Jr., and L. Ritzman. "Strategies for Service Systems." *European Journal of Operational Research* 56, no. 5 (1992), pp. 241–303.

Tanriverdi, H., P. Konana, and L. Ge. "The Choice of Sourcing Mechanisms for Business Processes." *Information Systems Research* 18, no. 3 (2007), pp. 280–299.

Thomas, D. R. E. "Strategy Is Different in Service Businesses." *Harvard Business Review* 56, no. 4 (1978), pp. 158–65.

Towns, S. "Audit Report Criticizes Massive Virginia IT Outsourcing Plan." *Government Technology*, October 14, 2009. Retrieved from http://www.govtech.com/policy-management/Audit-Report-Criticizes-Massive.html (accessed on February 6, 2012).

U.S. Department of Commerce, International Trade Administration, Office of Service Industries. Retrieved from www.ita.doc.gov/td/sif/about.htm. U.S. Department of Commerce, Bureau of Economic Analysis, 2012.

Wessel, D. "Working Smart: With Labor Scarce, Service Firms Strive to Raise Productivity," *The Wall Street Journal*, June 1, 1989, pp. A1, A16.

Appendix A

FHWA Project Example *USDOT and NENA (National Emergency Number Association) Wireless Implementation Plan*

Parties interested in assisting in this first-ever Wireless Implementation Plan (WIP) program are encouraged to send their letter of interest to NENA Wireless Implementation Director James Burgin at Burgin@nena.org.

BACKGROUND AND INTRODUCTION

As part of its efforts to improve the safety and efficiency of surface transportation, the USDOT supports the implementation of National Wireless E9-1-1 capabilities. This contract is intended to facilitate the deployment of enhanced wireless E9-1-1 services by supporting the efforts of state and local public safety answering points (PSAPs) in coordinating and implementing the upgrades that will be necessary.

There are approximately 100 million wireless subscribers in the United States. These wireless subscribers call 9-1-1 an estimated 70,000 times per day, or 25–30 million calls per year. Wireless calls represent almost 40 percent of the 100 million calls to 9-1-1 each year. Many of the calls to 9-1-1 from wireless devices are calls from travelers on the nation's highways. Wireless calls currently present an immediate and growing challenge to the essential health of the nation's 9-1-1 infrastructure. Without location, these calls will continue to consume excessive amounts of call capacity and personnel resources in the 9-1-1 systems. Additionally, there is a related consumption of resources for police, fire, and EMS as the responders resort to heroic and costly efforts to locate callers. For these reasons, the implementation of wireless E9-1-1 location technology is a matter of growing importance and national interest, and may have the unintended consequence of creating a challenge to the effectiveness of 9-1-1 as perceived by the public.

The challenge of implementing caller location technology for wireless E9-1-1 is compounded by the fact that many stakeholders must collaborate for the process to move forward. The slow progress to date is due in part to these stakeholders—that is, wireless carriers, public safety answering points (PSAPs), incumbent 9-1-1 service telephone companies, third-party database vendors, and location technology firms—having little or no history of collaboration. A lack of regulatory clarity of responsibilities, a lack of central leadership within the stakeholder groups, a greater-than-expected growth in the wireless industry, and new and emerging location technologies all have contributed to a de facto delay in the implementation of wireless E9-1-1.

Currently, there is a movement throughout the country to implement the first phase (Phase I) of wireless service. The above challenges, coupled with budgetary, technical, and skills/training issues, serve to slow the progress, however. Consequently, there remain a large number of PSAPs and wireless carriers that are far from beginning their Phase I implementation.

No current activity of any single stakeholder can reach the desired outcome of full wireless implementation (including Phase II) on its own. In order to make significant progress in this area, a comprehensive and coordinated approach to implementation will be required.

This contract is intended to produce and carry out a comprehensive plan to help address coordination and implementation issues with the wireless carrier community, the major telephone companies that provide 9-1-1 service (and the host of small Telcos that provide 9-1-1 services), the public safety community, and telephone handset, hardware, and switch manufacturers that must develop technology to meet the new demand for wireless location technology.

CONTRACT OBJECTIVES

The objectives of this contract are to develop the necessary tools, technical guidance, and training and outreach materials to facilitate implementation of the wireless E9-1-1 services throughout the 50 states. A related objective is to foster coordination among the many players in this field to ensure efficient approaches to the implementation process.

SCOPE OF WORK

As a high-level summary, the activities of the contractor (NENA) shall include performing program management; developing a work plan; providing technical and operational assistance to public safety answering points (PSAPs); creating, and publishing on electronic and print format, a National Contract Clearinghouse including a database of forms and form clauses that have been agreed to by parties across the nation; developing and maintaining a tracking system that accurately depicts the current status of wireless E9-1-1 implementation across the 50 states; developing the wireless deployment profile; conducting the necessary analyses and evaluations of wireless location technologies to provide technical assistance and to gather the necessary operational and technical information and insights; developing a test program for wireless implementation; serving as a technical resource for PSAPs in planning for and implementing wireless E9-1-1 services; providing consultation to the government regarding wireless E9-1-1; developing training and outreach materials; and producing and distributing three targeted instructional videos.

DELINEATION OF CONTRACTOR (NENA) TASKS

Task 1: Program Management, Administration, and Reporting

Develop and submit to FHWA a draft work plan for this project, identifying major activities, organizational and staffing responsibilities for various tasks, as well as overall plans and schedules for accomplishing individual tasks. FHWA will review the draft work plan and provide comments within 30 days of receipt of the draft plan. Based on the input of FHWA, develop and maintain a final work plan to guide the remainder of the contract. Conduct meetings with APCO and NASNA and other stakeholders to facilitate program planning and travel planning as well as coordination and consensus-building activities. The contractor (NENA) shall also fulfill the reporting and administration requirements contained in this contract.

As to each deliverable item producible in paper form (such as plans, reports, and white papers), the contractor (NENA) shall deliver to the COTR: (a) five ordinary photocopies; (b) one camera-ready, reproducible copy; and (c) one electronic copy.

Task 2: Provide Operational and Technical Assistance

A. Develop/maintain a knowledge base in order to provide technical and operational assistance to PSAPs regarding the implementation of wireless E9-1-1 services. The contractor (NENA) shall maintain an understanding of the contracting processes necessary for the PSAPs to enter into service agreements with the wireless companies in their jurisdictions and establish a database of the various contract types and procedures that are being used to establish wireless location capabilities at PSAPs. Provide technical assistance, as necessary and appropriate, to help facilitate contract negotiation.

To achieve this aspect of the project, the contractor (NENA) shall create a national clearinghouse of legal contracts, forms, and trends that are occurring in the nation that would accelerate the implementation process in the scenario where a PSAP and wireless company are actively negotiating for the service.

The contractor (NENA) shall create, and publish in electronic and print format, a National Contract Clearinghouse comprising a databank of forms, and form clauses, that have been agreed to by parties across the nation. This databank will be a passive reference tool for both wireless company attorneys and local prosecutors and so on to review and get an industry practice orientation for their particular implementation.

The contractor (NENA) shall execute and create a second element to facilitate a contractor (NENA) supported format for contract essential terms, and even highlighting certain clauses that are too onerous or perhaps rendered meaningless by rule clarification or S800, or other local law development.

The contractor (NENA) shall confer with legal experts in all states to develop, gather, and distill common practices and methods of contract formation and project management. Key trends in Project Locate also will be incorporated in this work to the extent data are available through that effort.

The Contract Clearinghouse shall be initiated and available for use by April 15, 2002. The clearinghouse would be maintained dynamically thereafter during the contract period.

It is anticipated that a task force and electronic interface will be created for this aspect of the project immediately. It is anticipated that an electronic interface, which complements the National Deployment Profile, will be available for utilization by April 1, 2002. Once established, the Clearinghouse will be updated dynamically as component documents are modified.

Model contracts for each state and service area will be established. The national inventory of contracts will flow to the implementation step of the process in an orderly fashion, and will permit the parties to do effective project management for their respective roles in the wireless implementation process.

B. Develop and maintain a tracking system that accurately depicts the current status of wireless E9-1-1 implementation across the 50 states. The contractor (NENA) shall develop approaches for collecting implementation status on a national basis and for presenting/displaying this information in a graphical and interactive manner. NENA will provide access to this information through an Internet-based, point-and-click map of the nation, with state and county boundaries. Utilize this dynamic inventory to draw attention to key practical roadblocks in the implementation process.

To achieve this work, the contractor (NENA) shall develop the Wireless Deployment Profile that will enable all those responsible for or interested in wireless deployment to find out the status of wireless implementation throughout the United States. The profile will be maintained at the state and county level, accessible using a point-and-click map of the United States with state and county boundaries.

The contractor (NENA) shall develop, and will post the Web site described herein, and will keep its information current through a host of data collection efforts, including but not limited to

- Direct surveys
- Direct telephone calls
- E-mail surveys
- Web-based surveys
- Collaboration with secondary and industry resources for updates
- Collaboration with associations and statewide offices containing wireless implementation data

This deployment profile will be maintained and managed by the contractor (NENA), with the participation of other parties. The results of the inventory will be posted on the Internet for the benefit of all parties related to the wireless implementation project.

The following information elements will be included in the profile:

Wireless Phase II status. Over the next several years, each county or PSAP system will be in various stages of Phase II implementation. The profile will track that status on a quarterly basis and indicate in tabular form progress toward implementation.

Readiness level. A number of implementation steps are required for Phase II, as indicated on the NENA wireless checklist.

Information related to PSAP readiness includes but is not limited to

- PSAP capability to display X, Y coordinates
- Wireless carriers serving the area
- 9-1-1 service provider(s), including the incumbent or host company
- Third-party vendors
- Choice of location determination technology (LDT) by carriers serving the area
- The impact of wire line 9-1-1 on wireless deployment
- Type of wireless solution

The Wireless Deployment Profile will be updated on a recurring basis. PSAP system is obtained either through personal contact or by survey. The states and 9-1-1 systems that take the lead on Phase II will be the first entries into the profile.

The contractor (NENA) shall work closely with state 9-1-1 coordinators, NENA chapter presidents, county 9-1-1 coordinators, service providers, and wireless carriers to obtain current status.

This inventory will be created and posted in a skeletal format by April 1, 2002, and a comprehensive version of this inventory will be available and posted on the Web site on June 1, 2002. Once completed, this tool will be made available for each interested party to view their county/jurisdiction, and to point and click on a graphical interface that connects the viewer to a tabular database summary of the progress for that jurisdiction.

C. Conduct the necessary coordination with stakeholder organizations and other entities involved in the implementation of wireless E9-1-1 services. The contractor (NENA) shall establish mechanisms to facilitate coordination among various groups involved in the implementation of wireless caller location technologies. Wireless legislation in each state commonly includes the establishment of a state funding board charged with the responsibility of determining how wireless funds are collected and distributed in that state. The contractor (NENA) shall facilitate communication with (and between) the individual state funding boards to permit the exchange of useful information regarding what processes have been used by states to provide funding to the PSAPs for the implementation of wireless E9-1-1 services. This may include the conduct of a workshop meeting for state funding board representatives, with necessary follow-up communications to ensure the full exchange of information.

To complete this aspect of the project, the contractor (NENA) shall hold workshop meetings for state funding board representatives, with follow-up and ongoing communications via conference calling and Web conferencing. Summary information and feedback from the boards will help shape and resolve funding issues that emerge during wireless Phase II.

D. The contractor (NENA) shall develop, in cooperation with other public safety resource providers, a technical assistance component that can directly assist stakeholders in moving forward with wireless implementation. The component will be designed to rapidly and effectively deploy assistance as appropriate and necessary.

The contractor (NENA) shall ensure that technical assistance and outreach activities performed under this project are coordinated with the broader government activities envisioned within the DOT E9-1-1 initiative, such as the planned development of "expert assistance teams."

The contractor (NENA) shall make its technical staff available for direct consultation, and will facilitate technical forums on key issues facing the technical implementation of wireless 9-1-1 services. The contractor (NENA) shall lend technical support and advice through its staff and by collaboration of key members, and will utilize electronic meetings and white papers to frame the issues impacting the implementation process.

Task 3: Perform Technical Analyses and Evaluation of Wireless E9-1-1 Implementation Approaches and Performance Issues

A. Conduct the necessary analyses and evaluations of wireless location technologies, including handset, tower-based, and hybrid solutions, to be able to provide technical assistance (see Task 2 of this Statement of Work) to the PSAP community, to the government, and to other stakeholder organizations. This task is also structured to gather the necessary operational and technical information and insights needed for the contractor (NENA) to fulfill the activities identified in Task 4 ("Develop and Conduct Educational and Outreach Programs") of this Statement of Work.

To accomplish this portion of the contract, the contractor (NENA) shall develop a testing program for wireless implementation. Test parameters will be developed by the contractor (NENA) with input from DOT and appropriate public safety and industry contacts. The tests will be designed to answer questions identified by the contractor (NENA) review team.

These tests and technology parameters shall be conducted in the first and second quarters of the contract period. The contractor (NENA) shall develop and submit to FHWA a Technical Analyses and Evaluation Report of Wireless Location Technologies. FHWA will review the draft report and provide comments within 30 days of receipt of the draft report. The contractor (NENA) shall prepare a final

Technical Analyses and Evaluation Report of Wireless Location Technologies based on the input of FHWA.

B. The contractor (NENA) shall maintain a technical awareness of wireless implementation approaches and of performance and operational issues in order to serve as a technical resource for the PSAPs in planning for and implementing wireless E9-1-1 services in their local areas. The contractor (NENA) shall provide consultation to the government regarding wireless E9-1-1 implementation (including technical, regulatory, and rulemaking) issues, and shall provide recommendations and advice for expediting implementation of national wireless E9-1-1 services.

The contractor (NENA) shall maintain an awareness of telemetric devices and services that potentially will interface with PSAPs, and shall assess the implications of nontraditional access to 9-1-1 on PSAP operations. This shall include the monitoring of efforts aimed at answering any unresolved issues raised by the NMRI process. Include any technical, policy, and public education issues from this subject matter into the education and outreach program discussed in Task 4 of this Statement of Work.

The contractor (NENA) shall design this activity with a view towards answering the unresolved issues raised by the NMRl process. It is anticipated that the technical, policy, and public education issues will be addressed in concert with the wireless E9-1-1 program.

The contractor (NENA) shall write white papers, conduct surveys, and lead an issue resolution program regarding the integration of telemetric and intelligent transportation data transfer to public safety centers. In completing this objective of this contract, the contractor (NENA) shall distill results of other DOT initiatives such as the field operational tests and other outreach efforts and trials of "nontraditional" communications to the 9-1-1 system. Each white paper should be submitted to FHWA in draft form for review and comment. Each white paper will then be revised based on the input of FHWA.

For this portion of the program, a series of white papers shall be produced on a quarterly basis during the contract period.

As to each deliverable item producible in paper form (such as plans, reports, and white papers), the contractor (NENA) shall deliver to the COTR (a) five ordinary photocopies; (b) one camera-ready, reproducible copy; and (c) one electronic copy.

Task 4: Develop and Conduct Educational and Outreach Programs

A. The contractor (NENA) shall develop training and outreach materials that support the government efforts to facilitate implementation of wireless E9-1-1. These materials shall be in the form of instructional videos for PSAP personnel and other stakeholders, white papers, and presentation materials to be used at educational forums. The contractor (NENA) shall distribute appropriate training videos to the PSAP community and shall provide follow-up services to this community to resolve residual questions and issues that may arise. This activity is designed to ensure maximum exposure of educational materials to users who have time and travel (cost) limitations for attending national or regional level conferences and forums.

The contractor (NENA) shall submit white paper topics and content descriptions to the COTR for approval prior to the development of the white paper. COTR approvals also will be obtained regarding the topics and contents (storyboards) of the planned training videos before they are developed. This approval process will be informal in nature.

To address this objective of the scope of work, the contractor (NENA) shall produce three instructional videos for further training and orientation for key stakeholders in the process. The contractor (NENA) shall submit a draft storyboard and script to the FHWA for review and comment before production of any video. The final storyboard and script shall be approved by the FHWA before production of any video is initiated. The three required videos are further described below. Instructional videos remain an effective technology delivery method for widespread distribution of the knowledge, project planning, and industry insight.

The contractor (NENA) shall produce and distribute three targeted instructional videos for distribution to key parties in the implementation process, as follows:

> *Video One. For PSAPs*: The contractor (NENA) shall produce this instructional video by editing existing raw footage from four wireless critical issues forums (CIFs) previously taped by NENA.
>
> *Video Two. For wireless companies*: The contractor (NENA) shall produce this video by editing existing wireless CIF footage and adding elements from NENA's Introduction to Technology course to meet the fundamental needs of over 200 wireless companies.
>
> *Video Three. For states and the public*: The contractor (NENA) shall produce this video in such a way that it focuses on the states and the public sector as an audience.

The contractor (NENA) shall collaborate with key stakeholders in producing each of the three required videos.

It is anticipated that the video production will begin immediately upon contract award (or as soon thereafter as practicable) and that it will be completed by October 15, 2006, for videos one and three. It is anticipated that video two will be completed by January 15, 2007.

Contractor (NENA) shall provide two master copies of each video to the COTR upon completion of that video.

B. The contractor (NENA) shall sponsor educational sessions at stakeholder conferences and hold special forums among the stakeholder communities to ensure wide distribution of educational information and to permit a broad exchange of views among stakeholder organizations. The education forum component of this activity also will serve to bring together companies (e.g., wireless E9-1-1 service providers) who are users of the equipment with manufacturers of switches and handsets to foster discussion relative to (product) demand, technical, and schedule issues.

The contractor (NENA) shall work with all stakeholders to hold forums and develop white paper recommendations.

C. The contractor (NENA) shall work with all stakeholders to develop white paper recommendations. The contractor (NENA) shall create an industry white paper on product development, services, and technical issues associated with Phase II. The paper shall address issues of product choice, demand, and manufacturing cycle times in addition to any performance and implementation issues identified. Recommend other white paper topics considered appropriate to this effort.

The contractor (NENA) shall hold a technology summit in conjunction with the planned Technical Development Conference and address the specific aspects of technical interoperability addressed herein. The education forum component of this activity will bring together companies (e.g., 9-1-1 service providers) having demand requirements with manufacturers of switches and handsets to realistically assess product demand and schedule. This forum will be held during the first quarter of calendar year 2002, and the forum will lead to a white paper process of identifying and capturing the key cycle times of wireless location technology.

Each white paper should be submitted to FHWA in draft form for review and comment. Each white paper will then be revised based on the input of FHWA.

The contractor (NENA) shall develop and submit to FHWA a draft final report. FHWA will review the draft final report and provide comments within 30 days of receipt of the draft report. The contractor (NENA) shall revise the final report based on the input of FHWA and provide a final version to FHWA.

As to each deliverable item producible in paper form (such as plans, reports, and white papers), the contractor (NENA) shall deliver to the COTR (a) five ordinary photocopies; (b) one camera-ready, reproducible copy; and (c) one electronic copy.

As can be seen from the NENA project, it is easy to see the complexity of developing the scope of work, the selection of the contractor, the pricing mechanism, and the management of the project.

Appendix **B**

Fortune 500 Company Example *Document Destruction Services Example*

With growing attention to protecting competitive information and increasing awareness of consumers regarding privacy, the demand for document destruction services has grown substantially over the last five years. As the demand has increased, so have the number of companies offering the service. There are over 600 firms nationally in the business of destroying discarded documents. This expanding market share will attract both new demand and new suppliers. Processes and technology have been improved along with improved logistics strategies. These improvements have led to significant cost reduction.

INDUSTRY SPECIFICS AND LEGISLATION

Recent legislation has resulted in an increased demand for destruction services. This legislation is largely a reaction to the exponential growth of identity theft and other forms of information-based fraud. Often it turns out that the information used to commit the fraud was obtained from casually discarded documents containing personal data.

The Gramm-Leach-Bliley Act—also known as the Financial Modernization Act of 1999—enacted by the federal government, went into effect in July 2004. This law mandates that all financial institutions must establish procedures for protecting personal information, including the protection of discarded information. The

Gramm-Leach-Bliley Act consists of three principal parts: the financial privacy rule, the safeguards rule, and the pretexting provisions.

Financial privacy rule. This rule applies to all financial institutions requiring them to provide customers with a detailed explanation of the management of information sharing and collection practices within the institution. This rule also allows for customers to request the confidentiality of specific information, which limits the amount of financial information that outside companies can access.

Safeguards rule. This rule is enforced by the Federal Trade Commission to require financial institutions to implement a method for maintaining and safeguarding customers' private financial records. This rule would include a need for document destruction after a required holding period.

Pretexting provision. This provision prohibits the act of obtaining or requesting an individual's financial information under false pretenses—this includes the act of impersonation or the use of fraudulent statements.

There has been a substantial growth in the numbers of firms requesting document destruction services because of the abundance of laws that have been passed along with the Health Information Portability and Accountability Act, or HIPAA, requirements. As a result of HIPAA, institutions were required to have a program in place to protect patient information at every point by April 2003.

The third act of legislation that plays a role in document destruction is the passing of the Sarbanes-Oxley Act of 2002. This act requires all public corporations to follow very specific guidelines regarding the correct auditing and accounting practices. With this act comes the need for confidential accounting and auditing practices. Certain information that should not be released or reach the wrong audiences also will need to be destroyed in a confidential and reliable manner. Once again, this act of legislation requires further expansion of the document destruction industry.

The Economic Espionage Act is another example of the need for confidential document destruction services. This act states that once property is released for trash pickup, it is no longer private property. This means that anyone who may come across confidential papers in the trash or actually choose to seek them out has legal rights to that information. This act makes it necessary for corporations with confidential information to appropriately dispose of these documents so as not to break laws of confidentiality.

Finally, the Fair and Accurate Credit Transactions Act (FACTA) of 2003 is important legislation for Nationwide to familiarize them with. This act encompasses virtually every business organization. It was passed to combat crimes such as identity theft and other consumer fraud. This act requires the destruction of all private consumer information and holds a company responsible for any known consumer information that gets into the wrong hands. FACTA and all other outlined legislation are reasons why it is very important for a financial institution, such as Nationwide, to be prudent about the abundance of private consumer information maintained by the company.

Because of the increasing legislative requirements, there has been a new attraction for firms to enter the document destruction business. Many of these new entrants are smaller companies. In order to compete on a national basis with the large suppliers, smaller suppliers have established a network of facilities in order to gain more business. The abundance of suppliers has led to a significant decrease in the cost of implementing a document destruction program. Smaller suppliers have been able to compete with larger suppliers using a lean business model (i.e., reduced overhead and technology). For example, larger suppliers have increased their overhead by acquiring small document destruction businesses. On the other hand, smaller document destruction suppliers have syndicated to create a national network of document destruction companies. This allows the smaller suppliers in the industry to effectively compete for national contracts.

Scope of Activity for Document Destruction Sourcing

- Documenting business requirements.
- Identifying savings opportunities.
- Assessing business risks.
- Obtaining supplier information.
- Estimating total costs. The project team conducted diligent research throughout the industry and realized that there was an opportunity for a minimum savings of 30 percent with local suppliers.
- Specifying service levels.
- Assessing supplier diversity implications.
- Preparing and issuing an RFP.
- Awarding contract; negotiating.
- Developing a scope of work; issuing contract.

Obtaining supplier information involves the prequalification of potential suppliers, narrowing the field from possible suppliers to acceptable suppliers. More importantly, depending on the nature, size, and importance of the purchase, it is during the inquiry phase that decisions are formed concerning future projections on the potential for extended relationships, given the increased importance of relationships in the context of managing an entire supply chain.

With particularly large purchases, the review scope during the inquiry phase can extend to the supplier's supplier. Regardless of the relationship sought, a critical analysis by the Acquisition Project Team is needed to gather more specific information in the following areas: financial stability—analyzing financial statements; service quality and quality philosophy—establishing quality reputation and TQM; major customers and suppliers—obtaining names and contacts; minority business commitment—reviewing track record; technological expertise—meeting both current and future requirements; cost and shortage conditions—handling rush, weekend, and urgent requests. The aim is to identify those suppliers who are capable of providing a continuous source of supply. Three suppliers were selected at the identification stage. The suppliers included Royal Document Destruction (RDD), AllShred, and the current supplier, Iron Mountain.

After identifying the suppliers, a risk assessment was conducted to determine which suppliers would be acceptable. The following provides an overview of risks to be considered when making the document destruction decision:

- *Strategic risk.* The degree to which the proposed investment will align with the company's strategic direction and integrate into the existing business
- *Financial risk.* The probability that the project will deliver on the proposed financial benefits

- *Technology risk.* The degree to which the investment must rely on new or untested technologies, including hardware, software, and networks.
- *Organizational impact or operational risk.* The amount of change needed within the business unit to benefit from the new investment, as well as the effort required to continue operations once the investment is implemented.

RESULTS OF SOURCING

RDD was awarded the contract. The three-year contract resulted in a savings of approximately $707,000. The results are given below.

Location	Annual Savings
Home office	$62,088.00
Dublin	15,750.00
Grove City	3,570.00
Service centers	76,500.00
Field offices	77,730.00
3-year total costs	$(671,710)
Annual savings	235,638
3-year savings (estimated)	706,914

Case 1

Advanced Computer Logic[1]

Eleanor Jamison, the director of purchasing for Advanced Computer Logic (ACL), Inc., was becoming increasingly concerned about the large number of orders placed for some of the company's least-expensive component parts.

ACL was a $100 million multinational firm that manufactured customized automated assembly equipment. The manufacturing operation was divided into two separate divisions: fabrication and assembly. The fabrication division consisted of 10 departments and the assembly division was a paced assembly line consisting of 95 workstations.

Last year while reviewing the purchasing process for the electronic actuator components, Eleanor discovered that each of the departments in the fabrication division was purchasing the same actuator components but from nine different suppliers. Seven of the suppliers were local and two were located within 100 miles of the facility. Last year the total purchases for the 10 departments were $967,000.

Eleanor called Tom Camp, the electronic component buyer, and expressed her concern. "Tom, investigate why we are buying the same inexpensive components from nine different suppliers. There should be no more than three suppliers for these components. Provide me with data and your suggestions at your earliest convenience."

The following day at lunch, Tom informed Eleanor that each department manager had different reasons for using specific component suppliers. The reasons ranged from delivery performance to informal engineering advice.

Eleanor interrupted, "How much is it costing the company to order the same components from nine different suppliers?" Tom responded, "Last year it cost the company approximately $185,000 to place individually triggered orders." The average component unit values range from a low of $0.75 to a high of about $133.00. The value of the combined inventory holding costs across the 10 departments is $306,000 with an average obsolescence rate of 30 percent. The cost of holding one component in inventory for one year is 25 percent. The obsolescence rate was high because the customers sometimes changed the engineering design before the equipment was shipped.

Tom asked, "Why do we need so much inventory that may quickly become obsolete? Do you believe a *systems contracting* arrangement with one of the suppliers would work better for us? From experience, a systems contracting arrangement would reduce ordering cost by more than 70 percent. On the other hand, maybe we should consider a reverse auction."

[1] Names and data have been disguised.

Case 2

The Allen and Gary Show[1]

Allen Construction and Gary and Sons Construction are fierce competitors. The president of Allen is so excited about the growth that he is considering adding two new crews for the 2012 construction season. In 2011, Allen successfully won four out five jobs for which they have competed. Mr. Allen stated that he has revised the financial targets to account for the unexpected growth that they experienced in 2011. During the same period, Gary Construction won only one out of seven jobs. In 2010, Allen Construction and Gary and Sons Construction were successful bidders on the projects given in Table C2.1. The overhead for each firm is also given in Tables C2.2 and C2.3.

TABLE C2.1
Market Data

Customer Number	Winning Bid ($)	Successful Bidder	Total Direct Cost ($)
101	109,000	Gary	83,450
101	167,200	Gary	138,023
101	72,600	Allen	69,567
101	134,700	Allen	130,567
101	108,600	Allen	106,356
101	141,700	Allen	138,945
101	77,000	Allen	75,782
101	193,458	Allen	192,890
101	119,900	Allen	120,875
101	63,700	Allen	75,673
102	91,700	Allen	87,456
102	122,000	Allen	117,234
102	99,100	Allen	95,783
102	88,700	Allen	85,982
103	147,100	Gary	118,934
103	78,000	Allen	74,673
103	97,100	Allen	92,783
105	118,900	Allen	113,892
105	132,800	Allen	128,903
107	87,600	Allen	84,675
107	123,700	Allen	120,987
109	111,200	Gary	93,200
109	76,300	Gary	65,090
109	104,700	Gary	91,400
109	112,346	Gary	99,200
109	137,600	Allen	136,784
110	141,000	Allen	138,934
110	92,600	Allen	91,653
110	108,200	Allen	107,634
110	111,700	Allen	113,456
112	178,800	Allen	170,987
112	133,400	Allen	128,764
112	117,100	Gary	96,234
118	80,800	Allen	82,894

TABLE C2.2
Allen Construction Company Home Office Overhead Expenses

Overhead	Expense ($)
Management wages	140,000
Estimating (part-time)	20,000
Office Mgr./Sec./Acct.	28,000
Payroll taxes (Mgt.), 25%	47,000
Hospitalization (5 families @ $500 per month)	30,000
Office rent	2,400
Telephone	2,400
Postage	1,200
Office supplies	1,800
Legal	1,000
Accounting	7,000
Interest	16,000
Travel (mileage)	6,000
Mobile phone	2,400
Pager—rental	600
Association dues	500
Marketing	2,000
Estimating—Cost of plans	2,400

TABLE C2.3
Gary and Sons Construction Company Home Office Overhead Expenses

Overhead	Expense ($)
Management wages	140,000
Estimating (Part-time)	20,000
Office Mgr./Sec./Acct.	18,000
Payroll taxes (Mgt.), 25%	44,500
Hospitalization (4 families @ $500 per month)	24,000
Office rent	2,400
Telephone	1,200
Postage	350
Office supplies	450
Legal	750
Accounting	4,000
Interest	3,890
Travel (mileage)	2,430
Mobile phone	650
Pager—rental	600
Association dues	500
Marketing	3,500
Estimating—Cost of plans	1,800

Assignment Questions

1. Analyze the performance for each firm. Your analysis should be as *thorough* as possible given the data and your assumptions.
2. What are the strengths and weaknesses of each company?
3. Write a memo outlining your recommendations for each of the businesses.

Case 3

AMD Construction Company: Negotiating the Old-Fashioned Way[1]

In June, AMD Construction Company was awarded a $120 million contract for building a section of I-65 near Birmingham. The contract called for clearing, tunneling, paving, bridge building, blasting, and landscaping 85 miles of roadway, two lanes in each direction. The contract also required a 10 percent DBE (disadvantaged business enterprise) goal.

Over a period of six months prior to the bid opening, Jane Axle, salesperson for Allen Manufacturing Company, had been calling on AMD to sell it the CAT-1 horizontal boring machine. Ms. Axle joined Allen about eight months ago. She had been the sales manager at a well-known fashion house in New York for the past 10 years. Although AMD had used the older labor-intensive models of horizontal boring machines, the company had no experience with the newer, fully automated boring machines. In September, Jane convinced Tom Reed, president of AMD, to witness a demonstration of the CAT-1. Because Mr. Reed's time was limited, the demonstration's sole purpose was to acquaint him with the general operating procedures for the boring machine.

Prior to the initial sales interview, Jane had searched the Internet to familiarize herself with the highway market. In her research, she compared Allen's equipment prices with other distributors in the industry. If successful, this would be her first sale in the highway market. In addition, she had familiarized herself thoroughly with the industry jargon.

The following interview occurred the day after the product demonstration. Jane had learned on the same morning that the contract in question had been awarded to AMD.

Jane: Good morning, Mr. Reed.

Reed: Good morning, Jane.

Jane: I understand you have received the I-65 contract.

Reed: That's right. All we have to do now is finish it under budget.

Jane: This appears to be the biggest project since 9-11.

Reed: Yes. However, we did have a similar project three years ago in Montgomery. We had major design problems on that job, and we missed our estimate by $344,000.

Jane: Doesn't the state pay for any errors or mistakes they make in their design work?

Reed: Yes, they pay for their mistakes. However, that mistake was ours and we didn't get paid for it! You know, Jane, the highway business is unforgiving and you make a large enough mistake on one job, you will go belly up.

Jane: That's exactly why I'm here this morning, Mr. Reed, and that is why I gave you the demonstration yesterday. I am here to show you how to make money by saving on construction costs right down the line. We realize that you have been in business many years and have the

[1] Names and data have been disguised.

know-how, or you wouldn't still be operating today. But I have studied your problems and believe we have a machine that will reduce your tunneling labor costs by 25 percent.

Reed: Well, at the present, I have two horizontal boring machines and two three-person tunneling crews, and can't see how your boring machine will benefit me at all. I did like your demonstration yesterday, but, of course, the tunneling operation is only one category of work and I have the crews and the equipment to get it done.

Jane: That's true, Mr. Reed, but remember that the new CAT-1 can easily produce two times the rate of your current equipment. What's more, the CAT-1 requires only one two-person crew. Believe me, we can get the dirt flying. Isn't it true that the tunneling operation must stay on schedule in order to bring the job in under budget.

Reed: Yes.

Jane: Well, the CAT-1 is capable of operating 2,000 hours at 80 percent capacity without maintenance. Two operators versus six is a significant savings. There is no loading or unloading to consume time that runs up the cost. The loading and unloading operation has been automated. The CAT-1 is ready to go.

Reed: I don't see how your product can live up to all of those specs.

Jane: Let's see. You will get two times the production rate and save two-thirds of your estimated labor cost. This savings goes straight to the bottom line.

Reed: That does sound interesting, but you have no real data to support your claim. You are aware that all projects are different.

Jane: I have factored all of those concerns into my calculations. The numbers never lie.

Reed: Numbers don't lie, but productivity can't be predicted. If the CAT-1 is so good, why do my competitors not use it?

Jane: In the demonstration yesterday, you were able to see that dirt flying. Dirt flying is productivity.

Reed: How long does it take to train a crew on the CAT-1?

Jane: It takes approximately two days to train an experienced operator on the CAT-1.

Reed: I understand that there is a comparable boring machine sold by one of your competitors. I will call them tomorrow for a demonstration. How does your machine compare to the B-34?

Jane: Yes, there are other machines we compare with. However, ours can compete with all of them. It is efficient and productive. Most of the other machines have some of our features but not all of them. Our machine is appropriate for your project.

Reed: Well, Jane, the CAT-1 certainly sounds economical.

Jane: It is economical, Mr. Reed. Two people operate the CAT-1 generally. The machine has digital hydraulic controls and a wide-vision cab that gives the operators clear vision and maximum flexibility at all times. It has a 350-horsepower GMC engine that operates at five different speeds. Perhaps the maintenance efficiency is also an attractive feature. There is a computerized cylinder cooling system that prevents damage to the cylinder walls. This feature is a significant improvement over your current boring machines. The machine can bore 5½ feet below ground level and can bore up to 30 linear feet at a time. The total height of the machine is 10 feet. What's more, it passes all of ALDOT's (Alabama Department of Transportation) requirements for highway projects.

Reed: Do you have any figures on the actual operating costs of your boring machine?

Jane: We have. We figure average operating cost per year (1,500 hours) for the CAT-1 is approximately $296,000 (without operators) or $371,000 with two operators.

Reed: What is the purchase cost?

Jane: I have it right here. The purchase cost for the CAT-1 is $895,233.

Reed: Your cost figures seem rather high since our estimate for tunneling is $676,000.

Jane: No, Mr. Reed, experience has shown that it is possible to amortize the cost of our machine over a two-year period. In addition, when you calculate the productivity and labor savings . . .

Reed: Jane, in this business, you have to plan one year at a time. I am not sure when I will get the next tunneling job. My current problem is my . . .

Jane: Of course, there is also a lease option. We currently offer a three-year open-end lease with the following conditions: no down payment, free maintenance, $25,000 per month, and a salvage value of $100,000 after three years.

Reed: I will have to get back with you next week. I need to take a closer look at our alternatives. I am also in the process of determining how our 10 percent DBE goal will be satisfied. Only then will I be able to move forward.

Jane: Mr. Reed, you are in luck. According to CFR 49 part 26, a portion of your DBE goal can be satisfied with the purchase of the CAT-1. We are partners with a certified DBE firm in another business. We can run the sale through his company.

Reed: If this is acceptable, I will get back with you tomorrow. This purchase could easily kill two birds with one stone.

Jane: Thank you and I look forward to meeting with you tomorrow.

Reed: Goodbye, Ms. Axle.

Case 4

The ARMS Procurement System at Tustin State University[1]

Christina Abrams angrily pushed the purchasing audit reports to the back of her desk. As director of purchasing for Tustin State University's purchasing department, she knew she could not avoid studying the reports. But for a moment she needed to cool off before she had a meltdown. Walking across the campus, she remembered how, for the past two years, the consultants told her that the new Administrative Resource Management System (ARMS) procurement system would solve her procurement concerns.

The ARMS procurement system went live at the beginning of May 2009. Since then, many problems have come to light from the various departments using the system.

BACKGROUND

With the start of the year in 2006, three administrative managers pulled together to work on improving the computer information system used by the university. The existing system was cumbersome and inaccurate. A new computerized information technology–based system was expected to reduce a significant number of errors in the process. It was decided that a supplier would be chosen through the competitive bidding process. Peoplesoft was awarded the contract to implement the new purchasing information system.

Shortly after the human resources department implemented ARMS, the TSU purchasing department analyzed its computer systems. The purchasing department discovered that it was using at least seven different ways to purchase items. Purchasing realized that this was confusing and difficult for its customers and felt that it was very important to identify the customers' needs. The customers responded by stating they wanted an integrated purchasing system that included reconciliation of outside orders and internal orders. In addition, the customers wanted a system that would reconcile emergency departmental purchases with a procurement card to the purchasing system. With the knowledge of the customers' needs and an idea of successful purchasing systems, a TSU purchasing evaluation team was formed. In cooperation with Andersen Consulting, a conceptual design was developed for an integrated purchasing system. For the next year, a team was set up to study, review, and make changes to the newly designed integrated purchasing system. The team developed two major interrelated forms of purchasing—the ARMS system and the procurement card—to solve the procurement problems at TSU.

THE OLD PROCUREMENT SYSTEM

Order Processing

The ordering process under the old procurement system contained several steps. The first step was for each department to identify a need. This would be accomplished through at least eight different sources, including vendor catalogs, shopping

[1] The author expresses appreciation to Ladonna Thornton for her contributions to this case. Names and data have been disguised.

trips, sales representatives, knowledge from past usage, yellow pages, colleagues, magazines, and newspapers. The method used varied by department and was based on individual preference. The next step was to identify the issuance method. There are seven different methods available. One such method is the paper 1303, which is a requisition for materials from outside vendors. An alternative to the paper 1303 is the online 1303, which is essentially the same. The third option available is the paper 100W. The paper 100W is for internal orders from inventory. The comparable alternative to the paper 100W is the online 100W. The next choice available is a low-dollar-amount purchase order, or LOPO. This is used for purchases of $400 or less. Another option is through reimbursements by accounts payable, or reimbursements by stores. This is used when a department purchases item(s) through petty cash that should have been purchased with a 100W or 1303. Once the issuance method is identified, an order is placed.

Assuming an outside vendor order is placed, the department must complete a paper 1303. (See Figure C4.1.) Next, department approval must be obtained. After the proper approval is acquired, the data are entered into a shadow system by the department. The shadow system is an internal departmental system that contains the department's purchasing records. It is important to note that this system varies by department and does not share information between departments. Next, the requisition is entered into the centralized system by the department, so that purchasing can process the information.

FIGURE C4.1 Requisition Form

Linda Jones Room 606 MRF
Phone: 310-5641 Fax: 310-8500

Attn: Team Tom Crawford and Jane Marlowe Exhibit 2

Human Cancer Genetics 8850
EFFECTIVE 11/01/06
DEPARTMENT NUMBER IS
2516

Requisition

2516 (Dept. Number) | D0001 (Dept. Req. Number) | Requestor ID | Date Required | New Item | P.O. Number | Agent

315197333 (Account & Subcode)

Dept. Name Human Cancer Genetics 8850
Room: 606 MEDICAL RESEARCH FACILITY
Deliver to 420 W. 12th Ave.

GENR (User Reference)

Ship-To | Ship Via | F.O.B | Terms | G/S | PO Type | Chg. Order or Release

Vendor Number | Itm Spec | Req Spec | PRIO | Blkt Type | Delivery or Expiration Date

Suggested Vendor
KENDRO LABORATORY PRODUCTS
31 PECKS LANE
NEWTOWN CT 06470-
phone (800) 522-7746 fax **(203) 270-2166**

Page 1 of 1

DO NOT WRITE IN SHADED AREAS

Lin	Qty	Unit	Line No.	Catalog Number	Product Name	Dept. Est. Unit Cost	P.O. Unit Price	Type
	3	Pail		91245	O-Ring, SA-300 Rotor	$4.00		
	3	Pail		60810	O-Ring, SA-600 Rotor	$13.50		

Vendor Quote No	Contract	Contract Number		Dept. Est. Total	
				$52.50	

Fiscal Contact:
Initiated by: ______ (Date)
Approved: ______ (Date)
______ (Date)

Inquiry Out ______ Due ______
Approved for Order ______ (Date) ______ (Agent)
Order Issued ______ (Date) By ______

P.O. Total
$52.50

CCCACL Version 10

When the requisition is entered into the central system, it must remain in a queue and print overnight for the purchasing department. The *requisitions* are sorted and distributed to the appropriate buyer. The buyer then verifies pricing with the selected/preferred vendor. Once the price is verified, the buyer reviews the paper/online requisition and creates the vendor's purchase order. (See Figure C4.2.) Similar to the requisitions, the purchase orders must remain in a queue

FIGURE C4.2 Purchase Order

PURCHASE ORDER

Ship To: Medical Research Facili-606
420 W 12th Ave
Tustin, CA 92782

Business Unit	Purchase Order	PO Date	Change Order
UNIV		07/23/09	
Payment Terms Net 30 Days			
Freight Terms			
Ship Via BEST			
Buyer:			Phone:
Direct all correspondence relative to this order to Purchasing Department, 2650 Kenny Road, Tustin, CA FAX Refer to Purchase Order number.			

Vendor:

KENDRO LABORATORY PROD
31 PECKS LANE
NEWTOWN, CT 04670-2337

Send Invoices in duplicate
Accounts Payable
1800 Cannon Drive
Tustin, CA 92782

Contract:

Line-Schd Item	Description	Quantity	UOM	Unit Price	Extended Amt	Due Date
1- 1	O-Ring, SA-300 rotor, #91245	3.00	Pail	4.00	12.00	07/23/09
2- 1	O-Ring, SA-600 rotor, #60810	3.00	Pail	13.50	40.50	07/27/09

Department Contact:

using the above 'ship to' address.

*** This purchase order is issued subject to the terms and conditions attached which are hereby incorporated.

Total PO Amount 52.50

Correct purchase order and stock numbers must appear on all packages, invoices, shipping papers and correspondence. Additionally, invoice must match on line-by-line basis, quantity, unit of measure, description unit price, total amount used on this purchase order. If invoice must differ, do not ship; contact the purchasing buyer immediately. Packing slips must accompany all shipments. Note: no substitutions, alterations, or additions are authorized to this order without consent of Purchasing Department.

[redacted]

Director of Purchasing

and print overnight. The purchase orders are sorted and distributed to the appropriate buyer. The buyer then signs and prepares the purchase order for mail/fax.

This ordering process was used by Tustin State for many years. However, there were several problems associated with the old purchasing system. The first issue is the number of sources that the department must reference to determine what is needed. This creates difficulty for the department to select the best vendor. The next issue is the large number of issuance methods. The departments must understand the stipulations for all seven methods to place the proper order. This is confusing to the departments and employees who did not have constant interaction with the system. In some departments, specific employees became experts on the process. Another problem is the shadow system and the central system. Each department maintained its own internal computer system where purchasing records were maintained. This creates an issue because the shadow system is not standardized across the university. In addition, entering data into two different systems increases the chance for errors. Posting errors cannot be detected unless a manual audit of all of the departmental purchase orders is conducted. A final problem with the old system is the purchase documents are handled too many times. The information is repeatedly sorted and distributed. This handling increases the possibility of a purchase order or requisition being lost.

Invoice Process

The invoice process is another costly and drawn-out procedure. The invoice process is manual with a lot of duplicate entries and reviews. The invoices are manually maneuvered through the system by handling and mailing. A typical invoice transaction would first be sent from a requisitioner to his or her department. After opening the invoice, the department will approve or not approve the invoice. If the department approves the invoice, then the invoice will be mailed to accounts payable. Accounts payable will then open and sort the invoices. A photocopy of the invoices will be made at this time by accounts payable. This is done to keep a record of all invoices. Accounts payable then previews and prepares the invoices for data entry. After entry into the computer system, accounts payable are manually verified. Then, the invoice is sent back to the originating department. The originating department then receives its returned invoice. At this point, the department will correct any differences between the original invoice and the current invoice. The invoice is approved if there are no changes to the invoice. The department then enters all invoices into its shadow system. The purpose of the shadow system is to keep track of all invoices received by the department. The final step is filing the invoices into the department's file cabinets. The total invoicing process takes from 30 to 90-plus days to complete.

ADMINISTRATIVE RESOURCE MANAGEMENT SYSTEM (ARMS)

Order Processing

The first step in the process requires the department to identify a need and source through the vendor catalog. The vendor catalog contains approximately 280,000 inventory items and represents "one stop shopping." Next, a requisition is created through the ARMS system. (See Figure C4.3.) The first required information is the vendor name, which is obtained by using the vendor database. The requisitioner

FIGURE C4.3 **ARMS Requisition Form**

Requisition

Business Unit: UNIV	APPROVED	
Req ID	Requisition Date	Page
25160D0001	07/20/09	1
Requestor		Phone
Organization: Human Cancer Genetics		

Ship To: Medical Research Facili-606
420 W 12th Ave
Tustin, CA 92782
USA

Vendor: KENDRO LABORATORY PROD
31 PECKS LANE
NEWTOWN, CT 04670-2337
USA

Location: Medical Research Facili-606
420 W 12th Ave
Tustin, CA 92782
USA

Buyer:

Line#: 1 **Item#:** **Descr: O-Ring, SA-300 rotor, #91245** **Category: LABOS**

Sched#: 1	Dist#: 1	Due Date: 07/20/09		
Qty: 3.00	UOM: Pail	Unit Price: 4.00	Ext Price: 12.00	
Organization: 2516	Fund: 315197	Account: 333		Function:
PRJ/GRT:	Program:	User Def: GENR		BY: 2000

Item Total:O-Ring, SA-300 rotor. #91245 **12.00**

Line#: 2 **Item#:** **Descr: O-Ring, SA-600 rotor, #60810** **Category: LABOS**

Sched#: 1	Dist#: 1	Due Date: 07/20/07		
Qty: 3.00	UOM: Pail	Unit Price: 13.50	Ext Price: 40.50	
Organization: 2516	Fund: 315197	Account: 333		Function:
PRJ/GRT:	Program:	User Def: GENR		By: 2000

Item Total:O-Ring, SA-600 rotor. #60810 **40.50**

Total Requisition Amount: **52.50**

Send Comments to Vendor:
Department Contact:

using the above 'ship to' address.
Do Not Send Comments to Vendor:
Purchasing: Please allow for shipping and handling charges on the Purchase Order.

Approval Signature	Approval Signature	Approval Signature

enters the vendor name, and the ARMS system will provide all applicable options. (If the requisitioner wants to give special instructions to the buyer and/or vendor, he or she can put them under the header comments of the ARMS form.) Once all of the information has been verified and approved, it is sent to the buyer via ARMS. The buyer receives the requisition and verifies the price and selected vendor. The requisition is sent to the director of purchasing for online approval. Once

FIGURE C4.4 ARMS Purchase Order

PURCHASE ORDER

Ship To: Medical Research Facili-606
420 W 12th Ave
Tustin, CA 92782

Business Unit	Purchase Order	PO Date	Change Order ???
UNIV		07/23/09	
Payment Terms Net 30 Days			
Freight Terms			
Ship Via BEST			
Buyer:			Phone:
Direct all correspondence relative to this order to Purchasing Department, 2650 Kenny Road, Tustin, CA FAX Refer to Purchase Order number.			

Vendor:

KENDRO LABORATORY PROD
31 PECKS LANE
NEWTOWN, CT 04670-2337

Send Invoices in duplicate to:
Accounts Payable
1800 Cannon Drive
Tustin, CA 92782

Contract:

Line-Schd Item	Description	Quantity	UOM	Unit Price	Extended Amt	Due Date
1- 1	O-Ring, SA-300 rotor, #91245	3.00	Pail	4.00	12.00	07/27/09
2- 1	O-Ring, SA-600 rotor, #60810	3.00	Pail	13.50	40.50	07/27/09

Department Contact:

using the above 'ship to' address.

*** This purchase order is issued subject to the terms and conditions attached which are hereby incorporated.

Total PO Amount 52.50

Correct purchase order and stock numbers must appear on all packages, invoices, shipping papers and correspondence. Additionally, invoice must match on line-by-line basis, quantity, unit of measure, description unit price, total amount used on this purchase order. If invoice must differ, do not ship; contact the purchasing buyer immediately. Packing slips must accompany all shipments. Note: no substitutions, alterations, or additions are authorized to this order without consent of Purchasing Department.

[redacted]

Director of Purchasing

the requisition is approved, the buyer creates a purchase order. (See Figure C4.4.) It is then sent to the vendor through the ARMS system by fax.

The end user can track the status of the requisition through the ARMS system using the master inquiry panel. The master inquiry panel provides departments with information on the status of open requisitions/purchase orders. The user can confirm that the requisition has been approved and whether a purchase order has been created. The end user also can print out the purchase order once it has been created. If there is a problem with the requisition, there will be notes in the requisition activity section.

Invoice Process

The ARMS system has simplified the invoicing process by eliminating many cumbersome steps. Accounts payable receives the invoice via electronic data interchange (EDI). The system then automatically matches the purchase order to the invoice received. Next, accounts payable reviews and approves the invoice online. Once the invoice is approved, payments are generated and issued through electronic funds transfer. Despite the convenience of this process, there are several difficulties. If the invoice does not match the purchase order exactly, the account clerk and purchasing must research the purchase order and identify where the error occurred. If the two departments cannot determine what caused the error, the department must amend the purchase order. This requires many additional steps by all parties involved.

Procurement Card

Another feature of the ARMS procurement system is that it allows reconciliation of the procurement card, which deals with emergency orders. (See Figure C4.5.) The procurement card is issued through the First Chicago Bank and is facilitated locally with World Bank in Tustin, California. The account can be assigned to either a department or a specific member of the university's faculty. The credit limit is $1,000 per purchase and $5,000 per month. Individual departments also can change these limits, if additional purchases are needed.

Simply stated, the procurement card is a credit card for special circumstances with special limits imposed on it. This card is used as an alternative to the university's original LDPO. This gives the department authority to approve purchases that do not exceed $400. It is also an alternative for formal requisitions that are below $1,000 per purchase. To ensure security of the procurement card, there are certain items that cannot be purchased with the procurement card. Some of the restricted items are given below:

- Airline tickets
- Capitalized equipment
- Cash advances
- Controlled substances
- Gasoline
- Guns and weapons
- Moving expenses

These items are declined if the card user attempts a transaction. If abuse of the card is suspected, the department head can inform the purchasing department to suspend usage of the card. Currently, the procurement card allows the user great flexibility with low-dollar purchases. The department only needs to reconcile the charges to the ARMS system when the bill is received.

The university has seen a boom in growth with the card since the introduction of the ARMS system; there are approximately 2,000 active cards. This is primarily because of the ease of using a credit card: A simple order can be placed without a purchase order. To obtain a purchase order, the department must wait approximately one week. However, the procurement card offers immediate purchases. Figure C4.6 is an example of a procurement card report.

FIGURE C4.5
Procurement Card

Department of Athletics
Marching Band Account

Departmental Procurement
Card Program
Receipts and Approvals

Contacts:
Athletic Dept.
4-4589
Marching Band
2-5969

Card User (last name-printed):

Date Card Used:

Vendor:

City/State:

General Description of Purchase:

Check here if purchase included alcohol

0 0

FY Dept Account

Sub Code User Ref # of Receipts

Charges to account TWO:

FY Dept Account

Sub Code User Ref # of Receipts

Total Amount of Receipts: $
Approvals:

Reviewed by Key Contact Person:

Date:

Area Head/Director

Date:

Dcan (for purchases of alcohol)

Date:

THE DECISION

The first problem Christina needed to solve was the problem with searching through 280,000 vendor catalogs. There are also a significant number of errors in the vendor database. The ARMS system cannot decipher between a vendor's billing address and its shipping address. Despite the convenience of this process,

FIGURE C4.6 Procurement Card Report

DISTRIBUTION NUMBER: DO5414	ACCOUNT SUMMARY BY SUBCODE	REPORT PAGE: 01 REPORT: AM090
COMPUTER DATE: 09/23/09	BUDGET VS. ACTUAL	ATHLETICS
BEGIN DATE: 07/0177	REVENUES & EXPENSES	ATHLETICS-BAND
VP: 45 S139 DISTRIBUTION NU Y	AS OF 08/31/09	ACCOUNT TYPE: BKSTRS, ATHLTCS, OTHER

		BUDGETS				ACTIVITY			
Subcode	Description	Original	Carryforward	Revisions	Current	Month	To Date	Open Commitments	Budget Balance
160	BDGT ONLY-OTHER SALS	4,000			4,000				4,000.00
170	BUDGET ONLY-WAGES								
171	STDNT NON-GA/NONFWSP	25,000			25,000	7,293.30	7,293.30		17,706.70
175	STUDENT OVERTIME					34.65	34.65		
170–179	WAGES	25,000			25,000	7,327.95	7,327.95		17,672.05
* 110–189	PERSONNEL	29,000			29,000	7,327.95	7,327.95		21,672.05
200	EMPL BENEFITS	300			300				
205	STD SPEC BENEFITS					80.61	80.61		
200–219	EMPLOYEE BENEFITS	300			300	80.61	80.61		219.39
250	BENEFITS-OTHER								
299	STUDENT PERS NO ABR					776.60	776.60		
220–299	FEE AUTHORIZATION					776.60	776.60		
300	SUPPLIES & SERVICES								
300	SUPPLIES								
333	EDUC & SCI SUPPLIES					23.62	23.62		
335	OTHER SUPPLIES	16,000			16,000	3,043.18	3,043.18	5,827.54	7,129.28
340	GAME EQUIPMENT	16,600			16,600	2,609.85	2,609.85	9,806.45	4,183.70
330–359	SUPPLIES	32,600			32,600	5,676.65	5,676.65	15,633.99	11.289.36
361	POSTAGE	1,500			1,500				1,500.00
421	REP & MAINT - EQUIPMENT	2,100			2,100	85.73	85.73	1,914.27	100.00
441	BLDG & GROUNDS R&M	1,500			1,500	284.00	284.00		1,216.00
461	RENTAL OF EQUIPMENT	4,000			4,000			500.00	3,500.00
501	COPY SERVICES	9,000			9,000	773.96	773.96		8,226.04
502	PHOTOGRAPHIC SERVICE	1,000			1,000			1,000.00	
504	PRINTING	9,000			9,000	288.56	288.56		8,711.44
500–519	REPRODUCTION SERV	19,000			19,000	1,062.52	1,062.52	1,000.00	16,937.48
533	TRAV OUT-OF-STATE S	38,000			38,000	726.00	726.00		37,274.00
570	GENERAL SVCS PURCH	28,000			28,000	1,320.00	1,320.00	12,880.00	13,800.00
608	BUSINESS MEALS	13,000			13,000			7,000.00	6,000.00
630	LODGING	3,000			3,000			13,000.00	10,000.00-
600–649	GENERAL	16,000			16,000			20,000.00	4,000.00-
667	MEDALS & PRIZES	3,000			3,000			2,800.00	200.00
*300–699	SUPPLIES & SERVIC	145,700			145,700	9,154.90	9,154.90	54,728.26	81,816.84
700	EQUIPMENT PURCHASES								
707	CAP EQUIP-OTHER	2,000			2,000				2,000.00
700–739	EQUIPMENT PURCHAS	2,000			2,000				2,000.00
760	INVALID SUBCODE								
767	NONCAP EQUIP-OTHER							2,723.00	
*700–789	EQUIPMENT TOTAL	2,000			2,000			2,723.00	723.00-

there are several difficulties. If the invoice does not match the purchase order exactly, the account clerk and purchasing must research the purchase order and identify where the error occurred. If the two departments cannot determine what caused the error, the department must amend the purchase order. Her walk was completed. Ms. Abrams returned to her office to begin looking for alternatives.

Case 5

The Auction Case[1]

EDI Associates is a small distributor with two full-time and five part-time consultants. Revenues during the past three years were approximately $10 million. EDI Associates packs and exports commodities to the Asian market. EDI has provided logistical services for the KACI Corporation for the past three years. Each year EDI negotiates transport and shipping rates with a variety of carriers. Recently, KACI decided to conduct a reverse auction for all packing and shipping services. The current contract with EDI was valued at $1.6 million per year. EDI Associates outsources approximately 80 percent of the contract to a major shipping company.

THE AUCTION

KACI contracted with Auction.com, a multinational, market-leading, e-commerce company specializing in e-procurement and auctions. Auction.com has approximately 1,000 employees worldwide and has conducted auctions for 140 large multinational clients. They have conducted about $21 billion in auctions, resulting in savings of about $6 billion. KACI is a global organization based in the United States. KACI was undergoing financial strain due to increased worldwide competition. In order to reduce costs, KACI turned to Auction.com to conduct a reverse auction. The auction event was a global procurement exercise focusing on logistics and transport. The auction event consisted of five stages:

1. Making the market (client).
2. Prequalification (supplier).
3. Preauction planning (supplier).
4. Auction-strategy (supplier).
5. Postauction analysis (client).

Making the Market

Shortly after the notification from KACI, EDI Associates began to prepare for the upcoming reverse auction. EDI received a CD with the documentation of the reverse auction process. This documentation consisted of over 50 files including tender documents, quote spreadsheets, specifications, and other relevant information. There were at least four updates prior to the final auction. The deluge of information was overwhelming.

Prequalification

The nonperforming suppliers are eliminated from the auction at the prequalification stage. At this stage, Auction.com must ensure that there are an adequate number of bidders remaining. EDI Associates had no idea how many other companies had been prequalified. Prequalification also introduces some financial parameters for the event. Auction.com set the switching cost at $1.3 million; that is, the price when KACI would consider awarding the contract away from the EDI supplier. The difference between the switching and existing contract prices was approximately

[1] Adapted from Andrew Stein and Paul Hawking, Southern Cross University, "Reverse Auction e-Procurement: A Supplier's Viewpoint," as published at www.hedgehog.com.

19 percent. This figure is very important as much of the advertising material by Auction.com quotes savings of 19 percent. EDI Associates again expended considerable resources at this stage: two site visits, four subcontractor meetings, 200 phone calls, 45 e-mails out, 15 e-mails in, 30 hours of the managing director's time, and 20 hours of the consultant's time. EDI's setup costs for the reverse auction were increasing.

- EDI Associates' market entry price: $2 million.
- Existing contract price: $1.6 million.
- Reserve (switching) price: $1.3 million.

For EDI Associates, the setup for the new quoting process was impressive.

Auction Strategy

Waiting for the auction was stressful for EDI. What strategy should be adopted? What would happen if the power failed, or the ISP went down? What would be the lowest position EDI Associates would take in the auction? Would they be swept up in the auction dynamic? Who would press the buttons? Would they hold their nerve? Auction.com conducted a training session from their Asian headquarters and EDI Associates soon mastered the auction interface. EDI established three strategies for the auction: entry, middle, and end strategy. The entry strategy was to come in at the high prequalification bid after about three minutes and then watch the market develop. The middle strategy was to maintain control on the screen and drive the bids down in a controlled manner. It is important to understand that, in the auction event, you only see bids and do not know where they come from. The only strategy was to be in the end game and, if EDI Associates did not win, they wanted to be under the switching cost at the end. This would show KACI that EDI Associates was a serious bidder. EDI Associates had seen sample auction events where the end game was frantic.

The Auction Event

The auction was delayed a week and, with a late flurry of updates and clarifications, EDI Associates waited until 10:33 to press the bid accept button. In five seconds, the early and middle strategies were destroyed. There were three other bidders and one bidder came in right on the switching price. This was felt to be a ploy to scare off other bidders; it was felt that this was the existing contractor.

Early Action

Where did that bid come from? (See Figure C5.1.)

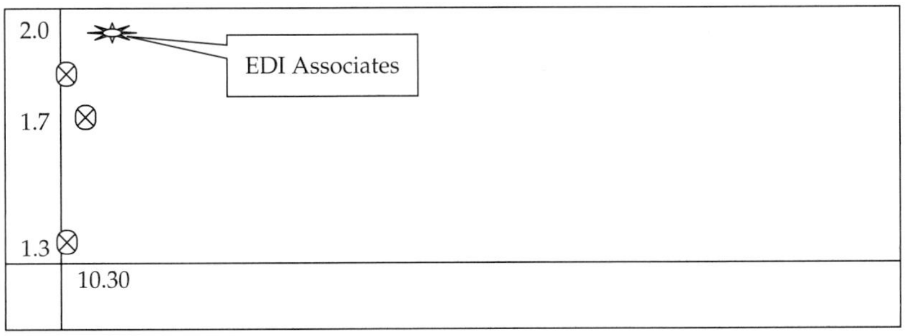

FIGURE C5.1
Start of the Auction

FIGURE C5.2
One Hour into the Auction

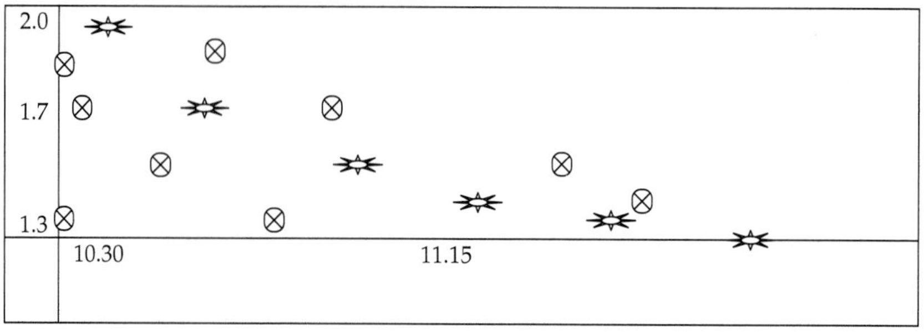

Middle Game (A Sinking Feeling)

After about half an hour, another bidder entered and soon started to drive down. (See Figure C5.2.) EDI Associates' strategy was to drive down to the reserve price.

End Game (A Dog Fight)

At this stage (see Figure C5.3), it is fair to say that the phones were put on hold. As the scheduled auction time elapsed, the bidding intensified. A bid in the last minute extends the auction by one minute. There were three bidders left. The original button presser passed to the managing director when the low position previously agreed upon was passed. The auction entered the phase that Auction.com calls the auction dynamic, the dynamic that drives the price down. The reserve was driven down $90,000 in seven minutes. The number of bids in the last seven minutes tripled all bids in the previous 1.5 hours. The managing director started to lose some semblance of control as he did not want to lose to the other bidders. The agreed low margin of 12 percent was reduced to 5 percent. *EDI Associates did not win the auction;* they were in the game at the end and drove the market down to inflict some pain on the other bidders.

Postauction Analysis

After the auction, EDI Associates was told they would have to wait five weeks for the result; it came much earlier. EDI Associates lost the contract they had at the start. The managing director took about two weeks to get over losing to the competition. There are several issues that need to be discussed concerning the reverse auction results.

FIGURE C5.3
End of the Auction

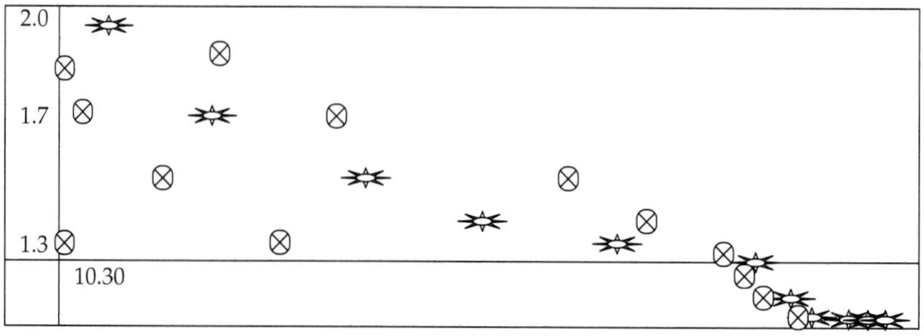

Case 6

Austin Wood Products[1]

Dave Pope, plant manager for the doors and molding department at Austin Wood Products (AWP), was very concerned about the company's lumber stockroom operations. There is no way to know what is available before you get to the storage area. There is usually a 50 percent chance of obtaining the needed lumber for a job. The stockroom situation is interfering with productivity.

COMPANY BACKGROUND

Austin Wood Products was started in 1981 by Michael Price (see Figure C6.1). With the fast-growing building industry in Texas, he realized the need for custom-manufactured doors. He began manufacturing doors in his garage up until 1982, when he moved to the facility in Belton. As the company began to grow, Price relocated to downtown Austin in 1983, and then to the present location, 1165 Guadalupe Road in Austin. The current facility has over 90,000 square feet of production, warehouse, and showroom space, and employs 130 people. The production process is shown in Figure C6.2. The 7,000-square-foot showroom displays their vast selection of quality handcrafted and manufactured products, which include a complete line of doors, moldings, decorative hardware, and entry systems. They are the only company in Austin that builds custom doors.

AWP's primary customer base is composed of custom builders in Austin, Dallas, Houston, and Fort Worth. AWP has their sales staff for in-stock and special orders, and a fleet of delivery trucks that deliver within a 50-mile radius of Austin. They also make regularly scheduled visits to the Dallas–Fort Worth area and Houston.

[1] The author expresses appreciation to Allison Buckner, Maya Dewi, and Seth Gernot for their contributions to this case. Names and data have been disguised.

FIGURE C6.1 **Organizational Chart**

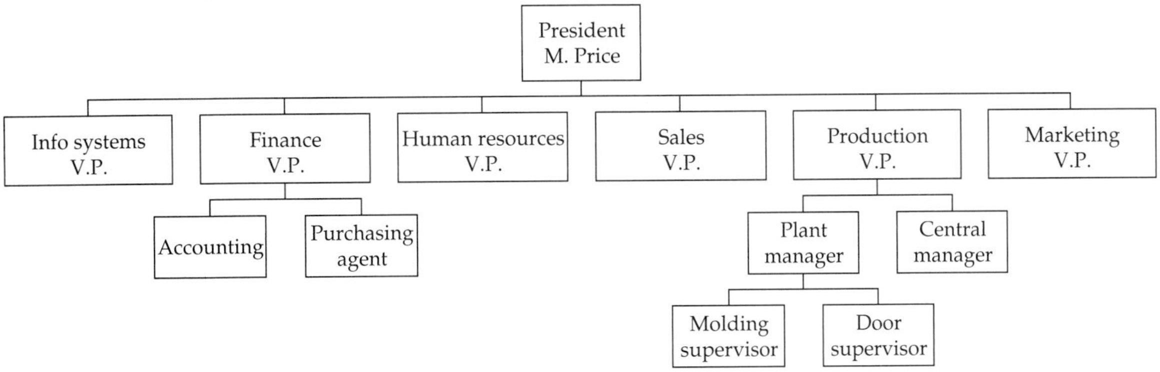

FIGURE C6.2 **Process Flowchart**

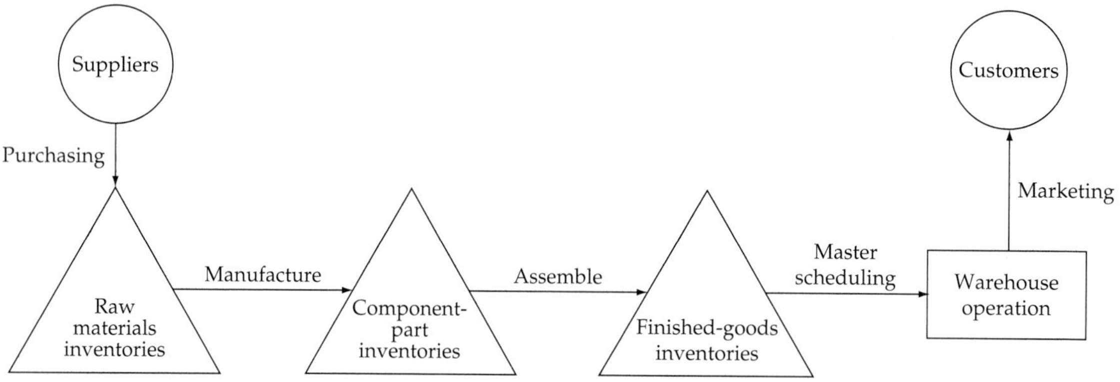

COMPETITIVE PRIORITIES

AWP products compete on a high level of service and the idea that they are very flexible. If it can be made of wood, then they will produce it. Plant manager Dave Pope prides himself on the fact that a customer can ask them for anything and he or she will receive it. For example, a customer last year asked them for three insulated redwood doors. Not only did Dave know what these doors were, but he has a regular supplier that would send the material promptly. It would utterly be impossible to walk into a large home improvement store and find anyone with the knowledge or resources to fit such an order. In addition to custom-made doors, AWP can make any type of wood molding. For about $300, anyone can have special knives made to make custom molding to fit the décor of his or her house.

AWP feels that along with this "anything for the customer" attitude is an exceptional sales and service staff. They have their own in-house sales staff that can assist customers in choosing the products they need. They also provide delivery for their products; this can lead to shorter lead times and more reliable shipment when everything inside the plant is running smoothly.

To ensure that the customers have everything they need with their doors, AWP sells a large amount of hardware with their doors. They stock many items from hinges to locks, all that a contractor or customer would need to install their door. AWP knows from experience that the quicker the door is sent and installed, the less likely it is to be damaged and sent back to the factory. No company wants returns, so they do all they can to ensure that their product is sent and installed correctly.

AWP is also very innovative when it comes to how they make their molding and what kinds of doors they can produce. Five years ago, they purchased a new molding machine that allowed them to make an unlimited number of varieties of molding. These new machines could make a larger style of molding, and the cutting knives could be custom cut to fulfill the customers' needs. The workers were sent to Florida to be trained on how to use and maintain the new machines. This may be looked upon as an unnecessary cost to some manufacturers, but AWP wanted to provide the customers with the opportunity to have individualized custom molding.

The peak manufacturing period is from February to November. The highly seasonal and cyclical product line is closely tied to the construction industry in Texas.

During this time, the company operates a 10½-hour shift for four days per week, Monday through Thursday. Each production worker is paid for 10 hours. The 120 production workers are paid, on the average, $16.35 per hour. Fringe benefits are about 30 percent.

AWP also installs the glass in the doors as they are being manufactured; a lot of other companies do not do this. In fact, other door manufacturers will have subcontractors install the glass in the field. Mr. Pope stated that the manufacturer cannot control the quality and workmanship that subcontractors do. AWP sends their doors with the glass, so that others will not damage AWP's high-quality doors.

CURRENT INVENTORY SITUATION

AWP currently does not have a formal inventory management system for the raw materials and finished goods that they maintain in their warehouse. AWP conducts a complete inventory of raw materials and finished goods once each year. It requires 47 workers to count the items. The inventory count takes two days to complete, from seven o'clock in the morning to five o'clock in the evening. After speaking with the plant manager, Dave Pope, it has become clear to Dave that AWP does not place a heavy emphasis on maintaining accurate inventory records. The president, Mr. Price, believes that since AWP is the only custom-door manufacturer in the city of Austin, they do not need to compete on costs; therefore, there is no heavy concern about reducing inventory costs. The 2008 sales revenues were $25,000,000. The average price per door assembly ranged from $450 to $1,250.

A second reason not to worry about the lumber stockroom is based on the nature of the demand. According to the vice president of production, Mary Smith, the demand for the different types of wood varies from one year to the next. Since approximately 95 percent of their sales come from custom orders, it is difficult for AWP to predict what styles and types of wood will be in demand for any given year. Custom order sales depend on the trends and preferences of the market. This factor makes it difficult for AWP to predict which types of wood to maintain in stock on a consistent basis and which ones to special order. Inventory turnover is the most important measure of inventory performance because it relates inventory levels to the product's sales volume. Mary Smith estimates that inventory was turned one and three-quarter times each year.

LUMBER PURCHASING

Lumber purchases represent 87 percent of all purchases and dollar value; fasteners, hinges, and miscellaneous materials represent the remaining 13 percent of annual purchases. Wood is purchased based on discounts, deals, and rebates that are offered by lumber yards. As orders are received, the wood is then allocated to the various orders. The estimated value of the wood inventory is approximately $3.5 million.

A TYPICAL DAY'S OPERATION

The production shift begins at 7:00 a.m. Those workers needing lumber at this time request permission to pick up lumber from the lumber store. In most cases, the lumber and other items have been kitted for the specific job catalog. If no kits have been prepared, the workers usually take the necessary items without bothering to record the withdrawals. Approximately 63 percent of the kits are available for the workers. All workers are required to return the remnants from their kits of materials before the end of the shift.

THE DECISION

At a recent management meeting, the president announced that the production levels would increase by 20 percent during the next month. Dave was anxious to resolve his production problems.

Case 7

Butler Systems[1]

Butler Systems is a manufacturer of environmental control systems and power conditioning equipment. Butler is the world's leading supplier of computer support systems and the largest supplier of precision air-conditioning and power protection systems. Butler sales exceed $1 billion. The HD-5 battery is the primary component for the EPS (emergency power supply) system.

INFLUENCES TO PRODUCT REQUIREMENT

The HD-5 battery is used in 80 percent of the emergency power supply systems. The EPS is a backup system designed to prevent glitches and ride out temporary power outages in computer network systems. The EPS allows for an orderly shutdown from the servers in order to avoid data loss as well as damage to critical hardware. The design engineering department specifies the customer requirements for the EPS. The purchasing department then develops the appropriate request for quotes (RFQ) as shown in Figure C7.1.

AVAILABLE PRODUCTS

The EPS falls into two categories: the flame-retardant category and the non-flame-retardant category. The flame-retardant battery can be used in place of the non-flame-retardant; however, the non-flame-retardant battery cannot be used in place of the flame-retardant battery.

SPECIFICATION AND SUPPLIER SELECTION

Product specifications are defined based on the customers' needs and requirements. The design information includes voltage, current rating, dimension, physical size, and battery duration time. For the HD-5 12-volt battery, the float voltage has to be between 13.5 and 13.8 VCD/unit average. Furthermore, the shell container and cover made of polypropylene plastic should meet flame-retardant specifications.

The reputation of Butler's battery suppliers is critical in the selection process. The battery supplier must be reliable and carefully selected. SDX Chemicals is the

[1] The author expresses appreciation to John Bingham and Pooja Arora for their contributions to this case, Names and data have been disguised.

FIGURE C7.1 Request for Quotes Process

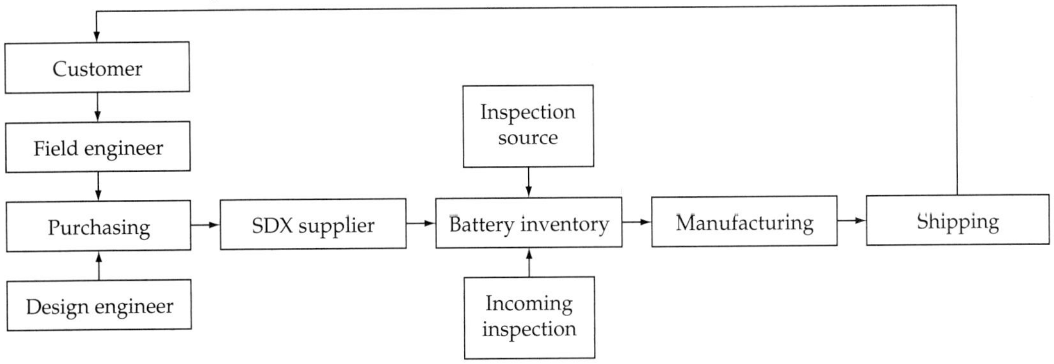

current supplier for the HD-S. Butler selects its battery supplier through the competitive-bidding pricing process. After the best suppliers are identified, a formal negotiation is conducted with at least two suppliers. The contract terms are given in the next section.

CONTRACT TERMS AND TYPE

The current five-year contract agreement with SDX has been in effect since January 2005. Upon the expiration of the initial term, the agreement will renew for successive one-year periods, unless either party informs by written notice of its intention not to renew 60 days prior to the expiration of the initial term.

The key terms of the current contract with SDX are given below:

1. *Product changes*. Once SDX is selected, and the agreement date is in effect, the battery specifications cannot change unless approval is given by Butler.
2. *Pricing*. Product prices are fixed for the term of the agreement. Sixty days' notice must be given before a price change can occur.
3. *Delivery*. On-time delivery is defined as shipment received by Butler four days after the order is placed. The supplier is required to pay for late charges and the cost of expediting.
4. *Delivery performance measures*. The supplier is expected to achieve a 100 percent service rate.
5. *Quality standards and goals*. Quality measures are expressed as nonconforming parts per million (PPM).
6. *Indemnification*. Supplier shall indemnify Butler against any and all losses, damages, liabilities, costs, and expenses.
7. *Insurance*. Supplier shall, at its sole cost and expense, maintain for the term of this agreement and for the period of any obligation general liability insurance. General liability insurance shall cover bodily injury, property damage, and personal injury in the amount of $1,000,000.
8. *Acceptance*. The current five-year agreement with SDX has been accepted and signed by the authorized representatives of each party.

Butler's current battery-buying process is efficient. Maintaining good supplier relationships with its suppliers is critical to Butler's success. Quality, price, delivery, flexibility, and service are considered in making sourcing and purchasing decisions. Butler remains competitive in the increasingly global and competitive markets.

RECENT DEVELOPMENTS

The vice president of operations is concerned about the low HD-5 battery inventory. There is currently a 20-day supply of batteries. A 90-day supply is the normal inventory level. Butler has not received a battery shipment in two months. Last week when the buyer discussed the problem with SDX, it was revealed that the contract price would be doubled and that the current contract with Butler is null and void.

The buyer also found out in his conversation with SDX that the battery industry has been experiencing significant shortages. The demand has been larger than expected based on the increased demand from China. Chinese auto manufacturers have been specifying the HD-5 battery for the new electric-powered cars. According to the SDX salesman, if electric cars become popular, SDX is expected to allocate more of its capacity to support the Chinese automotive industry.

Case 8

Camp Bowie Technologies, Inc.[1]

In June 2009, John Lane, having recently graduated from the University of North Texas, accepted a purchasing agent position at Camp Bowie Technologies (CBT). John received his first assignment from the purchasing manager, Mary Tobias. His initial project was to purchase 2,120 cell phones for the CBT field technicians. The field technicians used cell phones to receive job assignments, get directions, and digitally process payments. These tasks are accomplished by the implementation of smartphone software customized especially for CBT. To be able to use the smartphone software, the cell phones must be equipped with GPS technology.

COMPANY BACKGROUND

The CBT corporation, located in a suburb of Fort Worth, Texas, was one of the successful enterprises that had expanded suddenly with the dot.com boom that hit the Dallas/Fort Worth area in the late-1990s. CBT provided a wide range of computer and server systems services for the commercial sector, which included banks and a variety of corporate clients. CBT's sales had grown from $5.3 million in 2000 to $55.2 million in 2009. The company operated exclusively in the Dallas/Fort Worth metroplex. CBT currently employs 302 technicians. The CBT home office computer system must be able to transmit and receive data from the cell phones. According to Mary Tobias, replacing the current Nextel 7100i phones with the new generation of cell phones will result in an annual savings of $1 million if the target price of $150 per unit is achieved.

THE CURRENT CELL PHONE TECHNOLOGY

The current cell phone platform is the Nextel 7100i. In general, the company has been satisfied with its features, customer service and pricing contract. However, the phones are increasingly out of date.

THE PURCHASING PROCESS FOR THE NEW PHONES

In order to gain first-hand usage knowledge, John interviewed the field service director, the mobile resource manager, the network analyst, and some of the technicians. John also participated in ride-alongs with five field technicians. After collecting data from these sources, John assigned priority weights to each suggested function based on a 100-point scale. As an example, the push-to-talk function was one of the highest weighted features. Although the push-to-talk feature does not directly add value to customer service, John had observed that the technicians really enjoyed the push-to-talk feature. John concluded that technician satisfaction would have an indirect effect on customer service. A weight of 25 was assigned to the push-to-talk feature. Durability was assigned a weight of 14, since it was observed that the field technicians occasionally dropped their phones. Battery life also was assigned a relatively higher weight, 15. The most important external criterion was the quality of the service provider. The current agreement with Nextel supports 1,546 field technicians and is competitively priced. Also, the

[1] Names and data have been disguised.

TABLE C8.1
Feature Priority

Feature	Weight	Priority
Push-to-talk	25	High
Service provider quality	20	High
Durability	14	High
Battery life	10	High
Price	10	High
Bluetooth	4	High
Ease of use	4	High
GPS	4	High
Display	2	Medium
Life expectancy	2	Medium
Keyboard type	1	Low
Maximum data speed	1	Low
RAM	1	Low
Trackball or roller wheel	1	Low
Voice quality	1	Low
Total	100	

telecom network analyst who measures service provider effectiveness on a daily basis said that Nextel has great customer service and fast delivery times. Both of these features are very important because when technicians need a new phone, they are able to get their phone in a timely manner. In other words, fast delivery times will lead to improved customer service. Quick response is a competitive priority for CBT. Nextel's major shortcoming is that their network is not as large as some of their competitors in the metroplex, forcing CBT to use other service providers in certain segments of the market. A weight of 20 is assigned to service provider quality. The remaining feature weights are given in Table C8.1. All of the medium- and low-priority criteria are standard features for each of the competing service providers. Finally, John compiled his initial criteria assessment of the alternative phone and service providers in Table C8.2.

THE DECISION

John carefully assessed and reviewed the compiled data. On Wednesday morning, John sent Mary Tobias an e-mail with Tables C8.1 and C8.2 as attachments. Ten minutes later, he received the following reply from Mary:

> John, you are off to an excellent start. It appears that you have done your homework. It is easy to see that this is not going to be an easy decision. When buying cell phones, I am not sure about what it is we are buying. How do you plan on comparing the features, cost, and service quality? Do we have leverage with our current service provider? Should we receive a discount since the order is so big? How will we know if we are getting a good value? Is it possible to do a reverse auction for this spend? Cell phones are commodities. I would like your recommendations in a memo by tomorrow evening. I will be leaving town on Friday, and I would like to meet with you.
>
> Thanks,
> Mary

TABLE C8.2 Cell Phone and Service Provider Alternatives

Model	Service Provider	Description/Features
BlackBerry® 8820	AT&T	The unit cost is $249.99. It has adequate durability. Features include push-to-talk and trackball; 64MB RAM; 320 × 240 pixels resolution display; extended battery life—up to 5.5 hours of talk time; BlackBerry program type; Edge high-speed data network. It has a QWERTY keyboard, Bluetooth, and AT&T Navigator (GPS). Additional features include music, messaging, e-mail, video & Web, Media Mall, Productivity, and Wi-Fi.
BlackBerry Curve 8330	Nextel	The unit cost is $99. It has adequate durability. Although price is not a huge factor, this low pricing option will definitely play a role in the decision-making process. It has adequate durability that can potentially be upgraded, along with the valued trackball feature. However, one key missing element is the push-to-talk feature, which does not come equipped with this phone. The battery life of this phone is exceptional as compared with some of the other options, allowing for 5.9 hours of talk time without recharge. Another additional benefit is the sophisticated BlackBerry operating system. The phone also comes with Bluetooth and GPS capacity, and a standard QWERTY keyboard.
MOTO Q 9c	AT&T	The unit cost is 99.99. It has adequate durability. The Moto Q 9c is a smartphone produced by Motorola. The Q comes equipped with a trackwheel that is supported by our program and a quality display that can be easily read. The Q also has a battery life of 7.2 hours of talk time. There is no push-to-talk feature. This makes it one of the better performers we have researched in that category. The Q supports GPS and Bluetooth. One of the few drawbacks of the Q is a relatively low amount of RAM. However, the device does have enough RAM to meet the minimum specifications.
Samsung Epix™	AT&T	The unit cost is $199.99. It has adequate durability. It has no push-to-talk. It has no trackball or roller wheel. It has 150 MB RAM and 320 × 320 pixels resolution display. It has excellent battery life—up to 7 hours of talk time. It has a Windows Mobile 6.1 program type, 3G max data speed, QWERTY keyboard, Bluetooth, and GPS. Additional features include camera, music, messaging, e-mail, video & Web, Media Mall, and Productivity.
Samsung BlackJack™ II	AT&T	The unit cost is $79.99. It has adequate durability. There is no push-to-talk, trackball, or roller wheel. It has 256 MB RAM, 320 × 240 pixels resolution display, and excellent battery life—up to 7 hours of talk time—as well as Windows Mobile 6, 3G max data speed, QWERTY keyboard, Bluetooth, and GPS. Additional features include camera, music, messaging, e-mail, video & Web, Media Mall, and Productivity.
BlackBerry® Bold™	AT&T	The unit cost is $249.99. It has adequate durability. There is no push-to-talk, but it contains a trackball. It has 150 MB RAM, 480 × 320 pixels resolution display, and an adequate battery life—up to 4.5 hours talk time—as well as BlackBerry program type, QWERTY keyboard, 3G max data speed, Bluetooth, and GPS. Additional features include Wi-Fi, camera, music, messaging, e-mail, video & Web, Media Mall, and Productivity.

(continued)

TABLE C8.2 Cell Phone and Service Provider Alternatives *(continued)*

Model	Service Provider	Description/Features
BlackBerry® 8700c	AT&T	The unit cost is $49.99. There is no push-to-talk, but it contains a trackwheel. It has 150 MB RAM, 240 × 320 pixels resolution display, an adequate battery life—up to 4 hours of talk time—and a BlackBerry program. It also has Edge high-speed data network, QWERTY keyboard, Bluetooth, but no GPS. Additional features include messaging, e-mail, video & Web, Media Mall, and Productivity.
AT&T Tilt™	AT&T	The unit cost is $199.99. It has adequate durability. It has push-to-talk but no trackball or roller wheel. It has 256 MB RAM, 240 × 320 pixels resolution display, an adequate battery life—up to 4 hours of talk time—the Windows mobile 6 program type, 3G max data speed, QWERTY keyboard, Bluetooth, and AT&T Navigator (GPS). Additional features include Wi-Fi, camera, music, messaging, e-mail, video & Web, Media Mall, and Productivity.
CENTRO	AT&T	The unit cost is $79.99. It has adequate durability. The Centro by Palm is another phone that we decided to research for this project. The device comes with 128 MB of RAM, which is more than enough to execute our program, and is also equipped with a high-speed network. Another good feature of the Centro is the full QWERTY keyboard. This configuration eliminates any multiple tapping and makes data entry much easier. The Centro does have some drawbacks, however. One key feature missing is the push-to-talk capability. The device also lacks GPS capability.
Treo 800w	Nextel	The unit cost is $249. It has adequate durability. This phone comes with many attractive features, although they come at a price. It lacks the push-to-talk capability. However, it does have the trackball feature and 4.5 hours of talk time available. It is run with the Palm operating system 6.1 and has the necessary Bluetooth and GPS capabilities. The keyboard comes as the standard QWERTY, which is also desirable.
Verizon 700wx	Verizon	The unit cost is $299. It has adequate durability. In the past, CBT has not experienced good customer service and relations. However, the potential for this could change in the future, so Verizon phones should be considered. It lacks the push-to-talk capacity. It is equipped with the trackball feature and a qualified 4.7 hours of talk time. It has a Palm operating system 5.2.2, QWERTY keyboard, and Bluetooth capabilities. It does not have GPS capabilities. GPS can be added for $100 per phone. It also has questionable life expectancy at this point since it has been around for over two years already.
AT&T Moto Global	AT&T	Priced at $99.99, it has adequate durability, no push-to-talk feature, 96 MB RAM, a trackball, an excellent display and battery life—with 9 hours of talk time and 720 hours standby—and a Windows Mobile program type. It also has 3G max data speed, QWERTY keyboard, Bluetooth, and GPS.

Case 9

The Capital State Arena[1]

The Capital State Arena, located on the Capital State University (CSU) campus, is a new 20,000-seat arena that is a multipurpose building. Mainly for men's basketball, there are also plans to hold commencement there and other university sporting events and functions. A theatrical lighting system is obviously needed to offer the flexibility to light these events correctly. As a main component to a top-quality lighting system, a controller or "console" is needed. The console is the brains of any lighting system, whether it has 10 lights or 300 lights.

The new arena will take the place of St. Patrick Arena, which was built in the 1960s. Although there periodically has been renovation to St. Patrick Arena, a theatrical lighting system has never been implemented.

NEED RECOGNITION

There is a need for a lighting console for the new facility. A professional theatrical lighting system was specified by the planning committee. Having the ability to conveniently adjust the lights to accommodate different events and different moods during events is a strong competitive weapon for selling the arena during the off-season. This type of lighting adjustment is driven by a computer-controlled console. The most current technology was specified; the system will be leased out at a rate of $2,000 per day plus operator expenses.

AVAILABLE PRODUCTS

The process began when the purchasing department received the requisition. Two suppliers were contacted via telephone: CAE, manufacturer of Leprecon LP-3000, and Electronic Theatre Controls (ETC), manufacturer of ETC Obsession II. A review of the trade journal *Lighting Dimensions* was used to search for other sources. The review uncovered a third possible supplier: Strand, manufacturer of the Strand 520.

A search of the World Wide Web provided additional information on the three console choices. The Web pages also provided dealer network information, a warranty repair station list, and specification information for each console.

CONSOLE FEATURES

The three consoles had many similar features. The glossy product sheets provided by each manufacturer were used in writing the specification for the console purchase. The resident lighting designer from the theater department also was consulted on the specifications. In addition to this information, the list below helped in the decision-making process:

1. The console must be user-friendly. Programming should be able to be accomplished with just a few keystrokes on the console. This will eliminate the need to have a technician on retainer just to program or get the system turned on.

[1] The author expresses appreciation to Tami Reinhart and Bill Schwertfoger for their contributions to this case. Names and data have been disguised.

2. The console also should be accessible to the theater department as a teaching aide. When the arena and lighting system are not being used, teaching personnel should have the opportunity to sign up for hands-on console training.
3. The console should be expandable. With the increased use of moving lights controlled through lighting consoles, the console should have a few hundred channels that are unused. With extra control space, touring productions might want the opportunity to rent the "house console" and run their lights in conjunction with the in-house system.
4. Console software should be upgradeable. Since lighting consoles are now computer-driven, upgradeability is a factor. Each of the three consoles is upgradeable.
5. Equipment chosen must be manufactured in the United States, or the dealer must have the ability to get any warranty/repair parts in less than 24 hours. This criterion ensures that the console will be repaired in a timely manner.
6. The console should be purchased from a dealer within a 25-mile radius of the arena. The contract terms should include at least a two-year warranty on all parts and workmanship. The dealership also should accept the responsibility of installing "loaner" equipment if the original system fails and needs service. This is done so that any scheduled event that rents the system can still use the system without a loss of income to the arena.

VENDOR MARKET SHARE

The 1995 sales and market share history for each of the companies is illustrated in Table C9.1.

TABLE C9.1
Sales and Market Share History

Company	Sales	Market Share
Electronic Theatre Controls	$19,000,000	59%
Strand Lighting	9,500,000	29
Leprecon	3,700,000	11

BID ANALYSIS

The request for quote was sent out to the three manufacturers mentioned earlier: ETC, Leprecon, and Strand. The results of these requests are shown in Table C9.2.

TABLE C9.2
Quote Request Results

Vendor	Representative	Location	Console	Cost
ETC	Audio Image	Columbus, Ohio	Obsession II	$96,777
Leprecon	Audio Image	Columbus, Ohio	LP-3000	86,697
Strand	Vincent Lighting	Cleveland, Ohio	Strand 520	59,997

NEGOTIATIONS

Although Strand was the low bidder, the purchasing team ranked the Strand 520 as the best value. The theater department ranked the ETC as the best value based on the ease of use and service. The LP-3000 was ranked last by both the purchasing team and the users.

THE DECISION

The purchasing agent knew that the differences in opinion between the university purchasing team and the ultimate users posed a complicated purchasing decision. He realized that his decision on the purchase would involve both qualitative and quantitative trade-offs. One nagging thought in the back of his mind was that no matter which console/vendor he chose, he might never know the impact on either of the disagreeing parties.

Case 10

Carter Systems Canada, Inc.[1]

Mr. Travis received a purchase request from the operations manager for 12,000 GMT-680 housing assemblies. The engineering department had made the necessary design changes submitted by GM. One month ago, a purchase order for a similar design for the same auto platform was $27.88 per unit for 8,000 units.

BACKGROUND

Mr. Travis, the supply manager at Carter Systems Canada, was responsible for the purchase of the GMT-680 housing assembly. The GM-680 housing assembly was the major component part for automobile seat warmers for the GM luxury product line. Seat and steering wheel warming technology is complex and the manufacturing process is wrought with quality problems. It is not unusual to receive a sourcing shipment with a yield of 70 percent good housing assemblies. The source of the quality variation was traced to the numerous engineering changes that were submitted by the auto manufacturers. In other words, each new housing assembly purchase represented a new design. Mr. Travis found it useful, therefore, whenever he was required to issue a request for quote (RFQ) for housing assemblies, to make an estimate of the probable cost of the item from historical costs of similar equipment and from his experience with previous cost-adjusted engineering changes. He would estimate the new housings by adjusting the previous housing assembly cost with the new design estimated costs. This analytical approach required Mr. Travis to use his engineering and business school skills. This way he was well prepared to better evaluate the supplier quotes. This approach also could result in more effective negotiation sessions with successful suppliers. Mr. Travis determined the change in materials costs by analyzing the engineering changes. See Table C10.1.

[1] Names and data have been disguised.

TABLE C10.1
Engineering Changes

Added Components	**Estimated Yielded Materials Cost/Unit**
Terminal pin	$0.53
Cap Cermult1006-03 15uf xrt	1.08
Diode rectifier	1.28
Cap Tantalium 4.7	5.6
ASIC	1.89
Cap Electric 22uf	0.9
Unit cost of added materials	$11.28
Removed Components	
Zener diode	$0.89
Mosfet 174a 55v	5.73
Res 50803 40%	1.86
Cap Electric 47uf	0.3
Unit cost of deleted materials	$8.78

Mr. Travis realized that prospective suppliers for the procurement would include a group different from his usual suppliers and decided for that reason to make an extremely careful estimate of the probable cost.

After analyzing the engineering changes, Mr. Travis used his business skills to prepare the estimate shown below. The engineers' estimate generated by Mr. Travis will serve as a baseline for the negotiations process. As shown below, the estimated price is $28.26.

Direct Materials (DM)	Direct Labor (DL)	Manufacturing Overhead Estimated 100% of DL	Tooling	General and Administrative Estimated 5%	Profit Margin 10%	Estimated Selling Price
$7.30	$5.09	$10.18	$2.00	$1.23	$2.46	$28.26

Meanwhile, requests for proposals were sent out to 12 suppliers. Mr. Travis received eight responsive quotes, of which three were in the range from $29.78 to $33 per unit, and three ranged from $35.60 to $42.00. The last two bids were $22.14 and $24.68. Mr. Travis evaluated each supplier's cost breakdown with the others and compared each cost with his estimated costs. Mr. Travis was impressed with the quality of the two proposals that came in below his estimate and was surprised that both firms had each supplied similar housings during the past year. Both companies were well-established component engineering companies with good reputations for satisfactory performance on previous contracts. The cost breakdowns for the two low proposals are reproduced in Table C10.2.

TABLE C10.2 Cost Breakdowns

	Direct Materials (DM)	Direct Labor (DL)	Manufacturing Overhead (Estimated % of DL)	Tooling	General & Administrative (Estimated %)	Profit Margin (%)	Estimated Selling Price
Mr. Travis	$7.30	$5.09	$10.18 (100%)	$2.00	$1.23 (5%)	$2.46 (10%)	$28.26
Bell Systems	6.20	4.35	8.48 (75%)	3.22	0.88 (4%)	1.76 (8%)	24.68
D&G Technologies	5.90	4.00	8.40 (110%)	2.20	0.62 (3%)	1.03 (5%)	22.14

After investigating the cost breakdown, Mr. Travis wondered why the other five responsive quotes were significantly higher than the Bell and D&G quotes. He decided to call San Onofre Technologies (SOT) to discuss their $29.78 quote. After his conversation he reevaluated the SOT quote. The SOT cost breakdown is given below:

SOT Direct Materials (DM)	Direct Labor (DL)	Manufacturing Overhead Estimated 100% of DL	Tooling	General and Administrative	Profit Margin 5%	Estimated Selling Price
$7.02	$4.50	$7.20	$8.35	$1.35	$1.35	$29.78

Assignment Questions

1. What factors might have caused the variance between D&G Technologies' quotation and Mr. Travis's estimate? Between D&G Technologies' quotation and Bell Systems' quotation? Between SOT and the two lowest quotes?
2. In light of your answer to the above question, what conclusions can you draw concerning (a) the reliability and usefulness of cost estimates made by the buyer and (b) the value to be gained from the comparison of one supplier's quotation with the others?
3. Write a two-page memo justifying your recommendations.

Case 11

Eastern Waves, Inc.[1]

Mr. Paul Patton, Vice President of Purchasing for Code C, Inc., hung up the phone and shook his head. "How can Eastern Waves double prices on our fabricated steel purchases? Last summer we were celebrating a 60-percent cost reduction based on replacing our major domestic supplier with Eastern Waves, in Kuantan, Malaysia. We cannot compete if we source our angle steel products domestically." Mr. Patton phoned Jon James, the director of global sourcing. "Jon, I want you to hop on a plane to Kuantan and save our rear ends." "We have a contract." "What are our legal rights? Is our contract enforceable?" Prior to leaving, Jon requested assistance from one of the company's strategic partners in Asia. A synopsis of the situation in Malaysia follows.

BACKGROUND

Eastern Waves, Inc. is a steel manufacturing company located in Kuantan, Malaysia. The most recent balance sheet for Eastern is presented in Figure C11.1. In 2009, Eastern Waves' cash on hand was 188 ringgits (RM), which is equivalent to US$50. In the previous year, they had an even lower cash balance of RM118. This problem is very pressing because, without cash, they are unable to purchase raw materials from the local raw material supplier. Eastern currently has a joint venture relationship with Jinan & Iron Steel Corp., which enables Eastern to buy scrap steel on credit from the Jinan plate mill operation. This scrap steel is crucial to Eastern's success given the market price of the purchased raw steel billets. However, the scrap steel is of a lower grade than the standard raw steel billet.

One of the government's most recent import policies on steel will make doing business increasingly difficult. This policy is common in many developing countries. The new policy is expected to generate more business for local and government suppliers. As an example, purchasing steel from China is significantly cheaper. Since Eastern must purchase steel at a higher price, they are at a competitive disadvantage and have decided to pass the price increase to their customers.

The Malaysian Business Environment

Malaysia is located in Southeast Asia with neighboring countries of Singapore, Thailand, and Indonesia. Since gaining its independence from Great Britain in 1963, the Malaysian government has been committed to maintaining a supportive government policy to promote opportunities for growth and profits for local businesses in order to attract investors. Recently, Malaysia has transformed itself from a producer of raw materials into an emerging multisector economy. The Malaysian economy has continued to improve and the country recorded an increase in GDP of 4.2 percent in 2008. Malaysia currently has a workforce of 9.9 million people employed in various industries.

In 1997, Malaysia was hit hard by the Asian financial crisis. The manufacturing sector, which formerly employed 27 percent of the labor force, was one of the most affected industries. In order to rescue some of the largest state-owned companies, the government imposed several strict trade barriers on certain goods. Included

[1] The author expresses appreciation to Biao Yan for his contributions to this case. Names and data have been disguised.

FIGURE C11.1 Eastern Wave Balance Sheet

Balance Sheet as of 31st December, 2008

	Group		Company	
	2008 RM	2007 RM	2008 RM	2007 RM
ASSETS				
Property, plant and equipment	94,557,256	96,118,112	92,621,271	94,148,166
Subsidiary	—	—	1,585,944	931,639
Goodwill arising on consolidation	684,659	684,659	—	—
CURRENT ASSETS				
Stocks	1,199,424	—	1,199,424	—
Trade debtor	485,745	3,076	485,745	3,076
Other debtors and deposits	7,100,809	5,694,447	7,046,055	5,639,693
Cash and bank balances	381	1,221	118	938
	8,786,359	5,698,744	8,731,342	5,643,707
Less: CURRENT LIABILITIES				
Trade creditors	778,383	2,696,412	778,383	2,696,412
Other creditors and accruals	19,975,160	17,612,754	19,708,645	17,057,553
Hire purchase creditor	—	3,007	—	3,007
Amount owing to directors	582,220	96,709	495,255	9,744
Long-term loans	2,800,000	2,800,000	—	—
Bank balance overdrawn	611,089	669,282	611,089	669,282
	24,746,852	23,878,164	21,593,372	20,435,998
NET CURRENT LIABILITIES	(15,960,493)	(18,179,420)	(12,862,030)	(14,792,291)
	79,281,422	78,623,351	81,345,185	80,287,514
Financed by:				
SHARE CAPITAL	12,000,000	12,000,000	12,000,000	12,000,000
RESERVES	(9,389,295)	(7,554,834)	(7,325,532)	(5,890,671)
	2,610,705	4,445,166	4,674,468	6,109,329
LONG-TERM LOANS	76,670,717	74,178,185	76,670,717	74,178,185
	79,281,422	78,623,351	81,345,185	80,287,514

under law in these protected goods are steel billets, the raw material for use in the downstream steel industry.

The Steel Industry

The steel industry in Malaysia is divided into two subsectors, namely, the manufacture of long steel products and the manufacture of flat steel products. Long products include billets, bars, and wire rods and are widely used in the construction industry. Flat steel products include tin plates, galvanized sheets, metal sheets, and fabricated sheets. These forms of steel are used in the construction, oil, and manufacturing sectors of the economy. Mega Steel controls the flat steel segment while the long-product segment (billets) is dominated by six large manufacturers. All six manufacturers are government-owned. The big five include Amsteel, Malayawata Steel, Perwaja Steel, Antara Steel, and Malaysian Steel Works Inc.

In 2008, the Malaysian downstream steel millers prefered to pay slightly more for domestic billets. The primary reason for the inflated price was the restrictions placed on imports to protect the local economy. However, with the price gap continuing to increase due to falling international steel prices, the local difference was beginning to eat into profitability. Domestic billets were priced at approximately RM760 per metric ton (MT), while international were priced between RM600 and RM680 per MT F.O.B. Malaysia's consumption of billets is on average about 2.7 million MT annually. The protection of the Malaysian upstream steel industry was affecting local downstream steel millers as they were forced to buy from the more expensive domestic suppliers. The raw material price variances were putting Malaysian steel millers at a competitive disadvantage with Thailand and Indonesia.

Labor Issues

The government's primary reason for a new labor policy is to ensure sustained economic growth for a favorable investment climate. They are attempting to promote cordial relationships between employers and employees and industrial harmony based on social justice and equity. The Employment Act of 1955 regulates the minimum terms and conditions of service of an employee earning less than or equal to RM1,500 per month. The labor regulations attempt to protect the domestic workers, especially the majority ethnic group of Malay, who are stereotyped by the business elites as less efficient, nondisciplined, and favored by the government. As a result, the Malaysian industries still rely heavily on cheap foreign workers from countries such as Indonesia, Thailand, Philippines, and Sri Lanka. In order to reverse the dependency on foreign workers and promote domestic workers, the government has recently imposed an annual levy of RM125–1,500 on each foreign worker and limited their work stay to only two years per permit.

Eastern Wave Manufacturing

Eastern Wave is a small steel manufacturing company in Malaysia (see Figure C11.2). It has several plants in Malaysia and China and produces various downstream steel products such as angle steel (see Figure C11.3), I-beam, and round bar. The angle steel plant is located in Kuantan, Malaysia. The production method of the angle steel is called continuous rolling, and the key raw material ingredient for angle steel production is billets. When operating at full efficiency, the annual capacity of the angle steel production is 10,000 MT.

FIGURE C11.2
The Eastern Wave Company's Structure

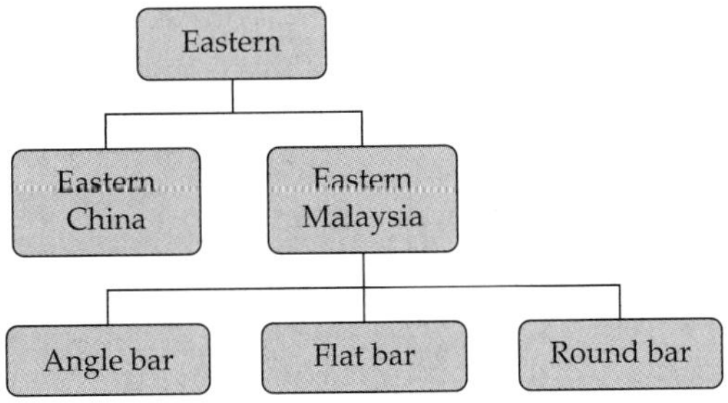

FIGURE C11.3
Angle Steel Bars

THE PROBLEM STATEMENT

The Malaysian government's trade barrier on billets in order to protect the domestic billet producers has greatly affected the bottom lines of the downstream steel manufacturing companies. The domestic billet price is 15–25 percent higher than the international billet price. On the other hand, the government allows import of the downstream products from other countries, such as Indonesia, in order to reduce domestic supply shortage of the downstream steel products and their prices' inflation. As a result of these two policies, many of the small to medium-sized downstream steel companies were forced to cease operations. Many other steel companies are struggling to survive in this government-controlled steel industry.

The supply problem is not the only serious problem that Eastern faces. Eastern is having difficulty with the governmental labor department. The domestic workers are protected under very strict labor laws and are generally difficult to manage because of the worker-friendly laws. There is a large supply of local workers; however, it is difficult to terminate them. While there is difficulty in firing the workers, the workers are free to resign or quit at any time they feel necessary. The local workers demand to be paid in full each month whether they work or not, and if their pay is delayed at all, most of the time the workers will strike. These strikes are becoming increasingly difficult to extinguish and are becoming more prevalent with Eastern's cash-flow problem. Eastern's difficulty in controlling their labor situation makes it very difficult to adjust to the demand fluctuation of angled steel.

Direct Raw Material Problem

Due to the increase in steel prices over the past few years in Malaysia, Eastern has been searching for solutions to their raw material problems. Instead of buying standard billets from the local billet suppliers, Eastern has been researching alternative

FIGURE C11.4 Trimmed Steel Plates

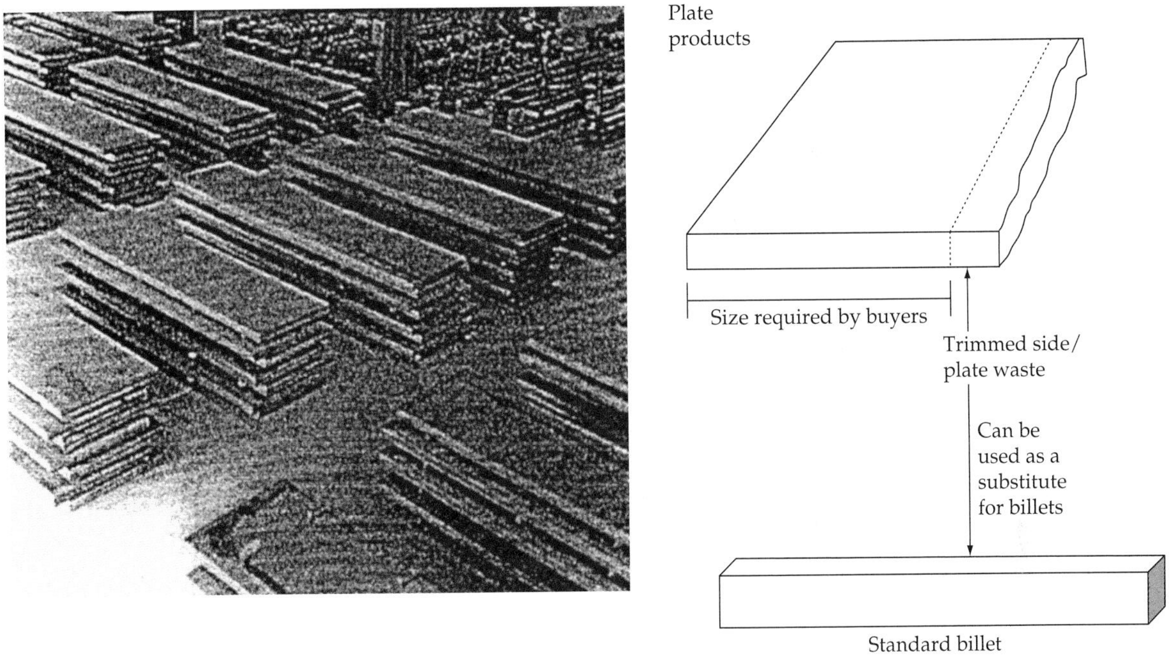

sources or a billet substitute. One suitable substitute is the trimmed sides of the steel plates, which are waste by-products. These ends are not the same quality steel as the billets. The cost of this scrap steel is now increasing because it is no longer considered to be scrap and because of the billet price inflation. In 2008, Eastern China started a joint venture with Jinan Iron & Steel Corp. Jinan Iron & Steel Corp. is one of the largest steel companies in China that produces stainless composite steel. The key factor to this joint venture is that Eastern had bought the patent to the production of stainless composite steel. As one part of the joint venture agreement, Jigang Steel Plate, Jinan Iron & Steel's subsidiary in Malaysia, has agreed to provide trimmed sides of the steel plates (Figure C11.4) at a favorable price. While this seems like a great deal on the outside, there are several difficulties that remain. The first is that the scrap steel that they are purchasing from Jinan is of a lower grade. However, this is overlooked because the steel does meet all of the requirements to produce angled steel for most of their customers. The one other glaring problem is the fact that Eastern will be receiving Jinan's waste products.

This means that if Jinan is not producing at a high level, Eastern will not be receiving enough raw materials to increase their production. With this agreement, Eastern is relying heavily on the increased demand and production of steel plates. If Jinan is not producing at a high level, Eastern might be forced to buy the billets at a higher price from a government-regulated supplier.

Direct Labor Problem

In the past, Eastern has hired mostly foreign workers from either China or Thailand. Even though the workers are foreign, they are still paid at the same rate as domestic workers. However, with the hiring of foreign workers, Eastern now incurs many additional expenses. These expenses include half of the airfare that the foreign workers demand in a year's time. They also will incur government taxes on foreign workers and immigration expenses. The company also has to provide housing for these workers while they pay for their own food. There are some advantages associated with hiring foreign laborers: They are usually under contract for two years. Not only are they under contract for two years, their working visa expires after the two years. Because the quality of life and the pay are better in Malaysia than their homeland, they usually are reluctant to quit. Another advantage is that they are not protected under the labor laws. Finally, when demand is low or the company is not producing at full capacity, the company could dismiss them without any legal problems. This also would save money and help increase profits during low demand. Although the labor cost is higher, the company believes that increases in labor control could stabilize production flow and thus reduce costs in other areas.

ASSUMPTION

The price of steel has been as unstable as the stock market during the past few years. The price is mainly determined by the market demand and supply. In order to conduct an analysis on steel prices, Eastern has assumed that the price of steel is set at RM1,300 per MT.

The strategic partner collected the data based on phone conversations with Eastern's production manager. Eastern operates on a 17-percent profit margin. The daily production output of angle steel is 15 MT, which is only half of the capacity. Currently, Eastern employs 40 workers, all of whom are foreigners earning a RM1,500 basic monthly wage. The mill operates only one eight-hour shift a day, 25 days a month.

The raw material (plate waste) currently costs RM495 per MT. The domestic standard billets cost RM760 per MT, while international billets cost RM600 per MT. Inventory holding cost is about 15 percent of the raw material price. However, around one-third of the total holding cost is spent on segregating qualified raw materials from disqualified raw materials (about 50 percent of the input) prior to production. The company has to do this because the raw material is plate waste, not the standard unit used to make angled steel. Only steel with a thickness above 120 mm is suitable for production of angle steel. The disqualified plate waste is not scrapped but sold to the market at RM525 per MT; daily sales are about 15 MT.

The output is 85 percent qualified angle steel, 10 percent semiqualified steel, and 5 percent scrap. The prices of these three outputs are RM1,300, RM1,000, and RM380, respectively. The production manager is confident that if standard billets are used for production, the qualified products will be 95 percent of the output; 4 percent is semiqualified while 1 percent is scrap. The supply of the plate waste is not stable and depends on the production schedule of the plate mill, which has a very irregular market demand. Sometimes, there is a shortage of the raw material supply when the plate mill has a slowdown of production. As a result, Eastern is currently operating at half of its capacity. There is no problem with the supply of standard billets in the market; however, the inflated price level makes purchase of the standard billets difficult.

THE DECISION

Jon phoned Mr. Patton immediately after the briefing. Mr. Patton responded, "Jon, please write a critique analyzing the situation in Malaysia as soon as possible." Eastern is under contract to ship 2,000 MT of steel to Code C during the next six months.

Case 12

Firebird Electric, U.S.[1]

In 1994, Firebird Electric, U.S. (Firebird), was the first foreign supplier to relocate to the United States to supply the Road-Master Car Company. Located in Columbia, South Carolina, Firebird supplies headlights, taillights, lid lamps, center high mounts, and front-turn assemblies to Road-Master. Road-Master sales account for 98.5 percent of Firebird's revenues. Original equipment manufacturing (OEM) lighting is supplied to the Orangeburg plant, the Columbia auto plant, and the Columbia motorcycle plant. In addition, service (aftermarket) products are made for foreign and domestic demands. Weekly shipments go to Road-Master Canada Manufacturing and Road-Master De Mexico. Service models also are shipped to Germany, Brazil, and Japan.

Firebird Electric, U.S., exports components from the molding division to sister and parent companies. Molded parts also are supplied to Road-Master.

OPERATIONS AT FIREBIRD U.S.

Firebird has five distinct operations centers. The East plant manufactures light assemblies and units. Manufacturing I produces headlights and front-turn assemblies. Manufacturing II assembles taillights, lid lamps, center high mounts, and aftermarket products. The West plant provides components to assembly and external sales. Manufacturing III is a sanitization and coating process for lenses, reflectors, and extensions. Manufacturing IV is a die injection molding facility producing reflectors, lenses, and housings. A halogen bulb department provides the majority of the bulbs used in production.

Assembly in the East Plant

Approximately 40 lines supply different makes, models, and types of lighting for Road-Master vehicles. Dedicated lines run multiple shifts to meet OEM production for current year A-car and B-car models. OEM production for the Avenger and Odyssey Minivan runs on one-shift dedicated lines. OEM requirements may exceed 1,200 units daily. Fourteen lines run to meet aftermarket demand. These lines are interchangeable among different models. Aftermarket assemblies and units are made 10–20 years after OEM production. Service requirements range from 30 to 10,000 units per month.

West Plant Operations

Manufacturing III is an isolated sanitization area for coating processes. Products are cleaned, prepared, and either aluminized or hard-coated. Aluminization provides a reflective coating to components such as reflectors and extensions. This process allows a plastic-molded part to reflect the light at the designed angles. Lenses are hard-coated to protect against chips and cracks.

Manufacturing IV, the focus of the upcoming make-or-buy decision, molds parts for finished assembly and sales. Lenses, reflectors, and housings are molded from resins and fiberglass-reinforced plastics. Die injection molding machines range from 60 to 900 tons of pressure. These machines are adaptable to produce

[1] The author expresses appreciation to Brandon Smeul for his contributions to this case. Names and data have been disguised.

multiple parts by interchanging the die molds. Firebird Electric has recently acquired the two largest molding machines in the world. The productivity of these machines will aid in the upcoming decision regarding further expansion. Firebird is reducing inventory in the West plant Material Order Center (WESTMOC) to possibly expand operations by three machines.

Firebird Electric manufactures halogen bulbs for in-house production and external sales. The halogen bulb (HB) department is capable of producing 60,000 bulbs per week. HB runs a continuous three-shift operation until weekly production quotas are met.

PURCHASING AT FIREBIRD

Purchasing for Firebird Electric is decentralized. The purchasing department at Firebird U.S. consists of nine full-time associates. The purchasing manager assists in decision making and controls administrative duties. Six buyers are responsible for obtaining materials to meet production requirements. One buyer supplies the HB department and one is solely responsible for MRO purchases. The other four buyers are responsible for specific vendors. Each buyer oversees all products purchased from 8 to 10 different suppliers. The two other purchasing associates are specifically assigned to supplier evaluation and incoming quality conformance.

Firebird Electric has been awarded OEM production for the lighting on the 2005 model two-door B-car. This report focuses on the procedures and decisions involved in supplying the housing for upcoming production.

HOUSING DEFINITION AND SUPPLY

Housings are fabricated through die injection molding. A resin is melted, injected, and stamped into the die mold. The housing's function is to attach to the body of the vehicle, protect internal components (cords, bulbs, etc.), and hold components in place so that the light functions as designed. Each make/model has unique housing specifications with regard to size, durability, holes, and necessary attachments to perform these duties.

As stated earlier, Firebird has the ability to produce housings in the molding division; however, of the approximately 240 parts presently molded in Manufacturing IV, only 11 are housings. Firebird also outsources production of housings to four central South Carolina molding firms: FPE, The South Carolina Plastics Company (TOPCO), Central South Carolina Plastics (COPCO), and Charleston Custom Plastics (WCP).

NEW PRODUCT DEVELOPMENT: DEFINING REQUIREMENTS

The customer, internal departments, and potential suppliers contribute to designing quality into molded parts. Due to Road-Master's strict quality requirements and just-in-time inventory systems, nonconformance results in high costs, hinders customer relations, and endangers prospective contracts. Departments included in the product definition and development stages include product design, purchasing, quality assurance, sales, die molding, engineering, manufacturing, plant management, quality control, production control, and materials management.

The first stage in new housing development is gathering model information from the customer via the sales department. Based on this information, the first drawings of the housing are completed and evaluated. Firebird considers the application of new technology, alternate manufacturing processes, and new inputs to production for all new model components. Project leaders and project members, representing the aforementioned departments, are selected for the development team.

Quality assurance reviews the initial drawings. The review encompasses simplifying fabrication by eliminating components and processes, and searching for alternative methods of tooling and production. The design review is then sent to manufacturing departments, die mold, purchasing, quality assurance, and quality control. A follow-up meeting is conducted involving representatives from all departments.

Development conferences with manufacturing personnel are held to inform team members of schedule updates, quality targets, costs, and responsibilities. The periodic meetings are held as needed to ensure that members are aware of revisions to plans. A constant flow of information is emphasized to continuously improve processes.

After product development is completed, Firebird defines the specifications for the fixture (die mold) measurements. The fixture is designed for accuracy, ease of use, and cost efficiency. A rough sketch of the fixture and the required materials is drawn. Purchasing and engineering personnel from Firebird and Road-Master must approve the concept. Upon approval, the fixture manufacturer submits a design drawing to quality assurance. Firebird purchases and retains ownership of the die mold fixture regardless of the outcome of the make-versus-buy decision.

The initial trial run of the product, always performed in-house, is done to verify that the fixture is capable of meeting drawing specifications and minimizing the rejection rate. Statistical process control charts are kept for resin input and output quality. If the process is deemed out of control, a modification schedule for a new trial run is scheduled. An evaluation meeting is held to inform all departments about potential problems. Cause-and-effect judgments are made and reconciled via modification request sheets. Target finish dates also are established at this meeting.

THE MAKE-VERSUS-BUY DECISION

As can be seen, new-product development is an involved process. Recently, more and more of Firebird production is outsourced. Using the assumptions given below, please analyze the make-or-buy decision. Please write a detailed report recommending either the make or buy decision.

Assumptions

1. Make and buy information is shown in Figure C12.1. Internal production costs were obtained from manufacturing and cost accounting; information on the cost to buy was gathered from journals, historical pricing, supplier information, and engineering estimates.
   - OEM demand is estimated at 250,000 units over the next year (1,000 units/day, 250 working days/year).
   - The resin usage is 454 grams (1 pound). Actual product weight is 432 grams with a spru weight of 22 grams.
   - Variables include cycle time, labor costs, overhead costs, material costs, transportation costs, and profit margins.
   - Difference in quality levels of in-house and procured parts is negligible.

FIGURE C12.1
Manufacturer Data

Overhead	General Allocation Base	Direct Labor
	Rate allocated	115%
Output	Units/day	1,000
	Work days/year	250
Resin	Resin/unit	455 g
	Resin cost/unit	$1.00
Molding unit	Precision 1 cost	$285,000.00
	Capital allocation/year	1
	Residual value	0
Labor	Employees/molder	2
	Wages/hour	$18.00
	Work hours/year	2,083.00
Plant	Size/square foot	100,000
	Space required for precision 1	1,000
	Cycle time	30
	Output	$8,000,000.00

	General	
Housings	Units purchased/year	250,000
	Cost/unit	$3.00
Purchasing	Cost per order release	$50.00
	Lot size	2,500
	Order releases/year	100

- The F.O.B. purchase price is $750,000; receiving and inspection cost is $35,000.
- Annual order processing cost is $5,000.

2. What are the costs to society when well-established firms like Firebird outsource even though they clearly have the capability to produce the good or service?
3. How should the suppliers be selected if the buy option is chosen? Please give a step-by-step approach to the selection and evaluation process.

Case 13

Great Lakes University[1]

In May 2012, Joan Middleton took over as director of purchasing at Great Lakes University (GLU), a large state university located in Cleveland, Ohio. Ms. Middleton is a 2005 graduate of The Ohio State University, where she majored in purchasing. Joan worked for seven years as a buyer for Honda. Upon arrival at GLU, she discovered that her staff was spending too much time and money on more than 180 spend categories. Consequently, she wanted to develop methods of increasing the effectiveness and the efficiency of the 180 spend categories. To accomplish this goal, she plans to move down the list of the spend categories beginning with the highest spend category, and ending with the least significant spend category.

THE UNIVERSITY

Great Lakes is a metropolitan university providing a rich environment for engaged learning in a dynamic location. Great Lakes' students consider the entire city as their campus for study, practical experience, and recreation. And the university's pledge to each student is an engaged learning experience in the real world, for the real world, among a diverse student body. More than 1,000 courses support 200 major fields of study at the undergraduate and graduate levels, as well as professional certificate and continuing education programs. Programs are offered in business administration, education and human services, engineering, law, liberal arts and social sciences, science, and urban affairs.

As nearly 60 percent of Great Lakes' students work full- or part-time, flexible academic programming and convenient class times are offered. Of the institution's 25,000 students, approximately one-third are in graduate-level programs and about half attend on a part-time basis.

THE PURCHASING DEPARTMENT

The purchasing department is directed by Ms. Middleton. Her primary responsibility is to manage the acquisition of the services and materials requested by all university departments. Ms. Middleton's current purchasing staff consists of herself, her administrative associate, and 10 buyers—three senior buyers and seven junior buyers. All three senior buyers applied for the director of purchasing position. The senior buyers frequently had lunch with some of the larger lawn care suppliers. Within the first few weeks on the job, she found it difficult to do her work well and decided to take action. In order to understand 180 major purchasing categories, Joan decided to start with a category near the middle of the list of the 180 spend categories. Joan selected the lawn care category. The 2012 lawn care subcategories and spend are shown in Table C13.1. The purchasing staff processes approximately 4,000–5,000 requisitions per month for more than 2,000 suppliers. The lawn care suppliers and spend are given in Table C13.2.

Lawn Care and the Spend

Joan's research, covering a 12-months period of the university's purchasing activity, revealed that more than 2 million dollars were spent for lawn care services and that

TABLE C13.1
Categories/Spend

Category	Spend
Irrigation and drainage	$ 177,878.00
Snow	435,990.00
Machinery and maintenance	263,890.00
Lawn care services (basic landscaping)	288,054.00
Chemicals/Foods	11,040.00
Gravel/Mulch/Soil/Turf	69,173.00
Plants/Shrubs/Trees/Seeds	460,332.00
Landscape design and construction	134,804.00
Athletic field	52,753.00
One-stop-shop (3+ services provided)	25,623.00
Supplies and equipment	89,669.00
	$2,009,206.00

TABLE C13.2
Suppliers/Spend

Supplier	Spend
Bogner Construction Co.	$242,776.43
Field Turf	153,019.90
Advanced Turf Solutions, Inc.	110,064.49
Agrium Advanced Technologies	103,662.35
Enviroscapes	84,538.25
Arms Trucking Co, Inc.	60,449.87
Petersons Lawn Care & Landscape Maintenance	56,393.42
Ahlum & Arbor Tree Preservation	54,830.00
Contemporary Tree SVC	52,783.21
John Deere Landscapes	47,545.08
JA Hitchcock Excavating	47,175.00
Impullitti Landscaping, Inc.	40,860.00
Winnscapes, Inc.	39,953.09
Precision Mulching, Inc.	39,015.00
Berta's Lawn Service	38,486.64
Vermeer Sales & Service	35,137.58
Hill Co., LLC	33,960.00
Century Equipment, Inc.	33,791.61
Central Farm & Garden Inc.	26,487.46
Buckeye Landscape SVCS, Inc.	26,173.84
Taylor & Sons Equipment Co.	25,979.90
Kurtz Bros, Inc.	24,849.98
Proscape Landscaping	24,347.50
Arms Turf Products	24,343.60
JD Equipment, Inc.	22,063.23
Delhi Landscape	20,065.00
Helena Chemical Co.	18,600.00
Barnes Nursery, Inc.	18,188.00
Oakland Design Associates	17,567.55
Michaels Lawn Care	14,935.00
Briarwood Landscape Service Inc.	12,392.50
Ohio Mulch	12,362.50
Dryject Ohio	12,021.09
Enviro Recycling Group, LLC	11,685.00
Turfgrass Inc.	11,340.00

TABLE C13.2
(continued)

Supplier	Spend
Reynolds Farm Equipment	11,236.72
Golf Preservations	11,040.00
Hilliard Lawn & Garden	10,949.00
Rausch Enterprises	10,710.70
Fred Azar Landscaping	10,648.00
Rico Construction, Inc.	10,012.50
Boyd Turf, Inc.	9,950.00
Oberfield's, Inc.	9,839.18
Greenscape Horticultural Services	8,920.22
Shearer Equipment	8,588.77
Tag Lawn Services, LLC	8,410.00
Edge Group	8,075.00
Brickman Group Ltd.	8,026.50
R&R Products Co.	7,944.54
Harrell's, LLC	7,770.95
Klingstone Paths, LLC	7,394.30
Schmidt, Thomas	7,152.20
Shepherd's Shoreline Construction	6,810.00
On-Course Management, LLC	6,745.00
Acorn Farms, Inc.	6,709.90
Wyandot Tractor & Implement Co.	6,281.65
Clark's Wood Recycling, Inc.	5,955.00
Midwest Turf Consultants	5,810.00
Columbus Equipment, Inc.	5,795.89
Willoway Nurseries, Inc.	5,699.64
Jones Fish Hatchery	5,636.18
Baker Vehicle Systems	5,563.25
Estate Lawn Care, Inc.	5,465.65
Buckeye Tractor & Implement	5,120.41
PRM Enterprises, LLC	5,056.00
Daniels Landscaping	5,000.00
Adgate Garden Center	5,000.00
Deep Roots Aerification Services	4,875.00
Hill, Michael R.	4,575.00
LESCO, Inc.	4,321.62
Franklin Equipment	4,167.94
Mccoy Landscape Services, Inc.	4,074.86
Orrville Trucking	4,032.56
Greenscapes Landscape Co.	3,946.00
Jarvis Outdoor Services	3,800.00
Fast Eddys Ground Maintenance	3,782.28
Nationwide Exterior Solutions	3,675.00
Sunbelt Rentals	3,371.22
Trupointe Cooperative	3,302.46
Mulch 1st Ltd.	3,285.00
WOW Painting & Contracting, LLC	3,200.00
Lavy Enterprises Turfgrass	3,146.50
EE Johnson Property Services, LLC	3,021.80
Park Enterprises Construction	3,000.00
Hudson Landscaping	2,950.00
Harold Tatman & Sons	2,822.50
Forestry Suppliers	2,718.08

(continued)

TABLE C13.2
Suppliers/Spend
(continued)

Supplier	Spend
Treeline Products Co, Inc.	2,664.00
Pat's Lawn Care Service	2,652.50
Seed Center	2,525.00
Straders Garden Centers, Inc.	2,499.50
Central Power Systems	2,414.16
Textron Financial Corporation	2,367.00
TurfTec International	2,285.94
Central Farm And Garden I	2,247.50
CLC Labs	2,226.15
Dayton Garden Labels	2,093.56
Fred C. Gloeckner & Co.	2,006.65
AG Design	2,000.00
Ohio Valley Teen Challenge	1,935.00
AM Leonard	1,932.82
Bearing Distributors	1,919.97
Wolf Creek Co.	1,771.55
KLYN Nurseries. Inc.	1,568.70
Lang Stone Co.	1,507.50
Strategic Turf Systems, Inc.	1,500.00
Fox Stone Products, Inc.	1,417.87
Vinecourt Landscaping	1,407.04
Sabic Polymershapes	1,388.20
Murphy Tractor & Equipment	1,353.35
Davis Tree Farm & Nursery, Inc.	1,305.00
Mid-Ohio Electric Co., Inc.	1,260.93
East of Eden	1,236.25
Woodland Mulch	1,234.40
Green Thumb Gardening	1,220.00
Mid-Amer Sports Advantage	1,219.00
Shemin Nurseries, Inc.	1,142.00
Prairie Creek Lawnscapes	1,130.00
WG Dairy Supply, Inc.	1,129.86
Walker Brothers Lexington	1,125.00
Stabilizer Solutions, Inc.	1,080.00
Vinyl Guard	1,061.00
Buckeye Power Sales	1,054.66
Hawksridge Farms	1,029.00
Willoway Wholesale Distribution Center	993.05
Feikert Sand and Gravel	979.01
Zarlinski Landscape Service	914.25
Mid-West Landscape, Inc.	903.00
Romich Sales and Service, LLC	895.84
Shamrock Asphalt Sealcoating & Repair	880.75
Piskula, Sean	870.00
Menards	861.42
BFG Supply Co.	844.14
Baker Vehicle Systems, Inc.	826.87
Orlo Auto Parts	823.44
Silico Turf	800.00
Trugreen Chemlawn	800.00
Total Tennis, Inc.	750.00
Wrights Tree Service, LLC	750.00

TABLE C13.2
(continued)

Supplier	Spend
Tanks, Leonard	747.00
AM Leonard, Inc.	727.00
Lifetime Fencing	711.50
Davey Tree Expert Co.	685.31
Contracting Solutions	675.00
MTC Horticultural Services, LLC	666.59
Herman Losely Son	607.75
Mid Ohio Tree Service	600.00
JW Raden Enterprises, Inc.	600.00
Shaefer Landscaping NUR	596.50
R&B Supply Co., Inc.	566.93
Lakeside Greenhouse	554.00
Trent, Charles	512.77
Mast-Lepley AG Hardware	503.77
Reel Turf Equipment Co., LLC	493.00
United Rentals	489.45
Herman Losely & Son, Inc.	472.50
W W Grainger 916	447.50
Columbus Fasteners Corp.	429.08
Freestyle Consulting	399.98
Dayton Nurseries	394.11
Smith Material Supply, Inc.	386.44
Jones Topsoil	377.82
Stone Creations	375.00
Fore-Par Group	366.43
Frye, Brandon L	360.00
Miller Lawn & Power Equipment	359.30
Dannaher Landscaping, Inc.	359.00
Interstate Battery System of Columbus	339.00
Lowes #01696	331.06
Lowes #00264	329.17
Golden West Industrial Supply	319.22
Morrison Custom Welding, Inc.	293.92
Discount Drainage Supplies	288.00
Olena Sales	282.04
Michigan Co., Inc.	262.14
Interstate Batteries	252.90
Zollinger Sand & Gravel	246.75
CWS	245.00
Mcdonnell Sales & SVC Co.	242.85
Tractor Supply Co. #0675	215.33
Como Mower Service	206.05
Knot and Rope Supply, Inc.	201.15
Stone Creation	200.00
Kauffman Tire Center	185.00
Wooster Rural King Supply	179.80
The Home Depot #3866	172.99
Barnes Nursery-Huron 2	145.96
Hite Parts Exchange, Inc.	145.00
Nortrax	126.00
Paradise Lawn Care, Inc.	107.25
Jurkiewicz, Michael	105.00

(continued)

TABLE C13.2
Suppliers/Spend
(continued)

Supplier	Spend
Ditch Witch of Ohio	103.25
Walmart	101.86
Olen Corporation Plant 1	72.33
H and H Lawncare Equipment, LLC	69.80
Ramco Rental, Inc.	65.00
OSU Petty Cash-Fawcett Center	64.41
Madison SWCD	60.00
Derringers, Inc.	60.00
Johnston Supply-Ashland	56.44
Columbus Builders Supply, Inc.	54.00
Nourse Farms, Inc.	53.05
Lake County Nursery	51.00
Ads, Inc.–Wooste	50.00
Sherwin–Williams Co.	49.86
Corso's Flower & G	49.00
Wayne's Country Market	48.00
The greenhouse Shoppe	47.99
Irrigation Supply of Columbus	47.60
Pymnt to Employees	44.80
Brown County–OSU Extension	41.20
Lowes #01175*	31.40
Fackler Equipment Company	29.44
Schlabach Engine Ltd.	21.00
WW Grainger	20.50
Grand Total	**$2,009,209.11**

the control and coordination for these service purchases was uneconomical. Joan discovered that there were no performance criteria associated with spend category. In some cases, the work was never formally finalized or documented, even though the invoice was paid. There was very little internal or external accountability. In an attempt to gain control of the purchasing department, Joan formed a committee that consisted of two buyers and two associates from the accounting department. She informed the committees that the report from the committee would serve as a model for the evaluation of the remaining spend categories.

While considering possible alternatives, Joan recalled how in a recent seminar she learned that service purchasing may be more difficult for people to visualize and to measure. In general, "service-level agreements" and "statements of work" may not have been as precise and finely tuned as specifications for manufactured goods. There is a general belief that service quality and performance are not as easy to measure and specify objectively as product quality and performance. However, service suppliers are frequently relied upon to create the statements of work. There were no statements of work between GLU and its service providers. Within the realm of lawn care purchasing at Great Lakes, there is also little reference to what the other spend categories are doing. This lack of a unified approach makes it difficult to understand the true scope of services purchases or to improve the management of materials and services purchases at GLU.

Case 14

Hoosier Pride Construction, Inc.[1]

Janice L. Edwards is president and CEO of Hoosier Pride Construction, a highway construction contractor. The company was started by Edwards and her husband in 1995 and now employs 15 people. Revenues and profits increased steadily from 1995 until 2005. Both were down in 2005 and 2006. During the last three years, both were erratic as a result of increased pressure on profits.

THE PROBLEM

Edwards recently met with her chief estimator (Shawn Edwards) and her accountant (Deon Houston) to determine how costs could be cut so the company could become more competitive in the market. At this meeting, she learned that employee benefit costs increased at approximately three times the rate of increase for wages alone (19 percent versus 6 percent yearly) from 2006 to 2008. In particular, the employee health insurance costs increased from $2,584 per employee per year in 2006 to $4,316 in 2008. The insurance premium to cover these costs increased 21.4 percent in 2008 and 22.6 percent in 2009. From 2006 to 2009, premium increases averaged 12.2 percent per year and the average health cost per employee was $7,212 in 2009. Edwards expressed frustration at these increases and asked what could be done.

Shawn and Deon invited Mrs. Edwards to a meeting of health care providers, insurers, and employers scheduled for the following week. At this meeting, they learned that their problem was quite common and being experienced by most other construction companies in the area. One consultant who surveyed construction firms in the region found "controlling employee benefit program costs" to be the most critical issue facing the business owners. Another national survey found that health benefit costs amounted to a whopping 26 percent of earnings. Moreover, health care costs have grown faster than overall inflation and faster than any other segment of the economy every year since 1998.

They also learned more about the nature and causes of this problem. Many of the speakers at the conference cited large catastrophic-illness claims, increased use of medical services, high-technology medicine, cost shifting from government programs (Medicare and Medicaid) to private insurance, high physician fees, drug abuse, mental illness, the AIDS crisis, and the recession (which has increased the number of high-user older workers among the insured and stimulated the use of elective procedures). One speaker noted: "If businesses in the private sector don't make a profit, they are not going to exist. The continuing escalation of health care costs is threatening the very survival of some companies, particularly small construction companies." Smaller businesses increasingly bear the brunt of the spiraling costs because they have no one else to turn to so they can shift their costs.

Several possible solutions were discussed, although there was no consensus regarding their effectiveness or applicability to particular situations. Among the cost containment suggestions were self-insurance, utilization review, managed care (i.e., health maintenance organizations, preferred provider organizations, and the new health savings accounts), wellness programs, flexible benefits, voucher

[1] Names and data have been disguised.

accounts, cost sharing (i.e., higher deductibles and coinsurance), and insuring of ambulatory alternatives to hospitalization.

Many speakers emphasized that employers should not wait passively for the government to solve the problem because that was unlikely to happen anytime soon. In addition, health care reform raises fundamental questions regarding societal priorities, and there is currently no consensus regarding these questions.

THE CHALLENGE

Edwards came away from the conference with a greater appreciation of the complexity of the problem and a greater determination to do something about it. However, she wasn't sure what to do. She viewed her company as a "preferred employer" because its benefits were always more liberal than those of other companies in the area, and particularly other construction companies. Edwards did not want to do anything to jeopardize her company's advantage in attracting and retaining high-quality personnel. At the same time, she realized that if no changes were made, her health insurance premiums would be greater than her total projected earnings by the year 2014.

Hoosier Construction's present health insurance plan (American Health) is a traditional indemnity insurance plan. All employees have one plan, which makes no effort to control the health care services provided. Employees select whatever services are provided at whatever price the particular provider charges. Neither physicians nor employees have a financial incentive to economize in the use of services or to seek out low-cost providers.

Edwards decided to establish an employee health benefits committee that would report to her in one month with recommendations for containing health benefit costs while minimizing adverse employee reaction. Membership on the committee consisted of Shawn, Deon, and the company superintendent. You have been asked to serve as an employee member of this committee.

The committee has recommended that Edwards consider three general options for the future: (1) stay with the current traditional indemnity policy with an average cost of $7,212 per year; (2) offer an HMO option in addition to the current plan; and (3) establish a health savings account (HSA) plan.

The committee members are split on the three options. The superintendent wishes to continue with the current plan. Deon wants to adopt the HSA and Shawn wants to offer the HMO option. All three are looking to you to make a recommendation and help them reach a consensus.

Case 15

Hudson Fabricators, Inc.[1]

Josh Keeler sat at his desk thinking about how to transform Hudson from a family-owned seat-of-the-pants business to a competitive ongoing concern. Josh was a recent graduate of Texas Christian University, where he majored in purchasing and supply management. He was hired by Hudson last week. He has been working closely with Mr. Emmons, who has been with the company for more than 25 years. After reviewing the new INE job, Josh realized that he must quickly implement a system for purchasing.

BACKGROUND

Founded in 1976, this small fabrication firm produces various items such as conveyors, platforms, supports, frames, hoppers, and light building steel for many major companies around central Ohio and even spanning the globe. They employ about 12 full-time people and up to, varying with production, a maximum of 40 people. Although the company lacks technology, they still wring out a profit year after year.

PROCESS

Hudson operates in a job-shop environment. Their clients include Rockwell International, Marzetti Foods, and Anheuser-Busch, and their products include condensers, conveyors, and industrial storage systems.

Hudson only uses materials certified by the American Society of Mechanical Engineers (ASME). In order to maintain the certification of the ASME, Hudson is required to furnish certain information to the society, and whenever they purchase steel, it has to have been chemically tested to meet the ASME codes. If the vendor's steel does not meet the ASME codes, Hudson would be required to find a new source within a certain number of days or else they would lose their ASME certification. Hudson contracts with a third-party supervisor to inspect their steel materials, and every three years they must pay $3,000 to $5,000 to get an ASME audit. Although costly, it is deemed well worth it to maintain the ASME certification.

PURCHASING AT HUDSON

The purchasing person, Tim Emmons, pointed out that since they are a job-shop organization, they cannot afford to buy in large enough quantities. Ninety percent of the steel is purchased through a broker. According to Mr. Emmons, it makes more sense for small firms to order through a broker. Hudson maintains an excellent relationship with their brokers. Emmons has negotiated with the steel broker to get the price based on the annual usage of steel rather than on an individual order. The lead times are also remarkable, being only, on average, one to three days.

He later explained, "Hudson's main competitive advantage is high service, as we can serve our customers a lot faster. A good relationship with our suppliers

[1] The author expresses appreciation to Brian Handke and Bayu Sudjumo for their contributions to this case. Names and data have been disguised.

also allows us to use an inventory-less shop. Given the job-shop technology, it is not economical to keep excess inventory on hand. Having a manufacturing plant of 30,000 square feet, we do not want to be holding inventory in space that we could be using for other operations; hence, we alleviate the holding expense by simply maintaining good supplier relations."

Hudson's production process is straightforward. Emmons also said that "under the conditions of a job shop, it is impossible to forecast our annual usage; there is no way to tell." Purchased materials are obtained on a job-by-job basis. Stating that they rarely know their workload two months in advance, forecasting does not work. There are significant swings in the number of production workers during the month. When the shop is at maximum capacity, due dates cannot be maintained.

THE ESTIMATING AND BIDDING PROCESS

The first step in the bidding process is initiated by a request for quote (RFQ). As an example, recently INE released an RFQ to Hudson to bid on a three-piece stainless steel multibin shelf system. The drawing shown in Figure C15.1 was attached to the RFQ. Next, a Hudson design engineer develops a set of drawings from the initial illustration. The material and labor requirements are determined next. Emmons then releases an RFQ to ACME Steel, the company's major steel distributor.

FIGURE C15.1
Three-Piece Stainless Steel Shelf System

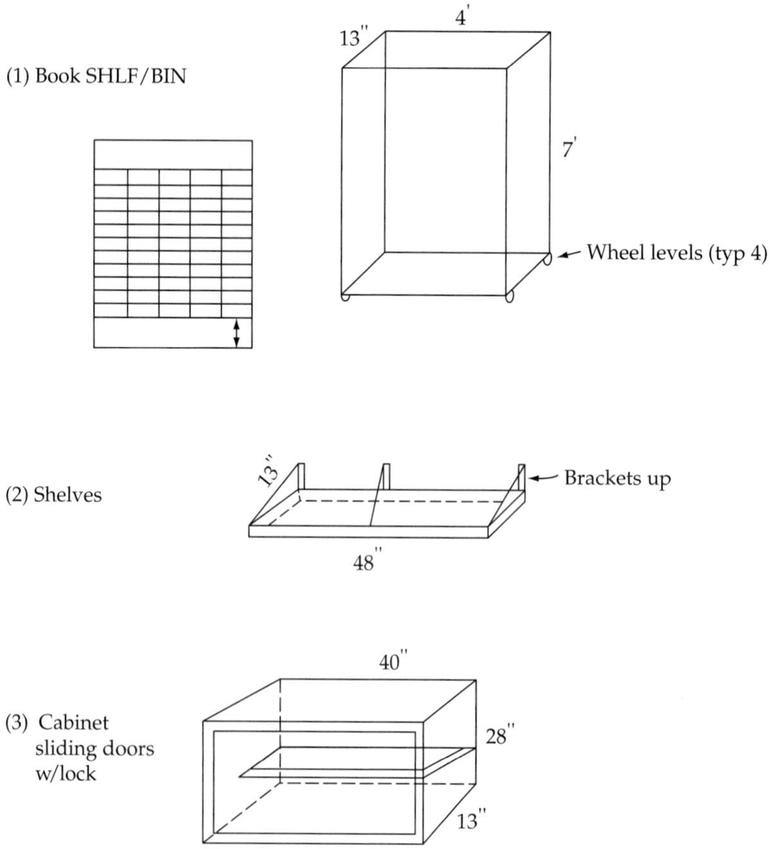

FIGURE C15.1 *(Continued)*

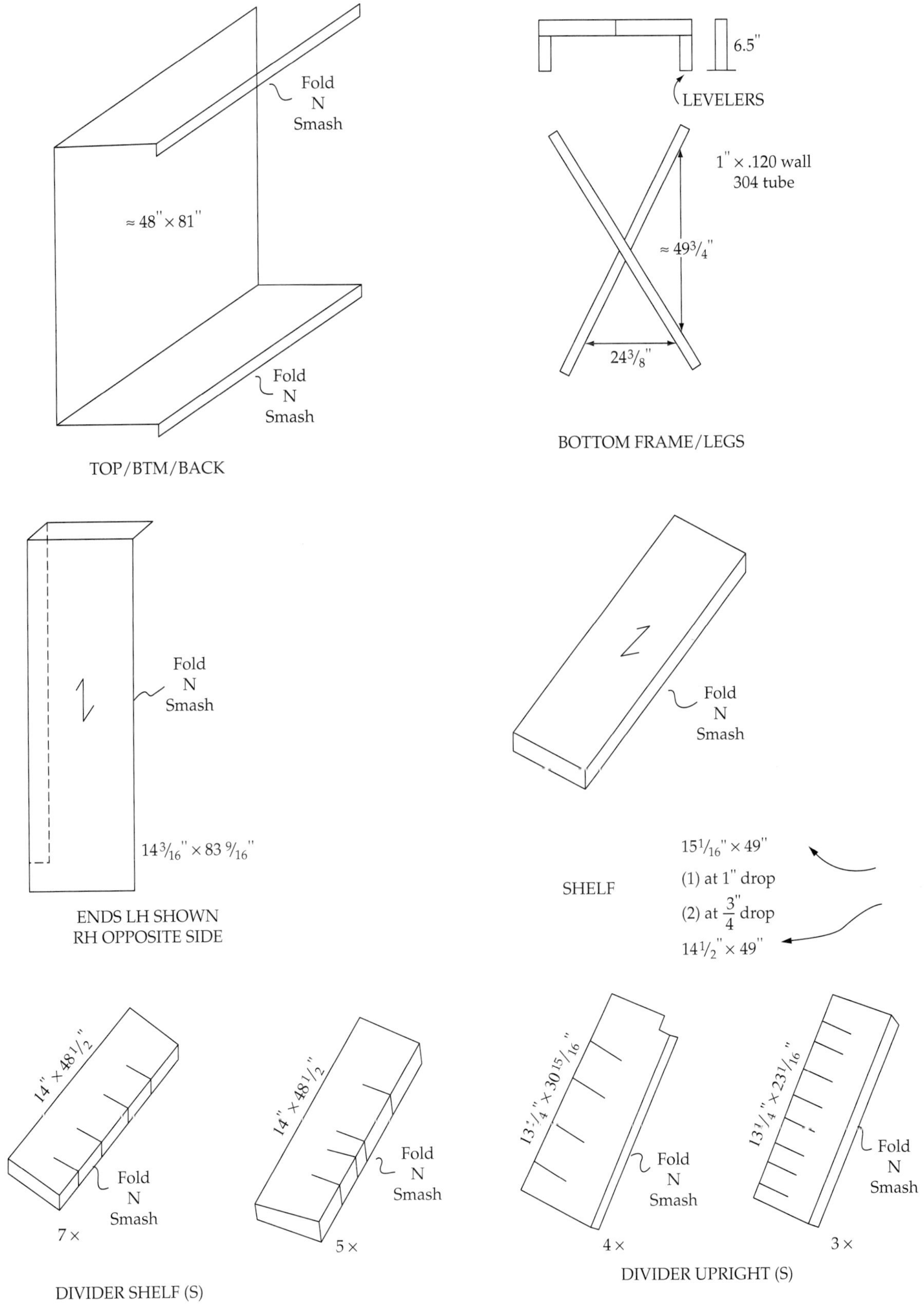

FIGURE C15.1 *(Continued)*

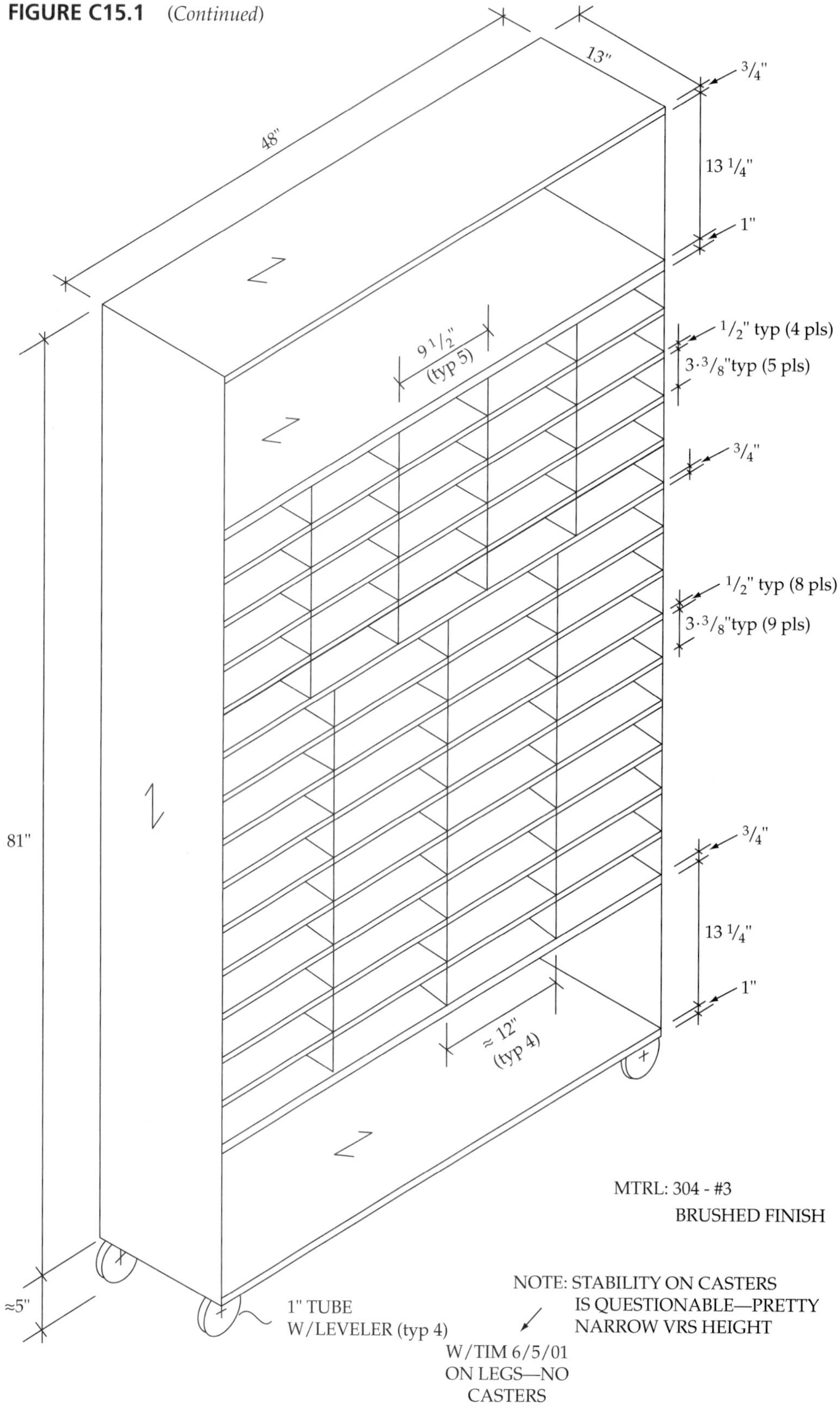

The following is a summary of the itemized material costs and labor times for the INE job.

Number of Pieces	Description	Weight (lbs.)	Price/100 wt.	Extended Cost
1	16-gauge stainless steel, sheet, polished, 48″ × 144″	121	$ 95	$114.95
1	16-gauge stainless steel, sheet, polished, 36″ × 120″	76	122.32	92.9632
5	16-gauge stainless steel, sheet, polished, 48″ × 120″	504	102.94	518.8176
1	16-gauge stainless steel, square tube, polished, 20′		186 (per 100 ft.)	37.2
1	Wear strip	NA	NA	10
1	Levelers	NA	NA	12
1	Lock	NA	NA	25
1	Track	NA	NA	10
1	Package and protect		20	20

Labor Summary: Bin System

Action	Time (minutes)	Repetitions	Total Minutes
Shear	2	50	100
Notch	1	75	75
Form	3	122	366
Saw	3	68	204
Weld	3	298	894
Cut	2	14	28
Set up	60	5	300
Assemble	60	4	240
Touch up	60	6	360

Labor Summary: Cabinet

Action	Time (minutes)	Repetitions	Total Minutes
Shear	2	14	28
Notch	1	20	20
Punch	1	4	4
Form	3	36	108
Weld	3	37	111
Set up	60	4	240
Assemble	60	6	360
Touch up	60	2	120

Labor Summary: Wall Shelf

Action	Time (minutes)	Repetitions	Total Minutes
Shear	2	14	28
Notch	1	16	16
Punch	1	16	16
Form	3	56	168
Weld	3	44	132
Set up	60	4	240
Assemble	0	0	0
Touch up	60	1	60

Total Labor Summary

Action	Time (minutes)	Hours
Shear	156	2.6
Notch	111	1.9
Saw	204	3.4
Punch	20	0.3
Form	642	10.7
Weld	1137	19.0
Cut	28	0.5
Set up	780	13.0
Assemble	600	10.0
Touch up	540	9.0
Lay out/fit	300	5.0
Travel	180	3.0

Hudson marks up all materials 35 percent and has a labor rate of $75 per labor hour. They also expect between a 25- and 50-percent profit on each job, depending on the total number of bidders. INE offers a bonus to the winning bidder of $1,000 for each day the project is completed in less than 21 days. On the other hand, a penalty of $500 per day is charged for each day beyond 21 days.

After Hudson Fabrication places its purchase order, the job fabrication sheet is developed. Similar to the materials estimate sheet, the job fabrication sheet's purpose is to give information about the description of the materials that are needed in the process in a very specific way. These are the documents that the workers will use as a guide for fabrication. One function of these plans is to show the "nesting" of components to be cut from the stainless steel sheets to minimize scrap. Also, they list the specific measurements of the subcomponents, the type of bending and forming required, and details such as whether or not the surface will be polished. The job fabrication sheet also serves to give visual drawings of the product that will be made in a step-by-step process, so that it will not mix the subcomponents from the different components. Once all requirements have been determined, it is up to the workers to produce the job to specifications under budget standards and on time.

CONCLUSION

On Friday, Josh will be meeting with the company owner to discuss an implementation process for developing a purchasing department. One of his assignments is to use the INE job as a base case to determine the positive and negative aspects of the current operation. The owner also is interested in how a purchasing system will improve profitability. Josh wonders what he should recommend.

Case 16

KACI Products, Inc.[1]

COMPANY BACKGROUND

The KACI Products Company is a manufacturer of high-quality small hand tools intended for consumer use. Its current product line includes drills, a small hand-held nail gun, and a number of carpentry tools such as power saws, electric planes, generators, and portable workstations. KACI Products has a strong research and development department that continually searches for ways to improve existing products as well as develop new products.

Currently, the research and development department is working on the development of a portable workstation that will have a built-in CAD-CAM system, although the technology involved is quite different. Tentatively named the Portable CAD, the product will initially be sold for around $575 and, therefore, the target market consists of upper-income baby boomers who are interested in staying busy. At this price, profits will be attractive. Last month KACI rolled out a working prototype and is satisfied that, with cooperation from the production and marketing departments, the product can be ready in time for the Christmas buying season. A target date that is 22 weeks away has been set for the product introduction.

CURRENT PROBLEM

KACI Products' Marketing Vice President, Simone Spruell, has recently learned from the company's marketing intelligence consultant that a competitor is also in the process of developing a similar product, which it intends to roll out for the Christmas buying season. In addition, the consultant also indicated that the competitor plans to sell its product, which will be somewhat heavier than the Portable CAD, for $499.95 in the hope of appealing to upper-middle- as well as upper-income groups. Simone, with the help of several of her key people who are to be involved in marketing the Portable CAD, has decided that in order to compete, the selling price for the Portable CAD will have to be lowered to within $50 of the competitor's price. At this price level, it will still be profitable, although not nearly as profitable as originally anticipated.

However, Simone is wondering whether it would be possible to expedite the usual product introduction process in order to beat the competition to the market. If possible, she would like to get a six-week jump on the competition; this would put the product introduction date only 16 weeks away. During this initial period, KACI Products could sell the Portable CAD for $575, reducing the selling price to $550 when the competitor's product actually enters the market. Since forecasts based on market research show that sales during the first seven weeks will be about 2,000 per week, there is an opportunity for considerable extra profit if the early introduction can be accomplished. In addition, there is a certain amount of prestige involved in being first to market. This should help enhance the Portable CAD's image during the anticipated battle for market share.

[1] Names and data have been disguised.

TABLE C16.1
List of Activities

Activity	Description	Immediate Predecessor
A	Select and order equipment	—
B	Receive equipment from supplier	A
C	Install and set up equipment	A
D	Finalize bill of materials	B
E	Order component parts	C
F	Receive component parts	E
G	First production run	D, F
H	Finalize marketing plan	—
I	Produce magazine ads	H
J	Script for TV ads	H
K	Produce TV ads	J
L	Begin ad campaign	I, K
M	Ship product to consumers	G, L

DATA COLLECTION

Since KACI Products has been through the product-introduction process a number of times, the R&D department has developed a list of the tasks that must be accomplished and the order in which they must be completed. Although the times and costs vary depending on the particular product, the basic process does not. The list of activities involved and their precedence relationships are presented in Table C16.1. Time and cost estimates for the introduction of the Portable CAD are presented in Table C16.2. Note that some of the activities can be completed on a crash basis, with an associated increase in cost.

TABLE C16.2
Time and Cost Estimates

Activity	Normal Time (weeks)	Normal Cost	Minimum Time (weeks)	Crash Cost ($/week)
A	3	$2,000	2	$4,500
B	8	9,000	6	9,000
C	4	2,000	2	7,000
D	5	1,000	3	4,000
E	2	2,000	1	3,000
F	5	0	5	—
G	6	12,000	3	12,000
H	4	3,500	2	8,000
I	4	5,000	3	10,000
J	3	8,000	2	35,000
K	4	100,000	3	160,000
L	8	10,000	8	—
M	1	5,000	1	—

Case 17

MARS, Inc. (D)[1]

In January 2009, Tom Sosa, the purchasing manager, received a telephone call from their Columbus, Indiana, diesel engine supplier informing him that effective June they were no longer producing the D-342 diesel engines at the Columbus plant. The D-342 engine sales were decreasing and would no longer be in their product line. Tom was in shock. He was now forced to deal with the sole supplier of the D-342 located in Portland, Oregon. The most recent price schedule submitted by the Oregon engine supplier is given below:

Units per Order	Unit Price
Less than or equal to 100	$ 4,800
Between 100 and 200	4,700
Greater than 200	4,550

The prices had been basically the same as the Columbus supplier except that they are F.O.B. Portland. The traffic department informed Tom that the transportation cost per hundredweight is $10 for carload lots of 50,000 pounds. The less than carload rate is $15 per hundredweight. The replenishment cycle normally takes one week.

BACKGROUND

Tom Sosa, the supply manager for MARS, Inc. was contemplating several significant changes in the D-342 diesel engine market. Mr. Sosa was concerned because in its production of the 98-D loader, MARS used 10 diesel engines each working day of the month. (MARS operated on a 20-day-per-month schedule.) Each engine weighs 500 pounds. Engine orders are currently placed every Monday morning. For the past 10 years, the D-342 engines had been produced in only two locations in the United States, one in Columbus, Indiana, and the other in Portland, Oregon. Mr. Sosa felt fortunate that the Columbus producer was located approximately 30 miles from his facility. The Columbus supplier offered just-in-time delivery service at no charge to MARS.

MARS implemented lean manufacturing in 2002. The kanban-controlled JIT production system was implemented based on the premise of minimizing work-in-process inventories (waste) by reducing lot sizes in order to increase production efficiency and product quality.

ACTION TAKEN BY TOM

Mr. Sosa compiled cost and warehouse capacity data on the D-342 engine from the accounting department. See Table C17.1.

Mr. Sosa wonders what effects these new developments will have on his cost structure.

Assignment Questions

1. What were MARS's total costs per year prior to the new price structure when the diesel engine price was $4,800? Was MARS using the EOQ method?

[1] Names and data have been disguised.

TABLE C17.1
Cost and Warehouse Capacity

Cost of unloading engines into warehouse	$0.25 (per 100/wt)
Order processing cost per requisition	$100
Warehouse capacity	200 units
Outside warehouse costs	$39 per year per unit*
Expediting cost per requisition	$50
Inventory carrying cost	38%

*There is existing space in the warehouse for 200 units. Additional space must be leased for a year. If an order is more than 200 units, part of the order must be stored in leased space.

2. With volume discounts and warehouse constraints, what is the best ordering quantity?
3. With purchase discounts and different rates, how are costs and EOQs affected?
4. How will these changes impact the lean manufacturing philosophy at MARS?
5. Determine the cost impact of using the Portland supplier. How will the change in supplier for the D-342 diesel engine affect sales for the 98-D loader?

Case 18

McGruder Pavers, Inc.[1]

McGruder Pavers is a family-owned company that was incorporated in 2003. The founder, David McGruder, works in the general Cleveland area. The office and equipment is located in North Olmstead, Ohio. The company employs 20 laborers, 5 working supervisors, and an office manager. During the peak construction season, the company has four construction crews working.

The company's primary focus is heavy highway, but it also does city work and an occasional commercial job for Cleveland State University. McGruder construction is known for high-quality work that is finished on time. In January 2012, McGruder was low bidder on a curb and gutter job for the city of Cleveland. The $689,030 project is significantly larger than the average job size of $219,000. The project is scheduled to begin on July 19, 2012 and must be completed by September 1—prior to the first Browns regular season football game. There is a liquidated damages clause in the contract that requires McGruder construction to pay $30,000 per day for every day beyond September 1, if the job is not finished. In order to achieve the appropriate level of productivity, David decided to purchase a curb and gutter machine. The machine selection was narrowed down to the 5700-C Concrete Curb and Gutter machine. The 5700-C Curb and Gutter machine is considered to be the number one curb and gutter machine in the world.

THE CURB MACHINE ACQUISITION PROCESS

The 5700-C machine's compact size and versatility allow contractors to achieve high levels of productivity. It gets in and out of tight spots quickly, making tight radius work in parking lots much quicker. In addition to curb and gutter work, the machine pours highway safety barriers, bridge parapets, sidewalks, golf cart paths, agricultural foundations, irrigation ditches, and stadium risers. According to the sales literature, the 5700-C will triple a normal day's production with "less work." Less finishing results in reducing manpower from behind the machine.

There is also an addition feature that could boost productivity even higher. The 5700-C is equipped with a **Smart Amp™ control system package** that offers the simplicity of an analog system but with the features of a digital system. The operator has greater flexibility for sensitivity adjustment. Display screens on the operator's panel will show fault codes if there is a problem with a sensor, cord, or amplifier. Of course, the operators will require a two-week, on-the-job training course.

PRICING SCHEDULE

The pricing schedule for the lease and purchase options is given below.

	Purchase	Monthly[a] lease	Monthly maintenance
Curb machine	$203,300	$15,300[b]	$1,000
Smart amp	$ 70,030		
Total	$273,330	$15,300	

[a]A minimum of 12 months.
[b]Includes the smart amp.
[c]Training—To be determined.

DAVID McGRUDER'S VIEWPOINT

As he examined the pricing data, David considered the lease versus purchase choice as a subsidiary consideration. He focused on understanding the cost structure and the expected operating environment as a means of establishing a range for negotiating down the published price schedule. If he was able to make a recommendation in favor of acquiring the smart amp, he wanted the contract to reflect the best possible terms for McGruder Construction. He speculated that the supplier's costs were essentially sunk costs, and that, if purchased, the supplier had agreed to extend the warranty to 12 months. Therefore, under a lease, the seller should be willing to absorb maintenance costs. The initial purchase was planned to be for the Cleveland job. His colleagues expected a recommendation within a few days.

Assignment Questions

1. Should the 5700-C Curve machine be acquired for the Cleveland job?
2. Should the 5700-C be leased or purchased?

Case 19

Medical Laser Equipment, Inc. (B)[1]

"Helen, I've been thinking about our procurement policies on those VA 22 beam laser assemblies."

Dr. Wilson was speaking to his production manager, Helen Gellar. Dr. Wilson had been reviewing the purchasing procedures on one of the company's strategic components.

Medical Laser Equipment (MLE) was a small (138 employees) producer/distributor of laser equipment and supplies, located in Columbus, Ohio, founded five years earlier by Dr. Wilson. Current sales volume was approaching $7,000,000 annually. The prosperity of MLE was fostered partly by the increasingly aging baby boom generation. It also was due in no small measure to the personality and managerial capability of Dr. Wilson. A resourceful surgeon of great drive, Dr. Wilson is also a successful and well-known surgeon in Columbus. He realized that just because he knew how to repair heart valves did not qualify him as an effective manager, so he decided to attend the executive business program at the Dublin College of Business.

The VA 22 beam laser assembly, which he was discussing with Helen, was a component of one of MLE's best-selling line of five different portable laser units. Allen Enterprises manufactured the laser platform in Fort Worth, Texas. At MLE, the platform, along with other components, was assembled to form the complete device, which consisted of chassis, chip assembly, laser/generator and controls, cable, the grip, and wiring.

Wilson continued, "I think we have too much money tied up in the VA 22 assembly inventory. Helen, please explain how you determine when to place orders. How much do you order at one time? How many assemblies are we using per year? Are we getting any discounts? Should we be using a just-in-time system?"

Helen Gellar replied, "At the current time, I do not know the answer to any of your questions. I will collect the relevant data and address your concerns in a memo by Friday."

The next morning, Helen pulled out a stack of old purchase orders for the VA 22. She was able to estimate that the direct labor cost for placing an order was approximately $95. Next she obtained the following costs from the accounting department: cost of capital, 10 percent; obsolescence, 5 percent; handling percentage, 15 percent; and annual storage cost, 20 percent. The VA 22 cost $1,000.

It is now Thursday; Helen is completely confused and wondering how to analyze the data she has collected. She then remembers a concept, called the EOQ, that she studied at City College. Helen reviews her old textbook and realizes that she is missing one vital component needed for the EOQ approach. She needs to estimate annual demand.

During the afternoon, Helen collects data on the VA 22 beam laser assembly. The inventory database for the first 100 working days is shown in Figure C19.1. She estimates that this sales rate is typical of what could be expected for the 150 remaining working days.

From the records, she also determines that the inventory policy for the VA 22 beam laser assembly consists of examining the level of assemblies every Monday

[1] Names and data have been disguised.

FIGURE C19.1 Inventory Database

Day	Beginning Inventory	Order Received	Demand	Ending Inventory
1*	4	0	0	4
2	4	0	0	4
3	4	0	0	4
4	4	4	1	7
5	7	0	1	6
6	6	0	0	6
7	6	0	1	5
8	5	2	2	5
9	5	0	1	4
10	4	0	0	4
11	4	0	0	4
12	4	0	0	4
13	4	0	2	2
14	2	4	0	6
15	6	0	1	5
16	5	0	0	5
17	5	3	1	7
18	7	0	2	5
19	5	0	2	3
20	3	0	0	3
21	3	0	0	3
22	3	5	0	8
23	8	0	1	7
24	7	0	0	7
25	7	0	1	6
26	6	0	2	4
27	4	0	0	4
28	4	0	0	4
29	4	2	0	6
30	6	0	2	4
31	4	0	0	4
32	4	0	1	3
33	3	0	0	3
34	3	4	1	6
35	6	0	0	6
36	6	0	2	4
37	4	0	0	4
38	4	2	1	5
39	5	0	2	3
40	3	0	2	1
41	1	0	1	0
42	0	7	1	6
43	6	0	0	6
44	6	0	0	6
45	6	0	0	6
46	6	0	0	6
47	6	0	0	6
48	6	0	0	6
49	6	2	1	7
50	7	0	0	7
51	7	0	1	6
52	6	0	0	6
53	6	1	2	5
54	5	0	0	5
55	5	0	1	4
56	4	0	0	4
57	4	0	0	4
58	4	0	0	4
59	4	4	1	7
60	7	0	0	7
61	7	0	0	7
62	7	1	1	7
63	7	0	0	7
64	7	0	2	5
65	5	0	2	3
66	3	0	2	1
67	1	5	1	5
68	5	0	1	4
69	4	0	0	4
70	4	0	0	4
71	4	0	2	2
72	2	0	0	2
73	2	0	0	2
74	2	4	1	5
75	5	0	0	5
76	5	0	0	5
77	5	0	0	5
78	5	0	2	3
79	3	3	1	5
80	5	0	2	3
81	3	0	0	3
82	3	5	1	7
83	7	0	0	7
84	7	0	0	7
85	7	0	2	5
86	5	0	0	5
87	5	3	1	7
88	7	0	0	7
89	7	0	0	7
90	7	0	1	6
91	6	0	1	5
92	5	0	0	5
93	5	2	0	7
94	7	0	2	5
95	5	0	0	5
96	5	0	1	4
97	4	3	2	5
98	5	0	0	5
99	5	0	1	4
100	4	0	1	3

*Order placed.

morning and placing an order (by the Internet or phone) to raise the level of laser assemblies on hand to 8 units. If a stockout occurs, enough VA 22's are ordered to eliminate the backlog and bring the level to 8 units. She notes that the assemblies ordered on a Monday always arrive in one, two, or three days. A stockout results in production delays, rescheduling of work crews, and delays in shipments of completed laser devices. The shipment time depends on weather, traffic, and other factors. Therefore, she also assigns a stockout cost of $250.

Case 20

Microfuse, Inc.[1]

Time: 3:42 p.m.
Date: Thursday, April 22, 2009
Place: Office of the VP for Manufacturing

> Val, our orientation has always been one in which control is a critical part of maintaining our market leadership position, hence vertical integration. The guiding belief throughout the company is that by being able to say that we actually make the products we are selling implies a certain level of proficiency and expert knowledge that customers themselves lack and thus look for when choosing a supplier. In addition to using our vertical structure as a marketing tool, we at Microfuse also regard ourselves as the best providers of quality manufacturing because of our long-standing quality and reliability tradition. Such control translates into greater power, especially in terms of profits, yet it comes at a cost. I understand that our inventory levels are too high. High inventory levels are a price we pay for us to add value to our vertically integrated business model. It should be noted that Microfuse operates a very efficient inventory system, but there is always room for improvement in this area. Although in general the company is open to outsourcing, until a supplier comes along that can provide more value than our current operation, our vertically integrated orientation will remain intact. So, Valerie, get together with Bob James to develop a business case for a limited outsourcing strategy for some of our noncore products. I would like a report on my desk by May 1.

As stated, Tom Cecil, VP of Microfuse's manufacturing division, asked Valerie (Val) Simmons, purchasing manager, to investigate the implementation of an outsourcing approach to solve a problem that had rapidly become the center of attention of the company's operating executives. Ms. Simmons would be working with Bob James, the plant superintendent.

The problem was this: All of the major competitors have cut costs by outsourcing more than 40 percent of their manufacturing capabilities. In the past year, XFfuse, Microfuse's closest competitor, has reduced their labor force by 50 percent.

THE MICROFUSE INDUSTRY

In order to truly understand the operational decisions Microfuse makes, it is necessary to be familiar with the industry. Microfuse is facing increased competition and significant pressures to remain innovative and efficient. The industry is technology driven. Microfuse's primary industry is circuit protection. It is a highly competitive industry that attracts firms from around the world. The companies that survive in the industry must compete not only on quality and value-added functions, but also on price. This translates into a need to be innovative and competitive at the same time. There is always a threat of becoming viewed as a commodity product; thus, the goal of many companies is to provide unique and valuable products that attract and retain customers. Obsolescence is the norm for the industry.

[1] Names and data have been disguised.

FIGURE C20.1 **Competitor Comparison**

Company	Fuses	Polymer PTCs	MOVs	Gas Tubes	Diodes	Thyristors	Polymer ESD	Total Technologies
Microfuse	×	×	×	×	×	×	×	7
XFfuse		×		×		×		3
Bussman	×						×	2
Raychem		×				×		2
EPCOS			×	×				2
AVX	×		×					2
St. Micro					×	×		2
Vishay					×			1
Teccor						×		1
Wickmann	×							1
Bel Fuse	×							1

COMPANY BACKGROUND

Microfuse is the industry leader, offering the broadest line of circuit protection in the world. They offer seven major circuit protection technologies (more than twice their nearest competitor) that span three industries: electronics, automotive, and electrical. See Figure C20.1. Microfuse technology is a critical component in many of the products we use on a daily basis, from cell phones and digital cameras to nearly 90 percent of automobiles, industrial machinery, computers, and virtually any other devices using electrical energy. The diverse product line is coupled with a presence throughout the world.

WEDNESDAY, APRIL 29—NEW INFORMATION

During the data collection phase of Val's research, she discovered that Microfuse currently has one site in central China and, through a recent acquisition, another facility located in southern China. Initially, the Chinese acquisition was driven by the fact that many more customers are setting up in China. For instance, the automotive sector in China alone is expected to increase from 4.4 million automobiles sold this past year to 10 million in 2010. Val was wondering how this new information would impact the outsourcing business case. The company also was projecting that almost all European functions may be moved to lower-cost sites in the near future. More specifically there appears to be an increased focus on moving the European division to Vietnam. Because of increased global business, Microfuse expects that in the future, 70 percent of production will be done abroad. Domestically a reduction in operations is forecasted. According to Val's interviews with some of the operating executives, most of the forecasted shifts in manufacturing are contingent on many factors, but that it is a possibility. There is a common belief that the Foundry site in Champaign-Urbana, Illinois, will never be completely relocated due to the fact that it is the base for planning and development and is heavily involved in the manufacturing function. Due to the control-orientated mentality of the company, moving all manufacturing away from headquarters seems unlikely, but not impossible.

Case 21

NEP: The Art and Science of Purchasing Coal[1]

Deon Houston, vice president for the National Electric Power (NEP) Commodity Trading Division, was in the process of producing her annual sourcing report for the company's three-year plan. While NEP seems to have had success using the competitive bidding process, reverse auctions may be the wave of the future. Ms. Houston was wondering if the reverse auction sourcing approach would work for purchasing the company's coal requirements.

Recently, labor shortages of qualified experienced workers in the eastern United States, Wyoming, and Montana have caused some production problems. With changing labor force safety concerns, and fewer new workers entering the mining industry, mining companies are faced with significant production problems in times of increasing demand for coal. At the same time, the demand for electricity is increasing at a rapid rate.

COMPANY BACKGROUND

National Electric Power is a multinational energy company with a variety of energy assets. NEP is headquartered in Columbus, Ohio, and has a service area of approximately 197,500 square miles in Arkansas, Indiana, Kentucky, Louisiana, Michigan, Ohio, Oklahoma, Tennessee, Texas, Virginia, and West Virginia. In 2001, NEP had revenues of $61.3 billion and carried $47 billion in assets, making them the largest electricity generator in the United States.

NEP utilizes several different fuels in generating electricity. Today, coal-fired plants account for 68 percent of NEP's generating capacity, while natural gas represents 22 percent and nuclear power, 8 percent. The remaining 2 percent comes from wind, hydro, pumped storage, and other sources. Since most of NEP's electricity is generated through the burning of coal, coal is the most important commodity that NEP uses. NEP owns and operates coal mines in Ohio, Kentucky, and Louisiana, which produce approximately 10 million tons of coal each year. While this does make them one of the top 20 coal producers in the United States, it is not nearly enough to fulfill their annual need of 75 million tons to support the 80 coal-burning plants that provide electricity to almost 7.3 million customers.

In order to obtain the additional coal needed to support operations, NEP has established a division of commodity traders, more commonly referred to as "coal traders." Coal traders are responsible for identifying sources of coal, negotiating prices, securing contracts with suppliers, and monitoring the current coal commodity market. In general, the factors that affect coal trader purchasing fit into three major categories:

- How coal affects the operations of NEP.
- Supplier selection and relationships.
- General market conditions and coal prices.

[1] The author expresses appreciation to Adam Rutan and Greg Williams for their contributions to this case. Names and data have been disguised.

COAL AND THE OPERATIONS OF NEP

Coal is used by NEP at approximately 80 power plants in the United States. All of the coal-burning stations operate by burning the fuel (coal) in a boiler to produce steam. The steam passes through a turbine to spin a generator that creates the electricity. This process converts the coal's energy content, British thermal units (Btus), into usable energy (kWhs).

The Btu of the coal is very important to the purchasing process. Power plants are designed to only burn fuel of one Btu level. When designing a station, the type of fuel to be used must be decided in order to determine which type of boiler is to be used. Boilers cannot be adapted to burn a different type of coal. The same fuel specifications also are set forth for the material-handling equipment. For example, a plant that is designed to burn coal of 12,000-Btu cannot burn 10,000-Btu coal efficiently. Coal with 12,000-Btu content will produce more electricity than 1 ton with 10,000-Btu content.

In order to optimize their capital equipment and operate as near to capacity as possible, coal traders must be aware of the limitations of the plant for which they are buying fuel. They must be aware of the production rate of the plant (how much coal is being used) in order to keep the plant from running out of coal. Coal traders are able to estimate the amount of coal the plant has used by monitoring the plant's energy output, as well as forecasts of output generated by other departments. A sample of the energy outputs of several plants is given in Figure C21.1

Another important factor in the operations of NEP is the type of coal to purchase. Similar to energy content, each plant is designed to burn a specific type of coal. There are three primary types of coal used in the power-generating process: bituminous, subbituminous, and lignite. Each coal has different physical characteristics that differentiate it from the others. Four primary criteria are used to distinguish the type of coal and evaluate its quality. Quality evaluation is important

FIGURE C21.1
Energy Output

Coal-Fired Plants		*Megawatts*
John E. Amos	West Virginia	2,900
Gen. James M. Gavin	Ohio	2,600
Rockport	Indiana	2,600
Mitchell	West Virginia	1,600
Conesville	Ohio	1,504
Muskingum River	Ohio	1,425
Mountaineer	West Virginia	1,300
Big Sandy	Kentucky	1,060
Phillip Sporn	West Virginia	1,050
Tanners Creek	Indiana	995
Clinch River	Virginia	705
Kammer	West Virginia	630
J.M. Stuart	Ohio	608
Cardinal	Ohio	600
Kanawha River	West Virginia	400
Glen Lyn	Virginia	335
Zimmer	Ohio	330
Picway	Ohio	100
Beckjord	Ohio	53
Total coal-fired		*20,795*

to coal traders as they attempt to obtain a high-value product. Coal traders must be aware of the following quality standards:

- *Moisture content.* This is expressed as the percentage of the coal's weight that is water. Moisture content below 20 percent is desirable for both bituminous and subbituminous, but exceptions can be made for lignite, which sometimes carries moisture levels as high as 45 percent.
- *Ash.* This is measured as a percentage of the coal's weight not burned. Typically, desired ash is between 6 and 8 percent of the coal's weight for all types of coal. This number is frequently changed based upon where the coal is mined. For example, Ohio coal mines typically average around 11 percent ash, which is relatively high. On the other hand, Wisconsin averages around 5 percent. The amount of ash required depends on the operations of the plant, as the ash can be reused and sold in a secondary market.
- *Sulfur.* This is measured in number of pounds per MM Btu. Due to emissions regulations set forth by the EPA, it is desirable to achieve low sulfur content. Coal traders must be aware not to purchase coal with high sulfur content for a plant with machinery that does not operate efficiently; otherwise, the plant may not meet EPA standards and may be forced to shut down.
- *Caloric value.* This is the Btus per ton. This will change based upon for which plant NEP is purchasing supplies. One ton of coal with 12,000-Btu content will produce more electricity than one ton with 10,000-Btu content.

Coal traders also must be aware of the region from which the coal is mined. A sampling of different mines and the amount of coal available from each mine are given in Figure C21.2. Since the coal must be transported to the plant, the distance the coal must be taken is an important factor in determining the price of shipping. For example, bituminous coal is found across the nation, primarily in New Mexico, Colorado, and Oklahoma. Subbituminous coal is mined in Wyoming, New Mexico, Arizona, Montana, and Colorado. The third type of coal, lignite, is mined in North and South Dakota, Arkansas, Montana, Louisiana, and Texas. Ideally, shipping costs can be minimized by purchasing coal from a mine close to the power plant.

SUPPLIER SELECTION AND SUPPLIER RELATIONS

NEP's preferential method of supplier selection is competitive bidding. When possible, NEP prefers to examine at least three bids. Contracts are granted based on quality, value, delivery schedule, service, and any other necessary conditions to meet their needs. Competitive bidding is not always required; however, coal traders are required to document why a competitive bid process was not ideal for that situation.

NEP does not have a quantitative method to prequalify suppliers. The factors that weigh most heavily in selection are experience and reputation. NEP relies heavily on past dealings with companies to make purchasing decisions. It is for this reason that NEP specifies in their request for proposals that they must be made aware if the bidder plans to subcontract any part of the bid to another contractor. NEP also maintains a policy of granting no preference based upon location or union/nonunion status.

Since NEP does provide service to government agencies, they are considered a government contractor. Based upon their status as a government contractor, under certain conditions, they must award contracts to minority or disadvantaged

FIGURE C21.2 South Powder River Basin Mine Capacities (tonnage in thousands)

Company	Mine	1995 Production	EVA Estimate		Air Permit	Notes
			Equipment	Loadout		
Zeigler	Buckskin	11,616	12,000	24,000	22,000	
Peabody	Rawhide	15,354	20,000	24,000	24,000	
Cyprus-Amax	Eagle Butte	16,941	19,000	24,000	24,000	
Western Fuels	Dry Fork	3,587	4,000	7,000	15,000	*Extreme Btu disadvantage, mothballed*
Kerr-McGee	Clovis Point	409	0	7,000	4,150	*Extreme Btu disadvantage, no equip.*
Drummond	Fort Union	—	0	2,000	9,400	*Extreme Btu disadvantage, no equip.*
Peabody	Caballo	18,357	23,000	24,000	35,000	
Cyprus-Amax	Belle Ayr	18,772	20,000	20,000	25,000	
Drummond	Caballo Rojo	16,808	18,000	30,000	30,000	
Kennecott	Cordero	14,608	18,000	24,000	24,000	
ARCO	Coal Creek	4,199	6,000	12,000	18,000	*No sales commitments, contract miner*
Subtotal below 8,600 Btu		**120,651**	**140,000**	**198,000**	**230,550**	
Kerr-McGee	Jacobs Ranch	24,639	25,000	39,000	35,000	*Adjusted for plant expansion*
ARCO	Black Thunder	36,099	37,000	44,000	55,000	*Applied for 55.0 MMT permit*
Zeigler	North Rochelle	664	2,000	16,000	8,000	*Planned, not under const., contract miner*
Peabody	Rochelle	26,035	30,000	30,000	30,000	
Peabody	North Antelope	21,248	21,000	35,000	35,000	
Kennecott	Antelope	10,866	12,000	20,000	30,000	*Adjusted for announced expansion*
Subtotal above 8,600 Btu		**119,551**	**127,000**	**184,000**	**193,000**	
Total commercial mines		***240,202***	***267,000***	***382,000***	***423,550***	
Black Hills P & L	Wyodak	2,838	3,000	3,000	10,000	*Captive, no loadout, Btu disadv.*
PacificCorp	Dave Johnston	3,312	4,000	4,000	—	*Captive, no loadout, Btu disadv.*
Subtotal captive mines		**6,150**	**7,000**	**7,000**	**10,000**	
Total SPRB		***246,352***	***274,000***	***389,000***	***433,550***	

bidders. NEP has implemented several measures to encourage coal traders to purchase from a variety of diverse suppliers. Perhaps the most important program for ensuring diversity is the Supplier Diversity Program. To be eligible to participate in the NEP Supplier Diversity Program, a company must be certified as a disadvantaged business enterprise.

While qualifying for the Supplier Diversity Program does not guarantee that NEP will select a company's bid, this practice was established in order for NEP to carefully monitor suppliers and the negotiations NEP's traders set forth. Energy is heavily regulated by the U.S. government; therefore, it is essential for NEP to make sure they are in compliance with the government regulation and not violating any antitrust laws.

After a bid is accepted, NEP proceeds with a contract for services. NEP follows the bid specifications and may enter into one or more agreements based upon forecasted need. Each contract is for a minimum of 10,000 tons of coal per month. NEP attempts to negotiate contract prices for a term of one, three, or five years at a fixed or escalating price. Typically, NEP specifies the method of delivery in the contract as well, requiring that delivery be made by rail or barge to reduce uncertainty in the delivery schedule. The primary focus of the contract is to specify minimum quality standards for the coal and control price in order to properly forecast financial activity. The contracts for coal also cover many nonquality standards for the coal and control price in order to properly forecast financial activity. The contracts for coal also cover many nonquality measures. Some other items covered in the contract are listed below:

- *Definitions.* Explanations of key terms in the contract.
- *Effective date and terms of agreement.* When the contract is to begin and criteria for nonperformance.
- *Quantity.* The amount of coal they wish to purchase.
- *Schedule of delivery.* Dates for shipments to be delivered.
- *Base price of the coal.* Price of the coal before shipping. Shipping prices change frequently so, therefore, are not included in the bid.
- *Conditions for price adjustments.* Protects the supplier from selling drastically below market value if a major supply shock occurs.
- *Sampling and analysis.* Specifies the responsibilities for testing the coal to make sure it meets minimum standards.
- *Records; inspection; audit.* Requires suppliers to make all records of transactions with NEP available to NEP.
- *Compliance with laws and regulations.* Protects NEP from any illegal transactions they might not be aware of.
- *Dispute resolution.* Arbitration in the case of disputed performance.

Case 22

Pendleton Construction, Inc.[1]

Henry Royce, purchasing agent for Pendleton Construction, Inc., is currently in the process of selecting a steel supplier/fabricator for a major highway project.

COMPANY BACKGROUND

Pendleton Construction, located in Bloomington, Indiana, is one of the largest heavy-highway construction firms in the Midwest. Additionally, the company builds bridges, high-rise office towers, power plants, government buildings, and roads. Pendleton has a reputation for high-quality standards, on-time project completion, and reasonable prices. The company has expanded rapidly during the past 20 years, keeping pace with the heavy-highway sector.

REINFORCED STEEL FABRICATION

Reinforced steel is used in almost all of Pendleton's projects. The steel itself is purchased from one of several large steel mills in the region. During the past 18 months, the fabrication (bending) required in preparation for steel placement had been done by Mohawk, a small local disadvantaged business enterprise (DBE) specialty steel fabricator. Pendleton's total steel-bending requirement for the most recent fiscal year was approximately 5,000 tons. Mohawk had charged identical prices per ton for both small and large steel fabrication jobs. Prior to bidding on a project, Royce requests a telephone quotation from Mohawk, and, invariably, the price per ton quoted is the same as the previous bid. Mohawk is also a supplier of specialty steel. Royce has an exclusive agreement with Mohawk to supply specialty steel items on short notice. This arrangement has worked very well for Pendleton. Mohawk also owns a major share in a detailing firm that did approximately 70 percent of the reinforced detailing work for Pendleton. According to Royce, Mohawk has done an excellent job supplying high-quality specialty steel to Pendleton. At the same time, he stated that Mohawk's fabrication work was pretty good.

Recently, Pendleton was awarded a mega highway project in southern Indiana that will require more than 9,780 tons of reinforced steel for three consecutive years. Because of the size of the project, Royce decided to solicit quotes from other sources for the fabrication work. However, Pendleton bid the project using Mohawk's fabrication estimates. Royce received three quotes for the fabrication work item. All three estimates were lower than Mohawk's bid quote. The quotes were $7, $8, and $9.50 per ton lower than the Mohawk estimate. The company with the best estimate, which was $9.50 lower than Mohawk's estimate, had recently filed for bankruptcy. However, the remaining two suppliers checked out as being well run and financially healthy. Baker Steel quoted a price that was $8 lower per ton F.O.B. the job site. Baker was a major steel fabricator located in Cleveland, Ohio, which is approximately 350 miles from the project site. The quote was made on the condition that all transport shipments be full loads, with no emergency

[1] Names and data have been disguised.

short shipment transport charges. Royce had carefully checked out Baker's business capability and reputation and found that it had performed quite well throughout the Midwest.

Royce felt that he needed to make a rational decision. He now wondered if he should place the steel-bending contract with Baker or whether he should stay with the Mohawk bid. What are the implications of his decision?

Case 23

Point Clear, Inc. (B)[1]

Horace Canti, the production control manager at Point Clear, decided to implement a time-phased requirements planning (MRP) system. In May he had attended a short course on world-class manufacturing. He now needed to convince the plant manager that requirements planning could work for Point Clear's concrete mixer assembly operation. Horace decided that a simple example was needed to illustrate his ideas.

Horace prepared a master schedule for one of the engine types produced by Point Clear—the J750 turbo mixer. The resulting master schedule is shown in Figure C23.1. This 12-week schedule shows the number of units of the J750 mixers to be assembled. Horace also decided to consider two "A" items to represent the projected requirements for the J750. The two "A" items were representative of the many other components. These two components, the turbine housing and the 562 turbine assemblies, are shown in the product structure diagram in Figure C23.2. Horace noted that the turbine housing is purchased from a tier-one supplier and is shipped to the main mixer assembly plant. The manufacturing stages that are involved in producing a J750 mixer involve the mixer assembly department, the purchased turbine housing, and the paint shop.

The manufacturing and purchase lead times required to produce the turbine housing and the turbine assembly components also are indicated in Figure C23.2. Note that two weeks are required to purchase the turbine housings and that all of the turbine housings must be delivered to the turbine assembly plant before Monday morning of the week in which they are to be used. It takes three weeks to produce a lot of turbine assemblies, and all of the assemblies that are needed for the production of turbine housings for a specific week must be delivered to the subassembly department stockroom before Monday morning of that week.

FIGURE C23.1
J750 Mixer Master Schedule

Weeks	1	2	3	4	5	6	7	8	9	10	11	12
Quantity	75	25	35	50	0	45	100	50	0	40	10	80

FIGURE C23.2
J750 Mixer Product Structure

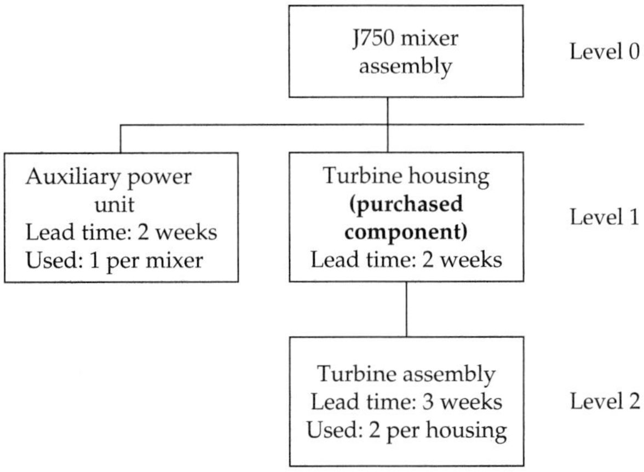

FIGURE C23.3
J750 Assembly Master Schedule

J750 Mixer Assembly Master Schedule

Week	1	2	3	4	5	6	7	8	9	10	11	12
Quantity												

FIGURE C23.4
Turbine Housing Requirements

Turbine Housing Requirements

Week	1	2	3	4	5	6	7	8	9	10	11	12
Gross requirements												
On-hand inventory *												
Scheduled receipts **												
Net requirements												
Planned order release												

*Measured at the end of each week.
**Received at the beginning of each week.

In preparing the MRP example, Horace planned to use worksheets (see Figures C23.3 to C23.5) to make the following assumptions:

1. Eighty-five turbine housings are on hand at the beginning of week one, and 25 turbine housings are currently on order to be delivered at the start of week two.
2. Two hundred turbine assemblies are on hand at the start of week one, and 120 are scheduled for delivery at the beginning of week two.

FIGURE C23.5
Turbine Assembly Requirements

Week	1	2	3	4	5	6	7	8	9	10	11	12
Gross requirements												
On-hand inventory*												
Scheduled receipts**												
Net requirements												
Planned order release												

*Measured at the end of each week.
**Received at the beginning of each week.

Case 24

Sage Imaging Center, Inc.[1]

The Sage Imaging Center is a multi-hospital system located in Columbus, Ohio. Over the past 10 years, Sage has grown from 2 radiologists to 15. Today, Sage specializes in imagining services, which include MRI and CT scans. In 2012, Sage performed an average of 200 images per day. Eighty percent of the images were from referrals from physician offices. Another 15 percent of the image work was outsourced from The Ohio State University, Wexner Medical Center. The remaining 5 percent were walk-in patients who practiced non-traditional healthcare. Sage currently has three CT scanning machines and MRI machines. Sage bills approximately $1,000 per image. The fee for service includes diagnosis and the required report by the radiologists. The Sage CEO has projected a 20-percent increase in imaging based on the health care reform. The board of directors recently approved the acquisition of another MRI machine.

Sage Imaging has two choices: (1) buy a refurbished MRI machine or (2) lease a new MRI machine for three years. The MRI machine has a useful life of seven years and costs $500,000. The Franklin County Bank is willing to loan Sage Imaging $450,000 at 7 percent interest and requires a down payment of $50,000 and annual payments due at the end of each of the next seven years. Since Sage Imaging does not have the proper maintenance capabilities, the bank will require Sage Imaging to sign a maintenance contract with Wade International. The contract, good for seven years of maintenance, requires annual payments of $10,000. Wade International made Sage Imaging a proposal that competes with the bank's offer. Wade International is willing to lease Sage Imaging the same MRI machine for five years. Since Sage Imaging's cash situation is very tight, Wade International has structured the lease with the $120,000 payment due at the end of each year. In addition, Wade International is agreeing to:

- Perform all of the maintenance during the lease period.
- Give the contractor the right to purchase the MRI machine at the end of five years for the prevailing market price (estimated to be $200,000).
- Allow the organization to buy a maintenance contract for two years on the MRI machine for $36,000 annually, paid at the end of years six and seven.

Case 25

Swisher Systems[1]

"Mike, this is Bill Simpson from engineering. What's going on with the prices of the 541, 234, 567, and 876 capacitors this year? At this rate, we're spending the department's budget twice as fast as we did last year."

"Look, Bill, we got an excellent price on several solenoid parts from a new supplier, but we had to accept higher prices for your components. Overall, the company will save more than 60 percent on more expensive components."

"Thanks for the lesson in purchasing. For your information, we don't use solenoids. Furthermore, I can get better prices online. I thought the purchasing department was supposed to save us money."

"Bill, you are correct. Purchasing must look at the overall budget, not just yours."

Mike Watkins is the director of purchasing for Swisher Systems Corporation. He is solely responsible for purchasing all material items throughout the company. Mike has had various experiences in materials management prior to joining Swisher Systems. After earning a bachelor's degree in business management with an emphasis in retailing at Crawford State University in West Texas, Mike went on to gain more than 35 years of industrial purchasing experience.

As a summer purchasing intern with Swisher, Todd Evans was assigned to shadow Mr. Watkins.

COMPANY BACKGROUND

Swisher Systems Corporation is an industrial heating company that was established in 1949. The company is an innovator of flexible heating products, especially with its knit and braided heating element. This heating element is a multistranded resistance wire that is knit and braided with fiberglass and is the base technology for almost all of Swisher Systems' products. The company also produces control devices and heating cable and is known throughout the industry as being the highest-quality flexible heat supplier. Swisher Systems has enjoyed first-mover advantages for quite some time, and the industry recognizes Swisher Systems as the innovator of flexible heat. It has several patents that support the company in sustaining market share, while its patented grounded heating element provides additional safety that other flexible heating elements cannot provide. Swisher Systems' competitive advantage stems from the quality of its products, which are able to maintain higher, safer temperatures that are more flexible than other products on the market.

PRODUCTS AT SWISHER SYSTEMS

All products that Swisher Systems produces are solutions to industrial heating applications. Swisher Systems manufactures roughly 50 percent standard products and 50 percent custom orders. Each product line can be designed to meet

[1] The author expresses appreciation to Craig Wilson for his contributions to this case. Names and data have been disguised.

custom applications. While variability of materials is substantial between product lines, all products essentially perform the same function. Swisher Systems' custom products can be applied to virtually all industries that require heating products.

The standard products can be divided into eight basic product lines. Most of the product lines are enhanced versions of an existing product line. For example, a silicone heating blanket is several flexible heating tapes sandwiched together between layers of silicone. This blanket can be used in areas where more coverage is needed, for example, a hopper tank. Each product line can be associated with a particular application; for example, flexible heating tape and heating cable are ideal solutions for freeze protection. The product line from Swisher Systems that contributes the greatest portion of sales revenue is the cloth heating jacket. This product is commonly used in the semiconductor industry to prevent condensation in the gas pipes that are critical in the semiconductor process. Swisher Systems' heating jacket can maintain higher temperatures than the competition's and is superior in a clean room setting. However, the silicone heating jacket alternatives offered by competitors are less expensive. This is mainly due to how the two products are produced. The cloth heating jacket requires intensive labor to sew the cloth, whereas the silicone jacket is manufactured with the help of machines.

Cloth heating jackets are the most labor-intensive and costly item to produce but, at the same time, are the largest revenue producer for Swisher Systems. The labor required to produce a cloth heating jacket is highly skilled, thus making it difficult for other companies to duplicate the quality achieved at Swisher Systems. In addition, since the product is made to fit, the cloth heating jackets tend to be custom-designed, resulting in added engineering costs.

Swisher Systems operates mainly in a business-to-business environment, supplying the semiconductor, food processing, medical, and petrochemical industries. The main focus of its business had been on the semiconductor industry, which went into a serious downturn with the recession in 2000. As a result, Swisher decided to place more emphasis on other industries.

Swisher Systems has multiple competitors, which vary among different industries. The companies that it competes with generally offer less expensive substitutes that tend to be of lower quality. Mateen Electric Manufacturing Company, Bailey Heating, and Cole Heating are a few of its many competitors.

Swisher Systems has annual revenues of approximately $20 million. Of that $20 million, $8 million, 40 percent of revenue, goes into the purchasing of material items. Another 20 percent of the revenue goes to direct labor. Overhead takes up the majority of the potential profit margin: 20 percent for direct overhead and 5 percent for indirect overhead, which includes selling and administration. The high overhead is a concern but appears to be unavoidable for a small company trying to grow. A sales call center was implemented over a year ago, which adds 10 more members to the payroll along with a marketing person who creates all of the written literature and designs marketing campaigns. This leaves a margin of about 15 percent for profit. This number can fluctuate due to negotiations with customers. Swisher Systems keeps approximately $12,000,000 of supply inventory on hand at any given point. This gives Swisher Systems approximately two inventory turns per year. Swisher Systems is constantly looking for ways to improve its financial status but appears to be overall stable with over 55 years in the business.

PURCHASING ACCORDING TO MIKE WATKINS

"Todd, I will teach you everything I know about purchasing during your internship… We will first start with an overview of purchasing at Swisher."

"Mr. Watkins, thanks for allowing me to learn from you." Todd pulled out his pad and began to take notes.

Todd observed that Mike Watkins was a one-man purchasing department. Over the past 35 years, Mike has formulated an opinion of how materials management and purchasing should be conducted. For instance, he outlined for Todd his five most important criteria for qualifying a supplier. The number one criterion is *on-time delivery*. His belief is that if the product is not in possession of the manager, the other factors are irrelevant. The second criterion is *quality*. Mike's definition of quality refers to both *material quality* and *information quality* from the supplier. He then restated that the number one criterion is *on-time delivery*. The third criterion is *value*. The fourth criterion is the *responsiveness of the supplier's organization*. According to Mike, supplier responsiveness is based on how quickly and accurately the supplier can change the order to meet Swisher Systems' requirements. Finally, Mike places emphasis on the supplier's *financial stability*. What good is it to develop a relationship with a supplier if that supplier will not be around tomorrow?

Mike views partnerships as an important part of materials management and purchasing, especially with small companies. With partnerships, Swisher Systems is able to call on short notice and have its orders fulfilled, a lot of the time without expediting charges. Companies would be less likely to help Swisher Systems if it was not for Mike taking the time to get to know the suppliers' representatives on a personal level. Mike gave as an example the time he was in the hospital, when many of his suppliers' representatives actually visited him. He stated that "this kind of a relationship is not made overnight" and even though he has personal relations with his vendors, he is still stern and fair in negotiations. He said this is done through honesty and integrity, which he claimed as the secret ingredient to being an effective purchasing manager.

Mike's enthusiasm for purchasing and supply chain management was easily observed by Todd. Mike's views on purchasing standards continue in the following section.

PURCHASING PROCESS AT SWISHER SYSTEMS

Mike is the only person who handles purchasing at Swisher Systems, which is allright with Mike since he likes the power. Typically, Mike sends out approximately 50 purchase orders a day. He bases his OEM purchase decisions on the following:

1. *MRP action report*. The primary method used to determine what needs to be ordered is based on Swisher Systems' MRP system, SIM 4500, and its MRP action report. Each morning when Mike arrives at his office, he prints the MRP action report, which is typically around 8–10 pages, and manually reads it. His decisions are driven exclusively by the MRP system report actions:
   - Cancel: No purchase is required.
   - Purchase requisition: Purchase order should be placed.
   - Slide: Purchase could be pushed back.
   - Short—no open orders: Parts are needed and suggested order date is due.

Mike then looks at the report for things that jump out at him, such as accelerate, low number of inventory, high number required, and so forth. Once he has a grasp of what needs to be ordered, he will print out a material analysis report that gives detailed information about each product. This report can be up to 80–100 pages. He then will manually go through both reports to sort out the requirements with different vendors and then create the purchase order for each supplier. He prefers to go through this process manually because the SIM 4500 system has its limits as to listing the primary and secondary suppliers, which may create problems later. He also likes to be in control and see which supplier should get the business and not let the computer decide it. After completing the manual analysis, he then prioritizes which suppliers should be called first. He will manually phone, fax, or e-mail his purchase order to the supplier.

2. *Current inventory level.* Mike stated that every few days, he performs a detailed analysis of inventory in addition to the MRP action report. He looks for trends that may constitute larger-volume buying or reduction in inventory that the MRP action report would not recommend. Sometimes when a volume discount exists, he then consults with the CFO, since it involves a significant amount of capital. Swisher Systems might have to carry additional inventory, but the cost may be offset by an attractive purchase price. According to Mike, every discount decision is the same. Mike, along with the CFO, decides the most profitable alternative for the company.
3. *Interaction with people who use the parts.* Mike is not one who likes to stay in his office. He spends a great deal of time on the plant floor talking to the production workers. If a need exists, a requisition form will be filled and the purchase will be made. The key players who typically requisition are members of the engineering team, especially for custom products; each engineering manager is responsible for forecasting, quality, and controlling cost for his or her specific section.

He does this routine everyday; not only is it very time-consuming, but a lot of paper is being wasted as well. Although the use of the SIM 4500 MRP program helps by preparing the MRP reports, ultimately, Mike relies on his memory to make decisions.

INVENTORY MANAGEMENT

Since on-time delivery is critical, having products in inventory is important. Along with this, it is also important that the inventory be accurate in the computer system. The inventory part activity can be checked on the computer. A manual count of inventory is necessary to ensure its accuracy. Material is constantly being used, and it is important to keep track of where the inventory is going and how much is used. Swisher Systems remedies this situation with an inventory requisition form that is manually filled out by anyone who takes material out of the stockroom.

Recently, the material manager requested 25 pounds of a specific chemical substance, based on the bill of materials. The price at this level would have been $93 per pound. Mike purchased 500 pounds at only $45 per pound. According to Mike, this was successful because the product would not become obsolete and it is used on a regular basis. "This points out the disadvantage of SIM 4500; it is not able to recommend volume buying because it looks solely at the bill of materials."

SUPPLIER RELATIONS

Currently, Swisher Systems maintains more than 1,000 suppliers in the database system. However, there are approximately 150–200 active suppliers. Some component parts and materials are acquired from more than one supplier. Mike does keep very good relations with his suppliers; oftentimes they will expedite their orders for him at no charge.

Swisher Systems, more specifically Mike, has the philosophy that multiple sourcing is better than single sourcing. Since it is a small company with little buying power, a competitive environment is the key to negotiating better prices. According to Mike, there are two dilemmas with single sourcing. On one side, by maintaining single sourcing, you can cut down on administrative costs, have better integration with suppliers, and receive larger quantity discounts. However, when uncertainty occurs and the supplier cannot fulfill the requirement, the buyer is scrambling to fulfill the requirement with an alternate supplier that has been cut off from the supply chain. Since on-time delivery is so critical to Mike, he chooses to pay the premium to have a stable of suppliers. In addition, with 150–200 active suppliers, keeping relationships with all of them is not impossible or excessively expensive.

When it comes to qualifying suppliers, Mike uses his five criteria, as mentioned earlier: *on-time delivery, quality, value, responsiveness,* and *financial stability*. Mike has a clear idea who will be included in Swisher Systems' supplier base. Mike uses his judgment, intuition, knowledge, and network to qualify a supplier. He will then look for the criteria mentioned above in the supplier. If it fulfills all the criteria, then the supplier is qualified.

NEGOTIATIONS

According to Mike, to be a great purchaser, you must be a great negotiator. Mike explains that a purchasing agent is measured on price variance. In other words, this is the difference in what the cost was and what the cost is now with savings. He has a goal to save at least 10 percent annually. An example at Swisher Systems is the cost negotiated from the printer of its catalogs. In 2004, it cost $1.86 for each catalog. Currently the cost is $1.38 and the quality has dramatically increased. This was a savings of $10,000 a year. Inexperienced buyers may not be aware that costs also can be negotiated with companies such as the United Parcel Service if a large volume of shipping is done. Swisher Systems uses UPS for inbound and outbound; therefore, it was able to negotiate better prices.

Mike emphasized that honesty and integrity are the most important characteristics when negotiating with suppliers. This comes along with the quality of communication. Not only is it important for the supplier to communicate honestly, but it is also important that the purchaser is honest too. This allows both sides to know exactly what is expected, and then can be gained. In addition, Mike says it is necessary to become an expert on what you buy. The more you know, the easier you can negotiate.

Another scenario where Mike used negotiation had to do with heating cable. When he first arrived at Swisher Systems, the current supplier was charging $1.10 per foot. He first began reducing cost by using a volume discount. Then he began researching and found another reliable supplier that was less expensive. He used this information to negotiate an even more favorable price with the current supplier. The result was a huge cost saving while still keeping the reliability of the current supplier.

CONCLUSION

This is precisely what happened in the case of Bill Simpson's situation earlier today. Total annual usage of the solenoid amounted to $120,000. The total usage of capacitors was $32,000. A new low-cost supplier, B&B, was selected to supply the solenoid component. Mike also agreed to add the capacitor requirements to the deal. The annual total for the combined purchase contract was $150,000 [$100,000 (solenoid) +$50,000 (capacitors)]. The company also will receive a 10-percent rebate at the end of the year.

Case 26

The Tank Case[1]

On May 5, 2008, Santiago Menendez, vice president and general manager of American Pride Molded Plastics, located in Whiting, Indiana, was shocked and surprised by a prequalification application and price schedule he had just finished reviewing. Hsu & Hsu, a Chinese company, will guarantee a quote of $0.22 per pound F.O.B. for the carbon black tank rubber. This price represents a 50-percent cost reduction.

GENERAL INDUSTRY BACKGROUND

Since 1835 rubber has been used to create a wide variety of products ranging from shoe soles to tank track assemblies. Rubber is defined as a substance that can be stretched to at least twice its original length and then returns to approximately the same shape at room temperature. American Pride Molded Plastics is a medium-sized company that makes a wide range of products for the government and private entities. The company processes the rubber specified for the M1 Abrams tank tires.

CLIENT INFORMATION

American Pride's primary client is the U.S. government. They were recently awarded the contract to produce the tire assembly for the M1 Abrams tank. The M1 Abrams (Figure C26.1) is the main battle tank for the U.S. Army. It is designed for use in a wide range of climates and terrain, such as the desert in the Persian

[1] The author expresses appreciation to Mike DeGroff and Kurt Dickman for their contributions to this case. Names and data have been disguised.

FIGURE C26.1
M1 Abrams Tank

FIGURE C26.2
Tank Wheels

Gulf or the countryside in Europe. It also is designed to take a lot of punishment, so its component parts must be able to perform. The tires for the tank also must be easy to replace when necessary but still be able to function adequately under duress until replacement. The wheels for the tank are called road wheels and idler wheels (Figure C26.2), which are located around the inside of the tread. The tank wheels are made of solid rubber and are used like a gear to assist in turning the tank. The tank tread provides a surface for seven road wheels and one idler per track per tank. There are a total of 16 tires per tank assembly.

Selling to the U.S. government is significantly different from selling to the private sector. The government is a large bureaucracy that is focused on getting the lowest price. However, the quality expectations and specifications remain. Supplying tank track rubber to the government, especially to the military, may result in federal charges and negative publicity (e.g., the army's Sergeant Bradley and the Marine Corps' Osprey helicopters). Governmental contractors must meet specifications in an efficient low-cost manner.

THE RUBBER-MAKING PROCESS

Natural rubber comes from the tree *Hevea brasiliensis* as a liquid consisting of cis-polyisoprene and water. The fluid flows from a cut in the tree and is collected in a cup. This is what we refer to as latex. The latex is coagulated (curdled), shaped into sheets, and then dried to form crepe rubber. The rubber also can be dried in the presence of smoke. This process changes the color to a light brown and is then called a smoked sheet. Base polymers, however, are not suited for production into the final product in which they are intended. Their properties have to be refined through compounding. Compounding consists of the following:

- Fillers—carbon black and finely ground silica used to provide reinforcement.
- Oils, waxes, and fatty acids—used to improve processability.
- Pigments—used to add coloring to the rubber.

The rubber specified for the M1 Abrams tank is called carbon black masterbatch. A rough formula for this synthetic rubber is as follows:

- Natural rubber: 57.21 percent
- Carbon black: 31.14 percent
- Oil: 4.03 percent

FIGURE C26.3
The Natural Rubber Industry

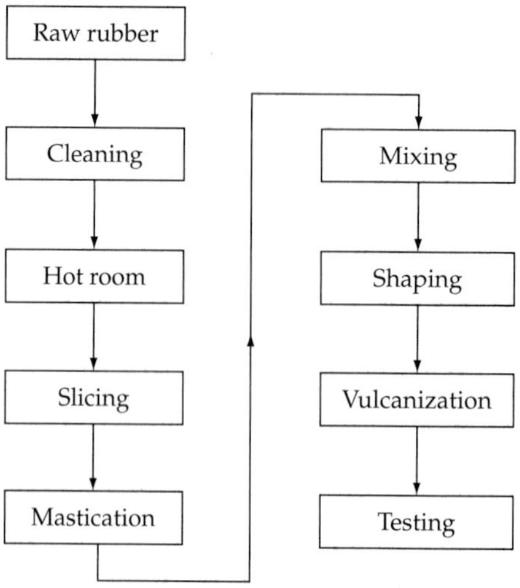

- Ash: 4.02 percent
- Residue: 3.60 percent

A flowchart illustrating the stages from raw rubber to finished goods is given in Figure C26.3.

Processing

There are two ways to achieve rubber compounding (processing):

1. Open rubber mills.
2. Large internal mixers.

An *open mill* is composed of two rollers that are 2 meters across and 0.6 meter in diameter. The rollers rotate in opposite directions and are heated and cooled as needed. The rubber is placed on the rolls and mixing is accomplished through the shearing action produced by the "nips" between the rollers. Compounding materials are added during the mixing process; after mixing is complete, the rubber is extracted from the mill in the form of a sheet.

An *internal mixer* is an enclosed chamber with two blades that are spiral in shape. The helical blades turn in opposite directions and at slightly different speeds. The compounds are added and the material is mixed to produce a homogeneous rubber. The temperature is controlled with cooling water or steam that is pumped through the blades and the chamber casing. After mixing is completed, the batch is dropped from the bottom of the mixer onto an open mill, where the rubber is formed into sheets.

Once the rubber has been compounded, it must be vulcanized (cured). Vulcanization solves the biggest problem encountered when producing rubber products: susceptibility to the elements. Rubber has a tendency to melt in the sun/heat and becomes rigid in cold weather. These problems are eliminated after the rubber is vulcanized. This method creates *crosslinks* within the molecular structure. This affords the necessary physical properties and provides the finished rubber with chemical and thermal stability.

American Pride doesn't possess the capabilities to compound their rubber. Therefore, the responsibility is passed to their suppliers. The mix, processing methods, and vulcanization methods used by the supplier to produce the carbon black masterbatch must be laid out in the specifications established by American Pride. Both methods stated above are standard and will satisfactorily meet processing requirements. One method is not preferred over the other.

Molding

There are three methods of molding used in the rubber industry:

1. *Compression*. Compression involves placing a blank between the two halves of the cavity mold. The halves are then compressed together; under temperature and pressure, the blank is shaped into the form of the cavity. Average temperatures range from 150 to 180 degrees Celsius. Average pressures range from 7 to 15 Mpa of projected mold cavity area. The blank also is vulcanized during compression and from there it is trimmed and ready to use.
2. *Transfer molding*. Transfer injection involves placing a blank in a container of the mold cavity. The rubber is then forced using pressure through a sequence of feed gates into the cavity. Once finished, the rubber is removed and ready for use.
3. *Direct injection*. Direct injection is similar to transfer molding. However, instead of placing the rubber blank into a container, the blank is fed into a screw extruder. The extruder forces the rubber using pressure through a combination of runners and feed gates into the mold cavity. Once finished, the rubber is removed and ready for use.

American Pride produces products using all three techniques. Direct injection molding is specified for the M1 tank.

Tests

There are four tests specified for measuring the quality of the carbon black masterbatch produced by the supplier:

1. *Durometer*. The durometer test is used to measure the hardness of the rubber. A sample is placed against an indentor point, which pushes back into the casing against a spring. The harder the sample, the farther the indentor point will push back against the spring and the greater the reading on the dial.
2. *Tensile strength*. Tensile strength measures the maximum tensile stress reached in stretching a sample to its breaking point. The strength is written as the force per unit of the original cross section of the sample length.
3. *Elongation*. Elongation measures the expansion created by a tensile force. The measurement criterion is the percentage of the original cross section of the sample length. Ultimate elongation is the elongation at the point of breaking.
4. *Tensile modulus*. Tensile modulus is a combination of tensile strength (stress) and elongation. It measures the stress required to achieve a certain elongation.

Tensile tests are used to indicate the effect of various compounding materials. The tests are sensitive to shifts in manufacturing conditions. They can be used to identify

- Under- or overvulcanization.
- Poor blending.
- The presence of foreign materials.

An example of a testing machine for tensile stress-strain can be seen in Figure C26.4.

FIGURE C26.4
Testing Machine for Tensile Stress-Strain

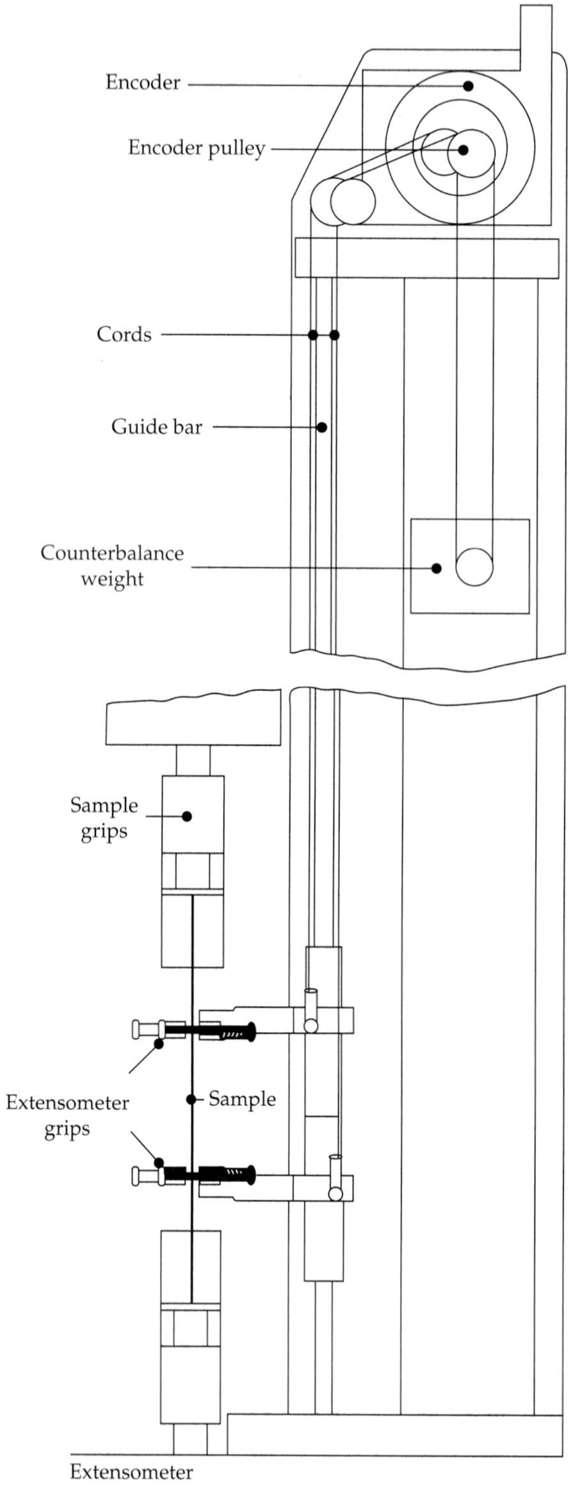

FINAL PRODUCT SPECIFICATIONS

The U.S. Army requires the following specifications for the tire to be acceptable:

- Tire for an M1 Abrams tank: 6″ wide × 25″ circumference × 1″ thick
- Total number of tires required: 15,000
- Tests to be performed on random tire selections:
  1. *Puller test*: For 6″, the tire must be able to pull at least 600 psi on a tire puller.
  2. *Mileage test 1*: The tire must run for six hours on a flywheel at 35 mph. The load of the tank also is simulated during testing. When finished, the tire must be free from blemishes (cracks, scratches, etc.).
  3. *Mileage test 2*: The tire must run for 48 hours on a flywheel at 15 mph. The load of the tank also is simulated during testing. When finished, the tire must be free from blemishes.

In addition to the above tests, samples must be cut from random tire selections and tested to meet the following specifications:

- Sample size: 6″ wide × 7″ long × 1″ thick
- Durometer: 65 ± 5
- Tensile strength: 6 Mpa or 870 psi
- Elongation: 200 percent

Raw Material Specifications

In order to produce a tire to the client's specifications, American Pride will need to purchase raw materials to the following specifications:

- Rubber required: Carbon black masterbatch
- Delivery units: Bales of 75 pounds in weight
- Line call out: ASTM D-2000 M 2 AE 707
- Durometer: 70 ± 5
- Tensile strength: 7 Mpa or 1015 psi
- Elongation: 200 percent

The three potential suppliers (Goodyear, Dunlop, and Bridgestone) have been qualified by the government and thus are legitimate candidates, as given in Figure C26.5. As a contractor for the government, American Pride Molded Plastics is required to go with the lowest bidder in order to provide the lowest possible cost to the U.S. Army. The company submitting the lowest quote is Goodyear. Their cost is $20,475 lower than Dunlop's and $6,825 lower than Bridgestone/Firestone's. The contract to be awarded to Goodyear is for 341,250 pounds of carbon black masterbatch at $0.43 per pound, with a total cost of $146,737.50. The contract will be signed one week from the award date on May 10, 2009.

FIGURE C26.5
Current Buying Alternatives

	GOODYEAR	DUNLOP	BRIDGESTONE
Quoted price/pound	$0.43/lb.	$0.49/lb.	$0.45/lb.
Quoted total cost	$146,737.50	$167,212.50	$153,562.50

Type of rubber required	Carbon black masterbatch
Tire requirements (lbs.)	22.75 lbs.
Total tires required	15,000
Total pounds required	341,250 lbs.

Case 27

TEMKO Earthmovers[1]

The TEMKO Company encountered the problem of defects in some of its purchased tractor short-block castings. The short-block castings are used to build the R-208 tractor engines. TEMKO installs the heads, manifold, carburetor, and other engine parts, which consist of approximately 13 percent of the short-block casting purchase price. When the defects are discovered, the short blocks have to be disassembled and repaired. It takes approximately eight hours per repair. Even with this process, almost 4 percent of the incoming short blocks end up as scrap. In other words, approximately 10 out of every 100 units are repaired and 40 percent of the repaired short blocks are scrapped. Each short-block casting costs between $1,550 and $1,700 depending on the supplier. There is also a cost of downtime associated with interruptions on the shop floor.

The internal labor cost of assembling each incoming short-block casting and repair as necessary is approximately $878 per short block. The estimated overhead, which is 150 percent of direct labor, consists of 33 percent variable and 67 percent fixed costs; the shop floor disruption cost is estimated to be $500 per disruption.

Recently, James Sun, the purchasing manager, released a request for quote (RFQ) for the short blocks to three prequalified suppliers of assembled tractor engines. However, only one supplier, ACE Manufacturing, Inc., showed an interest. ACE was a small startup company that was looking for work. In order to produce assembled R-208 engines, an investment in precision machinery of more than $1,500,000 would need to be made. ACE was willing to both invest in the necessary machine and guarantee at least 100 engines per month—provided TEMKO would contract with it as a **sole source** for the engines for the next three years. The price per engine would be $3,500 the first year, with an annual increase of 3 percent. TEMKO anticipated that they would need at least 1,000 *finished* engine assemblies per year for the next five years. As the purchasing manager for TEMKO, how would you analyze this outsourcing decision? (Make sure your analysis is complete.)

[1] Names and data have been disguised.

Case 28

Tom & Jerry (T&J) Construction, Inc.[1]

T&J finished its fifth year in business and have completed nearly 48 jobs. The company specializes in excavating, concrete, and trucking. The company is certified as a disadvantaged business enterprise (DBE) by the Indiana Department of Transportation (INDOT). However, T&J has worked primarily in the private sector. The company has done some trucking jobs for the INDOT market, but it's very seldom that T&J work as a contractor on INDOT projects. The company currently has 12 full-time employees including the owner, six employees in the field and five in the home office. There are also two estimators who work as independent contractors and get paid a flat 5-percent commission on all sales that meet a minimum 8-percent net profit. As independent contractors, they don't receive company benefits. Subcontractors are used for at least 30 percent of the work on all of the projects.

Last year, the company did $2,124,945 in good, solid business. Next year T&J is projecting a 10-percent increase in sales. Last year T&J estimated an 8-percent net profit, but actually made only 3.8 percent. The goal for next year is to meet that 8-percent profit.

The good news is that Tom is in excellent health, and he is now the sole owner of the business. Of course, this came about because of the unfortunate death of Jerry last December. Tom & Jerry Construction is known throughout Indianapolis for quality work at competitive prices. Tom stated that he does not believe in recessions and had never participated in one. Tom and his late partner made the business what it is, and it's considered a model construction company. The additional case facts follow:

- Tom is married with five kids, and is expecting twins! Last night, Tom's wife told him that she's signed them up for marriage counseling. She thinks there should be something more to life than having and raising children. The two youngest children got bad grades on their most recent report cards, and the 15-year-old son received a three-day suspension from school for acting like a bully. Tom's wife thinks that he needs to spend more time at home with the children and less time working.
- T&J's best working foreman, Sam Jones, who has been with the company since day 1, came into Tom's office yesterday morning requesting a 10-percent raise. His current salary is $60,000. He says if he doesn't get the 10-percent raise, he's moving on. One of the female employees that work for him is considering filing a sexual harassment suit against the foreman and the company. In the middle of his conversation with Sam, the phone rang and Tom promised to get back with Sam next week.
- The phone call was from a Huntington Bank loan officer. Just a friendly reminder that the payment on the 2012 Mercedes is two months late!
- Last Thursday Tom was notified that the building that his office is in has been sold. The company must be out in 45 days. T&J have been paying $1,200 a month rent, and Tom knows that the rent anywhere else will be at least 35 percent higher. Tom estimated that it will cost him approximately $7,500 to move the business to comparable location.

- Jerry died suddenly on December 31 last year, leaving several hundred thousand dollars of personal bills, and the only asset that his estate shows is 49-percent ownership in Tom & Jerry Construction. Fortunately, Tom and Jerry had a buy-out agreement that guaranteed the surviving partner could buy out the other partner's stock in the company for $1. Tom executed the contract clause on the day before Jerry's wake. At the time of his passing, Tom and Jerry were each paid an equal salary.
- The attorney for Jerry's estate called to say that it would not be wise to use money from Tom & Jerry Construction, Inc. to pay any more company bills until he has had a chance to audit the corporate books. He did not explain why; he just mumbled something about illegal agreement and the IRS. He stated that he could work the audit into his schedule sometime in the next three to four weeks.
- The company had Key Person Insurance, but Tom did not know whether the bookkeeper paid the premiums when they were due last year. Furthermore, Tom cannot find the file for the insurance policies. Jim Sousa, the bookkeeper, is on vacation in Jamaica and cannot be reached. He has been gone for five weeks, and will not return for another two weeks. Tom wondered how he can afford such a trip on what he earns as a full-time bookkeeper.
- A local truck dealership called yesterday morning to tell Tom that he just got a two-year-old tri-axle dump truck with only 10,342 miles on it. He only wants $85,000 for it, and the company desperately needs another dump truck. Tom didn't plan for a new dump truck in the current budget. The loan officer says he can make a loan to Tom for a payment of $1,435 per month for five years, with a 10-percent down payment. The truck dealer also offered to arrange a three-year lease for about $1,746 per month, and it would have a $53,000 buyout after three years.
- The company was recently been hit with two lawsuits for separate auto accidents. Both of the company drivers were cited. Tom's attorney says both accidents will cost a minimum of $10,000 in legal fees, which she wants upfront. Both lawsuits are frivolous, so says T&J's attorney, and he is advised not to worry about them. . . . yet!
- The insurance agent that handles the company's Workers' Compensation insurance just called. He said T&J's rates will be 80-percent higher next year. Tom had a brief discussion about why that would be; since T&J has a relatively good safety record, he said he would look into it. He told Tom not to worry. However, he was going on his three-week vacation Wednesday. The new premiums are due next week.
- The company's top estimator, Bob, has been having some personal problems lately. Tom noticed that Tom's late partner Jerry approved a couple of draws against future sales, and Bob's account is now $11,500 in the red. He has not estimated a job for almost four weeks, and has not been the successful bidder in over three months. Tom has been looking for Bob's contract with the company, but cannot find it. The bookkeeper is in Jamaica!
- The company picnic is scheduled for two weeks from Saturday, and the event will cost at least $2,500.
- The company has three jobs in progress, with a total volume of $420,934 when completed.

- Tom has decided that since he has the full burden of running the company, he will give himself a raise, his regular owner's salary plus one quarter of Jerry's late partner's salary, starting immediately.

Table C28.1 shows the overhead costs for the company as of December 31, 2011 of last year, as best as Tom can determine without the assistance of the bookkeeper.

TABLE C28.1
Overhead Review: Tom & Jerry Construction Company

Overhead	Expense ($)
1. Advertising	52,899
2. Sales and Estimating	125,146
3. Office Expenses	
Office staff	155,544
Rent	7,200
Office equipment	22,645
Computer and peripherals	15,290
Telephone	1,629
Office supplies	1,323
4. Job Expenses	
Construction equipment (trucks/excavator etc. utilized 100 hours per year)	327,772
Job supervision	198,696
Tools and equipment	27,192
Customer service	9,257
Cell telephone	6,116
5. General expenses	
Owner's salary (as partner)	105,798
General insurance	18,515
Interest expense	7,290
Bad debts	15,000
Contractor's association	6,500
Licenses and fees	5,290
Accounting fees	5,819
Legal fees	14,232
Education/Training	4,761
Entertainment	3,645

Case 29

Trip 7 Screen Printing[1]

Recently, Mike Kitchen, the production manager for Trip 7 Screen Printing, has been having problems with the company's main supplier of t-shirts. For several years now, Mr. Kitchen has ordered t-shirts from American Apparel, the largest t-shirt vendor in the United States, located in Los Angeles, California. He is preparing for a telephone conversation with the sales manager at American Apparel. Two days ago, he called customer service, and they put him on hold for 90 minutes. According to Mike, "It is now time for results."

COMPANY BACKGROUND

Trip 7 Screen Printing started in 1991. The company is located in Columbus, Ohio. Trip 7 Screen Printing specializes in custom screen printing and embroidery of textile products such as t-shirts, golf shirts, dress shirts, hats, bags, and sweatpants. The company also offers common promotional items such as pens and coffee mugs and even some unique items such as custom chocolates and Swiss army knives.

The company prides itself on pleasing its customers. Trip 7 Screen Printing offers free consultation services on artwork, garments, retail programs, and uniform programs. It also promises timely delivery of the finished products to the customer by trying to meet each individual customer's deadline. In order to accomplish such a demanding task of meeting each and every customer deadline, Trip 7 Screen Printing uses forecasts based on past sales history. The company's overall goal is to focus 99.99 percent on customer care.

Trip 7's screen-printing facility offers up to six colors per item on a wide variety of textile products. Also, Trip 7 Screen Printing uses only Tajima embroidery equipment, which has long been the forerunner in the embroidery industry.

Trip 7 has done screen printing and/or embroidery products for several companies, restaurants, organizations, schools, and so forth. Some of these include FedEx, Ballet Met's performances, The Blue Bird Club, Buckeye Café, Byrne's Pub, Children's Hospital, and the San Quinton baseball team; Trip 7 also provides services to walk-in customers.

PROCESS OF SCREEN PRINTING

Screen printing is a print process where a design is transferred to a substrate by way of a screen. Inks are transferred through a screen to the garment to achieve the desired result. This involves exact pressures, specialized inks, and heat curing. The result of these processes is a long-lasting design.

The following is a step-by-step procedure of the screen-printing process:

1. Conceive artwork and send it to the computer for processing of a composite proof that specifies the colors, size, and location.

[1] The author expresses appreciation to Sunny Reelhorn and Scott Stevens for their contributions to this case. Names and data have been disguised.

2. Create output film on vellum paper and make into screens.
3. Preregister artwork and check it for detail and quality.
4. Coat the screens with photosensitive emulsion.
5. Dry the screens and place them on a vacuum light table, which exposes the screens to a 3,000-watt metal halide light that burns the image onto the screen.
6. Wash out the screen with a pressurized washer at around 1,300 psi.
7. Double-check for accuracy.
8. Block, tape, set up, and squeegee press the design onto the garment by color (each color utilizes a separate screen).
9. Flash (dry) ink between each color layer, which takes about one to two minutes per shirt.
10. Repeat steps seven, eight, and nine for each color in the design.

CURRENT SITUATION

In the past, Trip 7 Screen Printing has had strong relations with American Apparel. American Apparel offers a wide variety of products, and even carries some not-so-common products such as the fitted ladies' polo t-shirt. With a wide variety of products from its supplier, Trip 7 Screen Printing is able to accommodate the various requests from its own customers. Trip 7 Screen Printing provides American Apparel with a considerable amount of business, over $250,000 in sales per year.

But within the past couple of months, Mr. Kitchen has been unhappy with the growing number of backorders American Apparel has had on Trip 7's orders. The situation has become such a problem that Mr. Kitchen has estimated that at least 25 percent of his t-shirt orders are backordered through American Apparel. He has contacted the American Apparel customer service representatives several times and has not received the results that he had expected. As a result, Trip 7 Screen Printing has had trouble making customer deadlines. The company also is incurring extra costs from its growing number of expediting orders from American Apparel and having to pay its employees overtime.

Mr. Kitchen knows that when Trip 7 Screen Printing fails to meet a customer's deadline, the company is breaking its promise to provide 99.99 percent customer care. If American Apparel cannot deliver its t-shirts to Trip 7 Screen Printing in a timely fashion, customer service will diminish. Being able to promise timely deliveries to its customers is a key competitive advantage for Trip 7 Screen Printing. Supply chain quality is the most important aspect of the business.

During the past two days, you were able to research alternative suppliers for Mr. Kitchen. The results of the study are shown in Figure C29.1.

FIGURE C29.1 **Comparison of T-Shirt Suppliers**

Company	American Apparel	Bodek & Rhodes	Broder Bros.	Virginia Tees
History	Started in 1978	Started in 1939	Started in 1919	Started in 1984
Location	Los Angeles, CA	Philadelphia, PA	Plymouth, MI	Petersburg, VA
Mission	Provide best products with refined styles, finest cuts, and most vibrant colors	Be the best supplier for customers and be an innovator	They succeed in helping their customers succeed	Customer satisfaction is top priority and to have the inventory in stock for its customers
Brands offered	4 brands with 16 types of t-shirts	32 brands	27 brands	31 brands
Shipping policies	5 days UPS Ground; same day if order before 5 p.m.	1-day UPS Ground; same day if order before 4 p.m.	1–2 days UPS Ground; same day if order before 3 p.m	1–2 days UPS Ground; same day if order before 5 p.m.
Special facts	All fabrics 100 percent cotton; sweatshop free	Over 500,000 square feet of inventory space	Private label brand called Luna Pier	Warehouse in Evansville, IN
Advantages	Custom colors and sizes; 29 color choices; organic brand; quantity discounts	Exclusive distributor of Ultra Club; quantity discounts	Order tracking online	No minimums; special orders accepted
Disadvantages	12-piece minimum; piece price (cannot mix)	Must have insurance for shipping and handling	Slow Web site; orders in boxes of 36 or 72 t-shirts	No exclusive or private labels
Price of 72 base t-shirts* plus shipping	$183	$165	$168	$168.28

**Base t-shirts* refer to only white t-shirts sizes S–XL ($1.99 × 72 = $143.28).

Case 30

Two-Bucks Wine Operation[1]

BACKGROUND

The Two-Bucks Market is a small specialty market located in a Fort Worth suburb. Between September 1, 2012 and September 30, 2013, this market generated $4,860,816.68 in sales. The grocery department contributed approximately 90 percent of the sales. However, the wine department generated $546,233 in sales during the 12-month period. The wine department manager, Tommy Ray, is actually an expert on wines. He has written a popular book entitled *Texas Wine Country*. There are also two part-time employees who work between 20 and 30 hours per week. Both part-time employees split time between the wine department and the liquor department. The part-time work duties include wine tasting, stocking, and setting up wine displays. This particular store is not part of the larger Two-Bucks chain network, although it is operated by a company that operates three other specialty markets in the state. It is easy to see that by being an independent store, it does not have the purchasing power of large retail giants, and cannot offer customer benefits like discounted gasoline. Consequently, Two-Bucks Market takes an approach to operations based on superior customer service. As an example, if a new wine is purchased, they will sometimes inform specific customers based on knowledge of their preferences. Any competitive advantage is thereby gained through quality service and the offering of unique products enhanced by unmatched customer service. Tommy also conducts weekly wine tasking sessions from 6:00 to 8:00 p.m. on Fridays.

Tommy is in charge of all wine, beer, and low alcohol spirits (under 44 proof) purchasing. According to Tommy, wine purchasing is a unique art-based taste, a high level of customer interaction and discussions with knowledgeable sales representatives. Although 3–5 distributors account for a large portion of the wines carried, there are roughly 16 vendors who supply different wines to Two-Bucks.

Major deliveries are received on Wednesdays and Fridays, but some additional wine is delivered on Thursdays. Specialty orders are delivered throughout the week. All wine orders are stocked when received. It is common practice for all orders to be in by 3:00 p.m. and stocked by 5:00 p.m. All wine orders were personally placed by Tommy Ray. Sales representatives visit the store Monday to Friday with samples. Orders are usually placed during these visits. The wine representatives were also invited to attend the wine tasting sessions on Fridays. Sales representative for large distributors scan the sales floor inventory and discuss the observed needs with Tom. Based on information from the sales representatives, Tommy decides whether or not to place an order. Purchasing deals are also common, and Tommy is alerted of these opportunities by the various sales representatives. The large distributors usually initiate the various purchasing deals. Also, Two-Bucks Market accepts special customer orders from the Texas elite. As an example, some customers order 6–10 cases per month.

THE WINE DEPARTMENT OPERATIONS

The wine department is divided into three different sections (Wine, Bottled Wine, and Jug Wine). Table C30.1 consists of a sample of the SKUs, a description of the

TABLE C30.1
Sample List of Wines

SKU	Description	Quantity	Average ($)	Amount ($)
075008498700	MACROSTIE CHARD 2	261	21.96	5,731.56
002010650180	AVANTI PINOT GRIGIO	523	7.99	4,178.77
008689102287	STA MARGHERITA	140	27.03	3,784.20
075360620810	PERRY CREEK	249	9.99	2,487.51
067880100004	LUZON 05	241	9.99	2,407.59
009792177010	ROMBAUER CHARD	49	34.99	1,714.51
8600387388	WOODBRIDGE CHAR	107	14.99	1,603.93
018474500020	EVE CHARD	119	12.99	1,545.81
070343200047	CONTRADA CHARD	127	11.99	1,522.73
008224259103	KINGFISH CHARDON	249	5.99	1,491.51
075062565101	ROOT1 CAV SAV	107	12.86	1,376.02
072117000400	HERON CHARD	114	11.99	1,366.86
061364902003	FOXGLOVE CHARDO	85	15.99	1,359.15
068935200961	KIM CRAWFORD 5 BI	70	17.92	1,254.40
089991100046	NEW AGE WHITE	129	9.49	1,224.21
067308776182	VILLALTA VALPO	102	11.99	1,222.98
008981901086	COLORES DEL SOL M	110	10.99	1,208.90
009870943620	KRIS PINOT GRIGIO 2	89	13.10	1,166.11
008105439440	CRANE LAKE CHARD	233	4.99	1,162.67
001144326010	CB CHARDONNAY	83	13.99	1,161.17
008372203835	CLARET	55	20.99	1,154.45
080614500003	ALTOS BONARDA	124	8.99	1,114.76
009870920131	VITIANO ROSSO	104	10.47	1,088.88
075772501800	STEVE VINCENT CRI	99	10.99	1,088.01
085955100103	MATCHBOOK BLOCK	82	12.99	1,065.18
008858649895	COLUMBIA CREST G	86	12.25	1,053.50
074715405881	LAN RESERVA RIOJA	50	20.99	1,049.50
008158401310	KJ CHARD	62	16.07	996.34
008735651012	CLOS DU BOIS	78	12.08	942.24
001813820102	EDNA VALLEY VYD CI	71	12.99	922.29
008711040057	TOASTED HEAD CHAR	72	12.49	899.28
852000005G	SUTTER HOME CHAR	68	12.99	883.32
008841578055	SIMI CAB	38	22.23	844.74
008308530058	ESTANCIA CHARD 200	70	11.99	839.30
071432013550	OGIER CDR BLANC	69	11.99	827.31
008981984389	BOHO CHARDONNAY	117	6.99	817.83
008175305020	VEUVE CLIQUOT NV	15	54.19	812.85
008981906008	MERIDIAN VYDS CHA	87	9.22	802.14
001690106112	STELZNER CLARET	43	18.57	798.51
008981984387	BOHO MERLOT	114	6.99	796.86
068453000011	POMELO SAUV BL	72	10.99	791.28
0089819005509	CHAT ST JEAN CHAR	60	13.06	783.60
001813836502	MOON MTN CAB	96	7.99	767.04
008500001623	GHOST PINE CAB	37	20.53	759.61
001235407144	PPEN KOONUNGA SHI	76	9.99	759.24
0674116307372	NELMS CAB	32	22.99	735.68
071140871365	TOAD CHARDONNAY	52	13.99	727.48
074265113519	FC CAB	24	29.99	719.76
008364887131	ELK COVE PINOT GRI	36	19.99	719.64
1235408185	LINDEMANS CHARD E	55	12.99	714.45

TABLE C30.1
(continued)

SKU	Description	Quantity	Average ($)	Amount ($)
008088749392	BOGLE CHARD 2000	64	11.12	711.68
080614500001	ALTOS MALBEC	58	12.25	710.50
008853400138	ST FRANCIS CAB	31	22.64	701.84
076961145444	SONOMA CUTRAR C	27	25.99	701.73
009224200400	BONANNO CAB	35	19.99	699.65
071788852002	HESS SELECT CHARD	56	12.40	694.40
008105419440	HACIENDA CHARD 19	94	7.34	689.96
072566720022	BELLE VALLEE P NOI	34	19.99	679.66
081945100700	GARNACHA DE FUEG	75	8.99	674.25
008308561129	VERAMONTE SAUV B	39	10.99	428.61
008981900848	BOHO SAUV BLANC	61	6.99	426.39
008105439427	CRANE LAKE PINOT	85	4.99	424.15
070343200094	POZZAN ANNABELLA	26	16.22	421.72
008051640494	CENTINE BIANCO	35	11.99	419.65
001208696531	CLOUDLINE P NOIR	19	21.99	417.81
008224259753	KINGFISH MERLOT	69	5.99	413.31
8273400101	CONCHA CAB 01	41	9.99	409.59
008841578405	SIMI CHARD	23	17.77	408.71
008500004528	PINOT GRIGIO	58	6.99	405.42
008308520022	FRANCISCAN CAB SS	14	28.85	403.90
074021612604	BR COHN SILVER	20	19.99	399.80
001813836102	MOON MTN CHARD	50	7.99	399.50
8072000057	GLEN ELLEN CHARD	49	7.99	391.51
008956913198	BOUCHAINE CHARD	17	22.99	390.83
078577400021	BENZIGER CHARDON	23	16.99	390.77
069224200683	CA TULLIO PINOT GR	39	9.99	389.61
074265110719	FERRARI CARANO CH	16	24.24	387.84
071090970614	MER SOLEIL SILVER	9	42.99	386.91
008682830003	SKETCHBK CHARD	23	16.77	385.71
072869184621	RABBIT RIDGE MERLO	35	10.99	384.65
074936221005	LOBSTER CHARD	32	11.99	383.68
008121800779	BURGESS MERLOT	17	22.40	380.80
0084689244134	CHIARLO BARBERA	27	13.99	377.73
001235419922	LINDEMAANS	47	7.99	375.53
008364801212	ELK COVE ROSE	25	14.99	374.75
008500001593	CODAX ALBARINO	25	14.99	374.75
087739700040	OBERON CAB	17	21.99	373.83
008069691633	BV CHARD	34	10.99	373.66
085455800620	BURCH HILL CAB	34	10.99	373.66
8520091874	SUTTER HOME WHITE	53	6.99	370.47
063778933674	BURGANS ALBARINO	26	14.18	368.68
008678518013	MAS DE LA DAME	23	15.99	367.77
008254496105	WHITE TAIL CHARD	52	6.99	363.48
008682830035	SKETCHBOOK P NOIR	18	19.99	359.82
087517400048	FOOLS BAY SHZ GREN	18	19.99	359.82
008912128812	J LOHR CAB	20	17.99	359.80
008469246084	PIGHIN P GRIGIO	24	14.99	359.76
078458500856	REGUSSE P NOIR	30	11.99	359.70
008500001591	CODAX ERGO TEMP	36	9.99	359.64
083954300102	MOM TIME OUT RED	40	8.99	359.60

(continued)

TABLE C30.1
Sample List of Wines *(continued)*

SKU	Description	Quantity	Average ($)	Amount ($)
081945100500	JUAN GIL JUMILLA R	21	16.99	356.79
008500001647	BRIDLEWOOD CHARD	27	13.06	352.62
001208693421	NOVELTY CAB	14	24.99	349.86
008739600458	POUY CTE GASCOGN	35	9.99	349.65
067508000617	MMCMANIS PG	35	9.99	349.65
8520061874	SUTTER HOME CHARD	50	6.99	349.50
080234900092	LEONE ROSSO	29	11.99	347.71
005161208113	ROSA DI ROSA	23	14.99	344.77
074773625935	REUSCHER HAART R	23	14.99	344.77
008941900611	DONA PAULA MALBE	23	14.95	343.85
008088749023	BOGLE PHANTOM	17	19.99	339.83
009870952004	COOPERS SB	34	9.99	339.66
8520000054	SUTTER HOME MERLOT	26	12.99	337.74
087801600207	CLAIRE MEURSAULT	6	55.99	335.94
001147250757	FLORA SPRINGS CAB	12	27.99	335.88
076315912012	BORGIA CAMPO DE B	48	6.99	335.52
008043234007	JACOBS CREEK CHA	46	7.19	330.74
089450900058	BANDIT CHARD	41	7.99	327.59
008775400015	HOGUE RIESLING	27	11.99	323.73
081945100725	ATTECA	17	18.99	322.83
008858640284	COL CREST MERLOT	23	13.99	321.77

TABLE C30.2
Unknown Wine Products

SKU	Description	Quantity	Average ($)	Amount ($)
002793960563	WINE	18	9.99	179.82
003410072874	26	3	14.99	44.97
008254400457	WINE	1	8.99	8.99
008739600433	WINE	26	7.99	207.74
019873001016	WINE	2	16.99	33.98
032568350411	WINE	4	15.99	63.96
032628440397	WINE	2	12.99	25.98
067081599999	WINE	1	14.99	14.99
068365200001	WINE	1	14.99	14.99
078603025900	G	14	22.20	310.80
081665000305	SHIRZ	12	9.99	119.88
304620930592	WINE	14	14.99	209.86
331276000014	WINE	9	10.99	98.91
410061012225	WINE	4	9.99	39.96
413354089119	WINE	20	8.99	179.80
421478750150	WINE	4	23.99	95.96
437001433209	WINE	104	12.99	1,350.96
490920000117	WINE	1	35.99	35.99
798096630609	WINE	33	6.99	230.67
804606600335	WINE	59	11.99	707.41
Total		**332**		**3,975.62**

products, the quantity that was purchased during the year, the average price, and the number of items sold. As can be seen in Table C30.1, Two-Bucks carries an extensive number of SKUs. From September 1, 2012 to September 30, 2013, over 1,200 different items were sold under the classification of bottled wine. Additional products were also sold under the other classifications. There were also 11,580 items sold, totaling $158,200, which were not scanned by their SKU at the time of purchase, and therefore could not be accounted for accurately in the sales record. There are a variety of different reasons that a bottle of wine was not scanned by SKU; the item's label did not have a printed barcode, the cashier chose to enter in the item by price rather than SKU, or the item's barcode would not scan, thus forcing manual price entry. Additionally, some non-wine products such as drink mixers are sometimes classified as wine, and sometimes classified as grocery items. See Tables C30.2 and C30.3.

TABLE C30.3
Non-Wine SKUs

SKU	Description	Quantity	Average ($)	Amount ($)
000945005237	SARNAC GINGER BEER	27	5.99	161.73
002858804582	YELLOW PAINT CHIP	9	2.99	26.91
002858804583	RED PAINT CHIP WINE B	16	2.99	47.84
002858804603	WINE BAG	7	2.99	20.93
002858804606	WINE BAG	4	2.99	11.96
002858804659	DOG WINE BAG	13	3.99	51.87
002858804661	CAT WINE BAG	5	3.99	19.95
007775783043	WINE SPIRITS CHAR	1	8.99	8.99
007775791160	BTL OPENER	2	2.99	5.98
008862166010	EMERGENCY KIT	2	7.99	15.98
009492270141	Q TONIC	63	8.49	534.87
009530113148	DOUBLE DEAD GUY ALE	1	9.99	9.99
061600379011	ZING ZANG 64	32	9.99	319.68
061600381422	ZING ZANG BLOODY	52	5.49	285.48
071023406000	WINE MULLING SPICE	2	3.49	6.98
085252700012	STEIEGL PILS	19	0.63	11.97
087671800131	WINE BAG	4	3.99	15.96
087671800132	WINE BAG	3	3.99	11.97
087671800143	GARDEN BLOOM	5	2.99	14.95
087671800225	WINE PAG	5	3.99	19.95
087671800227	POLKA DOT	11	3.99	43.89
087671800229	POLKA DOT	11	3.99	43.89
087671800637	POLKA BAG	2	3.99	7.98
087671800863	BLUSH	2	3.99	7.98
087671800872	WINE BAG	3	2.99	8.97
087671800873	WINE BAG	6	2.99	17.94
087671800877	CHEEKY CONGRATS	10	2.99	29.90
087671800879	SPARKLING GREEN	3	3.99	11.97
087671800919	WINE BAG	1	3.99	3.99
087671800958	PICK ME	3	3.99	11.97
089819500101	FEVERTREE TONIC	38	5.99	227.62
089819500105	FEVER TREE BITTER	55	5.99	329.45
089819500109	FEVER TREE GINGER	12	5.99	71.88
089819500113	FEVER TREE CLUB S	19	5.99	113.81
089819500127	FEVER TREE GINGER	5	5.99	29.95
070436130001	GREAT LAKES BURN	2	1.99	3.98
Total		**455**		**2,569.11**

THE WINE PURCHASING PROCESS

The top-selling wine was Macrostie Chardonnay, and it is well known that a very large portion of these sales came from a regular customer who buys this wine in large quantities on a weekly basis. Also, three of the top five wine sellers launched significant promotions during the year. The promotions ran for a few months at a time, and sales greatly increased during the promotion period. The wine purchasing process is driven by wine promotions, discounts, and deals they can receive from distributors. According to Tommy, the promotions were accurately correlated with sales and eliminated the need to develop a forecast. Weekly sales information is shown in Table C30.4. Tommy uses the information in Table C30.4, and input from the sales representatives, to roughly estimate purchasing amounts based on previous seasonal sales revenues to determine order quantities.

THE OCTOBER 5, 2013 MELTDOWN

On September 3, 2013, Tommy had knee surgery. Beverly Jones, the assistant store manager, was assigned to fill in for Tommy for the next two months. One month later, she is literally pulling her hair out trying to manage the purchasing, inventory, and customer service activities in the wine department. During the month, there have been significant stockouts, increased inventory costs, and dissatisfied customers.

TABLE C30.4
Weekly Sales

Week Ending Date	Sales ($)	Week Ending Date	Sales ($)
9/3/2011	12,803.08	3/17/2012	11,170.51
9/10/2011	0	3/24/2012	11,419.25
9/17/2011	2,788.18	3/31/2012	10,584.89
9/24/2011	12,683.1	4/7/2012	15,256.1
10/1/2011	13,446.87	4/14/2012	10,014.5
10/8/2011	13,309.42	4/21/2012	12,872.14
10/15/2011	12,398.04	4/28/2012	13,206.5
10/22/2011	12,924.28	5/5/2012	13,924.4
10/29/2011	15,777.85	5/12/2012	14,199.63
11/5/2011	14,456.13	5/19/2012	13,511.79
11/12/2011	12,069.85	5/26/2012	14,406.58
11/19/2011	14,266.77	6/2/2012	13,751.1
11/26/2011	24,741.76	6/9/2012	15,140.25
12/3/2011	14,762.22	6/16/2012	15,055.12
12/10/2011	20,961.76	6/23/2012	14,550.5
12/17/2011	21,619.99	6/30/2012	14,024.56
12/24/2011	30,401.07	7/7/2012	12,956.21
12/31/2011	19,751.23	7/14/2012	13,361.24
1/7/2012	13,328.64	7/21/2012	13,404.63
1/14/2012	12,647.94	7/28/2012	16,370.24
1/21/2012	10,597.29	8/4/2012	15,929.06
1/28/2012	12,285.99	8/11/2012	14,147.58
2/4/2012	11,090.74	8/18/2012	15,894.59
2/11/2012	15,138.55	8/25/2012	17,347.75
2/18/2012	12,393.37	9/1/2012	16,678.79
2/25/2012	13,382.52	9/8/2012	17,227.61
3/3/2012	13,054.52	9/15/2012	13,162.3
3/10/2012	12,121.55	9/22/2012	12,966.84

Purchasing Glossary

A

acceptance A draft on which the debtor indicates by the word "accepted" his or her intention to pay or honor.

account number Number assigned to a specific type of service or commodity. It coincides with category code.

acknowledgment A standard form used by a vendor or supplier to advise that the purchase order has been received.

actual weight Gross shipping or transport weight.

addendum A document used to modify bid documents prior to receipt of bids. An addendum is incorporated into the formal contract.

ad valorem The total value of goods or materials against which tariff rates are imposed.

advice of shipment A notice sent to the purchaser from the seller advising that the shipment has gone forward; usually contains details of packing, routing, delivery date, and so on.

agency Implies a relationship between two parties in which one is empowered to perform certain functions or business transactions for the other.

agent An agent is authorized by the principal to act in the principal's behalf and interest. An agent's actions generally bind the principal as if the principal had acted directly.

agreement A consensus by two or more parties. The term is synonymous with contract. An example of this is the agreement between owner and contractor.

airbill A shipping or manifest document used by airlines for air freight; contains shipping instructions to the airline.

air freight To transport or ship goods by air.

airway bill Document used for shipment and transport of air freight by air carriers; lists the materials shipped along with instructions, costs, and other specific details.

amendment A revision or change made to a document.

approve To accept and endorse as satisfactory; implies that the object approved has the endorsement of the approving agency or body. However, the approval may still require confirmation by another party.

arbitration The process by which parties agree to submit their disputes and claims to the determination and resolution of a third, impartial, and unbiased party (referred to as the arbitrator), rather than pursuing their claims in a court of law.

as is Indicates that the materials and equipment offered for sale are without warranty or guarantee. The purchaser has no recourse on the vendor or supplier for the quality of the materials and equipment.

assignment The transfer of rights or title to another party, frequently involving rights originating from a contract.

B

back order The part of an order that cannot be delivered at the scheduled date, but will be delivered at a later date.

banker's acceptance draft A document or draft used in financing a foreign transaction, making possible the payment of cash to an exporter, covering all or part payment for a shipment made by the exporter.

bargain Agreement on the terms and conditions of a purchase. Purchase of articles at a price favorable to the buyer.

barter The process of exchanging one kind of article for another, as opposed to trading by use of money.

bid A complete and properly executed proposal to perform work or supply goods or services that have been described verbally or in the bidding documents and submitted in accordance with instructions to bidders. A bid is an offer.

bid bond A form of bid security purchased by a bidder; provided, subject to forfeit, to guarantee that the bidder will enter into a contract with the owner for construction of the facility within a specified time period.

bidding documents Documents that typically include the advertisement or invitation to bidders, instructions to bidders, bid form, form of contract, forms of bonds, conditions of contract, specifications, drawings, and any other information necessary to completely describe the work for which bidders can prepare bids for the owner's consideration.

bid opening A formal meeting held at a specified place and time at which sealed bids are opened, tabulated, read aloud, and made available for public inspection.

bill An invoice the freight carrier uses to show consignee, consignor, shipment description, weight, freight charges, and other relevant information.

bill of exchange A formal written document used to settle and pay for an existing obligation.

bill of lading A transport company's contract and receipt for materials and equipment; agreement to transport from one location to another and to deliver to a designated individual or party.

bill of materials A list of all permanent materials required for a product on a construction project. The bill of materials list consists of all items described on a drawing and specification.

binder A temporary but binding commitment by an insurance company to provide insurance coverage.

blanket order Provides for the vendor or supplier to furnish certain materials for a certain period of time and at a predetermined price; acts as a master purchase order, reducing the number of smaller purchase orders.

boiler plate A term used to describe the terms and conditions on the back of a purchase order or the specific clauses described in a contract.

bonds Formal documents given by an insurance company in the name of a principal to an obligee to guarantee a specific obligation. In the construction industry the main types of bonds are the bid bond, performance bond, and payment bond.

breach of contract The failure to perform any of the obligations that are stated within the terms and conditions of the contract.

budget year The company's fiscal year.

bulk materials Materials bought in lots; purchased from a generic description or standard catalog description and bought in medium to large quantities for issue as required. Examples are pipe fittings, conduit, cable, timber, and stone.

bulletin A document used to request pricing for a modification to the design after a contract is issued. If pricing is acceptable, a change order to the contract incorporates the requirements of the bulletin into a project.

burden In construction, the cost of operating a home office or field office with staff other than operating site personnel. Also means federal, state, and local taxes, fringe benefits, and other union contract obligations. In manufacturing operations, burden typically means operating overhead costs.

buyer The buying staff negotiates and processes purchase orders, providing assistance to end users. Their mission is to support the departments in obtaining the best products for the best price. Their role in the procurement processes can include troubleshooting vendor, invoice, and payment problems where appropriate.

buying green Buying products that are made from recycled or remanufactured materials.

C

cancellation of order Annulment or cessation of order.

certificate of material compliance A written statement signed and approved by an authorized person stating that the materials comply with the material specification.

certificate of origin A document, issued by the appropriate authority in an exporting country, that certifies the origin of the equipment, materials, or labor used in the manufacture of the equipment or materials being exported to another country.

certification letter A form completed by vendors that supplies the company with key vendor information, including taxpayer ID, remit-to address, type of business, and minority status.

claim A request for additional payment.

COD Cash on delivery.

comment A brief statement intended as an explanation or illustration.

commercial terms The terms and conditions of a purchase order or contract that relate to the business and commercial aspects of the purchase order or contract. The price, quantity, and delivery date are the main elements covered under the commercial terms.

commodity A standard article of trade or commerce. Similar goods or services purchased within the company. Excellent candidates for reverse auctions.

compensatory damages Damages awarded to compensate the injured party by granting a monetary value equal to the loss or injury encountered.

competitive bidding The offer of proposals by individuals or organizations competing for a purchase order or contract to supply specific materials, equipment, or services.

conditional sale A sale made with the knowledge that title will not pass to the buyer until some stated condition has been achieved.

conditions of the contract A document describing the rights, responsibilities, and relationships of the parties to a contract.

conflict of interest When an employee is in a position to influence the conduct of a project for personal gain due to responsibilities or to arrangements with an outside entity.

consequential damages Payment for loss or damage that is not directly attributable to a wrongful action on the part of another party, but is the result of one or more of the consequences of the action.

consideration A term used to describe the value that shall be reimbursed to one party to a contract by another party in return for services or articles rendered.

consultant A participant, either internal or external to the company, whose participation requires a subcontract.

containerization The use of road and marine transportation containers normally 20 or 40 feet in length. Shipment of large sealed freight containers via rail, air, truck, or water to optimize transit time, security, packaging, and turnaround time.

contract An agreement between two or more parties that is written and enforceable by law.

contract administration Administering contracts and purchase orders to protect the interest of a specific organization and to satisfy the conditions and requirements of the contract and/or purchase order.

contract documents A term applied to a collection of related documents (contract, specifications, drawings, and any additional data) that define the extent of an agreement between two or more parties.

contribution To give or supply for a common purpose.

cost plus A contract or pricing method in which the purchaser agrees to pay the supplier an amount determined by the actual cost incurred by the supplier to provide the materials, equipment, or services purchased, plus a fixed percentage of that cost or a fixed sum as profit.

counteroffer To decline an offer by submitting a new offer with conditions or terms different from the original offer.

customs-duty fee entry The process to procure an instrument or apparatus from another country that must pass through U.S. customs.

D

debit notice An invoice used to offset a previous overpayment, showing the difference between the previous invoice and the payment.

deliverable A product or report that must be delivered to satisfy a contractual obligation.

delivering carrier The carrier that transports and delivers the materials and equipment to the purchaser.

delivery The act of transferring possession; applied to shipping, occurs when lading is surrendered and title, materials, and equipment pass to the receiving party.

demurrage A charge made on freight cars, vehicles, or ships held by or for a consignor or consignee for subsequent loading or unloading.

department A distinctive division of a large organization.

detail specification A description of the requirements for a specific item or material or equipment.

direct materials A group of materials finally incorporated or part of the finished product or project.

discount An allowance or deduction given by the seller to the buyer that reduces the cost of the item purchased when certain conditions are met by the buyer (e.g., prompt payment within a stipulated period).

dispatch The process of releasing the order to the vendor. Dispatch methods include printing the purchase order for mailing, faxing the purchase order, and placing the order by phone.

distribution The broad range of activities targeted at the efficient movement of finished materials and equipment from the end of the production line to the eventual end user or consumer.

dock (1) The loading or unloading ramp or platform at an industrial facility or factory. (2) Pier, jetty, or wharf for the receiving and embarking of ships.

draft A legal document instructing one individual to pay another.

due date The date when purchased materials and equipment will be available for installation at the project location.

dunnage Protective matter used around materials or equipment to prevent movement, damage, or breakage while in transit.

durable goods Consumer products that are used repeatedly over a period of years (e.g., household appliances, vehicles).

duty The charge assessed by a government on materials and equipment imported or exported.
An obligation established by law or contract is not formalized.

E

early purchasing involvement (EPI) A practice that involves purchasing professionals in the purchasing process or in a new product development process from the beginning.

early supplier involvement (ESI) A practice that brings together one or more selected suppliers with a buyer's product design team early in the purchasing process or in a new product development process. The objective is to utilize the supplier's expertise and experience in developing a product specification that is designed for effective and efficient purchasing.

earnest money Money that one party gives to another at the time of entering into a contract to "seal the deal." Earnest money can be forfeited if a contract is not formalized.

end-user The person in the unit who is responsible for obtaining goods and services.

error and omission excepted Printed on invoices or other statement(s) to safeguard the originator's right to amend or modify the value if found to be incorrect.

escalation The value of adjustment permitted by an escalation clause. An allowance for an anticipated increase in the cost of equipment, materials, and labor as a result of continuing price inflation experienced over time.

escalation clause A contract clause that provides for a price adjustment based on specific changes.

Ex (Ex mill, Ex factory, Ex warehouse, Ex dock) Prefix used to denote point of origin. When a seller quotes a price Ex, the seller proposes only to make the materials and equipment available at the Ex point of origin and includes no transportation costs in the quoted prices.

excess freight Freight in excess of that indicated on the original freight carrier billing.

exchange bill of lading A bill of lading compiled and exchanged for another bill of lading.

excise tax A tax on the manufacture, sale, or use of certain articles made, sold, or used within a country.

export Shipment of materials or equipment to a foreign country.

export permit A permit given by the government of an exporting country allowing a party within that country to export the materials and equipment to another country.

F

fabrication Manufacturing operations for materials or equipment as opposed to the final installation operation.

facilitation A system to decrease the time of international cargo transportation through the use of the latest customs methods, duty and tariff collection, and other related functions of international traffic activities.

factor An agent selling goods or materials on a commission basis for his or her principal.

fair and reasonable A determination that a price is fair and reasonable is really a conclusion that the proposed price is fair to both parties, considering the quality, delivery, and other factors.

fair market value The value of an article as determined by negotiation between buyer and seller; considered acceptable as a basis of a purchase and sale of the particular article.

FAS (free alongside) When a seller quotes a price FAS, the price includes the cost of transportation and delivery alongside the oceangoing vessel and within reach of the vessel's loading equipment. The price does not include costs for any export permits or the payment of any export duties or tariffs.

field inspection A thorough examination of the equipment and materials shortly after delivery to determine if they meet the requirements of the specifications and to find any hidden defects or damage.

field purchase order A purchase order used in field construction situations where authority to make the type of purchase involved is usually restricted or has a predetermined not-to-exceed value.

FIFO An accounting procedure based on a first-in, first-out treatment of stock or inventory; the articles that are received earliest are used first. The opposite of this procedure is LIFO (last-in, first-out).

firm offer A definite proposal or offer to buy or sell some article on stated terms and conditions. Such an offer binds the proposal for a stipulated time period.

F.O.B. A delivery term meaning "free on board" at a named place. The named place is where merchandise title passes from the seller to the purchaser. This is an important, and often negotiated, aspect of the purchase agreement because whoever holds title in transit is responsible for damages and losses and the filing of claims.

F.O.B. destination The most desirable term for the purchaser. Title is held by the vendor until merchandise is delivered to the purchaser or dock area. The vendor is responsible for damages and losses and the filing of claims up to the time of delivery. A separate freight bill will be submitted for payment.

F.O.B. destination, freight prepaid, and charged back Title of merchandise passes to the purchaser at the time of delivery; however, transportation and freight charges are prepaid by the vendor and added to the invoice.

F.O.B. origin Title of the merchandise passes from the vendor to the purchaser at the moment of delivery to the freight carrier. The purchaser is liable for freight charges and must file all claims for loss or damage.

F.O.B. origin, freight prepaid A delivery term that places liability with the purchaser once the freight leaves the dock, but the vendor is going to pay the shipping costs.

F.O.B. shipping point The location at which title to the articles passes from the seller to the buyer. The seller is liable for transportation costs and the risks of loss or damage to the goods up to the point where title passes to the buyer. The buyer is liable for such costs and risks after the passing of the title.

F.O.R. Free on rail.

force majeure Circumstances beyond an individual's control; pleadable as an excuse for the nonfulfillment of a contract or purchase order.

forward purchasing The purchase of quantities exceeding the immediate requirement, that is, in anticipation of any significant price increase or market shortage.

F.O.T. Free on truck.

freight forwarder Some freight forwarder organizations act as agents on behalf of shippers in organizing the transportation of articles without handling any of the articles. Others act as freight carriers in consolidating small and midsized shipments and delivering them to the purchaser.

G

general liability insurance A broad form of liability insurance covering claims for bodily injury and property damage.

generic A term used to generally describe a group, type, or class of materials and equipment, rather than name a specific trade name or source of manufacture.

goods received note A document detailing all equipment and materials after they have been audited and checked for quantity at the receiving point.

gross ton 2,240 pounds of weight.

gross weight The total weight of a shipment, including containers, packaging, and miscellaneous materials.

guarantee A promise, pledge, or formal assurance given as a pledge that another's obligation or debt will be fulfilled.

H

hedging A method of selling for future delivery whereby the parties protect themselves against potential loss.

hold order A purchaser's order to hold a particular delivery at a designated location for a specific period of time.

hold points Inventory or warehouse areas set aside for storing semicomplete articles.

hundredweight In U.S. measurement and domestic transport, 100 pounds; in U.K. measurement, a hundredweight, or "cwt," is 112 pounds or one-twentieth of a long ton of 2,240 pounds.

I

implied contract A contract formed when parties express, through their conduct, their agreement to be bound to its conditions and terms. An agreement is inferred and understood without express statements.

indemnification An obligation contractually taken on or legally imposed on one party to protect another party against any loss or damage from specific liability.

indemnity A responsibility of one person to make good a loss or damage incurred by another. A payment for damage, loss, or expense incurred.

indirect cost Also known as facilities and administrative costs. The cost of operations that cannot be assigned to specific projects, such as electricity and central administrative services; sometimes referred to as *overhead*.

indirect materials A group of materials used in making a product that are not incorporated into or part of the finished product.

inland bill of lading A bill of lading used in transporting materials and equipment overland to the exporter's international transporter. A through-bill of lading can be used in some circumstances; however, it is usually necessary to prepare both an inland bill of lading and an ocean bill of lading for foreign export of materials and equipment.

inland carrier A transportation organization that moves export or import materials and equipment between seaports and inland locations.

inquiry A request for information related to the schedule, location, availability, interest, cost, or quantity of construction-related items.

inspection plan A procedure that defines the material or equipment requiring inspection and describes the method and order of performing the tests or inspections.

Institute for Supply Management A professional association with a mission to provide national and international leadership in purchasing and material management, particularly in the areas of education, research, and standards of excellence. Membership is individual, not institutional, with local affiliates in Southwest Michigan and Central Michigan. See http://www.ism.ws.

instructions to bidders A document that is part of the bidding requirements, usually prepared by a design professional, architect, or engineer. Instructions to bidders describe specific instructions to the potential contractors on procedures, requirements of the owner, and other necessary information for the preparation and submission of bids for consideration and review by the owner.

inventory Items of materials and equipment that are in the storeroom or warehouse, or work-in-progress consisting of raw materials, fabrication elements, components, parts of intermediate materials and equipment, and finished materials and equipment ready for distribution and sale. Physical inventory is ascertained and established by actual count. It includes materials and equipment that are physically available for allocation and distribution, and stored and controlled in a warehouse.

invitation to bid Written notice of an owner's desire to receive competitive bids for a particular construction project where a select number of contractors are invited to submit bids.

invoice The seller's itemized bill of quantities and prices of materials, equipment, and/or services that have been delivered to the purchaser.

J

joint agent An official designated to act for two or more principals.

joint venture An organization in which two or more parties join together to form a business operation with the legal characteristics of a partnership to achieve a specific goal.

just-in-time (JIT) system System in which materials are purchased, transported, and processed "just in time" for their use in a subsequent stage of the manufacturing process; an operations management philosophy whose objectives are to reduce waste and cycle time. Operationally, JIT minimizes inventory at all levels.

justification A statement of account to demonstrate or prove to be just, right, or valid.

K

kitting The process of sending components of a total assembly to another location in a kit form for assembly.

L

labor and material payment bond A contract between a contractor and a surety in which the surety, for a premium payment by the contractor, agrees to reimburse subcontractors, vendors, and material suppliers any amounts due for their materials and services, should the contractor default in payment to them.

lading The act of loading, or the contents of a specific shipment.

lead time The period of time required to perform a specific activity of work.

lease A contract whereby an individual or organization lets another use property or equipment for a definite term and for an agreed rental cost. The lessor retains title to such property or equipment.

legal tender Money issued by the government to satisfy a debt or obligation.

letter of credit A letter addressed by a bank to a correspondent bank certifying that an individual or organization named therein is entitled to draw upon an account.

liability A state of being under obligation; exposure to a potential claim by which an individual or organization may be subject to pay for compensation for loss, damage, or other acts to another individual or organization.

lien A legal claim on the assets or property of another.

LIFO (last in, first out) An accounting practice of determining the cost of stock inventory used in a manufactured product or process.

liquidated damages A sum of money agreed to by the contracting parties as to damages to be given in case of a failure to meet the obligations of the contract.

litigation To engage in a lawsuit; the process by which parties submit their disputes to the jurisdiction of federal or state law courts for resolution.

lot size The amount of specific materials and equipment items ordered from a vendor.

LTL Less than truckload.

lump sum An amount or value used in a proposal, bid, or contract representing the total cost that an organization is prepared to contract to perform an item of work.

M

manifest A list of the cargo loaded in ships, trucks, containers, and the like; an oceangoing transportation, referred to as a ship's manifest.

markup A percentage that can be added to the total of all direct costs to determine a final price or contract sum. Allows the contractor or subcontractor to recover the costs associated with overhead.

materials management A concept whereby all materials and equipment procurement functions are combined under one management function, including contracting, purchasing, quality assurance, quality control, inspection and expediting, trafficking, and receiving.

mechanic's lien A type of lien filed by an individual or organization that has performed work for which payment is either in dispute or remains unpaid.

minimum carload weight A minimum weight for which a carload of materials and equipment can be charged.

minority business enterprise A company that is at least 51 percent owned, managed, and controlled by one or more minority persons. Minority means being African American, Hispanic American, Native American, or Asian American.

mixed truckload rate A rate applied to a truckload shipment made up of two or more different materials.

multiple consignee A container car, truck, or ship loaded with materials and equipment for two or more consignees.

multiple-source buying A container car, truck, or ship loaded with materials and equipment for two or more consignees.

N

negligence Under the law, failure to exercise the care and consideration a prudent person would exercise; lack of care and attention.

negotiation The process by which a buyer and seller reach an agreement on the terms and conditions regarding the purchase of materials, equipment, or goods.

net price The price reached after all allowable discounts, rebates, and the like are deducted from the original selling price.

net ton 2,000 pounds.

net weight The weight of the materials and equipment without the shipping container and dunnage.

noncompetitive purchase award A purchase from the only available supplier of a product or service. Therefore, no bids or proposals can be obtained. Formerly known as sole source.

O

OBL Ocean bill of lading.

obligation A duty that is the result of a promise or contract; an agreement that an individual or organization is responsible to fulfill.

obsolete Outmoded, worn out, discarded, or no longer in use.

offer A proposal or bid made by an individual or organization to another individual to perform a service or action; the acceptance of such an offer results in a contract. The individual or organization that makes the offer is called an offeror, and the individual or organization that receives the offer is called an offeree. A bid or proposal is an example of an offer.

open-end order Purchases made against the buyer's purchase order or contract. The purchase order or contract contains price, conditions, and terms. The purchase order or contract may not specify the final quantity to be purchased.

order lead time Period of time required to obtain an item from a vendor or supplier once the purchase order requirements are known.

overhead A cost inherent in the operating of a business. A cost that cannot be charged to a specific part of the work, materials, or equipment.

P

packing list A document or log prepared by the shipper to indicate in detail the particular package contents.

partial payment A stage payment made upon delivery of one or more completed units.

patent A government grant to an inventor by which he or she is the only person allowed to make or sell the new invention for a certain number of years.

P-card Master card used for quick transactions that cost $5,000 or less and for hosting functions, dues, memberships, conference registration, subscriptions, and travel expenses.

penalty clause A clause in a contract that stipulates the sum of money to be forfeited in the case of nonperformance of the terms and conditions of the contract.

performance bond A bond obtained in connection with a contract; ensures the performance and completion of all the scope, terms, conditions, and agreements contained within the contract.

physical distribution (warehousing) A range of materials management activities that involve taking care of shipping, receiving, internal movement, and storage of raw materials and finished goods.

piggyback The carrying of anything that usually moves alone by a large vehicle, such as the transportation of highway trailers or containers on specially equipped railroad flat cars.

pledge To bind by a promise.

point of origin (1) The location at which a shipment is received by a transportation company. (2) The actual location of origin of an article.

port of entry A port designated by a government as the entry point for materials, equipment, and services from an overseas country.

prebid conference A meeting with interested suppliers prior to the submission of bids. Its main purpose is to clarify specifications and answer questions from suppliers in an open and equitable manner.

prefabrication A manufacturing or fabrication technique, generally taking place at a location other than the construction site, in which various materials and equipment are combined to form a larger component element for final installation at the construction location.

price/cost analysis A powerful approach to pricing that allows the buying organization to determine what prices should be based on industry norms for direct cost, indirect cost, and a reasonable profit margin.

procurement All of the processes involved in requesting, ordering, auditing, and paying for goods and services.

procurement lead time The time required by a buyer to select and negotiate with a vendor or supplier and place a purchase order.

promissory note A written pledge or promise by one individual or organization to pay another unconditionally a certain sum of money (principal and interest) at a specified time.

purchase Obtaining an article for money; something acquired for a specific amount of money or its equivalent.

purchase order Authorizing document for provision of goods or services from a supplier; becomes a legally binding contract on acceptance by the supplier.

purchasing The act of buying materials, equipment, and services that conform to the correct quality, in the correct quantity, and at the market price, and are delivered in accordance with the promised delivery date.

purchasing cycle The activities in the acquisition of materials, equipment, and services.

purchasing manual An operating guide that explains the policies and procedures for purchasing personnel to follow in the performance of their work activities.

Q

quality The essential attributes that permit materials and equipment to function in the desired manner.

quality assurance A formal procedure that ensures that the materials and equipment will perform satisfactorily when installed.

quality control The procedure and activities that ensure adequate quality is maintained in the materials and equipment utilized in the manufacturing process.

quantity The amount of equipment or material units required.

quantity discount The reduction in unit price cost established by a predetermined minimum number.

quasi-contract An obligation under which an individual or organization that received a benefit must pay the individual or organization that gave the benefit, despite the absence of a contract.

quotation A summary of price, terms of sale, and general description of materials, equipment, or services offered for sale by a contractor or vendor to a potential buyer. When issued in response to a purchase inquiry, it is considered an offer to sell.

quotation expiration date The date after which a quotation is no longer valid.

quote To state a price for securities, goods, and services.

R

rate of exchange The rate at which the currency of one country is exchanged for the currency of another country.

rebate The amount refunded to a purchaser for the purchase of an agreed quantity or value within a stipulated period of time.

receipt inspection An audit and examination of materials and equipment prior to acceptance; to review the completeness of the delivery and to note any obvious damage.

receipt of bids The action of an owner in receiving sealed bids that have been invited or advertised in accordance with the owner's intention to award a contract.

receiving and storage The action of processing materials and equipment from vendors and suppliers, including maintaining and controlling all elements in storage, and the eventual distribution of the materials and equipment.

receiving report A form or log used by an organization's receiving department for recording the materials and equipment received and the differences, if any, from the quantities indicated on the purchase order.

request for information Vendors give information on a particular commodity or service. RFIs are often used as "brainstorming" tools to meet a particular situation (e.g., "provide audio/visual system for auditorium") and rely more on the expertise of the vendors to meet a need.

request for proposal (RFP) Vendors are asked to meet a need or set of needs. Unlike the request for information, criteria are more developed and specifications are given that the proposed commodity or service must meet or exceed. Most, but not all, of the proposals will spell out the equipment/labor/services needed to complete the project.

request for quotation (RFQ) Specific pricing and delivery information on listed products or services. Quotations are requested for exact quantities and products may be specified by make/model number, batch number, industry specification, and so forth.

requisition An internal form that an individual or department sends to the purchasing department requesting materials, equipment, or other services.

reverse auction A reverse auction is an online, declining-price auction between one buying organization and a group of prequalified suppliers. The bidding process is in real time. In most cases, the supplier with the lowest total cost bid is awarded the contract.

S

sales price The value received for items sold. Gross sales price is the total value paid. Net sales is the gross value less discounts, rebates, and freight costs.

salvage The material or equipment that is saved after damage or demolition has been completed.

salvage value The value recovered or realized when an article or facility is demolished, scrapped, or sold.

samples Examples of completed materials, products, equipment, or workmanship that establish standards by which the installed work will be evaluated.

seller's lien The seller's right to withhold or to lay claim on materials or equipment sold, giving up these rights upon receipt of payment.

short ton 2,000 pounds.

single source A purchase from a supplier who is the only respondent to a competitive bid, for example, request for quote.

sole source A purchase from the only available supplier of a product or service. Therefore, no bids or proposals can be obtained. Also referred to as a noncompetitive purchase award.

sourcing The process of researching and determining qualified sources of materials and equipment.

specifications A precise, detailed description and presentation of a component part or purchased item.

standard The requirements of a specific standardization method approved by a recognized and approved authority.

standardization The process of agreeing on a common specification. This process can take place at different levels: (1) across an organization, (2) throughout an industry, (3) across a nation, and (4) around the world.

strategic supplier The strategic supplier program is a unit within purchasing, stores, and auxiliary services. Its primary responsibility is negotiating high-valued contracts with key suppliers.

subsystem A group or set of assemblies, components, or elements that when combined perform a single function.

supplier Vendor, seller, or manufacturer.

supplier evaluation The procedure of evaluating a supplier's ability to perform the required quantity, quality, and scheduled requirements.

supply chain management The design and management of seamless, value-added processes across organizational boundaries to meet the real needs of the end customer. The development and integration of people and technological resources are critical to successful supply chain integration.

surplus The usable materials, equipment, components, or parts that are in excess of the requirements.

T

tariff, freight A listing of duties or taxes on imports or exports.

tax-exempt Not subject to taxes.

tax-exemption certificate A document given by the purchaser to the seller with the purchase order to indicate that the transportation is not subject to sales tax.

technical bid evaluation The ranking of vendor or supplier bids based on the quantity, cost, compliance with specifications, and delivery requirements.

terms and conditions (Ts and Cs) Specific requirements a buyer makes upon a supplier in the performance of work.

terms of payments The method of payment for materials, equipment, and services stipulated in a contract.

testing Confirming an article's ability to meet preestablished requirements by subjecting the article to a set of physical, chemical, or operating evaluations.

title The legal right to the possession of property.

total cost of ownership (TCO) The purchase price of a product and its transportation cost, plus indirect handling, inspection, quality, rework, maintenance, and all other "follow-on" costs associated with the purchase, including costs of disposal.

tracing Locating the current position of a shipment after it has entered the delivery and transportation phase.

trademark A mark, picture, name, or letters owned and used by a manufacturer or merchant to distinguish his or her goods from the goods of another.

traffic The action of transporting materials and equipment by a freight carrier.

transit charges Costs of services rendered while a shipment is being transported.

transit rate A rate applying to traffic stopped en route for milling, painting, packing, treating, storage, and so on.

transload Shipment stopped while being transported in order to be partially unloaded.

transmittal A form or letter indicating the action to be taken on an article being transmitted from one party to another.

U

Uniform Commercial Code (UCC) A codification of law that clarifies and regulates the rights and obligations of buyers and sellers engaging in commercial transactions. It has been adopted by all states except Louisiana.

unit cost contract A contract in which reimbursement is based on a preestablished cost per unit of measured for the quantities produced or installed.

unit load Several articles that are loaded on one pallet, or placed in a crate, enabling transportation of the items at one time, as one unit.

unit of issue A unit of measurement in which an item is issued from stock.

unit of measure Used to specify the number of units or items to be purchased.

unit train Freight trains that move large quantities of bulk materials between two or more locations.

usage The number of units or articles of an inventory item consumed over a period of time.

use tax A tax imposed on the user of materials and equipment.

V

valuation The appraisal of the value of exported or imported materials and equipment.

value The real worth of an article; marketable price; the intrinsic worth of an item. The value of an article is determined by the lowest cost at which a satisfactory supply of materials and equipment or services can be obtained.

value analysis The application of techniques that establish a value for a necessary action at the lowest evaluated cost.

value engineering A discipline that reviews the real value of various life cycle costs, materials, equipment, and manufacturing techniques. Value engineering reviews the initial cost of design, coupled with the costs associated with maintenance, energy use, and life cycle.

variable costs The costs associated with raw materials and all manufacturing operating costs, which vary with manufacturing output.

VAT Value added tax.

vendor An individual or organization that sells something to a purchaser.

vendor diversity program The purchasing staff that expend the effort to identify minority- and women-owned businesses and those classified under the Americans with Disabilities Act, who deal at the appropriate level of distribution to foster and develop these sources within policies and procedures of the company.

vendor maintenance Vendor specialists maintain the vendor database by adding to and updating current vendor information (1099 tax information, remitting address, government reporting date, etc.). They gather this information through the vendor certification process. The vendor database is the foundation of the procurement system; no transaction can be processed unless a vendor has been correctly entered into the database.

vendor performance evaluation A ranking and evaluation of vendors' and suppliers' performance based on quality of work, compliance with specifications, delivery, and cost.

vendor's lien A seller's right to retain possession of materials or equipment until he or she has received payment.

verification Witnessing of certain steps in the fabrication and manufacturing process, such as metallurgical analysis, hydrostatic performance, or operational tests; review and audit of nondestructive testing, x-rays, and bench tests.

vessel-ton One hundred cubic feet of volume.

visual inspection Manual inspection of materials and equipment.

volume discount A reduction in unit cost predicted on the size of a particular purchase.

voucher A document that serves as proof that the terms of a transaction have been met.

W

waive To give up a right or claim; to refrain from claiming or pressing.

warehouse receipt A document given by the warehouseman as a receipt for materials and equipment placed in the warehouse.

warranty A promise or pledge that something is what it is claimed to be. The seller makes a specific assurance concerning the nature, quality, and character of the goods.

waste The refuse from the fabrication and manufacturing process that cannot be reclaimed or reused.

weight, gross The actual combined weight of the item, container, or any dunnage materials.

weight, net The actual weight of the item; does not include the container or any dunnage materials.

weight, tare The difference between the gross weight and the net weight of an item being shipped; weight of the empty container, including dunnage packing material used in transport.

wholesaler An individual or organization that acquires products, materials, and equipment for resale to retailers or other users.

Index

Page numbers followed by n indicate footnotes.

D

F

J

K

L

M

N

O

P

Q

R

S

U

V

W

X

Y

Z